D1553847

DIFFERENTIATION THEORY AND SOCIAL CHANGE

DIFFERENTIATION THEORY AND SOCIAL CHANGE

COMPARATIVE AND HISTORICAL PERSPECTIVES

Jeffrey C. Alexander and Paul Colomy, Editors

Columbia University Press
New York

Columbia University Press
New York   Oxford
Copyright © 1990 Columbia University Press
All rights reserved

Library of Congress Cataloging-in-Publication Data
Differentiation theory : problems and prospects / Jeffrey C. Alexander
and Paul Colomy, editors.
p. cm.
Includes bibliographies and index.
ISBN 0–231–06996–0 (alk. paper)
1. Differentiation (Sociology) 2. Social change. 3. Social
systems. 4. Social structure. I. Alexander, Jeffrey C.
II. Colomy, Paul Burbank, 1952–
HM101.D535   1990
303.4—dc20   89–17382
                                                          CIP

Casebound editions of Columbia University Press books are Smyth-sewn
and printed on permanent and durable acid-free paper

Printed in the United States of America

c 10 9 8 7 6 5 4 3 2 1

Contents

13 Differentiation, Rationalization, Interpenetration: The
Emergence of Modern Society 441
Richard Münch

CONCLUSION
Revisions and Progress in Differentiation Theory
Paul Colomy 465

About the Contributors and Editors

Jeffrey Alexander is professor of sociology and chair of the Sociology Department studies at the University of California at Los Angeles. He earned his Ph.D. at the University of California at Berkeley. He has been a Guggenheim fellow and a member of the School of Social Sciences at the Institute for Advanced Studies in Princeton. Author of the *Theoretical Logic in Sociology* (University of California Press, 1982–1983), *Twenty Lectures* (Columbia University Press, 1987), *Action and Its Environments* (Columbia University Press, 1988), and *Structure and Meaning* (Columbia University Press, 1988). He has also edited several books and contributed numerous articles to scholarly journals.

Duane Champagne is assistant professor in the Department of Sociology at the University of California at Los Angeles. He received his Ph.D. in sociology from Harvard University in 1982 and has published articles on education, social movements, and social change. He is currently completing a book on the formation and institutionalization of states in four southeastern American Indian societies during the nineteenth century.

Paul Colomy is assistant professor in the Department of Sociology at the University of Denver. He earned his Ph.D. at the University of California at Los Angeles and was a postdoctoral fellow at Stanford University. He is the author of a number of articles in the areas of social change, social theory, social stratification, and social psychology. He has also edited *Functionalist Sociology* and *Neofunctionalist Sociology*, both published by Edward Elger Press. His current work examines recent theoretical and empirical contributions to the neofunctionalist tradition.

S. N. Eisenstadt is professor of sociology at the Hebrew University of Jerusalem. He has served as visiting professor at numerous universities, including Harvard, Stanford, MIT, Chicago, Michigan, Washington, Oslo, Zurich, and Vienna. His publications include *The Transformation of Israeli Society* (Weidenfeld and Nicolson, 1985), *Society, Culture and Urbanization* with A. Schachar (Sage, 1987), *The Origins and Diversity of Axial Age Civilizations* (State University Press, New York, 1986), and *Centre Formation, Protest Movements and Class Structure in Europe and the United States* with L. Roniger and A. Seligman (Frances Pinter, 1987). He is also the editor of the two-volume *Patterns of Modernity* (Frances Pinter, 1987).

Frank J. Lechner is assistant professor in the Department of Sociology at Emory University. He received his Ph.D. from the University of Pittsburgh in 1985, and has published articles on sociological theory, fundamentalism, ethnicity, and world system theory. His current research focuses on problems in sociological theory and world system analysis and on the comparative study of social movements and solidarity.

Niklas Luhmann has been a lawyer and civil servant, and is currently professor of sociology at the University of Bielefeld. He is a member of the Rheinisch-Westfalische Akademie der Wissenschaften, and was awarded an honorary doctorate from the University of Gent. Among his books published in English are *Trust and Power* (John Wiley, 1979), *The Differentiation of Society* (Columbia University Press, 1982), *Religious Dogmatics and the Evolution of Societies* (E. Mellen, 1984), *A Sociological Theory of Law* (Routledge and Kegan Paul, 1985), and *Love as Passion* (Harvard University Press, 1986).

Leon Mayhew is professor of sociology and dean of the College of Letters and Sciences at the University of California at Davis. He is the editor of *Talcott Parsons: On Institutions and Social Evolution*. His recent work focuses on the development of institutions of solidarity in modern society.

Richard Münch was born in West Germany and is currently professor of sociology at the University of Dusseldorf. Earlier he served as dean of the School of Letters in Dusseldorf. He was a consulting editor for the *American Journal of Sociology* from 1982 to 1984, and is presently coeditor of *Current Perspectives in Social Theory*. His most recent publications include *Theorie des Handelns* (1982), *Die Struktur der Moderne* (1984), and two volumes of *Die Kultur der Moderne* (1986).

Gary Rhoades is assistant professor at the Center for the Study of Higher Education at the University of Arizona. After receiving his Ph.D. in sociology at the University of California at Los Angeles he was a postdoctoral research scholar in Burton Clark's Comparative Higher Education Research Group at UCLA. He has published articles analyzing institutional change in educational systems, focusing particularly on educational professionals' roles in shaping their instititions. He is currently working on a book, *The Profession and the Laity*, which examines change in four higher education systems.

David Sculli is assistant professor of sociology at the University of Delaware. The conceptual bases of societal constitutionalism and its applications—to professions and organizations and to corporate crime— are currently being explored in several essays and grant proposals and a forthcoming book entitled, *Theory of Social Societal Constitutionalism: Foundations of a Non-Marxist Critical Theory.*

Neil J. Smelser, professor of sociology at the University of California, Berkeley, is the author of many books, including *Social Change in the Industrial Revolution, Theory of Collective Behavior,* and *Comparative Methods in the Social Sciences.* He is former chair of the theory section of the American Sociological Association and is cochair of the Committee on Basic Research for the Behavioral and Social Sciences, National Academy of Sciences/National Research Council.

Preface

This collection of essays presents provocative new work by leading proponents of differentiation theory. Simultaneously a theory of social change and a theory of modernity, differentiation theory, like its intellectual cousin functionalism, is currently experiencing a significant resurgence. Initially formulated by Talcott Parsons and his students in the late 1950s and early 1960s, the modern version of differentiation theory was met with increasing skepticism in the tumultuous years that followed. It appeared—to many critics at least—that the perspective was destined for the proverbial graveyard of history.

The prediction was wrong. Recent advances in differentiation theory have outstripped the criticisms issued over a decade ago. In organizing this volume, our aim has been to assemble contributions that accurately reflect new developments. We believe that the essays featured here not only invalidate earlier critiques but also supercede earlier efforts by revising, extending, and applying differentiation theory in innovative and important ways.

Whereas the initial formulation of differentiation theory rested upon the identification of a master trend of change toward greater institutional specialization, the current volume supplements that master trend with the description and analysis of several distinct patterns of change, particularly backlash movements against differentiation. These essays also directly revise the explanatory framework of differentiation theory itself, replacing a problem-solving and societal need approach with a more political model that emphasizes group conflict, power, and contingency. Third, the benign assessment of the consequences of differentiation, which stresses adaptive upgrading and greater efficiency, is balanced by the recognition that differentiation often generates discontents. In addition, differentiation creates groups with vested interests in particular institutional configurations, and the protection and advancement of those interests often produce rigidity and inflexibility rather than efficiency. Finally, the liberal optimism that infused Parsons' treatment of differentiation is replaced with a "critical modernism," which provides a standard for evaluating and criticizing existing societal arrangements.

These essays reflect not only theoretical progress and revision but also a large expansion of empirical scope. The range of substantive topics is considerable: higher education in Europe and the United States, the public sphere in seventeenth-century England, Axial-Age civilizations, and the Tlingit society in southeast Alaska, to mention only a few. Certainly, the range and depth of these discussions belie the common complaint that differentiation theory lacks historical specificity. Yet these empirically disparate essays represent far more than a collection of case studies. Each essay is informed by and extends differentiation theory in important ways. Any successful general theory must be able to prove itself capable of guiding wide-ranging empirical research, and the substantive depth of these contributions highlights the breadth of the differentiation approach to social change.

In addition to the individual essayists, there are others whose contributions we would like to acknowledge. At Columbia University Press, Louise Waller, executive editor, has gone above and beyond the call of duty in ensuring the quick and successful publication of this book. Susan Hopkins quickly and skillfully edited the manuscript copy, and Leslie Bialler navigated it through the galley proof stage. At an earlier stage of preparation, Bernard Barber provided an extremely helpful commentary on the entire manuscript. The contribution by Niklas Luhmann, originally written in German, was superbly translated by John Bednarz. Invaluable research assistance was provided by Alberto Arroyo, Sree Subedi, and Gretchen Wenner. Finally, the volume was typed and retyped by Irene Fort, Pat Conley, and Beverly Riggin of the University of Akron and by Dorene Miller and Andrea Reed Silverstein of the University of Denver.

Jeffrey C. Alexander   **Paul Colomy**
LOS ANGELES, CALIFORNIA   DENVER, COLORADO

DIFFERENTIATION THEORY AND SOCIAL CHANGE

Introduction

Differentiation Theory: Problems and Prospects

Jeffrey C. Alexander

The essays in this volume explore how social change can be seen as a process of differentiation. In its general outlines, this process is fairly well understood. Institutions gradually become more specialized. Familial control over social organization decreases. Political processes become less directed by the obligations and rewards of patriarchy, and the division of labor is organized more according to economic criteria than by reference simply to age and sex. Community membership can reach beyond ethnicity to territorial and political criteria. Religion becomes more generalized and abstract, more institutionally separated from and in tension with other spheres. Eventually cultural generalization breaks the bonds of religion altogether. Natural laws are recognized in the moral and physical worlds and, in the process, religion surrenders not only its hierarchical control over cultural life but its institutional prominence as well.

But to know the general outlines of this process, and even to be able to show how this general process is at work in "typical episodes" of social change, is not enough. If the general perspective of differentiation is going to produce a theory of social change, it must be brought down to earth. Obviously, not all social change is differentiation. Sometimes societies stagnate; often they become brittle and reactionary, concentrated and inflexible. Why do these responses happen? Why, by contrast, is differentiation sometimes able to proceed?

Merely to describe differentiation as a general process, moreover, makes it appear to be an automatic equilibrating mechanism, something that occurs whenever adjustments must be made to conflict and strain. This is not the case. The social processes that produce differentiation can and must be described in specific concrete terms. When they are, the contingency of differentiation will be more clearly understood and, therefore, its responsiveness to historical variation as well. Is a certain kind of ideology necessary for differentiation to occur? Is a particular kind of interest and group formation? What kinds of societies and historical developments are likely to produce these?

Finally, what is the relation between differentiation and the historical formations that are the traditional objects of classical change theory? Do feudalism, fascism, capitalism, and socialism represent a continuum of differentiation, or do they represent amalgamations of institutions that are differentiated in varying degrees? Would differentiation theory conceptualize the strains and conflicts in these formations in significantly different ways than traditional approaches do?

These questions demarcate the frontier of differentiation theory. They arise not just from scientific curiosity but out of theoretical competition. They are the questions that other theories put to theorists who think they see differentiation in social change. If the theory is to be maintained, it must be improved, and these questions must be answered.

In conclusion to this volume, Paul Colomy shows in an unusually clear manner how theoretical competition has developed in the field of social change, and formulates quite precisely the questions that have formed its core. He shows, moreover, that these are the very questions that have motivated the essays that have been written for this book. By pushing differentiation theory to provide answers, these essays not only raise this particular research program to a new level but, in doing so, initiate a new round in the theoretical competition that characterizes this substantive field.

In this introductory essay I will provide some background for these new developments. I begin by suggesting that the problems that these essays address have been at least implicit in differentiation theory from its origin in Durkheim's classical work. These problems, I try to show, can be seen as generic issues that every theory of social change must address. On the basis of this framework I present an historical account of social change theory in the postwar period. I place Parsons' renewal of differentiation theory in this context, and explain how the reaction against this renewal set the stage for the revision of differentiation theory today.

Durkheim's Problem

Although the notion that society changes through a process of institutional specialization can be traced back to ancient times, the modern theory of social change as differentiation may be seen as beginning with Durkheim. In *The Division of Labor in Society*, Durkheim (1933 [1893]) put Spencer's earlier theory in a new form and began a research program that extends to the present time. While Durkheim's first great work has, of course, become one of the classics of Western social science, the association with differentiation theory has not usually been made. For this reason, *Division*'s role in the present discussion is of particular interest; the problems I will describe in this classical work have been noted before but, because they have never been understood by reference to differentiation theory, their interrelation has been impossible to see.

Durkheim's first great work serves as an exemplar of differentiation theory in several different ways. It can be considered the first and still one of the most powerful applications of the theory itself. It can also be seen as embodying some of this tradition's most typical and debilitating weaknesses. In other words, Durkheim's early work presents in a nutshell the achievements of differentiation theory and the difficulties it often creates.

In Book One of *Division*, Durkheim outlines a general portrait of social change as differentiation. Societies were once mechanically organized. They had repressive laws and were dominated by a particularistic and omnipresent collective conscience. Gradually they have moved toward organic solidarity, where laws are restitutive and collective morality is generalized and abstract. In terms of institutional references, Durkheim focuses here primarily on economic change on the one hand and, on the other, on the separation of religion from political and legal functions. There is also a brief but important discussion of cultural generalization as indicating the increasingly person-centered character of the collective conscience.

This initial discussion, however, is highly abstract and general. While this broad sweep confers power and scope, it makes it difficult to incorporate any real analysis of particulars: distinct historical phases through which differentiation proceeds, select institutions and sectors upon which different periods of differentiation depend, historically specific social problems that differentiation systematically might generate. Durkheim's argument in Book One is evolutionary rather than developmental in the sense (Gould 1985) that there are no phase-specific strains outlined; functional in the sense that there is no theory of how particular structures are involved; and ideal-typical in the sense that there is no account of how a given episode of social differentiation actually occurs.

What is fascinating—and portenous—about this work, however, is that Durkheim goes on to try to supply such particulars in Books Two and Three. Book Two is his effort to supply a theory of social process. He argues that population growth leads to greater density and, hence, to greater specialization in order to create a more adaptive and efficient distribution of resources. His third book is an effort to discuss a particular historical phase of differentiation and the problems it typically engenders. He suggests that because industrial society is not yet fully differentiated, the division of labor is coercive and disruptive. When birth is further separated from wealth and political from economic organizations, industrial organization will be mature and society less conflictual.

The fatal weakness of *The Division of Labor in Society* is that its three books cannot be related to one another in a systematic way. That demographic pressure is the principal process through which differentiation proceeds, as Durkheim asserts in Book Two, is in itself open to doubt. More significant from a theoretical point of view is that this emphasis seems to directly contradict the notion that differentiation involves cultural and political phenomena, which Durkheim argued in Book One. What either demographics or systemic differentiation, more generally understood, have to do with the forced division of labor—Durkheim's topic in Book Three—is also problematic. For if the division of labor is, indeed, anomic and coercive in 1890, there is nothing in Durkheim's general theory, or in his specific account of social process, to supply an explanation. What is necessary is a more phase-specific model of general differentiation and of social process as well. Only with such a theory would it be possible to stipulate criteria for predicting "normal" and "pathological" outcomes of a particular social formation.

To establish links between the three parts of Durkheim's great book, in other words, would require a detailed account of structures and processes and a systematic effort to link these theories to the general theory of differentiation. This is precisely the goal toward which contemporary differentiation theory must strive.

In order to relate this agenda for a particular research program to issues about social change as such, one must recognize that Durkheim's problem was not simply his own. Through the lens of differentiation theory he was groping with issues that are generic to the study of social change. Each of *Division*'s three parts represents one important way in which social change has been conceptualized—through the construction of general models, through developing accounts of social process, and through historically specific analyses of tensions and strains. Durkheim's problem is an enduring one from which all students of social change can learn. The most important lesson, perhaps, is that rather than forming the basis for perspectives among which theorists are expected to choose, the validity of each part should be recognized. Rather than concrete empirical alternatives, they should be converted into analytic levels of the same theoretical model. In this way they can become different moments of ongoing empirical analysis, and the results of each level can be systematically related to the other.

The History of Social Change Theories

I would like to suggest, indeed, that the generic status of Durkheim's problem can be pushed even further still. The shifts of focus in his first great book can be seen as representing not only different empirical levels in the study of social change but also alternating phases in intellectual history. There is a dialectic in the history of social science between general theories of change, which are simplified models of an all-encompassing nature, and specific theories, which try to do more about less. The general theories of change put forward sweeping accounts of history as such. The most important ones for social science have been Marx's theory that all history is the history of class conflict, Weber's account of civilization as rationalization, and, of course, Durkheim's vision of development as differentiation.

It is impossible to do without these very general guiding rubrics. They are normatively significant, and they provide a base upon which every specific form of explanation must be built. On the other hand, while they are necessary, they are not sufficient. Whenever a general theory is forcefully articulated, or rearticulated, specific theories evolve in its wake. In part these are offshoots and elaborations of the general theory—efforts to elaborate and extend the research program (Wagner 1984; Wagner and Berger 1985) that has been forcefully set out. They are also and increasingly, however, challenges to generalizing effort per se. Arguments begin to be made that general theory as such cannot explain very much, and scientific prestige and attention shifts toward specific theories that explain more about less. Eventually the dialectic comes full circle. A new general theory of change emerges, both as an effort to tie these particular challenges together and as a protest against the specific approach to change itself.

In the 1930s, general theories of a Marxist bent about change gained wide influence (e.g., Lynd and Lynd 1937). They were challenged, in due course, by theories at a more middle range, which, it was argued, could present better explanations precisely because of their more specific focus. These specific theories challenged the sweep of Marxism by focusing on particular spheres instead of on social systems as such, by insisting on the uneven "application" of general laws (like those that Marxism formulated about class conflicts in capitalist societies), and by challenging the ideological implications that, Marxism assumed, followed from the laws of history.

The details of this response to Marxist change theory are worth noting because they began a chain reaction which continues today. Against broad claims for the undermining of political scope by forces of class, Selznick (1948, 1952, 1957) and Lipset (1956) argued for specifically political determinations of politics and, on this basis, for the possibility of democracy in the postwar world. Lipset (1963) later elaborated this argument by insisting on the specificity of values vis-á-vis class relations as well. Insisting on the particular and idiosyncratic nature of prestige as compared to class, Lipset (1955), Hofstader (1955), and Bell (1955) developed an account of status conflict in the postwar era that explained the emergence of McCarthyism and anti-democratic politics generally. Thinkers like Riesman (1950), Aron (1967, 1968), and Bell (1965) developed much more phase-specific analyses of capitalism that emphasized internal discontinuities and abrupt internal transitions. Once again, armed with these more explanatory theories, they could argue for specific strengths or weaknesses of societies in the postwar era.

Finally, a wide range of nation specific change theories emerged. These argued that the differences created by each nation's customs, religion, economy, and state were more significant in affecting the course of national change than the laws of history that Marx discovered. On the basis of "American exceptionalism," Hartz (1955) and Lipset (1963) explained the resilience of American democracy, and Bailyn (1967) explained its suspicious and antiauthoritarian style. Dahrendorf (1979) explained Nazism on the basis of German national specificity; Landes (1951) explained the decline of France's economic position by pointing to its peculiar pattern of family ownership and control; Bendix (1964) explained English stability by pointing to its ability to embrace industrial citizenship.

Each of these theoretical challenges to Marxism was tied not only to empirical objections but to objections about its abstract, general approach to change. Yet the major effort to tie the implications of these challenges together ended up shifting the terrain of change theory back to a generalized direction. In the late 1950s Parsons produced an extraordinarily sweeping theory of change as differentiation. Though it developed in part from Parsons' own internal theoretical momentum and from challenges that he had personally experienced, it was also a response to the specific findings that had emerged from the challenge to Marxian theory described above. Parsons' differentiation theory can be seen as incorporating the insights about bureaucratization, democratization, status conflict, and American exceptionalism that were achieved in the late 1940s and 1950s. It also responded to the demand to reconceptualize the "capitalist" phase.

Most of the insights for these specific theories had been drawn from Weber, but it was to Durkheim that Parsons turned for a general framework within which they could be placed. Parsons claimed that in the course of history each sphere of society gradually becomes more independent of all others. The power of economic forces to dominate other spheres is markedly diminished. Politics can constitute itself through its own organizational choices. Religious beliefs become more tolerant because they do not control power or community membership. Status anxiety increases because the distribution of rewards depends on individual achievement rather than group membership and ascribed status. Conflicts are more frequent but more constrained, because they are insulated from immediate contagion by other spheres. In one sense, then, differentiation theory can be seen as inductively arrived at. At the same time, of course, it was an attempt by Parsons to renew the very kind of sweeping historical account that anti-Marxist theorists had challenged.

The achievements of Parsons' new general theory can be seen in the way it wove together the more specific anti-Marxist theories I have described. Parsons' theory succeeded in making these appear to be manifestations of a general tendency that seemed to many to be eminently sensible at the time. There were also, however, enormous difficulties attached to Parsons' effort. In part because he had one hand resting on Weber's shoulder, Parsons was able to describe the actual course of differentiation with much more precision and concreteness than one can find in Durkheim's earlier work. Even so, Durkheim's problem remained. For if Parsons had taken his general bearings from Durkheim, it was only from *The Division of Labor in Society*, Book One. Like Durkheim's before him, Parsons' theory lacked a developmental notion of particular phases. While he plausibly argued against the feudalism-capitalism-socialism trichotomy of Marx, he did not distinguish clearly coherent historical phases of his own. Distinctive developmental tendencies were not articulated, and endemic problems were not identified for the contemporary era. The general theory did not, moreover, develop an account of change in particular sectors or institutions. On the contrary, although certain possibilities for sphere-specific theories were implied, Parsons insisted that the same general theory could be used to explain change in every institution and sphere. He did not see that specifying different concepts for different spheres does not necessarily challenge a more general theory of underlying tendencies. The challenge is to interrelate these specific theories rather than choose between them.

Differentiation theory as Parsons developed it also failed to incorporate national or regional specificity. Nor—and this is perhaps its most debilitating problem—did the general theory develop a conception of the processes that lead to differentiating change. As a result, Parsons' theory could not describe how particular conflicts and modes of collective action were linked to particular phases of social development or to the structural characteristics of different institutions. For example, in Parsons' (1966, 1971) most important monographic elaborations of his general theory, he barely noted the fact that the transitions between various phases of differentiation have frequently been carried out by war. Parsons emphasized, for example, that in early societies upper-class lineages typically depended on religious legitimation to maintain their domination. An exception, he acknowledged, were cases "in which a group subordinates another group by military conquest" (Parsons 1966:44). He went on to argue, however, that while domination through conquest may have "played an important part in *processes* of social change," this cannot be considered "*differentiation* in the present sense" (italics added). That in Parsons' hands differentiation theory is not intended to include processes of change could not be more clear. What follows from this is obvious as well— some of the most significant dimensions of social change fall by the wayside.

This excessive insistence on generality was responsible, in my view, for much of the criticism that Parsons' differentiation theory received. Its lack of phase-specific analysis, its failure to address institutional and structural levels, its negation of process—all contributed to the ahistorical, idealistic aura of this very sophisticated but still quintessential "modernization theory." The work of various students of Parsons can be seen as efforts to address these problems. Smelser (1959) and Eisenstadt (1963) wrote about distinctive historical phases and about the nature of differentiation processes; Bellah (1959) and Smelser (1963) tackled the problems of specific spheres. These revisions did not go far enough. Only later did these students become fully aware of the weakness of Parsons' general level of theorizing.

In the course of the 1960s, this theory was challenged—much as the preceding Marxist general theory had been—in the name of the greater utility of specific theories (see Nisbet 1969; Smith 1973; and, for a summary, Colomy's Conclusion, this volume). Theorists wanted to speak of specific events, like the French Revolution (Tilly 1967), and of precise variations in national outcomes (Moore 1966). They wanted to differentiate specific phases and uneven development—for example the emergence of the world capitalist system in the early modern Europe (Wallerstein 1974) or the monopoly phase of industrial capitalism (Baran and Sweezy 1966). They wanted also to be able to talk specifically about how change processes created problems and strains (Gusfield 1963; Gouldner 1979). Symbolic interactionists and resource mobilization theorists developed explanations of collective behavior that went far beyond anything in Parsons' work and were far more predictive than Smelser's. Conflict theorists (Collins 1975; Skocpol 1979) developed theories of state building and revolution that were much more historically specific and comparatively precise than Eisenstadt's. Finally, the ideolgical tone of these more particular theories was more critical and sober about the possibilities for satisfactory change.

Eventually, the dialectic through which change theories proceed produced, in turn, a new general theory. Marxism drew on many of these particular theories and challenged differentiation theory on its own most general grounds. The way in which Marxism has been able to correlate general and specific theories of change, and to do so in a systematic way, has made it the most fully developed approach to change in the history of the social sciences.

What Does a General Theory Do When It Is Challenged?

The empiricist philosophy of science, which continues to legitimate most social science today, holds that theories live and die through falsification. Kuhn (1970), Lakatos (1969), and other postpositivist philosophers and historians of science, however, have shown that falsification cannot—or, at least, in practice usually does not—disprove a general theory, even in the natural sciences. Lakatos (see Wagner 1984; Wagner and Berger 1985) has developed the most plausible account of how the resistance to falsification occurs. Theories differentiate between core notions, which are positions considered essential to the theory's identity, and others that are more peripheral. Faced with studies that throw some of their important commitments into doubt, general theories can sustain their vivacity by discarding peripherals and defending their core. They seek to incorporate challenges by reworking and elaborating new peripheral points. Of course, this kind of vivacious defense is no more than a possibility. Whether an effective shoring-up process actually occurs depends on the empirical actors and the social and intellectual conditions that exist at a particular time.

When differentiation theory first encountered challenges to its predictions and its mode of explanation it seemed that no successful defense would be made. Parsons himself was never able to throw the weaker points of his general change theory overboard or to expand it in an ambitious way. Faced with the choice of abandoning the theory or changing it, many functionalists simply left it behind. A theory can be abandoned even if it is not refuted; the effect on the course of scientific development is much the same.

In the polarized political climate of the 1960s and early 1970s it was hard to make the effort to sustain differentiation theory. A few theorists did try to build new circles around the inner core; Eisenstadt was the most important of these. From his first papers, he insisted (Alexander and Colomy 1985) that it was impossible to conceive of general differentiation and specific social process in isolation from one another. There are particular carrier groups for particular kinds of differentiation, and it is their interest structures and ideological visions that determine the actual course that differentiation will take. Smelser also initiated a fundamental critique from within. In his work on higher education on California, in connection with which he confronted directly Parsons' evolutionary neglect of institutional actors and contingent interests, Smelser (1973, 1974) insisted on studying resistance to differentiation. In the process he began to develop a plausible theory of the relationship between differentiation and self-interested elites.

These internal revisions were scattered and few, and at first they were hardly recognized by the social scientific community at large. Differentiation theory was given up for dead. By the late 1970s, though, this situation began to change. Several factors were involved: (1) The glow began to fade from the particular theories that had challenged differentiation in the first place. Neo-Marxist theories of the world capitalist system were challenged, for example, by rising economic growth in some third world nations and by the fact that the threat of a world economic crisis, which once seemed imminent, had receded. Conflict perspectives appeared increasingly to have underestimated the resiliency of capitalist and democratic institutions. (2) These developments appeared to weaken the specific explanatory power of Marxism; ideological events lessened the political attractiveness of its more sweeping conclusions. The cooling of the ideological climate made even nondogmatic Marxist social science seem less compelling. (3) A new generation of theorists emerged that had not personally been involved in the break from differentiation theory and did not, therefore, have a personal stake in continuing the controversy.

By the late 1970s and early 1980s an ambitious revision of differentiation theory had begun. Most of this work first emerged in Germany (e.g., Schluchter 1979 and Luhmann 1982) and the United States (e.g., Alexander 1978, 1980, 1981a, 1981b), though it appeared elsewhere as well, for example in England with the work of David Lane (1976). While the movement has a research program of its own, it can also be linked to the more general development in sociology of what has been called "neofunctionalism" (see Alexander 1985).

The essays in this volume deepen this development and indicate just how far-reaching it may become. On the one hand they engage the external challenges to differentiation theory from other traditions. On the other, they seek to overcome the internal problems of the initial model—what I have called Parsons' failure to overcome Durkheim's problem. I will not discuss here the degree to which the essays that follow succeed in these tasks. Colomy makes a detailed assessment in this volume's conclusion. I will finish, instead, with some final thoughts on the value of differentiation theory as such.

The Promise of Differentiation Theory

It seems to me that differentiation comes closer than any other contemporary conception to identifying the actual texture, the imminent dangers, and the real promises of modern life. While differentiation is certainly a powerful development on the modern scene, it is less primordial and fused than it is bureaucratic and specific. It is experienced, moreover, not as all-powerful but as a development that challenges the existence of deeply entrenched centers of private and public activity, centers that Habermas has somewhat loosely called life-worlds. It is because differentiation exists, Michael Walzer (1983) has shown, that justice in modern societies demands for these life-worlds ever greater autonomy and self-control.

Differentiation theory provides the same kind of nuanced self-reflection vis-á-vis theories of cultural change. In the last few years cultural fragmentation has received increasing attention from critics of modern society. Habermas (1984), Schluchter (1979), Bellah (1985), MacIntyre (1981), and Lyotard (1984) have condemned this fragmentation as alienating and oppressive. Yet the fragmentation of a meaning system can also be seen as its differentiation, as the growing autonomy, in relation to each other, of cognitive, affective, moral, and metaphysical versions of truth. Certainly anxiety and dislocation are attendant on such differentiation, but there is freedom and rationality to be gained, and the possibility of continuing cultural coherence as well. If the psychological and social environments of cultural differentiation are taken into account, it is clear that "fragmentation" rarely occurs without the possibility for corresponding increases in ego capacity and moral development and without the extension and proliferation of opportunities for meaningful solidary communities. Where Weber posited rationalization and depersonalization as the central characteristics of modernity, and neo-Marxist critical theory followed his path, differentiation theory offers an opportunity to describe modernity in a more ambiguous and, I think, realistic way. It would seem that it is the very pluralization of life-worlds, not their colonization, that creates the distinctive opportunities and pathologies of modern life.

Differentiation theory also promises a more discriminating approach to the issues of commodification and domination that Marxism has raised. Markets are dangers wherever they are allowed to exist and their specialized, purely instrumental rationality can be wielded for the self-interest of any group that commands the monetary medium of exchange. But markets, particularly in capitalist societies, are enmeshed within finely spun webs of quite differentiated controls, and these did not only begin, as Karl Polanyi assumed, in reaction against capitalist markets themselves. Differentiation goes back thousands of years. It can, indeed, partly be seen as a protective process, but one that proceeds in response to attempts at domination in every sphere (Walzer 1983). In the course of world history entrepreneurial groups have made dramatically more autonomous the distribution of grace and knowledge, power and citizenship—not just economic wealth. Each effort has produced a new basis for domination in turn. Differentiation continues to provide the resources for new efforts at domination today, and the abrupt discontinuities of contemporary social development often seem to invite domination as an equilibrating response. It is in communist—not capitalist—countries that groups have been able to institutionalize this omnipresent possibility for domination in long-term, apparently self-generating ways.

These remarks point to the promise of differentiation theory. Most of this introduction has focused, by contrast, on the problems confronted in any serious effort at using differentiation theory. It is from the intersection of problems and promises that the following essays proceed.

References

Alexander, Jeffrey C. 1978. "Formal and Substantive Voluntarism in the Work of Talcott Parsons." *American Sociological Review* 43:177–98.

——1980. "Core Solidarity, Ethnic Outgroups and Structural Differentiation: Toward a Multidimensional Model of Inclusion in Modern Societies." In Jacques Dofny and Akinsola Akiwowo, eds., *National and Ethnic Movements*, pp. 5–28. Los Angeles, Calif. and London: Sage.

——1981a. "The Mass Media in Systemic, Historical, and Comparative Perspective." In Elihu Katz and Thomas Szecsko, eds., *Mass Media and Social Change*, pp. 17–52. Los Angeles, Calif. and London: Sage.

——1981b. "Revolution, Reaction, and Reform: The Change Theory of Parsons' Middle Period." *Sociological Inquiry* 5:267–80.

——1982–1983. *Theoretical Logic in Sociology*. 4 vols. Berkeley and Los Angeles: University of California Press.

Alexander, Jeffrey C., ed. 1985. *Neofunctionalism*. Los Angeles, Calif. and London: Sage.

Alexander, Jeffrey C. and Paul Colomy. 1985. "Towards Neofunctionalism. Eisenstadt's Change Theory and Symbolic Interactionism." *Sociological Theory* (fall), 3:11–23.

Aron, Raymond. 1967. [1962] *Eighteen Lectures on Industrial Society*. London: Weidenfeld and Nicolson.

——1968. *Progress and Disillusion*. New York: Encyclopedia Britannica.

Bailyn, Bernard. 1967. *The Ideological Origins of the American Revolution*. Cambridge, Mass.: Harvard University Press.

Baron, Paul and Paul Sweezy. 1966. *Monopoly Capital*. New York: Monthly Review.

Bell, Daniel, d. 1955. *The New American Right*. New York: Criterion Books.

——1965. "The Disjunction of Cultural and Social Structure." *Daedalus* 94:208–222.

Bellah, Robert N. 1957. *Tokugawa Religion*. Glencoe, Ill: Free Press.

——1959. "Durkheim and History." *American Sociological Review* 24:447–61.

Bellah, Robert N. Richard Madsen, William M. Sullivan, Ann Swidler, and Steven M. Tipton. 1985. *Habits of the Heart*. Berkeley and Los Angeles: University of California Press.

Bendix, Reinhard. 1964. *Nation-Building and Citizenship*. New York: Wiley.

Collins, Randall. 1975. *Conflict Sociology*. New York: Academic Press.

Dahrendorf, Ralf. 1979. *Society and Democracy in Germany*. New York: Doubleday.

Durkheim, Emile. 1933 [1893]. *The Division of Labor in Society*. New York: Free Press.

Eisenstadt, S. N. 1963. *The Political System of Empires*. New York: Free Press.

Gould, Mark. 1985. "Prologomena to Future Theories of Societal Crisis." In Alexander, *Neofunctionalism*, pp. 57–71.

Gouldner, Alvin W. 1979. *The New Class*. New York: Seabury.

Gusfield, Joseph. 1963. *Symbolic Crusade*. Urbana-Champagne: University of Illinois Press.

Habermas, Jurgen. 1984. *The Theory of Communicative Action*. Vol. 1. Boston, Mass.: Beacon.

Hartz, Louis. 1955. *The Liberal Tradition in America*. New York: Harcourt and Brace.

Hofstadter, Richard. 1955. *Anti-Intellectualism in American Life*. New York: Knopf.

Kuhn, Thomas. 1970. *The Structure of Scientific Revolutions*. 2nd Edition Chicago, Ill.: University of Chicago Press.

Lakatos, Imre. 1969. "Criticism and the Methodology of Scientific Research Programmes." *Proceedings of the Aristotelian Society* 69:149–86.

Landes, David S. 1951. "French Business and the Businessman: A Social and Cultural Analysis." In Edward M. Earle, ed., *Modern France*, pp. 334–53. Princeton, N.J.: Princeton University Press.

Lane, David. 1976. *The Socialist Industrial State*. Boulder, Colo.: Westview Press.

Lipset, Seymour Martin. 1955. "The Sources of the 'Radical Right.'" In Daniel Bell, ed., *The New American Right*, pp. 166–233. New York: Criterion Books.

——1956. *Union Democracy*. New York: Free Press.

——1963. *The First New Nation*. New York: Basic Books.

Lynd, Robert and Helen Lynd. 1937. *Middletown in Transition*. New York: Harcourt and Brace.

Lyotard, Jean-François. 1984. *The Postmodern Condition*. Minneapolis, Minn.: University of Minnesota Press.

Luhmann, Niklas. 1982. *The Differentiation of Society*. New York: Columbia University Press.

MacIntyre, Alistair. 1981. *After Virtue*. Notre Dame, Ind.: Notre Dame University Press.

Moore, Barrington. 1966. *The Social Origins of Dictatorship and Democracy*. Boston, Mass.: Beacon.

Nisbet, Robert. 1969. *Social Change and History*. London: Oxford University Press.

Parsons, Talcott. 1966. *Societies: Evolutionary and Comparative Perspectives*. Englewood Cliffs, N.J.: Prentice-Hall.

——1971. *The System of Modern Societies*. Englewood Cliffs, N.J.: Prentice-Hall.

Riesman, David with Nathan Glazer, and Reuel Denney. 1950. *The Lonely Crowd*. New Haven, Conn.: Yale University Press.

Schluchter, Wolfgang. 1979. "The Paradoxes of Rationalization." In Guenther Roth and Wolfgang Schluchter, *Max Weber's Vision of History*, pp. 11–64. Los Angeles and Berkeley: University of California Press.

Selznick, Philip. 1948. "Foundations of the Theory of Organizations." *American Sociological Review* 13:25–35.

——1952. *The Organizational Weapon*. New York: McGraw-Hill.

——1957. *Leadership in Administration*. Evanston, Ill.: Row, Peterson.

Skocpol, Theda. 1979. *States and Social Revolutions*. New York: Cambridge University Press.

Smelser, Neil J. 1959. *Social Change in the Industrial Revolution*. Chicago, Ill.: University of Chicago Press.

——1963. *The Sociology of Economic Life*. Englewood Cliffs., N.J.: Prentice-Hall.

——1973. "Epilogue: Social Structural Dimensions of Higher Education." In Talcott Parsons and Gerald M. Platt, *The American University*, pp. 389–422. Cambridge, Mass.: Harvard University Press.

——1974. "Growth, Structural Change, and Conflict in California Higher Education, 1950–1970." In Neil J. Smelser and Gabriel Almond, eds., *Public Higher Education in California*, pp. 9–141. Berkeley and Los Angeles: University of California Press.

Smith, Anthony. D. 1973. *The Concept of Social Change*. London: Routledge and Kegan Paul.

Tilly, Charles. 1967. *The Vendee*. New York: Wiley.

Wagner, David. G. 1984. *The Growth of Sociological Theories*. Beverly Hills, Calif., London, and New Delhi: Sage.

Wagner, David G. and Joseph Berger. 1985. "Do Sociological Theories Grow?" *American Journal of Sociology* 90:697–728.

Wallerstein, Immanuel. 1974. *The Modern World System*. New York: Academic Press.

Walzer, Michael. 1983. *Spheres of Justice*. New York: Basic Books.

ONE

Resistance, Culture, and Uneven Forms

I

Modes of Structural Differentiation, Elite Structure, and Cultural Visions

S. N. Eisenstadt
with **M. Abitbol, N. Chazan, and Arie Schachar**

Theoretical Introduction: The Social Division of Labor, Differentiation, and the Structure of Elites

Drawing from my research on comparative civilizations, this paper extends some analytical considerations of evolutionary theory in the social sciences and expands the concept of differentiation. (Eisenstadt 1964, 1968a).

In the 1960s I essayed two central criticisms of evolutionary theory and the concept of differentiation as they were employed in the structural-functional school. The first criticism held that not all social change necessarily leads to differentiation. The second, and more important, maintained that institutional developments that take place at seemingly similar "stages" of differentiation may nevertheless lead in different directions. In other words, the patterns of integration—the institutional responses to the problems of differentiation—that emerge in different societies at seemingly similar stages of differentiation may vary considerably across societies.

Thus, to quote from some of the earlier formulations:

Recognition of the integrative problems that are attendant on new levels of differentiation constitutes the main theoretical implication of the concept of differentiation, and it is in the light of the analytical problems raised by this implication that the various questions pertinent to a reappraisal of the evolutionary perspective in social science have to be examined. . . .

The passage of a given society from one stage of differentiation to another is contingent on the development within it of certain processes of change which create a degree of differentiation that cannot be contained within the pre-existing system. Growing differentiation and the consequent structural break-throughs may take place through a secular trend of differentiation, or through the impact of one or a series of abrupt changes, or both. These tendencies may be activated by the occupants of strategic roles within the major institutional spheres as they attempt to broaden the scope and develop the potentialities of their spheres. The extent to which these changes are institutionalized and the concrete form they take in any given society necessarily depend on the basic institutional contours and premises of the pre-existing system, on its initial level of differentiation, and on the major conflicts and propensities for change within it.

We need not assume that all changes in all societies necessarily increase differentiation. . . .

Even when social change increases differentiation, the successful, orderly institutionalization of a new, more differentiated social system is not always a necessary outcome. Moreover, at any level of development, response to the problems created by the process of differentiation may take one of several different forms. The most extreme outcome is failure to develop any adequate institutional solution to the new problems arising from growing differentiation. . . . Aside from biological extinction, the consequences may be total or partial disintegration of the system, a semiparasitic existence at the margin of another society, or total immersion within another society.

A less extreme type of response tends to lead to "regression," that is, to the institutionalization of less differentiated systems within the more differentiated system that has broken down. . . . Many such regressive developments are only partial, in the sense that within some parts of the new institutional structure some nuclei of more differentiation and creative orientations may survive or even develop. . . .

Another and perhaps the most variegated, type of response to growing differentiation consists of some structural solution that is on the whole congruent with the relevant problems. Within this broad type a wide variety of concrete institutional arrangements is possible. Such different solutions usually have different structural results and repercussions. Each denotes a different structure crystallized according to different integrative criteria and is interpenetrated in a different way by the other major social spheres. . . .

One very interesting structural solution is the development of a relatively stable system in which the major institutional spheres *vary* in degree of differentiation. . . . In cases of such uneven differentiation the more differentiated units of such related societies (for example, the church in feudal or patrimonial systems) often tend to develop a sort of international system of their own, apart from that of their "parent" societies.

The variety of integrative criteria and institutional contours at any level of differentiation is, of course, not limitless. The very notion of interdependence among major institutional spheres negates the assumption that any number of levels of differentiation in different institutional spheres can coalesce into a relatively stable institutional system. The level of differentiation in any one sphere necessarily constitutes within broad limits, a precondition for the effective institutionalization of certain levels of differentiation in other social spheres. But within these broad limits of mutual preconditioning a great deal of structural variety is possible. . . .

Thus, at any given level of differentiation, the crystallization of different institutional orders is shaped by the interaction between the broader structural features of the major institutional spheres, on the one hand, and, on the other, the development of elites or entrepreneurs in some of the institutional spheres of that society, in some of its enclaves, or even in other societies with which it is in some way connected.

The variability in the concrete components of such interaction helps to explain the great (but not limitless) variety of structural and integrative forms that may be institutionalized at any given level of differentiation. Although different societies may arrive at broadly similar stages of evolution in terms of the differentiation of their major institutional and symbolic spheres, yet the concrete institutional contours developed at each such step, as well as the possible outcomes of such institutionalization in terms of further development, breakdown, regression, or stagnation, may differ greatly among them. (Eisenstadt 1968a)

My previous work did not, however, fully and explicitly address the problems of whether the different types of integrative solutions create different degrees of differentiation, types of uneven differentiation, or different modes of differentiation, with different institutional dynamics.

Similarly, that work only touched upon the crucial importance of different types of institutional entrepreneurs or elites. To continue the quote:

The crucial factor is the presence or absence, in one or several institutional spheres, of an active group of special "entrepreneurs"—that is, an elite that is able to offer solutions to the new range of problems. Among modern sociologists Weber came closest to recognizing this factor when he stressed that the creation of new institutional structures depends heavily on the "push" given by various "charismatic" groups or personalities and that the routinization of charisma is critical for the crystallization and continuation of new institutional structures. The development of such "charismatic" personalities or groups constitutes perhaps the closest social analogy to genetic mutation. It is the possibility of such mutation that explains why, at any level of differentiation, a given social sphere contains not one but several, often competing, possible orientations and potentialities for development. (Eisenstadt 1968a)

I also noted the importance of several preconditions, especially the presence of internal or international enclaves, in the development of such entrepreneurs.

I have not, however, fully explored the basic characteristics of these entrepreneurs, or elites, the dissimilarities between them and the modes of their institution-building efforts, or the importance of the cultural dimension in their activities.

My earlier work was presented, in part, as a critique of classic evolutionary theory. Nevertheless, it also accepted, implicitly and with many reservations, several assumptions about the nature and construction of institutions. Four such assumptions, most fully articulated by the structural-functional school, informed many theoretical formulations and comparative studies published in the 1950s and 1960s.

The first assumption presumed that structural differentiation is manifest in the development of relatively specialized roles which organize the flow of resources and the consequent social division of labor in all institutional spheres—technological, economic, political, religious, and the like.

Second, the classic approach accepted a relatively closed systemic view of society. It strongly emphasized the social division of labor as manifest in different degrees of structural differentiation and the development of specialized roles and institutional spheres which organize the flow of resources. It was argued that these features explain the basic characteristics and dynamics of any given institutional structure.

Third, it was maintained that criteria similar to those already employed in the study of institutional differentiation could be readily applied, without modification, to examinations of the cultural sphere.

Fourth, it was assumed that there is a "natural" tendency toward the parallel development of differentiation in all such spheres. Exceptions to this tendency, such as partial or delayed differentiation, were usually treated as unusual or problematic.

Thus both the "classical" approaches and earlier critiques shared a strong emphasis on the organizational aspect of the social division of labor. This emphasis reflects one important direction of classical sociological analysis that analyzes social structure and the mechanisms of the social division of labor—i.e., the allocation and distribution of resources through different social groups, positions, roles, and institutions.

At the same time they neglected other crucial insights of classical sociological analysis that constitute the core of the sociological tradition as crystallized by the founding fathers—Marx, Durkheim, and Weber. As is well known, these founders rejected the assumption, implicit in both utilitarian ethics and classical economics, of the predominance and sufficiency of different mechanisms of the social division of labor, especially the market, as regulators of social order. (These problems are more fully analyzed in Eisenstadt, 1985).

Sociology's founding fathers, while not denying the importance of the market as one regulative mechanism, nevertheless argued that the very organization of the social division of labor—of social exchange in general and the market in particular—generates several problems that render problematic the functioning of any concrete social division of labor. To different degrees, each stressed three aspects of the social order that cannot be adequately explained by an analysis of "organizational" mechanisms such as the market. The first aspect, examined primarily by Durkheim and to a lesser extent by Tonnies, was the construction of trust and solidarity. The second referred to the regulation of power and overcoming the attendant feeling of exploitation, and was studied mainly by Marx and Weber. The final element, the provision of both meaning and legitimation to social activities, was stressed in different ways by all of the founders, but perhaps especially by Weber. Each emphasized that while the construction of the social division of labor generates uncertainties with respect to these dimensions of social order, no concrete social division of labor can be maintained if these problems are left unattended.

The founding fathers stressed the great tension between the organizational division of labor, on the one hand, and both the regulation and legitimation of power and the construction of trust and meaning, on the other. The focus on such tension has been one of the most important legacies of the classical period of sociology.

The tensions between these different dimensions of social order has been somewhat neglected in later developments in sociology—especially in the structural-functional school, where the emphasis on structural differentiation has become central.

Neglect of these tensions has led sociologists to ignore the possibility that the construction of each dimension of social order can be carried out by different actors, or may involve different types of activities. Second, that neglect produced a scholarly insensitivity to the possibility that such activities can influence the construction of institutional structures and the flow of resources not only—not even mainly— by organizing the social division of labor in terms of the structural differentiation of roles, but also by creating various specific types of institutional formations. These formations cannot be subsumed under the rubric of structural differentiation. Nevertheless, they may effect the structuring of differentiation, producing not just different degrees but also distinctive modes of differentiation. Consequently, these formations may have a far-reaching impact on the institutional dynamics of their respective societies.

The impact of these assumptions on comparative analysis can be illustrated by referring to my earlier work, *The Political Systems of Empires* (Eisenstadt 1963). In that volume I assumed, implicitly, that different political systems can be distinguished by the degree to which they develop specialized political roles or subroles. The book also assumed that the major dynamics of those political systems are explainable in terms of differentiation and the problems it engenders.

Further, while I fully recognized that distinct imperial systems exhibited different dynamics and although these differences constituted the major focus of my analysis, the different dynamics were explained primarily in the conventional terms of differentiation.

Finally, while my book asserted that different values or goals— cultural, political, military, and the like—strongly influenced the dynamics, and even the ultimate destiny, of imperial systems, that insight was not fully explicated.

Thus, *The Political Systems of Empires* did not explore the possibility that the overall patterns of institutional integration and dynamics, which arose in systems characterized by relatively similar degrees of differentiation, could be explained not only in terms of levels of structural differentiation but also in terms of the relations between such differentiation and different elite activities. In particular, although they are essential to institutional formation and dynamics, the articulation of the boundaries of collectivities, the regulation of power, the construction of meaning, and those elite activities that are centered around the construction of trust were not carefully examined. These types of elite activities, it must be emphasized, cannot be explained solely in terms of structural differentiation. On the other hand, they did affect the structuring of social differentiation in the empires and, ultimately, their very destinies.

In more general terms, even the earlier criticisms of structural differentiation did not adequately consider the possibility that various institutonal complexes, as developed by the interaction between major elites and various social groups, arise not only in response to problems attendant upon the greater complexity of the division of labor, but also constitute an autonomous dimension of institutionalization, which may be closely connected to the different cultural orientations carried by such elites. It is also possible that these orientations may, in turn, generate different specific types of institutional formation and different modes of social differentiation and institutional dynamics.

To overcome these deficiencies, it is necessary to return to the analysis of the regulation of power and construction of trust and meaning. The investigation of these core dimensions of social order must include the examination of their relation to the social division of labor and explore the connections between the symbolic dimension of human activity and power relations, on the one hand, and the shaping of institutional contours, on the other.

This approach to the construction of social order, institution building, and elite social actors emphasizes the point that the establishment of any institutional setting is effected by a combination of several major components. One critical factor is the level and distribution of resources among different groups in a society which, in turn, are strongly influenced by the predominant type of division of labor. A second component consists of the institutional entrepreneurs or elites who are available (and who may be competing) for the mobilization and structuring of resources and for the organization and articulation of the group interests generated by the social division of labor. A final component is the nature of the conceptions (or "visions") that inform the activities of these elites and that are largely derived from the major cultural orientations prevalent in a given society. The institutionalization of these visions provides for the concretization of the charismatic dimension of social order, or the quest for a meaningful social order, and is usually crystallized by the activities of major elites.

There are three major types of elites. The first type, political elites, deals most directly with the regulation of power in society. The second formulates models of cultural order and is primarily concerned with the creation of meaning. The last type articulates solidarity relations between major groups and addresses itself to the construction of trust. The structure of these elites is closely related to the basic cultural orientations or codes prevalent in a given society, and these distinct elites are carriers of different types of orientations. These elites also tend to exercise different modes of control over the allocation of basic resources in a society. Through those different types of control they combine the structuring of trust, the provision of meaning, and the regulation of power with the division of labor in society, and thereby institutionalize the charismatic dimension of the social order.

Coalitions of these elites exercise control through their ability to manipulate access to major institutional markets (e.g., economic, political, cultural, etc.) and to convert resources between these markets. In addition, they control the production and distribution of information central to the structuring of cognitive maps of the members of their society in general and orientations of specific reference groups in particular. (This point is more fully worked out in Eisenstadt 1968b, 1982). In conjunction with their structuring of a social order's cognitive maps and social groups' major reference orientations, elites exercise different types of control through a combination of organizational and coercive measures.

Different coalitions of elites and their diverse modes of control shape the major characteristics and boundaries of their respective social systems, including the political and economic systems, the system of social stratification and class formation, and the overall macrosocietal system. Differing modes of control influence the central aspects of institutional structure in different societies. In addition, elite activities create specific loci of institutional structure, including the boundaries of different collectivites and the centers of societies or sectors thereof, which cannot be subsumed under the conventional rubric of differentiation. On the other hand, those loci are of great importance for understanding the institutional dynamics of their respective societies in general and the impact of structural differentiation in particular.

The central point of the approach developed here is that students of social differentiation must distinguish between the organizational dimensions of the structuring of resource allocation and the social division of labor, on the one hand, and the patterning of elite functions (i.e., the regulation of power, the construction of trust, and the provision of meaning), on the other. Special attention should be given to the ways in which combinations of these activities inform the institutional contours and dynamics of different societies.

Social Differentiation and Comparative Analysis of Civilization

In an effort to concretize the preceding discussion, this section applies the conceptual scheme devised above to several empirical investigations that have been undertaken by my colleagues and me. Three issues will be explored: first, a reconsideration of the origins of the early state, based primarily on African materials (Eisenstadt, Abetbol, and Chazan 1985a); second, an examination of cities and urban hierarchies in historical societies (Eisenstadt and Schachar 1985); and last, an analysis of the so-called Axial Age civilizations (Eisenstadt 1986).

Origins of the State and Early State Formation

Criticism of Evolutionary Approaches. We begin with an analysis of the formation of early states, concentrating primarily on Africa. Our point of departure is the inadequacy of those mostly evolutionary approaches premised, in principle, on defining the state in terms of different degrees of structural differentiation. On the basis of such a definition these approaches proceed to explain the great variety of early state formations.

Such analyses have their roots in the classical evolutionary studies of the origins of the state—whether those of Marx and of Engels (1942), Herbert Spencer (1925–1929), or the earlier anthropologists (e.g., Oppenheimer 1926; Lowie 1947). Several contemporary scholars have continued this tradition, including: the neo-Marxists J. Friedman and M. J. Rowlands (1977) and M. Godelier (1973), whose work indicates intriguing if somewhat paradoxical parallels to some of Parsons' schema; G. Balandier (1969) and his more differentiated comparative studies undertaken over several decades; and, more recently, R. Cohen and H. Claessen, and P. Skalnick (1978).

These latter studies have made substantial contributions to the analysis of the formation of early states. However, the quest for the specific characteristics of the early state pursued by the classic evolutionary approach does not take into account the great amount of variability that concrete forms of sociopolitical organizations exhibit at each so-called "stage of development" of the state. The dual assumption of universal stages of development or differentiation in all societies and the concomitant manifestation of similar institutional qualities at each stage has minimized the importance of certain elements in the internal structure of respective polities. That assumption

also fosters the perception that variations at each level of development are secondary to the major characteristics of the overall stage.

For instance, from the study of African materials one can readily
identify examples of different types of breakthroughs, from chieftain-
cies to early states and from early states to states. Because the transition between different types or stages did not invariably follow a
given linear progression, it did not always result in identical outcomes. R. Horton (1971), for example, details several different ways
in which stateless societies in West Africa assumed characteristics of
chiefdoms. In the same vein, the early Akan states possessed marked
similarities to each other which distinguished them from other early
states, such as Onitsha or the Hause city-states. When the Akan states
themselves underwent the breakthrough from early states to states,
the subsequent formations also diverged.

Closely related is the fact that much of this literature is unable to
explain why certain early states, such as Egypt and Ethiopia, developed into more differentiated or archaic states, whereas others, such
as the Sudanese empires of Ghana, Mali, and Songhai, did not, by
their own impetus, go beyond more rudimentary phases. These comparisons within Africa and others beyond the continent—expanding
into the Mediterranean New East and fertile crescent as well as the
Far East (Service 1975; Cohen and Service 1978)—cannot be explained in terms of the variables derived from classic evolutionary
theory.

Societal Centers and Their Dimensions.   The major differences among
these societies can be found in the structure of their respective centers. The crucial importance of these centers attests to the inadequacy
of an unreconstructed evolutionary approach which analyzes political
institutions solely in terms of their relative structural differentiation.

This difference in the structure of the center—a difference that
becomes even more visible in other (especially the Axial Age) civilizations to be discussed later—clearly indicates that such centers cannot
be viewed only in terms of the relative specialization of political roles
and organizations. Rather, these centers also have to be regarded as
among the most important of the institutional loci in which the charismatic dimension is articulated (see Shils 1975a, 1975b; Eisenstadt
1968b). These centers are, indeed, very closely related to the political
sphere and to political rules and authority. However, the dimension
of centrality is *not* tantamount to the organizational differentiation of
the political sphere or of political-administrative rules. This critical
fact has not been sufficiently recognized in the existing literature on

the origins of the state. This literature has not recognized that the process of control exercised from within the center, or centers, of a society deals not only with the organizational aspects of the social division of labor but also, and perhaps foremost, with their connection to the charismatic dimensions of the social order—i.e., the construction of trust, the regulation of power, and the provision of meaning. Further, each dimension may be articulated within different centers to different degrees, thereby giving rise to the exercise of different modes of control. These differences, in turn, are closely related to the nature of the coalitions of the elites predominant in a particular center and to the cultural orientations they articulate. As a result, different centers exhibit diverse structures and dynamics.

These centers can be distinguished in terms of their structural and symbolic autonomy and distinctiveness; the nature and types of activities undertaken by the center; and their relationship to the periphery, patterns of elite coalitions, and the nature of the systematic tendencies and capacity for change that develop within different types of centers.

These three dimensions need not always go together, as our cases indicate, and in different societies the extent of the development of each dimension may vary.

First, the autonomy of the center is manifest in the degree to which the center is organizationally differentiated from the existing social division of labor and, specifically, from various ascriptive units, such as territorial or kinship ones, and the extent to which it develops symbolic autonomy.

Second, cutting across the various types of distinctive centers, the nature of center activities may be identified by referring to several major dimensions. The first dimension designates the areas of social life where a center's activities are concentrated. These areas can be distinguished according to the major aspects of social order analyzed above: the creation of values and models of cultural and social order; the articulation of solidarity and collective identity; the regulation of power relations; and the regulation of the social division of labor and, especially, economic activities.

Regarding all of these activities another distinction, cutting across the former, is concerned with the degree to which the center's activities regulate and possibly exploit existing social arrangements in the periphery, or construct new types of structures in the periphery.

Closely related to the preceding distinction, yet also cutting across it, is the degree to which centers expand their activities beyond their original territorial boundaries.

Thus, different centers can be distinguished, as our case studies indicate, according to the types of activities they perform. The constellation of these activities, together with the relative distinctiveness of the centers, produce different types of respective contours and dynamics.

Organizational and Model Centers. Distinctive types of political dynamics closely related to different structures of centers can be identified in the two developmental stages of early states in Africa. However, these political dynamics become most fully articulated in the second, more developed, phase of state formation.

The first stage involved the symbolic separation of center functions from other spheres of activity. Such a breakthrough was usually characterized by the emergence of a sense of community that incorporated several broad kin groups and/or by the explicit elaboration of a cultural mythology that bound several such groups together. These dual processes, occurring either separately or jointly, often culminated in the emergence of identifiable articulators of solidarity and/or meaning. Most of the early state or proto-state configurations in Africa, such as Onitsha, Bono-Manso, Adanse, and the Manding *kafu*, had in common the relative enmeshment of their centers in broad, ascriptive primordial (usually either kin or age) settings.[1]

Even at this early stage some of the dissimilarities between different types of centers became apparent. Whereas the early Akan states evinced a communal solidarity that adhered to kinship divisions, in the first Manding agglomerations, *kafu*-related activities were kept symbolically and to some degree organizationally distinct from specific kin and economic concerns.

The second stage, which developed only among a small number of centers, occurred when the consolidation of the state's tasks were formalized through elaborate institutional arrangements and the construction of special centers. Usually it was at this historical confluence that a phase of state "irreversibility" was achieved.

More significantly, it was during this second stage, when the structural differentiation of the centers began, that the articulation of the center evolved along quite different paths. Two major types of state centers arose, and within each of these types many subvarieties appeared. As indicated above, each major type was characterized by different patterns of internal organization, divergent types of coalitions among elites, the prevalence of distinctive cultural orientations, and different types of political dynamics. "Organizational" centers, one type of such centers, were structurally much more elaborate and powerful than the units of the periphery, but were not highly distinct symbolically from the periphery. In other words, they did not articulate symbolic models of the cultural order or of solidarity that were different from those current in the major units of the periphery.

Attendant on growing social differentiation, the crystallization and restructuring of these centers were based on the reorganization and consolidation of family, kinship, and territorial structures. The state center became articulated through the ordering of broader primordial criteria—especially familial, kinship, and territorial—and, at times, through the actual redefinition of kin and territorial bases. In these cases there was almost no separation between religious or cultural and political or economic centers. The location of symbolic meaning, regulatory trust, and expansionary power functions also overlapped. Asante, the city-state of Ibadan, the Kongo center, and the Zulu in the days of Shaka all intertwined symbolic and institutional arrangements within a core group that exhibited only a low level of symbolic distinctiveness.[2]

These centers tended to be relatively congruent with the degree of structural differentiation in a society, giving rise to the construction of collectivities based on a diffuse symbolic identity. Depending on the degree of organization of tasks and the hierarchization of functions among kin groups, these centers engaged in a variety of activities, many of an expansive nature. Political elites could enter into coalitions with a variety of other elements such as military elites, economic groupings, and religious functionaries, who were, however, usually subordinated to the leadership of the kin-based potentates. Consequently, the symbolic dependence of the periphery on the center was kept to a minimum, while its instrumental dependence was more pronounced.

The central element of the coalitions in these societies was the various leaders of ascriptive units who articulated the solidarity of their respective groups and concurrently performed other, especially political (or military), elite functions. They evinced only a small degree of specialization and were, for the most part, firmly embedded in the same broadened kinship and territorial units. Power and authority and, in some measure, wealth were to a large extent, mutually convertible.

Whatever the extent of their organizational compactness and strength, "model-based" centers, in contrast, were characterized by a much greater degree of symbolic differentiation from the periphery. In these centers some or even most elite functions were organized in distinctive ways, and elite functions and structural differences developed in divergent directions. Consequently, state centers with different structures and emphases emerged.

In these instances, the development of centers and different elite functions did not occur through the reconstruction of primordial familial, kinship, or territorial groups in a larger and more differentiated symbolic and territorial scale. Rather, they arose primarily through the disembedment of some or most elite functions from the scope of such groups and through the crystallization of centers defined in relatively autonomous ways, i.e., according to criteria and modes of mobilization and structuring distinct from those of the periphery. These centers formulated, at a relatively early stage, some measure of distinct articulation of models of the cultural order.

In model-based centers, the articulators of meaning tended to be organized in different associational, kinship, and territorial settings. In these circumstances, power and authority were not easily convertible, nor was task specialization or wealth accumulation readily convertible into the symbolic functions linked to center consolidation. Consequently, as role differentiation increased, so did the mutual dependence of the separate elites on each other and, above all, of the periphery on the center. The periphery's dependence is evident in its high degree of subordination to the center's charismatic institutions.

In these societies, this separation of the center from the organization of tasks in the social division of labor opened up possibilities for the differentiation of elite functions and the consequent development of a variety of charismatic visions and their institutionalization in a multitude of ways and frameworks. These constituted the nuclei of a variety of center activities. The range of possible coalitions that could develop in these circumstances was great. In most of these centers, however, relatively autonomous articulators of models of the social and cultural order were dominant in the ruling coalitions.

Congruent and Noncongruent Societies.   Such variations in the structure of these centers and in institutional dynamics are found in societies at similar stages of structural differentiation. Accordingly, that variability cannot be explained adequately by conventional differentiation theory.

The clue to understanding such differences resides in the different elites, the visions they articulate, the coalitions they enter into, and the relation of such elites to other groups or strata in the society, especially their autonomy or embedment in broader ascriptive units. In other words, the crucial difference lies in the distinction between the degree of congruence between the specialization of tasks in the social division of labor, on the one hand, and elite functions (i.e., the articulation of power and political distinctiveness, the creation of trust, or the provision of meaningful models of the cultural order), on the other. Only in terms of this distinction is it possible to account more fully for the different paths of political dynamics in general and the diverse patterns of state formation in particular.

With regard to the relations between organizational specialization and the articulation of elite functions, two distinct patterns that are almost ideal types and between which some overlap naturally developed can be identified in historical Africa. These patterns, it should be noted, follow the distinction between the different types of centers analyzed above.

The first pattern encompasses those societies in which a relative congruence was prevalent between the specialization of the social division of labor and the articulation of elite functions. The second consists of those societies in which a dissociation or a noncongruence between elite functions and the organizational differentiation of society prevailed.

Good illustrations of the first type can be found among the Asante, the Kongo states, the Zulu, and the Ibadan Yoruba (see the references in note 1). In the first two cases congruence developed in kin and territorially based societies. In the latter two, universalistic (age or economic achievement) developments were prevalent alongside those of kinship.

The overlapping of elite functions and structural differentiation which was prominent in Asante (Chazan 1985), also existed in other early African states. The Kongo states exhibited a system of pacts under the kinship umbrella: traders and slave raiders were subordinated to lineage heads; military organization was defined by kin ties; and military functions were allocated, according to ascriptive formulas, to the heads of kinship units. Thus, existing social divisions were expanded to undertake new tasks commensurate with the crystallization of new centers (Chazan 1985).

A variant of such general congruence between organizational specialization and the articulation of elite functions can also be found in societies in which universalistic primordial and achievement criteria were prevalent alongside those of kinship. The Zulu, who developed very strong age regiments directly subordinate to the king alongside a parallel clan structure, evinced a preference for the concentration of elite solidarity and power functions within these two separate social organizations (Jatsy 1965; Ritter 1956; Thomas 1950). So did the

Ibadan Yoruba, whose lineage structure and military apparatus combined to create a center in which solidarity and power directly reflected the structural division of the society. In this case, the leadership of the city-state was drawn from kin leaders who had proven their military prowess or who had been among the military founders of the state (Henderson 1972).

A more complicated instance of such congruence was found among the Bambara (Apter 1967; Low 1971). Alongside age differentiation, other forms of association and secret societies appeared, such as the hunters' association *(donzo-ton)*, which, by virtue of their members' military training and their links with the bush spirits, performed an integrating role during sociopolitical disturbances and natural crises.

These institutions became the nuclei for the articulation of elite solidarity functions, with strong emphasis given to the task of expressing the solidarity of different collectivities.

In all of these instances, the basic elite functions corresponded to the principles of structural differentiation, and gave rise to a situation where the articulation of elite functions was deeply enmeshed in existing social structures and in the organization of the social division of labor.

In stark contrast, other African societies manifested a pattern of noncongruence between the articulators of elite functions and the organizational differentiation of society. Several types of noncongruence may be distinguished. One type, which is possibly the initial kind of separation between the structural differentiation of the social division of labor and elite functions, was evident in the crystallization of distinct articulators of existing kin-based models of cultural order in societies that had undergone processes of task specialization.

The Buganda, for example, were characterized by an organizational division of labor that increasingly diverged from the clan-based social foundation of the society—a distinction that, at the inception of the state, carried ethnic as well as ascriptive overtones. In that society distinct occupational groups, very salient bureaucratic functionaries, economic entrepreneurs, and kin leaders who progressively assumed specialized tasks reflective of the key areas of daily life emerged. Simultaneously, however, the articulators of meaning and the holders of power were concentrated in a single royal clan. This clan's leader, the Kabaka, was believed to have descended from the heavens and to embody in his person the major tenets of Buganda's cultural order. At the same time and despite horizontal hierarchies, the articulation of solidarity was vested in other clan leaders who maintained control in their areas and sent representatives to the *lukiko* (parliament).

In effect, then, the distinction between the articulation of solidarity and cultural models arose in contradistinction to the economic divisions between agriculturalists and pastoralists, between traders and producers, and between soldiers and citizens who effected major activities (Chazan and Abitbol 1985). It should be noted that distinct patterns of noncongruence were also apparent among the Oyo, Ife, Egba, Bambara, and Manding (see the literature cited in note 2; also Atanda 1977; Chazan and Abitbol 1985).

Conclusion: The Pattern of Center Formation, Elite Coalitions, and Cultural Orientations in Africa. Thus the distinction between structural differentiation and the differentiation of elite functions has helped to solve some of the problems for which the classical evolutionary approach is inadequate. First, this distinction has enabled us to analyze in greater detail both the variability of state forms in each stage of social differentiation and the relations of such variability to the transition between stages. Second, we have emphasized the importance of center formation as an autonomous dimension of social structure and have seen that different types of centers with distinct types of institutional dynamics, entailing different *modes* of differentiation, developed in congruent and noncongruent societies.

Different constellations of types of center distinctiveness and of center activities are closely related both to the patterns of elite coalitions that predominate in the centers and to the characteristics of their major elites, i.e., the degree to which they are autonomous or embedded in ascriptive units, or even act as representatives of such units in the society. The number of possible coalitions among various elites is, of course, very great.

The crucial aspect in the structure of these elites is the extent of their autonomy, especially in terms of self-identity and recruitment as against their being embedded in various narrow or broad ascriptive settings.

The elites' relative autonomy is very closely related to different types of cultural and societal visions. Here, a crucial advantage of our analysis is that it underscores the importance of cultural orientations, which are "carried" by various types of elites and coalitions, in shaping different patterns of centers and of institutional dynamics. Our approach is particularly sensitive to the distinction between perceptions of low or high degrees of tension between the transcendental and mundane orders, and to the direct or mediated access to the transcendental in shaping the contours and dynamics of different centers.

Thus, in most of the congruent societies in which embedded elites were predominant, the most prevalent cultural orientations emphasized a very low degree of tension between the transcendental and the mudane orders, whereas in most of the noncongruent societies the modal perception was of a very high degree of tension.

The impact of such cultural orientations or visions does not, however, occur through some direct "emanationism" but only through the activities of the different elites who carry these orientations, the structural characteristic of these elites, and their place in the coalitions dominant in particular centers. Thus, at least one crucial difference between the indigenous Islamic states and the jihad states was the internal structure of the Islamic elites, as well as their place in the ruling coalitions of their societies. Thus, in the Islamic states, Islamic elites were nonautonomous, secondary partners in existing coalitions, and highly embedded in ascriptive communities of their societies, while in the jihad states they were highly autonomous, independent partners in coalitions of relatively autonomous elites. Similarly, the relatively muted impact of the perception of tension between the transcendental and mundane orders on the structure and dynamics of the center in Solomonic Ethiopia was very closely connected to the vary limited autonomy of the Church in Ethiopia and the distance of Ethiopia from the centers of Christianity.

Finally, these factors are closely related to the ability of various states to generate and sustain different types of change which can be, at this stage, compared according to at least two criteria. First, model-based centers attempt to transform the existing social order, whereas organizational ones mainly regulate existing social relations, although they also develop new types of activities and extend their scope. Second, some states develop a capacity to sustain or absorb change over time, while other states do not exhibit a similar capacity.

These different patterns and dynamics of centers are also closely related to two closely interconnected analytical problems that we have touched upon above: the degree of convertibility of the major types of resources—wealth, power, and prestige—that develop in each of these resources and their capacity to incorporate such change.

Here it is interesting to note that the less autonomous the centers— especially in terms of their structural and symbolic dimensions—the stronger the tendency within them to convert resources between the different social units, and the easier it is for such units to convert the resources at their disposal into access to the center and to its power. This is, of course, closely related to the fact that within these centers there appeared only a few entirely autonomous criteria, or mechanisms, for structuring and controlling the flow of resources.

In contrast, the more structurally and symbolically autonomous the centers become the more there develops a distinct ruling class, which devises its own autonomous criteria and mechanisms for structuring and controlling the flow of resources. This development makes it more difficult for different sectors of the periphery to convert their resources into those of the center, especially in terms of power and prestige.

These different patterns of convertibility are also closely related to the modes of incorporation of change in different centers. The organizational centers of congruent societies are capable of absorbing a relatively wide range of new units or activities, either by incorporating them into existing units or by segregating them into distinct frameworks under their control.

The more autonomous centers become, the more they tend to concentrate on the restructuring of what can be called potential candidates for incorporation according to their own criteria. Consequently, they may become much more rigid in their attitude toward such units, often creating great tensions, conflicts, and opposition.

Thus the overall conclusion that emerges from this analysis is that the origins of the state are related not only to structural differentiation but also to its combination with the institutionalization of changes in the world view of a particular social group or society. It is the combination of symbolic and structural shifts that not only enables the initial breakthrough from a prestate to a state formation, from "early states" to more fully developed archaic ones, but also shapes the specific contents of the symbolic premises and institutional structures. These, in turn, are closely related to the degree to which congruent and noncongruent patterns subsequently evolve.

These closely connected cultural, social, and ecological changes are produced through the activities of different coalitions of elites. The articulators of models of cultural order and solidarity and the types of coalitions they form with political elites are of special significance.

The central importance of these articulators in the transition from one stage to another makes their specific characteristics and the nature of their position in the social system vital to understanding both the type of state (and its scope and further dynamics) that ensues and its ability to initiate, effect, and implement various types of change that are inherent by-products of state crystallization.

Comparative Urban Structure: Constantinople and Istanbul. The importance of these variables—of the distinction between the differentiation of the social division of labor and the articulation of coalitions of elites, cultural orientations, and *modes* of institutional differentiation and integration—is also evident in the analysis of cities and urban hierarchies in general, and particularly those of the historical civilizations (Eisenstadt and Schachar 1985).

Many classical sociological-anthropological analyses of cities and of urban hierarchies described differences between cities in terms of structural differentiation, focusing primarily on various urban zones and seeking to explain these differences largely in terms of evolutionary stages.[3]

The comparison between Constantinople and Istanbul, one of the most fascinating possible comparative cases, will be used to demonstrate the inadequacy of such an approach (see, for greater detail, Eisenstadt and Schachar 1985). The fascination of this comparison is twofold. First, we are examining two cities that, because they are in the same location, can also be seen as one city: the latter being built, despite the partial destruction, on the former; and both being in the same geopolitical zone and confronting many similar spatial and geopolitical problems. Both cities were capitals of great agrarian empires that shared many characteristics. The similarities of their agrarian and urban structures are especially significant in terms of structural differentiation (Eisenstadt 1963).

Yet despite these great similarities, there are very significant differences in some aspects of the structuring of urban space in these two cases. Moreover, these variations cannot be easily subsumed under the conventional rubric of structural differentiation, and highlight the need for revision of the classic model.

For the purposes of this comparison, the most important aspects of urban space are: first, the degree of centralization of city life and governance; second, the nature of the distinction between private and public space; and third, some aspects of residential and commercial quarters (see, for greater detail, Esienstadt and Schacher 1985).

The Conception of Cosmos and Empire and the Internal Structure of Constantinople. Constantinople (and later Istanbul) provides a very informative example of urban development under an imperial regime because, in many respects, it constituted the ideal type of an imperial city. Its imperial features were decisive in all phases and facets of its urbanization: in its origin, in the forces shaping its growth, in its plan and ecological structure, in its daily life, and in its relationship with the Church.

Constantinople's creation, its physical pattern, and its symbolic metaphors all stemmed from a relatively specific view of the cosmos —one perceived as a unitary political framework in which the empire was all-encompassing. The empire was headed, embodied, and represented, iconically and symbolically, by its center, the capital city, and by its creator and ruler. As an artifact, the city reflected the imperial cosmic pattern. Being created by the emperor, who was regarded as the representative of God on earth, the city became the holy center of the cosmos on earth. Its imperial character was mainly reflected by its size and the mode of control of the urban space. Its unparalleled size, both in area and in population, was due to the city's mastery over the empire's material resources. The effective control of urban space was realized physically through the planning of the city, its major outlines and areas being preserved and executed according to the imperial will.

The internal structure of Constantinople was defined by the various functions fulfilled by the city. As the imperial capital, the most important of the city's functions were: the protection of the regime and of the population; the provision of goods and services, as an expression both of the emperor's wealth and his responsibility for his subjects' welfare; the control of movement and activities within the urban framework; and, lastly, the symbolic-ritual role of structuring the environment, in which the emperor figured as God's representative on earth.

The protective role of Constantinople as an imperial city was manifest both in the physical features of the triangular site—the Sea of Marmara and the Golden Horn surrounding the peninsula on two sides—as well as by the complex system of walls, towers, and fortifications on its western land side. Walls built along the sea side of the city to offset any maritime attack provided additional strength to the city's defensive system. The walls also constituted a major source of control over the urban population. Movement into and out of the city through the gates could be channeled and supervised, and this allowed the imperial authorities to check and regulate the flow of travelers and merchants into the capital.

By residing in the imperial capital, inhabitants acquired the privilege of satisfying some of their basic needs through the generosity of the emperor. *Philanthropia* was one of the major traits of the emperor; the distribution of rich gifts in the wake of the ritual coronation ceremonies and the daily provision of food and water in several parts of the city were two of its manifestations. The most visible expression of the imperial city's role of provider was the great aqueduct of Valens, which cut through the city on a longitudinal axis from the Andrinople gate in the west through to the palace area at the eastern apex of the urban space, transporting water from Thrace over a long distance.

Similarly, the street pattern of Constantinople had two distinct levels. The upper one, planned and directed by the central authorities, was clearly demarcated and well maintained and provided the main arteries for processions and traffic in the city. This upper level array of main streets wedged in from the various city gates, focusing on the *Augusteum*, the apex of the the triangle, at the meeting point between the palace and Haghia Sophia. This street pattern, with the *Mese* forming its backbone, comprised the ceremonial sacred route, the governmental administrative axes, the specialized commercial avenues and the major squares, and the main points of interaction in the city. This wide avenue ran all the way from the main royal gate on the western wall—the Golden Gate—through the entire city, reaching the apex of the triangle at the *Augusteum*, the most important forum area, located between the royal palace and the church of Haghia Sophia.

The major functional and symbolic significance of this central avenue was enhanced by several fora placed at intervals along its length. Built as large squares surrounded by colonnades, the fora gave Constantinople a definite Greco-Roman character. These large, well-defined spaces were the main public meeting points of the urban population, preserving the old Roman traditions and providing the physical setting for the exhibition of the most prominent symbols of imperial power and authority: triumphal arches and tall columns supporting statues of the emperor. The fora were central points of interchange, interaction, trade, and entertainment as well as the foci of major political symbolism and participation. All of these activities were concentrated within a controlled space and under the symbolic supervision of the emperor. The fora represented, then, a special type of public space that combined the functions of centrality with a relative openness of public access and participation.

Toward the third side of the *Augusteum* was an entrance to the great hippodrome and its adjacent public baths. As the main center for public gatherings, ritual convocations, public protests, and all types of entertainment, the large hippodrome played a major role in the life of the population of Constantinople. It was here that the major factions *(demes)* waged their battles and organized their demonstrations.

From the Constantine Forum, the *Mese* led to a series of public squares where the numerous activities of the city's daily public life were held.

Branching out from the broad avenues of the upper level were the alleys that served the various neighborhoods and constituted the lower-level street system. Due to the scarcity of space and to the structures protecting the population from the severe climate and from intrusion by foreign elements, these alleys were narrow, winding, and tortuous but well fitted to the topography and the needs of the local population. These lower-level streets did not form a complete urban network, since they were used only by the local inhabitants, and did not connect the different neighborhoods.

From Constantinople to Istanbul. After fierce battles and a long siege Constantinople was taken over in 1453 by the forces of the Ottoman Sultan Mehmet II ("El Fatih"—The Conqueror), bringing to an end the long and illustrious history of the Byzantine Empire. Sultan Mehmet II transferred his government from Edirne (Andrinople) to Constantinople and made that city the capital of the Ottoman Empire. The imperial character of the city was thus preserved, although Constantinople changed from a Christian to a Muslim city.

Making Istanbul the capital of the Ottoman Empire and resettling its population brought about changes in the structure of the city and in its basic design and architecture.

The simplest and most natural of these various changes, and also the one that had the most visible effect, was the substitution of Islamic religious buildings, especially mosques, for the Byzantine churches. On occasion this was accomplished by the direct conversion of churches into mosques; more often it involved building new mosques. This type of substitution, though visible and impressive, was not a purely "external" one. It was connected to far-reaching changes in crucial aspects of the internal structure of the city, especially in the degree of centralization of and central control over its public spaces and in the structure of these public areas and their interrelation with private ones. These transformations were closely connected both with the basic Islamic religious and sociopolitical conceptions and with the structure of the elites and their modes of control, which contrasted sharply with those of the Byzantine Empire.

Concomitantly, a rather far-reaching transformation of the whole pattern of control over public lands and institutions occurred. This change was fully evident in the fact that most of the mosques and *madrassas* became *waqf*—public or private—foundations established (in most cases by the sultan) in perpetuity for these specific purposes. Taken away from the direct control of the central bureaucracy, these foundations became semiautonomous and were administered by special notables. The foundations combined both public and private functions in a manner typical, as we will see later, of most Islamic lands.

The establishment of these mosques and *madrassas* thus gave rise to a growing decentralization of urban life, particularly of public urban life. It also changed the relations between public and private land, weakening the distinction between them. By contrast, the Byzantine emperors had attempted to maintain that distinction.

In a parallel fashion, the functional structure of the city underwent a significant change with the transfer of commerce and shopping activities from the fora and the *Mese* to the covered bazaars, which were mainly situated north of the former Constantine Forum. These bazaars formed a unique concentration of thousands of shops and workshops offering an immense variety of goods unparalleled elsewhere in the Ottoman Empire and possibly the entire world. While the Suleymaniya complex fulfilled the central need for public services, the bazaars became the major center for commercial and economic activities.

The transformation of the street network was the last change brought to the city structure. While a relatively clear distinction existed in the Byzantine period between the upper level of streets—mainly the Mese and the wide avenues branching off it—and the alleys of the lower level, this distinction became blurred in the Ottoman period.The construction of private houses encroached on public space and narrowed the major arteries. With the deterioration of the broad avenues, the city lost its monumental axis. The emergence of the multicenters— the various imperial mosques and the bazaars—rendered the pattern of accessibility much more uniform; the network of alleys expanded and encompassed the whole city.

Concluding Remarks. Thus, despite the continuity of the imperial center and spatial locations, the transition from Constantinople to Istanbul produced a far-reaching transformation of several crucial aspects of the city's internal structure. Changes in the structure of public spaces as well as in the relations between the public and the private ones were especially significant.

First, a change occurred in the pattern of centralization of the imperial city, which transformed the overall centralization and control of the public spaces in Constantinople into a pattern of great decentralization around the different mosques and the sociocultural complexes surrounding them. Accordingly, the imperial palace lost its central controlling position.

Second, the nature of the public spaces was modified. During the Byzantine Empire, the overall character of public spaces was rooted in the combination of classical city-state and centralizing imperial traditions which included, in principle, all strata of the population and gave them the possibility of participating in public life. These public places assumed the more communal religious pattern characteristic of so many Islamic cities. These contrasting features of public space were intimately connected to the different relations existing between the political and religious elites in these two civilizations.

Third, change occurred in the relations between the public and the private spaces and was evident in the transformation of the street pattern as well as of the public spaces. These alterations were closely tied to the general pattern of decentralization and the establishment of *waqfs*.

These innovations indicated a general inward-turning tendency toward the closed family dwelling places, on the one hand, and, on the other, toward the communal-religious pattern, with the result that little space was left for specific overall urban, municipal—and imperial—public places.

Finally, there were modifications in the structure of the city's commercial pattern. The linear pattern, with a marked concentration in the fora along the main monumental axis, was transformed by the creation of a few bazaars whose location was strongly related to the main mosques. Each bazaar included a large number of commercial and artisanal enterprises that evinced a high degree of specialization.

On the whole, these changes were consistent with the general Islamic pattern of construction of urban life. At the same time, among all of the Islamic capitals, Istanbul probably stands out as the most imperial and the most centralized. This is probably closely connected to a tighter control over the *ulema* (to a degree unparalleled in any other Islamic state), and over the mostly foreign merchant and artisan groups.

The Axial Age Civilizations. The so-called Axial Age Civilizations (see Eisenstadt 1986) provide an unusually instructive substantive arena for the examination of both a) the difference between structural differentiation and the differentiation of elite structure and b) the variety of possible elite coalitions carrying different cultural visions or orientations. In addition, the impact of these elite coalitions on the institutional structure of their respective societies, on the *modes* of structural differentiation, and on the dynamics of these societies can also be assessed.

The term "Axial Age Civilization" (coined by Karl Jaspers) refers to those (great) civilizations that emerged in ancient Israel, in a variety of Christian settings, in ancient Greece, partially in Zoroastrian Iran, in China during the early imperial period, in Hindu and Buddhist South and Southeast Asia, and much later, beyond the Axial Age proper, in the Muslim world. These civilizations were characterized by the development and institutionalization of basic conceptions of tension and by a chasm between the transcendental and mundane orders.

These basic conceptions developed initially among small groups of "intellectuals" (who constituted, at the time, a new social element), and were closely related to very autonomous elites in general and to carriers of models of cultural and social order in particular. Ultimately, these conceptions were institutionalized in all of the Axial Age civilizations and became the predominant orientations of both the ruling and many secondary elites. These cultural visions were also fully institutionalized in their respective centers or subcenters. Such institutionalization made the intellectuals or cultural elites relatively autonomous partners in the central coalitions. Diverse clusters of intellectuals were transformed into more fully crystallized and institutionalized groups, especially groups of a clerical nature as exemplified by the Jewish prophets and priests, the great Greek philosophers, the Chinese literati, the Hindu Brahmins, the Buddhist Sangha, or the Islamic *ʾulama*. At the same time, the political elites were also transformed.

It was these autonomous elites that constituted the crucial new element in the institutionalization of these civilizations.

From our analytic perspective, the most central aspect of the Axial Age civilizations was that they exhibited, even if in different ways, noncongruent characteristics: they were characterized by a sharp distinction between the differentiation in the social division of labor and that of the articulation of elite functions.

In this regard they differed from the other "congruent" types of more "developed" or archaic societies that existed in many ancient patrimonial societies—e.g., ancient Egypt, which is probably the best illustration; city-states such as those of ancient Phoenecia; and various more decentralized tribal federations (Eisenstadt 1972). In such congruent societies the transition from one stage of political development to another (e.g., from early state to archaic kingdom) has usually been connected with the reconstruction and widening of the kinship and/or territorial elements and ascriptive categories and symbols, with the growing importance of territorial units as opposed to purely kinship ones, and with what may be called the qualitative extension and diversification of basic cosmological conceptions. It was also characterized by the increasing specialization of elites (who have, on the whole, been embedded in various—and even very complex and wide-ranging—ascriptive units), by a close correspondence between structural differentiation and the differentiation of elite functions, and by the prevalence of cultural models and conceptions containing relatively low levels of tension between the transcendental and mundane orders.

The mode of social differentiation that developed in these congruent societies featured the crystallization of centers that were ecologically and organizationally, but not symbolically, distinct from the periphery. Such patrimonial centers crystallized around elites who were enmeshed in various types of ascriptive units, often broad and reconstructed ones, and who carried cultural orientations characterized by a relatively low degree of tension between the cosmic and the mundane orders (see Eisenstadt 1970).

In contrast, the Axial Age civilizations were marked by growing distinctions, even discrepancies, between the structural differentiation of the social division of labor and the differentiation of elite functions. In addition these societies witnessed the emergence of autonomous elites and concomitantly more radical developments or breakthroughs in cultural orientations, especially in the direction of the radical conception of the tension between the mundane and the transcendental orders. At the same time, different modes of social differentiation appeared and were characterized by the restructuring of many crucial institutional formations, including: special, distinct, civilizational, or religious collectivities; different types of autonomous centers distinct from their peripheries; and ideological politics.

The Variety of Axial Age Civilizations.   Congruent patterns could be found in a great variety of societies and regimes. However, an even greater variety of centers existed in the noncongruent societies that developed in the Axial Age civilizations: full-fledged empires (e.g., the Chinese, Byzantine, or Ottoman); rather fragile kingdoms or tribal federations (e.g., ancient Israel); combinations of tribal settings of city-states (e.g., ancient Greece); the complex decentralized pattern of the Hindu civilization; or the complex imperial and imperial-feudal configurations of Europe.

But, and perhaps even more important from the point of view of our analysis, many far-reaching differences in institutional structures, the modes of structural differentiation, and institutional dynamics appeared within the different patrimonial settings but especially in the Axial Age civilizations.

The major difference, especially among Axial Age civilizations, was of course between imperial and more decentralized systems—of which India and feudal Europe, respectively, are the most important illustrations. However, great differences also arose within each of these types, with each general type denoting different patterns of structural differentiation and its relation to the articulation of elite functions (for further analysis and documentation see Eisenstadt 1978).

In India a very high degree of differentiation of the religious elite and a lower degree of differentiation of the political elite appeared. By contrast, there was a relatively small degree of differentiation of political roles of the broader strata. Similarly, within the imperial agrarian regimes far-reaching differences in the structure of their centers and the mode of their differentiation emerged, despite the fact that they shared rather similar degrees (and relatively high ones for historical societies) of structural and organizational differentiation in the economic and social spheres.

Thus, when we compare the Byzantine Empire and the Ottoman Empire—although, as distinct from patrimonial regimes, the degree of structural differentiation and of specific elite activities was very high and to some extent similar for these two civilizations—far-reaching differences between these empires in the structure of their centers and different elite functions are readily apparent. Thus, in the Chinese empire there was no distinction between administrative-bureaucratic and religious elites. In the Byzantine empire the differentiation between state and church and also that between the civil and military autocracy, as well as the autonomy of agrarian and some urban groups, were relatively great. In the Ottoman Empire the division between church and state was structured in a different way; it did not exist as an ideal but was, de facto, very important.

The concrete contours of these centers and their dynamics varied considerably according to the precise structure of the predominant elites, the cultural orientations they carried, and the modes of control they exercised. They also varied, of course, according to different organizational, economic, technological, and geopolitical conditions.

Of special interest from the standpoint of our discussion is the fact that it is possible to identify some similarities between the varieties of elites and coalitions and the dynamics of centers in these more developed societies and those identified in the various African cases.

Thus, in the noncongruent societies of the Axial Age civilizations, such as India, we find strong symbolic centers coupled with relatively weak political centers, as in Africa, but with a very sharp articulation of models of cultural order and a strong emphasis on the maintenance of the solidarity of ascriptive units. Similarly, many of the Islamic centers developed characteristics similar to those we have identified in some of the Islamic states in Africa. (Needless to say, in the whole realm of Islamic civilization a greater variety of centers developed than we found in Africa.)

Conclusion

One starting point of the present discussion—as against that of the 1960s—was to emphasize the importance of (a) the analysis of institutional structure in general and of social differentiation in particular and (b) the distinction between the differentiation of the social division of labor and the articulation of the various elite functions. We also asserted that the different patterns that that distinction can assume may have far-reaching repercussions on the institutional formation of different societies and the modes of differentiation within them.

Thus our analysis indicated, first, that at all levels and in all types of technological and economic development and structural differentiation it is the interaction between these aspects of the social division of labor and the activities of the major elites that generates the different patterns and dynamics of centers and institutional formations. Second, at any given level or in any given type of differentiation or social division of labor there may have developed, in different circumstances, a very wide variety of such patterns. Third, the differences in such dynamics are principally shaped by the crystallization of different coalitions of elites. Finally, some aspects of such dynamics may be relatively similar (even if they can never be exactly the same) across different levels and types of the social division of labor and social differentiation.

All of these considerations are closely related to the distinction between the social division of labor and the articulation of elite functions. In this presentation we have focused primarily on the impact of the construction of meaning by—especially, but not only—cultural elites. Parallel analyses could be attempted with respect to the construction of solidarity, the regulation of power, and their respective careers.

Thus the central point in our analysis is that each aspect of construction of social order, including "culture," has its own "symbolic" tendencies toward differentiation, and each possesses its own tendency toward autonomous development. These tendencies cannot be assumed either to be always concomitant with those that develop in the social division of labor, nor can they be subsumed under it. Instead, this very aspect of the institutional structure may, as we have seen, give rise to different *modes* of social differentiation and different types of institutional dynamics. It may also well be the case that they serve as independent causes of differentiation, not only in their respective spheres but also in the overall institutional structure. But this is already beyond the scope of the analysis presented in this paper; it should, however, constitute a central problem for theoretical and comparative sociological analysis in the future.

Notes

1. Chazan and Abitbol (1985). For good material on the Manding, see Hodge (1971). The best work on the Samori is Person (1968).
2. Busia (1953). See also Wilks (1975, 1977); Quartey (1977); Henderson (1972); and Gluckman (1975).
3. See, for instance, Childe (1950, 1954); Kraeling and MacAdams (1958); MacAdams (1966); Park, Burgess, and McKenzie (1925); and the analysis of this literature in Eisenstadt and Schachar (1985), ch. 1 and Sjoberg (1960).

References

Apter, D. 1967. *The Political Kingdom in Uganda*. Princeton, N.J.: Princeton University Press.

Atanda, J. A. 1977. *The New Oyo Empire*. London: Longman.

Balandier, G. 1968. *Daily Life in the Kingdom of the Kongo from the Sixteenth to Seventeenth Centuries*. New York: Pantheon.

——1969. *Anthropologie Politique*. Paris: Presses Universitaires de France.

Busia, K. A. 1968. *The Position of the Chief in the Modern Political System of Ashanti*. London: Frank Case.

Chazan, N. 1985. "The Early State in Africa: An Asante Case." In Eisenstadt, Abitbol, and Chazan, *The Origins of the State*.

Chazan, N. and M. Abitbol. 1985. "Myths and Politics in Pre-Colonial Africa." In Eisenstadt, Abitbol, and Chazan, *The Origins of the State*.

Childe, Gordon V. 1950. "The Urban Revolution." *Town Planning Review* (April), 21:3–17.

——1954. "Early Forms of Society." In C. Singer et al., eds., *A History of Technology*. Oxford: Clarendon Press.

Cohen, R. 1978. "State Origins: A Reappraisal." In H. Claessen and P. Skalnik, eds., *Early State*. The Hague: Mouton.

Cohen, R. and E. R. Service, eds. 1978. *Origins of the State; The Anthropology of Political Evolution*. Philadelphia, Pa.: Institute for the Study of Human Issues.

Eisenstadt, S. N. 1963. *The Political Systems of Empires*. New York: Free Press.

——1964. "Social Change, Differentiation, and Evolution." *American Sociological Review* 29(3):395–96.

——1968a. "Social Evolution." *International Encyclopedia of the Social Sciences*, 5:227–34. New York: Collier MacMillan.

——1968b. "Charisma and Institution Building: Max Weber and Modern Sociology." In S. N. Eisenstadt, ed., *Max Weber on Charisma and Institution Building*, pp. xi–lvi. Chicago, Ill.: University of Chicago Press.

——1972. *Traditional Patrimonialization and Modern Neo-Patrimonialization*. Beverly Hills, Calif.: Sage.

——1978. *Revolution and the Transformation of Societies*. New York: Free Press.

——1982. "The Axial Age: The Emergence of Transcendental Visions and the Rise of Clerics." *European Journal of Sociology* 23(2):294–314.

——1985a. "Macro-Societal Analysis—Background Development and Indications. In S. N. Eisenstadt and H. J. Helle, eds. *Perspectives on Macrosociological Theory*, vol. 1, pp. 7–24. Beverly Hills, Calif.: Sage.

Eisenstadt, S. N., ed. 1970. *Political Sociology*. New York: Basic Books.

Eisenstadt, S. N., ed. 1986. *The Origins and Diversity of Axial Age Civilizations*. Albany: State University of New York Press.

Eisenstadt, S. N., M. Abitbol, and N. Chazan 1985a. "Considerations and Introduction to African Cases. In Eisenstadt, Abitbol, and Chazan, *The Origins of the State*.

——1985b. *The Origins of the State*. Philadelphia: Asili.

Eisenstadt, S. N. and H. J. Helle, eds. 1985. *Perspectives on Macrosociological Theory*. Beverly Hills, Calif. and London: Sage.

Eisenstadt, S. N. and J. A. Schachar. 1985. *Society, Culture, and Urbanization*. Beverly Hills, Calif. and London: Sage.

Engels, F. 1942 (1884). *The Origins of the Family, Private Property, and the State.* New York: International Publishers.

Friedman, J. and M. J. Rowlands, eds. 1977. *The Evolution of Social Systems.* London: Duckworth.

Gluckman, M. 1940. "The Kingdom of the Zulu." In M. Fortes and E. E. Evans-Pritchard, eds., *African Political Systems*. pp. 25–55. London: Oxford University Press.

Godelier, M. 1973. *Horizons, Trajets Marxistes en Anthropologie*. Paris: Maspero.

Guy, T. 1979. *The Destruction of the Zulu Kingdom*. London: Longman.

Henderson, R. N. 1982. *The King in Every Man. Evolutionary Trends in Onitsha Ibo Society and Culture.* New Haven, Conn.: Yale University Press.

Hodge, T., ed. 1971. *Papers on the Manding.* Bloomington: Indiana University Press.

Horton, R. 1971. "Stateless Societies in the History of West Africa." In J. P. A. Ajayi and M. Crowder, eds., *History of West Africa*, vol. 1. London: Longman.

Jatsy, Marie-France Perrin. 1965. "Un Etat Militaire: Cas des Zoulou." Paper presented at the Centre d'Etudes Africaines, Paris, March 5, 1965.

Kraeling, Carl H. and R. MacAdams, eds. 1958. *City Invincible*, Chicago, Ill.: University of Chicago Press.

Low, D. A. 1971. *Buganda in Modern History*. London: Weidenfeld and Nicholson.

Lowie, R. H. 1947. *Primitive Society*. New York: Liveright.

MacAdams, R. 1966. *The Evolution of Urban Society.* London: Weidenfeld and Nicholson.

Oppenheimer, F. 1926. *The State: Its History and Development Viewed Sociologically.* New York: Vanguard.

Park, Robert E., Ernest W. Burgess, and Roderick D. McKenzie. 1925. *The City,* Chicago, Ill.: University of Chicago Press.

Parsons, T. 1966. *Societies: Evolutionary and Comparative Perspectives*. Englewood Cliffs, N.J.: Prentice-Hall.

Person, Y. 1968. *Samori: Une Revolution Ryula.* Dakar: Memoires de l'Institut Fondamental de l'Afrique Noire.

Quartey, S. M. 1977. "Developments of the Social Geography of Ahanteland Before 1600." *Ghanga Social Science Journal* 4(1):117–27.

Ritter, E. A. 1956. *Shake Zulu: The Rise of the Zulu Empire.* London: Green.

Roberts, B. 1974. *The Zulu Kings.* London: Hamilton.

Service, E. R. 1975. *Origins of the State and Civilization: The Process of Cultural Evolution.* New York: Norton.

Shils, E. 1975a. "Charisma." In E. Shils, ed., *Center and Periphery: Essays in Macrosociology*, pp. 127–35. Chicago, Ill.: University of Chicago Press.

——1975b. "Charisma, Order, and States." In E. Shils, ed., *Center and Periphery: Essays in Macrosociology*, pp. 256–76. Chicago, Ill.: University of Chicago Press.

Sjoberg, G. 1960. *The Pre-Industrial City.* New York: Free Press.

Spencer, H. 1925–1929 (1876–1894). *The Principles of Sociology.* 3 vols. New York: Appleton.

Thomas, A. 1950. *A History of the Zulu and Neighboring Tribes.* Ann Arbor, Mich.: University Microfilms International.

Vansina, *Kingdoms of the Savanna.*

Wilks, I. 1975. *Asante in the Nineteenth Century: The Structure and Evolution of a Political Order.* London: Cambridge University Press.

——1977. "Land, Labour, Capital, and the Forest Kingdom of Asante: A Model of Early Change." In Friedman and Rowlands, *The Evolution of Social Systems,* pp. 486–534.

2

Culture, Differentiation, and Environment: Social Change in Tlingit Society

Duane Champagne

There are presently sixteen thousand natives of southeast Alaska, primarily Tlingit, who have during the present century responded to world market incorporation and colonial domination with increased political and economic differentiation, while preserving core aspects of their traditional culture, values, and social organization. For over two centuries southeast Alaska natives have participated in world economic markets. During the present century the Tlingit have organized a political center and formed a separate bureaucratic-political institution that manages their political relations with the U.S. government. Furthermore, since the early 1970s the southeast Alaska natives have controlled a multimillion-dollar corporation with sales that have in recent years placed it on the Fortune 1,000 list. Nevertheless, Tlingit social and ceremonial relations continue to be upheld by traditional kinship groups and contemporary potlatch ceremonies. How is it possible to account for the pattern of differentiation, dependency, and sociocultural continuity in Tlingit society?

In order to account for social change in the Tlingit case, a comprehensive argument involving internal cultural, political, economic, and

I gratefully acknowledge research and writing support from the Rockefeller Foundation and National Science Foundation grant number RII 85-03914.

social relations must be combined with an analysis of geopolitical and dependency relations. Several recent theories of social change, both Marxist and functionalist, have moved toward convergence on the issue of using both exogenous and endogenous variables in an explanation for social change. Neo-Marxists have criticized functionalist theory for its primary emphasis on internal variables. Wolf (1982) argues that anthropology and sociology analyze societies as autonomous entities that do not have important interrelations or dependencies. He emphasizes that societies are open systems and that because of the rise in the last several centuries of world economic trade and markets, societies, especially those outside the Western world, must not be considered as isolated, integrated, and bounded systems that have few relations with other equally bounded and integrated societies or social systems (Wolf 1982:4–6). Furthermore, Giddens (1979:222–24) argues that Parsonian functionalism presents an "unfolding" model of social change, a model that "treats social change as the progressive emergence of traits that a particular society is presumed to have within itself from its inception" (Giddens 1979:223). Unfolding models of social change concentrate on endogenous factors as causes of social change. In many respects, Parsons' theory of societal evolution is an unfolding model, since it views social change as increasing specialization and the autonomy of primary subsystems' functions. Nisbet (1969:251), rejecting the unfolding model, argues that significant social change derives only from external events. Giddens argues, however, that an emphasis on exogenous sources of social change tends to treat societies as internally closed systems.

Neo-Marxist dependency and world system theorists have taken an externally open system approach to the study of social change. The neo-Marxist arguments, however, have concentrated on analyzing the internal relations of dependent societies in terms of class structure or mode of production. While such an approach presents an interesting hypothesis, it leaves the analysis open to the functionalist criticism that a Marxist class or mode-of-production argument treats societies as internally closed systems. Eisenstadt and Curelaru (1976:95) argue that Marxist theory has the characteristics of a closed rather than an open system approach because it tends to assume a relatively invariant relation between modes-of-production and political power and other aspects of the societal superstructure. An internally open system approach would allow norms, values, cultures, and political systems to have variable relations with the mode of production or the economic organization of a society.

An analytical framework that incorporated the open system aspects of dependency theory and the functionalist open system approach to the study of internal societal relations would have the potential to account for a greater amount of variation in social change than can either the neo-Marxist and functionalist theories, taken individually. Both the neo-Marxist and functionalist theories are currently exploring the possibilities of a more internally-externally open system of theory of social change.

Neo-Marxist Theories

Much recent sociological theory has emphasized the primacy of economic dependency and location within the world market system as major determinants of economic and political organization in less developed or peripheral societies (Bollen 1983; Amin et al. 1982). Recent criticism of the dependency approach within the Marxist tradition has emphasized that dependency theory, like earlier theories of imperialism, has failed to provide an adequate understanding of the impact of the world market on the internal sociopolitical order of non-European societies (Chilcote 1983:20, 25). Major criticisms of the dependency argument have suggested that it is overly economistic and conceptualizes "the colonized/imperialized world [as] a mere object of external determination, and not as a variegated system of historically constituted and very real social formations" (Ahmad 1983:40). Some recent theoretical trends have shifted their emphasis from external world market relations toward internal class and mode-of-production arguments (Wolf 1982; Quijano 1983; Chilcote and Johnson 1983). Furthermore, these arguments more closely approximate an internally-externally open system approach by their analytical consideration of international economic processes that account for the formation of new classes—new local capitalist classes, proletarians, and semiproletarians (Veltmeyer 1983:204). Chinchilla (1983:163) approaches a more internally-externally open system argument: while she suggests that the overall determinant for a change is economic, she allows for the possibility that political and ideological structures may make independent contributions to change and that precapitalist cultural and collective institutions may persist and become associated with the new capitalist formations introduced by the interpenetration of international capital. She argues that the articulation of the mode of production approach, which focuses on how internal social structures (classes and states) are influenced by dependency relations, is more capable of explaining the variation of social formations in third world societies than are the evolutionary Marxist mode of production argument, the externally deterministic world system argument, or the unilinear convergence arguments of modernization and Parsonian theory.

Skocpol (1979), following Hintze (1976), argues that uneven development within the world division of labor is a secondary factor in determining the causes of social revolutions. For Skocpol, situations in a society's geopolitical environment (defeat in war, imperial invasion and subordination) are major causes of crisis that can lead to loss of legitimacy by groups critical to the state's capacity to cope with competition from other nation-states or with tasks thrust upon it by changing world political and economic conditions (Skocpol 1979:32). The specific outcome of a state crisis will depend on the organization of the state, the internal class structure, and state and society relations.

Thus some neo-Marxists have moved toward a systematic consideration of both internal and external forces within the same framework in order to more adequately understand the empirical variation in the economic and political formations in third world societies. The neo-Marxist arguments of Skocpol and the articulation-of-production argument emphasize dependency and geopolitics while attempting to utilize a more open system approach to state and class relations. Generally, however, there is little systematic analysis of culture, values, and norms as independent variables in the neo-Marxist theories; a comprehensive internally-externally open system argument must at least consider these as potential explanatory variables.

Differentiation Theory

While neo-Marxist theories have emphasized world market and geopolitical perspectives, functionalists have continued to stress the primacy of social structure and culture in social change processes. Although Parsons does not provide a theory of societal change as a response to changing geopolitical and economic conditions, he does offer a relatively comprehensive theory of social action and an evolutionary theory of functional differentiation. Parsons (1977a:285–86) argues not only that more modern societies are more differentiated or complex, but, more specifically, that they differentiate according to system functions. Thus societies will tend to develop by forming increasingly autonomous and specialized cultural, political, economic, and integrative institutions. More differentiated societies will have greater capacities to mobilize resources and effect collective goals and will develop increasing autonomy in relation to environmental contingencies (Bellah 1964). The appealing aspect of Parsons' theory, from the point of view of the search for an open internal-external argument, is that his theory specifies a relatively comprehensive set of interrelated factors. Parsons' framework allows for the potential mutual differentiation of all four major functions of the social system: the polity, the economy, the societal community, and the pattern maintenance system, as well as the differentiation on the general action level between the social, cultural, and personality systems. Such an argument approaches the internally open system approach, since it conceptualizes more relations as potentially variable.

In several ways, however, Parsons' theory conceptualizes a limited view of the environment. Using a biological analogy, Parsons' paradigm assumes that more internally stable social systems react to their environments through interchanges and adjustments of internal functions in order to accommodate and adapt to changing conditions in the external environment. Parsons (1977a:230) tends to conceptualize a physico-organic environment as devoid of other social, political, or economic systems. Parsons' social system operates in a transsocietal vacuum, where its interchanges with the environment are primarily concerned with physical inputs. The personality system and the adaptive and goal attainment functions manage relations with the environment, but Parsons does not systematically analyze the possibility that more than one social system is active in the environment, or that some societies may be politically, culturally, and/or economically subordinated or dependent on other societies.

While Parsons tends to ignore unequal development and geopolitical relations, he (1977a:51–52; 1977b:114) argues, following Weber, that cultural systems can gain relative autonomy from particular societies and have influence on societal developments across history and territory. Parsons' main examples are the influence of secular Greek philosophy, the Greek notion of citizen within the city-state polis, rational Roman law, and the Hebrew concept of moral religious community, all of which contributed to the formation of modern secular culture, nationalism, and normative order. Parsons' main contribution to understanding external influences of social change derive from the cultural sphere. Not all functionalists have neglected the relations between internal and external sources of change; Johnson (1966:65–67, 92) argues that changes in the environment (colonial domination, market incorporation, the introduction of new value systems, demographic changes) will create demands that the system be adjusted through political action. Johnson's theory of disequilibrium and readjustment handles transsocietal "environmental" relations more concretely than Parsons, but Johnson does not concern himself with processes of differentiation.

Badie and Birnbaum (1983:58–59) argue that the concept of differentiation is not itself an explanatory variable, but rather that specific modes of differentiation are determined in precise historical contexts, which are related to the combined impacts of market and economic transformations, the breakdown of traditional forms of authority, international market relations, and the resistance of traditional elements of the society. A proposed differentiation, however, may not be accepted at all, and its introduction may lead to conflict between proponent and opposition groups (Eisenstadt 1964:246–47). For Eisenstadt, the process of differentiation is carried out by specific groups, who must rely on other groups to provide resources and commitments to newly differentiated and institutionalized structures. Since commitments to similar values and norms may not be equally shared between rival groups, differentiation is beset with conflict, since some groups may not be willing to contribute to the new structure. The innovators must solve the problems of creating and maintaining new levels of social integration through the creation and maintenance of cultural legitimation for their proposed change. Innovators may be countered by competing groups or fundamentalists, who wish to resist change or propose alternative solutions, or wish to accept a slower rate of change (Eisenstadt 1964:246–47). Thus the process of differentiation involves specific historical conditions and direct struggles between groups, who carry alternative cultural models as solutions for change.

Thus some recent work on the theory of differentiation indicates that the unfolding or evolutionary theory of societal differentiation must be extended beyond conceptualization of the environment in terms of the physico-organic environment; it must also include consideration of the impacts of transsocietal economic, political, and cultural relations as potential causes of differentiation. Furthermore, the process of differentiation and institutionalization must be explained by specific historical causal sequences that result from the interaction or struggles of groups within the society.

Culture

Eisenstadt (1978:196–204) argues that world political competition, a changing world capitalist economy, and internal pressures and conflicts can give rise to loss of legitimacy or conditions of relative deprivation that are associated with a variety of societal outcomes such as the collapse of regimes, revolutions, or relatively smooth transitions to modernity. He argues, however, that in addition to analyzing the specific historical conditions of changing state and world market relations that can lead to a widespread loss of legitimacy in existing sociopolitical institutions, an analysis of major cultural orientations and world views, in addition to the structural organization of society, will lead to a theory that will be capable of explaining more variation in the empirical range of societal change responses. Eisenstadt argues that within a given level of structural differentiation there is considerable variation in cultural orientations and world views. Accordingly, a predominantly structural argument (class, division of labor, level of structural differentiation) cannot support a general theory of social change. This view claims that there is a close connection between basic cultural orientations, the organizational basis of society, and the type of response a society will have to modernization problems, or to incorporation into transsocietal economic or political systems.

Weber and Eisenstadt (Eisenstadt 1978:13) focus on how cultural orientations provide guidelines for the participation and organization of political and economic institutions. For example, Weber argues that Calvinist doctrine created new orientations that gave religious legitimation to acceptance of a calling and the ascetic accumulation of wealth for economic reinvestment, both of which contributed to the breakdown of traditional capitalism and the development of rational capitalism. Weber (1981:369) indicates, however, that by the beginning of the nineteenth century Western economic behavior had been stripped of its religious foundations. While the Protestant Ethic thesis may be appropriate for understanding the initial breakthrough to rational capitalism or modern society, the features of non-Western cultural systems that support market participation, social solidarity, and political centralization may be more appropriate areas of focus in a world where capitalism already prevails and transsocietal political and economic relations have become increasingly dominant.

In summary, recent literature suggests the possibility of constructing an internally-externally open system framework for analyzing social change. Such a framework must include consideration of transsocietal geopolitical relations, incorporation of the world economy, and the interpenetration of transsocietal cultural systems. Furthermore, while not denying the Marxist mode of production hypothesis, an internally open system must consider the independent analytical contribution of culture, values, norms, and social integration. More specifically, I have tried to combine differentiation theory with an externally open system argument, which requires consideration of world economic market incorporation, geopolitical relations, and transsocietal cultural relations as conditions that may contribute to further societal differentiation. In the case study of social change in Tlingit society, I wish to show that the dependency, geopolitical, and unfolding differentiation theories cannot, individually, account for the economic and political differentiation of Tlingit institutions and, at the same time, account for the centrality and continuity of core aspects of Tlingit culture and social organization. It is suggested that an internally-externally open system model will be more appropriate for understanding social change in Tlingit society.

The Tlingit Case Study

There are considerable ethnographic and historical materials on the Tlingit. Much of the analytical work on the Tlingit and other northwest Alaska societies has focused on explaining the economic behavior of the potlatch or "giveaway." In exchange for social prestige, a host chief distributed blankets, copper plates, and slaves, often leaving himself and family with few worldly possessions. For a recent review of the literature on explaining potlatch behavior see Sequin (1985). The interpretation of potlatch behavior given in the present paper, which draws its inspiration from Weber and Parsons, focuses on culture and values. The Tlingit potlatch is seen as a cult for honoring clan ancestors.

Kinship groups formed the societal community of early Tlingit society (de Laguna 1952:2–7). There were two matrilineal exogamous moieties—Raven and Eagle (some groups use Wolf)—and both contained about twenty-five clans. The clans and moieties were distributed over villages and thirteen territorial groupings or "tribes." Both moieties were represented in every village, although a clan was often represented in only one or two villages. Moieties regulated marriage and ceremonial obligations. Clan members considered themselves descendants of a single maternal line that shared a common name and historical-mythological tradition (de Laguna 1977:451). The clans were further divided into one or more houses which included from two to eight families. The ties between villages and between houses even in the same clan were relatively weak (Oberg 1973:40). The house groups were the major political, economic, social, and ceremonial units in Tlingit society. Each house held territory and owned myths, crests, songs, dances, and other distinctive ensignia.

Tlingit social order was maintained by mutual reciprocities and obligations between moieties, clans, and houses. The moiety-clan organization and reciprocal relations were directly legitimated by Tlingit myths (McClellan 1954:83–86, 96). The mythical figure Raven is credited with creating the moiety system and for instituting the potlatch ceremonies which, as will be seen, bind the houses, clans, and moieties into economic, social, and cultural reciprocities.

The shared culture, myths, and norms of moiety-clan relations did not, however, necessarily ensure harmonious relations between the Tlingit clans and houses. Relations between the clans and territorial groups were often antagonistic and competitive. During potlatch ceremonies, if proper respect was not shown or one house humiliated the other by gifts that were too small, by incorrect dancing, or by knowing more songs than the other houses, potlatches could break into open conflict between antagonistic houses. On such occasions the host house would try to stop the fighting by intervening with a display of its moiety crest, either Eagle or Raven, while imploring the combatants to respect this common symbol of peace and solidarity (Billman 1969:60). Past incidents of humiliation, disrespect, and feud were incorporated into the traditions of each clan and caused friction whenever members of traditionally antagonistic clans came together. Similarly, villages were not necessarily harmonious social groupings but were composed of politically and economically autonomous houses that jealously protected their social, economic, and political prerogatives. House, clan, and territorial antagonism toward outside groups served to intensify within-group identity and clarify group boundaries (Coser, 1956:33).

Clans, houses, and individuals were ranked in Tlingit society, and all ranks were validated through distributions of wealth in potlatch ceremonies (Rosman and Rubel 1972; Averkieva 1971). Consequently, the accumulation of wealth—copper plates, blankets, slaves, and certain kinds of shells—were a necessary condition for a man, and his house, to properly legitimate social status and succession in rank. The distribution of wealth through the potlatch ceremony was a primary criteria for legitimating individual and house rank. Without enough wealth to properly legitimate succession to chieftainship, both the new chief and the house lost rank and prestige (Olsen 1967:6). Many men could not give a potlatch during their lifetimes, and for some men the giving of one potlatch might be the high point of their lives. Men of wealthy or aristocratic lineages might give several potlatches, while a man who gave eight potlatches was considered a "prince" (Salisbury 1962). The social standings of individuals and houses were open to change and depended on the individuals' and houses' ability to distribute wealth in fulfilling their potlatch obligations.

Culture and the Social Community

Tlingit society was characterized by social and economic inequality at both the individual and house levels. Rank and hierarchy in Tlingit society were legitimated by the value of honoring clan ancestors with a potlatch, and by the Tlingit world view, which incorporated a belief in rebirth.

Weber (1958:18ff) and others (Coser 1956:37) argue that the belief in rebirth in Buddhist and Hindu religion serves to legitimate inequalities in political and social organization. Although caste relations may be antagonistic, members of the lower caste groups perform their caste duties (dharma) in the belief that in their next rebirth or reincarnation they will be born into a caste of higher rank. To neglect caste obligations threatens the individual with a decline in caste rank or even nonhuman rebirth. Compared to Tlingit society, the Hindu belief system legitimizes a vastly more differentiated economic division of labor and much greater differentiation of political and cultural roles. In Tlingit society there were shamen, but there was no specialized priesthood who rationalized the meaning of the rebirth belief, and there were no centralized political structures or differentiated leadership that materially and politically benefited from the social stability that accompanied the rebirth belief, as did the upper warrior castes and patrimonial political structures of ancient India (Weber 1983:89). Nevertheless, the Tlingit belief in rebirth serves a similar role in legitimizing social and economic inequality.

The Tlingit believed that the soul of the deceased returned to earth and was reborn as a female of the same clan. There was the possibility of social mobility through rebirth, since one could be reborn into a house or lineage that had higher rank and wealth; "therefore some Tlingit who are dissatisfied with their lot are supposed to express the wish that they may die soon so that they can start over again under more favorable conditions by being born into the clan of some envied chief" (Krause 1956:193; see Stevenson 1966a:234). Individuals of wealthy and prestigious lineages needed to make sure, through properly performing clan obligations, that they were reborn within the same family and thus again under favorable social circumstances (Stevenson 1966a:231). Men who sacrificed their lives in war could be assured of a higher rebirth and a relatively quick return to earthly existence. To be killed in battle or to allow oneself to be executed in fulfillment of clan obligations to the law of blood ensured that one had a happy situation in the next world and a speedy return to a socially favorable earthly existence (Stevenson 1966a:234, 1966b:197; Oberg 1960:290–95). According to the Tlingit law of blood, the victim's clan, in cases of murder, would demand not necessarily the life of the murderer but the life of a man of social rank equal to that of the victim. Any man who allowed himself to be executed in fulfillment of clan obligations to the offended clan was given a highly honorable funeral and was said to have entered "highest heaven." Thus, in the latter instance, the belief system directly legitimated the performance of clan roles and obligations with promises of both otherworldly and this-worldly rewards. The Tlingit belief in rebirth provided a theodicy or rationalization and legitimation of rank, inequality, wealth, and misfortune. If a man faithfully performed his clan obligations and continued to suffer earthly misfortunes or low caste, he could expect a better social situation in his next rebirth.

Tlingit rebirth beliefs had a strong this-worldly orientation. The primary goal was not to achieve salvation in heaven, as in Christianity, or to escape the wheel of life, as in the Hindu religion, but rather to use the rebirth mechanism for social mobility within one's clan. One hoped to be quickly reborn within an aristocratic lineage in order to command social prestige, wealth, and honor. The Tlingit did not have a conception of salvation as a means to escape earthly life and imperfections, but rather affirmed enjoyment of this-worldly social position as a greater good than otherworldly existence.

In addition to the belief in rebirth, the potlatch validated individual, house, and clan rank. In Tlingit society potlatches served to honor the dead and provide payment for funeral services performed by members of the opposite moiety (de Laguna 1977:611). Whenever someone died, relatives from houses of the opposite moiety managed the funeral rites and the cremation of the body. The deceased's house and moiety were not allowed to handle the remains. The related houses of the opposite moiety provided food, clothes, and comfort to the bereaved house. The deceased was symbolically prepared for travel in the next world and had to be supplied with appropriate food, clothes, shoes, and weapons, all of which were cremated with him and were considered to aid him in his extraterrestrial travels.

After a period of mourning, during which the bereaved house gathered wealth, the houses that contributed to the funeral expenses were invited to a potlatch. If a house chief had died, his successor would hold a major potlatch. The potlatch ceremony itself lasted eight days, and the invited guests might remain for another two weeks if they found the hospitality congenial. Furthermore, if a new chief was raised to succession, the related house of the opposite moiety constructed a new house or refurbished the old house, and raised a totem pole. The contributions of each individual were carefully noted. Those who contributed the most to the funeral expenses, totem raising, and house building were rewarded accordingly in honor and gifts in the potlatch. A man who wished to be publicly distinguished in a potlatch had to make substantial material and/or service contributions to the bereaved family. Men of rank were obliged to make large contributions in order to preserve their rank, while aspiring men might wish to make contributions that would enhance their social standing and honor during the potlatch giveaway (Salisbury 1962:43)

The Tlingit potlatch, however, was more than a repayment of services and gifts provided during the mourning period. The potlatch giveaway was the primary means by which the Tlingit honored the deceased members of their clan.

The putting up of a house or pole, and the secret society performances, feasts, and distributions of property which accompanied it, were all undertaken for the sake of the dead members of a man's clan, and to them every blanket was given away and a great deal of food that was put into the fire was supposed to go. (Swanton 1908:343).

During the potlatch, the souls of the dead were believed to partake of the spirit of the goods, clothes, and food that were given away (Swanton 1908:343,462). When a gift was given away, the giver might announce the name of a deceased ancestor in whose honor the gift was given and to whom the spirit of the gift was sent. While the houses of the opposite moiety received the material embodiments of the potlatch gifts for their funeral and other services, the souls of the deceased ancestors were honored by each giveaway (Swanton 1908:463). In fact, "what is consumed is thought to be for the benefit of the deceased, indeed, for all the dead of the host sib" (de Lagune 1954:185–91). The guest houses in the potlatch represent their own deceased ancestors, who come to "show respect" and comfort the mourning house (McClellan 1954:80). The house chiefs were considered representatives of the clan ancestors and in this relation were invested with the management of the house economic estate and were the keepers of the house totems and emblems (Averkieva 1971:331). Consequently a Tlingit potlatch or feast was an occasion of communion between the dead and living members of related houses from both moieties.

The primary purpose of the potlatch was to honor and show respect for the dead members of one's clan. The means of honoring the dead were to give away gifts and food. Not to give a potlatch or to give away few gifts was to show disrespect for the clan ancestors, and was accompanied by loss of individual and house standing in the community (Salisbury 1962:210). Individual and house rank was determined by how much was given away at potlatches. Rich men were in the best material circumstances to undertake elaborate potlatches and earn the higher-ranking potlatch titles. Wealth was easily translated into rank in Tlingit society, but material accumulation was a means to an end. A man did not consume his wealth, but accumulated it in order to honor clan ancestors in the potlatch and make his name and house honorable within the community (Oberg 1973:103). The more wealth given away the greater the extent to which reciprocal obligations to the related houses of the opposite moiety were fulfilled, and the greater the honor to the individual, house, and clan ancestors.

Individual and house rank in Tlingit society was linked to the moral obligation to honor clan ancestors with feasts and giveaways (Salisbury 1962:215). Men who were active in obtaining and managing wealth had the means to fulfill the morally necessary and community monitored potlatch obligations. Individual achievement, social mobility, and the accumulation of wealth were sanctioned by the Tlingit sociocultural system. Houses and individuals who showed the greatest respect and honor for the ancestors were accorded the highest moral and social prestige. In Tlingit society, moral and social standing was contingent on accumulated wealth, since only the wealthy could show proper respect for the clan ancestors. A person whose actions did not conform to the moral standards of the community was considered to be of low caste (Swanton 1908:427). Since only through the accumulation of wealth could individuals or houses advance or maintain their social rank, the primary Tlingit value of honoring ancestors legitimated clan and individual rank based on differential capabilities to materially underwrite potlatch giveaways. The accumulation of wealth was not an end in itself, but a means of fulfilling Tlingit values and moral obligations.

While some aspects of Tlingit society—the accumulation of wealth, competition, and social mobility—appear similar to those of Western societies, the Tlingit value of honoring the clan dead through the potlatch giveaway gave a very different orientation to Tlingit norms in comparison to Western culture. Tlingit material accumulation cannot be defined as rational capitalism in the Weberian sense or as capitalism in the Marxist mode-of-production sense. Economic production in Tlingit society was based primarily on the house-kinship group. There was no formally free labor force that was required to sell its labor power on the market in Tlingit society. There were slaves, who were captured in warfare, and their labor was exploited to increase wealth, but such a labor form is not capitalistic for Marx or rational capitalism for Weber. While the Tlingit traded luxury goods with interior tribes, most Tlingit economic activity was devoted to subsistence and the accumulation of luxury goods for exchange in the potlatch. The Tlingit did not accumulate wealth as a means to reinvest capital in economically productive enterprises that might result in more profits and more reinvestment in the means of production (Spencer and Jennings 1965:188–90). Although there was rational calculation, amassing of wealth, and exploitation of slave labor, Tlingit values and culture directed that wealth be expended for the purpose of honoring clan ancestors rather than for economic investment and further accumulation. Perhaps Tlingit material accumulation can be termed a form of "social capitalism," since the distribution of wealth in a potlatch was the means of gaining moral approbation, social prestige, and rank (Salisbury 1962:40).

Polity and Economy

The Tlingit polity and economy were not differentiated from the Tlingit kinship system. The primary political and economic units in Tlingit society were the house matrilineal kinship groups. The house economic estate consisted of territory that gave the house access to fishing, hunting, and gathering grounds. The house chief was responsible for managing the house economy (Tollefson 1977:17–20). Similarly, there was no political center in traditional Tlingit society. The Tlingit did not have an institutionalized national council or political hierarchy that made binding decisions on matters of national interest. There was no formal political organization beyond the authority of the house chiefs (Oswalt 1978:335), except perhaps the village headman who was the chief of the highest rank in the village. The village chief was chosen according to his rank within the kinship system or societal community, and consequently there was little indication of a political system that was differentiated from the rank and kinship relations of the Tlingit societal community. Primary political commitments and loyalties were reserved for the household kinship group (Oberg 1973:24, 30). The Tlingit polity consisted of segmentary house-kinship groups that were organized into clans and moieties. The clans and moieties, however, never functioned as collective political groupings (Olsen 1967:1; Oberg 1973:48).

In summary, traditional Tlingit society was relatively nondifferentiated. The cultural system defined social rank and explicitly legitimated the kinship organization of the societal community, which dominated the organization of the Tlingit polity and economy. In the precolonization period, Tlingit culture, values, and norms did not support political centralization or any significant forms of economic or political differentiation. Therefore the nondifferentiated Tlingit social structure and Tlingit culture and norms cannot, by themselves, provide an explanation for the political and economic differentiation in the postcolonial period. Nevertheless, the nonascriptive, achievement, and acquisitive norms of Tlingit society may help us to understand the potential of further societal differentiation of the post–Western contact period. An explanation for Tlingit social change, however, cannot depend only on internal social and cultural variables, but must also look to the impact of world economic markets, colonization, and the interpenetration of Western values for an explanation for the political and economic differentiation of Tlingit society in the postcontact period.

Differentiation Before 1912

Early Tlingit contacts with Europeans centered around the fur trade. Europeans traded metal goods, tools, guns, and other articles of manufacture for otter and seal skins, which found a lucrative market in China. Through the fur trade the Tlingit and other northwest Alaska coast societies were drawn into the world economic system (Wolf 1982:182–94). The Tlingit were active and shrewd traders, and some houses controlled monopolies on internal trade routes. By acting as middlemen between the Europeans and the interior tribes, some Tlingit houses gained significant profits. Houses that monopolized trade routes used the new economic opportunities afforded by the fur trade to increase their wealth and, through giveaways in the potlatch, to increase their social and political prestige in Tlingit society (Olsen 1967:4; Klein 1980:94, 96). The houses that resided farther from the trade routes were less able to accumulate wealth and tended to be of lower caste rank (Swanton 1908:427). The fur trade increased both the availability of wealth and competition for social rank. "The Tlingit were well adapted to compete with the Europeans at their level of interest. Europeans wanted furs and the Tlingit wanted prestige items, and both wanted to increase their own wealth and social standing" (Klein 1980:96). Wealthy lineages, which controlled house chieftainships, were now more easily challenged by men with lower birthrights. Competition increased between houses and among individuals as the new wealth gathered from the fur trade was channeled into more elaborate potlatches (Averkieva 1971:334).

Between the early 1800s and 1867 the Russians maintained two settlements in southeast Alaska at Sitka and Wrangell. The Russians, however, were not able to politically dominate the Tlingit, although efforts were made to incorporate the house chiefs into a system of indirect rule and to curtail Tlingit clan feuds and the sacrifice of slaves at potlatches. At Sitka, the Tlingit traded foodstuffs at a daily local market on which the Russian settlement depended for survival (Golovin 1983:82–85). The material life of the Tlingit, however, changed with the fur trade economy. There was increased economic effort to produce for a market, and new demand and dependency on externally produced manufactured goods, especially metal goods, guns, and, later, traps. By the 1820s, the Tlingit had overexploited the local supply of fur-bearing sea animals, and were forced to hunt land animals in order to supply European traders. Some Tlingits converted to the Russian Orthodox religion, and the population declined owing to the introduction of new diseases associated with contact with Europeans. During the Russian period, the Tlingit did not institutionalize a political center or societywide political organization. While the Tlingit were incorporated into the fur trade they did not, however, abandon their subsistence economy, which continued to rely on fishing, hunting, and gathering. Much greater change in Tlingit society came after the U.S. purchase of Alaska in 1867.

The U.S. government did not assume administration of Alaska until 1877, after which the forces of change in Tlingit society were greatly accelerated. The Tlingit became politically subordinated to U.S. law and administration, incorporated into U.S. commercial and labor markets, and interpenetrated with U.S. values from missionaries and schools. By 1900, many Tlingit were absorbed into the U.S. economy. Tlingit men began working in the Alaskan gold mines, fished for the canneries, cut timber, hunted and trapped, worked on steamships, packed for mines, worked as guides and interpreters, and made traditional crafts for the tourist trade. Tlingit women worked in the canneries and salteries, did laundry, and made baskets and beadwork (Wyatt 1984). In the late 1870s two commercial fishing and canning companies moved into southeast Alaska, and by 1914 there were forty canneries. The canneries provided the Tlingit with opportunities for wage labor employment and also created a demand for a commercial fishing market. The canning industry, however, usurped control over the better salmon streams and monopolized most of the salmon harvest. Tlingit landownership was not recognized in the transfer of territory between Russia and the United States. Hence the Tlingit houses were denied legal rights to traditional salmon streams, which formed a large part of their subsistence economy. By 1910 the Tlingit had lost control over most of their traditional subsistence base resources (Tollefson 1977:21). Tlingits found it difficult initially to finance fishing boats, but increasingly fishing became the primary economic occupation of the men in the outlying villages. The canneries provided seasonal work from April to September for whole families, who migrated to the canneries when work was available and returned to their winter villages when the work season was over. Most Tlingit were unskilled laborers and few were engaged in capitalistic entrepreneurial activities (Looff 1980:209). Commercial fishing with boats, besides providing a marketable product, also allowed the Tlingit to sustain a subsistence-level economy by fishing, which was also supplemented by hunting subsistence activities (Federal Field Committee 1968:283). Consequently the Tlingit were not completely disassociated from the means of production. In Marxist terms, many Tlingit were semiproletarianized, meaning that part of their livelihood was earned in the subsistence economy while they sold their labor power to the canning industry.

There are no statistics available on the extent to which the Tlingit were absorbed into the southeast Alaska labor and commercial economy; historical reports indicate that many Tlingit were active participants in the new commercial fishing and wage labor markets. Shortage of labor in Alaska made the Tlingit an attractive labor source. Efforts by the canneries to import Asian workers were opposed by the Tlingit on the grounds that the Tlingit were willing to supply the labor needs of the canneries. "Within a few years after United States acquisition of the territory, the Tlingit were busying themselves with every job they could get" (Drucker 1958:10).

While the loss of traditional house salmon runs was a push factor for the Tlingit to enter the commercial fishing and wage labor markets, Tlingit sociocultural orientations provided additional impetus for the Tlingit to seek material gain in the newly available U.S. markets. The Tlingit, with their traditional emphasis on individual achievement and accumulation of wealth as a means to validate social rank, actively participated in the new markets (Drucker 1958:9–10). House chiefs, who were the traditional economic managers in Tlingit society, were themselves early engaged in the fur trade and in trade with the Americans. House leaders did not significantly resist Tlingit participation in the new markets, but rather encouraged participation in commercial fishing and cannery labor. There was little dispute as to whether or not the Tlingit would participate in the commercial economy (Drucker 1958:38–40).

As commercial fisheries took over their source of wealth, they could at least find employment utilizing their traditional skills of sailing and fishing. Because their basic attitude toward economic competition had much in common with that of their new masters, they had less difficulty in substituting the new system of wage earning and profits for the old system of subsistence and barter by which they had lived for many generations. (Rogers 1960:179)

In general, the Pacific northwest cultures adapted to the discipline of wage labor and a market economy more easily than Native Americans of other cultures (Drucker 1965:211–14).

Wyatt (1984) argues that there are several reasons within Tlingit society and culture that motivated the Tlingit to seek economic gain in U.S. commercial and labor markets. While the Tlingit were eager to earn cash in order to purchase commodities and raise their material standard of life, the Tlingit also sought to acquire wealth in order to uphold traditional institutions. Although U.S. authorities tried to curtail the blood revenge and settlement of civil infractions between the clans, these institutions continued informally in some villages into the 1920s. Settlements often required payment from the offending clan, and cash or goods purchased by cash were one way to settle accounts. The potlatch continued to attract Tlingit attention and wealth. The new economy presented new opportunities to acquire wealth that was necessary for potlatch distributions. For example, a Presbyterian lay worker at one village noted in 1904 that "a few years ago the only ambition of many a native seemed to be to earn a few hundred dollars that he might give a big feast to his friends, and so make his name 'high' among the tribes, even though he might have to live the remainder of his days in poverty" (Wyatt 1984). Giving potlatches was one motivation to earn money among the Tlingit, and large potlatches continued into the first decade of the present century despite U.S. government and missionary opposition. The payment of shamen for medical services also constituted an additional need to earn cash income within the traditional society.

Incorporation in markets contributed to the increased differentiation of economic organization from Tlingit kinship structure. The primary economic unit, the traditional communal house, began to break up into nuclear family units. Younger Tlingit protested against the social constraints of the traditional communal houses, and during the 1890s many preferred to move into single-family U.S.-style houses, which were considered more comfortable and prestigious. Many Tlingit migrated in search of employment to nearby towns such as Sitka, Wrangell, Juneau, and Ketchikan, where they moved into single-family houses (Olsen 1967:v; Tollefson 1978:10). During the 1880s and 1890s the Tlingit, because of missionary influence and a declining population (a drop from 10,000 to under 5,000 by 1912), began to concentrate into year-round villages. Missionaries, with the intention of proselytizing and bringing education to the Tlingit, persuaded the Tlingit to gather near the missions and live in nuclear family houses. The missionaries encountered difficulties when they tried to locate a mission near a particular group of houses because the other houses in the territory refused to relocate or attend mission activities at the site of other house groups. Consequently, missionaries were forced to seek neutral locations for their missions that were acceptable to all of the rival house groups in the area. By the early 1900s, the Tlingit were concentrated in thirteen villages and towns. They left their old communal houses and either migrated to nearby towns or formed permanent villages consisting of single-family houses that were congregated around Protestant missionary churches and schools.

Tlingit economic activity became more individualistic. Oswalt (1978:365) argues that the shift to a trapping trade economy led to increased economic individualism and the relative decline of the house as a primary economic unit. Individual trappers moved onto house lands and staked out exclusive trapping territories. Similarly, Tollefson (1978:5) and Oberg (1973:60–61) agree that the fur trade trapping economy obligated individual men to occupy trapping territories within the house domain. House economic activities became less important after the fur trade and the dissolution of the house economy was further accelerated during the 1880s and 1890s with the introduction of commercial fishing and wage labor forms of economic activity. Economic activity became an individual and nuclear family matter (Stanley 1965:19–21; Drucker 1965:221).

U.S. political domination and administration led to increased differentiation of education and judicial functions from the Tlingit societal community. After 1880, the Alaska territorial government took over control of Tlingit judicial affairs and imposed U.S. laws over Tlingit society. Informally, however, Tlingits preferred to settle their own affairs within the clan-based retributive system of justice. As late as the 1920s, many Tlingit secretly continued traditional forms of justice, while at the same time outwardly conforming to U.S. law and procedures. It is doubtful that during this early period that most Tlingit internalized U.S. law and procedures (Salisbury 1962:228). Furthermore, just as U.S. law and administration refused to recognize Tlingit kinship-house claims to territory, the U.S. government refused to recognize Tlingit clans and houses as political units. U.S. law recognized villages as political units, although villages were not well-defined groups in Tlingit society (Stanley 1965:5–6).

Protestant missionaries lauded Tlingit willingness to work for pay, but discouraged the potlatch as a waste of money. Nevertheless, some Tlingit maintained a belief in witchcraft and animism well into the 1920s, and a general belief in rebirth was held by most of the older generations into the 1960s (Stevenson 1966b:192; Olsen 1967:v). The Tlingit, while not willing to surrender their own culture, were willing to adopt education and some Christian practices, which they believed facilitated absorption into the U.S. occupational structure. Missionary contact coincided with Tlingit dispossession and incorporation into commercial fishing and wage labor markets, and the Tlingit house leaders were, generally, willing to accept the aid and advice of the missionaries as a strategy of adapting to changing economic and political conditions (Drucker 1965:218). Education offered by the missionaries provided linguistic and cultural skills such as reading and arithmetic that were necessary for obtaining jobs in the U.S. economy (Wyatt 1984). Schools were welcomed and students encouraged to study as a means to enhancing the prospects of future material gain (Krause 1956:230–31).

While traditional clan judicial functions were absorbed by U.S. courts and economic and education activities were increasingly differentiated from the moiety-clan system, the Tlingit societal community continued to operate. Missionaries and U.S. government agents attacked Tlingit beliefs and the potlatch, but did not directly threaten the kinship system. Most Tlingit retained identifications to house, clan, and moiety groups (Drucker 1965:218; Tollefson 1977).

Differentiation of a Political Center

In 1912, a group of twelve Tlingit and one Tsimshian[1] formed the Alaska Native Brotherhood (ANB). The organization had a constitution, bylaws, elected officers, and within a few years formed local camps, which sent three delegates to an annual grand camp meeting. Business was conducted according to strict rules of parliamentary procedure. An auxiliary, the Alaska Native Sisterhood, was organized on similar principles a few years later. By the mid 1920s, most native communities in southeast Alaska had ANB chapters (Drucker 1958:21).

The formation of the ANB was a response to the declining social, economic, and political conditions of the indigenous societies in southeast Alaska. As indicated earlier, the Organic Act of 1884 gave Alaska territorial status, but did not define the civil, legal, and land rights of the Alaska natives. Alaska natives were not granted U.S. citizenship, nor were their rights to traditional kinship fishing streams and territories recognized by U.S. courts. Consequently, by the 1890s the U.S. fishing industry had appropriated the most productive Tlingit salmon-fishing streams and relegated the Tlingit to smaller streams, commercial fishing, and wage labor as a means to gain a livelihood. Furthermore, the Tlingit were reduced to minority status as U.S. citizens began to outnumber the native population in southeast Alaska. The Tlingit also felt culturally oppressed since U.S. officials and missionaries were attacking Tlingit beliefs and agitating for an end to potlatches (*Alaska Fisherman* 1980:2). By 1910, "The Indians regarded their economic problem as their major one, but the question of their civil rights was related" (Drucker 1965:222). The primary goals of the early ANB were to provide an organizational basis for Alaska natives to gain U.S. citizenship, equal civil rights, and a return of dispossessed territories (Tollefson 1978:1; Hope 1975:2).

The initial formation of the ANB had few roots in traditional Tlingit culture (Case 1978:142). The ANB was formed by a group of Christianized and acculturated men who strongly identified with the values of U.S. society and firmly rejected traditional culture and society. The ANB founders received education from Presbyterian missionaries at the Sitka Training School or were active in the Presbyterian or Russian Orthodox church. "It is doubtful that the organizers could have done as effective a job or sacrificed so much without the religious commitment and personal dedication that they had to their cause" (Hope 1975:2). The founders were joined by others, who were educated on the U.S. mainland, and together they encouraged Christian, morality, education, civil government, and the participation in commerce, preservation of Indian history; they also worked against social discrimination and moved to improve health and labor conditions (*Alaska Fisherman* 1980:1). "(T)he Christian perspective of the Brotherhood, then as now, formed a common bond among the members" (*Alaska Fisherman* 1980:3–4). Grand camp meetings were opened with the singing of "Onward Christian Soldiers," and in the early days the Bible was read and interpreted to the annual convention. All prayed together as a unified community, "which was reflected in a standard of selflessness that put aside all meanness" (*Alaska Fisherman* 1980:28). "This period of time is fondly remembered by old time members as a time of action comparable to a religious revival" (Hope 1983:14).

Between 1912 and 1920, the ANB leadership favored the abolition of traditional customs, which were considered a bar to U.S. citizenship. The leadership of the ANB remained acculturationist throughout the history of the brotherhood. The executive committee vetoed traditional dancing at ANB meetings until the early 1950s, and then relented only after bitter opposition. The early assimilationist orientations of the brotherhood, however, encountered opposition from local house leaders, who were not eager to abandon Tlingit traditions but favored and encouraged participation within the ANB as a means to form a collective organization that could combat social discrimination and pursue native political and economic goals. After 1920 the ANB central leadership agreed to a policy of preserving traditional customs. Nevertheless, it was Christian values, organization, and procedures that dominated the ANB, while local house leaders upheld more traditional values.

Changes in Tlingit social solidarity were associated with the development and organization of the ANB. The concentration of the Tlingit into permanent villages led to changes in clan-moiety and potlatch relations. The disintegration of the communal house, relative Tlingit impoverishment, and population decline all contributed to the pooling of wealth among clans in order to maintain potlatch obligations. Moiety unity and moiety participation in the potlatches became more emphasized as opposed to traditional house participation (Tollefson 1977:23–24). Tlingit moieties came to play a central role in Tlingit potlatches. After 1912 every clan in the community participated in the potlatch. This more broadly based potlatch system served to create greater solidarity between the clans and ameliorate internal conflicts between rival clans and houses. The ANB stressed brotherhood and moiety unity. Now moiety groups were hosts in the potlatch, while the guests in the potlatch were the members of the opposite moiety (Tollefson 1977:23–24).

The ANB was differentiated from the Tlingit societal community in the sense that the Tlingit kinship system had no formal role in the organization and operation of the ANB. The Tlingit clan and moiety categories of social organization were not recognized by the ANB, which as a voluntary organization recruited its membership according to individual commitment. Clan and moiety rank did not carry over into rank and office in the ANB. Nevertheless, there are affinities between ANB and Tlingit norms. Tlingit norms of individual achievement, nonascriptive leadership criteria, rank, and competition favored the Tlingit in adopting the procedures and organization of representative government (Rogers 1969:453–54). For example, the Tlingit do not necessarily vote for fellow clansmen or moiety members and often fellow clansmen compete for the same office. Past service, education, ability to manage one's affairs in the U.S. economy, and willingness to assume non-self-interested leadership are criteria for gaining office in the grand camp or local camps of the ANB. At least one past president of the ANB credits the wisdom of the Tlingit ancestors and elders for the emphasis on achievement criteria in the selection of ANB leadership (Champagne 1982).

The ANB became an influential force in Alaska politics; it lobbied for passage of the act that granted U.S. citizenship to Native Americans in 1924. In 1928, the ANB test case guaranteed Tlingit and native children access to public schools in Alaska. An ANB boycott in 1929 led to the gradual removal of discriminatory signs from public facilities. The ANB worked for passage of the Alaskan Antidiscriminatory Act of 1946, as well as for extended workmen's compensation legislation, aid to dependent children, and relief for aged Alaska natives. It represented Alaskan fishermen and cannery workers in labor negotiations until the union was consolidated with the CIO in the mid-1940s. Through ANB efforts the Indian Reorganization Act of 1936 was extended to Alaskan villages. The Alaskan villages were then enabled to organize legal claims against the United States for lands lost during early colonization. Between 1929 and 1971 the ANB supported legal cases and provided political support to a variety of land suits against the United States. In 1965, the Tlingit and Haida won a joint suit against the U.S. for lands taken to create the Tongass National Forest. Furthermore, the ANB provided scholarships to students, worked to preserve the Indian subsistence economy from U.S. intervention, assisted the elderly and destitute, and contributed other social benefits to southeastern Alaska natives (*Alaska Fisherman* 1980:1–2; Tollefson 1977:13–17). In effect, the ANB became a powerful political force that provided the southeastern Alaska natives with a collective political organization that could effectively compete and protect their social, political, economic, and cultural interests within the framework of U.S. society.

In summary, the formation of the ANB, or Tlingit political center, was dependent on a variety of factors. U.S. political combination and associated legal, social, and political subordination of the southeast Alaska natives, as well as the dispossession of southeastern Alaska native land and economic resources, were all structural conditions that threatened economic, political, and social interests of the southeastern Alaska natives. However, such an argument by itself cannot account for the formation of the ANB. Why didn't the Tlingit fragment politically like so many other American Indian societies have done before the onslaught of U.S. political domination and market economy? An answer to this question lies in the continuity and strengthening of the solidarity of the Tlingit kinship moiety system. Given that the Tlingit solved the problem of integration, what traditional values legitimated collective political organization beyond the house group? There were none. The cultural models and values that uphold the ANB were introduced externally by Protestant missionaries and the U.S. school system. A highly acculturated Presbyterian Christian group of southeastern Alaska natives formed the ANB and they took their values, procedures, and models of collective organization from their missionary mentors. Thus, the interpenetration of new values and models of political organization, increased solidarity within the societal community, the structural conditions of political and social subordination, and economic dispossession combine to explain the formation and institutionalization of a differentiated political center in Tlingit society.

Further Economic and Political Differentiation

Since the formation of the ANB two new organizations have been formed by southeastern Alaska natives, the Tlingit-Haida Central Council (THCC) and Sealaska Corporation, both of which represent further developments in political and economic differentiation.

In 1929, the ANB decided to pursue the right to sue the U.S. for loss of territory. After ANB lobbying efforts, the U.S. Congress passed the Jurisdictional Act of 1935, which granted the Tlingit and Haida the right to present a land claims case against the U.S. government. Between 1935 and 1939, a specially appointed ANB committee failed to develop a case. The ANB convention of 1939 decided to form a political organization, the THCC, to prepare the claim against the U.S. Between 1941 and 1956, the THCC was led by an experienced ANB leader, and a case was presented in 1947. After twelve years the THCC won recognition of ownership of traditional lands under U.S. law. Since the ANB was an organization whose membership was not restricted to the Tlingit and Haida, the U.S. government ruled that the ANB could not represent the Tlingit and Haida in court, nor could the ANB manage the distribution of proceeds connected with the case. In 1959 the THCC was recognized by the U.S. as manager of the funds ($7.5 million) awarded in the land claims suit. In 1965 the U.S. government recognized the THCC as the governing body of the combined Tlingit and Haida tribes of southeast Alaska (Metcalf 1981:1–10). The following year a convention was held to reorganize the THCC. A movement emerged to demand a 100 percent per capita distribution of the land claim funds, but ultimately the money was kept as an endowment to finance the THCC. The THCC became a nonprofit organization dedicated to improve the social and economic welfare of the Tlingit and Haida. The THCC administers economic development, employment, housing, and education programs. Between 1966 and 1985 the THCC administered and contracted for numerous government aid and Bureau of Indian Affairs programs and built a small-scale bureaucracy that was financed by the claim's endowment and Alaska state and federal sources. Currently the THCC has twenty-one local community councils, which elect one delegate for every hundred registered Tlingit and Haida voters. The delegates meet at an annual convention to elect officers and an executive committee, which governs when the convention is not in session. The THCC has the power to manage Tlingit and Haida affairs and property (THCC 1982:30–31).

Between 1966 and 1971 the THCC represented the southeast Alaska natives in a movement of Alaska natives that was aimed at regaining rights to traditional territory.[2] With the enactment of the Alaska Native Claims Settlement Act of 1971 (ANCSA), the U.S. Congress legislated a compromise solution between the state of Alaska, interested oil companies, and the united Alaska native groups, who were called the Alaska Federation of Natives (AFN). ANCSA granted to the Alaska natives nearly one billion dollars in compensation, the right to select forty million acres of land, and provided for the establishment of thirteen regional profit-making corporations and numerous village corporations. The regional corporations were to manage the land estates and administer the distribution of funds. The ANCSA plan allowed native leaders to control economic and financial resources free from administrative constraints of the U.S. government and the Bureau of Indian Affairs. According to the ANCSA, the regional corporations are not required to pay income tax for twenty years and the stock in the corporations was not transferable until 1991. After 1991, new transferable stocks are to be issued and the regional corporations will lose their tax-exempt status. The threat of massive sales of stock by native shareholders or corporate takeovers present new threats to the Alaska native control of regional corporations and reclaimed land and resources. Much of the action of the AFN is currently directed toward securing a method to ensure native control of the regional corporations, land, and resources after the expiration of the 1991 protection of the ANCSA.

The THCC was designated to form the regional corporation in southeast Alaska, and the Sealaska Corporation was incorporated in June 1972. According to the regulations of the ANCSA, Sealaska would eventually receive $200 million; about half of this would be redistributed to the village corporations or passed out as per capita distributions. Sealaska received $100 million as capital and was given control over the mineral rights of the native land in southeast Alaska. The Sealaska Corporation was initially owned by nearly 16,000 southeast Alaska natives, each of whom owned 100 shares in the corporation.

By 1982 Sealaska operated much like a holding company, having either bought existing companies or organized new companies. Sealaska owned a large fish-packing subsidiary, a construction company, a sea transportation company, a timber subsidiary, and a business loan company. Furthermore, Sealaska owned small percentages of oil lease tracts off the North Slope of Alaska, and owned some real estate. In 1981 Sealaska had sales of $224 million and was ranked 745 on the Fortune 1,000 list (*Sealaska Shareholder* 1982). In subsequent years, sales have advanced at a slower rate to nearly a quarter of a billion dollars, although profit margins have been meager owing to a sluggish U.S. economy and the strong U.S. dollar which discourages the export of Sealaska's major products of fish and timber.

Contemporary Tlingit Society

The four major institutions in current Tlingit society are the Sealaska Corporation, the THCC, the ANB, and the moiety-clan system. The

ANB, the "grandfather" institution, is considered to have the most prestige, and is viewed as the structure that laid the foundations for the creation of the THCC and Sealaska. While the ANB is considered the seminal institution, its actual political influence has declined in recent years as the other, more specialized institutions have taken over some of its former tasks. Sealaska, with its substantial concentration of economic resources, is not the most powerful Tlingit-Haida institution. Nevertheless, as a voluntary association the ANB is free to pursue political goals and engage in political activities that are not proper for both the THCC and Sealaska. The ANB endorses political candidates, campaigns on political issues that affect its membership, organizes and mobilizes voter participation, and presents arguments before state and federal commissions and committees. The ANB continues its role as guardian of the southeast native political, economic, and cultural interests. The THCC administers social programs designed to aid the Tlingit and Haida, while Sealaska has the task of managing and developing land and resources. A division of labor has emerged among the differentiated institutions, and activities are consciously coordinated by the leadership in order to maximize the possibility of attaining Tlingit—Haida goals (*Sealaska Shareholder* 1981:8).

The THCC, Sealaska, and the ANB are specialized institutions that manage Tlingit-Haida relations with the U.S. economic and political system, but the core of Tlingit society remains in the clan-moiety system and the potlatch complex. While the ANB, the THCC, and Sealaska are differentiated from the clan-moiety system in the sense that their operations are not organized or determined by kinship or ceremonial prerogatives, there is, however, a complex and intimate relation between the kinship system and the differentiated institutions.

As noted earlier, at the turn of the twentieth century and in association with the new collective solidarity espoused by the ANB, Tlingit potlatches were transformed from events involving related lineages to events that included community members of both moieties. The clan-moiety system continues to operate in the organization and obligations of the potlatch. Clan and house groups, however, do not openly participate in political activities, do not own land (villages now control land as ANCSA corporations), are not economic units, and are functional primarily in the ceremonial activities of funerals and potlatches. Contemporary potlatches are one- or two-day affairs, often held on weekends. The larger potlatches are held by the northern villages of Hoona, Angoon, and Juneau. The southern and Haida villages have less elaborate potlatch ceremonies. Death, funeral obligations, and honoring the dead remain central features of Tlingit culture. The contemporary potlatch is focused on honoring dead clan relatives (de Laguna 1977:531, 611; Champagne 1982). The Tlingit are still conscious of their obligations to give a potlatch and conscious of the value of the things that are given in a potlatch. Families that give small potlatches are not highly regarded. The total value of goods given away in a potlatch are compared, and more prestige is associated with the giving away of larger amounts of money and goods. Individual achievement is recognized by potlatch rank. Contributions to a funeral or potlatch are recorded and announced publicly and outstanding material or service contributions are specially honored with potlatch gifts and attention (Champagne 1982). Nevertheless, potlatch rank is not exclusively given to men who participate actively in the ceremonies. Men who have shown leadership ability and gained private economic success are sometimes drafted into potlatch (clan) rank, despite their lack of knowledge of potlatch etiquette. A former president of the THCC and chairman of the board of Sealaska informed me that he was instated as a house chief although he had little traditional knowledge and had participated sparingly in potlatch ceremonies.

Traditionally the potlatch signified solidarity between related lineages. During the present century, however, the Tlingit have increasingly emphasized moiety participation in the potlatch, although related households continue to make up the core of a potlatch distribution and associated mutual obligations. The unity of the clans and moieties is tied directly to the potlatch ceremony in the mutual endeavor to fulfill the value of honoring the clan ancestors. In traditional society a show of disrespect might trigger open conflict and revenge on the part of the offended house, but in contemporary society a show of disrespect results in dissatisfaction with the potlatch and a tendency to grant the hosts less esteem for their potlatch efforts. If the potlatch is satisfactory for the guest moiety, the honor and reputation of the host clan is increased and good feelings prevail between the houses and clans. Rivalries and competition between clans and houses continue in Tlingit society, especially in the isolated village communities where clans and houses can influence the management of ANCSA village corporations and village government (Champagne 1982).

While the solidarity of the clan-moiety system, or Tlingit societal community, is tenuous and culturally grounded, the combined moiety figures of the Eagle and Raven are used as symbols of collective identity. The logos for both the ANB and Sealaska are the joined figures of a Raven and Eagle, which symbolize the unity of the two

Tlingit moieties or whole society. Furthermore, as both the Haida and Tsimshian have Eagle and Raven moiety systems and associated pot-latch cultures, the joined Eagle and Raven is a symbol of unity for all three major southeastern Alaskan societies. The use of the joint symbol as the logo for the ANB and Sealaska is a means of symbolically integrating these differentiated institutions with the societal communities of the southeastern Alaska native societies.

The leadership positions of the ANB, Sealaska, the THCC, and the moiety-clan system operate like interlocking corporate directorates. Many members of the Sealaska board of directors have held prominent positions within the ANB and THCC and are from large families of high caste within the traditional kinship system. For example, in 1982, thirteen of eighteen board members were leaders within the traditional tribal system or had strong family support for their election to the board. Four persons were considered contemporary leaders who were elected to the board based on their abilities as businessmen or political leaders. Six members of the board had played prominent roles in the ANB or Alaska Native Sisterhood, and at least four members served in prominent leadership positions in the THCC. One board member, who had been on the board since Sealaska's incorporation, was serving a second term as president of the THCC, was a past president of the ANB grand camp, and was serving on the ANB executive committee. He also participated with his clan in potlatch ceremonies (Champagne 1982). Most members of the board participated to some extent in each of the major Tlingit institutions.

All leadership positions in the ANB and the THCC and on the board of Sealaska are elective. Several criteria play a role in gaining access to prominent positions of leadership in any one of these organizations. Family support, caste, economic success, and visible leadership ability are all criteria that are important in the selection of Tlingit leadership. Members of upper-caste lineages still tend to dominate leadership in Tlingit institutions. A man who is born into a prominent lineage has access to power if he shows ability and leadership qualities. Being born into a commoner lineage is not, however, an ascriptive bar to leadership if the person shows visible leadership capabilities. A man (or woman) can gain visibility through willingness to work for Tlingit goals in the ANB, where people can see his or her commitment and leadership qualities. Service in the ANB is often considered a training ground for future leaders. Personal economic success in the U.S. economy is another criteria for leadership, since a man who cannot manage his own personal economic affairs will not be entrusted with managing Tlingit collective affairs. The Tlingit continue to equate leadership, wealth, and wisdom. The achievement criteria of proven leadership capabilities and personal economic success are more salient than knowledge and participation in traditional Tlingit social activities. For example, one board chairman of Sealaska had little knowledge of or willingness to participate in traditional Tlingit social institutions such as potlatches. This was a source of grumbling among people from his home village, but he was nevertheless generally considered to be the man most capable of managing Sealaska. Another board member, who was from the small Tsimshian group, did not have strong family support, but had a past record of leadership in the AFN and in the movement that led to the ANCSA.

Support from one's clan and village does play an informal role in the selection of leadership for Tlingit institutions. Candidates for office do not openly rally for support from their clan or village. Informally, however, clan leaders and elders may endorse a candidate and inform their kinsmen of the choice. The clan elders, however, can only endorse a candidate; each person decides independently how to vote in any given election. For example, a THCC president informed me that his sister, who was an influential member of his matrilineal clan, rarely gave him her political support. If a clansman is running for an important office, clan membership may be one criteria for voting for him, if the man is capable and respected. The influence and relation of the traditional clan system to the differentiated institutions of the THCC, the ANB, and Sealaska play themselves out primarily through informal networks of votes. Clan elders and prominent clan matrons can have an impact on the selection of Tlingit leadership through use of their influence to support specific candidates and issues (Rogers 1960:257; Stanley 1965:40–53; Hope n.d.).

In summary, contemporary Tlingit is composed of differentiated economic and political institutions, while at the same time the Tlingit societal community remains undifferentiated from the Tlingit cultural and value system. Tlingit culture and values continue to motivate participation in the potlatch ceremonies, provide a sense of common identity, and legitimate the moiety-clan organization of the Tlingit societal community. The Tlingit emphasis on individual achievement, competition, economic success, rank, and individual mobility continue to operate within the potlatch complex and are also operative within the frameworks of the differentiated economic and political institutions.

Discussion

A dependency argument would emphasize that the Tlingit, starting with the earliest fur trade era, became increasingly incorporated into the world economic system. The Tlingit increasingly produced for markets, and, especially in the present century, have come to rely primarily on commercial fishing and seasonal labor. Tlingit villagers have been semiproletarianized since they rely on fishing for part of their subsistence requirements. Tlingit village economics are subject to variations in fish markets, which affects both the price of fish sold to canneries and the demand for Tlingit wage labor (Looff 1980; Averkieva 1971). The Sealaska Corporation is dependent on the production of primary goods such as timber and canned fish. Furthermore, the Tlingit were subject to colonial political and cultural domination by the U.S. There can be no denying the economically dependent and politically subordinate nature of Tlingit society. Nevertheless, a dependency argument does not explain the formation of a Tlingit political center (ANB), the formation of the THCC and Sealaska, or the continuity and importance of Tlingit cultural and clan-moiety institutions.

On the other hand, the differentiation and institutionalization of Sealaska, the THCC, or the ANB did not derive from an unfolding of preexisting structures within the Tlingit societal community or from the generalization of Tlingit values. The Tlingit clan-moiety system did not provide the organizational base or collective solidarity for any of the differentiated institutions. The Tlingit values of honoring the clan ancestors did not legitimate the organization and goals of the ANB, the THCC, or Sealaska. The ANB was formed in 1912 to struggle against loss of Tlingit land, loss of civil rights, and changing economic conditions. These conditions, however, were not sufficient, since Tlingit kinship organization and tenuous social solidarity did not enable the Tlingit to form a concerted collective political organization. The founders of the ANB rejected traditional culture and tried to form an organization based on Protestant values, rules, and forms of organization. Protestant Presbyterian values were instrumental in the formation of the ANB, and it was these values, not traditional Tlingit values, that supported the collective instrumentality of the ANB and its derivative organizations, the THCC and Sealaska.

Nevertheless, many central aspects of traditional culture persisted. The increasing social solidarity of the Tlingit societal community and the support of the newly differentiated institutions by the clan and house leaders were critical to their institutionalization and continuity. The ANB leadership has been more acculturated than the rank-and-file membership. Early conflict between kinship leaders and the ANB leadership centered on the place of traditional culture in Tlingit affairs. Ultimately, the ANB leadership was forced to tolerate and help preserve traditional culture. The more traditional clan leaders gave their consent to the new institutions because they were seen as instruments for preserving Tlingit culture and for regaining land and civil rights.

While Tlingit culture and values did not directly legitimate the differentiation of political and economic institutions, Tlingit belief in rebirth and a nonsalvation world view legitimated this-worldly orientations and social inequality, while the Tlingit value of honoring the dead legitimated rank based on individual economic achievement. Tlingit acquisitiveness was a "pull" factor in the readiness of the Tlingit to accept wage labor employment and participate in the U.S. economy. Tlingit culture does not, however, legitimate capitalist accumulation in the sense of rationally organizing the means of production in response to market demands (*Sealaska Shareholder* 1981). Tlingit accumulation was oriented toward honoring the deceased clan ancestors in potlatches, since this was the route to honor and high caste in Tlingit society. Furthermore, the principles of leadership selection in the three differentiated institutions continue to follow the traditional emphasis on economic success and proven leadership ability. These nonascriptive and achievement-oriented criteria for leadership supported the organizational and instrumental requirements of the THCC, Sealaska, and the ANB.

In conclusion, both dependency and functional differentiation arguments are not sufficient, by themselves, to account for Tlingit political and economic differentiation. Tlingit political and economic differentiation was not the result of a natural unfolding of the societal community, but rather was created in direct response to specific conditions of political, economic, and social subordination in combination with the acceptance of Protestant values by a leadership group, increasing social solidarity, and cultural orientations that legitimated individual achievement and material accumulation. Although Tlingit society represents a small-scale case, it illustrates the need for analyzing social change with a consideration for endogenous factors of culture, social solidarity, and processes of differentiation in conjunction with the exogenous factors of market incorporation, geopolitics, and the interpenetration of new values and belief systems. Because of the increasing importance of transsocietal political, economic, and cultural relations in recent world history, such a comprehensive internally-externally open framework will be necessary in order to more fully understand contemporary social change processes.

Notes

1. The Haida, Tlingit, and Tsimshian are relatively similar northwest Alaska coast societies. They share the potlatch complex, belief in rebirth, and the dual kinship structure between the Raven and Eagle moieties. While the man who originated the ANB was a Tsimshian, most of the members of the ANB have been Tlingit, mainly because the Tlingit are the largest group in the area. Today the three groups share and participate in the potlatch complex, the ANB, and several other organizations. There are some subtle differences in the culture and social organization of each group, but a comparison of the three societies is beyond the scope of the present paper. The Tlingit dominate the ANB, but the two other groups are represented and integrated politically and socially. Nevertheless, clear distinctions remain and it is difficult for the Haidas and Tsimshian to gain the very highest positions in the institutions shared by all three groups.

2. A discussion of the social movement that led to the enactment of the Alaska Native Claims Settlement Act of 1971 (ANCSA) is beyond the scope of the present paper. The interested reader should consult Arnold (1978) and McBeath and Morehouse (1980).

References

Ahmad, Aijaz. 1983. "Imperialism and Progress." In Ronald Chilcote and Dale Johnson, eds. *Theories of Development*, pp. 33–73. Beverly Hills, Calif.: Sage.

Alaska Fisherman, The. 1980. Special Edition. Juneau. Tlingit-Haida Central Council.

Amin, Samir, Giovanni Arrighi, Andre Gunder Frank, and Immanuel Wallerstein. 1982. *Dynamics of Global Crisis.* New York: Monthly Review Press.

Arnold, Robert. 1978. *Alaska Native Claims.* Anchorage: Alaska Native Foundation.

Averkieve, Julia. 1971. "The Tlingit Indians." In Eleanor Leacock and Nancy Lurie, eds., *North American Indians in Historical Perpectives*, pp. 317–42. New York: Random House.

Badie, Bertrand and Pierre Birnbaum. 1983. *The Sociology of the State.* Chicago, Ill.: University of Chicago Press.

Bellah, R. N. 1964. "Religious Evolution." *American Sociological Review* 29:358–74.

Billman, Esther, ed. 1969. "A Potlatch Feast at Sitka, Alaska." *Anthropological Papers of the University of Alaska* 14:55–64.

Bollen, Kenneth. 1983. "World System Position, Dependency and Democracy." *American Sociological Review* 48:468–79.

Case, David. 1978. *The Special Relationship of Alaska Natives to the Federal Government: An Historical and Legal Analysis.* Anchorage: Alaska Native Foundation.

Champagne, Duane. 1982. *Field Notes: Interviews and Observations.* Unpublished Data Source. Department of Sociology. University of California, Los Angeles.

Chilcote, Ronald. 1983. "Introduction: Dependency or Mode of Production? Theoretical Issues." In Chilcote and Johnson, *Theories of Development*, pp. 9–30.

Chilcote, Ronald and Dale Johnson, eds. 1983. *Theories of Development*. Beverly Hills, Calif.: Sage.

Chinchilla, Norma. 1983 "Interpreting Social Change in Guatemala: Modernization, Dependency and Articulation of Mode of Production." In Chilcote and Johnson, *Theories of Development*, pp. 139–180.

Coser, Lewis. 1956. *The Functions of Social Conflict*. New York: Free Press.

de Laguna, Frederica. 1952. "Some Dynamic Forces in Tlingit Society." *Southwestern Journal of Anthropology* 8:1–12.

——1954. "Tlingit Ideas About the Individual." *Southwestern Journal of Anthropology* 10:172–191.

——1977. *Under Mount St. Elias: The History and Culture of the Yakutat Tlingit*. Washington, D.C.: Smithsonian Institution Press.

Drucker, Philip. 1958. *The Native Brotherhoods: Modern Intertribal Organization on the Northwest Coast*. Bureau of American Ethnology Bulletin 168. Washington, D.C.: U.S. Government Printing Office.

——1965. *Cultures of the North Pacific Coast*. San Francisco *Calif.: Chandler.*

Eisenstadt, S. N. 1964. "Institutionalization and Change." *American Sociological Review* 29:235–47.

——1978. *Revolution and the Transformation of Societies*. New York: Free Press.

Eisenstadt, S. N. and M. Curelaru. 1976. *The Form of Sociology: Paradigms and Crises*. New York: Wiley.

Federal Field Committee. 1968. *Alaska Natives and the Land*. Washington, D.C.: U.S. Government Printing Office.

Giddens, Anthony. 1979. *Central Problems in Social Theory*. Berkeley: University of California Press.

Golovin, Paul. 1983. *Civil and Savage Encounters*. Portland: Oregon Historical Society.

Hintze, Otto. 1976. *The Historical Essays of Otto Hintze*. Felix Gilbert, ed. New York: Oxford University Press.

Hope, Andrew III. 1975. *Founders of the Alaska Native Brotherhood*. Sitka, Alaska: Special Edition.

——n.d. *Modern Tribes*. Xerox. Unpublished.

Hope, Herbert. 1983. "An Overview of ANB History." *The Alaska Native News* 1(12):13–15, 41.

Johnson, Chalmers. 1966. *Revolutionary Change*. Boston, Mass.: Little, Brown.

Klein, Laura. 1980. "Contending with Colonization: Tlingit Men and Women in Change." In Mona Etienne and Eleanor Leacock, eds., *Women and Colonization*, pp. 88–108. New York: Praeger.

Krause, Aurel. 1956. *The Tlingit Indians*. Seattle, Wash.: American Ethnology Society.

Looff, David H. 1980. "Growing Up in a Dying Community." In Art Gallaher and Harland Podfield, eds., *The Dying Community*, pp. 207–236. Albuquerque: University of New Mexico Press.

McBeath, Gerald and Thomas Morehouse. 1980. *The Dynamics of Alaska Native Self Government*. Lanham, Md.: University Press of America.

McClellan, Catherine. 1954. "The Interrelations of Social Structure with Northern Tlingit Ceremonialism." *Southwest Journal of Anthropology* 10:75–96.

Metcalf, Peter. 1981. *The Central Council of the Tlingit and Haida Indian Tribes of*

Alaska: An Historical and Organizational Profile. Juneau: Central Council of the Tlingit and Haida Indian Tribes (THCC).

Nisbet, Robert. 1969. *Social Change and History.* New York: Oxford University Press.

Parsons, Talcott. 1977a. *Social Systems and the Evolution of Action Theory.* New York: Free Press.

——1977b. *The Evolution of Societies.* Englewood Cliffs, N.J.: Prentice-Hall.

Oberg, Kalevero. 1960. "Kinship Sentiment and the Structure of Social Action." In Walter R. Goldschmidt, ed., *Exploring the Ways of Mankind,* pp. 290–95. New York: Holt, Rinehart and Winston.

——1973. *The Social Economy of the Tlingit Indians.* Seattle: University of Washington Press.

Olsen, R. L. 1967. "Social Structure and Social Life of the Tlingit in Alaska." *Anthropological Records.* Vol. 26. Berkeley: University of California Press.

Oswalt, Wendell. 1978. *This Land Was Theirs.* New York: Wiley.

Quijano, Anibal. 1983. "Imperialism, Social Classes, and the State in Peru, 1890–1930." In Chilcote and Johnson, *Theories of Development,* pp. 107–38.

Rogers, George W. 1960. *Alaska in Transition.* Baltimore, Md.: Johns Hopkins University Press.

—1969. "Party Politics and Protest: Current Political Trends in Alaska." *The Polar Record* 14:445–54.

Rosman, Abraham and Paula Rubel. 1972. "The Potlatch: A Structural Analysis." *American Anthropologist* 74:658–71.

Salisbury, Oliver. 1962. *Quoth the Raven: A Little Journey Into the Primitive.* Seattle, Wash.: Superior.

Sealaska Shareholder. 1981–1982. Juneau: Sealaska Corporation.

Sequin, Margaret. 1985. *Interpretive Contexts for Traditional and Current Coast Tsimshian Feasts.* Canadian Ethnology Service Paper No. 98. Ottawa: National Museum of Man.

Skocpol, Theda. 1979. *States and Social Revolutions.* New York: Cambridge University Press.

Spencer, Robert and Jesse Jennings. 1965. *The Native Americans.* New York: Harper and Row.

Stanley, Samuel. 1965. "Changes in Tlingit Social Organization." Xerox Unpublished.

Stevenson, Ian. 1966a. "Seven Cases Suggestive of Reincarnation Among the Tlingit Indians of Southeastern Alaska." *Proceedings of the American Society for Psychical Research* 26:191–240.

——1966b. "Cultural Patterns in Cases Suggestive of Reincarnation Among the Tlingit Indians of Southeastern Alaska." *American Society for Psychical Research Journal* 60:229–43.

Swanton, J. R. 1908. "Social Condition, Beliefs and Linguistic Relationship of the Tlingit Indians." In *Twenty-Sixth Annual Report of the U.S. Bureau of American Ethnology, 1904–05,* pp. 391–485. Washington, D.C.: U.S. Government Printing Office.

THCC (Tlingit-Haida Central Council). 1982. "The 'Tlingitization' of Social and Economic Programs." *The Alaska Native News* 1(2):29–31.

Tollefson, Kenneth. 1977. "A Structural Change in Tlingit Potlatching." *Western Canadian Journal of Anthropology* 7:16–24.

——1978. "From Local Clans to Regional Corporation: :The Acculturation of the Tlingit." *Western Canadian Journal of Anthropology* 8:1–20.

Veltmeyer, Henry. 1983. "Surplus Labor and Class Formation on the Latin American Periphery." In Chilcote and Johnson, *Theories of Development*, pp. 201–30.

Weber, Max. 1958. *The Religion of India*. New York: Free Press.

——1981. *General Economic History*. New Brunswick, N.J.: Transaction Books.

——1983. *Max Weber on Capitalism, Bureaucracy and Religion*. Stanislov Andreski, ed. Boston, Mass.: George Allen and Unwin.

Wolf, Eric. 1982. *Europe and the People Without History*. Berkeley: University of California Press.

Wyatt, Victoria. 1984. "History of Relations Between Indians and Caucasians in Southeast Alaska." Ph.D. dissertation. (Draft copy.) Yale University.

3

Fundamentalism and Sociocultural Revitalization: On the Logic of Dedifferentiation

Frank J. Lechner

Serious reflection on the legacy of Talcott Parsons is an important task for sociological theory; a reevaluation of the concept of differentiation and the way Parsons used it is in turn an important part of that task. In this paper I will not present an empirical or conceptual critique of differentiation as such but will follow a more indirect evaluation strategy. I will define and analyze a form of collective action which, while recognized by Parsons, goes against the grain of his analysis of differentiation and modernity in general, yet can be interpreted in terms of his later theoretical resources. Specifically, I will suggest that fundamentalism as an ostensibly antimodern phenomenon can be dealt with by applying Parsons' own theoretical tools to his substantive concerns more systematically than he himself has in relatively informal comments on that subject. Formally put, fundamentalism will be considered as the mode of collective action oriented to resolving problems inherent in value generalization by means of dedifferentiation across levels of action on the basis of pattern maintenance as the primary value principle. Dealing with fundamentalism in terms of a relatively abstract model may help clarify the

I am grateful to Rainer Baum, Burkart Holzner, Omar Moore, Roland Robertson, and Zdenek Suda for helpful comments on an earlier version of this paper.

"logic of dedifferentiation" and, perhaps, modify part of Parsons' work. One such modification may lie in an overall point that this paper will try to convey—namely that much attention needs to be paid to the actual problems of order and meaning in modernity, and that modernity is a rather more fragile and contentious affair than Parsons explicitly realized.

The argument will proceed as follows. First, I will briefly review some relevant statements by Parsons on differentiation and dedifferentiation/fundamentalism. Second, I will define in ideal-typical terms what will be called the fundamentalist "syndrome." Third, that syndrome will be interpreted as a form of sociocultural revitalization in modernity. Fourth, some empirical cases will be discussed by way of illustration. Finally, I will make some brief comments on fundamentalism in relation to the transsocietal arena.

Differentiation and Fundamentalism in Parsons

Differentiation has long been one of the master variables in Parsons' work, but he has actually used it in different ways. First, according to him, structural change of systems in response to external and internal challenges is likely to take the form of a binary split which leads to units with specific, different functions. The "classical" formulation, ultimately derived from Spencer, defines differentiation as an intermediate form of dynamic process (Parsons 1961a:37), by which roles emerge from a diffuse matrix to be oriented to specific functions by specific norms; occupation-kinship differentiation is the classic case (Parsons 1961a:76; Smelser 1959). Or, as Parsons says elsewhere, differentiation is the "division of a unit or structure in a social system into two or more [!] units or structures that differ in their characteristics and functional significance for the system" (1971:26); the differentiation of labor in the Industrial Revolution (1971:77) and the differentiation of family and educational roles in the educational revolution (1971:101) are examples. Earlier the economy as a whole subsystem had been the prototypical case—illustrating the tendency whereby "total societies *tend* to differentiate into subsystems (social structures) which are specialized in each of the four primary functions" (Parsons and Smelser 1956:47). Differentiation according to the binary principle (most likely on somewhat vague "good grounds" [1971:51]) is directional and operates within the framework of a system (Parsons 1977a:282ff). It has to do essentially with roles and social subsystems; it is differentiation from an undifferentiated social state. Modernity, then, is minimally characterized by high-level differentiation within societies.

But by the logic of the scheme a general variable like differentiation should apply at other levels as well. Parsons has paid particular attention to cultural system differentiation. For example, he has stated that cultures "also became differentiated on bases other than moral," which then crystallize as independent cultural subsystems; highly differentiated cultural systems are another hallmark of modern societies (1971). Cultural systems must have a capacity to parallel social system differentiation (1961b). For example, the educational revolution was accompanied by cultural system differentiation between two previously fused primary aspects of the "instrumental-rational orientation" (1978:124–26); that can be contrasted with attempts to dedifferentiate relatively independent forms of cultural orientation and action, as in attempts to impose *Gesinnungsethik*-like standards of relevance on cognitive-intellectual pursuits (1978:144ff). In more general terms, "in the course of such processes [of evolution] it is to be expected that both the religious and the secular aspects of both cultural and social systems should undergo differentiation within themselves and that there should be processes of differentiation between them" (1978:243).

The latter point is important in itself: differentiation as a process combined with the analytical "differentiation" of four-functional aspects of action-in-general suggests that in the course of evolution differentiation should also take place *between* system levels. Parsons has paid special attention to cultural system–social system differentiation in the case of early and late Christian culture (1971:29); the historic religions generally (1977:315) have achieved greater social system–cultural system differentiation. That has been elaborated further by Bellah (1964), Baum (1975), and Robertson (1978). In those cases, differentiation has come to refer to the autonomization of different "levels" of action and organization of action around differentiated objects of orientation. For example, Bellah (1964) has described the differentiation, by various "jumps," of culture, society, and self as different foci of action in the course of religious evolution from a relatively undifferentiated "primitive" condition to more fully differentiated early modern and modern patterns (see below). What remains less clear in all of these cases, as in Parsons' own relatively loose image of differentiation at the general action level, is how the totally undifferentiated origin can be described as well as the differentiation-from-what. Nor is it always possible to find specific social structures that carry each case of "higher" differentiation. Technically speaking, then, these treatments of more general differentiation may not measure up to the classical type. But the point to be derived from them is a different one—namely, that modernity can be characterized as the form of sociocultural order in which at least four levels of action acquire a certain autonomy, while all operating under the imperative of continuous self-reflection and self-revision. This point will be relevant later when I discuss dedifferentiation at this general level.

Finally, Parsons also uses differentiation in relation to the system of modern societies (1977a:292; 1971:40, 74, 139ff). Sociocultural evolution in Parsons' sense actually refers mostly to the evolution of that system, although his major "cases" have to do with internal societal differentiation and with America as the fully modern society. Hence there is no full account of how that "system of modern societies" as such has further implemented the various other evolutionary characteristics. Parsons limits himself to a rather arbitrary assignment of major societies to particular functions in that system. Although this move to the transsocietal level in dealing with evolution is clearly an advance, it has not been made in a technically satisfactory or sufficiently abstract way. In principle, however, it should be possible to apply the same general evolutionary categories to the emerging world system—perhaps more so than in the case of societies (the definition of which has been problematic especially because of the problematic direct application of abstract dimensions and "models" to concrete societies defined as relatively self-sufficient systems). At the very least Parsons has suggested that dealing with modernity now requires the consideration of societies as sociocultural systems in the context of an encompassing global system. Differentiation thus applies not only to societies and to the "general action system," but to the more concrete system of societies as well. It is a master variable that cannot be assigned to any one function; hence, in retrospect, identifying it with the goal attainment dimension seems rather arbitrary. It is indeed the "bottom line" in the evolutionary process.

Without criticizing Parsons' treatment of differentiation as such in this context (for sharp though very different critiques see Smith 1973 and Brownstein 1982), I suggest that while Parsons emphasized the "positive" side of differentiation as process and pattern, the counterpoints to it are equally important. In essence, I suggest that differentiation also entails fundamental problems in the meaningful organization of action as objectively possible outcomes of the evolutionary process. Such fundamental problems can be called "discontents." Those inherent in what Parsons called value generalization are relevant in this context. Value generalization implies that the bounds of a cultural tradition are loosened and that a more abstract interpretation is given to value principles. Hence beliefs can no longer be taken for granted but must be "held" (Geertz 1968); value implementation becomes a more critical, open process and thus less directly satisfying; new degrees of freedom are provided for action in various domains, which may thus be perceived to be less meaningful from the point of view of certain ultimate principles; and given greater cultural complexity, the meaningful coherence of culture itself can be perceived to be at stake. Although he never dealt with such discontents in a systematic or detailed fashion, the analysis of forms of "disorder" was in fact an important part of Parsons' voluntaristic theorizing. After a brief discussion of Parsons' treatment of discontents and responses related to value-generalization I will suggest that Parsons' discussions can be reformulated and extended more adequately by applying some of his own conceptual resources to his substantive concerns.

Discontents and antimodern movements were very prominent in Parsons' essays on national socialism in the 1940s (Parsons 1954). Influenced by Weber, Parsons interpreted modernization primarily as rationalization—a process by which rational-legal authority and economic rationality become dominant in society and traditional value patterns become disenchanted. It can lead to disorganization and anomie, especially insofar as its impact on a society is uneven. Two types of responses are to be expected. On the one hand, Parsons suggests, there is the rationalistic-utopian, superemancipatory response (1954:137), which takes the value pattern inherent in rationalization as the only possible one and becomes compulsive in debunking traditionalist residues (1954:119). But on the other hand, traditionalist parts of society—status groups whose prestige is threatened, regions that suffer from technological change, representatives of values that are being debunked—all experience insecurity. They will respond to such insecurity in an exaggerated, unrealistic, romanticist fashion and interpret certain values in a very absolute and literal way (1986b:114–45; 1954:120). Such responses aggressively turn to the things that symbolize rationalizing and emancipatory areas. They draw energy from the values of relatively particularistic social circles. National socialism operated in a society that experienced relatively intense disorganization, due to relatively rapid rationalization, and had many strong traditionalist pockets; it appealed to particularistic nationalist sentiments which cut across different parts of the social structure; and it combined traditional-fundamentalist and unrealistic-romantic elements. Hence national socialism, while not as such "fundamentalist," incorporated a "fundamentalist revolt against the whole process of rationalization" (Parsons 1954:123). Parsons thus systematically considers actual and potential disorganization in modernity and antimodern movements. The limitation of this part of his work lies primarily in the relatively one-dimensional, unidirectional view of modernization; the modernization-disorganization-antimodern response sequence was part of a relatively conventional *Gemeinschaft*-to-*Gesellschaft* theory. In *The Social System* (1951) the pattern variables helped spell out that process in terms of the transformation in institutionalized role expectations; fundamentalism is there presented again as an extreme response to scientific-technological rationalization on the basis of compulsive attachment to the primarily evaluative-expressive symbolism of traditional religions.

In his later work Parsons maintained that the transformation of Christian culture favored an increasingly liberal order. But as his view of evolutionary process became more fully multidimensional, his view of fundamentalism became more refined as well. Insofar as a modern sociocultural order is both differentiated and upgraded, more inclusive and generalized, efforts at dedifferentiation are possible that may produce a form of moral absolutism focusing on one essential moral commitment to which all others are to become subordinate (Parsons 1978:255). Intellectually, four absolutist tendencies can be distinguished, all of which deal with problems of modern sociocultural order in terms of a dedifferentiated view focused on particular societal subvalues (Parsons 1977b). Different values or subvalues can become the basis of fundamentalist views, but all share a tendency toward dedifferentiation and an exclusive focus on counterabsolutisms. More generally, Parsons (1966) can translate his early discussion of fundamentalism in more technical terms as the ideal-typical form of resistance to one particular aspect of evolutionary process, namely value generalization; to the fundamentalist such generalization appears as the abandonment of value commitment itself.

The specific sources of such fundamentalism may vary, but its "logic" is similar in different cases, as Parsons (1986b) argues, especially in the essay on value commitments. There fundamentalism is interpreted as the effort to "deflate" media, especially value commitments, by imposing tight restrictions on degrees of freedom in value implementation. Value absolutism is the common feature of all such deflation. It is "the assertion of sharp limitations on implementative flexibility, restricting the obligation to the most immediate, often most drastic, steps for implementing the pattern at the particular level of reference. Legitimation is thereby withdrawn from otherwise open ranges of flexibility with respect to more remote means of implementation of other subvalues within a larger system" (1968b:464). The demand for the security of "real" commitments also threatens to escalate conflict and exclude previously legitimate parts of the community. "Fundamentalism" is the appropriate prototype for such deflationary processes insofar as religion normally represents the highest level of commitment. But while fundamentalism is likely to be religious in origin the concept is more generally applicable (1968b:465). Fundamentalism normally entails *de*differentiation and "increasing unconcern for the exigencies of broadly differentiated implementation" (1968b:470). Movements in this general direction may be eliminated, split, or absorbed—or they may lead to a new level of generality in the prevailing value system which then includes the previously contending parties (1968b:470–72). However, such possible value generalization is again not without problems, since "the higher the level of generalization, the greater the scope for fundamentalist revolts against current patterns and levels of implementation, in the name of value-absolutism at various levels and in reference to various particular concerns" (1968b:472).

Thus we find several general features of fundamentalism in Parsons' work. Fundamentalism is a generic, theoretical concept referring to a particular type of value-oriented response to a fundamental dimension of evolutionary process. Operating from the highest cybernetic level, it represents the most comprehensive counterpoint to value generalization. While its sources may vary, its logic is similar in different cases and can be technically analyzed in terms of media deflation. Although such fundamentalist responses are to be expected in evolutionary process and can in fact make creative though unintended contributions, they entail further problems that make the full realization of a fundamentalist program difficult—especially where value generalization and a differentiated order have been firmly established and have placed the burden of proof on fundamentalist "revolts." But despite that unstable and uncertain course it is at least a theoretically important phenomenon, since the hierarchical element in action theory implies the inherent possibility of the escalation of protest to the highest possible level—which can then become a basis for a total but "overdetermined" reconstruction of meaningful order.

The latter point suggests a link with Smelser's (1962) theory of collective behavior. Specifically, fundamentalism appears as a major subset within the category of value-oriented movements. In Smelser the equivalent of dedifferentiation is short-circuiting—the process by which movements attempt to reconstruct meaningful order without appropriate specification of all dimensions and components in action. The highest cybernetic element in Smelser is generalized belief—legitimating such short-circuiting in absolutist fashion. In addition, in Smelser's scheme value-oriented movements are the most radical and encompassing of all. In both Parsons and Smelser it appears that while such movements may address fundamental problems in modernity they do so essentially by rejecting that very form of sociocultural order—*Gesellschaft* as such. And while fundamentalism will normally claim to reestablish an absolute, traditional value pattern, we may also infer that such claims will themselves be problematic and can by no means be taken for granted.

Combining Parsons and Smelser thus gives at least the contours of fundamentalism as a form of dedifferentiation. Applying a heuristic suggested by Münch (1980, 1982) and Parsons' general action scheme may help to make those contours clearer and analytically more compelling. Münch has suggested that the relations between subsystems can themselves be treated as variables. Interpenetration is both the analytical and substantive-theoretical baseline; but it is at least objectively possible for "dynamizing" subsystems to dominate "controlling" subsystems (or vice versa), or for subsystems to become isolated or embroiled in permanent conflict. Fundamentalism can then be seen as the mode of collective action that, given its emphasis on the highest "controlling" elements, is characterized by the domination of "controlling" over "dynamizing" subsystems—which leads to "oversteering." In functional terms, fundamentalism can be seen as an attempt at sociocultural revitalization by restoring pattern maintenance as the primary value principle in terms of which life is to become meaningful again. Meaningful order is thus to be reconstructed by means of the dedifferentiation of all dimensions of action in the direction of the pattern maintenance dimension. Without wishing to evoke negative medical connotations, fundamentalism can thus be called a "syndrome." Given the combination of emphasis on controlling elements, dedifferentiation, and a "constraining" attempt at the reconstruction of meaningful order, the thrust of fundamentalism can presumably be traced throughout the Chinese box structure of Parsons' AGIL scheme. Thus the next task will be to say in abstract terms what fundamentalism "means" at different levels of action.

The Fundamentalist Syndrome

What does fundamentalism "look like" in ideal-typical, action-theoretical terms? In order to spell out the "logic of dedifferentiation" the ideal-typical description will use as heuristic tools only Munch's rule, the so-called general action system (cultural system = L, social system = l, personality system = G, behavioral system = A), and its respective subsystems (hence, for example, moral culture = Li, societal community = li, etc.). The description follows fundamentalism as it "moves" across these various levels (see Gould 1976; Lidz and Lidz 1976; and Baum and Lechner 1981).

Let me start the abstract description of the syndrome at the cultural level. Here controlling-over-dynamizing means first of all that ultimate-constitutive culture comes to dominate moral culture, hence: the ultimization of moral culture (Ll>Li). This means that moral principles are treated as objective, ultimate truth. If that is so, one cannot take any liberties with morality: in principle there can be only "one right." As a result, any transgression against moral law must be regarded as a major sin. The ambiguity arising from the contingency of existential and ethical ideas, originally introduced by Judaism, is thus "resolved." If moral principles are thus treated as ultimate truth, autonomous secular moral culture or autonomous "civil religion" will be delegitimated (see Lidz 1979). Under ultimate pressure value generalization must be checked. Insofar as "generalized values" are characteristic of modernity in Parsons' view, this is a major source of fundamentalism's rejection of modernity. The same goes for expressive culture—it is ultimized as well (Ll>Lg). Art is, to coin a term, religionized or ideologized. It, too, must express ultimate truth. Substance takes priority over form, but the fixedness of the substance does not imply that one can take liberties with the form. Expressive models are grounded in a "deep" foundation. They thus become less a matter of private taste and more a set of collective aesthetic representations (which are likely to be inculcated in everyone by ritual).

Cognitive culture will be ultimized as well (Ll>La). One cannot let science or "reason" in general run an independent course; there must be "higher" constraints on them; they must fit into some grander design. Or rather, there is assumed to be unity between the Higher Truth and the specific truths that science might produce. If any conflict between specific and Higher Truth appears, religious-ideological revelation takes priority over the claims of reason per se. In addition, cognitive culture will be moralized (Li>La). This follows quite directly from its ultimization. It means first that noncognitive values will be imposed on science. Purely intellectual rationalization will be devalued. Generally speaking, an ethic of responsibility requires clear cognitive input to assess potential results; but since in fundamentalism cognitive input per se is devalued and moral principles have ultimate significance, the dominant ethic is likely to be an ethic of conviction. The contingency of ethical ideas and the (cognitive) conditions of their implementation, especially as fueled by the Reformation, are thus "resolved." And, finally, expressive culture is moralized as well (Li>Lg). Moral and expressive culture are pretty much fused. Expressive models come to have moral significance; there is always a lesson to be learned from art.

In general, then, fundamentalism as a movement at the cultural level attempts to put the burden of proof on attempts to differentiate spheres of culture.[1] But this does not mean that it simply "reduces" ambiguity or "rejects" reflexivity. While this may be the fundamentalist *self*-conception, in fact fundamentalism cannot be characterized either in terms of the content of specific ultimate values or as totally nonreflexive. In dealing with more or less differentiated spheres it demonstrates a certain *kind* of *reflexive capacity*. For example, a fundamentalist ethic of conviction may *define itself* as living by faith alone and not to be compromised. But *in fact* no ethics can be merely a matter of conviction. The difference between an ethic of conviction and others, then, may lie more in the *kind* of reflexiveness involved. The same goes for other aspects of reflexiveness and revision at the social and cultural level. It is this *kind* of capacity rather than mere unreflexiveness that distinguishes it from voluntaristic or utilitarian ways of handling the contingencies of modern sociocultural systems.

In the fundamentalist syndrome the relation between "culture" and "society" is a close one. The image of the good society is at least supposed to be clear; a direct realization of Higher Principles is at least considered possible and obligatory (L>I). Collective sentiments are felt to be derived from collective representations. There cannot be much room for societal experiments with available cultural resources. Social action is always in principle subject to Higher Criteria, and must thus remain within strict boundaries. Again, differentiation and value generalization, which would increase the "degrees of freedom" for social action, are checked. This cultural dominance is likely to be reflected most in the societal subsystem most directly related to the cultural system, namely the so-called fiduciary system. For example, if we locate education in this sphere, its moral task will come to be especially emphasized. Insofar as the family is generally regarded as the institution specialized in moral transmission, its moralizing role will be emphasized, while its independence and privacy will be relativized as being potentially dangerous.

At the social system level, again, controlling subsystems will come to dominate others. This implies, first of all, moralization of the societal community ($Il > Ii$). There will be strict religious-ideological criteria for full membership; the societal community comes to be defined more exclusively. Insofar as a broadened base of inclusion is characteristic of modernity, this is another antimodern feature of fundamentalism. There will be a demand for strict enforcement of moral precepts. Generally speaking, law mediates between overarching values and specific normative order; for fundamentalism, the emphasis will be on its anchorage in Higher Principles and on strict obedience to it. Substantive rationality comes to prevail in law as it does in the moral sphere; "mere procedure" becomes a secondary matter. In social action, value commitments take priority over "mere" influence; it is primarily on the basis of such commitments that one can forge communal bonds.

The polity will be moralized as well ($Il > Ig$). The importance of proper legitimation is emphasized over power or administrative performance per se. If the ultilitarian distortion of "modernity" is accepting legality only and denying the necessity of legitimacy/morality, fundamentalism tends to delegitimize legality per se. Authority is religionized or ideologized; it is to be used to carry out an established societal project. There is a tendency to establish religious-ideological criteria for political office. The symbolic aspects of politics come to carry as much weight as actual results. Similarly, the economic sphere will be moralized as well ($Il > Ia$). Economic development cannot become a value in itself but must be a means for a Higher Goal. Insofar as economic life operates by contract, contracts will have to fit into the framework of a Higher Contract. Commitment is never to economic activity per se but always on the basis of "Higher Criteria."

The "socialization" of polity and economy by the societal community ($Ii > Ig$, $Ii > Ia$) follows closely their moralization. "Society" takes priority over "state." This does not mean that the "associational" aspects of society dominate its "system" aspects but rather that the polity is seen as expressing the community as a whole. Insofar as political development involves bureaucratization, it has to be checked by a normative order. Similarly, mechanical solidarity takes priority over mere contractual relationships, as does the "social meaning" of status incumbents over their merit. In the distribution of rewards religio-moral criteria will count most; the honorable and the prestigious will form the major elite. Restructuring a stratification system along fundamentalist lines thus means making it more one-dimensional.

Society as such will try to incorporate the individual as tightly as possible (I>G). Only as a conscientious role player can the individual make a legitimate contribution. He has to let collective sentiment prevail over personal affect. At the same time the ultimately grounded expressive culture does not allow much freedom in the choosing of ego ideals (L>G), which will thus tend to be rather uniform. This reverberates at the personality level as well. On the one hand, the ego will be idealized (Gl>Gg). Ego interests are typically given up for a Higher Cause; the ego will develop in terms of a Higher Framework. "Selflessness" becomes a value. On the other hand, dominating collective sentiment translates into superego, keeping the lid tightly shut on the id (Gi>Ga). "Self-discipline" becomes the rule. Hence, insofar as modernity involves greater autonomy for the individual, fundamentalism also tends to go against the modern grain in this respect (even if it only serves to render individual autonomy more problematic rather than to destroy it altogether).

Finally, without going into the behavioral system (or intelligent problem-solving) level per se (Lidz and Lidz 1976), fundamentalism makes intelligence per se count less. If common sense is the product of expectational intelligence teaming up with collective sentiment, this means that it will be "commonalized" (I>A). In other words, if a conflict arises between the individual's understanding or expectations and those that collective definitions specify, the latter are to be followed. The utilitarian tendency is not to ask questions where common sense seems to be violated, because to worry about *common* sense is stupid as long as one remains cool-headed; the fundamentalist tendency is not to ask questions because that would be bad and because ultimately the very idea of cool-headedness is reprehensible. Again, this does not necessarily destroy the independent problem-solving capacities of individuals, but rather constitutes a particular way of channeling and constraining them.

Fundamentalism and Revitalization

Let us assume that the above section presents the form the fundamentalist syndrome takes ideal-typically speaking. In this section I will suggest that one aspect of the fundamentalist self-interpretation— namely, that fundamentalism is engaged in a process of sociocultural revitalization—can be treated more systematically in action-theoretical terms. Before considering how revitalization can take this particular, dedifferentiating form I will briefly deal with the link between current, more historical approaches to revitalization (e.g., McLoughlin 1978; Huntington 1981) and action theory, to make the point that action theory needs to posit processes of revitalization.

The reason for revitalization processes seems to be essentially the revisability of action systems that comes with modernity. No wonder: if, as many *Gesellschaft* theorists have argued, identities are now to be consciously constructed, they can be *re*constructed; if beliefs are "held," they can be changed (Geertz 1968). And not only do systems become revis*able*, actual revision, re-formation becomes the norm. That is, revitalization must be part and parcel of modernity. This is not to say that revitalization does not occur in "traditional" societies—Wallace (1956) indicates the contrary. Nor is it to say that revitalization does not have more general theoretical relevance, for example as a necessary element in *any* sociocultural order: Weber's concept of charisma, Durkheim's notion of effervescence, and the like already point to theoretical significance beyond the latest stages of evolution. However, in line with more conventional views of modernization, I would still argue that there is something qualitively different about "revisability" and "revitalization" in modernity, especially because they seem to have become the *norm*.[2]

In a very general sense the pressure toward revisability and revision seems to be a function of differentiation and generalization, coupled with the "need" for integration/implementation, in roughly the following way. Differentiation, insofar as it is the condition of a more elaborate division of labor and of rationalization within differentiated spheres, introduces a measure of certainty and predictability in sociocultural life, and if differentiation is seen only as the condition of the emergence of the iron cage, its relevance to the problem of revitalization must seem minimal. But differentiation also implies uncertainty; a purely stable arrangement of systems is impossible; one can give priority to one or the other, but one is always forced to move on the horns of a dilemma. This follows from Bellah's model of religious evolution (Bellah 1964), which points to the differentiation of self, culture, and society introduced in the historic stage; the Reformation stage then made conflicts between them inevitable. In particular, as Baum (1977a) emphasizes, conflicts are institutionalized among various elites, between the individual and society, and between ideas and institutions. The latter point is exacerbated by value generalization. Generalized values cannot be "realized"; one never quite lives up to them, there always remains a deficit. And yet activism has become the rule in modernity—one can no longer simply accept the dilemmas or the value deficit; one is obliged to live up to and implement one's standards. The fallout from the Reformation stage is indeed the requirement to deal with these problems actively. But this leads to problems. The conflicts (especially between spheres) are conflicts between various directions in the rationalization of the world, and thus no fully rationalized solutions are possible. Decisions must be made but rational necessity alone cannot be brought to bolster them. Hence there is a built-in danger of extremism in the pursuit of any rational reconciliation. The modern world has institutionalized tragedy as well as decisionism. There are tensions we must live with but at the same time experience as grave burdens.[3] In such a world, "order" can never be secure but must continually be (re)constructed. Although the standards may have become more general and the scene of action complex, there still is a "need," or at least a tendency, to construct normative order. And yet no particular order can be considered perfect. To sum up: differentiation introduces tension; generalization legitimates the tension, as it were; "adaptation" means drawing active-critical implications from this; and yet order needs to be (re)constructed while remaining inherently problematic—hence, revitalization must become the rule in modernity.

But what makes such revitalization *possible?* Here the more historical approaches to revitalization, like the ones taken by McLoughlin (1978) and Huntington (1981), in turn make action-theoretical assumptions. I suggest that some of the conditions they suggest for revitalization in America can be generalized and fit in with action-theoretical accounts of sociocultural order. First of all, there must obviously be something to be revitalized—essentially some "common cultural core" shared by many actors, which is *one* element in all social order according to action theory. Although Huntington criticizes a pure consensus theory of historical change and McLoughlin indicates that commonality cannot be taken for granted and that the "core" itself may change, the "core" assumption is made nevertheless.

But for such a core to make it through a process of revitalization some continuity through change must be guaranteed, encoded as it were. Huntington goes further than McLoughlin in assuming straight continuity of core values. But the purpose of both is not so much to emphasize continuity over change and consensus over conflict. Rather, the theoretical significance of their work may be that it shows how continuity makes change and how consensus makes conflict possible.

For a revitalization process to be more than an intellectual affair and to become societally relevant, there must be some intimate link between the cultural and the social-institutional level. In principle the society must be in some sense culturally defined; the societal community must be a "moral" one—as action theory has argued for social systems generally. McLoughlin and Huntington argue of course that America satisfies this condition—especially insofar as the nation came to be identified with a rather explicit set of ideas, a "creed."

If action is to be undertaken under these conditions, there must also be pressure to do so. In other words, the core must have ethical implications for individual and social action. The continuous tension between institutions and ideas that this involves has been character-istic of America according to McLoughlin and especially Huntington. The "interpenetration" of "ethics" and "action" has also been one of the keynotes in action-theoretical thinking about order, as I indicated above (see Münch 1980, 1982).

If, then, revitalization is undertaken, what can the revitalization trajectories be? First, if there is to be continuity through change, then some of the continuity should be found *in the pattern of revitalization.* Here we can take cues from Eisenstadt (1978), who pointed to deep-structural continuity in revolutionary transformation, from Martin (1978), who pointed to "frames" setting the boundaries to change fueled by differentiation, and from Baum (1977a, 1977b), who distin-guished between ex toto and ex parte codes as themselves stable grids of modernization trajectories. If such codes are to be used by more or less authoritative agencies as a basis for sociocultural revision, then we should find some such forms in the pattern of revitalization itself as well.

But another way of distinguishing between forms of revitalization may be more relevant here, namely to characterize processes of revi-talization on the basis of the direction in which they would typically go. From an action-theoretical point of view different syndromes are objectively possible, depending on their specific functional primacy; of course revitalization in a more complex, multidimensional mode is possible as well. Since only fundamentalism is of interest here, the question is: what values are the variables accounting for revitaliza-tion in general to take for an action complex to make a fundamental-ist move? The tentative heuristic to be followed here is relatively simple: "modernization" entails similar problems for all action com-plexes. While in Parsons' model of modernity "differentiation" and "integration" were really inseparable aspects of evolutionary process, we may distinguish between shared problems of "differentiation" and various "integrative" modes of dealing with them. Hence we should try to identify those points in an action complex where disturbance is most relevant to a fundamentalist mode of revitalization, and at the same time the conditions that must also prevail (i.e., the particular "values" of the revitalization variables) if there is to be a fundamentalist response.

First, fundamentalism as a value-oriented movement attempting some kind of cultural restoration requires, to use a term that has become rather problematic, "strain" at the cultural level. Erosion of the cultural framework should be noticeable from some point of view. More specifically, since fundamentalism attempts to reestablish absolute values, such strain should come in the form of value dissensus (whether such dissensus is objectively there or simply a plausible interpretation on the part of the actors involved makes little difference). At the same time, there should be common cultural resources available for a fundamentalist revitalizing response. As a value-oriented "movement," fundamentalism requires the availability of plausible, shared, generalized belief (Smelser 1962). More specifically, such belief should legitimate dedifferentiation.[4]

Second, fundamentalism as a value-oriented movement is more likely the more strain at the social level spills over to the cultural level. This is more likely the case the more sensitive a society is to infractions on its cultural definitions. To use Swanson's terms (Swanson 1967; see Bergesen 1978), the more corporate interests take priority over constituent interests, the more embedded collective representations will be and the more areas will be politicized. Hence, in more "immanent" societies fundamentalist revitalization is more likely.

Immanence signals relative nondifferentiation of culture and society and has implications beyond this particular zone of interpenetration. For fundamentalism as a reaction to differentiation partially depends on the extent and legitimacy of the differentiation accomplished. More generally speaking, then, to the extent that differentiation has been less pervasive and less legitimate, efforts at dedifferentiation will obviously be easier. Such efforts, like all revitalization movements, require that ethical implications of cultural principles are taken seriously. Thus immanence indicates the extent to which such activistic impulses will be sensitized while the extent and legitimacy of differentiation indicates the extent to which they will be facilitated in a fundamentalist direction.

But fourth, and more importantly, if Martin (1978) can treat the process of secularization as a function of a sociocultural "frame" and "differentiation," then we should be able to account for typical responses to secularization in similar terms. Since differentiation (as it often leads to delegitimation, destratification, and "alienation") is a constant, the frame has to be the differentiating factor. The frame, which guarantees continuity through change, is not only likely to be *reflected in* the pattern of fundamentalism, the *kind* of continuity it guarantees is also important. Generally speaking, fundamentalism is more likely the greater the elective affinity between it and the frame. I suggest that this affinity can be characterized most generally (though still only loosely) in functional terms. Fundamentalism is value maintenance and pattern maintenance oriented; it attempts stabilization (on the basis of absolute values) and "decomplexification" (by means of dedifferentiation). In action theory, this has also been regarded as the primary function of the L-G axis in the AGIL paradigm, as opposed to the A-I axis (see Baum 1977a, 1977b). Hence, fundamentalism is more likely where an L-G frame prevails. Baum's so-called ex toto codes, too, were assigned special L-G significance. And such ex toto codes were supposed to be applied in processes of revitalization, hence to "frame" modernization. So we may infer: ex toto/L-G frames, hence ex toto/L-G revitalization, hence fundamentalism.[5]

Finally, to return to the more general evolutionary perspective, there may be something qualitatively different about revitalization in modernity especially insofar as it has become the *norm*. I have also called fundamentalism a mode of revitalization and a mode of dealing with modernity. That suggests: fundamentalism is inherent in modernity. Just as the Bellah model of religious evolution has implications for revitalization generally, it has implications for fundamentalism. Essentially, the point is that fundamentalism, as a dedifferentiating response to differentiation, is only possible *after* some significant differentiation has taken place. So only after Bellah's historic stage are full-fledged value movements of a fundamentalist sort possible. In addition, the early modern inner worldly–activist Reformation and its fallout seem to constitute the condition that make such movements at all viable and likely to be undertaken. Given these prior evolutionary stages many modern societies have *some* capacity for fundamentalism. Given this and the points made above the problem now is to distinguish between forms of fundamentalism.

Empirical Variations

What variations can we expect *within* the general fundamentalist syndrome? Without claiming completeness and only in a very general vein let me suggest a few sources of variation—assuming for the moment that the "normal" preconditions of revitalization are present and that there are developments roughly conforming to the fundamentalist syndrome. Again, I follow the Martin (1978) heuristic—one source of variation having to do with aspects of the "frame," the other with aspects of "differentiation."

First we have, of course, the variables previously introduced to account for fundamentalism; they can have different "values."[6] The first of these suggests: fundamentalism requires shared belief legitimating dedifferentiation. The emphasis is on absolute values and on top-down constraints. We may thus find an important source of variation in the way dedifferentiation is initiated at the highest level of action, in the *kind of ultimization* attempted. I suggest that there are basically three ways: moral culture or "ideology" can be given ultimate status; a "traditional" religion can come to overwhelm all else; and a "traditional" religion can be pitted against a more or less autonomous moral culture and civil religion (see Lidz 1979; Markoff and Regan 1981).

The general implication of the immanence variable is: fundamentalism will flow more smoothly the more limited and the less legitimate differentiation is to begin with. Where differentiation is "more limited" it will also tend to be "less legitimate," so that one kind of fundamentalism can capitalize on it. But where differentiation has gone deeper and become more legitimate, fundamentalism will be in a more problematic position. In general we could say, following Martin, that the Reformation-plus-Enlightenment tandem supports differentiation most; in most other cases, as Parsons would have argued as well, it will be at least somewhat problematic.

Third, the specific frame variable suggests: the fundamentalism syndrome has greater affinity with some frames than with others. Hence high-level efforts at dedifferentiation should receive differential support lower down. Where authority and identity codes are more ex toto (that is, where collective interests and collective abstract ideals "normally" have priority in the legitimation of authority and the formation of individual identity—(Baum 1977a, 1977b), fundamentalism is more likely to receive support. Fundamentalism also tries to make stratification systems more one-dimensional by imposing religious-ideological criteria of evaluation as the only legitimate ones; hence support for fundamentalism will be greater the more there has historically been a one-dimensional stratification system. If, on the other hand, codes are more ex parte and stratification has tended to be more mixed or split (see Baum 1972), support will be harder to come by.

But these conditions only specify how a system is predisposed to fundamentalism; they do not by themselves indicate what fundamentalism is responding to. As I indicated above, "modernity" or "the impact of modernization" has to be the bottom-line shared experience. Hence there will obviously be differences related to the modernization/differentiation experience. Was it internal or external, gradual or sudden, early or late, deep or superficial, etc.?[7] An externally induced, sudden, late, and deep modernization experience is likely to present a more favorable environment for fundamentalist tendencies. At the same time revitalization processes and fundamentalism can be regarded as broad "value-oriented" movements, to use Smelser's (1962) term. They are therefore subject to the contingencies to which such movements are normally subject.

Two of the variables in Smelser's model are equivalent to the conditions mentioned above. "Conduciveness to strain" identifies the likelihood that conflicts will spill over to the value level. The immanence/limited differentiation variable described above already points to differential conduciveness. Smelser's "generalized belief" variable is equivalent to the belief-legitimating dedifferentiation variable. But Smelser adds three main contingencies: first, "strain" reflects the differential impact of modernization. Such strain can normally be expected to include value dissensus, the delegitimation of authority, destratification, "anomie," and the like. Societies can obviously vary in these respects. A fundamentalist effort at mending a shattered whole will be fueled when dissensus follows presumed value unity, where authority is supposed to be wide-ranging and have a "sacred aspect," and where modernizing changes cannot be handled by an open, multidimensional stratification system. Second, there are of course differences related to the influence of specific "precipitating events" and to the specific chances of the actual mobilization of resources and people by active leaders/elites.[8] Finally, "social control" denotes the differential capacity of responsible authorities to contain a movement (which provides the counterpoint to the differential support variable mentioned above). Obviously, if there are variations on these grounds, we should also expect different fundamentalist movements to have different foci and different typical ways of failing. But let me turn to some ideal-typical illustrations of the points made thus far (which are meant to serve as illustrations only). My cases will be Chinese, Islamic, and American fundamentalism.

The Chinese cultural revolution qualifies as a fundamentalist experiment, both at the cultural-ideological and at the social system level (see Huntington 1981). This fundamentalist experiment was characterized by the fact that the high-level impulse came in the form of the ultimization of ideology. It was facilitated by the fact that differentiation was limited to begin with: the social system had direct cultural significance; ideology and organization were ideally inseparable. In this case Maoism, however diffuse a set of beliefs it may in fact have embraced, served as the generalized belief legitimating dedifferentiation, and many fundamentalist themes can be found in it. For example, it implied that strict ideological constraints had to be put on the moral, aesthetic, and cognitive spheres; following the vision of the Great Leap it suggested that communization had to take precedence over economic development per se, that redness had to be valued more highly than expertness, that "politics" (= ideology) had to take command and that contradictions in society had to be "resolved" by means of class struggle; for individuals, full commitment and strict self-discipline were required (see Schurmann 1966; Dittmer 1974). Once a cultural revolution was initiated it could capitalize on a strong legitimation of wide-ranging central authority and the collectivity orientation of individuals.

The major modernization push after the Communist revolution came in the form of a fast and thorough politically controlled reorganization of economy and society and in the form of rationalization of the control apparatus. However, industrialization did not occur as expected, agriculture was hard to modernize, and the political reorganization was not based on a widespread consensus on the nature of its legitimacy (see Pepper 1978). Thus modernization took place primarily in the G-sphere, with the state functioning as the integrative mechanism, while adaptive upgrading and cultural restoration remained problematic. In the 1960s, according to standard accounts (e.g., Dittmer 1974; Lee 1978, 1979; Schram 1973), a split occurred in the Party —first of all at the level of value patterns—within the elite and between Liu and Mao, the latter emphasizing themes of struggle, solidarity, idealism, and the like. Along with this dissensus, which was of course especially significant in a centrally guided society, came destratification at the top insofar as the ideologically primary elite around Mao became relatively powerless (while retaining at least some cultural honor and prestige). The bureaucracy came to operate more in terms of functional criteria rather than under a sacred ideological canopy. Liu's efforts at "rationalization" could be seen as still quite limited attempts at differentiation. Since the power center could ultimately not answer the claims put forward by radical opponents, the mechanisms of social control at its disposal were undercut and conflict escalated to the value level. The burden of proof shifted dramatically; the fundamentalists could at least for a while take advantage of that shift.

The focus in the subsequent cultural revolution was of course first on the center of power, and secondly on reeducation. It was characterized by intense activity at the "center," with mainly indirect impact from there on the periphery by a cultural-ideological and in principle almost antiorganizational orientation and by the generality of its impact. The ideologically committed rose in the hierarchy. Thus at least initially the cultural revolution followed the fundamentalist program. Its failure was that "organization" had to be restored and the stratification system restructured on the basis of power. If we characterize the Chinese modernization process as G oriented and the ideological revitalization efforts as L oriented, its revitalization processes can perhaps be characterized as L-G oscillation.

The Iranian revolution is of course the most famous case of fundamentalist revitalization. It is characterized by the fact that ultimization came in the form of a traditional religion overwhelming everything else. Many fundamentalist characteristics can be found at the level of belief and consequently at the level of action. Using the constitution of the Islamic Republic of Iran as a representative document we can see, for example, that the revolution was thought to derive its strength from being "ideological" (i.e., Islamic), from striving for authenticity, thus cleansing the nation of "dust and impurities" and purging it of foreign ideological influences (Algar 1980:18). Of course the republic is supposed to be the embodiment of religious belief, and differentiation of the political and religious spheres is rejected (Algar 1980:107ff, Article 5). Economic development is supposed to take place within a framework of social justice; the societal community is tightly inclusive with respect to women, relatively exclusive with respect to (non-Islamic) minorities (see Algar 1980:21–22, Article 11). "Individualism" is seen as evil. Thus a generalized belief legitimating dedifferentiation was clearly available. At the same time, differentiation, for example between religion and state or between religion and morality, had remained relatively limited even before the time of the shah; at least the burden of proof had always been on the differentiators. The society had remained relatively immanent and was thus conducive to strain at the value level. Once begun, the movement could draw on the sacred aspect of religiously inspired authority and on the collective-idealistic orientation of individuals (that is, on the L-G aspects of the underlying frame).

The concrete background to the Iranian revolution is quite well known (see Akhavi 1980; Fischer 1980; Keddie 1980; for the Middle

East more generally see Esposito 1980). The shah's "revolution" consisted of a fast, politically organized attempt at radical adaptive upgrading by means of economic-technological progress (the national income and inflation rose fast; resources were developed; agriculture was modernized). At the same time the expanded state apparatus was to maintain tight control over the societal community. (Iran thus experienced both A- and G-oriented "modernization.") As a result substantial value dissensus and cultural bifurcation developed between the proponents of "modernization" and the majority of more tradition-minded opponents. Land, legal, and educational reforms cut into the structure of the societal community (anomie). While a "new class" rose on the scales of wealth and power, it did not do so on the scales of honor and prestige; the *ʾulama*, provincial elites, the *bazaari*, and even the peasants were at least relatively displaced in terms of stratification—a clear case of destratification. The attempted adaptive/goal attainment revolution certainly required drawing upon the legitimacy bank—which declared the shah's regime to be bankrupt. When the relatively independent religious elite began to lead to countermovement it could thus draw upon substantial dissatisfaction. The ensuing conflict quickly escalated to the value level, and the mechanisms of social control containing the movement were gradually undermined. The burden of proof was shifted completely.

The focus after the revolution itself was of course on "restoring" the Islamic nature of the society and taking over the center of power. Intense religiously inspired activity combined with an almost antiinstitutional orientation had a pervasive impact throughout the society. The most religiously qualified rose in the hierarchy. The fundamentalist program was in fact carried out in the personal, sociopolitical, and cultural spheres. If it fails in the longer run it will probably be because any conflict can now immediately become a value conflict because the original aura of authenticity cannot be maintained and because potential differentiation will put pressure on the more dedifferentiated mold, which may force it to move in a more authoritarian direction. The overall revitalization process can then perhaps be characterized as another case of L-G oscillation (with the content of L and G being quite different than in the Chinese case).

American fundamentalism is a case where the high-level impulse comes from a traditional religion pitted against a more or less autonomous moral culture and civil religion.[9] It follows the fundamentalist syndrome, for example, by efforts to ultimize/moralize science, to remoralize the society, to religionize politics, and to reintegrate individuals. A generalized, religiously grounded belief legitimating some dedifferentiation was thus available. Of course it had to do so in a context where differentiation had proceeded quite far and had itself become legitimate, so that normally the burden of proof was on the dedifferentiators. In addition the society was hardly immanent since constituent interests were at least on a par with corporate ones, and since American civil religion was sufficiently general and autonomous to not be directly affected by social conflict, which tended not to spill over to the value level per se. Once initiated as a more or less public movement fundamentalism in America could not draw on ex toto resources, but had to rely on its own constituent parts and on individuals committed to the specific cause, and, ironically, on elements of American civil religion and of the American tradition.

The major modernization push in late nineteenth- and early twentieth-century America was first of all a matter of adaptive upgrading by means of fast and thorough economic modernization (as measured in output, national income, productivity, and the like). At the same time an integrative revolution took place to increase the inclusion of members/citizens in the societal community, primarily by means of a universalistic legal system and a relatively open, multidimensional stratification system. The state's role remained limited. The American "creed" was not crucially involved although some cultural adjustments were of course necessary. Hence it is fair to say that America underwent primarily adaptive-integrative modernization in that pivotal period. While civil religion plus denominationalism (plus ethnic pluralism) actually limited value dissensus, some Protestants experienced what Marsden (1980) calls the internal American analogue to the immigration experience, insofar as they were culturally displaced and the burden of proof was shifted to them. On the other hand, given the open stratification system, destratification was unlikely, and consequently fundamentalism did not emerge simply as a movement of the "disinherited." When fundamentalism claimed a role in American revitalization both in the beginning of this century and in recent years, it could draw on cultural-moral dissatisfaction, but it could not dominate the process or succeed on its own terms, although a limited fundamentalist contribution remained legitimate.

The focus of American fundamentalism as a diffuse movement has been on bringing morality back in and on battling the impact of "secular humanism" in science and morality and in education and politics. It has been characterized by ambivalence insofar as it remained committed to (and was itself made possible by) some fundamental features of the very society it tried to fundamentally cleanse of impurities. While fundamentalists seem to have risen in terms of stratification since the beginning of this century, they have not done so on religiomoral grounds. The actual impact of the fundamentalist program has in fact remained limited. If anything, the trends provoking it to begin with have continued, while the burden of proof has been placed upon it even more firmly. But given the legitimacy of differentiation, the durability of civil religion and denominationalism, the inclusiveness of the societal community, and the limited range of political authority, fundamentalism in America is bound to fail on its own terms (and in fact seems to have liberalized under the pressure). If we characterize American revitalization processes as cases of A-I oscillation, some form of fundamentalism may still have an important contribution to make insofar as it keeps a certain "tension" in the system and helps prevent sliding into mere individualist utilitarianism.

Fundamentalism and Globalization

Thus far I have discussed fundamentalism in an intrasocietal vein, as if societal action systems were pretty much closed and pretty much followed their own logic. We know, however, that societies are now part of a *system* of societies. Parsons' own discussion of evolution focused precisely on that system. The question, then, is if developments at the inter- and transsocietal level have an impact on societal fundamentalism, if the terms of the discussion should therefore be changed, and if in the frame-plus-differentiation equation "globalization" should be introduced as a necessary third term. In very brief compass I suggest that "globalization" is indeed a crucial element in the analysis of fundamentalism and that the relation between the two can be stated in roughly action-theoretical terms.

Following Nettl and Robertson (1968), Robertson (1983), and Robertson and Chirico (1985) we can outline several aspects of globalization. To begin with societies, being part of a world system, now not only have to internally guarantee continuity over change, the priority of collective over individual interests, and the like, but also need to be concerned with the *relative* quality of their societal identity (L in the four-function paradigm) and the *relative* effectiveness of their societal goal attainment (G in AGIL). Societies, then, are now no longer culturally self-sufficient (if they ever were), and are thus forced to be more identity minded, to legitimate particular societal identities in more "global-universalistic terms, and to evaluate their performance in global-comparative terms. Global development thus intensifies the *empirical* problem of societal order and revitalizes it at the same time. With respect to the relation between individuals and national societies this implies a gradual drawing out of personality from the nation-state shell, and potentially a relating of the self to the more global category of humanity. It also suggests that in the present global circumstance the relationship of particular societies to their own cultural reservoir is rendered more problematic. And, finally, the world system itself, while often regarded in merely political-economic terms, now seems to be in the (conflict-ridden) process of being culturally "vitalized"; at least the *problem* of global order is high on the international agenda. It follows, as Parsons had already noted, that societal modernization is never merely societal, that the global system is an integral part of modernity. Insofar as we are witnessing an emerging differentiation between the societal and global spheres, accompanied by as yet problematic global value generalization, it may even be regarded as a new stage in sociocultural evolution (Robertson 1983). Important here is what this more global perspective adds to the analysis of revitalization: revitalization movements can now be seen at least in part as societal (not necessarily only internal-societal) modes of dealing with in part *globally* induced problems of order. We thus need to broaden our view of such movements.

Any revitalization theory, then, should be able to account for both global "vitalization" and societal revitalization (and, by implication, for fundamentalism). I would argue that only a *voluntaristic* theory of the world system enable us to do both (see Robertson 1983). The hallmark of such a voluntaristic theory (a "global extension" of action theory) would be the *interpenetration* of the societal and global spheres on the one hand, and of "ideal" and "material" spheres on the other. Only a world system theory of this sort can face the double task. Although such a theory is in fact only in its beginning stages, we can suggest a few things it would have to hold and a way in which it might shed light on revitalization and fundamentalism.

Such a theory would have to hold, to give only one example, that the "globe" is possible only if "society" is also possible. Thus a voluntaristic world system theory has to ask again, from a new point of view: how *is* society (now) possible? If there is to be some global-societal functional differentiation, an action-theoretical point of view would suggest that *some* value generalization should also be expected to balance and bridge it. Thus if a world system is to be possible we should postulate the emergence of global values in terms of which particular societies can construct and legitimate their identities. By analogy with Durkheim's conception of organic solidarity, a core element of the emerging global culture might well be the cult of the nation-state, or "institutionalized societalism." At the very least such a theory would have to postulate a global search for the legitimate terms of existence of particular societies and for criteria to evaluate proper societal functioning. (Particular societies, on the other hand, should be found to formulate their particular identities more explicitly and legitimate them in more transsocietal terms.)

More important in the present context is another implication of such a theory: for global vitalization to be possible, societal revitalization should also be possible. Indeed, the world system in this view *requires* societal revitalization (and seems to have made it almost *obligatory*). One indicator for this is the following. The "church"/ religion sphere in a society (L in AGIL terms) is often central to how a society defines itself and its quality, and the "state"/politics sphere (G in AGIL terms) determines the quality of societal goal attainment. Since these are also the "sensitive" spheres from a global point of view, it is not accidental that church-state and religion-politics tensions are prevalent worldwide (see Robertson and Chirico 1985; Robertson 1983). It is then especially this zone of interpenetration that is crucial to societal revitalization, although other zones are of course involved as well. But while the revitalization requirement in principle weighs heavily on all societies, it may not be equally heavy in all cases. One further task for revitalization theory, then, is to analyze the possible *differential* impact of globalization. Moreover, the actual nature of revitalization movements is likely to be the result of *interpenetration* of relatively transsocietal and relatively internal factors, hence of the general process sketched here and the variables of previous sections. Fundamentalism is a case in point.

Fundamentalism was described above as the revitalization mode characterized by handling problems in various zones of interpenetration by top-down dedifferentiation. In addition, there appeared to be an affinity between fundamentalism and L-G oriented immanentist societies. These characteristics by themselves make fundamentalism pattern maintenance oriented. Now a voluntaristic world system theory would suggest that since the problematic global impact is felt especially in the L and G spheres, and fundamentalism has affinity with L-G oriented systems, the latter will be more affected by the globalization process and will, given the presence of the factors outlined in previous sections, be likely to respond in a fundamentalist fashion. The globalization process thus reinforces internal tendencies toward fundamentalism. More generally, such a theory would suggest that especially in the face of global developments "relativizing" societal coherence and identity, more or less absolutist fundamentalist revitalization efforts aimed at reestablishing coherence, conflating different spheres of life, and "closing" the society are to be expected. In some societies revitalization will simply *be* fundamentalist, depending on conditions mentioned in previous sections. In most societies efforts at revitalization will at least have fundamentalist *aspects*. And at least in relation to global development particular societal revitalization efforts may *appear* to be fundamentalist. Generally speaking, then, fundamentalism can be seen as one kind of functionally appropriate response to globalization.

Conclusions

What can we conclude from the analysis presented in this paper? Even the limited empirical illustrations indicate that further testing of the present approach, with more and different empirical materials, is necessary. This paper will perhaps serve as a basis for more empirical work in this general area. In addition, the "fundamentalist syndrome" is sufficiently generally formulated to allow for further application to phenomena (especially social movements) that do not seem to be cases of full-fledged fundamentalism.

In terms of the theoretical thrust of this paper we can at least conclude that in principle only an integrated theoretical framework —capable of providing an abstract description of fundamentalism at different levels of action and an evolutionary, comparative-structural, and world systemic perspective—will do if we are to fully understand fundamentalism. While the task of developing such a framework has by no means been completed in this paper I hope that an adequate start has been made. In addition, I have also tried to show that it is possible to extend and modify Parsons' approach to take into account inherently problematic aspects of modern sociocultural order and to analyze, from within the action-theoretical framework, part of the "logic of dedifferentiation."

With respect to fundamentalism itself one important conclusion has to be that as analyzed in this paper it certainly is a quintessentially modern penomenon. In part this is the case simply by definition: fundamentalism is of course modern insofar as it is "a way of dealing with modernity." Beyond that, a general, value-oriented effort at dedifferentiation in response to differentiation is certainly distinctly modern. However problematic the notions of "tradition" and "modernity" may have become, it has traditionally been thought characteristic of a tradition that "order," though it may in fact change, is largely taken for granted. In modernity that, at least, becomes impossible. As Al-Ghazzali said long ago, once the glass of a tradition has been shattered it can never be put together *as* a tradition (quoted in Halpern 1965:30–31). Hence even those whose impulse it is to try and take order for granted in fact have to *work* for it and *worry* about it. Against their own sentiments they are forced to attempt active reconstruction. But an effort at sociocultural revitalization now requires a degree of reflexivity, of conscious selectivity that is at least distinctly nontraditional, in spite of the fundamentalist self-conception. This reflexivity even goes so far as to reject its very basis—and it is precisely characteristic of modernity that it allows one to choose the ultimate option of rejecting modernity as such. And finally, given the essentially global nature of the modern human condition, fundamentalist revitalization also appeared to play an important role in the modern world system. Hence fundamentalism is very modern indeed.

Notes

1. I suggest that the concept of "burden of proof" can fruitfully be used to describe the aspects of and movements in complex and changing sociocultural situations. In such situations various parties involved generally have different definitions of the situation and different proposals for reconstruction; cultural conflict is likely to follow from their different claims to legitimacy and their different relative strengths. Movements generally try to shift at least the "burden of proof."

2. This does not force us to fully accept Bellah's claim that action systems become *infinitely* revisable in modernity. For one thing, as Bellah himself has surely recognized, revisability is constrained by relatively invariant system identities. Second, just as it is only the deadline of death that makes the freedom and individuality of persons meaningful precisely because it restricts the capacity of individuals to infinitely revise their biographies (Baum 1982), so the capacity to revise and the identity maintenance of societies is perhaps only meaningful if societies can "die"—if they are *not* infinitely revisable.

3. Fundamentalism is important precisely as one way to try to "dissolve" such tensions that come with modernization.

4. Hence we should find parallels between the symbolic structure of a fundamentalist belief system and the fundamentalist syndrome outlined above. If such parallels are an important condition for the development of fundamentalism, then finding them can also serve as an indicator of its (at least potential) presence.

5. The previous point about the extent and legitimacy of differentiation produces an interaction effect here: in L-G frames differentiation probably has not gone as far, and has become less legitimate, than it was in A-I frames to begin with. So differentiation itself should vary with the nature of the frame. Second, the "hence" only indicates probabilities. An ex parte framework does not necessarily

make fundamentalism impossible; it does make it more problematic. A-I frames will vary in the extent to which they make room for some form of fundamentalism. Insofar as fundamentalism does play a part there, it will do so as a counterpart to the mainstream.

6. I suggest that we regard the ethical implications variable as a constant. There has to be some commitment to an innerworldly-activist orientation. In modernity this can perhaps be taken as a cross-cultural universal.

7. As Bendix (1967) has indicated, the speed and extent of modernization and the like are important variables if we are to interpret responses to it. Such specific variables have an important role to play in the analysis of such responses, but do so best *within* a general theoretical framework.

8. Here again more specific factors, the ones usually associated with the so-called resource mobilization perspective on social movements (see Zald and Mc-Carthy 1979), are seen to play an important role *within* a more general framework.

9. I rely on Marsden (1980) and McLoughlin (1978), among others. Fundamentalism as a theoretical category is here "operationalized" to include much of evangelicalism as well.

References

Akhavi, Shahrough. 1980. *Religion and Politics in Contemporary Iran*. Albany: State University of New York Press.

Algar, Hamid, tr. 1980. *Constitution of the Islamic Republic of Iran*. Berkeley, Calif.: Mizan Press.

Baum, Rainer C., 1972. "On Political Modernity: Stratification and the Generation of Societal Power." In Edward B. Harvey ed., *Perspectives on Modernization: Essays in Memory of Ian Weinberg*, pp. 22–49. Toronto.

—— 1975. "The System of Solidarities." *Indian Journal of Sociology* 16(1/2):305–53.

—— 1977a."Authority Codes: The Invariance Hypothesis." *Zeitschrift fuer Soziologie* (January), 6(1):5–28.

—— 1977b. "Authority and Identity: The Invariance Hypothesis II." *Zeitschrift für Soziologie* (October), 6(4):349–69.

—— 1981. *The Holocaust and the German Elite: Genocide and National Suicide in Germany, 1871–1945*. London: Croom Helm; Totowa, N.J.: Rowman and Littlefield.

—— 1982. "A Revised Interpretive Approach to the Religious Significance of Death in Western Societies." *Sociological Analysis* 43(4):327–49.

Baum, R. C. and F. J. Lechner, 1981. "National Socialism: Towards an Action-Theoretical Interpretation." *Sociological Inquiry* 51(3/4):281–308.

Bellah, Robert N. 1964. "Religious Evolution." *American Sociological Review* (April), 29:358–74.

Bendix, Reinhard. 1967. "Tradition and Modernity Reconsidered." *Comparative Studies in Society and History* 9(3):292–346.

Bergesen, Albert J. 1978. "A Durkheimian Theory of 'Witch Hunts' with the Chinese Cultural Revolution 1966–1969 as an Example." *Journal for the Scientific Study of Religion* 17(1)19–29.

Brownstein, Larry. 1982. *Talcott Parsons' General Action Scheme: An Investigation of Fundamental Principles*. Cambridge, Mass.: Schenkman.

Dittmer, Lowell. 1974. *Liu Shao-ch'i and the Chinese Cultural Revolution: The Politics of Mass Criticism.* Berkeley: University of California Press.

Eisenstadt, Shmuel N. 1978. *Revolution and the Transformation of Societies: A Comparative Study of Civilizations.* New York: Free Press.

Esposito, John L. 1980. *Islam and Development: Religion and Sociopolitical Change.* Syracuse, N.Y.: Syracuse University Press.

Fischer, Michael M. J. 1980. *Iran: From Religious Dispute to Revolution.* Cambridge, Mass.: Harvard University Press.

Geertz, Clifford. 1968. *Islam Observed: Religious Development in Morocco and Indonesia.* Chicago, Ill. and London: University of Chicago Press.

Gould, Mark. 1976. "System Analysis, Macrosociology and the Generalized Media of Social Action." In J. J. Loubser et al., eds., *Explorations in General Theory in Social Science,* pp. 470–506. New York: Free Press.

Halpern, Manfred. 1965. *The Politics of Social Change in the Middle East and North Africa.* Princeton. N.J.: Princeton University Press.

Huntington, Samuel P. 1981. *American Politics The Promise of Disharmony.* Cambridge, Mass.: Belknap.

Keddie, Nikki R. 1980. *Iran: Religion, Politics and Society.* London: Frank Cass.

Lee, Hong Yung. 1978. *The Politics of the Chinese Cultural Revolution: A Case Study.* Berkeley: University of California Press.

Lee, Hong Yung. 1979. "Mao's Strategy for Revolutionary Change: A Case Study of the Cultural Revolution." *China Quarterly* (March), no. 77, pp. 50–73.

Lidz, Victor M. 1979. "Secularization, Ethical Life, and Religion in Modern Societies." In Harry M. Johnson, ed. *Religious Change and Continuity,* pp. 191–217. San Francisco, Calif.: Jossey-Bass. (*Sociological Inquiry* [1979], vol. 49, nos. 2–3.)

Lidz, Charles W. and Victor Meyer Lidz. 1976. "Piaget's Psychology of Intelligence and the Theory of Action." In J. J. Loubser et al., eds., *Explorations in General Theory in Social Science,* pp. 195–239. New York: Free Press.

McLoughlin, William G. 1978. *Revivals, Awakenings, and Reform: An Essay on Religion and Social Change in America, 1607–1977.* Chicago, Ill. and London: University of Chicago Press.

Markoff, John and Daniel Regan. 1981. "The Rise and Fall of Civil Religion: Comparative Perspectives." *Sociological Analysis* 42(4):333–52.

Marsden, George M. 1980. *Fundamentalism and American Culture: The Shaping of Twentieth-Century Evangelicalism, 1870–1925.* New York and Oxford: Oxford University Press.

Martin, David. 1978. *A General Theory of Secularization.* New York: Harper and Row.

Münch, Richard. 1980. "Über Parsons zu Weber: Von der Theorie der Rationalisierung zur Theorie der Interpenetration." *Zeitschrift für Soziologie* 9(1):18–53.

—— 1982. *Theorie des Handelns.* Frankfurt am Main: Suhrkamp.

Nettl, J. P. and Roland Robertson. 1968. *International Systems and the Modernization of Societies.* New York: Basic Books.

Parsons, Talcott. 1954. *Essays in Sociological Theory.* New York: Free Press.

—— 1961a. "An Outline of the Social System." Talcott Parsons et al., eds., *Theories of Society,* pp. 39–79. New York: Free Press.

—— 1961b. "Introduction" (to section on culture). In Talcott Parsons et al., eds., *Theories of Society,* pp. 963–993. New York: Free Press.

—— 1966. *Societies: Evolutionary and Comparative Perspectives.* Englewood Cliffs, N.J.: Prentice-Hall.

—— 1968a. "Max Weber and the Contemporary Political Crisis." In Talcott Parsons, ed., *Politics and Social Structure*, pp. 98–124. New York: Free Press.

—— 1968b. "On Value-Commitments," In Talcott Parsons, ed., *Politics and Social Structure*, p. 439–72. New York: Free Press.

—— 1968c. (1937). *The Structure of Social Action*. New York: Free Press.

—— 1971. *The System of Modern Societies*. Englewood Cliffs, N.J.: Prentice-Hall.

—— 1977a. *Social Systems and the Evolution of Action Theory*. New York: Free Press.

—— 1977b. "Law as an Intellectual Stepchild." *Sociological Inquiry* 47:(3/4):11–58.

—— 1978. *Action Theory and the Human Condition*. New York: Free Press.

Parsons, Talcott and Neil Smelser. 1956. *Economy and Society*. New York: Free Press.

Pepper, Suzanne. 1978. *Civil War in China: The Political Struggle, 1945–1949*. Berkeley: University of California Press.

Robertson, Roland. 1978. *Meaning and Change: Explorations in the Cultural Sociology of Modern Societies*. New York and Oxford: University Press.

—— 1983. "The Relativization of Societies: Modern Religion and Globalization." In William Shepherd and Thomas Robbins, eds., *New Religious Movements and the Law* pp. 31–42. New York: Crossroads Books.

Robertson, Roland and JoAnn Chirico. 1985. "Humanity, Globalization and Worldwide Religious Resurgence." *Sociological Analysis* 46:219–242.

Schram, Stuart R., ed., 1973. *Authority, Participation and Cultural Change in China*. Cambridge: Cambridge University Press.

Schurmann, Franz. 1966. *Ideology and Organization in Communist China*. Berkeley: University of California Press.

Smelser, Neil. 1959. *Social Change in the Industrial Revolution*. Chicago, Ill.: University of Chicago Press.

—— 1962. *Theory of Collective Behavior*. Glencoe, Ill.: Free Press.

Smith, Anthony D. 1973. *The Concept of Social Change*. London: Routledge and Kegan Paul.

Swanson, Guy E. 1967. *Religion and Regime*. Ann Arbor: University of Michigan Press.

Wallace, Anthony F. C. 1956. "Revitalization Movements." *American Anthropologist* 57:264–81.

Zald, Mayer N. and John D. McCarthy, eds., 1979. *The Dynamics of Social Movements: Resource Mobilization, Social Control, and Tactics*. Cambridge, Mass.: Winthrop.

4

Uneven Differentiation and Incomplete Institutionalization: Political Change and Continuity in the Early American Nation

Paul Colomy

Sociology is a multi-paradigmatic discipline composed of several competing traditions. In this context, specific theories often grow and develop in response to criticisms formulated by those outside a particular theory group. Frequently, it is a school's competitors and critics who are especially attuned to the theoretical and empirical weaknesses of a given approach. Accordingly, critics often provide a school with a theoretical and research agenda, and a theory's progress can be partially determined by its ability to produce satisfactory revisions.

The multi-paradigmatic character of sociology is nowhere more evident than in the study of social change. This area features several competing schools including Weberian, conflict, structuralist, Marxist, world systems, and differentiation theory. Each of these paradigms grows, in part, by responding to its critics. Focusing on differentiation theory and acknowledging the partial veracity of the criticisms

The author thanks Shubhasree Subedi and Alberto Arroyo for their valuable assistance with this research. This study was supported by a University of Akron Faculty Summer Research Fellowship.

leveled against it, I revise crucial elements of this approach to social change.

Since the late 1960s, differentiation theory has been criticized for its lack of historical specificity, its reluctance to address the causes of differentiation, its failure to examine the role of concrete groups in promoting or resisting differentiation, its neglect of power and conflict, and its overemphasis on the integrative consequences of differentiation (e.g., Nisbet 1969; Turner and Maryanski 1979: 109–18; Smith 1973; Rueschemeyer 1977; Stinchcombe 1978:77–104; Granovetter 1979). Many of these criticisms are at least partially true, and if differentiation theory is to advance it must respond to those charges.

The revisionist work has already begun. Recent scholarship in this tradition has initiated examinations of the causes of structural change, the impact of power and concrete groups on institutional change, and the potentially disintegrative consequences of differentiation (e.g., Eisenstadt 1985; Smelser 1985; Prager 1985; Barber 1985; Lechner 1985; Colomy 1985; Alexander 1985; Alexander and Colomy 1985). In accord with this revisionist thrust, I aspire to lend differentiation theory greater historical specificity and to underscore the conflictual and continually problematic aspects of institution building. Toward those ends, the concepts of uneven differentiation and incomplete institutionalization are introduced and then applied to a substantive discussion of political change and continuity in the antebellum United States.

Uneven Differentiation and Incomplete Institutionalization

Differentiation theory is organized around a postulated master trend of change and an implicit model of institutionalization. The theory avers that the most significant feature of modern social change is the replacement of multifunctional structures by more specialized institutions and roles. This analytic characterization of change has been used to describe both transformations of entire sociocultural systems and alterations of distinctive institutional spheres (see Parsons 1966, 1971; Luhmann 1982; Bellah 1964; Smelser 1959; Keller 1963; Parsons and Platt, 1973; Eisenstadt 1969; Fox 1976; Alexander 1980, 1981).

Analytically, differentiation theory's postulation of a master trend is legitimate. Indeed, all of the most fertile macrosociological theories of change posit a distinctive master trend—e.g., Marx's emphasis on class struggle and the movement toward a classless society, Weber's depiction of rationalization, Tocqueville's description of an irreversible trend toward equality, and Durkheim's discussion of organic solidarity and the "cult of the individual." Moreover, contemporary students of change share with their classic forebears the same proclivity for organizing their analyses around the description of a master trend —e.g., convergence theory's description of the increasing similarities across industrial societies (Moore 1979), world system theory's discussion of the growth of a capitalist world system and the accompanying tensions between core and periphery (Chirot and Hall 1982), and conflict theory's depiction of a movement toward power as the primary distributive principle in modern societies (Lenski 1984).

Although there is not sufficient space to substantiate the argument here, my position is that these divergent characterizations of master trends are not equally valuable. Employing multidimensionality and level of abstraction as criteria for evaluating competing analytic descriptions, I am persuaded that differentiation theory's master trend is the more theoretically useful tool for characterizing the broad parameters of modern social change in a wide variety of social and cultural spheres. In principle, differentiation theory is capable of subsuming many classic and contemporary statements about the course of modern social change (Alexander 1983:128–50).

A second major assumption of contemporary differentiation theory is an implicit model of "complete institutionalization" (e.g., Smelser, 1959). The theory's concern with broadly conceived transformations of total societies and its penchant for highly abstract descriptions of change in particular institutional spheres focus attention on the dominant and most visible patterns of change. This one-dimensional view inadvertently implies a model in which fully legitimate traditional arrangements are supplanted by fully legitimate modern, albeit more specialized, structures. According to this perspective, "dissatisfaction" plays a transitional role in the drama, prompting replacement of a less effective, traditional institutional complex, and then subsiding once a more effective, differentiated structure is created. It is also presumed that more specialized institutions are legitimated as consistent specifications of a society's dominant value pattern (Smelser, 1959).[1] In my view, however, this approach suffers from an illusion of completeness and errs in exaggerating the amount of legitimacy accorded more differentiated institutions.

The analytic and empirical breadth of differentiation theory can be extended by treating the master trend and the model of complete institutionalization as useful analytic starting points that need to be followed with greater empirical specification of the actual contours of change. This recommendation suggests two types of elaboration.[2]

First, identification of the master trend must be supplemented with the description of patterned departures from that trend. The postulated trend is usefully treated as an orienting device that establishes ideal-typical starting and ending points. Actual episodes of change can be assessed against the ideal-typical conception, thereby generating the identification of analytically distinct deviations from the master trend. The ultimate product of this approach is a more empirically grounded conception of change.[3]

The concept of *uneven differentiation* provides a description of a patterned departure from differentiation theory's designated master trend. As a distinct type of change, uneven differentiation refers to the varying rate and degree of differentiation of a single institution or role structure within a given social system. Whereas differentiation theory's master trend assumes that institutional change occurs at a uniform rate and degree throughout a social system, uneven differentiation asserts that at any given time such change is often relatively more advanced in some sections of a society, while it is just beginning or is strongly resisted in other areas. Uneven differentiation suggests, then, that the master trend of change proceeds at an uneven rate and degree across the distinct regions of a society.

The notion of uneven differentiation is especially significant for the examination of structural change in decentralized and heterogeneous social systems. I hypothesize that the greater the dispersion of power and the higher the degree of subcultural and social diversity in a system, the more likely it is that uneven differentiation will occur. In social systems marked by these characteristics, the rate and degree of differentiation of any single institutional sphere is likely to vary across a system's geographic subunits.

In addition to the notion of uneven differentiation, a more complex conception of institutionalization is necessary. Heretofore, differentiation theory has concentrated on delineating abstract descriptions of master trends. This procedure prompts neglect of the opposing and conflicting currents associated with nearly every episode of institution building. In contrast, a more empirically grounded and processual approach to institutionalization exposes the rough underside of the apparently smooth surface of differentiation.

The establishment of more differentiated institutions invariably produces a cultural-ideological struggle centered around the legitimacy of the new structure. Even when the burgeoning institution acquires considerable acceptance and many adherents, several groups and individuals usually retain a critical stance toward it. Further, many critics, whether of the left or right, present their rebukes in a rhetoric that draws heavily upon a society's sacred principles and founders. In this fashion opponents challenge the institution's legitimacy by emphasizing fundamental inconsistencies between the emerging institution and the society's most cherished traditions. It is true, of course, that the voices of opposition may be muffled by an appearance of unanimous support for the new institution. Nevertheless, an institution's critics, even if they represent only a small minority, remain sociologically significant because they constitute a bastion of ideological resistance to the new order and render the institution's legitimacy problematic. Further, although these subterranean opponents may not be initially successful in their opposition to the new structure, they often leave a legacy of criticism which, if elaborated by later generations, serves as an important source of change. In short, the concept of incomplete institutionalization sensitizes students of change to an institutional "war of position"[4] that accompanies many episodes of differentiation.

In addition, more differentiated structures often pursue ends that conflict with the interests of other institutions and groups. Generally, newly created institutions seek to consolidate their position and authority. This drive toward institutional consolidation, however, frequently infringes upon the interests and authority of other established or emerging institutions and groups. In an effort to protect their own niche, a variety of groups may take steps designed to eliminate what they regard as the "excesses" of the new institution. Thus, the development of many institutions assumes the character of what has been described as a "double movement,"[5] wherein the drive for consolidation is opposed by a loose coalition seeking to defend both narrow group interests and the more amorphous public welfare.

It is reasonable to hypothesize that the breadth and intensity of opposition to institutional differentiation are greatest when the new structure has been most successful in its drive toward consolidation. A burgeoning structure's very success in extending its spheres of influence over domains previously controlled by other institutions and groups usually prompts vigorous counterattacks from those whose material and ideal interests are thereby threatened, and instigates a broadly based resistance designed both to temper the focal structure's perceived excesses and to undermine its legitimacy. Accordingly, even in those regions of a society where the master trend is most fully realized one can reasonably expect to discover evidence of incomplete institutionalization.

The double movement sequence just described presupposes a minimal level of cultural and social differentiation. When the drive toward consolidation occurs in a cultural and social context characterized by a relatively low level of differentiation, a sustained counterattack is less probable. However, the greater the degree of pre-existing social and cultural differentiation, the greater the probability that movement towards institutional consolidation will produce a strong counterreaction.

Denoting the contingent and continually problematic character of legitimation, incomplete institutionalization provides a more multifaceted conception of structural change. It suggests that beneath the master trend toward differentiation there lies opposition, and though that resistance may not fully impede the new structure's growth, it does affect the institution's stability and its capacity to exercise authority.

The utility of both the concept of uneven differentiation and a more supple understanding of institutionalization is illustrated below through a discussion of antebellum political developments. I describe, first, a master trend toward political differentiation that occurred in the United States between 1740 and 1850. Presented in ideal typical terms, this master trend depicts a shift in the structure of politics away from a traditional deferential pattern and toward a modern, mass party configuration. Subsequent sections of this paper describe the relative extent to which this trend was realized in four antebellum states and identify sources of resistance to its complete institutionalization. A concluding section suggests how the study of uneven differentiation and incomplete institutionalization opens up the explanatory framework of differentiation theory.

A Master Trend of Political Differentiation in the United States, 1740–1850

Several scholars, representing a variety of disciplines and employing diverse perspectives and methodologies, agree that during the Jacksonian period a significant transformation in politics occurred. Contrasting the structure of political rule evident in Jacksonian America with that of the late colonial and early postrevolutionary periods, these scholars depict a transition from a diffuse, deferential pattern to a more specialized and differentiated configuration of politics. The general pattern of change delineated in this literature is similar to master trends of differentiation described for other institutional spheres.

Focusing on political developments between 1740 and 1850, the following analytic summary describes a master trend of political differentiation along three interrelated dimensions: the social composition of the indigenous political elite, the dominant forms of political organization, and the hegemonic political culture.

By 1740, provincial politics in nearly every continental colony were dominated by an indigenous gentry (Berthoff and Murrin 1973:263–72; Greene 1961:461–62, 469–70; 1966:171–72; 1975:41–45; Gross 1976:12–14, 62–65, 156–70; Larabee 1948:1–31; Main 1966:391–97; 1967; Purvis 1980; Mills 1956:269–70; Dahl 1961:11–18; Grant 1961:115–53; Zemsky 1971; Willingham 1973). In each colony provincial political leaders (i.e., primarily those who held office in the colonial councils or assemblies) were drawn from the ranks of the relatively wealthy; they were well born, highly educated, and from among the dominant religious and ethnic groups. In areas where the necessary substratum of economic and social differentiation existed, the gentry also dominated important local offices.

Typically, provincial leaders were members of a larger self-conscious and fairly cohesive economic, social, and cultural elite that had emerged by the early eighteenth century in most colonies. The provincial gentries, composed of merchants, planters, and professional men, maintained their identity through intermarriage, informal, social relations, and an array of economic and political connections. The gentry tended to be concentrated in the eastern and more economically developed sections of each colony, frequently in or near major river valleys, or in the burgeoning colonial cities (Bridenbaugh 1938:96–100, 251–55, 411–18; Bridenbaugh, 1955:137–46, 334–50; Main 1965:7–67; Nash 1979). Largely because of shared economic and political interests, but also reflecting their cultural concerns, the gentry inclined toward cosmopolitanism and exhibited a greater preoccupation with the metropolitan "center," primarily London, and its ideals, customs, and conceits (Wright 1957:3–6, 19–20, 111–13, 126, 131–34, 137, 142–44, 196–97, 250; Greene 1969).

Although relatively well defined and possessing a sense of corporate identity, the gentry was not exclusive. Ambitious men occasionally broke into its circle by virtue of economic or political success (Bailyn 1967b). "Sponsored mobility" also occurred, with an established member of the gentry promoting the career of a talented and promising, but lowly-born young man (Hofstadter 1962:167–68; Sydnor 1953:75). In both cases these upwardly mobile individuals usually adopted the gentry's life-style and world view.

Late colonial politics exhibited a distinctive organizational pattern and were permeated by a relatively well-defined political culture. Although there were occasional efforts to create and sustain formal political organizations, especially in the middle colonies, gentry politics were overwhelmingly personalistic (Greenberg 1977; Greene 1966; Chambers 1963:26). The success of an aspiring candidate or an elected official largely depended upon his personal connections, especially the prestige and material resources of his friends and family (Sydnor 1952:60–85; Tully 1978:86–87). Such tasks as the mobilization of the electorate, nominations, securing funds for political "campaigns," and the distribution of appointive offices were carried out by informal cliques of notables, and considerations of personal character, honor, and status in the community were paramount (Aronson 1964:3–7, 140–43, 156–57; Crenson 1975:50–55, 72–103; Sydnor 1952:44–49; Chambers 1963:21–23; Tully 1978:90–92.

Personalism also informed the substance and organization of political conflict, which typically pitted one faction, identified with and usually led by members of the gentry, against another faction similarly constituted. Familial and court versus country factions were the dominant political forms of the period (Bailyn 1976b:106–25; Chambers 1963:17–21; Bonomi 1971; Greene 1966:163–72, 176–77). Though some of these factions persisted for many years, they possessed few of the characteristics associated with modern political organizations— separation of person from function, a rationalized division of labor, and established criteria for recruitment and advancement (Chambers 1963:45–50). Notions of party loyalty and personal subordination to a political organization were absent (Hofstadter 1969:1–73; Chambers 1963:24–25). The possibility that personalistic factions might evolve into formal political organizations was effectively inhibited by a traditional "consensus" political culture that denied the legitimacy of conflict and identified faction and party as threats to public welfare (Wallace 1969:471–76).

The dominant political ethos, derived both from the English "country ideology" and the broad ideals of the gentry class itself, held that the pursuit and protection of the public good was the highest political ideal. This was commonly identified with the preservation of liberty and freedom and a distrust of concentrated power, particularly executive power (Bailyn 1967a:55–93; Bailyn 1967b:41–58; Shalhope 1972). In pursuit of the public good, the elected or appointed official accepted a duty to use political expertise on behalf of all people. The ideal statesman should be "able," "independent," "courageous," "virtuous," and "public spirited" (Weir 1969:477; Schwartz 1983:25–27). In more concrete terms, the gentry's political ethic manifested itself in a vigorous antiparty and antifaction attitude and an insistence upon the right of the magistrate to follow his own reason and conscience (Greene 1975:43, 46–47).

In addition, traditional conceptions of stewardship and deference partially legitimated the diffuse pattern of gentry leadership. By the mid-eighteenth century gentry families regularly socialized their sons to the duty of public service and the obligation of securing the public good (Greene 1976; Greven 1977:286–88, 321–33). Aside from the considerable gratifications attendant upon living up to an exemplary role, upper class stewardship was also pursued as a means of promoting particular material interests, attaining social distinction, and enhancing the family name (Greene 1975:42–44; Williams 1959:342–45).

Further, by 1740 most colonies could be accurately characterized as "deferential societies" (Greene 1966:172–73; 1968:29–31; 1973:266–77). It was widely presumed that members of the gentry were the "natural leaders" of the community and the most qualified to hold public office and exercise political authority (Greene 1975:48–49; Bailyn 1959:91–92; Buel 1964; Pole 1962). This elitist conception of leadership partially explains why, despite a relatively expansive franchise (Brown 1955; Brown and Brown 1964; Williamson 1960:20–39), members of the gentry were regularly elected to public office (Murrin 1965).

The American Revolution had significant consequences for the structure of gentry rule in every state. Everywhere it sanctified libertarianism and egalitarianism and lent to those values a dynamism that was reflected in a variety of reforms, in occasional jibes at the deference ideology, and in an apparent increase in the rate of social and economic mobility (Bailyn 1967a:230–319; Lipset 1963:74–98; Foner 1976:19–144; Wood 1969:481–83; Nash 1979; Main 1965; Cooper 1983:30–35, 43–45). Further, in conjunction with the expulsion of the English and some loyalists, the creation of more equitable state constitutions created greater political opportunity for "new men" from the middle and lower social orders who, in the postrevolutionary period, were more likely to secure a seat in the states' lower houses and, on occasion, even in the upper chambers (Main 1966; 1967; Martin 1973; Wood 1969:476–78). Finally, a wide variety of significant postrevolutionary issues provided the bases for the development of somewhat more stable factions within state legislatures (Main 1973).

Nevertheless, postrevolutionary political life continued to be informed by the legacy of the colonial period. Many of the gentry had led the revolutionary struggle itself and, despite the conspicuous rise of new men into politics, continued to assume the bulk of leadership posts in the newly created state governments (Cooper 1983:45–46; Higginbotham 1974:96–97).

At the national level, the men who participated at the federal constitutional convention and took the lead in the constitution's ratification at the state conventions were overwhelmingly drawn from the ranks of the gentry (Brown 1976; Main 1961:116). Ideologically, the desire for a stronger centralized government partially represented a conservative backlash stimulated by the perceived fluidity, democratization, and restlessness that, to many, bordered on disorder and anarchy (Wood 1969:393–425). A national government was envisioned, in part, as a necessary mechanism for restoring order and social authority (Wood 1969:471–99; Heale 1982:10–11). The anti-Federalists, adhering to a localist and loosely democratic orientation, explained their defeat by the more adept political maneuvering and the greater prestige of those assembled in the Federalist camp (Wood 1969:486, 519–23; Main 1961:249–55; Kenyon 1955). The latter factor, of course, is testimony to the continuing influence of traditional conceptions of deference and upper class leadership (Pole 1967:6–7; Wood 1969:488–90).

In the long run, the most significant consequences of the American Revolution were not the political mobility of a few new men nor the sporadic diatribes against deferential ideology but the widespread acceptance of political structures and values and the stimulation of economic developments that were potentially incompatible with the earlier period's traditional assumptions and practices.

The revolution eliminated the royal connection, and the subsequent creation of a republican form of government made "the people" the sovereign source of political authority (Palmer 1959:185–238; Ellis 1971:268–99). The American system of institutional checks and balances, with each component of government deriving its ultimate authority from the people, reinforced the notion of popular sovereignty (Wood 1969:306–90, 519–64, 593–615; Morantz 1971:91–94). The acceptance of popular sovereignty portended the emergence of a mass politics inconsistent with the traditional pattern of rule. In addition, the revolution's institutionalization of a generalized value of equality lent legitimacy to efforts aimed at achieving greater political participation and the inclusion of ethnic, cultural, political, and economic out-groups (Lipset 1963; Glazer 1975:3–32; Morantz 1971:31–34; 55–58). Moreover, in the long run, independence encouraged the growth of a somewhat more autonomous economy, fostering the formation of domestic institutions for production, commerce, and credit and the emergence of new social cleavages inimical to traditional political structures (Egnal and Ernst 1972).

The federal constitution too had long-range consequences for the nature of political rule. By establishing a national political arena and introducing regular contests for national offices, the constitution spurred national party development (McCormick 1966). The constitution also unified into a single country diverse social and economic formations, thereby creating a need for mechanisms, including extra-constitutional arrangements such as political parties, to sustain a minimal level of coordination (Cooper 1983:47–56).

In most instances, however, these potentialities for the transformation of political rule were not realized, but became a central part of the revolutionary generation's legacy to the nineteenth century. In several states, the traditional pattern of rule established during the late colonial period survived the revolution and the divisiveness surrounding the ratification of the federal constitution; it remained battered but viable. The task of translating the revolutionary and constitutional heritage into a more full-blown critique and the transformation of traditional political arrangements was left to the next century.

During the 1790s a transitional stage in the movement from a traditional to a more modern structure of rule appeared (Formisano 1974). Emerging from debates within the national center over fiscal and especially over foreign policy and organized around contests for public office, the Federalist and Republican interests built relatively stable coalitions, appealed to the electorate for support, and vilified their opponents (Buel 1972:1–90; Charles 1956; Cunningham 1957, 1963; Chambers 1963:34–169; Goodman 1964; Fischer 1965; Banning 1978:179–269). Indeed, with the passage of the Alien and Sedition Acts in 1798 the conflict between these interests became so intense that contemporaries referred to Jefferson's subsequent election as the "Revolution of 1800" (Sisson 1974:343–437; Howe 1967).

Despite the great significance of these political contests, however, the Federalist-Republican battles did not generate a durable party system with a differentiated and extensive party organization and a normative structure supporting party and party competition (Formisano 1974, 1976:53–54; Hofstadter 1969:74–211; Young 1966; Chambers 1973). National organizations were incipient at best, coordination between federal, state, and local partisans was loose or nonexistent, party names remained uncertain throughout the period, Federalists and Republicans did not constitute stable political reference groups for the electorate, and a proparty ideology had yet to be articulated while political opposition continued to be denounced (Formisano 1974;

Heale 1982:29–30). Moreover, Federalist and Republican organizations did not endure. In several states, Federalist organization virtually crumbled after its defeat in 1800 and Republican partisans, without a significant Federalist opponent, dissolved into chronic and highly personalistic factionalism (Ellis 1971:19–35, 275–78).

Although noticeably weakened by the partisanship of the 1790s, the traditional structure of gentry rule survived well into the nineteenth century. Notables continued to dominate national, state, and local offices, their leadership partially legitimated by a persisting deference mentality (Formisano 1974:483–85; Buel 1972:75–90; Morantz 1971:43–55; Pessen 1973:296–88). Even in the face of incipient party organization, personalistic and familial connections strongly informed late eighteenth- and early nineteenth-century politics, and the traditional emphases on honor, prestige, and character figured prominently in elections and appointments to public office (Crenson 1975; Wiebe 1984:7–130 Morantz 1971:63–67). Finally, while considerably modified, an organic and hierarchical conception of society persisted along with a virulent antipartyism (Wallace 1973:1–183; Sisson 1974:23–69).

Although they did not destroy the structure of gentry rule, the struggles of the 1790s introduced and/or reinforced three developments that proved instrumental in establishing a more modern structure of political authority. First, the intense partisanship of the 1790s compelled elites to seek support from the mass electorate. These efforts underscored the political significance of popular sovereignty in a republican government and went far toward instilling a "habit of participation" (Formisano 1974). Second, although invariably on the periphery of power in the 1790s, "radical democrats" and Democratic-Republican societies, drawing sustenance primarily from the ranks of small farmers and the urban lower classes, became an important element in the Jeffersonian coalition (Ellis 1971; Link, 1942; Young, 1967). They lent that coalition a pronounced democratic and popular rhetoric, constantly contrasting the virtues of the people with the pretensions of a corrupt aristocracy (Wood 1974). These democratic sentiments were intrinsically hostile to notable rule and became an important element in the arsenal of nineteenth century mass politics (Sisson 1974:452–53; Morantz 1971:120–33, 244–61). Finally, memories of the Federalist-Republican struggle survived into the nineteenth century and became an integral part of a political mythology that shaped the subsequent perception of politics. The charismatic personages and principles of this era were constantly invoked in efforts to legitimate new political structures.

By 1850, the diffuse structure of notable rule had been severely weakened and largely supplanted by the more specialized pattern of party leadership (Nichols 1967; Formisano 1974). This more differentiated type of leadership reflected three inter-related transformations. Most conspicuous, perhaps, was the appearance of new types of men in positions of political power. While the wealthy and eminent continued to hold public office, several prominent local, state, and national party managers and political leaders came from less prestigious families, were less educated (or educated at less renowned institutions), and possessed less wealth than the leaders of the colonial and early national periods (Pessen 1973:286–88; Pessen 1978:171–96; Marshall 1967; Aronson 1964:56–157; McWhiney 1957; Thornton 1978:5–20; Watson 1981:213–45; Oakes 1982:138–47; Ridgway 1979). There was also a tendency for a larger number of more "peripheral" ethnic and religious groups to be better represented among the political elite (Kelley 1979; Watson 1981:131, 221). The cohesiveness of this emerging political stratum, largely composed of upwardly mobile, middle-class lawyers, was premised less on similar class position and more on the bases of commitment to party and the acceptance of political opposition as legitimate, a developing sense of American identity, and the realization that they were charged with the task of sustaining the great work of the revolutionary generation (Forgie 1979; Berens 1978:112–28, 165–70). Although many of these new men had other occupations, politics tended to be their primary vocation and, for some, a primary source of income (Marshall 1967).

The organization and ideals of politics also changed. Personalistic politics, of course, did not disappear in the Jacksonian period and connections and friends continued to be important in advancing a man's career (Hall 1979:174). Nevertheless, the distinctive feature of antebellum politics was the emergence of mass political parties (Silbey 1985:33–68). The party system of this era, unlike any before or since, was nationwide and competitive in virtually every state (Silbey 1967:18–34, 142–46; McCormick 1966; Chambers 1973:650). Parties, not friends and family, secured funds to support an individual's candidacy (Nichols 1967:340, 375–76; Chambers 1971:673; Pessen 1978:150). The party caucus and nominating convention largely replaced the discredited gentry clique and legislative caucus as the means for selecting candidates and devising party strategy (Chase 1973). The party press and cadre supplemented interpersonal communication in informing the electorate about government policies and personalities, and newspaper editors played an increasingly important political role (Heale 1982:157–87; Baldasty 1983:261–79;

Cooper 1978:38–42; Chambers 1971:674–77). Parties supplied the electorate with a cognitive map of the political universe, ordering their perception of political events (Holt 1978:35–37). Parties increasingly served as reference groups representing collective symbols and values that adherents incorporated in their individual identities (Formisano 1974:21–27).

Parties organized the conduct of officeholders, shaped policy, and influenced the distribution of patronage. Party discipline and loyalty enhanced the party caucus's role in organizing legislative voting. Accordingly, representatives in national and state legislatures increasingly voted along party lines (Levine 1975; Silbey 1967; Holt 1978:26–27, 34–35; Ershkowitz and Shade 1971). Parties also fostered greater coordination between national, state, and local governments as well as linking the executive and legislative branches (Jaenicke 1978:32). Finally, the salience of partisan affiliations in the dispensation of patronage increased significantly (Aronson 1964:143; White 1954:11–17, 302–9; Hall 1979).

The rise of mass party organizations was associated with a corresponding change in political ideals and conceptions of political leadership (Wiebe 1984:234–52, 291–320). Personal cliques and familial factions were increasingly condemned as aristocratic, while impersonal, party organization that transcended any single individual was approbated. Ideally, the party was responsive to the majority, and the party leader was an instrument of the organization. In addition, advancement to positions of political leadership was dependent not upon one's social status but upon dedication and service to the party (Hofstadter 1969:243–44).

With the emergence of the party, loyalty to the organization became a crucial element of the new political code. The new political ethos subordinated both independent judgment and rigid adherence to moral principle to party decisions. Central to this new creed was the belief that all politicians were required to sacrifice themselves to the party and not let either convictions or personal ambitions impede obedience to the will of the party's majority (Cooper 1978:198–200; Wilson 1984:31–32). This injunction was not simply tactical but ethical: the proper politician ignored restraining scruples when they conflicted with those of the greater number (Wallace 1969:461; Hofstadter 1962:154–66).

In contrast to the earlier period, when gentry leaders aspired to the ideals of "consensus" or "harmonious" politics, party competition and parties themselves were accorded a positive evaluation. This positive evaluation derived, first, from the claim that parties adhered more strictly to democratic principles, especially majoritarianism, than had previously political practice (Heale 1982:85–86). In addition, party advocates claimed that parties served valuable social functions.

These changes in social composition, organization, and ideology promoted the emergence of a more specialized political elite. The organizational and normative context of the new politics provided leaders with a distinctive power and resource base which became the infrastructure of a political oligarchy. Party managers and leaders, not the mass electorate, usually made the "big decisions" (Pessen 1978:156–58). However, the democratic legitimization of parties, and the two-party system itself, introduced a tension into the relation between the political elite and the electorate. In making decisions, political elites were constrained by possible reactions of constituents, those reactions invariably subject to manipulation by competing political leaders (Heale 1982:84–85).

The new politics led many notables to shun public life. Several were disenchanted with the new style and tone of campaigning and electioneering. Others, slandered as aristocrats, were defeated at the polls (Hofstadter 1969:165–66; Pessen 1973:290; Pessen 1978:174). Some descendants of the gentry remained politically active, but were compelled to observe, at least publicly, the new rules of the political game (Chambers 1972:646–47).

In sum, then, during the Jacksonian period the dominant trend of political change was toward more differentiated political elites, organizations, and ideals. This process resulted in a significant alteration in the social composition of political leaders—both party leaders and elected and appointed officials were more likely to be drawn from middle status groups than had been the case in the colonial and postrevolutionary periods. On the organizational level, the Jacksonian era witnessed the crystallization of mass political parties and new political roles. Finally, the new political orientations were evident, including a positive evaluation of parties and party activity, an emphasis on loyalty and subordination to the party, and a conception of the political leader as an instrument of the party.

In the following sections I describe the uneven realization of this master trend in four antebellum states—New York, South Carolina, Virginia, and Massachusetts.[6] The substantive discussion of politics in these states establishes two major points. First, these states differed in the rate and degree to which they realized the master trend. Second, even where the master trend was most fully evident, there was considerable resistance to modern mass politics, and such opposition impeded the complete institutionalization of the new structures.

Political Differentiation Approximated: New York

By 1850 the master trend toward political differentiation was clearly evident in New York.[7] A significant democratization of officeholding and party leadership had occurred, with increasing numbers of "new" men of nonnotable origins assuming positions as alderman, judges, mayors, state legislators, governors, congressmen, senators, cabinet officers, ambassadors, and other influential public posts in city, state, and federal administrations (Jaher 1982:215; Pessen 1973:284–87; Heale 1976:31; Bridges 1982, 1984; Johnson 1978:69–78). Increasingly, it was career politicians and other men of middle- and lower-class origins who ran for office, organized local party machinery, and mobilized grass roots support. Further, interested in constructing electorally powerful organizations, career politicians of both parties were led to ally themselves publicly with the "common man" and against the "aristocratic" element.

More so than in most other states, the leadership of both major parties in New York fell under the dominion of professional politicians. Typified by the Democrat Martin Van Buren and the Whig Thurlow Weed, these professionals were of middle- or lower middle-class origins and not connected to the state's leading families (Benson 1961:64–85; Hofstadter, 1969:240–43). Unlike the patrician statesman of an earlier era, these party managers discovered in the modern political party a creed, a vocation, and a congenial social world.

By the early 1820s the personalistic and familial character of late eighteenth- and early nineteenth-century politics was beginning to be supplanted by a mass party system. Unlike the "virtuous statesman" of the classic tradition, New York's professional politician evinced a passion for constructing and maintaining differentiated mass party organizations (Hofstadter 1969:247–49). By the early 1830s each of New York's major parties was led by a small group of party managers who, in turn, had connections with auxiliary agents in virtually every county. These statewide parties were tied together through an elaborate network of ward, city, village, county, and district committees that laced the state within a pyramidal party structure open to the public through most of its tiers (Wallace 1973:133–34). Regular consultation between state and local party leaders promoted cohesion and coordination. At the top, the state party caucus formulated broad party strategy, while nominations for many local offices remained the prerogative of local committees. Significantly, the tightly disciplined party apparatus just described was consciously conceived as a means of ending the rule of the old elite families (Heale 1976:32). Moreover, differentiated parties also provided an avenue of upward mobility, for these partisan organizations continually sought out young men who showed promise and groomed them for responsible positions in the party (Remini 1958:349–50).

By the mid-1820s, important political functions such as nominating candidates, mobilizing the electorate, and fund raising, which had previously been performed by informal ad hoc cliques of local notables and their families and friends, came under the purview of differentiated party organizations (Kass 1965). By 1826, the nominating convention had replaced the notable's legislative caucus as the primary means for selecting party candidates. Each partisan organization also printed and distributed the party ticket to ensure disciplined voting for all offices and measures. During election campaigns both parties organized large mass meetings in all of the large towns and in almost every county of the state. The parties also sponsored rallies, parades, pole raisings, musters, and picnics; created songs and emblems; and circulated pamphlets, handbills, and flyers and distributed hats, buttons, and vests with the candidates' features or names stamped on them. Another feature of modern electoral mobilization was the ward heeler who used the votes of recently arrived immigrants as potent political weapons (Heale 1976:32). As campaigns became more elaborate and expensive spectacles, party fund raising grew more systematic and rationalized.

Political parties in New York also exercised considerable control over the press (Kass 1965). The use of public contracts, postmasterships, contributions, loans and guaranteed subscription lists allowed parties to keep many editors subservient. In addition, the anticipation of a substantial amount of printing at election time in the form of issuing party handbills, circulars, and tickets enticed other editors to cast their lot with a particular party.

Finally, the adroit dispensation of patronage was essential for building statewide organizations and sustaining party discipline. The dominant party dictated appointments to many federal, state, and local offices, such patronage being understood as a legitimate reward for meritorious party service (Remini 1958). In fact, by comparison with New England states, Jacksonian New York was distinguished by its politicans' open avidity for the spoils of office, and the spoils system exerted a powerful influence on the state's politics (Mc-Cormick 1966). More generally, the "New York School of Politics" acquired a national reputation for wire pulling and unsavory political maneuvering.

Turnover in New York's assembly and senate increased substantially throughout the Jacksonian era, partially reflecting a substantial increase in voter participation and the emergence of two highly organized and competitive political parties (Gunn 1980:276–81). Within the legislature, the dominant party's caucus usually controlled the election of house speakers and filled the state offices that the assembly was authorized to appoint. Finally, roll call analyses reveal substantial divisions along party lines on key issues (Gunn 1980:284–86; Wallace 1973:128–30).

The "party-in-the-electorate" was also well developed by 1834 and party identifications were deeply rooted (Wallace 1973:131–34; Benson 1961:81, 124–207; McCormick 1966:123). Both parties espoused the principle of regularity, and all the available evidence suggests mass acceptance of party loyalty. Election returns at the state, county, town, and ward levels indicate a pronounced stability in party percentages between 1832 and 1853. That stability reflects both the continuation of partisan allegiances and the general inclination for sons to assume the political identities of their fathers. During this period a close, competitive balance obtained between the two major parties and this contributed to an extremely high rate of voter participation. Only once did participation in presidential elections fall below 80 percent in New York, and in those years when only a gubernatorial contest was held participation ranged between 71 and 74 percent. Finally, the electorate's strong identification with parties is also reflected in the virtually identical alignments that appeared in both state and national elections.

Ideologically, New York moved further and more rapidly than any other state toward the systematic justification of a differentiated party system. Two general types of arguments were presented in support of modern political organizations (Wallace 1969; Wallace 1973:111–183; Hofstadter 1969:212–35; 239–53). First, parties were tied to widely held social values. Proponents maintained that parties were democratic associations infused with the spirit of republicanism and majority rule. Second, a "lay functionalism" identified several useful services parties performed for the larger community, including: (1) protecting citizens' freedom by acting as a watchman on those in power; (2) enabling citizens to express divergent interests and opinions; (3) acting as a relatively accessible channel of upward social mobility for the lower and middle social orders; (4) binding the entire country together by crosscutting sectional cleavages; and (5) diffusing political knowledge and stimulating popular participation in government.

In addition, New York politicians went further than any other group in defending what some contemporaries regarded as the excesses of partisan politics. For example, an earlier argument that portrayed parties as essential means of preserving democracy was superceded by the contention that the party's preservation was a laudable end in itself (Wallace 1973:134–37). According to party proponents such organizational maintenance required obeisance to the directives of the party caucus and convention, and, above all, the subordination of individual judgment and ambition when they diverged from party policy. In short, party loyalty was elevated to a sacred principle and, as many critics have noted, this preoccupation with survival often promoted neglect of ideological objectives. Finally, in line with New York's vanguard role in building and defending differentiated party institutions, it was a New York politician who averred the most blatant defense of the spoils system: "to the victors belong the spoils."

Deferential ethos, the cultural bulwark of traditional politics, were subject to a relentless assault (Benson 1961:10–12, 355–58; Wallace 1973:139–42). Populist democratic rhetoric was widely employed by 1824, and thereafter all pragmatic politicians loudly proclaimed their devotion to political equality. With populism a standard feature of election campaigns, politicians of all feathers presented themselves as friends of the people and branded their opponents as aristocrats.

Although antebellum New York moved closer than any other state to the full realization of the master trend of political differentiation, even this politically innovative state did not completely institutionalize mass parties. The "new" politics did not, for example, totally displace the older elite. "Traditionalistic" enclaves persisted throughout the antebellum era, and in these areas men of fortune and those from prominent families were accorded deference from the electorate and assumed the most powerful local posts as their natural right (Zuckerbraun 1980). Further, several individual patricians continued to participate in municipal government, the state legislature, and various federal administrations (Jaher 1982:216). In addition, the wealthy and prominent played an important role in partisan politics by contributing to the formulation of local and national party policy, gathering funds for the parties, and maintaining state and national party ties (Bridges 1982; Gatell 1967). Finally, throughout the 1820s and into the 1830s, New York's professional politicians built their statewide machines by forging alliances with local notables in various communities (Johnson 1978:62–71; Kutolowski 1978).

Mass parties also confronted a substantial ideological resistance which impeded their full legitimation. In fact, by moving so quickly and forcefully to consolidate their position in New York, political parties stimulated resistance from a larger number of distinct opposition groups than appeared in other states. In New York mass parties' very success sowed the seeds of widespread opposition. There were five primary sources of the antiparty critique. First, Yankee Protestantism and pietism denounced the individual's subordination to a party as a restriction of the individual's freedom of conscience, as an illegitimate intercession between an individual and God, and as the unwarranted promotion of expediency over adherence to moral principle (Formisano 1969). Second, a displaced ruling elite revived the classic republican critique of parties and politicians and, in New York City during the early 1850s, began to build the "good government" groups which presaged the future struggle of the reformer against the boss (Bridges 1982). Third, a relatively differentiated intellectual elite, which rankled under the shackles of party loyalty criticized parties for debasing public discourse and ignoring principle (Spann 1972:64–121). Fourth, a burgeoning group of differentiated professional humanitarians asserted that the spoils system impeded the efficient and effective delivery of social services to the less fortunate (Heale 1976). Finally, in New York, as in many northern states, the apparent concentration of power in the hands of a few machine politicians and the seeming unresponsiveness of parties to popular sentiments (particularly, anti-Catholic and nativist prejudices, temperance, and anti-slavery) fueled the anti-party critique which, in turn, stimulated some of the rank and file of established parties to construct more democratic parties during the early 1850s (Holt, 1973; Gienapp, 1985).

In addition to the critique of parties, antebellum New York also witnessed the persistence of more traditional attitudes. Upper class notables often coupled their attacks on parties and the "excesses" of democracy with a reaffirmation of belief in the classic statesman ideal (Jaher 1982:216–22; Spann 1972:114–21). Remnants of deference, severely weakened by democratization, also persisted. As noted above, in some enclaves the electorate continued to defer to the community's "natural leaders" (Zuckerbraun 1980). Further, a wing of New York's Whig party sought to preserve and capitalize upon traditional political attitudes (Barkan 1971; Warner 1973).

In summary, antebellum New York moved farther and more rapidly than most other states toward the consolidation of mass parties. Nevertheless, even in the Empire state the new political institutions and ethos were never accorded total legitimation and the institutionalization of mass parties was never complete.

Political Differentiation Resisted: South Carolina

While New York most closely approximated the master trend of political differentiation, South Carolina most successfully resisted it. More so than any other state in antebellum America, South Carolina opposed the encroachment of a more differentiated pattern of politics. Unlike New York, South Carolina's traditional ruling class was not supplanted by a group of professional politicians. Notables were encouraged to assume public office and most fulfilled that responsibility. A study of South Carolina's 440 "great planters" of the antebellum era revealed that approximately 75 percent held at least one important public office—justice of the peace, state assemblyman or senator, governor, or United States representative or senator (Davidson 1971). More generally, political power remained "in the hands of the rich and the well-born" (Wooster 1969:5). The landed gentry dominated the state legislature (Wooster 1969:146–48), and given South Carolina's peculiar constitution, the legislature (politically) dominated the state. Moreover, the men who held other important public offices at both the state and local levels—governor, state supreme court justice, justice of the peace, sheriff, or commissioner of roads and bridges— were also typically drawn from the gentry and propertied classes (Wooster 1969:55, 64–65, 78–80, 88–89, 98, 100, 102–3; Freehling, 1965a:90–91). South Carolinians who served in either the United States Senate or House were also drawn almost exclusively from the patrician elite (Jaher 982:368–71).

South Carolina was the only antebellum state where even the semblance of a durable two party system did not appear. John Calhoun's 1849 boast that in South Carolina "party organization, party discipline, party proscription—and their offspring, the spoils' principle have been unknown" is accurate history. The usual practice of politics in the state was essentially factional and based on informal, unstable coalitions of various members of the political elite (Greenberg 1977:175). For the most part, elections and campaigns were organized casually and informally (Banner 1974:61–62). State legislative seats, if contested at all, normally fell under the control of local coteries with little stable association with cliques elsewhere in the state. Equally significant is that more than half of the 144 congressional races held in the state between 1824 and 1860 featured only a single candidate, offering no contest to the voters (Banner 1974:79–80). Political leadership within the state was largely factional and organized around leading personalities (Faust 1982:204–23). Temporary statewide organizations emerged in the face of crisis—e.g., the Nullification Crisis of 1832 or the early Secession Crisis of 1850—and their machinery bore similarities to stable party formations. Still, as these crises passed, that machinery was quickly dismantled (Banner 1974:63–65).

Despite the absence of well-organized parties within the state, South Carolinian politicians could not totally ignore the two national parties. The ascendance of the Democratic and Whig organizations compelled South Carolinians to give considerable attention to party machinations, and many loosely identified themselves with one of the major parties. However, whereas other states produced a relatively even, competitive balance between the Democrats and Whigs, South Carolina proved to be an exception. In the congressional elections held between 1824 and 1860, 29 percent of all candidates claimed *no* party label. Of those candidates who publicly declared a partisan identity, 71 percent called themselves Democrats, 10 percent called themselves Whigs, and 19 percent referred to themselves as "States Rights Nullifiers" or as "Union" men, the latter labels putting them clearly in neither Democratic nor Whig camps (Banner 1974:80–81). However, it must be noted that most South Carolinians who called themselves Democrats or Whigs had little to do with the day-to-day activities of those national party organizations (Greenberg 1977:166).

Although established partisan organizations did not emerge in antebellum South Carolina, there was substantial electoral participation in legislative and congressional elections. When two or more candidates competed for office, congressional contests produced a median level of voter participation of 69 percent with voting levels rising as high as 95 percent in individual districts. These figures indicate that when provided with a choice, the South Carolinian electorate voted with roughly the same willingness as voters in other states (Banner 1974:82–83).

As late as 1850, South Carolina's political leadership remained wedded to the eighteenth century ideals of gentry stewardship, statesmanship, independence, *noblesse oblige*, and personal honor (Freehling 1965b:37). These ideals enshrined the notion that leaders should "exercise their disinterested and enlightened judgment free from any pressure exerted by the multitude" (Faust 1982:42; also see Jaher 1982:370–71). It was widely argued that stability, public order, and the protection of liberty all required the enlightened rule of disinterested statesmen. Only the traditional pattern of leadership could ensure that the public welfare would be promoted and that liberty would be protected. James Hamilton Jr., a leading member of the state's elite, wrote, "The people expect that their leaders in whose public spirit they have confidence will think for them—and that they will be prepared to act as their leaders think" (Hamilton 1830).

Adherence to classic political ideals was matched by a vitriolic and pervasive antiparty cant. There was an almost primordial aversion to political parties in any form (Freehling 1965b:36–42). In South Carolina, the antiparty critique drew primarily on traditional republican tenets. Accordingly, the state's elite decried the party system for its putative promotion of a passion for federal patronage, the rule of party hacks, and the rise of inferior demagogues (Freehling 1956:38). In addition, South Carolinians condemned the appearance of party because it presented a threat to liberty, eroded the social and political authority of "men of high character," and undermined the cohesiveness of the community (Brady 1972:187–204).

In conjunction with this anti-party sentiment, leading Carolinians articulated a distinctive southern, regional interest largely manifest in the protection of slavery and in opposition to tariffs designed to protect northern manufacturing interests. National parties, they argued, were premised upon a series of compromises between northern and southern wings of the parties and posed a grave threat to "the southern way of life." According to this conservative world view, traditional politics were better suited than mass party politics to protect vital southern interests.

Along with this antipartyism and proSouthernism, deference to the "natural aristocracy" also persisted. For the most part, South Carolinians of middle and lower status assumed that the gentry were the most capable of exercising social and political authority and regularly returned them to elective office (Greenberg 1977: 102–4).

In brief, South Carolina's relative traditionalism provides a vivid contrast to New York's innovative political developments. Even as late as 1850, political authority in the Palmetto state continued to be exercised by a patrician elite, who vigorously opposed modern party organizations and clung tenaciously to the classic statesman ethos.

Political Differentiation Accommodated: Virginia and Massachusetts

Virginia. Jacksonian Virginia produced a "compromise" or "accommodationist" pattern of political differentiation which fell between the extremes of South Carolina and New York. During the Jacksonian era, Virginia politics became more differentiated from the traditional status and normative order than it had been in the colonial and Jeffersonian periods. However, traditional elements persisted and inhibited the full development of a specialized political stratum, differentiated party organizations, and a distinctive partisan ethic.

Virginia experienced a somewhat higher degree of political mobility in the Jacksonian period than in the colonial and Jeffersonian epochs (Colomy 1982; Sharp 1970; Sydnor 1948:50; Wooster 1975:39–40, 112–17; Kuroda 1969:46–47, 238, 257–58; Eaton 1966:297–98; Harrison 1970; Simms 1929). Still, despite a few exceptions Virginian congressmen and presidential cabinet officers continued to be selected from among members of the gentry class. None of the twelve Virginia governors who served between 1827 and 1852 were closely connected to well-established gentry families. However, five of those governors had Scottish ancestors and the same number came from the western, and less economically and socially developed, region of the state. In comparison to the "English" and eastern gentry's unquestioned monopoly of this office prior to the Jacksonian era, this indicates somewhat gender political mobility. State legislators of the period possessed more wealth than nonlegislators but, in line with the state's overall economic decline, were significantly less wealthy than colonial and early postrevolutionary legislators. At the local level, justices of the peace and sheriffs continued to be drawn from the ranks of local gentry families, though their power had been significantly reduced by the emergence of district courts and the professionalization of the bar. Finally, the Democratic and Whig party leaders were drawn overwhelmingly from the state's gentry class, and were often related by family connections.

Virginia politics were dramatically altered by the emergence of a well-organized two-party system (McCormick 1966:198–99). Parties assumed the tasks of nominating candidates, organizing campaigns, and mobilizing the electorate. By the late 1830s, the state's parties' conventions were nominating candidates and presidential electors, appointing correspondence committees throughout the state, circulating party pamphlets, and whipping up party enthusiasm. Political campaigns, particularly for national offices, were dramatic spectacles replete with mass rallies, barbecues, processions, banners, emblems, songs, slogans, and emotionally charged appeals to party loyalty. A partisan press flourished, and the leading Democratic and Whig papers exerted a significant impact on the state's politics. The party manager—a new type of actor on the Virginia scene—became a powerful political force, especially in his capacity as arbiter between conflicting wings of the party (Sharp 1970:15).

The distribution of federal and state patronage became largely a matter of rewarding those who rendered useful service to the party (Harrison 1970). Despite many publicly expressed reservations about the principle of rotation, both Democrats and Whigs adopted the practice of partisan patronage.

Party voting appeared in the Virginia legislature in the mid-1830s, and continued throughout the 1840s (Ershkowitz and Shade 1971). Legislators began to identify themselves as either Democrats or Whigs and to vote with their party on many issues, especially economic and "corporate" issues.

It must be emphasized, especially in the case of Virginia, that party organization and partisan considerations made initial forays into the traditional bastion of local authority—the county (McCormick 1966). Each party's state central committee appointed local county corresponding committees. Competing committees were often established in a single county and committee activities could be extensive and sustained. The most active local committees nominated candidates for the state legislature and for the House of Representatives and assumed partial responsibility for expenses incurred during campaigns for these offices.

Moreover, in spite of the local gentry's dominance of local politics, the age of parties introduced several new elements to the local political scene. First, many political decisions were partially premised on partisan criteria. Second, party organization and discipline, though by no means fully institutionalized, had become more salient, and local committee chieftains were obliged to consider the decisions of national and state party organizations. Finally, in some communities competing parties appeared and the local gentry was split by conflicting partisan loyalties.

As party organizations became more elaborate and tied national and local levels together through an extensive network of committees, as the nominating convention and partisan press became more important, and as political campaigns assumed the character of dramatic spectacles, voters began to acquire partisan identities (Kuroda

1969:179). Previously, voters had followed the lead of the local gentry. With the establishment of political parties, many voters employed partisan organizations and perspectives as political reference groups.

Party loyalty and discipline, the subordination of individual judgment to the party, and democracy were the "new" political ideals and they became an important part of Jacksonian Virginia's political culture. The new ideals were pronounced and reaffirmed in partisan conventions, parades, rallies, and newspapers. As in New York, parties were justified by reference to the valuable functions they performed for the community, state, and nation (Kuroda 1969:268). In addition, there was increasing acceptance of the legislators' right to instruct United States senators. Since the state legislature was usually controlled by one of the major parties, acceptance of the doctrine of instruction meant, in effect, an endorsement of a party's right to dictate the votes of an esteemed public figure (Eaton 1952). Finally, democratic sentiments were more widely espoused and accepted. Throughout the South substantial democratic reforms had modified state constitutions, the apportionment of state legislatures, and the mode of selecting state and local officials. Virginia reformers employed similar rhetoric to demand alterations in their own state's constitution. The growing appeal of democratic values did not eliminate the notion that the wealthy and well-born were obliged to render public service, but it did put those who blatantly espoused an elitist conception of social and political authority on the defensive. The successful public figure was increasingly obliged to employ a democratic rhetoric (Sydnor 1948:281–87).

In New York, political developments similar to the ones just described nearly eliminated more traditional political practices and ethos. By contrast, in Virginia these "modern" innovations functioned alongside more traditional elements in an uneasy accommodation.

Party leadership, for example, remained informal and secret, with its inner core held together not, as in New York, by professional politicians' passion for organization, but by overlapping family ties (Ammon 1953, 1963; Harrison 1970; Simms 1929). This informality, secrecy, and familialism forestalled the development of a party organization with a standardized division of labor, an identifiable hierarchy, and the specification of party service as a basis for promotion within the party.

In addition, Virginia Democrats, the state's dominant party, eschewed a "pure," democratic nominating convention and continued to employ a "mixed" caucus convention. Further, both members of the legislative caucus and the party's elite had much greater influence over the convention's proceedings than did the typical county delegate.

Moreover, while partisan considerations certainly shaped the behavior of Virginia's state legislators, party discipline was less exacting in Virginia than in New York and other states (Ershkowitz and Shade 1971). Several important state issues, including constitutional reform, state-sponsored internal improvements, and state supported public education were debated outside the party framework. Sectional groupings were the primary antagonists in these debates and each side included members of other major parties (Ammon 1946; Sutton 1972). The relative absence of partisan cohesiveness reflected both the inability of Virginia's nationally oriented parties to incorporate the state's sectional tensions and the persistence of an individualistic ethos antagonistic to party discipline (McCormick 1966:184–85).

The oligarchic structure of county government, consisting of life tenure in major county offices and the county court's control over local appointments, also impeded the full development of parties. Justices of the peace and other locally prominent citizens dominated party committees and there was little distinction between the community's larger status order and its political hierarchy. Moreover, unlike New York, Virginia's state parties did not enjoy the power to appoint men to the most important local offices. Rather, these offices were controlled by local gentry families, who usually did not invoke partisan criteria as the primary basis for distributing posts (Kuroda 1969; Porter 1947).

Modern political organization and practices, then, did not fully supplant more traditional patterns. Further, those modern elements that did appear were not fully legitimated. Jacksonian Virginia contained a virulent strain of antipartyism that denounced professional politicians as "hacks" and "collar men." Drawing inspiration from the classic republican tradition, ideological conservatives asserted that parties sacrificed the public welfare to the narrow interests of selfish partisans. These critics of political modernization praised the classic statesman ideal, celebrating the disinterested public servant whose deliberations were based on the rational assessment of the public good. The statesman ideal was inherently antiparty, for it obliged the public leader to hold himself above party and faction and maintained that only decisions based on virtue and the public interest, broadly conceived, could benefit the whole community (Brown 1980).

Other traditional political ideals also persisted. Members of the gentry continued to be socialized to the values of public service and *noblesse oblige*. Honorable public service was a mark of distinction and was considered, among the gentry, as the duty and right of a gentleman (Craven 1932:35–36; Burdick 1985:17–19). Commitment to stewardship was often reinforced by a family tradition of public service (Mitchell 1981:21–22). Finally, though weakened by the ascendance of democratic sentiment, deference to gentry claims to social and political authority continued to be an important element of Virginia's political culture. A deferential ethos was more widely diffused in Virginia than in New York, and partially reflected the paternalism of an established slave-based society (Sydnor 1948:290–91; Genovese 1972:97–98).

In short, Jacksonian Virginia produced an accommodation between modern and traditional components of political leadership, organization, and ideology which placed the Old Dominion between the extremes of New York and South Carolina. Further, those modern elements that did emerge were the object of a sustained ideological critique that prohibited their complete institutionalization.

Massachusetts. Like Virginia, Jacksonian Massachusetts produced a pattern of accommodation between a relatively differentiated party system and a traditional ruling class. While more differentiated party organizations enabled some "new" men to enter public office and assume influential positions within party organizations, both parties, but especially the Whigs, who dominated the state's public offices, allowed traditional elites disproportionate representation in leadership positions. The appearance of competitive partisan organizations, by contrast, constituted the most significant step toward political differentiation. Finally, the era also witnessed the wider acceptance of a proparty ideology, though throughout the period antiparty sentiment remained strong.

The creation of relatively differentiated party organizations coupled with the greater acceptance of a proparty ideology enabled new types of men, those without great wealth or status, to assume a more central role in the public life of Massachusetts. Accordingly, a more professional type of politician appeared during the late Jacksonian period and acquired substantial influence both as a party functionary and as an elected or appointed public official (Formisano 1983:246, 313–14; Schlesinger 1945:146–50, 257–60; Brauer 1967:20). Relative to the Jeffersonian era, a higher proportion of men from middling economic and social circumstances occupied important state and local offices in the Jacksonian period (Jaher 1982:54; Pessen 1973:282–89; Doherty 1977:82–102).

However, as in Virginia, the predominant pattern remained one of elite dominance. From the 1830s through the mid-1850s, Massachusetts' senators, representatives, and governors were drawn overwhelmingly from upper-class families (Baltzell 1979:374, 385–95, 399–400, 498). Although a few self-made men occupied the Boston's mayor's office during this period, most of the town's mayors had upper-class origins (Baltzell 1979:373). Other important city posts, including the Common Council and Board of Alderman, were dominated by the wealthy (Rich 1971:266). Leading positions in the state legislature were also assumed by the elite (Rich 1971:266).

Although the advent of mass parties afforded the professional politician and the man of middling economic circumstances greater political mobility than they enjoyed previously, bluebloods continued to play an important role in partisan affairs. Upper-class men figured prominently in the leadership ranks of both parties (Schlesinger 1945:254–57; Formisano 1983:313). The well-to-do were most conspicuous in the Whig party and served in a variety of capacities—as delegates to party conventions, as vote distributors during campaigns, and as directors of the party's state and county committees (Rich 1971:266). More significantly, however, members of the upper class shaped the party's policy.

Perhaps the most striking movement toward greater political differentiation was the elaboration of complex and durable partisan organizations (Formisano 1983:245–46; 263–64; 259–64; 305–9; McCormick 1966:25–50). By 1839 both the Democrats and Whigs were organized as "voter mobilizing machines," with state-directed local committees organizing the electorate in the towns and villages. Each party's state central committee convened monthly meetings and regularly consulted with county committees. Town committees generated lists of voters and during the balloting checked for illegal voters. In the 1840s, enterprising (and almost invariably Democratic) politicians aided Irish Catholic immigrants in securing citizenship and voting rights by drawing up papers and filling out forms in tacit exchange for political support (Handlin 1941:189–91). Both parties spawned associations that traveled throughout the state giving political and educational lectures and distributing pamphlets and partisan newspapers. The latter flourished in Jacksonian Massachusetts, with the Democrats publishing some twenty different newspapers while the Whigs controlled over fifty. Fund raising too, became more systematic with the party, rather than relatives or friends, serving as the primary agent for raising and dispensing campaign funds. Parties issued concerted appeals to the rich and middle classes alike requesting contributions to the parties' war chests (Rich 1971:266–67). The "expressive" features of politics were not neglected as each party sponsored huge political rallies, parades, and barbecues designed to reaffirm partisan commitments.

In the early 1840s both parties moved away from the traditional caucus of notables and toward the political convention (Formisano 1983:245–46). The modern convention system was organized throughout wards, towns, and counties and up to the state level. Delegate selection was increasingly based on the principle of democratic representation, with party representatives from each town attending a state convention where the party's ticket, its slate of presidential electors, and its address were selected. Though thousands of delegates attended these conventions, it must be acknowledged that real power resided in an inner core of party leadership which usually picked candidates and formulated the resolutions and addresses that were subsequently "passed" by the convention's delegates.

The partisan use of patronage also became much more systematic in this era (Darling 1925). Federal patronage was especially important to the Democratic party, stimulating its initial appearance in the early 1830s and continuing to provide it with sustenance during its maturation in the 1840s. The Whigs' dominance of state and important local offices supplied them with a valuable source of patronage.

The "party-in-office" emerged in the late 1830s. Prior to that time the Massachusetts legislature held few roll call votes. Only after the creation of mass parties did roll calls become more common and did voting on bills become organized along party lines. In addition, appointments to legislative committees and chairmanships increasingly reflected an acceptance of two party norms (Formisano 1983:307–9).

Voter participation rose in this period, although despite the exertions of party leaders and functionaries participation in Massachusetts remained below the national average throughout the Jacksonian era (Formisano 1983:33–34). Identification with political parties became more intense and widespread. Finally, partisan competition within towns also increased dramatically, reflecting the parties' penetration into local communities and the partial erosion of Massachusetts' consensual tradition (Formisano 1983: 45–53).

Elements of a modern political culture also appeared in Jacksonian Massachusetts. During the late 1830s and early 1840s, a proparty ideology became more widely accepted. A survey of religious, gubernatorial, and July 4th annual public addresses delivered between

1800 and 1844 revealed that by the late 1830s these ritualistic orations reflected a much more positive conception of parties and a greater recognition and appreciation of the functions they performed (Formisano 1983:84–106). Organized political opposition was also accorded greater legitimacy than it had received in the Jeffersonian period (Formisano 1985:309–10).

In the Jacksonian years, party loyalty was intense and party discipline more exacting (Formisano 1983:279–80). For most voters, party loyalty was regarded as a political virtue. Once party loyalties formed in the late 1830s, they exhibited remarkable staying power with families serving as the primary agents of political socialization.

The era's public rhetoric displayed a much greater acquiescence to egalitarian and democratic values. That the Bay State's Democratic party, whose following included ethnic out-groups and "honest" farmers, laborers, and mechanics, should adopt a populist rhetoric is not surprising. However, many prominent, conservative Whigs, who privately adhered to an elitist conception of social leadership, were also obliged, on occasion, to proclaim their support of democracy and political equality (Jacobson 1951; Hofstadter 1962:165–66; Jaher 1982:78–80).

As in Virginia, the growth of modern political organization and the appearance of more modern political culture did not totally displace more traditional structures. Despite the considerable modernization of campaign machinery, parties continued to rely upon influential people and the prestige of famous leaders to get the vote out. In comparison to New York, the political order was not as clearly differentiated from local communities' status orders (Formisano 1983:283–88). Traditional inhibitions against self-electioneering persisted and, unlike in Virginia and South Carolina, there was a deep-rooted resistance to stump oratory (McCormick 1966:39–40, 46–47).

As implied earlier, the substitution of the convention for the traditional notable caucus did not radically alter the locus of decision making authority. That power remained the property of a relatively small group of upper class men who, linked by family, social, and financial ties, exercised it informally and in private (Dalzell 1973:59–60).

More generally, Massachusetts' political parties, much like Virginia's, did not evince the same degree of autonomy from the larger status order that characterized the partisan organizations of New York. Noting that the Whig party dominated the state's politics throughout the Jacksonian period, the most meticulous study of antebellum Massachusetts politics observes, "Massachusetts' Whiggery especially was directed at its core by a Brahmin elite of merchant-manufactures and their lawyer-political allies" (Formisano 1983:324). It wasn't until the mid-1850s that the Brahmins began to lose their dominant position in the state's politics (Formisano 1983:315). Although their dominance of the Democratic party did not compare with their ascendance among the Whigs, various bluebloods types—the scholar-educator, the reformer-politician, and the old republican public servant—also figured prominently in the Democratic party (Formisano 1983:314; Schlesinger 1945:151–55, 170–74, 254–57; Brauer 1967:20).

The continuing, disproportionate political authority exercised by the Massachusetts gentry should not overshadow the significant change that had occurred. Though not proceeding as far in Massachusetts as in New York, political differentiation in the Bay State did produce a highly complex and durable organizational substratum of political authority. That development, in turn, created the possibility that other groups could appropriate the organizational machinery and exploit it for different purposes. In fact, toward the latter part of the nineteenth century, Irish-Catholics and elements of the lower class did obtain control over parts of the political machine and forced the gentry to share political power.

Although a proparty ideology became much more widely accepted, ideological conservatives in antebellum Massachusetts generated a sustained attack on the legitimacy of the party system which inhibited its complete institutionalization. Several prominent religious and intellectual figures, placing themselves above the partisan battles of the day, denounced the nefarious impact of parties on community life and mourned the loss of the classic public virtues (Howe 1970:205–11, 221–26). In addition, elements of Massachusetts' Whiggery continued to express an ambivalence about the effects of the party system. Throughout Whiggery's existence there was a wing within the party coalition that regularly voiced antipartisan sentiment and exhibited a reticence about several key elements of antebellum political modernity, including party patronage, "excessive" party loyalty and discipline (which purportedly detracted from personal responsibility), demagogic campaigning, and the stimulation of passion over reason (Howe 1979:50–55, 57–58, 280). Very prominent in Massachusetts Whiggery, this culturally conservative wing denounced the working components of the new political, and especially the Democratic, machines as slavish collar men who sold out liberty for patronage, who lacked personal merit and social distinction, and who, knowing that they had no claims upon the loyalties of the people, spread the blight of blind partisanship. However, this antiparty ideology was not confined to proper Bostonians for when the populist Know-Nothing movement, attracting primarily lower middle and working-class men, surfaced in the 1850s it, too, espoused an antiparty ideology (Formisano 1983:326–43, Baum 1978, 1984).

Massachusetts antipartyism displayed somewhat greater intensity than that which appeared in Virginia because it drew upon the New England heritage of "moralistic republicanism" (Kelley 1979:50–51, 83–84, 120–23). Massachusetts' Protestant heritage gave "a decidedly moralistic quality to Bay State politics" (Dalzell 1973:83). Many men active in public life were reticent about compromising principle to political expediency and those reservations fueled the antiparty critique. As the issue of slavery moved toward the center of the public stage, a split appeared within the Whig party between the conscience or moralistic wing and the cotton elements (Brauer 1967; Sewell 1976:139–42). Eventually this moralistic quality prompted defections from both major parties, dissidents moving initially toward the Liberty party and later to the Free Soil party. Both of these parties were premised on the principled rejection of slavery (Formisano 1983:329–39).

Finally, even though democratic and egalitarian sentiments had gained much ground in antebellum Massachusetts, deferential attitudes were still evident. Though not as pervasive as in the colonial era and although class and social resentments were now voiced more publicly, deference on the part of lower- and middle-status men toward the well-to-do did persist in the small villages, factory towns, and the largest cities of Jacksonian Massachusetts (Formisano 1983:283–88).

In brief, Jacksonian Massachusetts, like Virginia, exhibited a pattern of accommodation between a governing class and a more differentiated pattern of political leadership. In both states, the most significant development was the elaboration of mass parties and the adoption of modern campaign practices. Coupled with the growth of a proparty ideology and democratic values, these more modern political organizations provided for greater political mobility and inclusion. Still, these initial steps toward political differentiation did not completely uproot the upper class's traditional control over public authority. Rather, an uneasy compromise was struck between political tradition and modernity which persisted throughout the antebellum period.

Conclusion

The brief vignettes of political developments in antebellum New York, South Carolina, Virginia, and Massachusetts underscore the uneven realization of the master trend of political differentiation. While nearly every state in the nation experienced a minimal degree of political modernization, the rate and degree of change varied considerably. These accounts also indicate that in no state did differentiated political structures attain complete institutionalization. In every instance, the construction of relatively modern political institutions and ethos encountered opposition that, in turn, impeded full legitimation.

Earlier I argued that differentiation theory must supplement its postulated master trend of change with the identification of patterned departures from that trend. The concepts of uneven differentiation and incomplete institutionalization illustrated by the empirical materials presented above broaden the empirical scope of differentiation theory by describing theoretically significant departures from the master trend of differentiation and the implicit model of complete institutionalization. However, these concepts not only provide a more variegated conception of change, they also underscore the need for an elaboration of differentiation theory's explanatory framework.

Initial formulations of differentiation theory employed the theory's conceptual scheme as a classificatory device to order societies, institutional forms, or roles, on the basis of their relative complexity. Aside from an occasional reference to strain, societal needs, or increased efficiency, these initial statements gave little explanatory attention to how particular institutions actually moved from one level of complexity to another.

Clearly, global concepts such as strain, needs, and efficiency cannot fully account for either the uneven character of differentiation or the incomplete institutionalization of more differentiated structures. A more comprehensive and supple explanatory framework is necessary if patterned departures from both the master trend of differentiation and the implicit model of complete institutionalization are to be explained.

The rudiments of such a conceptual scheme are now beginning to crystallize in what can be called a structural voluntaristic approach (see Eisenstadt 1964, 1969; Smelser 1974; Colomy 1985). This incipient perspective maintains that institutional change is partially shaped by external, constraining social conditions such as the predominant socioeconomic formations (and the conflicts they engender), the prevailing political structures and distribution of power, the hegemonic cultural codes, and the pattern of solidary relations. Analysis of these conditions must be supplemented with the examination of how specific groups contribute to the differentiation process. This revisionist approach recommends that an adequate explanation of uneven differentiation and incomplete institutionalization must describe the confluence of structural and voluntaristic elements (see chapter 7 this volume).

The concepts of uneven differentiation and incomplete institutionalization, then, broaden the empirical scope of differentiation theory. These ideas give the approach greater historical specificity and highlight the often subterranean tensions and conflicts associated with structural differentiation. Finally, these notions encourage the elaboration of the theory's explanatory framework.

Notes

1. It must be noted that in a very interesting, recent paper, Smelser (1985) has revised his earlier conception of structural differentiation. A critical assessment of the model of complete institutionalization comprises a central part of his revisionist approach.

2. Our efforts to extend the empirical scope of differentiation theory and to lend it greater historical specificity can be regarded as an instance of "theory elaboration" (see Wagner 1984; Wagner and Berger 1985).

3. The first steps toward a more inclusive conception of change have already been taken. Several studies have focused on dedifferentiation, noting that in response to diverse structural strains a social system may retreat from relative complexity to a less differentiated level (see Parsons 1954:104–44, 298–322; Lechner 1984; Lipset and Raab 1970). "Unequal development," which refers to the unequal rate and degree of differentiation across distinct institutional spheres, has also been examined recently (see Smelser 1971; Eisenstadt 1973; Rueschemeyer 1976; Alexander 1981). It should be noted that my discussion of uneven differentiation extends the logic underlying the concept of unequal development.

4. The notion of a "war of position" is borrowed from Gramsci (1971), but it is used somewhat differently here. Gramsci's primary concern was with the transformation of an entire social and cultural system, and he coined the "war of position" concept to designate the cultural and moral struggle that necessarily preceded a successful armed insurrection. In my view, the concept is usefully elaborated by refracting it across distinct institutional subsystems. Accordingly, one anticipates that virtually every instance of institutional transformation will involve a war of position between the proponents of change and those resisting alterations. Although I find it useful to stretch Gramsci's concept in this way, I clearly run the risk of diluting its revolutionary thrust.

5. The notion of a "double movement" was developed by Polanyi (1944) to describe how the perceived excesses of a differentiated self-regulating market stimulated a countermovement aimed at protecting broad societal interests. Polan-

yi's notion is profitably generalized to describe how the drive toward institutional consolidation in a variety of institutional spheres is resisted by those seeking to protect vital group and societal interests.

6. These states were selected for three primary reasons. First, the theoretical argument required discussion of colonies/states that had been well established by 1740. Second, a concern for comparative analysis dictated examination of colonies/ states from each of the nation's major sections—New England, the Middle States, the Upper South, and the Lower South. Finally, we selected colonies/states for which a relatively extensive historiography was available.

7. In the following discussions of states the focus is on how closely each case followed the master trend by the late Jacksonian period. A full treatment would require that I discuss each state's development from 1740 to 1850; space limitations preclude such a lengthy exercise. In any case, since my primary concern is with the emergence of differentiated political structures, my exclusive focus on the late Jacksonian period is theoretically appropriate.

References

Alexander, Jeffrey C. 1980. "Core Solidarity, Ethnic Outgroup, and Social Differentiation: A Multi-Dimensional Model of Inclusion in Modern Societies." In Jacques Dofny and Akinsola Akiowowo, eds., *National and Ethnic Movements*, pp. 5–28. Beverly Hills, Calif.: Sage.

—— 1981. "The Mass News Media in Systemic, Historical and Comparative Perspective." In Elihu Katz and Thomas Szecsko eds., *Mass Media and Social Change*, pp. 17–52. Beverly Hills, Calif.: Sage.

—— 1983. *The Modern Reconstruction of Classical Thought: Talcott Parsons.* Berkeley: University of California Press.

—— 1985. "Introduction" In Jeffrey Alexander, ed., *Neofunctionalism*, pp. 7–18. Beverly Hills, Calif.: Sage.

Alexander, Jeffrey C. and Paul Colomy. 1985. "Toward Neofunctionalism." *Sociological Theory* 3:111–23.

Ambler, Charles H., 1910. *Sectionalism in Virginia from 1776–1861.* New York: Russell and Russell.

Ammon, Henry. 1948. "The Republican Party in Virginia, 1789–1824." Ph.D. dissertation. University of Virginia.

—— 1953. "The Richmond Junto, 1800–1824." *Virginia Magazine* 61:395–18.

—— 1963. "The Jeffersonian Republicans in Virginia." *Virginia Magazine* 71:153–67.

Aronson, Sidney. 1964. *Status and Kinship in the Higher Civil Service.* Cambridge, Mass.: Harvard University Press.

Bailyn, Bernard. 1959. "Politics and Societal Structure in Virginia." In James M. Smith, ed., *Seventeenth Century America*, pp. 90–115. Chapel Hill: University of North Carolina Press.

—— 1967a. *The Origins of American Politics.* New York: Random House.

—— 1967b. *The Ideological Origins of the American Revolution.* Cambridge, Mass.: Harvard University Press.

Baldasty, Gerald. 1982. "The New York State Political Press and Antimasonry." *New York History* 64:261–79.

Baltzell, Digby. 1979. *Puritan Boston and Quaker Philadelphia*. New York: Free Press.

Banner, James M. 1974. "The Problem of South Carolina." In Stanley Elkins and Eric McKitrick, eds., *The Hofstadter Aegis: A Memorial*, pp. 60–93. New York: Alfred A. Knopf.

Banning, Lance. 1978. *The Jeffersonian Persuasion*. Ithaca, N.Y.: Cornell University Press.

Barber, Bernard. 1985. "Beyond Parsons' Theory of the Professions." In Jeffrey Alexander, ed., *Neofunctionalism*, pp. 211–224. Beverly Hills: Sage.

Barkan, Elliott R. 1971. "The Emergence of a Whig Persuasion: Conservatism, Democratism, and the New York State Whigs." *New York History* 52:367–395.

Baum, Dale. 1978. "Know-Nothingism and the Republican Majority in Massachusetts: The Political Realignment of the 1850s." *Journal of American History* 64:959–86.

—— 1984. *The Civil War Party System: The Case of Massachusetts, 1848–1876*. Chapel Hill, N.C.: University of North Carolina Press.

Bellah, Robert. 1964. "Religious Evolution." *American Sociological Review* 29:358–74.

Benson, Lee. 1961. *The Concept of Jacksonian Democracy*. Princeton, N.J.: Princeton University Press.

Berens, John. 1978. *Providence and Patriotism in Early America, 1640–1815*. Charlottesville, Va.: University Press of Virginia.

Berthoff, Rowland and John Murrin. 1973. "Feudalism, Communalism, and the Yeoman Freeholder." In S. Kurtz and J. Hutson, eds., *Essays on The American Revolution*. New York: Norton.

Bonomi, Patricia H. 1971. *Factious People, Politics, and Society in Colonial New York*. New York: Columbia University Press.

Brady, Patrick. 1972. "Political Culture in the Early American Republic: The Case of South Carolina." Ph.D. dissertation, U.C.S.B.

Brauer, Kinley. 1967. *Cotton vs. Conscience*. Lexington, KY.: University of Kentucky Press.

Bridenbaugh, Carl. 1938. *Cities in the Wilderness: The First Century of Urban Life in America, 1625–1742*. New York: Ronald Press.

—— 1955. *Cities in Revolt: Urban Life in America, 1743–1776*. New York: Knopf.

Bridges, Amy. 1982. "Another Look at Plutocracy and Politics in Antebellum New York City." *Political Science Quarterly* 97:57–71.

—— 1984. *A City in the Republic: Antebellum New York and the Origins of Machine Politics*. Cambridge, Eng.: Cambridge University Press.

Brown, Richard. 1976. "The Founding Fathers of 1776 and 1787: A Collective View." *William and Mary Quarterly* 33:465–80.

Brown, Robert. 1955. *Middle Class Democracy and the Revolution in Massachusetts, 1691–1780*. Ithaca, N.Y.: Cornell University Press.

Brown, Robert and Katherine Brown. 1964. *Virginia, 1705–1786: Democracy or Aristocracy?* East Lansing, Mi.: Michigan State University Press.

Brown, Thomas. 1980. "Southern Whigs and the Politics of Statesmanship, 1833–1841." *Journal of Southern History* 46:361–80.

Burdick, John. 1985. "From Virtue to Fitness: The Accommodation of a Planter Family to Postbellum Virginia." *Virginia Magazine* 93:14–35.

Buel, Richard. 1964. "Democracy and the American Revolution: A Frame of Reference." *William and Mary Quarterly* 21:165–90.

—— 1972. *Securing the Revolution, 1789–1815*. Ithaca, N.Y.: Cornell University Press.

Calhoun, John C. 1853. *Disquisition on Government*. New York: Peter Smith.

Chambers, William N. 1963. *Political Parties in a New Nation*. New York: Oxford University Press.

—— 1967. "Party Development and the American Mainstream." In William N. Chambers and Walter D. Burnham, eds., *The American Party Systems*, pp. 3–32. New York: Oxford University Press.

—— 1971. "Election of 1840." In A. M. Schlesinger, ed., *History of American Presidential Elections*, 2:pp. 643–744.

—— 1973. "Politics in the Early American States." *Reviews in American History* 1:499–503.

Charles, Joseph. 1956. *The Origins of the American Party System*. New York: Harper and Row.

Chase, James. 1973. *Emergence of The Presidential Nominating Convention, 1789–1832*. Urbana, ILL.: University of Illinois Press.

Chirot, Daniel and Robert Hall. 1982. "World System Theory." *Annual Review of Sociology* 8:81–106.

Colomy, Paul. 1982. "Stunted Differentiation: A Sociological Examination of Political Elites in Virginia, 1720–1850." Ph.D. dissertation. Department of Sociology, U.C.L.A.

—— 1985. "Uneven Structural Differentiation: Toward a Comparative Approach." In Jeffrey C. Alexander ed., *Neofunctionalism*, pp. 131–156 Beverly Hills, Calif.: Sage.

Cooper, William. 1978. *The South and The Politics of Slavery, 1828–1856*. Baton Rouge, La.: Louisiana State University Press.

—— 1983. *Liberty and Slavery*. New York: Knopf.

Craven, Avery. 1932. *Edmund Ruffin: Southerner*. New York: Appleton.

Crenson, Matthew. 1975. *The Federal Machine*. Baltimore, Md.: John Hopkins University Press.

Cunningham, Noble E. 1957. *The Jeffersonian Republicans*. Chapel Hill, NC.: University of North Carolina Press.

—— 1963. *Jeffersonian Republicans in Power*. Chapel Hill, NC: University of North Carolina Press.

Dahl, Robert. 1961. *Who Governs?* New Haven: Conn.: Yale University Press.

Dalzell, Robert. 1973. *Daniel Webster and The Trial of American Nationalism*. Boston, Mass.: Houghton Mifflin.

Darling, Arthur. 1925. *Political Changes in Massachusetts, 1824–1848*. Cos Cob, Conn.: John Edwards.

Davidson, Chalmers. 1971. *The Last Foray: The South Carolina Planters of 1860*. Columbia: University of South Carolina Press.

Doherty, Robert. 1977. *Society and Power*. Amherst: University of Massachusetts Press.

Eaton, Clement. 1952. "Southern Senators and the Right of Instruction." *Journal of Southern History* 18:252–67.

—— 1966. *A History of The Old South*. New York: Macmillan.

Egnal, M. and J. Ernst. 1972. "An Economic Interpretation of the American Revolution." *William and Mary Quarterly* 29:3–32.

Eisenstadt, S. N. 1964. "Social Change, Differentiation, and Evolution." *American Sociological Review* 29:235–47.

—— 1969. *The Political System of Empires.* New York: Free Press.
—— 1973. *Tradition, Change and Modernity.* New York: Wiley.
—— 1985. "Systemic Qualities and Boundaries of Societies: Some Theoretical Considerations." In Jeffrey Alexander ed., *Neofunctionalism,* pp. 99–112 Beverly Hills, Calif.: Sage.
Ellis, Richard. 1971. *The Jeffersonian Crisis: Courts and Politics in the Young Republic.* New York: Norton.
Ershkowitz, Herbert and William Shade. 1971. "Consensus or Conflict: Political Behavior in the State Legislatures During the Jacksonian Era." *Journal of American History* 58:591–621.
Faust, Drew. 1982. *James Henry Hammond and the Old South.* Baton Rouge: Louisiana State University Press.
Fischer, David Hackett. 1965. *The Revolution of American Conservatism.* New York: Harper and Row.
Foner, Eric. 1976. *Tom Paine and Revolutionary America.* London: Oxford University Press.
Forgie, George B. 1979. *Patricide in the House Divided: A Psychological Interpretation of Lincoln and His Age.* New York: Norton.
Formisano, Ronald P. 1969. "Political Character, Antipartyism, and the Second Party System." *American Quarterly* 21:683–709.
—— 1974. "Deferential-Participant Politics: The Early Republic's Political Culture, 1789–1840." *American Political Science Review* 68:473–87.
—— 1976. "Toward a Reorientation of Jacksonian Politics: A Review of the Literature, 1959–1975." *Journal of American History* 63:42–65.
—— 1983. *The Transformation of Political Culture.* New York: Oxford University Press.
Fox, Renee. 1976. "Medical Evolution." In Jan J. Loubser et al., eds., *Explorations in General Theory in Social Science,* 2:773–87. New York: Free Press.
Freehling, William. 1965a. *Prelude to Civil War.* New York: Harper and Row.
—— 1965b. "Spoilsmen and Interests in the Thought and Career of John C. Calhoun." *Journal of American History* 52:25–42.
Gatell, Frank. 1967. "Money and Party in Jacksonian America." *Political Science Quarterly* 82:235–52.
Genovese, Eugene. 1972. *Roll Jordan, Roll.* New York: Free Press.
Gienapp, William E. 1985. "Nativism and the Creation of a Republican Majority in the North before the Civil War." *Journal of American History* 72:529–59.
Glazer, Nathan. 1975. *Affirmative Discriminations.* New York: Basic Books.
Goodman, Paul. 1964. *The Democratic-Republicans of Massachusetts.* Cambridge, Mass.: Harvard University Press.
Gramsci, Antonio. 1971. *Selections from the Prison Notebooks.* Q. Hoare and G. Smith, eds. and trs. New York: International Publishers.
Granovetter, Mark. 1979. "The Idea of Advancement in Theories of Social Evolution and Development." *American Journal of Sociology* 85:489–515.
Grant, Charles. 1961. *Democracy in the Connecticut Frontier Town of Kent.* New York: Columbia University Press.
Greenberg, Douglas. 1979. "The Middle Colonies in Recent American Historiography." *William and Mary Quarterly* 36:396–427.
Greenberg, Kenneth. 1977. "The Second American Revolution: South Carolina Politics, Society, and Secession, 1776–1860." Ph.D. dissertation. University of Wisconsin (Madison).

Greene, Jack. 1961. "The Role of the Lower Houses of Assembly in Eighteenth Century Politics." Journal of Southern History 27:451–474.

—— 1963. *Quest for Power.* Chapel Hill: University of North Carolina Press.

—— 1966. "Changing Interpretations of Early American Politics." In R. Billington ed., *The Reinterpretation of Early American History*, pp. 151–84 (San Marino Calif: Huntington.

—— 1968. "Introduction: The Reappraisal of The American Revolution in Recent Historical Literature." in J. Greene, ed., *The Reinterpretation of the American Revolution, 1763–1789.* New York: Harper and Row.

—— 1969. "Political Mimesis." *American Historical Review* 75:337–60.

—— 1973. "Revolution, Confederation, and Constitution, 1763–1787." In W. H. Cartwright and R. L. Watson, eds., *The Reinterpretation of American History and Culture*, pp. 259–95. Washington, D.C.: National Council for the Social Studies.

—— 1975. "The Growth of Political Stability: An Interpretation of Political Development in the Anglo-American Colonies, 1660–1760." in John Parker and Carol Urness, eds., pp. 27–52. Minneapolis: University of Minnesota Press.

—— 1976. "Society, Ideology, and Politics: An Analysis of the Political Culture of Mid-Eighteenth-Century Virginia." in R. Jellison, ed., *Society, Freedom, and Conscience*, pp. 14–76 New York: Norton.

Greven, Philip. 1977. *The Protestant Temperament.* New York: Knopf.

Gross, Robert. 1976. *The Minutemen and Their World.* New York: Hill and Wang.

Gunn, L. Ray. 1980. "The New York State Legislature." *Social Science History* 4:267–94.

Hall, Kermit. 1979. *The Politics of Justice.* Lincoln: University of Nebraska Press.

Hamilton, James. 1830. Letter. In James Hamilton Papers. South Caroliniana Library. Columbia, South Carolina.

Handlin, Oscar. 1941. *Boston's Immigrants.* Cambridge, Mass.: Harvard University Press.

Harrison, Joseph H. 1970. "Oligarchs and Democrats: The Richmond Junto." *Virginia Magazine* 78:184–98.

Heale, M. J. 1976. "From City Fathers to Social Critics: Humanitarianism and Government in New York, 1790–1860." *Journal of American History* 63:21–41.

—— 1982. *The Presidential Quest: Candidates and Images in American Political Culture, 1787–1852.* London: Longman.

Higginbotham, Don. 1974. "Military Leadership in The American Revolution," in *Leadership in The American Revolution* pp. 91–111. Washington D.C.

Hofstadter, Richard. 1962. *Anti-Intellectualism in American Life.* New York: Vintage.

—— 1969. *The Idea of a Party System.* Berkeley: University of California Press.

Holt, Michael. 1973. "The Politics of Impatience." *Journal of American History* 60:309–31.

—— 1978. *The Political Crisis of the 1850s.* New York: Wiley.

Howe, Daniel. 1970. *The Unitarian Conscience.* Cambridge, Mass: Harvard University Press.

—— 1979. *The Political Culture of the American Whigs.* Chicago, Ill.: University of Chicago Press.

Howe, John R. Jr. 1967. "Republican Thought and the Political Violence of the 1790s." *American Quarterly* 19:147–65.

Jacobson, Norman. 1951. "The Concept of Equality in the Assumptions and Propaganda of Massachusetts Conservatives, 1790–1840." Ph.D. dissertation, Univesity of Wisconsin.

Jaenicke, Daniel. 1978. "Theories of Political Parties as Theories of Politics." Paper delivered at the American Political Science Association Meetings, Washington D.C., August.

Jaher, Frederic. 1982. *The Urban Establishment.* Urbana: University of Illinois Press.

Johnson, Paul. 1978. *A Shopkeeper's Millennium.* New York: Hill and Wang.

Kass, Alvin. 1965. *Politics in New York State, 1800–1830.* Syracuse, N.Y.: Syracuse University Press.

Keller, Suzanne. 1963. *Beyond the Ruling Class.* New York: Random House.

Kelley, Robert. 1979. *The Cultural Pattern in American Politics.* New York: Knopf.

Kenyon, Cecelia. 1955. "Men of Little Faith." *William and Mary Quarterly* 12:2–43.

Kuroda, Tadahisa. 1969. "The County Court System of Virginia from the Revolution to the Civil War." Ph.D. dissertation. Columbia University.

Kutolowski, Kathleen. 1978. "The Janus Face of New York's Local Parties: Genesee County, 1821–1827." *New York History* 59:145–72.

Larabee, Leonard. 1948. *Conservatism in Early American History.* New York: New York University Press.

Lechner, Frank. 1984. "Fundamentalism and Sociocultural Revitalization: On the Logic of Dedifferentiation." Unpublished paper. University of Pittsburg.

—— 1985. "Modernity and Its Discontents." In Jeffrey Alexander, ed., *Neofunctionalism*, pp. 157–178. Beverly Hills, Calif.: Sage.

Lenski, Gerhard E. 1984. *Power and Privilege: A Theory of Stratification.* New York: McGraw-Hill.

Levine, Peter. 1975. "State Legislative Parties in the Jacksonian Era: New Jersey, 1829–1844." *Journal of American History* 62:591–608.

Link, Eugene P. 1942. *Democratic Republican Societies, 1790–1800.* New York: Columbia University Press.

Lipset, Seymour. 1963. *The First New Nation.* New York: Norton.

Lipset, Seymour and Earl Raab. 1970. *The Politics of Unreason.* New York: Harper and Row.

Luhmann, Niklas. 1982. *The Differentiation of Society.* New York: Columbia University Press.

McCormick, Richard P. 1966. *The Second American Party System.* Chapel Hill: University of North Carolian Press.

McWhiney, Frank. 1957. "Were the Whigs a Class Party in Alabama?" *Journal of Southern History* 23:510–22.

Main, Jackson T. 1961. *The Anti-Federalists.* Chapel Hill: University of North Carolina Press.

—— 1965. *The Social Structure of Revolutionary America.* (Princeton, N.J.: Princeton University Press.

—— 1966. "Government by the People: The American Revolution and the Democratization of the Legislatures." *William and Mary Quarterly* 23:391–407.

—— 1967. *The Upper House in Revolutionary America, 1763–1788.* Madison: University of Wisconsin Press.

—— 1973. *Political Parties Before the Constitution.* New York: Norton.

Marshall, Lynn. 1967. "The Strange Stillbirth of the Whig Party." *American Historical Review* 72:445–68.

Martin, James. 1973. *Men in Rebellion*. New Brunswick, N.J.: Rutgers University Press.

Mayo, Elton. 1979. "Republicanism, Antipartyism, and Jacksonian Party Politics: A View From the Natin's Capital." *American Quarterly* 31: 3–20.

Mills, C. Wright. 1956. *The Power Elite*. FairLawn, N.J.: Oxford University Press.

Mitchell, Betty. 1981. *Edmund Ruffin*. Bloomington: Indiana University Press.

Moore, Wilbert. 1979. *World Modernization: The Limits of Convergence*. New York: Elsevier.

Morantz, Regina. 1971. *"Democracy and Republic in American Ideology, 1787–1840."* Ph.D. dissertation. Columbia University.

Murrin, John. 1965. "The Myths of Colonial Democracy and Royal Decline in Eighteenth-Century America." *Cithara* 5:53–67.

Nash, Gary. 1979. *The Urban Crucible*. Cambridge, Mass.: Harvard University Press.

Nichols, Roy F. 1967. *The Invention of the American Political Parties*. New York: Macmillan.

Nisbet, Robert A. 1969. *Social Change and History*. New York: Basic Books.

Oakes, James. 1982. *The Ruling Race*. New York: Vintage.

Palmer, R. R. 1959. *The Age of the Democratic Revolution*. Princeton, N.J.: Princeton University Press.

Parsons, Talcott. 1954. *Essays in Sociological Theory*. New York: Free Press.

—— 1966. *Societies: Evolutionary and Comparative Perspectives*. New York: Free Press.

—— 1971. *The System of Modern Societies*. Englewood Cliffs, N.J.: Prentice-Hall.

Parsons, Talcott and Gerald Platt. 1973. *The American University*. Cambridge, Mass: Harvard University Press.

Pessen, Edward. 1973. *Riches, Class and Power Before the Civil War*. Lexington, Mass: D.C. Heath.

—— 1978. *Jacksonian America*. 2d ed. Homewood, Ill: Dorsey Press.

Polanyi, Karl. 1944. *The Great Transformation*. Boston: Beacon Press.

Pole, J. R. 1962. "Historians and the Problem of Early American Democracy." *American Historical Review* 67:626–46.

—— 1967. "Introduction: American Historians and the Democratic Process." In J. R. Pole, ed., *The Advance of Democracy*, pp. 1–12 New York: Harper and Row.

—— 1978. *The Pursuit of Equality in American History*. Berkeley: University of California Press.

Porter, Albert O. 1947. *County Government in Virginia, 1607–1904*. New York: AMS Press.

Prager, Jeffrey. 1985. "Totalitarian and Liberal Democracy: Two Types of Modern Political Orders." in Jeffrey Alexander, ed., *Neofunctionalism* pp. 179–210. Beverly Hills, Calif: Sage.

Purvis, Thomas. 1980. "High-Born, Long-Recorded Families: Social Origins of New Jersey Assemblymen 1703–76." *William and Mary Quarterly* 37:592–615.

Remini, Robert V. 1958. "The Albany Regency." *New York History* 39:341–55.

Rich, Robert. 1971. "A Wilderness of Whigs." *Journal of Social History* 4:263–76.

Ridgway, Whitman. 1979. *Community Leadership in Maryland, 1790–1840*. Chapel Hill: University of North Carolina Press.

Rueschemeyer, Dietrich. 1976. "Partial Modernization." in Jan J. Loubser et al. eds., *Explorations in General Theory in Social Science* 2 pp. 756–772. New York: Free Press.

—— 1977. "Structural Differentiation, Efficiency, and Power." *American Journal of Sociology* 83:1–25.

Schlesinger, Arthur M. Jr. 1945. *The Age of Jackson.* Boston, Mass: Little, Brown.

Schwartz, Barry. 1983. "George Washington and the Whig Conception of Heroic Leadership." *American Sociological Review* 48:18–33.

Sewell, Richard H. 1976. *Ballots for Freedom: Antislavery Politics in the United States, 1837–1860.* New York: Oxford University Press.

Shade, William G. 1981. "Political Pluralism and Party Development: The Creation of a Modern Party System, 1815–1852." In Paul Kleppner et al., eds., *The Evolution of American Electoral Systems* pp. 77–112 Westport, Conn.: Greenwood Press.

Shalhope, Robert E. 1972. "Towards a Republican Synthesis." *William and Mary Quarterly* 29:49–80.

—— 1980. *John Taylor of Caroline.* Columbia: University of South Carolina Press.

Sharp, James. 1970. *The Jacksonians vs. the Banks.* New York: Columbia University Press.

Silbey, Joel. 1967. *The Shrine of Party.* Pittsburgh, Pa.: University of Pittsburgh Press.

—— 1985. *The Partisan Imperative.* London: Oxford University Press.

Simms, Henry H. 1929. *The Rise of the Whigs in Virginia, 1824–1840.* Richmond, Va.: Price. pub?

Sisson, David. 1974. *The American Revolution of 1800.* New York: Knopf.

Smelser, Neil J. 1959. *Social Change in the Industrial Revolution.* Chicago, Ill.: University of Chicago Press.

—— 1962. *The Theory of Collective Behavior.* New York: Free Press.

—— 1971. "Stability, Instability, and the Analysis of Political Corruption." in Bernard Barber and Alex Inkeles, eds., *Stability and Change* pp. 7–29. Boston, Mass: Little, Brown.

—— 1974. "Growth, Structural Change, and Conflict in California Public Higher Education, 1950–1970." In Neil J. Smelser and Gabriel Almond, eds., *Public Higher Education in California* pp. 9–141. Berkeley: Uniersity of California Press.

—— 1985. "Evaluating the Model of Structural Differentiation in Relation to Educational Change in the Nineteenth Century." In Jeffrey Alexander, ed., *Neofunctionalism,* pp. 113–30 Beverly Hills, Calif.: Sage.

Smith, Anthony D. 1973. *The Concept of Social Change.* London: Routledge and Kegan Paul.

Spann, Edward. 1972. *Ideals and Politics.* Albany: State University of New York Press.

Stinchcombe, Arthur L. 1978. *Theoretical Methods in Social History.* New York: Academic Press.

Sydnor, Charles S. 1948. *The Development of Southern Sectionalism, 1819–1848.* Baton Rouge: Louisiana State University Press.

—— 1952. *American Revolutionaries in the Making.* New York: Free Press.

Thornton, John. 1978. *Politics and Power in a Slave Society, Alabama 1800–1860.* Baton Rouge: Louisiana State University Press.

Tully, Alan. 1978. *William Penn's Legacy.* Baltimore, Md.: John Hopkins University Press.

Turner, Jonathan and Alexandra Maryanski. 1979. *Functionalism.* Menlo Park, Calif.: Cummings.

Wagner, David G. 1984. *The Growth of Sociological Theories.* Beverly Hills, Calif.: Sage.

Wagner, David G. and Joseph Berger. 1985. "Do Sociological Theories Grow?" *American Journal of Sociology* 90:697–728.

Wallace, Michael. 1969. "Changing Concepts of Party in the United States: New York, 1815–1825." *American Historical Review* 74:453–91.

—— 1973. "Ideologies of Party in the Antebellum Republic." Ph.D. dissertation. Columbia Univesity.

Warner, Lee H. 1973. "The Perpetual Crisis of Conservative Whigs: New York's Silver Grays." *New York Historical Society Quarterly* 57:213–36.

Watson, Harry. 1981. *Jacksonian Politics and Community Conflict*. Baton Rouge: Louisiana State University Press.

Weibe, Robert H. 1984. *The Opening of American Society*. New York: Knopf.

Weir, Robert. 1969. "The Harmony We Were Famous For: An Interpretation of Pre-Revolutionary South Carolina Politics." *William and Mary Quarterly* 26:473–501.

White, Leonard. 1954. *The Jacksonians*. New York: Macmillan.

Williams, David. 1959. "Political Alignments in Colonial Virginia Politics, 1698–1750." Ph.D. dissertation. Northwestern University.

Williamson, Chilton. 1960. *American Suffrage: From Property to Democracy, 1760–1860*. Princeton, N.J.: Princeton University Press.

Willingham, William. 1973. "Deference, Democracy and Town Government in Windham, Connecticut." *William and Mary Quarterly*, 59:402–22.

Wilson, Major. 1984. *The Presidency of Martin Van Buren*. Lawrence: University Press of Kansas.

Wood, Gordon. 1969. *The Creation of the American Republic*. New York: Norton.

—— 1974. "The Democratization of the Mind in the American Revolution." in *Leadership in the American Revolution*, pp. 63–89. Washington D.C.: Library of Congress.

Wooster, Ralph. 1969. *The People in Power*. Knoxville: University of Tennessee Press.

—— 1975. *Politicians, Planters, and Plain Folk*. Knoxville: University of Tennessee Press.

Wright, Louis. 1957. *The Cultural Life of the American Colonies*. New York: Harper.

Young, Alfred F. 1967. *The Democratic Republicans of New York*. Chapel Hill: The University of North Carolina Press.

Young, James. 1966. *The Washington Community, 1800–1828*. New York: Harcourt, Brace and World.

Zemsky, Robert. 1971. *Merchants, Farmers, and River Gods*. Boston, Mass: Gambit.

Zuckerbraun, Matthew A. 1980. "Born to Rule: Aristocracy in New York Politics after Jackson: A Study of Westchester County, New York Families in Office, 1840–1920." Ph.D. dissertation. Columbia University.

TWO

Power, Conflict, and Social Groups

5

The Contest Between Family and Schooling in Nineteenth-Century Britain

Neil J. Smelser

In a recent essay (Smelser 1985) published in a volume with a spirit and intent similar to this one—namely, to explicate, debate critically, and elaborate a major sociological perspective—I reexamined the concept of structural differentiation. In that essay I argued that one assumption informing earlier differentiation theory was valuable but incomplete as an account of the motive force for differentiation; that assumption is that a more differentiated structure functions more effectively—mainly because it is more specialized—than a prior, less differentiated structure. More particularly, I argued that while the assumption might have validity, the process of emergence of more differentiated structures, as well as the contours of those structures, had to take into account both the political struggles among social groups (economic, ethnic, religious, etc.) who had vested interests in preserving or changing existing structures (and if changing, in what directions) and the political resolutions of those struggles. I illustrated this argument historically by attempting to suggest why the British and American primary education systems took such different lines of differentiation and segmentation in the nineteenth century.

In this essay I will attempt to fill in another piece of the puzzle that must be put together to understand the process of structural differentiation. Remaining with the same historical case—though this time only in Britain—I will attempt to show how the particular situation of the British working-class family in nineteenth-century British capitalism constituted one of the major obstacles to the differentiation of primary education at that social class level.

The Problem for This Essay

Of all the institutions that appear to "converge" in modernized societies, near-universal schooling is perhaps the most notable. Seemingly independent of religious system and political ideology, societies regularly invest some of their resources into the building of age-graded institutions in which children spend many of their waking hours, learn the elements of literacy and numeracy, and are exposed to the values, norms, and ideologies of their societies. And as Alex Inkeles points out, "[even] if they do not follow the same developmental sequences, industrial nations will converge at the same point on many dimensions. For example, in the United States, the extensive diffusion of primary schooling was reversed. Nevertheless, in common with other modern systems, both countries came to have close to 100 percent of school-age children enrolled in primary schools" (Inkeles 1981:6).

The two institutions we often associate with primary schooling are family and work. Formal schooling means that teachers take over a large part of the parents' socializing functions, and this results in a differentiating "out" of a large part of what was previously a part of the family life. Furthermore, we see schooling as preparatory to work, preceding full-time occupancy of a work role, and preparing future workers with requisite skills, attitudes of conformity, and discipline. Schools are generally thought to be functionally "better" than families for accomplishing these purposes in urban-industrial societies because of the specialized skills of teachers, as well as the range and generalizability of skills which can be imparted in schooling.

While challenging neither Inkeles' argument that modern societies tend to end with similar results in schooling nor the functional argument just enunciated, I would like to suggest that neither tells us very much about the social and political *process* by which schooling becomes established. In fact the historical agenda of those who were responsible for creating a schooling system very likely had a quite different agenda from that suggested by the end result. I will present this point of view in reference to the British experience in schooling for about a seventy-five-year period beginning in about 1810, which was the period of establishing the main lines of their system of primary schools. If I may telegraph my conclusion, I will argue how very much things *other* than the family and *other* than preparation for adult occupational roles were on the minds of both those who were attempting to provide the schooling and its customers.

Some Aspects of the Historical Heritage That Conditioned the Growth of Mass Schooling

The first observation to be made about British schooling is that its system grew in a way that made it a microcosm of the stratification system of that society. At the beginning of the nineteenth century Britain inherited a system of great public schools that were explicitly dedicated to a pattern of education that reproduced the ethic of aristocratic gentlemanliness and catered mainly to the aristocracy, as well as a complex system of grammar schools and private and proprietary schools, which served a clientele across the band of the middle classes. What little schooling was available to the poor in the eighteenth century was organized separately. (Scotland's parish school system, organized on a community basis and serving various classes, was an exception.) This tendency to stratify by class carried through into the twentieth century; it is one concern of current debates about the comprehensive schools in England.

The second general point to be made is that schooling for the poor was philanthropic, emanating from the ethic of "an open aristocracy based on property and patronage" (Perkin 1969:17) and a society based on leadership and responsibility on the part of the wealthy and ruling classes (answered by deference on the part of the lesser classes) —although utilitarian, democratic, and radical values, as well as the values of religious dissent, were already in a challenging position by the end of the eighteenth century. This philanthropic ingredient characterized the education of the poor in the eighteenth century and the growth of Sunday schools late in the eighteenth and into the nineteenth century. When the movement for day schools for the poor made its appearance early in the century, it was a strictly voluntary movement, carried out by the National Society (Church of England) and the British and Foreign School Society (largely but not exclusively Dissent), both of which attempted to raise subscriptions among the wealthy to establish schools based on their respective principles. When the state did enter the arena for the education of the poor in 1833, it did not establish its own schools, but rather set up an arrangement whereby subscriptions raised by the two voluntary societies would be matched by government funds. This "matching fund" principle dominated the primary educational scene until 1870, when legislation providing for "filling in the gaps" with state schools was passed by the Gladstone government. This philanthropic principle ran sufficiently deep that leaders attempted to impress it on others when education was seeming to "fail"; the child labor legislation of 1833 called for industrialists to establish schools "for" the children who worked in their mills, and as late as the 1850s the Newcastle Commission blamed the failure of education in remote agricultural areas and in urban centers on absentee landlords and irresponsible merchants and manufacturers who would not provide resources for schools "for" the poor (Parliamentary Papers 1861a:76–78).

The third historical point to be made is that schooling for the poor was, by and large, religiously based. Some High Churchmen claimed a complete monopoly on educating the young for the Church of England, and throughout much of the century the National Society called for the learning of the catechism on the part of its pupils and insisted that they attend a Church of England Sunday school on the sabbath. The British and Foreign School Society rejected the church's formularies, but nonetheless regarded its own schools as having a religious mission. There were some secularist voices such as the Society for the Diffusion of Useful Knowledge, the Mechanics Institutions, and some liberals who looked admiringly at the secular American experiment in education, but as far as the institution of actual schooling for the poor was concerned, these were comparatively minor forces.

The Major Pressures to Expand Schooling for the Poor

During much of the nineteenth century little was heard of the need to develop the skills or workers necessary for industry. Comparisons with supposedly superior European craftsmen were heard in the 1830s, after the Crystal Palace Exhibition of 1851, and after the Paris Exhibition of 1867, but technical education did not become a major political concern until the last decades of the century. Interviews with manufacturers found in a diversity of government reports showed them to be somewhat indifferent to the issue of literacy, some expressing the opinion that literate workers were better workers, others finding no difference, and still others expressing the belief that the ability to read and write made workers too independent. And in fact the level of skill required for both agricultural and industrial workers in that stage of industrialization (between 1780 and, say, 1850) required little literacy or numeracy on the part of the workers.

The much greater pressure to educate the poor came from two other sources. The first has to do with the great issue of "the condition of the people," which was prominent in the minds of the ruling classes in the politically turbulent years between 1815 and 1848 and, to some degree, later. The issue had two principal manifestations. The first, expressed mainly by persons and groups higher in the stratification system, was the idea that those lower in the system were not behaving as they should according to their position. One of the chronic concerns on the part of the British ruling classes throughout the nineteenth century was that others than the "industrious and respectable poor" did not live up to those expectations of industriousness and respectability. There was a continual concern with crime, vice, pauperism, drink, and idleness as threats to both the social order and the public treasury. Educational reformers could cite "ignorance" as a cause, and point to education as a preventative measure. (This theme, I should add, is the only place where I could read into history a criticism of the family; it was those very lowest orders who were unable to support or set examples for their own children who were the object of attack in the discussions of pauperism and its attendant vices. But the attack was always on the moral depravity of individuals; not in any sense was "the family," as an institution, said to be in any way faulty.)

Another closely related variant involves situations in which the social orders behave in ways that constitute a political threat to the social and political order. Crime, drink, and idleness are social but not directly political threats; rioting, demonstrations, political petitioning, and revolutionary activity are. Throughout the nineteenth century, and especially during its first half, episodes of political protest or revolt on the part of the working classes stimulated interest in supporting and strengthening the educational system as a direct instrument of social control: the Peterloo massacres and the general working-class discontent in northern England in 1818–1819; the reform agitation of 1831–1832 and the agricultural riots in southern England at about the same time; the Chartist agitation of 1839; the Newport and Rebecca riots in Wales in 1839; the Plut Plot of 1842; the agitation for repeal of the Union in Ireland in 1843; and the great national distress in the economy in 1846–1847. This kind of evidence suggests strongly that political-class (social order) rather than economic-competitive pressure was most important as a stimulus to popular education.

The second general pressure was competition, but it was religious, not economic, in character. Multidenominational in many cases in the early years of the movement, Sunday schools soon came to be identified either with the Church of England or with some kind of Dissent. The British and Foreign School Society formed in 1809, and within two years the Church of England had formed its own counterpart to encourage schooling for the poor. The "matching fund" legislation of 1833, greatly expanded in 1846, was unpopular with many Dissenters because the Church of England's access to subscription money was so great that it also received the lion's share of state funds. And in the 1840s, when the Church of England undertook to populate the primarily Dissenting Wales with National Society schools, the Dissenters countered with a similar campaign of their own. The National Society opposed inspection by state officials, and compromised with the government in 1839 by permitting inspection only if the appointments of the inspectors were approved by the church. Dissenters objected to having church-approved inspectors inspect their schools, and subsequently they came to an agreement with the state that non-church inspectors visit their schools. Ultimately there were separate and exclusive inspecting systems not only for the National Society and the British and Foreign School Society schools, but also for Wesleyan Methodist, Catholic, Scottish Presbyterian, Free Church of Scotland, and Jewish schools.

At the same time as this religious competition fostered the establishment of schools, it was also a source of paralysis with respect to state initiative in educational activity. Church and Dissent would scan the many legislative plans that were paraded through Parliament from the 1830s to the 1860s, and each proved an effective veto group, the church if state activity smacked of secularism, Dissent if state activity showed any sign of church control over the schools, or state preference for the established church.

Orientations of the Working Classes to Primary Education

So much for the main impulses on the side of the suppliers of schooling. They were mainly preoccupied with questions of moral, social, and political order and, except for a minority of Tory and High Church spokesmen who believed that education fostered unrealistic aspirations and political revolutionary ideas, most agreed that a religiously based education would have a pacifying and conservative effect on the working population. There was, of course, sharp disagreement about what kind of religion this should be, and as a result there was brisk competition for the souls of the young through the schools.

What of the potential customers? What were their main impulses with respect to education? The first thing to stress is a diversity of impulses, ranging from highly skilled, "respectable" workers who accepted the "civilizing" mission of the schools and regarded them as a form of self-improvement, on the one hand, to the underclass of the poor (labeled by Mary Carpenter as the "dangerous and perishing classes"), who had few contacts with any institutions, including schools, save for the poor law machinery. There were also a minority of politically conscious workmen who demanded a self-determined education more in keeping with their economic and political aspirations as workers. But despite this diversity, a single set of problems persisted throughout the century with such tenacity that it merits special consideration; this set of problems were what were referred to as the "twin evils" of irregular attendance and early withdrawal of children from schools. These two sets of problems, furthermore, were intricately associated with the family economy of the working classes, and put economic and family necessities and interests in partial war with the interests of the schoolers.

The tradition of utilizing the labor of children, even very young children, in economic activity is an ancient one in Great Britain (as elsewhere), and that tradition was embedded mainly in agricultural customs and craft apprentice systems. As the commercial and industrial transformation of England quickened in the eighteenth century, the principle of child labor was carried forward, though in somewhat altered form. The statutory seven-year apprenticeship declined as crafts were threatened by mechanized production and the proliferation of low-skill jobs requiring little training, and was repealed by law in 1814 (54 Geo. III, c. 96). Child labor continued to be used, however, in agriculture, in the burgeoning domestic industries buoyed by expanding trade, and in industries such as textiles and mining that prospered in the new industrial development.

In the late eighteenth century, when the first great impulse for popular education made its appearance in the form of the Sunday school movement, the pioneers of that movement took for granted the inviolability of work traditions by offering instruction on Sundays, the only day of the week on which it could be assumed that the potential clientele—both children and adults—would not be at work.

As such, the Sunday school movement avoided, to a degree, the possible conflict between work and schooling, except insofar as the working-class clientele for Sunday schools would be so exhausted on the sabbath as to prefer rest to yet more disciplined activity on that day.

When the movement to provide day schools for the working-class population began to spread in the early nineteenth century, that conflict came into the open. One of the activities undertaken in 1818 by the Select Committee Appointed to Inquire into the Education of the Poor was to send out questionnaires to clergymen in every parish in Britain requesting particulars relating to the education of youth. Each clergyman was also asked to add comments on the condition of his parish. The repetitiveness of the statement that the economic exigencies of the poor discouraged the education of their children is remarkable. Consider only a few:

> For the parish of Castle Rising, county of Norfolk: "There is a great reluctance among the lower orders to allow their children to receive instruction, unless they are paid the earnings which they would otherwise receive from the labours in the field."
>
> For the parish of Stowe, Nine Churches, county of Northampton, "All the children of the poor are admitted to the school, and most of them are desirous to benefit by it, but are unable, through poverty, to take advantage of the means sufficiently long to educate them properly."
>
> For the parish of Charterhouse Hinton, "The children of the poor are employed so many hours during the day in the clothing manufactories, that they have not the opportunity of educating them, otherwise they would be desirous of receiving instruction." (Parliamentary Papers, 1837; 585, 661, 778).

It is difficult to place quantitative significance on these comments, other than to note their frequency and to summarize the composite picture that emerges. That picture contains the following ingredients: the poor were generally described as favorably disposed toward the education of their children, but acting on this attitude was greatly impeded by the economic circumstances of that class. A few clergymen reported that because of dire circumstances parents could not afford the fees for day schooling; but the more frequent observation was that parents would not forego wages, even very modest wages, that children might be able to contribute to the family wage packet. The result was that many poor would take advantage of schooling— where it was available—only until there was opportunity for the children to contribute materially to the family's welfare.

This general assessment of the situation and of the motivation of the poor repeats itself with monotonous consistency in succeeding decades. Witnesses interviewed by the committees created to inquire into education in 1843 (Parliamentary Papers 1835) and 1837 (Parliamentary Papers 1837–1883) echoed the sentiments expressed by the curates two decades earlier. Factory inspectors and others reported that workers were indifferent or hostile to the educational clauses of the Factory Legislation of 1833 because schooling deprived them of their children's potential earnings (Smelser 1959: 297). And after the system of inspection of state-aided voluntary schools was established in 1839, the inspectors returned again and again to the themes of irregular attendance and early withdrawal. Commenting on the schools of London, the Rev. F. C. Cook complained,

We not only lose our children at a very early age, without any systematic means, or indeed, for the most part, without any kind of means of keeping up an intercourse with them after leaving school, but that a fearfully large proportion of poor children either do not enter our schools at all, or remain in them so short a time, that any expectation of their receiving real benefit from the instruction therein given must be a mere illusion. (Parliamentary Papers 1846: 311)

Seldom was irregularity of attendance or early leaving mentioned without referring to its economic causes. The Rev. H. W. Bellairs enunciated the principle simply: "The demand for juvenile labour being great, it follows that a large proportion of juveniles will be withheld from the day school" (Parliamentary Papers 1852–1853: 987). J. D. Morell summarized the main grounds on which children are kept from school: The need for girls to care for younger children or to help their mothers in various other ways, and the inability of boys to earn money very early (Parliamentary Papers 1850: 492). Economic opportunities appeared always to be at the heart of matters. In Wales, the Rev. H. Longueville Jones reported that

[the difficulty in attendance] which probably is met with more or less in all districts, has been increased during the last year . . . by the scarcity of adult labour, which certainly has not been equal to the marketable demand. In many localities I have found boys of twelve years old earning from 3*s.* to 3*s.*6*d.* a week; in some towns and mining districts, from 5*s.* to 6*s.;* and in a peculiar instance, in Flintshire, the managers informed me, last winter, that lads of this age were gaining no less than 9*s.* a week in colliery operations. Under such temptations as these, it is no wonder that children should be drawn away from school at a premature period of their physical as well as mental development. (Parliamentary Papers 1854:661)

The power of the marketplace—and families' willingness to react to that power by sending their children to work rather than school— is shown by two further lines of evidence. The first has to do with variations in families' behavior according to the kind of economic activity (and opportunities) peculiar to their region. Certain evidence gathered in Wales in the 1840s and 1850s is revealing in this regard. In North Wales children continued to be employed in agricultural pursuits, as was traditional, and when large-scale industry began to develop, boys between the ages of seven and twelve were sent to work in the copper mines, collieries, saltworks, ironworks, and quarries. Yet the demand for child labor in North Wales fell considerably short of that in South Wales, where the main industrial and extractive industries were located.

The commissioners of the state of education in Wales noted in 1847 the relationship between industrial activity and early withdrawal. Lingen, whose area of investigation included Carmarthenshire, Glamorganshire, and Pembrokeshire in South Wales noted that in all three of these counties more than half of the scholars were between five and ten years of age. He noted also, however, that in Glamorganshire the percentage of those under five years of age was larger, and those over ten years of age smaller than that in the other two counties. He accounted for this by noting that "in Glamorganshire labour very soon becomes valuable (a boy of 11 or 12 can earn from 5s. to 7s. per week), and manufacturing employment is not suspended by the vicissitudes of the seasons, so as to afford more leisure at one time of the year than at another for a person to go to school again" (Parliamentary Papers 1847a: 22). Lingen apparently accepted this fact as a given, for his only conclusion was that special efforts be made to stress infant schooling in the manufacturing districts when children would be available for attendance. Symons, investigating the central counties of Brecknockshire, Cardiganshire, and Radnorshire, noted the same early leaving age connected with employment in the iron and mining enterprises, and picked up a sex difference as well. Before the age of ten, male scholars exceeded females by 26 percent in the schools surveyed; after that age females exceeded males by 20 percent. His explanation was simply that "that labour of the boys becomes first available" (Parliamentary Papers 1847a: 275).

A similar but more comparatively documented result is found in the report of Assistant Commissioner John Jenkins, who was charged by the Newcastle Commission to make inquiries into the state of education in several Poor Law Unions in North Wales (Corwen, Dolgelly, Bala, and Ffestiniog) that were agricultural in character; in Neath, a mixed mining or manufacturing and agricultural section; and in Merthyr Tydfil, a mining and manufacturing section. To shed light on the early withdrawal problem, Jenkins compared the North

Wales unions with the other two with respect to the proportion of students of each age to the total number of students present. The results are shown in table 5.1. What is revealed is the enormous competition of the very young in the manufacturing unions, combined with the tendency for children to begin to fall out of school rapidly at around nine and ten years of age; in the agricultural unions, a much greater proportion of the children stay on to eleven, twelve, thirteen, and even fourteen years of age. Also, in the agricultural unions the sex differences are not really significant, whereas in the manufacturing areas a high proportion of females appear to be pulled out around the ages seven through ten (presumably to tend to younger siblings and assist the mother in the domicile), but from that point on the proportions begin to change, with more girls staying in school through ages thirteen and fourteen in the manufacturing districts (Parliamentary Papers 1861b).

Furthermore, while the average daily attendance did not differ greatly between the agricultural and manufacturing mining unions, Jenkins pointed out that occasions for nonattendance differed in the two types of region. In the agricultural areas withdrawal was more systematic, being closely associated with seasons of planting and harvesting; the main problem in the industrial districts was irregular attendance, as children were taken in and out of schools as demands of the family and the mines and industries fluctuated.

This last observation leads to the second line of supplementary evidence, namely that children's involvement in the economy (and their corresponding noninvolvement in the schools) was associated with the briskness of economic activity. Many observers pointed to the fact that when trade was brisk, school attendance suffered generally, and the average age of children in attendance dropped as older children left. If trade were to become brisk, said one schoolmistress in the Wolverhampton manufacturing district, "in a fortnight half the school would leave" (Parliamentary Papers 1843:168). For 1846, the Rev. F. C. Cook reported on the demand for juvenile labor in his district (Church of England schools in Middlesex, Cambridge, Essex Huntingdon, Norfolk, and Suffolk), and stated that it was "rare and exceptional" for a boy to remain in school beyond eight-and-one-half years of age in agricultural districts and that the straw-plaiting industry withdrew children of both sexes from school from infancy. "These are difficulties," he complained, "which it is impossible altogether to overcome" (Parliamentary Papers 1847b:161). In 1851 the Rev. Watkins blamed the "goodness of trade" and the fact that many children were withdrawn from Yorkshire schools to be sent to the Great Exhi-

TABLE 5.1

Students in Agricultural and Industrial Mining Poor Law Unions,

		Under 3 Years	3–6 Years Inclusive	7 Years	8 Years	9 Years	10 Years
Agricultural Unions (58 schools)	Males	.79	12.7	10.5	11.3	13.1	12.7
	Females	1.1	16.2	11.1	11.1	13.0	12.2
Industrial Mining Unions (59 schools)	Males	3.0	23.1	13.8	16.6	13.1	11.2
	Females	3.8	26.1	11.2	12.9	10.3	8.4

Source: Parliamentary Papers, 1861; p. 470.

bition in London for poor attendance that year. Two years later, the Rev. J. J. Blandford noted the same phenomenon and observed with respect to schools for the laboring classes, "the attendance is in an inverse ratio to the prosperity of the locality in which they are situated" (Parliamentary Papers 1854:346), making particular reference to the manufacture of lace. And the Rev. W. J. Kennedy noted that 1861 in Lancashire was a year of "greater unalloyed commercial success than any previous year in the memory of man,"; this brought "irresistible" opportunities for employment, even among very young children, and more frequent and stronger complaints than usual from teachers about attendance (Parliamentary Papers 1861b:119). When prosperity brought with it inflation—as in the Crimean War years— the motive for sending children out to work was strengthened, and parents' disposition to keep children in schools diminished accordingly (Parliamentary Papers 1856:464). Further confirmation of the association between employment opportunities and school attendance was given in the reports of the inspectors of the workhouse schools in the 1850s, who commonly reported that these schools emptied out in times of prosperity, so that the workhouse teacher was sometimes "left with a small number of minute and illiterate children, but little removed from the grade of infants" (Parliamentary Papers, 1852:56)

There is some evidence that the opposite effect—increasing attendance—was felt when trade was sluggish. Referring to northeast England, J. S. Laurie acknowledged that "even when the labour market

Wales, 1858

11 Years	12 Years	13 Years	14 Years	15 Years	Above 15 Years	Total No. of Children
10.9	9.0	8.4	5.0	2.1	3.4	1,772
9.6	9.5	7.0	4.8	2.2	12.	1,346
8.3	4.6	3.1	2.1	1.3	1.3	3,535
8.9	6.5	5.6	3.5	2.1	.92	3,137

is glutted by redundant supply, or somewhat depressed by slightness of trade, the attendance does not decline." The more provident parent, he concluded, acknowledges that schooling might be of some future material benefit and "prefers to renew or prolong the term of his children's schooling, at least till the avenues of employment be again fairly open" (Parliamentary Papers 1857:578). The most dramatic effect of this sort, however, was observed by the Rev. Kennedy when the cotton famine—associated with the northern states' blockade of southern ports during the American Civil War—struck Lancashire in 1862:

Hundreds of thousands are unemployed and penniless. [A year ago] the difficulty was to get persons to fill the schools. Now, schools have been thrown open freely, and the difficulty is to find rooms to hold the scholars, and teachers to instruct them. The contrast is one of the most striking that could be imagined, and especially impresses those who, like me, have it daily thrust upon their observation wherever they go. Most of the schools I go to are either crowded by scholars taken very obviously from the unemployed classes, or are partly turned into sewing schools, or into store-rooms for clothing, or into soup kitchens. (Parliamentary Papers 1863:102)

He noted, however, that this invasion of "strange, undisciplined scholars" disrupted the progress of the ordinary students.

Though the evidence establishing a connection between fluctuations in economic opportunity and fluctuations in school attendance is generally strong and consistent through the nineteenth century, it must not be concluded that this was a universal relationship, or, indeed, that it was the only kind of impact of economic conditions on educational conditions. For really marginal families, for example, the school fees (ranging from 2*d.* to 4*d.* per week) would make a real economic difference if their children were thrown out of employment; some children were no doubt withdrawn for this reason, and, in consequence, would be neither at work nor at school. Also, when the parents themselves were unemployed in sluggish times, some would leave the area in search of other work, withdrawing their children from school to take them with them (Parliamentary Papers 1864:161–62). And with respect to the possibly beneficial effect of prosperous times, one instructor suggested that in better times the feelings of self-respect of the entire family were increased and, moreover, the parent "begins . . . to feel more *ambition* for his family; he demands an instruction for them which goes beyond the bare elements; and if he cannot get it at one school, he feels no hesitation in paying twice as much to get it at an another" (Parliamentary Papers 1852–1853: 623–24). We will return to this theme later.

The evidence for the mid-nineteenth century, then, consistently and overwhelmingly suggests that the demands of the capitalist economy of that period undermined the efforts of educational reforms and politicians to secure the public order and reproduce Britain's class system through a mass primary educational system directed at the working classes and the poor. The effects of these contrary tendencies —effects that were generally described as a relative failure of the educational efforts—themselves become the basis of public commentary and controversy. There was, however, little consistency on the part of those who attempted to diagnose that failure. The Rev. J. P. Norris said that of all the hindrances to teachers' efforts to secure regular and prolonged attendance, the greatest is "the want of cooperation of the children's parents" (Parliamentary Papers 1852: 378). In a similar vein, the Rev. H. W. Ballairs argued that "juvenile labour and the indifferences of careless and dishonest parents are the causes of our schools being so imperfectly filled" (Parliamentary Papers 1857:263).

Among other causes, the Rev. Watkins believed that the supercession of the labor of the parent by the labor of the child led to a state of affairs whereby the child of the poor could successfully rebel against the parents:

What the [bread-winning] child wills, *that* the parent must do, and in fact *does;* and where there are three or four of these little tyrants in the family, who know their own value, and are determined to act upon it, the confusion that ensues is most miserable and degrading. Does the parent wish the child to be punctual at his half-school time? To attend the Sunday-school? Not to remain in the streets after dark? To go to bed betimes? To give up the company of wicked disreputable children? He may command all this, but the truth is, that the child will not obey him; and, moreover, glories in his disobedience. (Parliamentary Papers 1843–1844:473)

Other inspectors, especially when referring to the poor among the working classes, took a less moralistic view of the matter and regarded the situation as arising from necessity. The Rev. Watkins wondered "what can fairly be expected" other than defective education when "the mill, or the mine, or the loom, the 'care of younger children,' or 'assistance in the parents' labour,' carry away the child . . . ?" (Parliamentary Papers 1852; 118).

Still other inspectors suggested that the problems of early withdrawal and irregularity of attendance were matters neither of morality nor natural necessity but, rather, involved some kind of conflict or contradiction of principles abroad in British society in the mid-nineteenth century. The Rev. Stewart suggested such a conflict when he wrote that "every school that is worth its name represents . . . a hand-to-hand fight with the employers of labour" (Parliamentary Papers, 1845:355). Further insight into the nature of this fight was provided in a reflection by the Rev. H. W. Bellairs:

> I have never yet seen it laid down with sufficient clearness that there is this antagonism between the material interests of the poor, the laws of political economy in a mere productive point of view, and the objects of educationalists. Political economy would seem to require the greatest possible amount of goods at the least possible expense. Experience shows that, in some branches of industry, children are less expensive agents in production than men. Hence their selection by the producer. The earnings of the adult operative are insufficient to support himself and *children* up to fourteen years of age, hence the removal of them from school in order to meet the wants of the household. Compel them to go to school, and you drive the family to the workhouse. (Parliamentary Papers 1854:79–80)

To put this antagonism in slightly different words: given the reluctance of the government to intervene in the market for labor, given governing classes' traditional dread of pauperism and its supposed consequences (crime, idleness, destitution, and increased poor rates), given the structure of the labor market of the time, and given the drive on the part of working-class families to survive economically, it was impossible to expect any other results than voluntary withdrawal of many children from school when economic opportunity presented itself and the consequent failure to attain the educationalists' goals of spreading elementary schools as universally as possible among the masses.

A few years after the Rev. Bellairs made his observation, the government created the Newcastle Commission, the second of three educational commissions of the 1850s and 1860s, charged to study, diagnose, and generate recommendations for schooling for each of the three great class divisions of Victorian Britain. In considering the poor, the commissioners made a distinction between "the independent poor" on the one hand and "paupers" and "vagrants and criminals" on the other, acknowledging thereby that different considerations applied to these categories. In considering the "independent poor," the commissioners came up with the same range of facts reported repeatedly by the inspectors. They indicated "but little conflict of opinion" with regard to the motives of parents in removing their children from school at an early age. All agreed "that the children are removed for the sake of the wages which they earn, or of their services at home; the further inducement of fitting the children for some calling for which early training is required being alleged in some cases" (Parliamentary Papers 1861a:179). These motives operated in different ways in agriculture, manufactures, mining, and various urban occupations, and large portions of the commission's report are given over to documenting the importance of juvenile labor as a cause for irregular attendance and early withdrawal.

Moreover, the Newcastle commissioners confronted the same contradiction that the Rev. Bellairs had enunciated, and attempted to outline principles for dealing with it. In the first place, they said, "independence is of more importance than education; and if the wages of the child's labour are necessary, either to keep the parents from the poor rates, or to relieve the pressure of severe and bitter poverty, it is far better that it should go to work at the earliest age at which it can bear the physical exertion than that it should remain at school" (Parliamentary Papers 1861a:188). In the Rev. Bellair's words the "material interests of the poor" should take priority over the "objects of educationalists." Furthermore, the commissioners rejected any scheme of general compulsion (on the Prussian or American model), which they believed would come into collision with "the constitution of English society and habits and feelings of the people" (Parliamentary Papers 1961a:198). Furthermore, they rejected any compulsory education imposed by employers, unless it was contractually agreed upon by employers and employees alike (Parliamentary Papers 1861a:217). In these statements the commissioners were proclaiming that the "principles of political economy" (which include the noninterference of government in contractual arrangements) ought to have precedence over the "objects of educationalists." In voicing these priorities, the Newcastle commissioners were reaffirming that the wage structure and the freedom of the family to determine the economic (and educational) fortunes were inviolable parameters, and that whatever educational changes might be recommended should take place *within* the limits set by those parameters. It can be said, moreover, that the beginning of government support for voluntary education in 1833 until legislation was passed in the 1870s relating to compulsory attendance, government policy amounted to a kind of paradox: to encourage educational development mainly from the "supply side"—i.e., building schools, training teachers, supplementing teachers' salaries—yet to offer these educational services to the poor in circumstances under which, it was freely acknowledged, the poor would refuse or partake minimally of those services.

Efforts and Trends That Counteracted the Family-Economy Forces

While the forces emanating from the family-economy complex outlined in this essay appear to have been sufficiently strong to undermine much of the efforts of reformers and politicians in the first three-quarters of the nineteenth century, these efforts also continued to be significant forces and reformers were forever devising ways to make attendance more regular and extend it to later ages, although until late in the century these efforts by and large stopped short of compulsion. Among the efforts visible in the 1830–1860 period were the following:

- Child labor legislation of 1833 and subsequent years, which limited the hours of labor of children and young people, and called upon manufactories to provide part-time schooling for employed children.
- The legislation of 1842 prohibiting the labor of children under ten in deep-pit mining which, however, was partially undermined as the collieries continued to use their labor in other capacities.

Most of the efforts to deal with the twin evils of early withdrawal and irregular attendance had to do with adapting the schools and their practices rather than intervening in the labor market. Evans (1971) listed a number of such efforts initiated in Wales and parts of England during the period from the 1840s to the 1860s:

- The attempt to lay more stress on the infant schools, which served children at very young ages when the demands of the labor market were negligible.
- The practice on the part of some employers to appoint children to certain attractive posts, such as office clerkships, on the condition that they remain in school for a certain number of years.
- The practice of apprenticing promising pupils to special trades or processes in industrial works, on the condition that they improve their basic skills through schooling.
- The introduction of an educational test in some employs as a condition for employing children from ten to twelve years of age.
- The attempt to encourage students who had left school between eight and ten years of age to return for various periods between the ages of twelve and sixteen.
- The introduction of various prize schemes for rewarding outstanding performance on the part of children.
- The establishment of evening schools, which were also designed to remedy past deficiencies in schooling.

By and large, these various adaptations appear to have had minimal influence on parents with respect to foregoing opportunities for their children's earnings in the labor market.

Two further government policies of the period, not usually interpreted in this context, should also be mentioned:

- The development of capitation payments in the 1850s, by which local schools were given additional subsidies for every student attending a minimum number of days per year. One effect of these payments was to encourage managers and masters to urge regular attendance on the part of their pupils, since their own revenues were helped by doing so.
- The "payment by results" scheme associated with the Revised Code of 1862, which made payments to schools contingent on the numbers of students who passed annual examinations administered by school inspectors. This provision, usually interpreted as a way of holding down the increasing costs of primary education that characterized the 1850s and as a means of administrative simplification of schooling, nevertheless also constituted a "carrot" to managers to maximize the numbers of students attending regularly, so they could be properly prepared to be among those who passed at examination time.

All of these efforts did not solve "the education problem," which continued to be at the top of reformers' agendas through the 1860s;

the main complaint continued to be that too few children actually attended schools, and for periods that were too brief, and that this circumstance continued to constitute both an ineffective expenditure of public resources and a social evil. As I have argued in this essay, one of the main sources of this "evil" was to be found in the character of nineteenth-century British capitalism, which had a skill structure and a wage structure that made it both possible and necessary for the family to be a unit with multiple wage earners, including women and children. This "evil" was much abated in the last quarter of the nineteenth century, an effect that can be attributed in part to a number of other purposive efforts on the part of reformers and politicians and in part to a number of independent economic and social changes affecting the economy. Among the most important of these were the following:

- The Education Act of 1870 constituted a critical breaking point in the solution of the "religious problem" facing education, for it was at this time that the state was given formal power to establish schools on a nondenominational basis (even though the subsidized voluntary-denominational system also continued as it had existed before). This act, plus revisions of it in subsequent years, permitted a vast expansion in the supply of schools in areas where the voluntary-denominational system had failed to provide schooling.
- In the 1860s and the following decades the demand for child and juvenile labor diminished, partly as a result of the new levels of skill requirements called for in new industrial sectors (electricity, chemicals) and in the rapidly burgeoning service sector that included demands for clerks, secretaries, telegraphers, and, indeed, schoolteachers, and partly as a result of the spread of legislation limiting the working hours of children in many new industries.
- In the 1870s and 1880s the British authorities finally succeeded in making primary education compulsory—with some machinery to enforce compulsory attendance—and ultimately free of fees to be paid by the parents of pupils.
- The period of the great depression of 1873–1896, while occasioning many periods of unemployment for working classes, was nevertheless an era of improvement in their standard of living, based largely on reductions in the price levels of necessities.
- More than before, the late nineteenth century saw the further evolution of an occupational structure (with greater demands for literacy and numeracy) that made the education of one's children more than a provision of minimum but unhelpful skills—that is to say,

made it more frequently an opportunity for movement from manual into lower service occupations; this shift in occupational structure meant that a larger proportion of the working population could actually regard the education of their children as a source of possible economic and status betterment, whereas in earlier decades education lacked such expectations and existed as a narrower and less friendly institution dedicated to the moral betterment of the working classes as defined and insisted upon by their betters.

The consequence of these various developments in the last third of the century was to occasion a vast expansion in both the numbers and proportion of working-class children in the primary educational system, and to their attendance until substantially later ages.

A Concluding Remark

In closing, we might return to Inkeles' observation that, ultimately, mass education tends toward a common structure in all modern societies. Without challenging the accuracy of that assertion, it might also be said that much of what is historically and sociologically interesting about education is not found in that *result* as such so much as in the *process* by which the result comes about. And in this respect nineteenth-century Great Britain offers a very instructive example. The history of primary schooling in that country can be regarded more accurately as a process emerging in a complicated three-way tug-of-war among profound social forces pulling in opposite directions than as a series of functional adaptations as we usually understand them. The first set of forces were primarily economic, as these worked their way through the labor market and through that into the family economy; in the context of early British capitalism these forces seemed more hostile than conducive to the success of mass education. The second set of forces were rooted in considerations of reform, politics, and class, as ruling groups worked to sustain the evolving class system and keep it stable; in this connection they saw education, particularly moral education, as a valuable resource; as such, these forces were more conducive than hostile to the spread of primary schooling. And the third set of forces were religious and mainly conductive to working-class education, but there was such conflict between the Church of England and Dissent, as well as among other religious groupings, that they constituted an obstacle to massive state interventions in education because they feared that either their claimed monopoly or their religious position in society would be endangered. The fusion of religion and education was broken, and only barely, in 1870, only after three-quarters of a century of halting expansion within that fusion. The "break" in the dominance of economy-family conditions over primary education was attained only in the late nineteenth century, as a result of a series of economic and political developments that made the education of young children more nearly affordable and, at the same time, more difficult to evade. The fusion of education with class considerations was weakened only later, and one wonders even today how far that fusion has ultimately been dissolved in that country to this day. In any event, the British case provides a telling example of how stormy the history of a differentiating institution can be when so many deep social forces continuously drag it in different directions.

References

Evans, Leslie Wynne. 1971. *Education in Industrial Wales, 1799–1800: A Study of the Work Schools System in Wales During the Industrial Revolution.* Cardiff, Wales: Heanton Press.

Inkeles, Alex. 1981. "Convergence and Divergence in Industrial Societies." In Mustafa O. Attir, Burkhart Holzner, and Zdenek Suda, eds., *Modernization Theory, Research, and Realities.* Boulder, Colo.: Westview Press.

Parliamentary Papers 1817–1818. *Parochial Returns,* 11.

—— 1835. *Report of the Select Committee on the State of Education of the People of England and Wales,* 8.

—— 1837. *Report from a Select Committee on the Education of the Poorer Classes in England and Wales,* 7.

—— 1843. *Reports of Factory Inspectors,* 13.

—— 1843–1844. *Reports of Factory Inspectors,* 35.

—— 1845. *Reports of Factory Inspectors,* 37.

—— 1846. *Reports of Factory Inspectors,* 32.

—— 1847a. *Reports of the Commissioners of Inquiry Into the State of Education in Wales, XXVII,* part 2.

—— 1847b. *Reports of Factory Inspectors,* 45.

—— 1850. *Reports of Factory Inspectors,* 44.

—— 1852a. *Reports of Factory Inspectors,* 40.

—— 1852b. *Minutes of the Committee of Council,* 39.

—— 1852–1853. *Reports of Factory Inspectors, 80.*

—— 1854. *Reports of Factory Inspectors,* 52.

—— 1856. *Reports of Factory Inspectors,* 48.

—— 1857. *Reports of Factory Inspectors,* 33.

—— 1861a. *Report of the Commissioners to Inquire Into the State of Popular Education in England,* 1.

—— 1861b. *Reports of Factory Inspectors,* 49.

—— 1861c. *Report of Assistant Commissioners,* 21:2.

—— 1863. *Reports of Factory Inspectors*, 47.

—— 1864. *Reports of Factory Inspectors*, 45.

Perkin, Harold. 1969. *The Origins of Modern English Society, 1780–1880*. London: Routledge and Kegan Paul.

Smelser, Neil J. 1959. *Social Change in the Industrial Revolution*. Chicago: University of Chicago Press.

Smelser, Neil J. 1985. "Evaluating the Model of Structural Differentiation in Relation to Educational Change." In Jeffrey C. Alexander, ed., *Neofunctionalism*. Beverly Hills, Calif.: Sage.

6

Political Competition and Differentiation in Higher Education

Gary Rhoades

By and large, differentiation has been posed as a "free market" process. Following a Spencerian model linking differentiation to increased population size, some have characterized differentiation as continuous and inexorable, unfolding naturally through time. Others have adopted a Durkheimian approach, focusing on social factors generating differentiation—e.g., social density and technological developments (Schnore 1958; Lukes 1972). But for the most part sociologists have treated the process as if it were guided more by an "invisible hand" than by the state's and social groups' quite visible hands. General societal trends are adduced to explain differentiation; agency is relatively ignored (but see Eisenstadt 1964).

In part this is due to sociologists' principal concern with differentiation's effects rather than its causes. Attention is directed not to explaining concrete cases of differentiation, but to mapping it out and describing its outcomes. Causal explanations are derived from analyses of differentiation's consequences, its functional benefits (Merton 1968; Rueschemeyer 1977). As functionalists focus more on system

The author gratefully acknowledges the support of the National Institute of Education. A special debt of gratitude is due Professor Burton R. Clark, who has sponsored the author as a postdoctoral researcher since 1981 and has created and provided a research environment with the Comparative Higher Education Research Group at UCLA that has been rich with opportunities.

needs than on group demands and interests, explanations are couched in terms of the increased efficiency or adaptive capacity that accrues to the system.

Lack of concern with the political realm also stems from the nature of the mechanisms cited to explain differentiation. If it is not treated as a process of biological growth and/or of natural adaptation resolving "strain," then competition is invoked as the driving engine. In either case, political activity or regulation is regarded as an artificial intervention skewing differentiation, a *deus ex machina* (Rueschemeyer 1977). Naturalistic evolutionary models, for instance, ignore political factors' affects on demographics.[1] Focusing on competition has a similar effect; competition is posed as a natural state, a feature of societies' internal functioning that is "determined by social causes independent of individual men's wills" (Lukes 1972:169). Agency and political factors, as in Durkheim's "Two Laws of Penal Evolution," are considered derivative matters of secondary concern.[2]

Within such a conceptual framework, if the state is considered, it is generally conceived as a brake on differentiation or as a source of integration in an increasingly complex social world. This is particularly true in studies of higher education.[3] Conditions of political decentralization are linked to the establishment of universities (Ramirez and Meyer 1980:378). Smelser (1973, 1974) points to the state's role in restricting further differentiation in American higher education—e.g., between undergraduate and graduate organizational levels. And in applying a population ecology model, which emphasizes competition as a determinant of social organization patterns (Hannan and Freeman 1977), Birnbaum (1983) argues that state intervention decreases system diversity, making it less likely that new organizational forms will evolve in response to environmental pressures. As these models' exemplars lie in classical economic and natural science, it is hardly surprising that the state and *Homo politicus* are treated as unnatural factors that distort and hamper the natural process.

Contrary to differentiation theory's underlying logic, this paper suggests that differentiation in higher education is largely the product of political competition and state sponsorship, and that the "natural" trend is toward dedifferentiation. If general causes or mechanisms create the potential for differentiation, they are not sufficient to explain the extent to which and the particular way in which that potential is realized. Durkheim, Parsons, and subsequent sociologists have not offered detailed accounts of how differentiation is produced. They have cited mechanisms of competition or of strain but have said little about exactly how these translate into differentiation, or about other possible resolutions.[4]

Drawing on recent theoretical work I suggest that agency must be incorporated into explanations of differentiation if we are to understand particular cases of that process. The proximal cause of differentiation, in higher education systems at least, lies in state and group political actions.[5] And only through considering peoples' beliefs and actions can we explain the tendency toward dedifferentiation in higher education. Human agents determine both the pace and path of differentiation. They do not simply hinder the process, creating a disjuncture between general causal conditions (stimulus) and the institution's development (response). People chart the particular course of differentiation that evolves.

In concentrating on politics' shaping influence on differentiation this paper builds on Eisenstadt (1963, 1964, 1965, 1978) and Rueschemeyer (1977), both of whom urge a focus on interest groups and power. But it also seeks to go beyond them. Both Eisenstadt and Rueschemeyer emphasize the determining influence of select groups. Eisenstadt says "innovating elites" occupying strategic roles in an institutional sphere may activate differentiation.[6] Rueschemeyer's consideration of power translates more definitively into consideration of the interests of the powerful. This paper, on the other hand, attends to both the state and a wide range of groups acting through the state to affect differentiation. It also attends to the political competition between external lay groups and academics, instead of just to entrepreneurial leadership or the "powerful."[7]

But political competition, though it involves power, is not always *for* power, nor does it involve only material interests.[8] It can concern the role or function an institutional system performs. It can concern ideas and values from which are formed images of how an institutional system should be structured and of what work it should do.

I am interested more in various groups' competing images than in entrepreneurial elites' "cultural codes" or the dominant group's ideology. Competing definitions of the system are continually played out in the higher education arena. And the pattern of competition shapes differentiation's path.

Differentiation in Higher Education: Theses

This paper examines regularities in political competition's effects on differentiation in higher education across four national contexts—the English, French, Swedish, and American. The main thesis is that the central axis of competition is between academics and external lay groups, superimposed on inherent tensions between institutional insiders and outsiders.

Thesis 1: The more the academic/external lay group balance of power favors academics, the less open the system will be to differentiation.

Academic dominance inhibits the advancement of new or alternative images of and roles for higher education.[9] It encourages accommodation to change within existing institutional frameworks and according to prevailing predilections concerning the work of higher education.

But academia and external lay groups vary by nation—national academes, for instance, are neither monolithic nor equivalent (Neave and Rhoades 1987). Only a "centralized" academia and its institutional image impedes differentiation (Ben-David and Zloczower 1962). And different lay groups will provide a different counterbalance to academia. Analyses of academics and lay groups must attend to their historically and culturally specific features (Alexander 1984). To assume that such groups have standard orientations stemming from their structural position is to miss the features of political competition that determine particular patterns of differentiation. This culturally contingent element is embedded in my analysis of academia and lay groups' competition for meaning.

Agency must be linked to structural context. My focus is on political structure. State structures affect competing groups' input and influence in higher education policymaking and implementation. As higher education has become more bureaucratized, the state has become the central arena in which this competition is played out (Clark 1983:240). Thus, my second thesis.

Thesis 2: External lay group access to higher education policymaking and implementation is greater in systems in which the legislative branch is both relatively powerful vis-à-vis the executive branch and administrative bureaucracies and is active in higher education matters as an independent force.

The converse thesis is that academics' position as professional experts and institutional insiders gives them greater access and influence in countries in which strong administrative bureaucracies oversee higher education.

The premise is that new or alternative institutional images must be promoted or at least supported by external lay groups if differentiation is to proceed. External lay group access is necessary to counterbalance academics' influence, to provide the leverage to activate differentiation. For the widespread tendency in higher education is toward dedifferentiation, denoted by the phrase "academic drift." Newly created, initially innovative institutions, or less prestigious ones with alternative roles in higher education, drift toward traditional academic patterns of organization and work (Neave 1979). Routinization is often accompanied by gradual dedifferentiation, driven by upward mobility aspirations.

DiMaggio and Powell (1983) and Meyer and Scott (1983) point to the isomorphism characterizing organizational fields dominated by professionals. They call attention to professionals' ability to define "rational myths" and organizational models that promote homogenization within these organizational fields. Similarly, I suggest that academics are major definers and defenders of higher education images. They are the system's vested interests, and constitute an obstacle to further differentiation. Competition in higher education is for status and legitimacy, encouraging conformity to prevailing models rather than attempts by organizations to distinguish themselves from their competitors. Market models do not apply. Differentiation ensues not as a natural process but in response to the political actions of groups working through the state to challenge the prevailing institutional image(s) and promote alternative ones. Hence, my third thesis.

Thesis 3: Dedifferentiation is the "natural" trend in higher education: State action is necessary to prevent it. Challenging groups' political action and state articulation of new institutional images is needed to generate differentiation.

Differentiation is precipitated in the *political* marketplace.

There are, of course, different types of differentiation, but the standard definition is Smelser's (1959:2): "a process whereby one social role or organization . . . differentiates into two or more roles or organizations. . . . The new social units are structurally distinct from each other, but taken together are functionally equivalent to the original unit." Differentiation may be intrasectoral (within an established institutional sphere—e.g., splitting teaching and research functions into separate higher education units) or intersectoral (differentiation of one institutional sphere from another—e.g., education from the family). My concern is with the former, an important distinction as the factors shaping these processes are different (Ramirez and Meyer 1980).

Differentiation differs across institutional realms. I examine differentiation in a "public" institution open to conscious manipulation. Differentiation in "private" institutional realms like the family may be driven by different factors.[10]

There are also different types of dedifferentiation. It may involve return to the previous status quo—a new, differentiated unit fails or reverts to standard forms. Or it may denote "a structural fusion of functions"—institutions taking on functions normally performed in other realms, the opposite of differentiation's pattern of fission (Rueschemeyer 1977).

I refer to dedifferentiation in the first sense, for the notion of differentiation as fission and dedifferentiation as fusion is problematic. New, differentiated structures taken together are assumed to be functional equivalents of the old structure. But as functions become attached to relatively independent institutional frameworks the functions may be transformed, changing not just in external form but inner nature. In addition, this conception of differentiation affords no insight into the emergence of new functions—e.g., the development of the research function in universities. Further, the notion of dedifferentiation as fusion would classify the advancement of new interpretations of social justice into higher education and the corresponding development of distinct organizational structures geared to these concerns as a fusion of functions in that "political" purposes are attached to a "nonpolitical" institution. But this ignores mainstream and radical sociologists of education who indicate that educational systems have always had important political functions—whether assimilation, political socialization, or "reproduction." Society is less a conglomeration of dissociated spheres than an amalgam of institutions performing various and overlapping functions. With fusion as with fission the "same" function performed in different institutional realms is altered.

Change in higher education may involve the "infusion" of new concerns and the construction or recasting of organizational units to work in accordance with these. The institutional realm is filled with new principles, ideas, and images—imbued with new purpose as a whole or in new organizational forms. The system may structurally differentiate by reconstituting itself or by generating distinct organizations outside the existing framework. As I see it, infusion is a major type of differentiation within institutional spheres.

Episodes of potential differentiation in English, French, Swedish, and American higher education from 1960 to 1980 provide, in capsule form, insight into the forces shaping this process. In using critical episodes as a unit of analysis I am building on yet modifying Turner's (1972: 1974) concept of "social dramas." Turner's notion is consistent in three respects with my approach to differentiation. First, Turner's "root metaphor" is "a human esthetic form, a product of culture not of nature" (1974:32). Second, Turner focuses on both social dynamics and the structures that shape them. Finally, social dramas are as much about symbols and ideas as they are about power and material interests.

But the concept of social dramas carries some less attractive baggage. The metaphor of drama connotes successive phases and closure. Instead of climax and denouement I prefer to speak of episodes in an ongoing drama. In addition, Turner's language of "breach," "crisis," and "reintegration" refers more to the system than to groups. I am interested not in the breach of a system's norms but in groups' competition over norms, or in this case institutional images. Finally, the idea of drama implies a script, which for Turner is determined by social structure. I attend more to the willful activity of human agents who may step beyond and rewrite the structurally defined script in improvised and contingent episodes.

Before discussing these dramatis personae and their role in various critical episodes I first set the stage.

Setting the Stage

Given what they experienced between 1960 and 1980, the English, French, Swedish, and American higher education systems were prime candidates for differentiation. Demographic trends and social demand caused prodigious growth in enrollments and the number of higher education organizations. Subsequent downshifts in the economy created heightened strain and competition.

Higher education systems expanded dramatically in the 1960s and 1970s, particularly in the university sector. British higher education enrollments doubled, to 710,000 full- and part-time students. Full-time university enrollments nearly tripled, to 286,000. The age participation rate doubled, peaking at 14 percent in 1972/3 (Farrant 1981).[11] And the number of universities more than doubled, to 45.

Expansion in French higher education proceeded even faster, and from a larger baseline. Total enrollments doubled, to over one million. University enrollments nearly quadrupled, to over 850,000. The percentage of the relevant age group entering universities more than doubled, to almost 20 percent (Cerych and Colton 1980; Cerych, Colton, and Jallade 1981; Gruson and Markiewicz-Lagneau 1983). The university population tripled, to seventy-seven by 1977.

The smaller Swedish system also experienced considerable proportionate growth. Higher education enrollment tripled, to nearly 160,000. The percentage of the age cohort entering higher education also tripled, to over 30 percent (Lane and Fredriksson 1983). The organizational population grew less dramatically—from four universities in 1960 to six by 1976.

The American higher education system, already massive by 1960, with 3.2 million students and 2,040 institutions, still grew enormously. Enrollment nearly quadrupled, to 12.1 million. The percentage of the age cohort in higher education increased to 40.5 percent in 1980, from 26.1 percent two decades earlier (National Center for Education Statistics 1981, 1982). The organizational population increased to 3,273—doctorate-granting universities more than doubled, to 456, and two-year colleges increased from 593 in 1960/1 to 1,211 in 1978 (American Council on Education 1984).

These rapidly expanding systems experienced varying degrees of strain, expressed most publicly in student unrest in the late 1960s. The student revolt of May 1968 in France nearly toppled the De Gaulle regime. Student rebellion in the United States was nearly as demonstrative; though it was more dispersed, in selected sites and states it was no less disquieting. Student unrest in Sweden and Britain was more restrained but still occasioned political response and educational change (Lipset and Altbach 1969). If student protest was differentially motivated and oriented in these countries, it was nevertheless evidence of systems' growing pains. Whatever its cause, student unrest caught the attention of political leaders and the public, and precipitated political efforts to reform higher education.

Other strains afflicted higher education in the 1970s, particularly in Europe. After a decade of expansion, enrollment growth rates decreased, economies weakened, and governments tightened budgetary reins. Average annual enrollment growth rates of 8 and 9 percent from 1965 to 1970 dipped to less than 2 percent from 1975 to 1980 in England, France, and the United States, a trend that emerged in Sweden at the end of the 1960s (Premfors and Ostergren 1978; Neave 1982). This meant less money for higher education, as public appropriations are linked to student enrollment. The worldwide recession of the early 1970s further contributed to this. Between 1971/2 and

1976/7 English universities realized a 7 percent fall in average unit of resource per student (Williams and Blackstone 1983:13). The total higher education budget in France decreased between 1969 and 1975 (Bienayme 1978:20). Between 1970 and 1975 in Sweden public expenditure for higher education and research declined as a percentage of the national budget (Lane and Fredriksson 1983:35). And in the 1970s American higher education received a declining percentage of state spending (Bowen and Glenny 1976; Furman 1981).

Despite enrollments leveling off, the recession and governmental reductions generated concern about graduate unemployment. The sense in much of Europe was that student demand was outstripping employment opportunities, creating a national public problem. Already seen as a problem in France by the late 1960s, the situation worsened—by the end of the 1970s university graduate unemployment had nearly quintupled, to almost 15 percent (Patterson 1976; Geiger 1977; Paul 1981). In Sweden, graduate unemployment became a widely publicized issue around 1970 (Premfors and Ostergren 1978:18). The poor articulation between higher education and the labor market was an issue taken up by the government in Britain as graduate unemployment peaked in the mid-1970s (Lindley 1981).

Disjuncture between higher education output and labor market opportunities was worse in some fields. Engineering graduate unemployment in Britain peaked at less than 6 percent; for arts graduates it reached 16 percent. The problem was that in European systems much higher education output traditionally had been absorbed by the public sector. In the early 1970s the public sector took in 43.7 percent of all graduates in France, 53 percent of all young university graduates in the United Kingdom, and 75 percent of all graduates in Sweden (Organisation for Economic Co-operation and Development 1981). The drying up of many public sector occupational opportunities in the 1970s (e.g., in teaching) created a glut in arts and science fields that had long been geared to "internal reproduction"—educating people to staff state school and university systems.

These same enrollment and economic trends meant increased competition within higher education. Expanded organizational populations were confronted with a leveling off of potential students and financial resources. A likely response was increased competition between them.

Either heightened competition, strain, or growth should foster structural differentiation. Buffeted by the combined force of all three, it seems almost a foregone conclusion that these higher education systems would experience differentiation. One might expect a slower pace of differentiation in one country or another—e.g., the United States because of its relative lack of a graduate unemployment strain. But one would expect differentiation nonetheless. Conditions made these systems ripe for it.

The Political Articulation of a Challenge

If the situation was ripe, someone had to do the picking. Human agency and state agencies were the catalysts. Various branches of the state adopted a proactive role. In the 1960s states spawned or sponsored distinctive higher education organizations and sectors in England, France, and the United States. And the planning process that led to overhauling Swedish higher education in 1977 had already begun. In the 1970s states tried to alter work within existing organizations or create new structures within them to facilitate the achievement of new purposes.

These episodes held the promise of differentiation, but it need not have been that way. An expanded organizational population, for instance, could simply have been "more of the same." In Britain the university-dominated Robbins Committee in 1963 called for just this in an effort to create the framework for expansion. New organizations would be created in the universities' image or groomed for eventual promotion to that status. Nonuniversity organizations would be encouraged to emulate university work.

But the promise was made. The publicly professed purpose of the new structures was to promote alternative models of higher education. The Colleges of Advanced Technology (CATs) and polytechnics in England were developed as a more "vocational" model of higher education. The University Institutes of Technology (IUTs) in France were geared to a more practical training function, just as the 1976 reforms of "second-cycle" university study were aimed at vocationalizing university work. And the 1968 reform was intended to create new kinds of universities. The 1977 restructuring of undergraduate studies in Sweden recast higher education work into a more vocational model. And a more democratic admissions policy was advanced. The proliferation of community colleges in the United States was an intentional step toward opening the door of American higher education. Student aid and affirmative action policies involved stepping out of this door to pull in the disadvantaged, fashioning a proactive model of higher education.

The established academic image of higher education was being challenged though not necessarily replaced by competing images. The latter were derived from lay concerns, born of a new emphasis on, or a new interpretation of, certain values. Lay images were of a system oriented more to the needs of external society than to the self-defined interests of academics. New roles and functions were defined, or at least ones that in the laymen's view needed more emphasis. Higher education would be more accountable to clientele and public concerns and less an autonomously run professional guild. Finally, new and/or broader social justice concerns were advanced, demanding higher education's active role in ensuring and distributing social justice. Academic meritocracy was not enough.

The birth and sponsorship of distinctive structures was a matter of state action, but lay groups outside the state were also involved. Either they pressured the state or the state articulated reforms with public opinion in mind. The inspiration or incentive for state action often came from outside the state. But if states cannot claim paternity with respect to new higher education structures, they can often rightly take credit for influential and even essential patronage for these innovations.

The Episodes of Potential Creativity. In 1956 the British minister of education provisionally designated eight CATs (there would later be ten). Though new in concept almost all of the designated institutions had histories dating back to nineteenth-century part-time classes and mechanics institutes (Venables 1978). Old organizations and structures were infused with new work and purposes.

State action preceded growth, strain, and increased competition. Both universities and technical colleges had "empty places," and expected enrollment growth could have been accommodated in existing institutions. Comparisons with Western European countries' output of engineering graduates showed little shortage of technologists, nor was there overwhelming demand for them from British industry (Burgess and Pratt 1970: 1971). The government was trying to create, not respond to, demand for advanced technology. "Societal needs," then, are not objective social conditions; people perceive and translate them into incentives for action, and their meaning varies according to the translator.[12]

If there was demand, it was from those within "further education." This alternative, practical tradition was lay inspired, having originally developed in response to the demand of various lay constituencies, and expressing lay concern for economic and industrial relevance. So the state may sponsor alternative images that already exist, and the concrete form these take may reflect the wishes of those outside the Ministry of Education as much as of those within.

The formal origins of Britain's polytechnics also lie in state action. The secretary of state for the Department of Education and Science (DES) designated the first polytechnic in 1969. By 1973 the last of thirty had been formed from ninety existing institutions. Most were created by combining colleges of technology, art, and commerce (Burgess and Pratt 1971). With the polytechnics the government explicitly advanced a "binary policy," promoting a distinct "public sector" of higher education in opposition to the Robbins Committee recommendations.

This challenging image was articulated in a different climate than that of the CATs. Increased demand for higher education had made itself felt. Expansionism and a stronger notion of equality in education were in vogue.[13] Polytechnics were a response to this climate: they were to open up opportunities for part-time and nontraditional students with a more relevant education that was responsive to local needs.

The state also played the major role in promoting innovation in French higher education. A January 1966 government decree created the University Institutes of Technology (IUTs). Planned by a Ministry of Education commission, IUTs were created from scratch (Lamoure 1981). But they were patterned along the lines of *grandes écoles* with their small size, selective admissions, intensive instruction, use of many nonacademic teaching staff, and curriculum's direct linkage to labor market needs. The *grandes écoles* are a "nonacademic" tradition and model of higher education, having been created by the state or private industry to provide professional and utilitarian training (Zeldin 1967).[14] They embody a far more distinctive and prestigious alternative image than does the nonuniversity tradition in England. The pinnacle of French higher education is the Ecole Polytechnique, not the Sorbonne (Suleiman 1974).

IUTs were partly a response to a perceived labor market need. Government projections in the mid-1960s indicated a need for people with a different sort of technical training than was presently available —more concrete than that given engineers, but more general than that given lower-level technicians. IUTs would train middle-level personnel in technical and administrative fields (Van de Graaff 1976).

Private industry helped articulate this need. Employer representatives and state administrators on the parent "Commission of 18," and the subcommission that worked out the details of the IUTs, were its principal architects.[15] Private sector support and local political pressure spawned many IUTs (Van de Graaff 1976). If the state sponsored a new kind of higher education it was largely in response to or in conjunction with lay groups.

The organizational and internal governance structures of French universities were overhauled by the November 1968 Orientation Law. The law was drafted by Edgar Faure, appointed minister of national education with the task of ensuring that the fall reopening of the faculties would not see a repeat of the May student revolt. Civil servants had little to do with the reform. The minister, his cabinet members, and newly appointed ministry officials took the initiative over the heads of the entrenched bureaucracy (Formerand 1975; Salmon 1982).

The reform incorporated many of the protesters' demands, such as increasing student and nonprofessorial faculty participation in university governance.[16] But it also reflected preexisting reform currents. Colloquia convened at Caen in 1956 and 1966, and one at Amiens in March of 1968 promoted the "modernization" of French universities: increased university autonomy, multidisciplinary organizational units, and the replacement of the chair with the department system.[17] The reform coalition consisted primarily of university academics, largely from the science faculties. So the state responded less to external groups than to higher education's lay clientele (students) and would-be reformers within universities.[18] Though the state can claim credit for creating a new university system, much of the incentive and inspiration for change came from outside the state.

In 1976 the state renewed the technocratic modernization thrust of the mid-1960s, attempting to "vocationalize" the third and fourth years of university study (the "second cycle"), linking them to the private sector labor market. It both continued a reform process initiated a decade earlier, when the faculty course was reorganized into three cycles, and pursued some of the aims of 1968—giving universities some autonomy in planning their courses and making the curriculum "relevant" (Grignon and Passeron 1970; Cohen 1978). State action was driven not only by external events and demands, like graduate unemployment, but by an internally derived logic.

In Sweden the ad hoc royal commission, known as U68, which drafted a comprehensive reform law, was appointed in 1968 by the Ministry of Education. The four members of its central commission were higher civil servants. But in drafting the reform they were aided by three "reference" groups representing political parties, higher education interest groups (including students), and trade unions and employer associations (Ruin 1982). In 1974 the government appointed a working group of six Parliament members to hammer out a compromise bill from the raw and controversial material of the 800-page commission report. The educational bureaucracy took the lead, but the 1977 reform was not an inside job.

The 1977 reform was partly a response to student unrest and external lay groups' images and input. Experiments in student democracy at the departmental level, addressing the student demands of July 1968 for increased participation, were eventually combined with and expanded by the U68 enterprise, which overhauled the system's governance structure (Lane and Fredriksson 1983). Participation was extended not just to students but to nonprofessorial teachers, university staff, and outside interest groups. The professorial university was replaced by a system of external participation and group representation in various planning and governance bodies, inspired by a popular lay model of governance—industrial democracy (Ruin 1982).

But U68 and the 1977 Higher Education Act were also a continuation of educational reform that had reshaped lower and upper secondary education. Higher education was targeted by a reform coalition of major political parties, interest groups, and top-level bureaucrats that was committed to comprehensiveness and quality (Premfors 1981).

The vocational model was raised as an appropriate one for a comprehensive higher education system by combining nonuniversity institutions and programs with universities in an integrated system of higher education units.[19] The U68 commission responded to the vocationally slanted images of higher education held by manual and white collar workers' unions (the LO and TCO) and by the employers' association (the SAF).[20] Undergraduate education was changed accordingly. Programs of study were organized into five occupational sectors that would replace the university faculties. The working assumption was "that all higher education should prepare for future occupational activity" (Lane and Fredriksson 1983:186).

But the 1977 curricular reforms were also geared to the Social Democratic aim of increasing access to higher education. The new general, local, and individual programs of study were geared to attract first-generation university students. They received strong union support. To further open higher education to a new clientele the 1977 reform reduced the importance of formal education as a selection criteria. Work experience would be taken into account. One of four quota groups of applicants receiving places in relation to their size would be comprised of those who were at least twenty-five years old and had four years of occupational experience (Premfors and Ostergren 1978).

Access is also the issue over which state and federal government reoriented American higher education. In moving to not only open higher education's door but step outside it and escort people in, government changed the face and function of higher education.

In the 1960s states began sponsoring and coordinating the growth of community colleges. The idea was neither conceptually nor materially new. A 1947 President's Commission on Higher Education had proposed the idea of community colleges, and more than three hundred junior colleges whose history dated to the early 1900s provided an existing institutional base (Palinchak 1973). But states adapted the junior college idea to much broader purposes. Community colleges would not be "junior" copies of four-year colleges but instead would serve the community and meet a diverse clientele's needs by performing several educational functions—offering transfer, occupational, general, and adult education. They would make possible education for all and give "late bloomers" a second chance. States planned community colleges so that all high school graduates would be within commuting distance of one of them.[21]

States underwrote and contributed to this institution's proliferation. By the mid-1960s some type of community college education structure was operational in forty-three states. From 1963 to 1971 community colleges nearly doubled in number and tripled their enrollment (Palinchak 1973). State action and subsequent growth reflected tremendous grass roots demand for more higher education. One state legislature after another heard and heeded its constituents back home.[22]

The demand for increased access soon made itself felt at the national level. As education is a state responsibility, the federal government was only minimally involved in providing institutional aid. But it facilitated access with student aid and by requiring institutions to increase access for disadvantaged groups.

The 1965 Higher Education Act provided federal scholarships based for the first time purely on need, with no ability screening (Gladieux and Wolanin 1976). The educational issue had earlier been "talent loss" and the need for better education for the most academically able. But meritocracy gave way to a broader and stronger notion of equal educational opportunity, and the federal government responded to this political climate by taking responsibility for actively promoting such opportunity. With the 1972 education amendments grants for low-income students were greatly expanded and were allocated directly to students rather than through higher education institutions as had been true of 1965 aid programs.[23]

In the name of and at the behest of groups suffering discrimination, in the late 1960s and early 1970s the federal government tried to push all of postsecondary education to accept as a basic function the achievement of equal educational outcomes. Disadvantaged groups were to gain access proportionate to their numbers, not just to student places but to faculty positions. An affirmative action policy was built on the 1964 civil rights acts, presidential executive orders, and Title IX of the 1972 education amendments. Compliance was ensured by requiring any institution in receipt of federal funds to provide evidence that they were taking affirmative action (Carnegie Council on Policy Studies in Higher Education 1975; Shils 1982). Structures were also created within existing organizations (e.g., affirmative action offices) to operationalize this new function.

In all four countries, then, states advanced a lay-inspired challenge to prevailing academic images of higher education. In England, state initiative lay primarily in the DES. In France it was more the minister than the Ministry of National Education that took the lead. The legislative branch had an insignificant role in both cases. But in Sweden the Parliament played a major role in reform. And though bureaucrats directed the Ministry of Education's U68 they were advised by various lay groups. Finally, in the United States, which lacked a national ministry, reform was initiated in both state and federal legislative and executive branches. The different political structures and cultures reflected in these varied loci of state action affected whether differentiation's promise was achieved.

Vision and Reality

The promise was there. A new vision awaited realization. New images and the challenge they represented had been concretized in new organizations, structures, and laws that survive and remain in force. Each portended possible differentiation, moving beyond conventional academic work and purposes. What has been their fate?

CATs have been "upgraded" to university status. In making this transition they were subject to university tutelage. Academic advisory committees of eminent university academics planned the universities'/designates' curriculum, staffing, and organizational structure (Venables 1978).

Most people in the CATs were willing parties to this assimilation. The upgrading process merely accelerated drift. CATs had already virtually eliminated subdegree coursework, severely reduced part-time work, expanded to university-type coursework, and shifted to a national pool of students selected by university standards (Burgess and Pratt 1970). Anxious to join the university club, CATs planned charters that conformed to conventional notions of universities and university work (Venables 1978:49–50).

Drift was stimulated from above. Visiting committees of the National Council for Technological Awards (NCTA), an external body that approved some CAT courses and on which sat university representatives, encouraged shedding part-time work—it was believed to be not conducive to the atmosphere of a higher education institution. The DES also fostered drift, regarding upward mobility as a sign of success, academically defined.[24] It gave academics a greater role in governance by reducing local authority control, and it allowed CATs to undertake more advanced full-time work (Venables 1978). Institutions received 75 percent grants for advanced work. And enrollment-based institutional funding from the DES was biased against part-time study (Donaldson 1975; Fowler 1982).

Polytechnics have not yet been "upgraded" but have been accused of aping universities and abandoning their distinctive mission (Whitburn et al. 1976:6). Designed as vocationally and locally oriented teaching institutions offering subdegree and courses and concentrating particularly on part-time and nontraditional students, the trend in polytechnics is away from subdegree and part-time work. The growth area has been full-time students in degree courses. Eighteen polytechnics now have research degree committees. Students are selected largely by university standards and are increasingly drawn from a national pool. And proportionately fewer polytechnic students in 1978 were studying science and technology subjects than were university students (Scott 1983).

Polytechnic drift is generated from below and above. Staff prefer to teach full-time degree courses in disciplines. Less than a third believe that polytechnics should offer "more of an 'applied' education than generally available in universities," and 40 percent have an equal or greater interest in research than in teaching (Whitburn et al. 1976; Halsey 1981).

The Council for National Academic Awards (CNAA), which validates degree courses in nonuniversity institutions, and on which university academics were prominent in the early years, has used course approval as a lever to promote the university model of governance, academic staffing, and degrees.[25] It has promoted research in polytechnics as "essential for standards."

The DES also encouraged drift, minimizing local authority control and rarely exercising its veto over research appointments and courses that stray from polytechnics' original mission. The same administrative incentives that encouraged CATs to abandon part-time and sub-degree work apply to polytechnics; and the latter's salary system makes pay a positive function of the level of work being taught (Donaldson 1975).

DES practices reflect civil servants' acceptance of university academics' model of higher education. Certain kinds of coursework, students, and activities are defined as superior to others. The DES sees its function as encouraging this model to ensure "quality."

External lay groups can do little to counter this. They have very little input into policy formulation and even less into implementation. At the system level there is no mechanism for regularized lay input. At the individual institution level lay representatives sit on governing bodies but have little impact (Moodie and Eustace 1974).

The executive branch dominates in higher education matters. Parliament's role is minor at best. The executive branch proposes and disposes laws; strong parties make Parliament merely an opposition government waiting to get into power. Lay groups have little access to civil servants, whereas academics are their social colleagues and past classmates—Oxbridge graduates dominate the civil service (Perkin 1977). Britain's political culture promotes administration by institutional insiders instead of outside participation. External lay groups are not seen as "legitimate interest groups" in higher education policymaking (Kogan 1975). If the educational establishment dominates policymaking, implementation is left to the experts, academic professionals.

So when new structures are initiated in England dedifferentiation toward the prevailing academic image of higher education sets in. Push from below with no braking and even some pull from above fosters this.

In the presidentialist French Fifth Republic the executive branch dominates a weak parliament.[26] But academic input is not as influential as in England. The upper civil service is dominated by *grande école*, not university, graduates. On the other hand, a "Jacobin tradition" pervades French administration—it holds that public interests are best served by the guidance of independent, disinterested civil servants rather than by the efforts of narrow, self-seeking private interest groups (Suleiman 1974; Tarrow 1974). External interest group input is not highly regarded: until the 1980s it was hardly solicited. But professional input is seen as legitimate and can be considerable.

Many of Faure's chief assistants, for example, were university professors (Cohen 1978:49).

The Ministry of Education is neither as centralized nor all-controlling as it might seem. It does not oversee all of higher education, which includes most *grandes écoles,* and there is much room for maneuver at the university level. National and local academic bodies control academic appointments and curricula (Bienayme 1978; Salmon 1982). The ministry's directorate for higher education has much autonomy, and directors are virtually always university professors (Coombs 1978). And, paradoxically to Anglo-Americans, university professors' civil servant status provides freedom from instead of accountability to deans, presidents, and even the ministry. Universities are not autonomous, but professors are.

The IUTs reveal the limits of ministry control even outside the university. Their creators gave them autonomy from university faculties to ensure distinctiveness. But the title "university institutes of technology" reflected academics' input—employers preferred the title "institutes of higher technical training" (Lamoure 1981). A 1976 government commission criticized the IUTs' drift from vocational commitment. The IUT diploma was still not recognized in "collective conventions" negotiated between public and private employers and trade unions that would provide slots in the job hierarchy (Van de Graaff 1976:206). IUTs had failed to attract the intended number of students and many used them as a stepping stone to further study, diluting their original terminal mission (Neave 1976).

The IUTs' direct administrative connection to the ministry blocked organizational drift. But centralist arrangements restricted IUTs' regional mission of responding to local economic and manpower needs (Quermonne 1973; Van de Graaff 1976). Only 20 percent of coursework is free from national constraints, and IUT directors are appointed by the ministry.

In addition, drift at the classroom level is generated by academics and appointment/promotion practices. A third of IUT staff were to come from the private sector. Only 12 percent actually do, and more than was intended come from academia. The latter have demonstrated a preference for conventional university work(loads) and a desire to do research—not surprising since they are evaluated for promotion according to standard academic criteria by the national academic body overseeing all university promotions.

The ministry exercises less control over the university curriculum. In 1968, Faure could change structures but little else (Bourricaud

1982). And the 1968 Orientation Act provided a "framework" for implementation by academics. But if academics implemented its skeleton they largely undermined its intent. The new units of teaching and research (UERs) and universities were to be multidisciplinary, but many UERs are identical with traditional faculties, and less than twenty of seventy-seven universities are truly pluridisciplinary (Cohen 1978; Freville 1981). The goals of increased university pedagogical autonomy also foundered on the rocks of academic practice. The university curriculum remains constrained by the national diplomas that staff, students, and employers prefer.[27] The national civil service status of academics disposed and enabled them to resist any regional mission university presidents tried to develop. Finally, student and external group participation has been weak and has not reoriented universities' mission.

If academics undermined the 1968 reforms, they ignored the 1976 second-cycle reforms. Universities were to formulate vocationally relevant courses (left undefined by the ministry) and replace established courses with them. Following protest in the universities, a ministerial circular allowed universities to retain "existing fundamental programs." The committees intended to plan the new programs never formed (Bienayme 1978:31–32).

The absence of lay involvement in French higher education policymaking and implementation enabled academics to resist with considerable success efforts to promote differentiation.

Swedish academics were not enamored of state-initiated reform either (Lane 1982). The three political parties in which they were best represented opposed U68 (Ruin 1982). Saco/SR—the trade union of academics, persons with academic degrees, and professionals—voiced opposition throughout the U68 reform process not just to vocationalization but to representation for external groups on various planning and governance bodies. This led Parliament in 1975 to adopt a proposal giving representatives from inside the institutions a two-thirds majority. Academic lobbying also led Parliament to moderate U68 proposals by emphasizing the possibility for "planned diversity within a unified framework," allowing units to maintain their identity (Premfors 1981). Swedish academics resisted reform in the formulation stage and then tried to undermine its implementation.

But the competition between academics and lay groups was not one-sided as it was in England and France. Corporatist labor market groups were integrated into higher education policy and decision-making bodies in the 1960s. Higher education policymaking was permeated by the typical Swedish political culture that promotes consultation with and participation by designated interest groups. Lay groups came to be regarded as legitimate representatives of the "public interest" in higher education.

External lay groups' hand was strengthened by the Swedish Parliament's significant formal powers in higher education, actively exercised since the 1950s (Premfors 1980). Academics have not countered this by having the Ministry of Education's ear; the ministry and the National Board of Universities and Colleges were houses of reform.[28]

The key means of access for external lay groups was the state commission. In England, the classic parliamentary system, legislation is prepared within the executive branch and presented to Parliament. The opposition may take it or leave it; usually they prefer to leave it. In Sweden, the state commission system includes all of the political parties (including the opposition) and relevant interest groups in a forum for negotiation. (Kelman 1981:170)

Institutional insiders had no effective monopoly over planning policy. Outsiders were brought into a cooperative problem-solving process.

Outsiders also oversaw implementation, enabling them to ensure that reforms were not ignored or watered down. Lay group representatives were on both the central committee (H75) that carried out reform and the six regional committees overseeing implementation. They also had a major role in newly established central, regional, and local governance bodies.

Nevertheless, drift has ensued as old discipline-based courses have often been transplanted intact into new curricular structures. "By 1980 at least, the boards of study . . . suggest that traditional academic views continue to prevail and that the ideas of breaking the hold which separate academic disciplines and fields of study have traditionally maintained have been thwarted" (Boucher 1982:152). Students have favored single courses—intended as a complementary element to the vocationally oriented general lines of study. And three of four single courses are discipline oriented—through them the prereform academic curriculum lives.[29]

Such drift was possible because the reform act was a framework decision leaving much to be decided at the local level. The bodies overseeing and planning the undergraduate curriculum accorded one-third representation to academics, students, and external groups. But de facto power remained very much in professorial hands. Academics were adept at dominating the internal politics and ultimately the work of higher education's basic units.[30]

America lacks the political and professional structures that in England and France inhibit higher education organizations and sectors from seeking out distinctive niches. Higher education is overseen not by a strong national ministry that, as in France, emphasizes a common national mission, but by state legislatures, boards, and executive bodies that encourage regional and local missions. American academia is not a Jacobin body that as in France works according to nationally defined curricula and diplomas and is appointed and promoted nationally. Nor is it a body that as in England ensures adherence to national standards through rigorous self-regulation with mechanisms like the University Grants Committee, academic advisory committees, the CNAA, and external examiners. The diversity of their organizational homes reflects and recreates American academia's diversity.

American higher education is therefore pluralistic, with multiple hierarchies limited to the different leagues within which higher education organizations compete. Institutions' actual and preferred missions vary by league.[31] If there is much drift, with teachers' colleges becoming comprehensive universities, it does not mean as it has in England that old functions are shed. The common title "university" obscures the different—often unconventional—work activities of such institutions in America.

American academia is also distinctive in its political weakness. American higher education institutions were not the outgrowths of academic guilds; they built from the top down. The "American mode" of authority localized bureaucracy, providing a strong administrative component on campuses (Clark 1983). Unlike their European counterparts, American academics prefer it that way (Baldridge et al. 1978; Mortimer and McConnell 1979). More important, faculty do not have a direct line to state and federal officials and legislative representatives. The principal higher education lobbyists at the state level are presidents and systemwide administrators; at the federal level they are institutional, not academic, associations.

External lay groups, on the other hand, have multiple mechanisms by which to influence higher education, and much power. True to American political culture, which emphasizes openness and accountability, there is a long tradition across various educational levels of a broad range of groups becoming deeply involved in educational matters. And unlike lay access in Sweden, input is not regulated by the governmental bureaucracy and limited to corporatist group representatives on state commissions (Kelman 1981).

A commonly cited mechanism of lay oversight is trusteeship. But the evidence suggests that trustees act as business boards of directors, leaving most matters to the executive they have appointed (Clark

1983). As in Sweden, "amateur" outsiders rarely dominate institutional politics.

More important for lay influence is that state and federal legislators in the United States play a major and independent role in formulating policy and shaping higher education. Congress can not only prepare legislation and set its own agenda, it can also influence federal agencies and bureaucracies' implementation of legislation (Gladieux and Wolanin 1976:231). The 1972 education amendments were initiated by Congress and ran counter to the Nixon administration's legislative package. On the other hand, weak political parties and party discipline makes American legislators more responsive to constitutents and interest groups than are European members of Parliament (Kelman 1981:151–52).

Community colleges illustrate this lay influence. Though their balance of missions varies by state, if community colleges have drifted, it has been away from conventional academic transfer work and toward community service, continuing/adult, and vocational/technical education.[32] Local citizen advisory committees contributed to this (Zoglin 1981). Interest groups and state legislators also pushed the practical side of community colleges, calling for strengthened ties to business and industry (Eulau and Quinley 1970:117). Lobbying of local representatives by community colleges and their constituencies has enabled them to maintain and extend distinctive educational functions (Zusman 1978). And, as was intended, community colleges remain the basic mechanism of access for the disadvantaged (Astin 1982).

Federal legislation reveals the higher education community's weakness. In 1972 higher education institutional associations favored continued and/or increased institutional aid over a shift in emphasis to direct student aid. Congress overrode their opposition. Responding to the political climate of the times, legislators pushed open the door to higher education, asserting that a college education was a right (Gladieux and Wolanin 1976).

Institutional responsiveness to external demand to equalize educational outcomes is facilitated both by central administrators' control of admissions and by campus administrative offices that oversee efforts to broaden the social composition of the profession itself. These on-campus translators of lay concerns have gotten results. Minority representation increased by 50 to 100 percent among college entrants between the mid-1960s and 1970s and substantially increased among law, medical, and graduate students. Very moderate increases in minority and female faculty have also been achieved (Astin 1982; Amer-

ican Council on Education 1984). And universities and colleges continue to pursue affirmative action in the face of court challenges and
backsliding by the federal chief executive (Shils 1982:473).

Laypersons also have recourse through the judiciary. The courts
have played· a prominent role in affirmative action (Green 1981).
Lawsuits against institutions and departments have kept affirmative
action in the public eye and forced higher education to recognize the
realization of equal educational outcomes as a problem it must deal
with.

The relatively loose political structure that encourages niche finding is a powerful force encouraging adherence to that niche and its
mission. State master plans force institutions to adhere to certain
missions. State program review evaluations (undertaken by lay-dom-
inated state coordinating or governing boards) of new and existing
programs further encourage responsiveness to lay concerns and adherence to stated missions.[33]

In America, political structures, lay group strength, and a diverse
academic profession encourage differentiation and inhibit drift.

There was change in English, French, Swedish, and American higher
education. But there was also dedifferentiation and resistance to change.
Isomorphism marked these systems. Ex-CATs and polytechnics, whatever their differences from universities, moved closer to the "English
idea of a university" (Halsey and Trow 1971). French universities still
work principally to academically oriented and defined national diplomas. And even in IUTs, which were and are stamped by the compelling alternative *grande école* image in France, the coursework and
activity of students and personnel have become more like that of the
academic faculties to which they are linked. If the form of Swedish
undergraduate education has been reshaped according to lay images,
the academic model of coursework has nevertheless emerged with
much the same content. Only in America, which lacks a dominant
academic image, do lay as well as academic models thrive; and there
a nonacademic function now pervades the system as a whole. Elsewhere, new structures, organizations, and sectors tended to compromise their promise, gradually conforming to prevailing academic
practice rather than transcending or transforming it.

Conclusion

Conventional structural-functionalists characterize differentiation as
a natural market process guided by social systems' inherent propen-

sities and/or disjunctures. This paper suggests that in higher education if general trends have a broad predisposing influence their effects depend on how they are perceived and acted upon by human agents. Differentiation is activated and actuated through political competition between academics and lay groups. And an undertow drags the system toward dedifferentiation.

The predisposing climate did not yield the expected harvest. Differentiation proceeded in the four higher education systems at different rates and in different directions than might have been expected given the general trends they had experienced. Though French higher education's enrollment and economic trends, student unrest, and unemployment primed it for differentiation, little occurred. Despite its less dramatic growth and relatively quiescent students, Swedish higher education was infused with new purpose on a grander scale than was the case in either the French or English systems. Their participation rates seemed to make the Swedish and American systems least susceptible to the imposition of social justice functions. But such demands were made. In the English system, which was the least open, they were not.

The key to whether vision became reality was the political competition between academics and lay groups. If power is defined as influence in an institution and on state bodies that oversee that institution, then my first thesis is somewhat confirmed. Lay influence in higher education was quite weak in England and France, at both the organizational and national levels. In Sweden and the United States it was quite strong at both levels. Academic influence in England was very strong at both levels. In France it was strong at the national level; at the organizational level academics (and their work) were resistant to control, but academics did not control university structures. In Sweden academic influence was moderate at the national level and very strong at the institutional level. In America it was weak at both levels. Accordingly, higher education was marked less by differentiation than by dedifferentiation in England, and by somewhat more differentiation and less dedifferentiation in France. Swedish higher education was subject to more differentiation than either the English or French systems. And American higher education experienced the most differentiation and the least dedifferentiation of all four systems; only there did the lay challenge concern not only undergraduate but graduate education and academia itself. The balance of academic and lay power affected differentiation.

Academic and lay group influence varied in policy formulation versus policy implementation. The strongest lay challenge took place over the formulation and legislation of reforms—less a matter of lay groups facing off with academics than of each influencing state actors. But implementation in Europe was left to academics and was contingent on their cooperation. Academics twisted new structures to old academic purposes. In the United States, on the other hand, implementation was overseen by nonacademics—politicians and institutional administrators who were strong relative to academics, open to lay pressure, and sympathetic to lay concerns. American higher education was unique among the four systems in having nonacademic but professional components on campus (administrators) with significant powers relative to academia and interests distinct from those of academics. Referring to dichotomous competition between academics and external lay groups overlooks the key role played by internal nonacademic professionals.

Equally important, differentiation's path has been shaped by differences in lay groups and academics across the four countries. The main Swedish lay groups, for instance, were economic associations; they pushed vocationalization and increased access for those with work experience. Lay groups in the United States, on the other hand, were not designated by the state to serve on formal planning bodies. Various interest groups including local community and ethnic groups pushed for community colleges and affirmative action. Efforts to promote change sometimes came from segments of academia. But if the mechanisms differed, academia in England, France, and Sweden nevertheless was a centralized, self-regulating guild that minimized, isolated, and often reversed the efforts of wildcat academics trying to change the system or strike out on their own. The uniquely diverse, decentralized American academia, on the other hand, which was not committed to a single, pervasive image of higher education, facilitated differentiation.

Political structures and cultures influenced the contest between academics and lay groups. My second thesis also receives partial confirmation. In Sweden and the United States, where the legislative branch played an independent and powerful role, lay access to policymaking and implementation was far greater than in England and France, where the executive branch and ministries dominated higher education policymaking. But the legislative branches in Sweden and the United States are different, and the key mechanism by which lay input was incorporated in Sweden was the state commission, appointed by the Ministry of Education. In addition, although a strong legislative branch may facilitate lay access to policymaking it may be immaterial to lay involvement in implementation. Lay oversight of implementation in Sweden was through regional and organizational committees; in the United States it was through not only state legislatures but the courts, federal regulations, and campus bureaucrats. Finally, the cases of England and France reveal both that one has to distinguish between the executive and administrative branches' involvement, and that the former affords more lay access than the latter. So the second thesis somewhat oversimplifies state involvement.

The converse of the second thesis is also only partially confirmed. Academics had a greater voice in policymaking in England and France, where the executive branch was dominant in higher education. The administrative bureaucracies let academics implement reforms and were either unwilling or unable to overcome resistance and stem drift. But the administrative bureaucracy in Sweden was not so inclined, and consistent with Swedish political culture was quite receptive to the input and interests of certain corporatist lay groups. So the political structure's effects cannot be divorced from a consideration of political culture.

If the competition between academics and lay groups is "no contest," then inertia and/or drift ensue. My third thesis is also partially supported by the data. Lay challenges and state action were essential to promoting and preserving differentiation. Left to their own devices, higher education systems were both disinclined toward change and inclined toward isomorphism after change was externally induced. But states do not always prevent this. Administrative practices in England, for instance, encouraged dedifferentiation. Yet dedifferentiation is less a natural trend than the effect of a dominant institutional image that distorts new growth and engenders imitation.

In explaining the differentiation *of* institutional systems, Eisenstadt has identified institutional entrepreneurs as the catalysts. In explaining differentiation *within* established, bureaucratized institutions, I suggest that the key actors are "institutional image makers" and presenters of challenging images.

Academia is the linchpin. Academics have tried to define the nature of their professional service and the criteria for its evalation, claiming a "mandate" (Hughes 1958). They have tried to monopolize a market. Preservation of this monopoly is contingent partly on academia's political power and partly on its cultural authority (Starr 1982). Much of academia's power lies in its ability to influence other groups' belief systems. If academics can define and promulgate an image that dominates the screen, they can inhibit differentiation and make dedifferentiation palatable. The more a dominant institutional image defines their activity, the less academics and higher education will operate according to free market principles, moving to meet community and clientele demands.

The general cultural order, and changes in it, affect institutional images, just as general economic and social trends affect institutional structures. But features of this order are differentially specified by various groups in competing institutional images. It is not the "spirit of an age" that defines an educational system. Though Durkheim (1977) provides a fascinating analysis of educational ideals' social context and cultural origins, "he did not examine the extent to which educational ideals vary, not only with 'different periods and countries,' but with different social groups within a society" (Lukes 1972:132). It is the institutional images of particular groups that define higher education systems. In higher education, academics play the starring role, upstaged by lay groups in some episodes but prominent in every scene. An understanding of differentiation and dedifferentiation in higher education demands an appreciation of the political competition for meaning that takes place there—a competition that is not finally won or lost but is instead an ongoing process between a field of groups that can change over time and place.

Notes

1. Demographers have long been aware of these factors; Schnore (1958:625n).
2. Traugott (1978:17–18). Durkheim's work was largely in reaction to Comte's and Tonnies' (as well as Spencer's), including their views of the state and the need for state regulation; Lukes (1972:146–47, *passim*).
3. Some studies of educational expansion, such as status competition theory, do focus on political activity.
4. Smelser (1959) is an exception. Durkheim was aware of other possible resolutions but paid little attention to them; Lukes (1972).
5. The state should not be anthropomorphized as an individual. It consists of various branches, groups, and interests, and its actions are born of various peoples' efforts.
6. *May* is a critical verb, for Eisenstadt's argument is that conditions that make differentiation possible do not necessarily generate the process in a particular way or solve the problems that functionalists argue cause differentiation.
7. Eisenstadt tends not to focus on relations between entrepreneurs and other groups, overlooking not only how these relations affect whether the entrepreneurs' visions will be accepted, but how they affect the nature of those visions.
8. Giddens (1982:194–95). Social ideology affects structural differentiation; structures may be compromises between competing ideologies or responses to ideological pressures; Ramirez and Meyer (1980).
9. Dominance by one lay group may pose a similar threat; Rhoades (1983).

10. But political factors and the state can also affect private realms. Legislation and court rulings affect family issues, just as social movements affect family roles.

11. Cross-national comparisons are difficult because in some countries part-timers are converted into full-time equivalents, whereas in others they are not distinguished from one another.

12. Much of history is about "misperceptions"—which are often merely the different perceptions of different groups.

13. The strong concept assumes that poor backgrounds must be compensated for; the weak assumes that all can compete equally; Kogan (1978:31).

14. The "professional" training in the best *grandes écoles* involves generalist education rather than narrow training; Vaughan (1969).

15. Only four of the twenty members on the subcommission and seven of the Commmission of 18 were university academics.

16. Representation on various new bodies was organized into three strata in academia, and included students as well, Salmon (1982).

17. Cohen (1978); Bourricaud (1982). On chair and department systems see Clark (1983) and Neave and Rhoades (1984).

18. Faure responded more to the latter's concerns as reinterpreted by the May protesters, for whom many of the Caen reforms were anathema. This is why Faure abandoned much of Caen's technocratic language in promoting his reforms; Cohen (1978); Bourricaud (1982).

19. Unlike American comprehensive universities, Swedish comprehensive units are conglomerates of spatially disparate units—they are diverse in size, program, and function; Lane and Fredriksson (1983).

20. Many of the ideas that dominated U68 had first been formulated in a 1967 TCO policy document; Ruin (1982).

21. The President's Commission on National Goals in 1960 affirmed this goal of opening up education geographically.

22. Blocker, Bender, and Martorama (1975). States varied in the timing and rate of growth, and a few states, such as Indiana, did not develop community colleges.

23. Federal funding shifted toward student aid after 1965. In 1967 institutional support and student aid constituted 65 and 35 percent of federal outlays respectively; by 1975 the figures were 28 and 72 percent; Green (1981).

24. The one London CAT that was not upgraded had remained truest to the distinctive purposes of the CATs; Burgess and Pratt (1970).

25. University academics also often sit on polytechnic governing bodies and serve as external examiners (a system whereby academics from outside an institution are brought in to examine degree candidates' papers).

26. Premfors (1980). The French distinguish between "government" and "Parliament." Lay groups, as in England, have less influence over representatives than elsewhere due to the strength of party discipline.

27. Bienayme (1978). The 1968 law encouraged universities to develop "university diplomas," but these hold little attraction for students and staff and are little recognized by employers.

28. Ruin (1982); Premfors and Ostergren (1978). But there is not the social distance between university academics and civil servants that one finds in France. More than 80 percent of upper-level administrators hold university degrees; Anton (1980:24).

29. Boucher (1982); Lane (1983). The American pattern of students selecting

single courses lasting from 10 to 15 weeks was until the 1970s foreign to Europe, where students followed courses that were years long.

30. Premfors (1983:14). Swedish research points to the failure of the bodies planning the undergraduate curriculum. Academics dominated single departments and bodies overseeing graduate instruction and research; Lane and Fredriksson (1983).

31. Gross and Grambsch (1974:106). Johnson's (1978) survey reveals that institutions look to similar sorts of institutions (those in their higher education sector) as role models, and not to the most prestigious institutions.

32. The issue today is how to preserve or reinvigorate community colleges' liberal arts and transfer functions; Cohen and Brawer (1982).

33. State planning's rationale lay largely in blocking institutional drift—e.g., from junior to four-year colleges. On program review see Rhoades (1983:304–6).

References

Alexander, Jeffrey C. 1982. *Positivism, Presuppositions, and Current Controversies.* Vol. 1 of *Theoretical Logic in Sociology.* Berkeley and Los Angeles: University of California Press.

—— 1984. "Social-Structural Analysis: Some Notes on Its History and Prospects." *The Sociological Quarterly* (winter), 25:5–26.

American Council on Education. 1984. *1984–5 Fact Book on Higher Education.* New York: American Council on Education/Macmillan.

Anton, Thomas J. 1980. *Administered Politics: Elite Political Culture in Sweden.* Boston, Mass.: Martinus Nijhoff.

Astin, Alexander W. 1982. *Minorities in American Higher Education.* San Francisco, Calif.: Jossey-Bass.

Baldridge, J. Victor, David V. Curtis, George Ecker, and Gary L. Riley. 1978. *Policy Making and Effective Leadership: A National Study of Academic Management.* San Francisco, Calif.: Jossey-Bass.

Ben-David, Joseph and Avraham Zloczower. 1962. "Universities and Academic Systems in Modern Societies." *European Journal of Sociology* 3(1):45–84.

Bienayme, Alain. 1978. *Systems of Higher Education: France.* New York: International Council for Educational Development.

Birnbaum, Robert. 1983. *Maintaining Diversity in Higher Education.* San Francisco, Calif.: Jossey-Bass.

Blocker, Clyde E., Louis W. Bender, and S. V. Martorana. 1975. *The Political Terrain of American Postsecondary Education.* Fort Lauderdale, Fla.: Nova University Press.

Boucher, Leon. 1982. *Tradition and Change in Swedish Education.* Oxford, England: Pergamon Press.

Bourricaud, François. 1982. "France: The Prelude to the Loi d'Orientation of 1968." In Hans Daalder and Edward Shils, eds., *Universities, Politicians, and Bureaucrats,* pp. 31–62. Cambridge: Cambridge University Press.

Bowen, Howard R. and Lyman A. Glenny. 1976. *State Budgeting for Higher Education: State Fiscal Stringency and Public Higher Education.* Berkeley: Center for Research and Development in Higher Education, University of California.

Burgess, Tyrrell and John Pratt. 1970. *Policy and Practice: The Colleges of Advanced Technology.* London: Allen Lane/Penguin.

—— 1971. *Technical Education in the United Kingdom.* Paris: Organisation for Economic Co-operation and Development.

Carnegie Council on Policy Studies in Higher Education. 1975. *Making Affirmative Action Work in Higher Education.* San Francisco, Calif.: Jossey-Bass.

Cerych, Ladislav and S. Colton. 1980. "Summarising Recent Student Flows." *European Journal of Education* 15(1):15–34.

Cerych, Ladislav, S. Colton, and J.-P. Jallade. 1981. *Student Flows and Expenditure in Higher Education, 1965–1979.* Paris: Institute of Education.

Clark, Burton R. 1983. *The Higher Education System: Academic Organization in Cross-National Perspective.* Berkeley and Los Angeles: University of California Press.

Cohen, Arthur M. and Florence B. Brawer. 1982. "The Community College as College: Should the Liberal Arts Survive in Community Colleges?" *Change* 14(2):39–42.

Cohen, Habiba. 1978. *Elusive Reform: The French Universities, 1968–1978.* Boulder, Colo.: Westview Press.

Coombs, Fred. S. 1978. "The Politics of Educational Change in France." *Comparative Education Review* 22(3):480–503.

DiMaggio, Paul J. and Walter W. Powell. 1983. "The Iron Cage Revisited: Institutional Isomorphism and Collective Rationality in Organizational Fields." *American Sociological Review* 48(2):147–60.

Donaldson, Lex. 1975. *Policy and the Polytechnics.* Lexington, Mass. and Farnborough, Hants, England: Lexington Books/Saxon House.

Durkheim, Emile. 1977. *The Evolution of Pedagogical Thought.* London: Routledge and Kegan Paul.

Eisenstadt, S. N. 1963. *The Political System of Empires.* New York: Free Press.

—— 1964. "Social Change, Differentiation, and Evolution." *American Sociological Review* 29(3):375–86.

—— 1965. *Essays on Comparative Institutions.* New York: Wiley.

—— 1978. *Revolution and the Transformation of Societies.* New York: Free Press.

Eulau, Heinz and Harold Quinley. 1970. *State Officials and Higher Education.* New York: McGraw-Hill.

Farrant, John H. 1981. "Trends in Admissions." In Oliver Fulton, ed., *Access to Higher Education*, pp. 42–88. Guildford, England: Society for Research Into Higher Education.

Fomerand, Jacques. 1975. "Policy Formulation and Change in Gaullist France." *Comparative Politics* 8:59–89.

Fowler, Gerald. 1982. "Past Failure and the Imperative for Change." In Leslie Wagner, ed., *Agenda for Institutional Change in Higher Education*, pp. 80–99. Guildford: Society for Research Into Higher Education.

Freville, Yves. 1981. *Rapport à les ministre de la commission d'étude de la reforme du financement des universitaires (annexes).* Paris: Documentation Française.

Furman, James M. 1981. "State Budgeting and Retrenchment." In James R. Mingle et al., eds., *Challenges of Retrenchment*, pp. 243–58. San Francisco, Calif.: Jossey-Bass.

Geiger, Roger. 1977. "The Second-Cycle Reform and the Predicament of the French University." *Paedagogica Europaea* 12:9–22.

Giddens, Anthony. 1979. *Central Problems in Social Theory.* London: Macmillan.

—— 1982. *Profiles and Critiques in Social Theory.* Berkeley and Los Angeles: University of California Press.

Gladieux, Lawrence E. and Thomas R. Wolanin. 1976. *Congress and the Colleges.* Lexington, Mass.: Heath/Lexington Books.

Green, Kenneth C. 1981. *Government Support for Minority Participation in Higher Education.* Report prepared for the Commission on the Higher Education of Minorities. Washington, D.C.: Mimeograph.

Grignon, C. and J. C. Passeron. 1970. *French Experience Before 1968.* Paris: Organisation for Economic Co-operation and Development.

Gross, Edward and Paul V. Grambsch. 1974. *Changes in University Organization, 1964–1971.* New York: McGraw-Hill.

Gruson, Pascal and Janina Markiewicz-Lagneau. 1983. *L'enseignement superieur et son efficacité: France, Etats Unis, URSS, Pologne.* Paris: Documentation Française.

Halsey, A. H. 1981. *Higher Education in Britain: A Study of University and Polytechnic Teachers.* Report to the Social Science Research Council. New York: Mimeo.

Halsey, A. H. and Martin Trow. 1971. *The British Academics.* Cambridge, Mass.: Harvard University Press.

Hannan, Michael T. and John H. Freeman. 1977. "The Population Ecology of Organizations." *American Journal of Sociology* 82(4):929–64.

Hughes, Everett C. 1958. *Men and Their Work.* Glencoe, Ill.: Free Press.

Johnson, Richard. 1978. "Leadership Among American Colleges." *Change* (November), pp. 50–51.

Kelman, Steven. 1981. *Regulating America, Regulating Sweden.* Cambridge, Mass.: MIT Press.

Kogan, Maurice. 1975. *Educational Policy-Making: A Study of Interest Groups and Parliament.* Hamden, Conn.: Linnet Books.

—— 1978. *The Politics of Educational Change.* Manchester, England: Manchester University Press.

Lamoure, Jean. 1981. *Les Instituts Universitaires de Technologie en France.* Paris: Institut d'Education de la Fondation Européene de la Culture.

Lane, Jan-Erik. 1982. "Variety of Attitudes Towards the Comprehensive University." *Higher Education* 11(4):441–74.

—— 1983. "Higher Education: Public Policy-Making and Implementation." *Higher Education* 12(5):519–67.

Lane, Jan-Erik and Bert Fredriksson. 1983. *Higher Education and Public Administration.* Stockholm: Almqvist Wiksell International.

Lindley, Robert. 1981. "Education, Training, and the Labour Market in Britain." *European Journal of Education* 16(1);7–28.

Lipset, S. M. and Philip G. Altbach, eds. 1969. *Students in Revolt.* Boston, Mass.: Houghton Mifflin.

Lukes, Steven. 1972. *Emile Durkheim: His Life and Work.* New York: Harper and Row.

Merton, Robert. 1968. *Social Theory and Social Structure.* New York: Free Press.

Meyer, John W. and W. Richard Scott. 1983. *Organizational Environments: Ritual and Rationality.* Beverly Hills, Calif.: Sage.

Moodie, Graeme C. and Rowland Eustace. 1974. *Power and Authority in British Universities.* Montreal: McGill-Queens University Press.

Mortimer, Kenneth P. and T. R. McConnell. 1979. *Sharing Authority Effectively.* San Francisco, Calif.: Jossey-Bass.

National Center for Education Statistics. 1981. *Digest of Education Statistics, 1981.* Washington, D.C.: National Center for Education Statistics.

—— 1982. *Projections of Education Statistics, 1990–91*. Washington, D.C.: National Center for Education Statistics.

Neave, Guy. 1976. *Patterns of Equality*. Windsor, Eng.: National Foundation for Educational Research.

—— 1979. "Academic Drift: Some Views from Europe." *Studies in Higher Education* 4(2):143–59.

—— 1982. "On the Edge of the Abyss: An Overview of Recent Developments in European Higher Education." *European Journal of Education* 17(2):123–45.

Neave, Guy and Gary Rhoades. 1987. "The Academic Estate in Western Europe." In Burton R. Clark, ed. *National Disciplinary and Institutional Settings*. Berkeley: University of California Press.

Organisation for Economic Co-operation and Development. 1981. *Employment Prospects for Higher Education Graduates*. Report on intergovernmental conference on "Policies for the 80s." October 12–14, 1981. Paris: Organisation for Economic Co-operation and Development.

Palinchak, Robert. 1973. *The Evolution of the Community College*. Metuchen, N.J.: Scarecrow Press.

Patterson, Michelle. 1976. "Governmental Policy and Equality in Higher Education: The Junior Collegization of the French University." *Social Problems* 24(2):173–83.

Paul, Jean-Jacques. 1981. "Education and Unemployment: A Survey of French Research." *European Journal of Education* 16(1):95–119.

Perkin, Harold. 1977. *British Society and Higher Education*. Higher Education Working Group Working Paper no. 20. New Haven, Conn.: Yale University Press.

Premfors, Rune. 1980. *The Politics of Higher Education in a Comparative Perspective: France, Sweden, United Kingdom*. Studies in Politics 15. Stockholm: University of Stockholm.

—— 1981. *Integrated Higher Education: The Swedish Experience*. Group for the Study of Higher Education and Research Policy Report no. 14. Stockholm: University of Stockholm.

—— 1983. "Implementation Strategies in Higher Education." Prepared for conference on "Studies of Higher Education and Research Organization." Rosenon, Dalaro, Sweden, June 6–10, 1983.

Premfors, Rune and Bertil Ostergren. 1978. *Systems of Higher Education: Sweden*. New York: International Council for Educational Development.

Quermonne, Jean-Louis. 1973. "Place and Role of University Institutes of Technology (IUT) in the New French Universities." In Organisation for Economic Co-operation and Development, ed., *Short-Cycle Higher Education: A Search for Identity*, pp. 211–34. Paris: Organisation for Economic Co-operation and Development.

Ramirez, Francisco O. and John W. Meyer. 1980. "Comparative Education: The Social Construction of the Modern World System." In Alex Inkeles, Neil Smelser, and Ralph Turner, eds., *Annual Review of Sociology*, 6:369–99. Palo Alto, Calif. Annual Reviews.

Rhoades, Gary. 1983. "Conflicting Interests in Higher Education." *American Journal of Education* 91(3):283–327.

Rueschemeyer, Dietrich. 1977. "Structural Differentiation, Efficiency, and Power." *American Journal of Sociology* 83(1):1–25.

Ruin, Olof. 1982. "Sweden: External Control and Internal Participation: Trends in Swedish Higher Education." In Hans Daalder and Edward Shils, eds., *Universi-*

ties, Politicians, and Bureaucrats, pp. 329–64. Cambridge: Cambridge University Press.

Salmon, Pierre. 1982. "France: The Loi d'Orientation and Its Aftermath." In Hans Daalder and Edward Shils, eds., *Universities, Politicians, and Bureaucrats*, pp. 63–102. Cambridge: Cambridge University Press.

Schnore, Leo F. 1958. "Social Morphology and Human Ecology." *American Journal of Sociology* 63(6):620–34.

Scott, Peter. 1983. "Has the Binary Policy Failed?" In *The Structure and Governance of Higher Education*, edited by Peter Scott, pp. 166–95. Guildford, Eng.: Society for Research Into Higher Education.

Shils, Edward. 1982. "Great Britain and the United States: Legislators, Bureaucrats, and the Universities." In Hans Daalder and Edward Shils, eds., *Universities, Politicians, and Bureaucrats*, pp. 437–88. Cambridge: Cambridge University Press.

Smelser, Neil. 1959. *Social Change in the Industrial Revolution.* Chicago, Ill.: University of Chicago Press.

—— 1973. "Epilogue: Social-Structural Dimensions of Higher Education." In Talcott Parsons and Gerald M. Platt, *The American University*, pp. 389–422. Cambridge, Mass.: Harvard University Press.

—— 1974. "Growth, Structural Change, and Conflict in California Public Higher Education, 1950–1970." In Neil Smelser and Gabriel Almond, eds., *Public Higher Education in California*, pp. 9–142. Berkeley: University of California Press.

Starr, Paul. 1982. *The Social Transformation of Medicine.* New York: Basic Books.

Suleiman, Ezra N. 1974. *Politics, Power, and Bureaucracy in France.* Princeton, N.J.: Princeton University Press.

Tarrow, Sidney. 1974. "Local Constraints on Regional Reform." *Comparative Politics* 7(1):1–36.

Times Higher Education Supplement. 1983. "Public Sector Research 'Essential for Standards.' " No. 572, October 21, 1983, p. 1.

Traugott, Mark, ed. 1978. *Emile Durkheim on Institutional Analysis.* Chicago, Ill.: University of Chicago Press.

Turner, Victor W. 1972. *Schism and Continuity in an African Society: A Study of Ndembu Village Life.* Manchester, England: Manchester University Press.

—— 1974. *Dramas, Fields, and Metaphors: Symbolic Action in Human Society.* Ithaca, N.Y. and London: Cornell University Press.

Van de Graaff, John. 1976. "The Politics of Innovation in French Higher Education: The University Institutes of Technology." *Higher Education* 5:189–210.

Vaughan, Michalina. 1969. "The Grandes Ecoles." In Rupert Wilkinson, ed., *Governing Elites: Studies in Training and Selection*, pp. 74–105. New York: Oxford University Press.

Venables, Peter. 1978. *Higher Education Developments: The Technological Universities, 1956–1976.* London and Boston, Mass.: Faber and Faber.

Weber, Max. 1978. *Economy and Society.* Guenther Roth and Claus Wittich, eds. Berkeley and Los Angeles: University of California Press.

Whitburn, Julia, Maurice Mealing, and Caroline Cox. 1976. *People in Polytechnics: A Survey of Polytechnic Staff and Students, 1972–3.* Guildford, Eng.: Society for Research Into Higher Education.

Williams, Gareth and Tessa Blackstone. 1983. *Response to Adversity: Higher Education in a Harsh Climate.* Guildford: Society for Research Into Higher Education.

Zeldin, Theodore. 1967. "Higher Education in France, 1848–1940." *Journal of Contemporary History* 2:53–80.

Zoglin, Mary Lou. 1981. "Community College Responsiveness: Myth or Reality?" *Journal of Higher Education* 52(4):415–26.

Zusman, Ami. 1978. "State Policy Making for Community College Adult Education." *Journal of Higher Education* 49(4):337–57.

7

Strategic Groups and Political Differentiation in the Antebellum United States

Paul Colomy

This paper addresses the issue of voluntarism within the context of a neofunctionalist approach to social change. That issue is initially discussed in terms of the relatively autonomous levels of scientific discourse. Subsequently, an empirically specified model of the voluntaristic component is developed. Elaborating the concept of strategic groups, that analytic specification partially explains significant variations in the patterns of social change.

The theoretical argument is concretized by examining the development of mass political parties in the antebellum United States. The empirical discussion indicates how strategic groups contributed to the uneven pattern of political change and the incomplete institutionalization of modern political structures in antebellum Massachusetts, New York, South Carolina, and Virginia.

The author thanks Shubhasree Subedi and Alberto Arroyo for their valuable assistance with this research. This study was supported by a University of Akron Faculty Summer Research Fellowship.

The Scientific Continuum and Voluntarism: Toward an Empirical Specification

Scientific work is conducted at different levels of abstraction, and these distinct levels can be arrayed along an epistemological continuum in terms of their relative generality and specificity (Alexander 1982a:1–35). For the social sciences this continuum, ranging from the most general to the most specific, includes the following components: presuppositions, ideological orientations, models, concepts, definitions, classifications, laws, complex and simple propositions, methodological assumptions, and observational statements (Alexander 1982a:40).

The differentiated levels of science constitute analytic or quantitative distinctions, not concrete or qualitative ones. Further, these analytic levels are "interdependent," with every scientific statement containing implicit references to each level. However, every level of scientific activity also has its own partial autonomy. Each level possesses distinctive criteria of scientific merit and is best evaluated by reference to those criteria. The partial autonomy of those components helps to explain why scholars who violently disagree at one level of scientific discourse can be in full agreement at another level (Alexander 1982a:3–5).

To date, the most incisive treatments of voluntarism have been formulated at relatively general levels of scientific discourse. Three modal positions on this issue are identifiable. The fully determinist position maintains that patterned social action is the product of externally imposed constraints, and that voluntarism is a chimerical supposition (Mayhew 1980, 1981). At the other extreme, the completely voluntaristic stance asserts that individuals are free and autonomous actors, and that social regularities are the by-product of negotiations between such independent actors (e.g., Blumer 1969). Finally, a structural-voluntarist approach argues that while "collectivist," external factors largely account for social patterns, a degree of voluntarism exists (and is particularly pronounced in modern societies) and, moreover, is critically important for fully understanding the empirical processes of change and creativity (Parsons 1937; Alexander 1978, 1982b, 1984a).

Debates between these abstract positions on the status of voluntarism are evident in a variety of sociological traditions. For example, discussion over the relation between "human agency" and "objective structures" has split contemporary Marxism into two warring camps.

On the one side, voluntarists emphasize the importance of the individual agent as the creator of society. An opposing faction, by contrast, regards individual subjects only as the bearers of objective instances. A satisfactory synthetic position incorporating the useful elements of both camps has not yet been essayed (Bottomore 1982:30–31). Similarly, it is readily apparent that animating the interminable discussions over structure versus process, stability versus change, and scientific versus naturalistic methodologies in symbolic interactionism is the more general issue of reconciling voluntarism and social organization (Meltzer and Petras 1970; Maines 1977). These two instances reflect the general debate over voluntarism that permeates virtually every major sociological tradition (see Dawe 1978).

In my view, the structural-voluntarist position is the most persuasive. Moreover, it is possible that such a "synthesis"[1] could provide a strong link between diverse sociological paradigms that might be used to bridge the barriers between purportedly irreconcilable approaches.

Nevertheless, because the different levels of science possess a partial autonomy, successful resolution of the voluntarism issue at the more general levels of scientific discourse is not automatically translated into a series of illuminating insights at more empirical levels. The central task of this paper, then, is to present the rudiments of a more empirically specified version of structural voluntarism.

Toward that end, our discussion formulates an analytic description of how concrete social groups affect social change. More specifically, in an effort to explain the uneven character and the incomplete institutionalization of a master trend of political differentiation in the antebellum United States (see chapter 4), a model of "strategic groups' is constructed. Consistently attentive to the structural factors that condition strategic groups' orientations and activities, the model attempts to describe the impact of these groups on political change and continuity.

Finally, given the variety of competing theoretical approaches, initial efforts to grapple with voluntaristic considerations at the more empirical levels will be most fruitful if formulated within existing theoretical frameworks. Working within the neofunctionalist tradition, this essay indicates how one specification of structural voluntarism contributes to a more thorough understanding of institutional development.

The model of strategic groups was specifically devised to account for variations in the pattern of political change in antebellum America. Accordingly, preceding the presentation of that model a brief overview of antebellum political developments is necessary.

Political Development in America, 1740–1850: Uneven Differentiation and Incomplete Institutionalization

Much American historiography and political science depict a master trend of political change that occurred during an early period of the nation's history. Specifically, it is asserted that from 1740 to 1850 American political leadership moved from a traditional, deferential pattern to a modern, egalitarian mass party configuration.[2] According to this view, late colonial America produced a self-conscious, comprehensive, and relatively cohesive gentry class that dominated the cultural, social, economic, and political life of each colony and that survived, battered but intact, well into the early nineteenth century. In each colony/state, the gentry's dominance was legitimated, in large part, by an integrated set of traditional values. By 1850, however, this class had lost its predominant position. While many notables continued to be leading figures in the nation's history, the comprehensive pattern of gentry rule was supplanted by a more differentiated structure of politics and political leadership.

This master trend from a traditional politics to a more modern configuration featured three important developments. First, larger numbers of "new men," often of middle- or lower-class origins and responding to relatively more differentiated channels of political mobility, began to assume positions of political authority. Second, more specialized political organizations emerged. Most significantly, mass political parties replaced the "aristocratic" factions and cliques of an earlier era. Finally, new "rules of the game" appeared, with norms of party loyalty and discipline displacing the classic, independent statesman ideal.

However, the master trend of political change was unevenly realized throughout the United States. By 1850 this master trend was most fully realized in New York. South Carolina, by contrast, was singular in its near total rejection of differentiated political leadership and in its adherence to traditional forms. Virginia produced an accommodative pattern, wherein modern components of political organization and rules of the game as well as a slight increase in the political mobility of new men were combined with elements of a traditional ruling class pattern. Further, Virginia's modern political organization and ethos were considerably more developed with regard to national elections and issues than they were with reference to state and local contests. Antebellum Massachusetts, too, evinced an accommodative configuration, adopting many of the organizational and normative innovations associated with mass party politics and allowing for a slight increase in political mobility, while in several areas the population continued to exhibit deference toward a patrician class that assumed its traditional right to rule. In sum, the transformation of political structures in the antebellum United States can be characterized as an instance of uneven differentiation, that concept denoting variation in the rate and degree of differentiation within a single institutional sphere.

In addition, those modern political structures that did appear were incompletely institutionalized. Incomplete institutionalization refers to the contingent and continually problematic character of institutional legitimation, and emphasizes the currents of opposition associated with most episodes of institution building. Thus, even in New York, where the master trend of political differentiation was most evident, relatively modern political structures were not fully accepted. Remnants of the older, established gentry elite continued to attack the new political order, and the very successes of the mass parties in consolidating their position prompted opposition from religious groups, intellectuals, and a burgeoning stratum of professional humanitarians. These diverse sources of resistance resulted in the incomplete institutionalization of mass parties in antebellum New York. In the other three states where political leadership had not moved as far toward the modern pattern, resistance and opposition to the new politics were also evident. Accordingly, in these areas, too, the differentiated elements that did surface were characterized by incomplete institutionalization.

The patterns of change just described establish an explanatory agenda for differentiation theory. In addition to formulating useful descriptive concepts, such as uneven differentiation and incomplete institutionalization, differentiation theorists must also explain these types of transformation. One avenue for such theoretical elaboration is charted below.

Strategic Groups

There have been few attempts to develop adequate explanations of differentiation.[3] Several earlier statements (e.g., Parsons 1966, 1971; Bellah 1964; Keller 1963; Fox 1976) employed the differentiation schema as a taxonomic device to classify societies, institutions, and roles in terms of their relative complexity. However, the concepts of uneven differentiation and incomplete institutionalization underscore the need for an explanatory framework capable of accounting for both variations in the rate and degree of differentiation and the imperfect legitimation accorded newly differentiated structures.

A fully satisfactory explanation of uneven differentiation and incomplete institutionalization would explore both structural and voluntaristic factors. With regard to political change and continuity in the United States, the most pertinent structural elements include the pattern of cleavage structures, the constitutional opportunity structures, and the reigning cultural codes. A complete structural analysis would demonstrate how each state's particular configuration of these components influenced the rate and degree of political differentiation and the level of legitimation accorded differentiated structures. These factors have been more thoroughly examined elsewhere (see Colomy 1982, 1985), and my primary focus here is on the voluntaristic elements that shaped antebellum political development. At the same time, throughout the discussion there are references to the structural elements that conditioned the orientations and activities of the most important political actors.

Structural conditions establish broad limits on the types of new social arrangements that are likely to arise. Nevertheless, within these limits there are usually several different paths along which institutional change can evolve. In short, similar structural configurations can produce a variety of distinct institutional outcomes (Smelser 1974; Eisenstadt 1964:382–86, 1968:230–33). For example, although antebellum Virginia and South Carolina shared many of the same structural characteristics, including a similar pattern of cleavage structures between each state's eastern and western regions, a restrictive constitutional opportunity structure, and a traditional, deferential cultural code, the Old Dominion accommodated several components of relatively modern political institutions while the Palmetto state eschewed virtually every element of the politically modernist pattern.

Analytically, concrete groups pursuing specific material and ideal interests intervene between these "collectivistic," external, structural conditions and subsequent patterns of change. The groups' orientations and activities frequently function as "selective mechanisms" that determine which specific institutional formation, among the limited array of possibilities, becomes crystallized.

The study of how concrete actors influence the course of structural change has been most fully developed by Smelser and Eisenstadt. In an analysis of public higher education in California, Smelser (1974) identified several "academic estates" that figured prominently in the episodes of structural change and conflict that occurred on many campuses throughout the 1960s and into the early 1970s. In several substantive and theoretical treatises, Eisenstadt has developed the more general notion of institutional entrepreneurs, which he applied to those specific actors who direct the course of differentiation in a wide variety of institutional settings. More specifically, the concept of institutional entrepreneurs refers to small groups of individuals who formulate broad symbolic orientations, articulate innovative goals, establish new organizational and normative frameworks to pursue the goals, and mobilize the resources necessary to attain the goals (Eisenstadt 1964, 1965, 1971, 1973; Eisenstadt and Curelaru 1976).

Introducing sophisticated treatments of voluntarism and a measure of historical specificity, Smelser's and Eisenstadt's formulations constitute significant "breakthroughs" in differentiation theory. Theoretically, I seek to extend these advances by correcting certain omissions. In particular, while Smelser's analysis identifies very general collective interests and values that impel specific academic estates to support or resist institutional change, his discussion fails to distinguish between the elements of each estate who actively promote or oppose change and those who do not actively participate. Further, he does not account for conflicts *within* academic estates, nor does he discuss the consequences of those internal tensions.

Eisenstadt's model of institutional entrepreneurs also omits important considerations. First, the concept of the institutional entrepreneur is primarily designed to explain the master trend of differentiation; the formulation must be generalized if it is to account for uneven differentiation, incomplete institutionalization, and other patterned departures from the master trend. Second, his discussion of entrepreneurs' orientations is presented primarily in substantive terms and lacks analytic precision. Third, Eisenstadt does not give sufficient attention to the presence of conflict and divisiveness within entrepreneurial groups. Finally, he overemphasizes the impact of innovative groups in establishing new structural arrangements and neglects the processes by which groups initially opposed to an innovation can, subsequently, act to promote its institutionalization.

These omissions prompt, first, the generalization of the voluntaristic intent underlying Smelser's and Eisenstadt's models. In particular, I propose the more inclusive concept of strategic groups as an analytic means of incorporating a variety of more specific voluntaristic formations under a single rubric. Strategic groups designate the individuals and groups who assume leadership in directing the course of institutional development. Employing substantive and temporal criteria to elaborate the concept, I argue that strategic groups include several distinct types of collectivities, ranging from those who take the lead in introducing new levels of differentiation (who, following Eisenstadt, can be referred to as institutional entrepreneurs), to those who are attracted to the entrepreneurs' innovations and aspire to implement similar structures in their own communities (institutional followers), to those who assume leadership in protecting existing structural arrangements (institutional conservatives) and finally including those who forge working compromises between extant and newly proposed levels of differentiation (institutional accommodationists).

In very broad terms, this particular specification of voluntarism suggests the following scenario of how strategic groups shape institutional development. In a decentralized or "federalized" system (e.g., the antebellum United States), change in a particular institutional domain produces a "ripple effect." Often, institutional change is introduced in one unit (e.g., a state) and other units subsequently adopt similar innovations. Voluntaristically, entrepreneurs in the original unit initiate change and that pattern of innovation is then embraced and acted upon by institutional followers in other units.

Once a new level of differentiation is proposed or realized in one or several units of a decentralized system, the traditional character of previously established, diffuse structures is increasingly subject to critical scrutiny. Earlier, those arrangements had been partially legitimated because "they had always been that way." However, the ripple effect awakens a sense of alternatives and the possibility of transforming those time-tested arrangements. Consequently, the legitimation of these conventional structures moves beyond traditionalism to conservatism. That conservative defense is partly reflected in the active intervention of leadership groups—institutional conservatives—who seek to bolster up the old order, and to protect their particular interests.

Finally, once the innovative and conservative positions are solidified, the grounds for a "middle road" of institutional compromise are established. Accommodationists self-consciously promote institutional structures that combine new and traditional elements.

This scenario provides a cursory sketch of strategic groups' contributions to the pattern of uneven political differentiation in the antebellum United States. However, it is both possible and desirable to move beyond this abbreviated outline and toward a more empirically grounded treatment of strategic groups and their impact on political change and continuity. Therefore, in the more substantive discussion that follows I explore how New York's Albany Regency, South Carolina's Calhounites, Virginia's Richmond Junto, and Massachusetts's Boston Associates and their allies shaped political developments in their respective states.[4]

Further, through such a more detailed analysis one can begin to redress some of the omissions in Smelser's and Eisenstadt's pioneering efforts. Accordingly, I address three crucial aspects of strategic groups. First, the orientations of strategic groups are analyzed in terms of three mechanisms—an institutional project, prototypes, and generalized values. Second, the various grounds of diversity and coordination within strategic groups are explored. Finally, the coalitional and conflictual relations between strategic groups and their allies and opponents are examined.

Orientations.   The activities of strategic groups and their impact on the institutional order are partially determined by their orientations which, in turn, are the product of a combination of mechanisms. A fundamental component of strategic groups' orientations is adherence to a broad institutional project. Institutional models serving as prototypes further specify the project. Finally, the project is elaborated and legitimated by drawing an intimate connection between it and generalized value patterns.

Institutional Projects.   Central to strategic groups' activities is an institutional project or mission that combines ideological and normative commitments with the self-interested construction or preservation of a social niche.[5] The project identifies the social sector in which change is sought, resisted, or accommodated, and specifies those social functions to be satisfied by a new or existing institutional arrangement. While sharing these elements, the projects of institutional entrepreneurs, institutional conservatives, and institutional accommodationists display distinctive features.

Integral to the entrepreneurs' project is the delegitimation of established practices and the construction of new bases of legitimacy. In this regard, the project assumes the character of a "contrast conception" vis-à-vis established practices, which are denounced as inefficient, ineffective, and inequitable. The proposed institutional structure is promoted as a remedy for these ills. Finally, the institutional project identifies a potentially new source of material interest, viz., the construction of an organizational niche.

The project of institutional followers is proposed as a faithful reflection of entrepreneurs' innovations. Followers' projects, like the entrepreneurs', are also presented as contrast conceptions to established practices.

The conservatives' project is organized around a virulent defense of existing practices and a complementary critique of proposed alterations. The conservative project also assumes the form of a contrast conception, juxtaposing the sacred legacy of the founding fathers against the sacrilegious changes advocated by self-interested entrepreneurs. Existing practices are pronounced essential for stability, order, and harmony. Finally, the conservative project aspires to protect the myriad interests endangered by institutional change.

While the projects of institutional entrepreneurs and conservatives are relatively clear and, in many ways, are simply mirror images of one another, the institutional accommodationists' mission is fraught with ambivalence. Elements of established practices are condemned and certain reforms are suggested, but the critique is rarely generalized and the proposed alterations are usually piecemeal. In short, change is proposed so that continuity might be restored. Accommodationists resemble entrepreneurs "with the brakes on," sponsoring change, in part, to protect traditional interests. However, in contrast to conservatives, accommodationists also attempt to broaden the circle of interest, claiming that those previously excluded will have a stake in the modified institutional arrangements.

These general observations about institutional projects appear to make sense of the concrete projects of strategic groups in antebellum New York, South Carolina, Virginia, and Massachusetts.

The Albany Regency, the leading political party entrepreneurs in antebellum New York and the dominant entrepreneurial group behind the creation of the national Democratic party in Jacksonian America, promoted parties as effective instruments for increasing both political participation and voter control over government (Remini 1958, 1959; McCormick 1966:104–24; Wallace 1969, 1973; Hofstadter 1969:212–71; Niven 1983:23–155). The Regency's project included more specific goals such as keeping citizens informed about governmental activities and providing genuine political choices to the electorate. Mass parties were envisioned as permanent organizations independent of any one person, with a leadership responsive to their members. Mobility within the organization was to be dependent on dedicated service to the party.

The institutional project was presented, in part, as a contrast conception to the established modes of political organization which, according to the Regency, were personalistic, temporary, and aristocratic factions allocating political preferment on the basis of family pedigree. The advocacy of political parties as a virtual panacea for the problems engendered by such "aristocratic" domination subsequently became a source of disillusionment with that institution, figuring prominently in later efforts to reform the party system.

The Regency's institutional project acknowledged that significant interests were attendant upon creating mass parties. Patronage and the assumption of leadership within the party organization were the primary material rewards available to party entrepreneurs and their allies (Remini 1958).

In South Carolina, John C. Calhoun and his faction articulated a conservative project (Freehling 1965a:89–91, 330–33; Freehling 1965b; Schultz 1950:3–25; Brady 1972:187–208; Faust 1982:40–43). Reacting to the successes of party entrepreneurs throughout the nation and especially in New York, these institutional conservatives advocated a quasi-aristocratic version of democracy, envisioning a society ruled by gentlemen. Stability, public order, and the protection of liberty all required the enlightened rule of disinterested notables. Only these "natural aristocrats," it was asserted, would aspire to the highest ideals of statesmanship and promote a principled politics. Only the traditional pattern of leadership could ensure that the public welfare would be promoted and that liberty would be protected.

By contrast, the new politics threatened society's liberty and order by enshrining the rule of self-interested party managers and spoilsmen. Mass parties enriched the spoilsman at the expense of the public, and undermined statesmanship. The partisan dispensation of patronage invariably perverted power and, in the hands of unscrupulous demagogues, party patronage could become a source of dictatorial powers. Political parties also generated disorder that party hacks sought to exploit for their own advantage. Finally, parties minimized the effectiveness of men of high character and exceptional ability.

The Calhounites' defense of traditional modes of political organization and leadership was partially inspired by a concern for protecting material interests. First, these conservatives were the very natural aristocrats lauded in their approbation of conventional politics. Thus, their project was, in part, an assertion of their own political and social interests. In addition, these conservative South Carolinians articulated a distinctive southern and regional interest, largely manifest in the protection of slavery and in antiprotective tariff sentiment. For them national parties, premised on a series of compromises between northern and southern wings of the parties, posed a grave threat to the southern "way of life." In the conservatives' view, traditional politics were more adept than mass party politics at protecting vital southern interests.

In Virginia, the Richmond Junto, a group of institutional accommodationists, articulated a project that appropriated many elements of the Regency's innovative institutional vision, while tempering the rough democratic edges of that enterprise (Ambler 1913; Ammon 1948, 1953, 1963; Harrison 1970; Dent 1974; Remini 1959:29, 41, 64, 130–33, 192; Niven 1983:178–82; McCormick 1966:184–99). The Junto's primary concerns included the maintenance of Virginia's influence on the national polity and the protection of states' rights from illegitimate usurpation by the federal government. Toward that end, the Junto joined forces with the Albany Regency and thereby established the basis for the national Democratic party. This alliance of "southern planters and northern democrats" generated significant changes in Virginia's politics. Most significantly, presidential and congressional elections and, to a lesser extent, state assembly elections increasingly fell under the purview of the modern party, with organization and discipline the new watchwords. The Junto welcomed and promoted these changes, justifying them as essential for continued Virginian prominence in national affairs and the preservation of states' rights.

Still, unlike the institutional entrepreneurs in New York, the Junto did not couple these organizational innovations with a generalized critique of gentry political domination. To be sure, individual members of the Junto, especially editor Thomas Ritchie, often proposed reforms—e.g., an extension of the suffrage, more equitable apportionment of seats within the state assembly, a restructuring of the county court system, and educational reform. However, these reform sentiments were usually either ignored or opposed by other members of the Junto and, ultimately, were tangential to the construction of mass parties in Virginia. It is more accurate to say that mass parties were built alongside the structure of gentry rule and, on occasion, reinforced it and, at other times, opposed it. Moreover, unlike the Regency, the Junto itself remained oligarchic, closed, secretive, and premised on familial connections.

Finally, unlike the Albany Regency, the Richmond Junto did not envision a party organization that unified all levels of government. The Junto exhibited an almost obsessive fascination with national politics, while state and local disputes were usually resolved outside the (national) party framework.

Materially, the Richmond Junto sought to secure federal patronage for Virginians and to preserve Virginia's influence on national affairs. The Junto also desired to protect the relative freedom of the state and her institutions from federal encroachment.

In Massachusetts, the Boston Associates and their allies formulated an institutional project consisting of three primary components (Howe 1979:11–68; Darling 1925:183, 199–200; Dalzell 1973:30–34; Brauer 1967:7–29). First, they argued that economic and social development required rational guidance, which could be most effectively supplied by government. The latter, in turn, would be most judiciously directed by a society's natural leaders and notables. In concrete terms, these accommodationists strongly supported Clay's "American System," a political program that included national tariffs to protect domestic industry, various government-sponsored internal improvements (e.g., canals, roads, and bridges), and a national bank to regulate the currency.

Second, the inner circle of Massachusetts Whiggery emphasized morality. This was evident in an aggressive didacticism whose primary object was individual and social redemption. In this regard, these accommodationists advocated a variety of reforms and public works designed to uplift individuals and the community: educational and prison reform; care for the deaf, mute, and blind; the creation of libraries and hospitals; and a variety of philanthropic activities.

Finally, the Boston Associates articulated a theory of "natural harmonies," maintaining that all social classes, economic interests, and regions shared similar concerns and that aid to a particular class, interest, or region ultimately benefited the entire nation. Thus, in contrast to the Calhounites, these accommodationists adhered to a nationalistic outlook and labored incessantly to maintain a viable alliance between the northern and southern wings of the Whig party. They regarded national parties as essential to national unity and to the triumph of the Whig program. Consequently, between 1834 and 1854 the core group of Massachusetts Whigs opposed all programs that would alienate southern Whigs.

Massachusetts Whiggery sharpened the contours of its institutional project by contrasting it to the Democratic project. Whereas the Democrats held a laissez-faire attitude toward morality and economic development, the Boston Associates promoted a "positive liberal state" wherein the government assumed responsibility to regulate society in a manner designed to improve the general welfare, raise the level of opportunity for all men, and assist all individuals in developing their potential. In addition, Massachusetts accommodationists often presented themselves as an "antiparty" party that decried the Democrats' extreme partisanship and the excesses of their spoils system.

Materially, the Boston Associates, most of whom were intimately involved in manufacturing, derived direct benefits from the high protective tariffs, the internal improvements, and the national bank of the American System. In addition, despite the protestations directed against the Democrats, Massachusetts Whigs, when in office, practiced their own version of the spoils system, awarding attractive offices to themselves and their allies and promoting public policies that favored their own enterprises.

Prototyping.   Strategic groups' institutional projects are usually elaborated and further specified by the adoption of a prototype.[6] Prototyping denotes a general process whereby groups draw upon institutional exemplars from the past or present to supplement and extend their projects. Prototypes serve both cognitive and legitimating functions. Cognitively, prototypes function as metaphors that give direction to a strategic group's activities and provide potential constituents with an established frame of reference for interpreting their project. Further, institutional prototypes are usually imbued with value, and strategic groups often stress the apparent "isomorphism" (Meyer and Rowan 1977; DiMaggio and Powell 1983) between the prototype and the group's institutional project, with the aim of attracting greater support and defusing criticism.

It is useful to distinguish two types and two phases of prototyping. In the first type, strategic groups draw on historical, institutional exemplars from their society, stressing the continuity between what they advocate and what existed previously. This type of prototyping has a revivalistic character, with strategic groups claiming to seek only the resurrection of cherished and hallowed forms from the past. The cognitive and legitimating functions of revivalistic prototyping are clear—the older institutional exemplars provide a stable, cognitive frame of reference, while their putative sacred character lends legitimacy to the projects of strategic groups.

A second form of prototyping occurs when strategic groups use the arrangements of other institutional spheres within the same society as models. This cross-institutional prototyping is particularly salient in the metaphors strategic groups use to inform the orientations and participation of adherents to their enterprises. In adopting these institutional analogues, strategic groups may also alter them, infusing them with new meaning. Nevertheless, the adoption of metaphors and the employment of practices associated with revered institutions imparts a legitimacy to the efforts and projects of strategic groups.

In addition to revivalistic and cross-institutional prototypes, there are two phases of prototyping, viz., the innovative and the derivative. In the innovative phase, institutional entrepreneurs draw upon revivalistic and cross-institutional prototypes to construct and implement their vision of a more differentiated institutional order. In the derivative phase, the entrepreneurs' burgeoning structure is, itself, taken as a point of reference by other strategic groups. Institutional followers, inspired by the new institutional order, employ the structure as a prototype for their own innovative activities. Institutional conservatives treat the new structure as a negative reference institution, and seek to stifle developments within their own bailiwick and elsewhere that appear sympathetic to the new order. Finally, accommodationists selectively adopt elements of the more differentiated institution and fuse them with more traditional patterns.

In New York, the Albany Regency employed both revivalistic and cross-institutional prototypes to organize and legitimate their vision of a modern, differentiated party system (Remini 1959:23–26, 29, 30–42, 123–46, 196–98; Hofstadter 1969:226–31; Niven 1983:30–34, 178–80; Nichols 1967:264–65). Although Martin Van Buren and other members of the Regency introduced many significant changes in political organization and were among the first to build a genuine mass political party, they were forever claiming that their efforts were aimed at the simple restoration of the "old Republican party." One student of the antebellum New York political scene notes, "Martin Van Buren's rhetoric echoed constantly the belief that his activities involved no innovations but were designed to achieve a 'general resuscitation' for the 'old democratic party' " (Kass 1965:3). In his autobiography and his history of political parties, Van Buren continually refers to the continuity and intimate connection between the state and national party he helped to construct and the old Jeffersonian party (Van Buren 1867, 1920). Moreover, the Regency invariably presented itself to its followers and potential adherents as the "last authentic heir of the original Republican party" (Kass 1965:112). It is true that elements of the Regency's political organization were drawn from the old party—including the party caucus, the central committee, the corresponding committee, and the partisan use of patronage and the press. Less often acknowledged, however, was the fact that the Regency substantially refined and developed these elements and added new ones—especially the positive evaluation of the party system and its functions, the systematic elaboration of party organization throughout the state and local communities, the insistence upon party discipline and loyalty, and the acceptance of a legitimate opposition—so that the party system it sponsored was qualitatively different from the one created by Jefferson and Madison. In short, the old Republican party served as a prototype that shaped the vision and legitimated the project of the Albany Regency.

The Regency also drew on cross-institutional prototypes to create a differentiated party organization (Goldman 1970, 1972; Hofstadter 1969:244–45). These entrepreneurs relied on military rhetoric and imagery to shape their vision of modern political organization. For the Regency, the ideal party man was the "democratic soldier," who was characterized by a self-effacing attitude and voluntary self-sacrifice to party welfare. Party loyalty and obedience, the new political virtues, were modeled after the regimentation and discipline associated with military organization. Considerable concern was also expressed over "deserters" and "traitors." Moreover, partisan tactics and campaigns, party struggles, and notions of political opposition, victory, and defeat were conceived and expressed in the language of military warfare. The pervasive use of military imagery is largely explained by the fact that entrepreneurs and their supporters perceived and partially patterned political parties after combat organizations that required discipline and militaristic severity. Such rhetoric was useful, in part, because it resonated with a fund of shared military experience and because leading political personalities were often known for their military exploits and bearing.

Adopting revivalistic and cross-institutional prototypes, the Albany Regency constructed a mass party organization and a new style of politics that were clearly differentiated from traditional patterns. The Regency's success in creating this new organizational and normative framework marked the most innovative phase of institution building. Once constructed, New York's Democratic party began to serve as a prototype for followers in other states as the prototyping process entered its derivative phase.

The substantial progress of the master trend of political differentiation in antebellum America is partially due to the large number and relative success of those institutional followers who employed New York's Democratic party as a prototype for their own institution-building activities. Accordingly, "Regency style politics quickly traversed New York boundaries. The organization code, carried by New York emigres or imitated by local politicians across the country, powerfully altered the political culture of the middle period" (Wallace 1973:185). A sizable number of early nineteenth-century American institutional followers employed the Regency model as a prototype for transforming fledgling, informal political associations into disciplined, modern party organizations. For example, in Illinois Stephen A. Douglas, drawing on his knowledge of New York Regency politics, introduced the party nominating convention into Illinois' politics and thereby contributed to the emergence of a disciplined party apparatus (Capers 1959:14–15; Johannsen 1973:25–31, 38–49, 57–60; Johnson 1908:10, 24–29, 38–42; Douglas 1961 [1835, 1837]:24–31, 42–50). Though many traditional Illinois politicians initially opposed the innovation, Douglas successfully countered with the argument that having observed the operation of the convention system in New York, he was convinced that it was the only way to manage elections with success.

In South Carolina, however, the Regency and the new politics it inaugurated served as a negative-reference institution. Calhoun and his allies thundered against mass parties. In his *Disquisition on Government*, Calhoun ranted against the vices of party politics: "in the violent strifes between parties for the high and glittering prize of governmental honors and emoluments—falsehood, injustice, fraud, artifice, slander, and breach of faith, are freely resorted to, as legitimate weapons;—followed by all their corrupting and debasing influences" (Calhoun 1853:49–50; see also Freehling 1965a:331). And in his correspondence it is clear that Calhoun holds the "New York School of Politicks" in special contempt (see Calhoun's letter to Henry St. George Tucker, March 1843). Calhounites frequently contrasted the new politics' celebration of spoilsmen with South Carolina's pattern of gentlemanly rule in which "the best men" exercised public authority (Faust 1982:42).

Further, Calhounites disputed the Regency's claim to be the authentic heir to the old Republican party. They charged that the Regency, in fact, had actually distorted the genuine principles of the old party (see Calhoun's letter to Duff Green, October 2, 1844).

These institutional conservatives coupled their employment of the Regency as a negative-reference institution with their own version of a revivalistic prototype (Freehling 1965a:331, 1965b:36; Hofstadter 1969:252–56). The Calhounites argued that in the era of the founding generation, the dominant pattern of political authority was reign by "natural aristocrats." However, in the age of Jackson the philosopher-statesman had given way to the party manager and the demagogue. The Calhounites saw themselves waging a principled struggle to restore the founding fathers' principles and their pattern of deferential leadership. Thus, whereas the Regency saw the new parties as a resurrection of forms established by "the great generation," the Calhounites saw them as evidence of declension from the ways of the founding fathers.

The Richmond Junto was more receptive to the Regency's modern conception of the party. Indeed, the construction of the national Democratic party was partially premised on a Van Buren–initiated alliance between the Albany Regency and the Richmond Junto (Harrison 1956; Remini 1959:129–33). Integral to that coalition was the Junto's partial adoption of the Regency model of politics. By 1830, "the Richmond Junto had largely accepted Van Buren's view of party" (Dent 1974:195).

That acceptance was selective. In national elections, the Junto employed political strategies and organizational forms that had been refined by the Regency. The Junto, like the Regency, also insisted upon a degree of party loyalty and obedience. On the other hand, though, unlike the Albany Regency, the Junto did not fully embrace a military metaphor to organize and legitimate political participation, and the Junto and Virginian politics generally displayed a notably less disciplined politics: "Virginia politicians, because of the very nature of the state's political and social structure, were far more individualistic and independent of organizational control than the New York breed" (McCormick 1966:185). Further, the Richmond Junto never attempted to organize and integrate politically the Virginian Democratic party at the national, state, and local levels to the same degree evident in New York.

In addition to this selective adoption of the Regency model, the Junto's accommodationist vision entertained a distinctive version of a revivalistic prototype. The Junto envisioned itself and presented the state's Democratic party to others as the true heirs of the Jeffersonian-Madisonian legacy. Thus, Thomas Ritchie, chieftain of the Junto, "wanted to reconstitute the Old Republican party" (Dent 1974:58–59). William C. Rives, another central figure in the Junto, revealed that "we all look back to the administration of Mr. Jefferson as the golden age of the republic, and would eagerly catch at the faintest prospects of restoring it, and bringing back the maxims of his policy" (see Rives' letter to Thomas Gilmer, July 22, 1827).

This revivalistic prototype was partially based on ideological grounds, animated by a concern for resuscitating the old states' rights doctrine as penned by Jefferson and Madison in the Kentucky and Virginia resolutions of 1798 and the Virginia Report of 1799 and celebrated in the "revolution" of 1800. However, there was also an important organizational component to this prototype, for the Junto-Regency coalition was an effort to resurrect the old Republican party which had been built upon a New York–Virginia alliance (Niven 1983:178–82).

The Boston Associates, like the Calhounites, typically employed the Regency model as a negative-reference institution and attacked its nefarious influence on the republic. At the same time, however, this critique was combined with a less publicly avowed admiration for the Regency's organizational innovations (Formisano 1983:307–9). This ambivalence was reflected in the Boston Associates' creation of an antiparty party.

In addition to its ambivalent stance toward the Regency model, the inner core of Massachusetts Whiggery employed both cross-institutional and revivalistic prototypes (Formisano 1983:262–67; Howe 1979:32–33). The religious revival and the factory were utilized as cross-institutional prototypes. The Bay State's Whigs sought to duplicate the style and modes of religious revivals and tapped the wells of popular enthusiasm that animated revivalism. They imparted to their campaigns the flavor of religious revivals. In addition, the factory—harnessing the power of a permanent system with interchangeable parts—was also employed as a prototype. However, this machine metaphor had limits, and recognizing that not every part of the party system was equally interchangeable the Whig state central committee advised local committees in several communities that "nothing effectual can be done without the cooperation of influential persons in every town" (Formisano 1983:265).

The Boston Associates also employed revivalistic prototypes (Welter 1975:31, 191–92; Howe 1979:69–95; Formisano 1983:269). Like the Regency, the Calhounites, and the Junto, the Boston Associates claimed to be the true heirs to the Republican party. Thus Daniel Webster, leader of the Massachusetts accommodationists and an ex-Federalist, willingly aligned himself with Jefferson in his opposition to executive power. In fact, the historical allusions revived by the Whig appellation preceded the Republican-Federalist conflict. The term *Whig* drew upon an enduring "commonwealth" tradition, which heralded the "country party's" opposition to executive despotism. Such opposition rhetoric appealed strongly to the Whigs, who lost most of the presidential elections held between 1834 and 1854. In addition, the appellation was also an effort to claim kinship with the Whigs and patriots of the American Revolution, who had also fought against executive power. The Boston Associates and their allies frequently referred to their efforts as a second American Revolution, asserting that the great battle waged for human liberty in 1776 remained the battle that each generation must fight in order to be free. Finally, drawing on the rich rhetoric of the country party tradition, Massachusetts Whigs accused the Democrat Andrew Jackson of "Ceasarism," and argued that this "despot" was conspiring to enhance the power of the presidency (see Howe 1979:69–95).

Overall, then, the Regency, employing revivalistic and cross-institutional prototypes to supplement its institutional project, fashioned a differentiated organizational and normative framework for politics. Once created, this new political style and organization served as a positive-reference institution for many institutional followers across the country who constructed similarly differentiated political structures. The success of these followers partially explains the progress of the master trend of political differentiation. At the same time, however, the New York model served as a negative-reference institution for other groups. In South Carolina, conservatives denounced the new school of politics and, drawing on their own version of a revivalistic prototype, tenaciously clung to the traditional pattern of political leadership. Accommodationists in Virginia and Massachusetts adopted several elements of the Regency model and combined them with more traditional elements of each state's political culture. In this manner, then, prototypes shaped the orientations and activities of strategic groups and contributed to the uneven pattern of political differentiation in antebellum America.

Values. Both the institutional project and prototypes are supplemented with values. By "connecting" their institutional vision to a society's most central values, strategic groups seek to legitimate their projects and to attract a broad base of popular support.

Two aspects of culture are important for understanding the impact of values on institutional change. The first aspect is captured by the "cultural refraction" model of culture/society relations (Alexander 1984b). That model applies to societies where a comprehensive and integrated cultural system is subject to conflicting interpretations by competing social groups and interests. In the antebellum United States, republicanism exhibited this refracted character.

Crystallized in the writings of British opposition theorists, republicanism assumed a hegemonic position during the late colonial and revolutionary periods, and shaped American political thought and policy throughout the antebellum period. Republicanism viewed power with great suspicion. It was a commonplace that power, though necessary, posed a constant threat to liberty, which was the most highly cherished republican value. Any concentration of power, in any institution but especially in government, was a source of great danger. The preservation of liberty required both the establishment of different branches of government and the division of power between rulers and the ruled, the latter exercising ultimate authority over elected representatives. Liberty could also be weakened by corruption of the rulers or citizens. The republics would be preserved only if its citizens and officials adopted the traditional virtues of industry, frugality, simplicity, independence, and fortitude. In addition, there was an ambiguous egalitarian thrust in republicanism which on the one hand recognized social distinctions and on the other emphasized equal rights and dignity. Finally, republican doctrine identified public welfare as the exclusive end of good government and called for the sacrifice of individual interests to the greater needs of the whole. This republican tenet underscored an organic vision of society and was partially expressed in the frequent indictment of "selfish" factions and parties. (This brief summary of republicanism is drawn from Bailyn 1967:55–93; Wood 1969:46–90; Shalhope 1972, 1980:59–69; and Schwartz 1983.) The hegemony of republicanism and the political institutions founded in its name were buttressed by the deferential mentality of antebellum leaders and citizens to the standards and public achievements of the "founding fathers" (Forgie 1979).

The republican legacy strongly shaped party entrepreneurs' orientations, and elements of that cultural tradition were utilized to legitimate their institutional projects. Regency members envisioned their institutional innovations as concrete expressions of republican doctrine. For example, Van Buren, assuredly the single most important party entrepreneur, "was convinced that he represented the true (republican) inheritance of Jefferson and Madison" (Hofstadter 1969:227). The psycho-symbolic dimension of this republican revivification is partially evident in the political pilgrimage Van Buren undertook to Jefferson's Monticello, where he "soaked up the purest form of republicanism" (Remini 1959:60) and received the old republican's benediction for the burgeoning party structure (Van Buren 1920:182–88).

Finally, the republican antipathy to centralized power was integral to the new institution's imagery and the party's platform (Benson 1961:216–37).

In South Carolina, conservatives asserted that the New York school was antirepublican. Calhounites resurrected and repeated verbatim classic republicanism's antipathy toward the party system. Mimicking old republican doctrine, they contended that parties threatened the public welfare and were the artifice of deceitful demagogues (Freehling 1965b). These conservatives held that the enlightened leadership of the "best men," evincing a genuine and disinterested concern for the public good, was the true heritage of republicanism. On another level, they contended that their (extreme) interpretation of states' rights more nearly reflected republican strictures than the Regency's hypocritical and self-serving lip service to that doctrine (Freehling 1965a).

In Virginia, the states' rights element of republicanism was central. Although few Virginians carried the doctrine to the Calhounite extreme, by 1820 (and largely in response to the perceived decline of Virginia's economic and political power) the Junto and others revived old republican principles, which then acquired the character of a liturgy and intellectual orthodoxy (Risjord 1965). Assuming "the emotional power of a political religion," (Peterson 1960:37) the states' rights doctrine encouraged Virginians to be "jealous" of their liberties and rights and to scrutinize the policies of the federal government for signs of consolidation and usurpation. This doctrine, along with the notion of "strict construction," were the republican tenets the Junto most frequently drew upon in shaping its vision of Virginia's Democratic party.

The sacred texts of the states' rights dogma were the Kentucky and Virginia resolutions of 1798 and the Virginia Report of 1799, penned by Jefferson and Madison. In their hands, states' rights had been wedded to egalitarian sentiments and such specific reforms as popular sovereignty, an increase in the number of elective offices, and equitable apportionment premised on population. During the 1820s, however, as the states' rights doctrine assumed its sacrosanct status, Jefferson and Madison's synthesis became more problematic. Some members of the Junto did combine their commitment to states' rights with a concern for egalitarian values and measures, but others broke completely with the synthesis, embracing only states' rights (Peterson 1966:271–85).

The Boston Associates emphasized the organic, collectivistic nature of classic republicanism, arguing that on occasion the individual must sacrifice his welfare to the needs of the whole community (Kelley 1979:83–84, 95, 137, 271, 273; Howe 1979:18–21, 32–35; Formisano 1983:297–301). They stressed an individual's social duties and responsibilities rather than his rights or liberties. In addition to this organic conception of society, the Boston Associates highlighted the moralistic thrust of republicanism and asserted that the moral order must be vigilantly defended against a wide variety of contemporary vices and temptations. Finally, the Boston Associates constantly warned against the dangers posed by excessive executive power, and frequently championed congressional authority as a constitutional antidote to executive "despotism."

Within the expansive context of the republicanism the second aspect of culture, which symbolic interactionists refer to as "general movements," assumes significance. General movements are salient cultural themes and mass preoccupations with certain values such as equality or liberty (Blumer 1939:258; Turner and Killian 1972:281–82). While general movements lack organizational identity, they nevertheless exert a powerful influence by providing value orientations to organized collectivities mobilized in support of or opposition to change.

The Jacksonian era witnessed the birth of a general movement centered around egalitarianism. One well-informed student of the age notes: "Egalitarianism expressed the central tendency of the period. ... After 1815, not only in politics but in all spheres of American life, egalitarianism challenged elitism and, in most spheres and places, egalitarianism won" (Benson 1961:336). It is, of course, largely on the basis of observations gleaned from Jacksonian America that Tocqueville wrote of the irreversible trend toward equality; many other scholars have described the impact of a diffuse egalitarianism on intellectual, social, political, legal, economic, and professional life in the early national period (see Ward 1953; Welter 1975:77–104; Haskell 1977:63–90; Meyers 1957; Hofstadter 1962:145–71; Pole 1978:112–47; Schlesinger 1945: 306–90).

The Albany Regency borrowed elements from the egalitarian general movement to generate a blistering attack on the "aristocratic" character of traditional politics (Wallace 1969, 1973; Hofstadter 1969:212–71; Shade 1981:79). Concomitantly, the Regency affirmed the intimate connection between the new institutional order—mass party structures—and egalitarianism. The Regency held, for example, that parties were democratic associations responsible to the majority of the membership. As a popular organization, the party enabled men from all walks of life to participate in government.

Political officials and party representatives were to abide by the expressed will of the majority; political leaders were to consider themselves the instruments of the party organization. The proper criteria for advancement were not family pedigree or wealth, but faithful dedication to the party and long service in its support. Ideally, the modern party gave all members equal voices and equal chances to rise to positions of leadership. It also provided members with equal chances of receiving patronage. Unlike the aristocratic clique, the modern party was not the property of a man or a family, but transcended all of its individual members.

An equally significant cultural dynamic is the tendency for a general movement to generate a countermovement—a spirited defense of values and standards threatened by the ascendance of the initial movement (Alexander and Colomy 1985a, 1985b). This type of cultural reaction often shapes the orientations of institutional conservatives seeking to protect existing organizational and normative frameworks, and of institutional accommodationists interested in fashioning alternative institutional arrangements partially reflecting a cultural tradition that is losing widespread support in the face of an ascendant general movement.

Thus, the egalitarian general movement did not succeed in erasing all traces of traditional elitism. Although the strong current of egalitarianism placed elitism on the defensive, elements of the older cultural pattern persisted in many areas, especially South Carolina. In that state, the powerful Calhoun faction sought to design a political organization consistent with the tenets of traditional elitism. Accordingly, these conservatives emphasized the statesman ideal and deference toward notables. The latter enshrined the officeholder who displayed an unwillingness to subordinate self to party, majority will, or the expressed desires of constituents when these conflicted with his own reasoned judgment. Schooled in the elitist tradition, these South Carolinians eschewed the construction of an impersonal party organization and the celebration of egalitarian sentiment as a cynical means of garnering votes. This defense of elitism shaped the orientations and activities of the Calhounites and contributed to the state's more traditional organizational and normative framework for politics (Banner 1974; Faust 1982:39–45; Calhoun 1853:55–59).

Treading on the path toward accommodation, the Junto sponsored a party structure that included both elements consistent with the general egalitarian movement and features more in line with traditional elitism. On the one hand, several Junto members insisted upon such antielitist measures as party loyalty and discipline, the subordination of individual judgment to the party, the dispensation of state patronage on the basis of party regularity, and legislative instructions to senators (Eaton 1952).

Still, these accommodationists never completely abandoned traditional tenets of elitism—upper-class stewardship, *noblesse oblige*, and statesmanship. Though less likely than Virginia proto-Whigs to avow these sentiments publicly (Brown 1980; Marshall 1967; Bruce 1982), the Junto's reluctance to demand complete party discipline and loyalty and its willingness to accede to the partial "independence" of officeholders mirrored an accommodation to elitist standards (Sharp 1970:215–69). Further, while the "democratic" convention displaced the elitist caucus as a means of selecting candidates in most states, the Junto proposed, as a "compromise," the "mixed caucus-convention." Finally, the Junto itself was dominated by men well connected to the state's leading families (Ammon 1953, 1963; Harrison 1970).

Like the Junto, the Boston Associates wedded elements of egalitarianism to more traditional conceptions of social authority. The egalitarian sentiments voiced by Massachusetts Whiggery reflected a realistic adaptation to an increasingly popular egalitarian general movement. Although there were significant differences between the two movements, both the Workingman's party and the Anti-Masons reflected and reinforced egalitarian values. In an effort to secure a large popular base of support for their party, the Boston Associates appealed to these groups partly by co-opting elements of their egalitarian platforms and rhetoric (Formisano 1983:197–244). In a similar fashion, Whiggery's public debates with the spokesmen of the state's Democratic party, who were more fully committed to egalitarian values and policies, compelled the Boston Associates and their allies to adopt a more popular rhetoric and to support some egalitarian reforms (Schlesinger 1945:288–89).

At the same time, however, the Boston Associates continued to adhere to a traditional, unitary conception of authority. The Boston Associates and other Brahmins assumed it as their right and duty to assert authority in the economic, political, social, and cultural realms (Jaher 1982:44–87; Story 1981). Complementary notions of upper-class authority such a paternalism, stewardship, a hierarchical conception of society, and deference to the community's "natural leaders' were also expressed. On the other hand, class tensions were discounted, harmony between different social groups was emphasized, and the possibility of social mobility through diligence and perseverance was stressed (Howe 1979:213–14). This traditional notion of leadership partially reflected a modernizing elite's interest in economic expansion and the adoption of policies consistent with both economic development and social stability. In addition, however, other factors encouraged these traditional claims, including family tradition, a history of class authority, and a Calvinist-inspired sense of public responsibility (Baltzell 1979).

Internal Organization. A strategic group's pattern of internal organization shapes its activities and conditions their impact on the course of institutional development. In general, both the creation of more differentiated institutions and the maintenance of traditional structures (in the face of an increasingly realized master trend) require considerable internal cohesion. However, the sources of cohesion among entrepreneurs and conservatives are usually quite distinct. Broadly speaking, entrepreneurs rely on generalized commitments and a shared identification with the new institutional order as the bases of internal unity, whereas conservatives are more inclined toward personalistic and primordial sources of solidarity. Relative to entrepreneurs and conservatives, accommodationists typically exhibit less internal unity, and the sources of whatever unity appears tends to combine both primordial and more generalized commitments. These general patterns are reflected in the internal organization of the Regency, the Calhounites, the Junto, and the Boston Associates.

The Regency's original inner core included Martin Van Buren, William Marcy, Benjamin Knower, Samuel Talcott, Benjamin Butler, Azariah Flagg, Silas Wright, Edwin Croswell, Charles Dudley, Thomas Alcott, and John Dix. In origin these men were middle class or lower middle class, often self-made men or the sons of self-made men. They were moderately prosperous and respected but not rich during their early years. Finally, they were not connected to the leading families of the state (Hofstadter 1969:240–41; see also Benson 1961:65–70).

The Regency members' unpretentious social origins and the sense that they were "outsiders" to New York's traditional ruling circles gave their political organization and rhetoric a distinct "edge of class resentment." This was most clearly expressed in "their attitude toward patrician politicans who assumed that office was a prerogative of social rank" (Hofstadter 1969:241). Estranged from "aristocratic" politics and speaking in a voice littered with democratic sentiments, the Regency politician also began to develop a distinctive social identity, viz., the modern professional politician.

Perhaps the most salient characteristic of the Regency's organization was its high degree of cohesiveness. "Unity among the members of the Regency was the single most striking feature in the operation of this political machine. It was evidenced by the mutual confidence and trust they showed in each other's opinions and ideas. They rarely made important decisions without holding consultations beforehand" (Remini 1958:350). Further, "their deliberation, plans and formulations of policy, based on this mutual understanding and cooperation, rendered them invincible and gave to the New York Democratic party a singleness of purpose and action" (Remini 1958:351).

While regular consultation between Regency members clearly contributed to internal unity, the latter was also a product of a "passion for organization." Unlike the South Carolina political organization, the Regency's unity was not based on the authority of a brilliant, charismatic leader. And even though Van Buren assumed a first-among-equals status, the distinctive feature of Regency organization was individual subordination to the party. Indeed, loyalty and obedience to the party made organization an end in itself, and party loyalty occasionally supplanted issues as the basis for concerted action. In short, "party unity was the democrat's answer to the aristocrat's wealth, prestige, and connections" (Hofstadter 1969:246; see also Kass 1965:28–29).

The preoccupation with an organization deemed independent of any single man's will was also reflected in the attention Regency members gave to recruiting new men and promoting them to positions of authority within the party (Remini 1958:349). Specific impersonal criteria for advancement within the organization began to emerge and (political) mobility was increasingly separated from the larger status order (Kass 1965:31–33).

Like the Regency, the Calhounites in South Carolina exhibited a high degree of cohesion. The sources of that unity, however, differed significantly from those that bound the Regency together. The core group of Calhounites included John C. Calhoun, Robert and Alfred Rhett, Francis Pickens (a cousin of Calhoun), Franklin and Benjamin Elmore, Robert Hayne, James Hamilton, James Hammond, and George McDuffie. This group was united both by familial ties and through identification with the gentry-planter class and a commitment to its continued predominance (Faust 1982:206; Wiltse 1949:200).

Within this faction the dominant fact was subordination to Calhoun's leadership. Indeed, from 1832 to 1850 John Calhoun was "almost absolute master" of South Carolina (Wiltse 1949:394). "One man —John C. Calhoun—dominated politics in South Carolina to a degree unparalleled elsewhere" (Banner 1974:60). His leadership was largely a matter of charisma: "His experience, his sincerity, the tremendous force of his own convictions, raised him to a pre-eminence that could not, after nullification, be successfully challenged" (Wiltse 1949:294). Further, Calhoun "expected those who agreed with him to follow his lead. Those who did not agree were given an opportunity to change their minds, but if they proved obdurate they were eliminated" (Wiltse 1949:292).

Such personalistic authority produced some internal tensions. Perhaps most readily apparent was a tendency for jealousy and enmity to arise among Calhoun's lieutenants. Authority and prestige depended on one's relative proximity to Calhoun, and this generated much rivalry among the men under Calhoun's command (Schultz 1950:13; Faust 1982:212). Personalistic rule and the absence of an independent, permanent political organization produced much disorder after Calhoun's death in 1850 (Schultz 1950:12).

For the most part, the Calhounites overcame these intrafactional hostilities. First, Calhoun insisted upon at least the semblance of unity among his followers, and he quickly responded to any signs of dissension within the ranks. He often dictated policies without consultation, and he expected his policies to be accepted (Wiltse 1949:292). Internal unity was also achieved through the shared conviction that the Calhounites were protecting vital southern interests endangered by hostile groups from other parts of the country. The most important southern interests were slavery and free trade. Still, concern was also accorded to the preservation of other, putatively distinctive, southern institutions—e.g., traditional patterns of political leadership—that were threatened by the increasingly industrial and democratic north. Calhounites also feared that internal dissension within their ranks could be exploited by outsiders (Wiltse 1949:199–201, 203–4).

Finally, Calhounites were able to exploit South Carolina's historic commitment to harmony and unity, thereby generating a high degree of internal cohesion (Weir 1969).

The Richmond Junto displayed a lower degree of internal cohesion. Organizationally, the Junto did not move far beyond the traditional substratum of familial connections. It developed in the early nineteenth century out of a combination of two preexisting groups, each bound by kinship. Wilson Cary Nichols and Spencer Roane were the joint founders of the Junto, and the subsequent leadership of the group, whose core members never numbered more than twenty, remained the monopoly of their near relatives, either by blood or marriage (Harrison 1970:186; Ammon 1953:399–400).

After 1824 the inner circle of the Junto included nine men: Thomas Ritchie, John and William Brockenbrough, William Roane, Richard Parker, Philip Nicholas, Peter Daniel, William Selden, and Andrew

Stevenson (Dent 1974:27). These individuals, although residing in
Richmond for at least part of the year, were unequivocally linked to
Virginia's planter class and adopted many of its practices: "Functioning in an informal fashion without regular meetings and possessing a
membership drawn for the most part from the planter class, the Junto
was completely a part of the aristocratic framework of the past. Its
influence was derived from the wealth, social prominence, and untir-
ing political activity of its members. Political direction was still a
matter of personal influence, though now a trifle less casual and
haphazard" (Ammon 1953:395; see also Dent 1974:29; Harrison
1970:186–90).

In addition to familial connections, the unity of the Richmond
Junto was also premised on the promotion of the interests of the
state's Democratic party. From the presidential election of 1824 through
the election of 1844, the Junto invariably carried the state party
legislative nominating convention or Virginia's electorate for the
presidential candidate of its choice (Dent 1974:31). Further, the Junto
did discipline its own members: "Regarding national candidates and
national issues, the Junto assumed the right to speak for Virginia with
a single voice and it could be intolerant of dissent" (Harrison 1970:187).

Two factors account for the Junto's low degree of unity in comparison to that of the Regency and the Calhounites. First, the Junto was
primarily oriented toward national issues and presidential elections,
not to state issues. Indeed, the Junto developed no coherent or consistent policy on state questions and its members were allowed to disagree about many important issues. Unlike the Regency, the Richmond Junto made no real effort to develop a cohesive and disciplined
statewide organization. Consequently, Virginia politics often assumed
an individualistic character and were partially independent of partisan control (McCormick 1966:184–85; Harrison 1970:197; Dent
1974:31–33). Second, the Junto operated as a thoroughly secret and
informal group. "Secrecy was essential, for it would have been contrary to republican theory and to local practices to admit that a small
and fixed group of men ruled the party. At no time did any loyal
Republican acknowledge the existence of this inner council" (Ammon
1953:396). But such secrecy also meant that little could be done to
build a centrally controlled statewide party organization. In addition,
the informal, familial nature of the Junto forestalled the development
of a party that had a standardized division of labor, an identifiable
hierarchy, and the specification of party service as a basis for promotion within the ranks (Harrison 1970; Ammon 1963).

In many respects, the Boston Associates resembled the Richmond

Junto. The Associates were men drawn primarily from the upper class, and included several Brahmins and wealthy merchant-manufacturers and lawyers. Among the inner circle, the most influential figures were Daniel Webster, Abbot and Amos Lawrence, Robert Winthrop, Edward Everett, Harrison Gray Otis, Nathan Appleton, Rufus Choate, John Davis, Caleb Cushing (who left the party in the 1840s), Andrew Norton, Samuel E. Eliot, and Samuel Armstrong (Duberman 1960:56–109; Formisano 1983; Brauer 1967:7–29).

Much as was the case with the Junto, the bonds uniting the Boston Associates had less to do with a passion for organization and more to do with the informal ties of a private club (Dalzell 1973:59–60; Formisano 1983:313–15). The group was premised on a sturdy network of family, social, and financial ties, and the men who composed the inner circle were close personal friends. These men took shares in the same business ventures and supported the same public and philanthropic causes; their children married one another. Thus one observer notes: "In State Street offices and Beacon Hill drawing rooms they met daily, and out of quiet conversations in such places party policy and party strategy grew almost by accident" (Dalzell 1973:59). In addition to the bonds evident in such informal association, the Associates were bound together by their similar class position and by their shared views on politics, class authority, and morality.

Nevertheless, such unity was brittle and could not match that produced by the Regency. Because of the informal, intimate nature of the inner core, there was little more than personal relations on which to build party leadership and provide direction. Accordingly, differences of opinion between leading personalities could easily produce rifts throughout the entire organization. In fact, between 1838 and 1845 Massachusetts Whiggery was split between Daniel Webster and those who supported his ambition for the presidency and Abbot Lawrence and his allies who supported Clay's candidacy. Further, throughout its existence Massachusetts Whiggery experienced a divisive tension between, on the one hand, party construction and the development of an independent political organization that itself commanded loyalty and, on the other, Daniel Webster's charismatic personage. At times these two forces moved in complementary directions; on other occasions, however, they diverged and Webster threatened to use his popularity to build a following loyal to him and independent of the Whig organization.

Finally, the pronounced moralistic quality of Bay State politics weakened party organization. By the mid-1840s, a noticeable rift had appeared between the Young Whigs (including Stephen C. Phillips,

Charles F. Adams, Charles Sumner, Charles Allen, and John G. Palfrey) and the party's older conservative leadership. The Young Whigs demanded that the party take a principled position on the annexation of Texas and later on the slavery question. Party leaders equivocated, however, and this precipitated the Young Whigs' subsequent bolt from the party.

In sum, the internal organization of strategic groups contributed to the overall pattern of uneven political differentiation that appeared in the antebellum United States. The Regency was built around a passion for organization and the coordination of its efforts contributed to the construction of a modern party organization. In South Carolina, Calhoun's charisma and the Calhounites' deep antipathy to political parties effectively inhibited the development of even the semblance of modern political organizations. Both the Junto and the Boston Associates exhibited less internal unity, and even had they been fully committed to constructing modern differentiated parties it is unlikely that given their relatively low degree of internal cohesion their efforts would have compared favorably with the success of the Regency.

External Relations.   Any strategic group's impact on institutional development is shaped by its relations with other social groups. Therefore, an analysis of the types and consequences of coalitional and conflictual relations in conjunction with a discussion of the structural factors that condition these relations is necessary to understand uneven differentiation and incomplete institutionalization.

Strategic groups' coalitions with other collectivities are conditioned by two considerations. First, the social structures in which strategic groups operate set limits on the number and types of coalition partners. Further, the number, diversity, and nature of potential allies strongly affects strategic groups' ability to guide the course of institutional development. In general, the more decentralized and diverse the social structure in a given subunit, the more advantageous the bargaining position of entrepreneurs, followers, and accommodationists will be. Conversely, the more power and resources concentrated in a small number of groups, the more likely it is that entrepreneurs, followers, and accommodationists will have to modify their institutional visions in a manner acceptable to prospective coalition partners.

The New York Regency operated in a social context characterized by a relatively pronounced egalitarianism, a relatively expansive constitutional opportunity structure that opened most local and state offices to virtually all adult white males, and a considerably fragmented pattern of stratification that dispersed power across several distinct elites and even gave some power to the middle and lower classes (Fox 1965; McCormick 1966). Moreover, antebellum New York was characterized by incipient industrialization and a notably high degree of religious and ethnic group differentiation. In this context the Regency was successful in allying itself with the burgeoning working class and the religious and ethnic "out-groups" (Kelley 1979; Benson 1961). In forging these coalitions the Regency retained considerable autonomy and was able to realize its modern conception of party organization.

Institutional conservatives are more likely to secure support in social contexts in which power is concentrated in relatively traditional groups. The Calhounites organized in a state that continued to emphasize deference to traditional elites, possessed a restrictive constitutional opportunity structure that limited mass access to local and state political offices, and exhibited a pattern of economic and social stratification that concentrated power in the planter elite (Greenberg 1977). All of these factors worked to the advantage of the Calhounites, who were widely perceived as acting in the best interests of South Carolina. Accordingly, they were able to ally themselves with the state's powerful planters and also with the middling and poorer farmers (Banner 1974).

Institutional accommodationists in Virginia were confronted with a cultural, social, and political context much like that of South Carolina, and consequently their allies pulled them in a relatively conservative direction. In order to institutionalize its own restricted view of modern parties, the Junto allied itself with the dominant planter groups which, in turn, compelled the Junto to moderate its already temperate view of modern parties. At the same time, there was a sectional split within Virginia between the eastern and western portions of the state, which the Junto might have more successfully exploited to increase its autonomy vis-à-vis the planter class and to build more differentiated organizational and normative frameworks for politics. However, the Junto's preoccupation with national affairs, its close ties with the eastern gentry, and its own limited vision of party organization inhibited the use of this broad-based cleavage for the purposes of party building (Ammon 1963; Harrison 1970; Ambler 1910; Sutton 1972).

Throughout the early 1830s, Massachusetts was characterized by considerable ethnic and religious homogeneity, which was disrupted only in the 1840s by the large influx of Irish Catholics. In addition, the

Bay State experienced incipient industrialization with the growth of the textile industry. A modernizing economic elite acquired considerable power through its control over these new enterprises. The state's constitutional opportunity structure was relatively expansive, although the secret ballot had not been fully institutionalized. Finally, the cultural ethos combined a traditional deferential attitude toward elites with some growth of egalitarian sentiment. Confronted with this social configuration, the Boston Associates successfully allied themselves with a variety of groups—especially members of the dominant religious and ethnic groups, the relatively wealthy, and many native workers who felt threatened by immigrants. While these allies, especially the workers, compelled some democratization of the Associates' public rhetoric and style, the inner circle of that elite group was able to construct a powerful political base without promoting a fully modern conception of party and partisan organization.

A second condition affecting coalitional activity is control over the distribution of pertinent material resources. The nature of resources and the criteria for their distribution vary. Entrepreneurs and followers tend to employ specialized material resources (e.g., political office) and to use relatively specialized criteria (e.g., demonstrated loyalty to the organization) for their distribution. Conservatives, on the other hand, tend to use somewhat more diffuse material resources (e.g., political office, but also access to exclusive status groups) and to employ more general criteria (e.g., performance, but also "character") for their distribution. Finally, while accommodationists employ several types of material resources and use both specialized and general criteria for their distribution, the central dynamic is movement toward greater specialization in both the content and distributive criteria of resources.

Dominating the most important executive and legislative positions within the state, the Regency controlled appointments to many state, county, and local offices. The dispensation of patronage was guided by specifically political criteria, i.e., demonstrated loyalty and service to the party. "Those who stepped out of line were quickly noted and informed upon" (Remini 1958:344). In this way, the employment of patronage was subordinated to the purpose of sustaining a unified and disciplined party organization (Kass 1965:29–31).

More so than in any other state, political power and patronage in South Carolina were concentrated in the state legislature. Through their control of this epicenter of power, the Calhounites were able to bend other aspiring politicos to their will (Freehling 1965b:38). At the same time, Calhounites were especially sensitive to the character and status of those who received patronage. While loyalty to Calhoun was used as a criteron, it was also important that the potential recipients be either respected in their communities or sponsored by those who were (Banner 1974:76–79).

The Richmond Junto awarded patronage to those who rendered useful service to the Democratic party and those who exhibited deserving public character. As party competition intensified, the Junto increasingly relied on party service as the primary standard for distributing patronage (Kuroda 1969:50, 137, 140–41, 223–24). Virginia's constitution, however, placed insurmountable obstacles in the path of the Junto. Specifically, there was a state-county disjuncture in appointive power. While the Junto was able to influence the distribution of power and lucrative state posts and thereby sustain a substantial degree of party loyalty and discipline at that level, the Junto had considerably less authority over the distribution of powerful county offices. The latter remained securely in the hands of locally prominent men and families—relatively impervious to control by the Junto or the electorate (Porter 1947:182–96). This disjuncture between state and county patronage and, specifically, the decentralized and oligarchic character of local patronage, inhibited the full development of extensive party organizations throughout all levels of government during the Jacksonian era (McCormick 1966:180).

Throughout the Jacksonian period, inhibitions against using party service as the sole, explicit criteron for apportioning offices persisted in Massachusetts (Formisano 1983:248, 307, 311). Many who sponsored a man for appointive office pointed to his "good character" rather than to his party regularity. Nevertheless, as the era progressed, the dominant trend was toward the explicit and frequent invocation of loyalty and service to the party as a primary qualification for appointment. Increasingly, the Boston Associates demanded that aspirants to office and their supporters offer as evidence of their qualifications service as delegates to party conventions or as chairmen of town or county party committees. Finally, throughout this period the Whigs and Boston Associates controlled most of the major appointive state and local offices and used that control to make their influence felt throughout the state.

Even when successful in building powerful coalitions, strategic groups invariably encounter opposition. Conflict can have several consequences for differentiation and institutionalization. It can result in the defeat of strategic group and their institutional projects. Alternatively, even if strategic groups are relatively successful they may not completely dominate their opponents and the outcome can be a structure composed of diverse and contradictory elements.

When conflict between groups assumes a competitive form with clearly defined winners and losers, there is a tendency toward convergence and the acceptance of the initially victorious group's project. The tendency is the same whether entrepreneurs, followers, or conservatives emerge as decisive winners. In either case opponents, seeking a path to victory, often adopt the very organizational and normative framework they initially opposed. Therefore, when entrepreneurs and followers are clearly successful, competition tends to promote greater differentiation. However, when conservatives are clearly victorious, competition inhibits differentiation.

Two qualifications should be noted with regard to the institutionalization of differentiated structures. First, even though entrepreneurs and followers may emerge as decisive winners and most of their initial opponents eventually acquiesce to their innovations, a small number of disgruntled traditionalists may refuse to support the new structures and practices. Their continued criticism and occasional efforts to revitalize older forms inhibit the full institutionalization of more differentiated structures. Second, although entrepreneurs and followers may be successful in "persuading" many of their opponents in a given institutional sphere, criticism and delegitimation may still be directed at the new structures from other social spheres. These attacks, too, impede the complete institutionalization of differentiated structures.

In New York, the first attempts to build mass party organizations, to open up political offices to categories of men previously excluded, and generally to create a more inclusive polity were undertaken by the Regency (McCormick 1966:119–24; Benson 1961; Remini 1959:186–98). The incipient Whig leadership vigorously opposed these organizational and normative innovations and sought to mobilize a large constituency in defense of traditional deferential leadership patterns. However, adherence to conventional patterns of authority and the repudiation of populist egalitarianism were largely responsible for the Whigs' inability to compete effectively with the Democrats for political office. By 1834 important elements of the Whig leadership decided not merely to adopt but to improve the innovations introduced by the Democrats. The electoral campaign of that year marks the genuine ascendance of mass parties in New York. In this case, opponents who initially emerged to combat the Democrats' structural and normative innovations and defend traditional arrangements served, in the end, as agents of differentiation. Thus, countermobilization actually promoted the creation of more differentiated political structures.

At the same time, however, New York Whigs did not fully embrace the new party structures and many Whigs continued to harbor a profound ambivalence about the value of mass political parties. That ambivalence persisted throughout the antebellum period and impeded the complete institutionalization of differentiated political organizations. Moreover, opposition to the "new politics" also arose from religious and intellectual groups and an emerging group of professional humanitarians. That opposition, too, contributed to the incomplete institutionalization of more modern political structures.

In South Carolina, institutional conservatives established the terms of political conflict, and their political success enjoined their opponents to adopt a similar organizational and normative framework. Thus, the opposition to the Calhounites also publicly eschewed the party system, developed temporary and personalistic factions that dissipated after the resolution of a given issue, and avowed commitment to the traditional patterns of leadership that presumably distinguished the South from the rest of the nation. In short, the Calhounites' substantial political success inhibited the proposal of radical political innovations by their opponents. The overall effect of conflict, then, was to reinforce traditionalistic political leadership and impede the development of differentiated political institutions (Banner 1974; Freehling 1965b).

In Virginia the effects of conflict and competition were more ambiguous. On the one hand the leading Virginia Whigs, who opposed the Junto, were drawn primarily from among the gentry. These men were generally from well-established families, had superior educations, and were committed to traditional political ideals. They envisioned society as an organic order whose true interests could be determined only by its "natural leaders," and assumed that hierarchy and deference to the upper classes were necessary components of a well-ordered society (Brown 1980; Marshall 1967). Indeed the Virginia Whigs emerged, in part, in response to the new political practices and tactics introduced by the Junto and the Virginia Democrats; Virginia Whigs rallied around a defense of the traditional political ideals that they felt were threatened by the emergence of partisan politics and the rise of the political manager (Brown 1980:379). Consequently, during its inception the Whig opposition reinforced a traditional conception of politics. On the other hand, however, the emergence of sustained competition between partisan groups, even though their leadership was drawn primarily from the gentry, was an important impetus for greater differentiation. By 1834 the Whig opposition had secured a majority of seats in the state's legislature and was organizing at the national level to oppose the election of Jackson's successor, Van Buren (Cole 1912; Simms 1929).

Between 1836 and 1840 Virginia Whigs became better organized and by 1839 were able to agree upon a single presidential candidate. During the 1840 election it sponsored rallies, processions, and monster conventions. In short, the Whigs realized that if they were to win elections it would be necessary to adopt a more modern form of political organization and a more popularly oriented campaign strategy. Their political success also compelled the Democrats to become better organized. Thus, "between 1834 and 1839 both parties elaborated their organizations, increased their discipline, altered their campaign techniques, and broadened the nature of their appeal" (McCormick 1966:197). In brief, competition pushed both Virginia Democrats and Whigs toward greater political differentiation.

Nevertheless, despite increased competition Virginia Democrats and Whigs did not completely relinquish the older traditions, and conventional elements of leadership retained a vitality in Virginia that prevented the full differentiation of modern political forms (Dent 1974). It should also be noted that the persistence of these traditions among elite political figures and the criticism leveled against the new politics by a small group of southern intellectuals also impeded the complete institutionalization of those modern political structures that did appear in Jacksonian Virginia (Faust 1977).

In Massachusetts, competition had similar effects to those observed for Virginia—i.e., party competition promoted greater differentiation. However, the competition between parties in Massachusetts was not as pronounced as in Virginia. In the Bay State the Whigs won the vast majority of national and state contests. Between 1834 and 1848, with but two exceptions, the Whigs annually elected their candidate to the governorship, and in every year but one they controlled both the upper and lower houses of the state legislature. Twenty-seven of the thirty-one men who represented Massachusetts in the House of Representatives and all of the state's United States senators who served during this period were Whigs. In every presidential election the Whig candidate received all the state's electoral ballots (Brauer 1967:19). These facts should not be taken as evidence of the complete absence of competition, but it should be clear that the Whigs were the state's dominant party. The lack of consistently intense competition enabled many conservative Whig leaders to retain some of their traditional reservations about the party system and prevented the Bay State from producing a fully differentiated party structure (Formisano 1983:310–16). These reservations, in conjunction with the more fully developed indictment of the party system by an elite group of intellectuals and religious leaders, also impeded the complete institutionalization of modern political structures in Massachusetts.

Conclusion

The notion of strategic groups provides a partial explanation of uneven differentiation and incomplete institutionalization. It suggests that students of differentiation should give more detailed attention to voluntaristic elements in their explanations of social change. Specifically, the analysis of concrete leadership groups' orientations, internal organization, and relations with other collectivities is essential for understanding how institutions evolve and acquire their particular contours.

At the same time it is important to emphasize that the examination of strategic groups does not, and in principle cannot, provide a complete account of either the master trend of differentiation, uneven differentiation, or incomplete institutionalization. The analysis provided here is an effort to introduce a micro corrective into the explanatory scheme of differentiation theory. The construction of a comprehensive framework that links both micro and macro levels of analysis is a task those interested in elaborating differentiation theory must address.

Notes

1. I use the term "synthesis" in a very broad sense to suggest that both collectivistic and individualistic theories provide useful insights into the processes of social change. At the same time, I agree with Alexander's (1982b:2) position that strictly speaking a synthetic position with respect to the problem of order is not possible.

2. This is a very abbreviated discussion of the ideas presented in my paper "Uneven Differentiation and Incomplete Differentiation: Political Change and Continuity in the Early American Nation," which is included in this volume.

3. This discussion extends, theoretically and substantively, an earlier analysis (Colomy 1985).

4. My emphasis in what follows is on leadership groups that clearly exerted the most powerful impact on each state's political development. As the final section of the paper indicates, I do not argue that these particular groups are the only ones that exercised influence.

5. The term *project* is taken from Sartre (1968:91), who writes: "The most rudimentary behavior must be determined both in relation to the real and present factors which condition it and in relation to certain objects, still to come, which it is trying to bring into being. This is what we call a project."

6. The concept of prototyping was introduced into sociological discourse by Ralph Turner (1970), who developed it in the context of his interactionist role theory.

References

Alexander, Jeffrey C. 1978. "Formal and Substantive Voluntarism in the Work of Talcott Parsons: A Theoretical and Ideological Reinterpretation." *American Sociological Review* 43:177–98.

—— 1982a. *Positivism, Presuppositions, and Current Controversies.* Berkeley: University of California Press.

—— 1982b. "The Individualist Dilemma in Phenomenology and Interactionism: Towards a Synthesis with the Functionalist Tradition." Paper delivered at the tenth World Conference of Sociology, Mexico City, August 1982.

—— 1984a. "Social-Structural Analysis: Some Notes on Its History and Prospects." *Sociological Quarterly* 25:5–26.

—— 1984b. "Three Models of Culture and Society Relations: Toward an Analysis of Watergate." *Sociological Theory* 2:290–314.

Alexander, Jeffrey C. and Paul Colomy. 1985a. "Institutionalization and Collective Behavior: Points of Contact Between Eistenstadt's Functionalism and Symbolic Interactionism." In E. Cohen, M. Lissak, and U. Almagor, eds. *Comparative Social Dynamics.* Boulder, Colorado: Westview.

—— 1985b. "Toward Neofunctionalism." *Sociological Theory* 3:11–23.

Ambler, Charles H. 1910. *Sectionalism in Virginia from 1776–1861.* New York: Russell and Russell.

—— 1913. *Thomas Ritchie.* Richmond, Va: Price.

Ammon, Henry. 1948. *The Republican Party in Virginia, 1789–1824.* PhD dissertation, University of Virginia.

—— 1953. "The Richmond Junto, 1800–1824." *Virginia Magazine* 61:395–418.

—— 1963. "The Jeffersonian Republicans in Virginia. *Virginia Magazine* 71:153–67.

Bailyn, Bernard. 1967. *The Ideological Origins of the American Revolution.* Cambridge: Harvard University Press.

Baltzell, Digby. 1979. *Puritan Boston and Quaker Philadelphia.* New York: Free Press.

Banner, James M. 1974. "The Problem of South Carolina. In S. Elkins and E. McKitrick, eds. *The Hofstadter Aegis: A Memorial*, pp. 60–93. New York: Knopf.

Bellah, Robert. 1964. "Religious Evolution." *American Sociological Review* 29:358–74.

Benson, Lee. 1961. *The Concept of Jacksonian Democracy.* Princeton: Princeton University Press.

Blumer, Herbert. 1939. "Collective Behavior." In A. M. Lee, ed., *Principles of Sociology*, pp. 165–225. New York: Barnes and Noble.

—— 1969. *Symbolic Interactionism.* Englewood Cliffs, New Jersey: Prentice-Hall.

Bottomore, Tom. 1982. Introduction to Bottomore and S. Nowak, *Sociology: The State of the Art,* pp. 27–35. London: Sage.

Brady, Patrick. 1972. "Political Culture in the Early American Republic: The Case of South Carolina." PhD dissertation, University of California, Santa Barbara.

Brauer, Kinley. 1967. *Cotton vs. Conscience* Lexington: The University of Kentucky Press.

Brown, Thomas. 1980. "Southern Whigs and the Politics of Statesmanship, 1833–1841." *Journal of Southern History* 46:361–80.

Bruce, Dickson D. Jr. 1982. *The Rhetoric of Conservatism: The Virginia Convention of 1829–1830 and the Conservative Tradition in the South* San Marino, Calif.: Huntington Library.

Calhoun, John C. 1843–44. Letters: (a) to H. S. G. Tucker, March 1843; (b) to D. Green, October 1844. In Calhoun Papers, South Carolina Library, Columbia, South Carolina.

—— 1853. *Disquisition on Government.* New York: Peter Smith.

Capers, Gerald. M. 1959. *Stephen A. Douglas: Defender of the Union.* Boston: Little, Brown.

Colomy, Paul. 1982. *Stunted Differentiation: A Sociological Examination of Political Elites in Virginia, 1720–1850.* PhD dissertation, University of California, Los Angeles.

—— 1985. "Uneven Structural Differentiation: Toward a Comparative Approach." In J. C. Alexander, ed. *Neofunctionalism.* Beverly Hills, Calif.: Sage.

Cole, Arthur C. 1912. *The Whig Party in the South.* Washington, D.C.: American Historical Association.

Dalzell, Robert. 1973. *Daniel Webster and the Trial of American Nationalism.* Boston: Houghton Mifflin.

Darling, Arthur. 1925. *Political Changes in Massachusetts, 1824–1848.* Cos Cob, Conn.: John Edwards.

Dawe, Alan. 1978. "Theories of Social Action." In Tom Bottomore and R. Nisbet, eds. *A History of Sociological Analysis,* pp. 362–417. New York: Basic Books.

Dent, Lynwood. 1974. *The Virginia Democratic Party, 1824–47.* PhD dissertation, Louisiana State University.

DiMaggio, Paul and Walter Powell. 1983. "The Iron Cage Revisited: Institutional Isomorphism and Collective Rationality in Organizational Fields." *American Sociological Review* 48:147–60.

Douglas, Stephen A. 1961. *Letters of Stephen A. Douglas,* Robert W. Johannsen, ed. Urbana: University of Illinois Press.

Duberman, Martin. 1960. *Charles Francis Adams.* Stanford Calif.: Stanford University Press.

Eaton, Clement. 1952. "Southern Senators and the Right of Instruction." *Journal of Southern History* 18:252.67.

—— 1966. *A History of the Old South.* New York: Macmillan.

Eisenstadt, S. N. 1964. "Social Change, Differentiation, and Evolution." *American Sociological Review* 29:235–47.

—— 1965. *Essays on Comparative Institutions.* New York: Wiley.

—— 1968. "Social Evolution." *International Encyclopedia of the Social Sciences,* pp. 228–34. New York: Macmillan.

—— 1971. *Social Differentiation and Stratification.* Glenview, Ill.: Scott Foresman.

—— 1973. *Tradition, Change, and Modernity.* New York: Wiley.

Eisenstadt, S. N. and M. Curelaru. 1976. *The Form of Sociology: Paradigms and Crises.* New York: Wiley.

Faust, Drew. 1977. *A Sacred Circle: The Dilemma of the Intellectual in the Old South, 1840–1860.* Baltimore: Johns Hopkins University Press.

—— 1982. *James Henry Hammond and the Old South:* Baton Rouge: Louisiana State University Press.

Forgie, George B. 1979. *Patricide in the House Divided: A Psychological Interpretation of Lincoln and His Age.* New York: Norton.

Formisano, Ronald P. 1983. *The Transformation of Political Culture.* New York: Oxford University Press.

Fox, Dixon, Ryan. 1965 (1919). *The Decline of the Aristocracy in the Politics of New York: 1801–1840.* New York: Harper.

Fox, Rene. 1976. "Medical Evolution." In J. J. Loubser and R. C. Baum, eds. *Explorations in General Theory in Social Science: Essays in Honor of Talcott Parsons,* pp. 773–867. New York: Free Press.

Freehling, William. 1965a. *Prelude to Civil War.* New York: Harper and Row.

—— 1965b. "Spoilsmen and Interests in the Thought and Career of John C. Calhoun." *Journal of American History* 52:25–42.

Goldman, Perry M. 1970. "Political Rhetoric in the Age of Jackson." *Tennessee Historical Quarterly* 29:360–71.

—— 1972. "Political Virtue in the Age of Jackson." *Political Science Quarterly* 87:46–62.

Greenberg, Kenneth. 1977. "The Second American Revolution: South Carolina Politics, Society, and Secession, 1776–1860. PhD dissertation, University of Wisconsin.

Harrison, Joseph H. 1956. "Martin Van Buren and His Southern Supporters." *Journal of Southern History* 22:438–58.

—— 1970. "Oligarchs and Democrats: The Richmond Junto." *Virginia Magazine* 78:184–98.

Haskell, Thomas L. 1977. *The Emergence of Professional Social Science* Urbana: University of Illinois Press.

Hofstadter, Richard. 1962. *Anti-Intellectualism in American Life* New York: Vintage.

—— 1969. *The Idea of a Party System.* Berkeley: University of California Press.

Howe, Daniel. 1979. *The Political Culture of the American Whigs.* Chicago: University of Chicago Press.

Jacobson, Norman. 1951. "The Concept of Equality in the Assumptions and the Propaganda of Massachusetts Conservatives, 1790–1840." PhD dissertation, University of Wisconsin.

Jaher, Frederic. 1982. *The Urban Establishment.* Urbana: University of Illinois Press.

Johannsen, Robert W. 1973. *Stephen A. Douglas.* New York: Oxford University Press.

Johnson, Allen. 1980. *Stephen A. Douglas: A Study in Politics.* New York: Knopf.

Kass, Alvin. *Politics in New York State, 1800–1830.* Syracuse, New York: Syracuse University Press.

Keller, Suzanne. 1963. *Beyond the Ruling Class.* New York: Random House.

Kelley, Robert. 1979. *The Cultural Pattern in American Politics.* New York: Knopf.

Kuroda, Tadahisa. 1969. *The County Court System of Virginia from the Revolution to the Civil War.* PhD dissertation, Columbia University.

McCormick, Richard P. 1966. *The Second American Party System.* Chapel Hill: University of North Carolina Press.

Maines, David. 1977. "Social Organization and Social Structure in Symbolic Interactionist Thought." *Annual Review of Sociology* 3:235–60.

Marshall, Lynn. 1967. "The Strange Stillbirth of the Whig Party. *American Historical Review* 72:445–68.

Mayhew, Bruce H. 1980. "Structuralism versus Individualism: Part I, Shadowboxing in the Dark." *Social Forces* 59:335–75.

—— 1981. "Structuralism versus Individualism: Part II, Ideological and Other Obfuscation." *Social Forces* 59:627–48.

Meltzer, Bernard N. and John W. Petras. 1970. "The Chicago and Iowa Schools of Symbolic Interactionism." In T. Shibutani, ed. *Human Nature and Collective Behavior,* pp. 3–17. New Brunswick, N.J.: Transaction Books.

Meyer, John and Brian Rowan. 1977. "Institutionalized Organizations: Formal Structure ans Myth and Ceremony." *American Journal of Sociology* 83:340–63.

Meyers, Marvin. 1957. *The Jacksonian Persuasion.* Stanford, Calif.: Stanford University Press.

Nichols, Roy F. 1967. *The Invention of the American Political Parties.* New York: Macmillan.

Niven, John. 1983. *Martin Van Buren: The Romantic Age of American Politics.* New York: Oxford University Press.

Parsons, Talcott. 1937. *The Structure of Social Action.* New York: Free Press.

—— 1966. *Societies: Evolutionary and Comparative Perspectives.* New York: Free Press.

—— 1971. *The System of Modern Societies.* Englewood Cliffs, N.J.: Prentice-Hall.

Peterson, Merrill. 1960. *The Jeffersonian Image in the American Mind.* New York: Oxford University Press.

—— 1966. *Democracy, Liberty and Property.* Indianapolis: Bobbs-Merrill.

Pole, Jack. 1978. *The Pursuit of Equality in American History.* Berkeley: University of California Press.

Porter, Albert O. 1947. *County Government in Virginia, 1607–1904.* New York: AMS Press.

Remini, Robert V. 1958. "The Albany Regency." *New York History* 39:341–55.

—— 1959. *Martin Van Buren and the Making of the Democratic Party.* New York: Columbia University Press.

Risjord, Norman K. *The Old Republicans* New York: Columbia University Press.

Rives, William C. 1827. Letter to Thomas Gilmer, July 1827. In William Cabell Rives Papers, Library of Congress, Washington, D.C.

Sartre, Jean-Paul. 1968. *Search for a Method.* New York: Vintage.

Schlesinger, Arthur M. Jr. 1945. *The Age of Jackson.* Boston: Little, Brown.

Schultz, Harold S. 1950. *Nationalism and Sectionalism in South Carolina, 1852–1860.* Durham, N.C.: Duke University Press.

Schwartz, Barry. 1983. "George Washington and the Whig Conception of Heroic Leadership." *American Sociological Review* 48:18–33.

Shade, William G. 1981. "Political Pluralism and Party Development: The Creation of a Modern Party System, 1815–1852." In P. Kleppner et al. eds. *The Evolution of American Electoral Systems,* pp. 77–112. Westport, Conn.: Greenwood Press.

Shalhope, Robert E. 1972. "Towards a Republican Synthesis." *William and Mary Quarterly* 29:49–80.

—— 1980. *John Taylor of Carolina* New York: Columbia University Press.

Simms, Henry H. 1929. *The Rise of the Whigs in Virginia, 1824–1840*. Richmond: Price.

Smelser, Neil. 1974. "Growth, Structural Change, and Conflict in California Public Higher Education, 1950–1970." In N. Smelser and G. Almond, eds. *Public Higher Education in California*. Berkeley: University of California Press.

Snydor, Charles. 1948. *The Development of Southern Sectionalism, 1818–1848*. Baton Rouge: Louisiana State University Press.

Sutton, Robert. 1972. "Sectionalism and Social Structure." *Virginia Magazine* 80:70–84.

Turner, Ralph H. 1970. *Family Interaction*. New York: Wiley.

Turner, Ralph H. and Lewis Killian. 1972. *Collective Behavior*. Englewood Cliffs, N.J.: Prentice-Hall.

Van Buren, Martin. 1867. *The Origin and Course of Political Parties in the United States*. New York: Hurd and Houghton.

—— 1920. *The Autobiography of Martin Van Buren*. John C. Fitzpatrick, ed. Washington, D.C.: GPO.

Wallace, Michael. 1969. "Changing Concepts in the United States: New York, 1815–1825." *American Historical Review* 74:453–91.

—— 1973. *Ideologies of Party in the Antebellum Republic*. PhD dissertation, Columbia University.

Ward, John W. 1953. *Andrew Jackson: Symbol for an Age*. London: Oxford University Press.

Welter, Rush. 1975. *The Mind of America, 1820–1860*. New York Columbia University Press.

Wiltse, Charles M. 1949. *John C. Calhoun*. Indianapolis: Bobbs-Merrill.

Wood, Gordon. 1969. *The Creation of the American Republic*. New York: Norton.

THREE

Solidarity, Domination, and Responsibility

8

Core Solidarity, Ethnic Out-Groups, and Social Differentiation

Jeffrey C. Alexander

Theorists of Western development have been hard put to account for the ethnic and racial conflicts that have created the recent wave of nationalist and separatist movements in industrial societies. For developing nations, such conflicts are to be expected; they are part of the "transition" period. But after industrial society is firmly established, it is believed that such divisions will become residual, not systematic or indeed intensifying, contradictions (Marx 1955 [1848]; Toennies 1957 [1887]; Weber 1958 [1904]; Durkheim 1947 [1893]).

This theoretical difficulty is fundamental; its roots lie in the complex history of Western development itself. Theories of nation building are products of Enlightenment thinking, generated by the twin revolutions of political nationalism and industrialism. As the analytic translation of these social developments, such theories have been rationalistic in the extreme, sharing a utilitarian distaste for the nonrational and normative and the illusion that a truly modern society will soon dispense with such concerns.

One antidote to this theoretical failing is increased sensitivity to secular myths and cultural patterns, phenomena with which theorists

I would like to acknowledge the advice and helpful critical readings of a number of friends and colleagues: Jeffrey Prager, Seamus Thompson, Leo Kuper, Ivan Light, Dean R. Gerstein, and Ruth Bloch. I have also received invaluable aid from Maria Iosue, who was my research assistant for this project.

have been increasingly concerned (Geertz 1973a; Bellah 1970). But solidarity is the more crucial theoretical dimension for problems of emergent ethnicity and nationalist conflicts. Solidarity means the subjective feelings of integration that individuals experience as members of social groups. Given solidarity's phenomenological character, solidarity problems clearly diverge from those of economics and politics, which concern themselves, respectively, with scarcity and the self-conscious organization of goals. Yet solidarity also differs from problems of culture, which are oriented toward meaningful patterns relatively abstracted from specific time and space. Thus, although integrative exigencies are not generated by purely instrumental considerations, they are more concrete than "values." In contrast to values, social solidarity refers to the structure of actual social groups. Like religion, politics, and economics, solidarity constitutes an independent determinant of human societies and a fundamental point for sociological analysis (Shils 1975a; Parsons 1967a, 1971; Alexander 1978, 1983; see Nakane 1970 and Light 1972).

"Inclusion" and the Paradigm of Linear Evolution

Solidarity becomes fundamental because every nation must, after all, begin historically. Nations do not simply emerge out of thin air, for example, as universalistic, constitutional entities. They are founded by groups whose members share certain qualitatively distinct characteristics, traits around which they structure their solidarity. No matter what kind of future institutions this "core group" establishes, no matter what the eventual liberalism of its social and political order, residues of this core solidarity remain.

From the perspective of the integrative problem, national development can be viewed as a process of encountering and producing new solidary out-groups (see Lipset and Rokkan 1967; Rokkan 1975). With religious and economic rationalization, new sects and social classes are created. With territorial expansion and immigration, new ethnic groups are encountered (see E. Weber 1976). In response to these developments, pressures develop to expand the solidarity that binds the core group. In this way, nation building presents the problem of "inclusion" (Parsons 1967b, 1971).

I define inclusion as the process by which previously excluded groups gain solidarity in the "terminal" community of a society. Two points are crucial in this definition. First, inclusion refers to *felt* solidarity, not simply to behavioral participation. Pariah groups that fill crucial social roles—like Western Jews in the Middle Ages or Indians in postcolonial Uganda—are not "included."[1] Second, I am concerned here specifically with a society's terminal community (Geertz 1973b). A dominant focus of the American tradition of race relations and ethnicity studies has focused almost exclusively on the primary group level, on whether individuals join the same clubs, make the same friends, and intermarry (Gordon 1964). While such questions are certainly significant, morally as well as intellectually, they cannot provide the only important focus for historical and comparative analysis. In defining the terminal community as the widest solidary group with which individuals feel significant integration, I am referring to those feelings that, extending beyond family and friends, create the boundaries of acknowledged "society." The question of whether this terminal community is narrow and limiting or expansive enough to encompass a range of particular groupings is as ramifying an issue as the level of economic or political development or the nature of religious belief. Inclusion, then, refers to a change in solidary status. To the degree that individuals are felt to be full members of the terminal community they have been "included."

Inclusion can be measured by the degree to which the terminal community has become more "civil" and less "primordial." The latter refers to the given, seemingly natural ties that structure solidarity —race, territory, kinship, language, even religion (Geertz 1973b; Shils 1975b). People sharing any one of these traits will feel direct emotional bonds. Primordial ties are necessarily few. In aboriginal society, where the "world" ended at the farthest waterhole, sex, kinship, age, and territory presented the principal axes for solidary identification.

Civil ties, on the other hand, are more mediated and less emotional, more abstract and self-consciously constructed. Instead of referring to biological or geographic givens, they refer to ethical or moral qualities associated with "social" functions and institutions. The emergence of civil ties can be seen as a process of differentiation, one that parallels the movements toward economic, political, and religious differentiation that have been the traditional foci of modernization theory. Membership in the terminal community must, in the first place, be separated from membership in particular kinship groups and, more generally, from biological criteria. This community solidarity must also be differentiated from status in the economic, political, and religious community.

The primordial-civil continuum, then, provides an independent criterion for evaluating the inclusion process. This standard has, however, usually been applied in an artificial, linear way even by those theorists who have taken the integrative problem seriously. From Hegel and Tocqueville to Parsons, the transition from primordial to civil solidarity has been envisioned as rigidly interlocked with political and economic transformation. The ideal-typical point of origin is the narrow moral basis of Banfield's "backward society," a self-contained village where identification scarcely extends beyond the family to the town, let alone to occupation, class, or even religious affiliation (Banfield 1959). This primordial community is then transformed in the course of modernization into Durkheim's organic solidarity, Parsons' societal community, or Tocqueville's mass democracy; given the expansive civil ties in the latter societies, individuals "rightly understand" their self-interest (Durkheim 1947 [1893]; Tocqueville 1945 [1835]; Parsons 1971).

To a significant degree, such a universalizing transformation in solidarity has, indeed, characterized the modernization process. In the Western Middle Ages, the Christian Church provided the only overarching integration that bound distinct villages and estates. It was, after all, the papal bureaucracy that created the territorial jurisdictions of Gallia, Germania, Italia, and Anglia long before these abstract communities ever became concrete groupings (Coulton 1935:28–29). It did so fundamentally because Christian symbolism envisioned a civil solidarity that could transcend the primordial ties of blood (Weber 1958 [1904]. Similarly, alongside the officers of the Church, the king's henchmen were the only medieval figures whose consciousness extended beyond village and clan. To the degree that the king and his staff succeeded in establishing national bureaucracies, they contributed enormously to the creation of a civil terminal community, despite the primordial qualities that remained powerfully associated with this national core group (Royal Institute of International Affairs 1939:8–21; see Eisenstadt 1963). Economic development has also been closely intertwined with the extension of civil ties, as Marx himself implicitly acknowledged when he praised capitalism for making "national one-sidedness and narrow-mindedness . . . more and more impossible" (Marx 1955 [1848]:13; see Landes 1969:1–40).

Civil solidarity is, in fact, fundamentally linked to differentiation in these other structural dimensions. Only if religion is abstracted from the earthly realm and oriented toward a transcendent, impersonal divine source can "individualism" emerge—i.e., an accordance of status to the individual person regardless of social position (Little 1969; Walzer 1965). Only with political constitutionalism, which is closely related to such religious developments (Friedrichs 1964), can groups respond to injustice, not in terms of reasserting primordial unity but in terms of defending their rights as members of the wider community (Bendix 1977). Only with the functional, impersonal form of industrial organization can positions be awarded on the basis of efficiency rather than in terms of kinship, race, or geographical origins. Civil solidarity cannot, however, simply be considered the reflection of these other differentiations. Not only does it constitute an independent, nonresidual dimension with which these institutional developments interact but it occurs, in addition, through particular, concrete mechanisms that, in responding to these developments, create wider solidarity: through more efficient transportation and communication, increased geographical and cultural mobility, urbanization, secular education, mass and elite occupational mobility and intermarriage, and increasingly consensual civic ritualization (see E. Weber 1976; Goode 1963:28–80; Lipset and Bendix 1960; Shils and Young 1975:135– 52).[2]

But although these systemic linkages are certainly correct, there has been a strong tendency to conflate such abstract complementarity with empirical history. Theorists of solidarity have themselves been infected by Enlightenment rationalism. From the beginning of Western society, in fact, "progressive" thinking has confidently proclaimed purely civic solidarity to be the "future" of the human race, whether this future lay in the Athenian polis, Roman law, the universal brotherhood of Christianity, the social contract, the General Will, or classless communism.[3] But in historical reality differentiation is not a homogeneous process. It occurs in different spheres at different times, and these leads and lags have enormously complex repercussions on societal development (Smelser 1971; Vallier 1971; Eisenstadt 1973; E. Weber 1976). As an autonomous dimension, solidarity varies independently of developments in other spheres. As a result, civic integration is always unevenly attained. Indeed, the newly created, more expansive associations that result from differentiation will often themselves become, at some later point in time, narrowly focused solidarities that oppose any further development. This is as true for the transcendent religions and nationalist ideologies that have promoted symbolic and political differentiation as for the economic classes, like the bourgeoisie and proletariat, which after a triumphant expansion of cosmopolitanism have often become a source of conservative antagonism to the wider whole.

Most fundamentally, however, civil integration is uneven because even national society exhibits an historical core. While this founding group may create a highly differentiated national political framework, it will also necessarily establish, at the same time, the preeminence of certain primordial qualities.[4] While members of noncore groups may be extended full legal rights and may even achieve high levels of actual institutional participation, their full membership in the solidarity of the national community may never be complete (Lipset and Rokkan 1967; Rokkan 1975). This tension between core and civil solidarity must inform any theory of inclusion in industrial societies.

A Multidimensional Model: The Internal and External Axes of Inclusion

My focus here is on the problem of ethnic, not class, inclusion. I define ethnicity as the real or perceived primordial qualities that accrue to a group by virtue of shared race, religion, or national origin, including in the latter category linguistic and other cultural attributes associated with a common territorial ancestry (see Schermerhorn 1970:12).

Inclusion of an ethnic out-group depends on two factors: (1) the external, or environmental, factor, which refers to the structure of society that surrounds the core group; (2) the internal, or volitional, factor, which refers to the relationship between the primordial qualities of core group and out-group. The external factor includes the economic, political, integrative, and religious systems of society; the more differentiated these systems are, the more inclusion becomes a legitimate possibility. In contrast to this external reference, the internal factor is more volitional: to the degree that primordial complementarity exists between core group and out-group, members of the core group will tend to regard inclusion as a desirable possibility. Finally, although both internal and external factors can be measured behaviorally, their most significant impact is subjective and phenomenological. To the degree that the environment is differentiated and primordiality is complementary, the felt boundaries of the terminal community will become expansive and civil.

While remaining systematic, this general model takes into account a wide range of factors. Each factor can be treated as independently variable, and by holding other factors constant we can establish experimental control. Of course such a general model cannot simply be tested; it must also be specified and elaborated. This can be accomplished by at least two different strategies.

Taking a purely analytic approach, we may trace the effects of varying each factor in turn. We can demonstrate, for example, that in terms of the external environment, differentiation in every social sphere—not simply changes in solidarity itself—has consequences for the structure of terminal integration. In South Africa, for example, while the divergence among primordial qualities remained fairly constant, more differentiated *economic development* ramified in ways that enlarged core and out-group interaction and increased the pressures on the rigidly ascribed political order (see Kuper 1969). Similarly, while primordial anti-Semitism remained unchanged and legal restrictions were unaltered, European mercantilism created important opportunities for the exercise of Jewish financial expertise, the recognition of which eventually had wide-ranging repercussions. In nineteenth-century America, on the other hand, the black out-group was not drawn first into qualitatively more differentiated economic production. While the primordial separation between black and Caucasian Americans remained constant, the Civil War initiated changes in the *legal system* that differentiated some (if not all) individual rights from racial qualities. As an example of variation in the *political environment*, we can refer to the processes often initiated by the construction of certain great empires. By differentiating overarching bureaucracies and impersonal rules, conquerors like Alexander and Napoleon opened up opportunities for excluded groups, like the Jews, in nations where the primordial distinctions between core group and out-group, and other structural characteristics as well, had remained relatively unchanged.

Although the relative differentiation of religion constitutes another variable in the inclusion process, as I have indicated above and will illustrate further below, the contrast between Protestantism and Catholicism, both relatively transcendent religions, is instructive for the kinds of specifications that must be introduced in applying this model to the complexity of a concrete historical case. Whereas the greater symbolic abstraction and institutional differentiation of Protestantism, especially the Puritan variety, is generally more conducive to inclusion than Catholicism, in the exclusion produced by slavery the reverse has often been true, as the contrast between Anglo-Saxon and Iberian slave conditions has demonstrated (Elkins 1969). Indeed, in the particular conditions of slavery, two of the most traditionalistic aspects of Iberian Catholicism were particularly conducive to black inclusion: (1) its relative paternalism generated a greater concern for the well-being of out-groups than did the more individualistic voluntary principles of Protestant societies; and (2) the Catholic fusion of church and state encouraged religious interference in the political and legal order to an extent unheard of in Anglo-Saxon societies.

These broad structural changes in the "external environment" have affected solidarity through the kind of specific integrating mechanisms I outlined above: increased interaction as effected through geographic and economic mobility, increased economic and political participation, expanded education and communication, and intermarriage. Significant numbers of American blacks, for example, used their upgraded legal status to emigrate, especially after World War I, to urban areas, where the racially based qualifications for economic and political participation could not be so easily enforced. Small but influential segments of European Jewry (the *Schutzjuden,* or "protected Jews") used the limited political immunity generated by their economic prowess to gain access to the secular, homogenizing culture of nineteenth-century Europe. By the same token, it was participation in South Africa's differentiated economic life that produced for nonwhites increased access to universalistic culture through education and economic and geographical mobility through, in part, expanding urbanization (Doxey 1961:85–109; Van der Horst 1965; Van den Berghe 1965:86, 279–80). In fact, it was precisely to inhibit and control these mechanisms—to protect core group domination from the effects of societal differentiation—that Apartheid was first introduced by the Afrikaner Nationalist elite (Kuper 1960; Van den Berghe 1965; see Blumer 1965).

We may, on the other hand, hold environmental factors constant and trace the effects of variation in internal factors. Probably the most significant illustration of variation in primordial complementarity and its relation to inclusion is the widespread phenomenon of finely graded color stratification (see Gergen 1968). In Mexico, where a light Spanish or *criollo* complexion has traditionally defined the racial core, *mestizos,* or mixed bloods, are granted significantly more inclusion than the darker-skinned Indians. This continuum from light to dark color has created a finely graded series of "internal" opportunities for inclusion. The same kind of color gradation, from black to "colored" to white, affects access to the internal environment in South Africa. The rule in both cases is based on the complementarity criterion: members of a solidary out-group have access to the degree that their racial traits are seen as closer to those of the core group. Similar kinds of gradations could be established along the dimensions of religion and national origins, as I illustrate later in this paper. Variations in these internal factors facilitate inclusion by affecting the kinds of structural mechanisms I have cited above, and the latter, of course, affect in turn the way the complementarity criterion manifests itself. Thus, while Peru's population exhibits the same color grading as that found in Mexico, darker "mixed blood" has gained significantly less inclusion there. This variation can be explained by the interaction of color with the greater differentiation of the Mexican social structure, produced by the contrast between Mexican and Peruvian colonial development and by the impact of the Mexican revolution (Harris 1964:36–40).

Having outlined the major analytic features of this inclusion model, in the following I seek to demonstrate its applicability via a specific case study.[5]

The Model Applied: The Uneven Inclusion of Europeans, Asians, and Africans in the United States

In discussing the U.S. case, I compare levels of inclusion of European and non-European immigrants and consider, within each category, variations in both internal and external factors.

The social system that confronted mass European immigration after 1820 presented, by the standards of its time, an unusually "civil" structure. In large part this depended on America's historical past, or perhaps its lack of one (Hartz 1955; Lipset 1965:1–233). Without an American feudalism, there existed no aristocracy that could monopolize economic, political, and intellectual prerogatives on a primordial basis. Similarly, without the legacy of Catholicism and an established church, spiritual domination and monopolization were less viable possibilities than they were in Europe (Bellah 1970:168–89).

As a result of this and other historically specific factors, institutional life in America was either unusually differentiated or at least open to becoming more so. Schumpeter's notion of an open class system applies more to the early American nation than to Europe, for while geographical and economic mobility did not eliminate the American class structure, they guaranteed that actual class membership fluctuated to a significant degree (Thernstrom 1974). Although America had an unusually weak national bureaucracy, its political system was differentiated in other important ways. The combination of strong constitutional principles and a dearth of traditional elites generated early party conflict and encouraged the allocation of administrative offices by a "spoils system" rather than according to the kind of implicit kinship criteria inherent in a more traditionally status-based civil service. The wide distribution of property and populist opposition to stringent electoral qualifications meant a significant dispersion of the franchise. Finally, the diversity and decentralized

character of Protestant churches in America encouraged the proliferation of pietistic religious sects and voluntary denominationalism
rather than established religion (Miller 1956:16–98, 141–52; Miller
1967:90–120, 150–62; Mead 1963:12–37). The transcendent, abstract
quality of Anglo-American Protestantism also made it conducive to
the secularization of intellectual and scientific discussion and to the
emergence of public, nonreligious education.

This external situation must be balanced, however, against the
internal one. Despite its relatively civil structure, this American nation had been founded by a strong self-conscious primordial core.
White in race, Anglo-Saxon and English-speaking in ethnicity, intensely Protestant in religious identity, this "WASP" core group sought
to maintain a paradox that, though hypocritical, was rooted in the
historical experience of the American nation. They asserted that
American institutions, while differentiated and civil, were at the same
time permeated by certain primordial qualities (Jordan 1968). And,
indeed, although a basic factor in American race relations from the
outset, until the 1820s and 1830s this anomaly was not severely tested
within the white society. During the seventeenth century, European
immigrants were almost entirely English, and although the sources of
immigration varied more in the eighteenth century, the nation's English and Protestant primordial core could still conceivably be identified with the institutional structure of the nation (Hansen 1940;
Handlin 1957:23–39).

Between 1820 and 1920 America experienced massive immigration
from a wide variety of European nations. As the core group tried to
defend its privileged position waves of xenophobic sentiment and
exclusionary movements were produced (Higham 1969). Yet by the
middle of the present century, these out-groups had achieved relatively successful inclusion (Glazer 1975:3–32), at least within the
limits established by the necessarily historical roots of national identity (Gordon 1964; Glazer and Moynihan 1963).

In terms of the internal volitional factor in inclusion, the points of
conflict and accommodation in the immigration process must be assessed in terms of the congruence between primordial solidarities
(Hansen 1940; see Schooler 1976). While the Caucasian homogeneity
of the out-groups and the core group prevented racial conflict, significant polarization still occurred between the WASP core and non-
English immigrants. The division was most intense, however, between the core and northern European immigrants (siding together)
and southern European groups (Handlin 1957:75, 85; Higham 1969).
Southern Europeans, after all, differed more strikingly from the core

in national culture and language. Although this national conflict was partly offset by the Christianity that most immigrants shared, antipathy between Catholics and Protestants made the religious variable another significant point of ethnic cleavage.

In the actual empirical process of inclusion, these points of internal cleavage and convergence were combined in a variety of ways (Parsons 1967b; Blauner 1972:56, 68). The Irish, for example, played an important bridging role, for while sharing certain vital cultural and linguistic traits with the English core, their Catholicism allowed them to interpenetrate on the religious dimension with the later, more intensely excluded Catholic group, the Italians (Handlin 1973:116–24). Similarly, although the Jews were disliked for specifically religious reasons, this was partially offset by racial and national convergence, particularly in the cases of northern European Jews like the Germans. Between the Christian core group and eastern European Jewish immigrants, in fact, German Jews often played a mediating role like that of the Irish Catholics between the English core and the southern Europeans (Howe 1976).

After they had become naturalized citizens, and within the limitations established by their primordial divergence, these European immigrants took advantage of the openings presented by differentiation in the external environment to contest the privileged position of America's WASP core (Handlin 1973). According to their respective origins and special skills, groups took different institutional paths toward inclusion. Catholics used American disestablishment to gain religious inclusion and legitimacy, and Catholicism gradually became one Christian denomination among many (Ahlstrom 1972:546–54, 825–41). In the big cities, Catholics used America's party structure and spoils system to gain power. Jews, on the other hand, parlayed their urban-economic background into skills that were needed in the industrializing economic system (Blauner 1972:62–63). Later, the Jewish emphasis on literacy—which in its Old Testament emphasis on "the Word," which it shares with Protestantism, partly neutralized the religious cleavage—helped Jews to gain access to the intellectual and scientific products of America's secular culture.

The internal and external situation that confronted America's non-European "immigrants"—those from Africa and Asia—was strikingly different.[6] In terms of primordial qualities, divergence was much more intense. Racial differences created an initial highly flammable cleavage, one to which Protestant societies were (and are) particularly sensitized (Elkins 1969; Tannenbaum 1969; Bellah 1975:86–112). Asians and Africans were also distinguished more sharply in the religious dimension, for few shared the majority's commitment to Christianity. In fact, as "non-Christians," blacks were, in the seventeenth and eighteenth centuries, as often the butt of religious as of racial slurs. Superimposed upon these religious and racial dimensions was the sharp divergence between non-Europeans and the American core in terms of national origins, viz., long-standing American fantasies about "darkest Africa" and the "exotic Orient" (Light 1972; Blauner 1972:65). Further, there existed no common linguistic reference or (for Africans at least) urban tradition to bridge the gap (Blauner 1972:61; Handlin 1957; 80–81). The WASP core group, and indeed the new European immigrants themselves, reacted strongly against such primordial disparity: the history of mob violence against Chinese and blacks has no precedent in reactions against European immigrants.

Equally important in the fate of these immigrants, however, was the nature of the external environment they entered (see Blauner 1972). Entering as slaves in the seventeenth and eighteenth centuries, blacks were without legal rights. Because their participation in American institutional life was at every point legally fused with the biological criterion of race, they faced a closed, not an open and differentiated, social system. Although the circumstances were much less severe for the Chinese immigrants who entered *en masse* in the 1850s, their common status as indentured laborers sharply limited their mobility and competitiveness in the labor market (Bean 1968:163–65; Lyman 1970:64–77). This external inhibition exacerbated primordial antagonism, and the California state legislature passed a series of restrictive pieces of legislation that further closed various aspects of institutional life to the Chinese (Lyman 1970:95–97). Similarly, whereas the Japanese did not face any initial external barriers, the primordial reaction against the agricultural success of immigrant Japanese farmers produced California's Alien Land Law, which fused farm ownership with naturalized citizenship, a status denied to all non-Caucasian first-generation immigrants (Bean 1968:332–35; Modell 1970:106–10). This law partly undermined their agriculture production, forcing masses of Japanese into the cities (Light 1972:73–74). (External situations characterized by "fusion" of the type described above will hereafter be referred to as "fused.") At one time or another, then, each non-European group faced a social environment that was fused to one degree or another. Simply in terms of external factors alone, therefore, non-European immigrants could not as easily transform their numbers into political power, their economic talents into skills and rewards, and their intellectual abilities into cultural accomplishments.

Uneven institutional differentiation and internal primordial divergence together generated massive barriers to African and Asian inclusion that protected not only the WASP core group but also the partially included European immigrants. To the degree that American blacks and Asians have moved toward inclusion, it is the result of accommodation on both fronts. In terms of internal factors, widespread conversion not only to Christianity but also to "Americanism," the adoption of the English language, and the assumption of an urban life-style have had significant impact, as have the changing religious sensitivities of the Christian majority and the continued secularization of American culture.

On the external side, institutional differentiation has opened up in different dimensions at different times. With the legal shift after the Civil War, economic and cultural facilities (Lieberson 1980:159–69) began to be available for some blacks, particularly for those who immigrated to northern cities after World War I. Only after further legal transformations in the 1950s and 1960s, however, has political power become fully accessible, a leverage that in turn has provided greater cultural and economic participation. In the Asian case, discriminatory legislative enactments were gradually overturned in the courts and formally free access to societal resources was restored by the end of World War II. Two facts explain the remarkably greater rate of Asian as compared to black inclusion. First, their great "external" advantages allowed Chinese and Japanese immigrants to preserve, at least for several generations, the resilient extended-kinship network of traditional societies (Light 1972; see Eisenstadt 1954). Second, the core group's primordial antipathy was, in the end, less intense toward Asians (Lieberson 1980:366–67), whose racial contrast was less dramatic, traditional religion more literate, and national origins more urbanized and generally accessible.

A Note on the Model's Application to the Colonial Situation

Although I have developed this model specifically with reference to relatively modernized Western societies, I would like to comment briefly on its relevance to the colonial situation, both because the notion of "internal colonialism" has been recently applied to these Western societies (Blauner 1972; Hechter 1975; see also note 5, this paper) and because colonial and postcolonial societies have themselves been so vitally affected by the modernization process.

As a form of ethnic domination that usually combines a highly fused external environment with vast primordial disparity, the prototypical colonial situation must be viewed as the polar opposite of solidary inclusion. For this reason, and because colonization has involved the initial and often continual application of force, there has been a strong tendency to perceive colonization in a theoretically undifferentiated way, as initiating a system of total domination that can end only in secession and revolution. From the perspective developed here, this perception is in error: the colonial situation is subject to the same kind of analytic differentiation and internal variation as any other relationship between core group and subordinate out-group. Indeed, every core group, whether in the West or in the third world, rests historically upon some form of colonization. Early Parisians colonized the territorial communities that later composed France, much as the French later tried to incorporate, much less successfully, the North African Algerian community. Similarly, the difference is only one of degree between the aggressive nation building initially undertaken on the island now called England by the English core group; the subsequent domination by the English nation over its neighboring communities in the British Isles; and the later English colonization of the non-British empire.

Resolution of the colonial situation, then, varies according to the same analytic factors as does the inclusion or exclusion of out-groups in Western societies. Although the rigidity of later colonial situations has often produced radicalized nationalist movements for ethnic secession (see below), there have been alternative developments. The case of Great Britain is instructive in this regard (for background see Beckett 1966; Bulpitt 1976; Hanham 1969; Hechter 1975; Mitchison 1970; Norman 1968; Philip 1975; and Rose 1970, 1971). Although Wales, Scotland, and Ireland were all incorporated involuntarily, the nature of the external political factor by which this colonization was accomplished was crucial for later events. The early military domination of Ireland by the still highly traditional English state was far harsher than the later incorporation of Wales and Scotland by an English state much more committed to bureaucratic and, in the case of Scotland, constitutional organization. This initial political variation created a crucial context for the critical primordial relation of religion, helping to determine the relative success of England's attempts to incorporate these colonies into Reformation Protestantism. Scotland and Wales were successfully "reformed"; Ireland was not. In combination with the territorial discontinuity of Ireland, this religious situation created the basis for the much more passionate primordial antipathy that developed between Ireland and England. It also prevented the kind of elite intermingling that helped to further mitigate primordial antagonism between England and the other colonies. On the basis of this primordial religious antagonism, the relatively undifferentiated condition of English church-state relations became crucial to Irish development, producing the fusion of economic, political, and religious positions that was unknown to Wales and Scotland. This, in turn, set the stage for the harsh settlement communities that finally transformed the Irish-English relation into the kind of rigid and exploitative situation that is so close to the traditional colonial one. Finally, only in this multidimensional historical context can the divergent responses to English industrialization be properly understood. Whereas the vast differentiation of the English economy that occurred in the nineteenth century produced significant leverage for the Welsh and Scots, the Irish were unable to take advantage of this opportunity for inclusion to any comparable degree. Indeed, in Ireland this industrialization actually helped to create the internal resources for national emancipation.

In such rigid colonial situations, if economic and cultural mobilization do not lead to successful secessionist movements (see below), they may trigger instead extraordinary efforts at core group protection. In South Africa, Apartheid was instituted only in 1948 after intensifying economic, political, and cultural modernization threatened to open up various spheres to African participation (Doxey 1961; Van der Horst 1965). In terms of the model proposed here, Apartheid represents an attempt to isolate the "mechanisms" of inclusion— urbanization, geographical and economic mobility, education, communication, intermarriage—from the underlying processes of differentiation that produced them. Using formally legitimate coercion, Apartheid tries to link each of these mechanisms to the primordial dimension of race. It establishes racial "tracks" for job training, urbanization, education, intermarriage, sexual intercourse, spiritual action, public association, and communication (Kuper 1960). In this strategy of coping with increased differentiation through government-induced and government-legitimated racism, the Apartheid strategy resembles the Nazi one. Just as Nazism went beyond the merely conservative antidemocratic regimes of an earlier Germany because the latter could no longer manage the strains of a rapidly and unevenly differentiating society, so Apartheid is the kind of radical, violent response to a challenge to core solidarity that occurs only in an industrialized society undergoing rapid modernization. In both German Nazism and South African Apartheid, this more radical opposition to change was carried out by the more insecure older social groups—in Germany by segments of the lower middle class, and in South Africa by the Afrikaner (not the British) Nationalist party.

If traditional colonialism could create such different outcomes depending on the particular content of external and internal relationships, the fate of so-called "internal colonies" in contemporary industrial societies must surely be considered in an equally nuanced way. Only such a sensitivity to analytical variations, for example, can explain the kind of divergent experiences of the descendants of Mexicans, Africans, Indians, Japanese, and Chinese—all of whom have been considered colonized groups—in the United States today.

The Process of Inclusion and Ideological Strategies

Structural dislocations, of course, do not directly imply social mobilization. However, with the single exception of Diaspora communities, solidary exclusion will, eventually, provoke mobilization designed to equalize out-group positions vis-à-vis the core. The nature of these struggles and the kind of ideological strategies the out-groups assume will be related closely to the structural bases of their exclusion. Three ideal-typical strategies may be distinguished.

Assimilative Movements and "Equal Opportunity." Assimilation may be defined as the effort to achieve full institutional participation through identification with the primordial qualities of the core group. Significant movement in this antiethnic direction will be a viable strategy only under certain conditions. If inclusion is reasonably to be viewed simply as a matter of closing the "primordial gap," fairly substantial external opportunities must exist. Assimilation is not, of course, a rationally calculated strategy. It emerges rather from the experience of relative commonality and from certain levels of actual sociation in institutional life. In the American case, both Christian and Jewish European immigrants have followed this path as, more recently, have Asian-Americans. In Britian, although the Welsh and Scots have shown strong assimilative tendencies, these have been intertwined, as will be seen, with more primordially sensitive strategies.

The conflicts within assimilative groups are between "traditionalists," who wish to maintain strong ethnic identity and are usually regarded as politically conservative, and "modernists," who seek to adopt the dominant ethnic style and most often are viewed as politically progressive. As for conflicts between assimilationists and the host society, assimilating solidary out-groups produce significant independent social and political movements only in first generations. After this initial wave, however, they often constitute important cultural forces and produce widely influential ethnic spokesmen. The self-conscious stratificational principle that such assimilative spokesmen adopt is "equal opportunity" rather than "equality of results." The assimilationsists' drive for equality is expressed in the desire for "social rights" such as public education. Yet they simultaneously embrace the ideal of individual liberty for every member of the society, justifying their demand for limited egalitarianism on the grounds that it is necessary to sustain the principle of individual meritocratic competition. This commitment to liberty only reflects their structural experience: for assimilative groups constitutional, individualizing freedoms have been an effective lever in the inclusion process (Raab 1972; Glazer 1975).

Even in the limiting case of maximal external opportunity and internal complementarity, however, it is unlikely that the primordial gap will ever be completely closed—a fact that cannot, moreover, be attributed merely to the core group's historical advantage. Highly assimilated out-groups themselves often seek to maintain vestiges of primordial definition—what Weber cynically labeled ersatz ethnicity and what contemporary Americans admiringly call "roots." Solidary differentiation, after all, need not have a pejorative connotation; it is necessary for the construction of social identification as such. For this reason, the concept of civil society is limiting. Although an assimilating out-group disproportionately identifies with a core group, the definition of core primordiality may itself be subtly changed by the very process of assimilation (see Glazer 1975).

Nationalist Movements and Ethnically Conscious Inclusion. In groups that experience stronger primordial divergence from core groups and face more difficult structural barriers, assimilative strategies will not predominate. To be sure, assimilation will be one reaction to solidary exclusion, and as long as out-group efforts at inclusion continue it will remain, if only unconsciously, a significant and important strategy in breaking down the barrier of primordial divergence. Yet where solidary groups face significantly fused external structures or possess certain primordial qualities—like race, or origin in an autonomous territorial area—that cannot easily be mitigated, they will remain primordially sensitive to a significant degree. When these groups become mobilized, the stratificational principle that they advocate shifts from the "balanced" endorsement of equal opportunity to more group-oriented demands for preferential treatment. As the equality of results becomes more significant, the individual rights of the dominant core receive increasingly less attention (Hentoff 1964; Prager 1978); Glazer (1975) ignores these basic distinctions in his conflation of the European and non-European aspects of U.S. inclusion. This shift reflects, of course, the *relative* failure of differentiated constitutional principles and civil rights in effecting out-group inclusion. Such an ideological transition is manifest in the "affirmative action" demands of America's racial minorities and in the demands by groups like the Welsh and Catalonians for linguistic equality in public education.

Contrary to the assimilationists, these nationalist groups do form independent social movements. In terms of struggles for actual political power, however, they usually express themselves through institutionalized party structures and economic organizations, and only sporadically create vehicles that compete for power with these dominant institutions. While primordially sensitive, these movements still seek equal institutional access. Moreover, though self-consciously committed to maintaining ethnic distinctiveness, they continue to undergo a gradual process of primordial homogenization. For example, while there is significant support in Wales for linguistic autonomy—social-psychological studies indicate much higher rates of approval for Welsh over English accents (Bourhis, Giles, and Talfel 1973)—the actual number of Welsh speakers has greatly declined in recent years. This would seem to have been the inevitable result of meeting the other major Welsh nationalist demands, which have urged inclusion in the English core institutions of culture and economic life (Thompson 1978). Such unintended consequences will continue to be a source of tension in national movements as long as the primordially sensitive group remains committed to inclusion rather than to secession. Whether these movements continue to seek inclusion depends on the relative flexibility of the institutional environment. In the cases of American blacks, the British Scots and Welsh, and the Spanish Catalonians, these environments have either continued to be sufficiently flexible or have recently become so. Insofar as they are not flexible, secessionist movements develop (Shils 1975a). In the case of French-Canadian Quebecois, the issue remains unresolved; their situation indicates the independent impact that social mobilization has on basic structural dislocation.

Nationalist Movements and Ethnic Secession.   Whereas efforts at ethnically conscious inclusion are only rarely committed to independent party organization, secessionist movements create political organizations that subordinate not only traditional political disagreements within the out-group but economic divisions as well.

Although the line should not be drawn too sharply, two general factors are crucial in facilitating this movement toward secession. The most basic one is unusual rigidity, in terms either of internal primordiality or the external environment. Among primordial qualities, independent territory seems to be the most significant factor; hence the radical nationalism so often associated with the ideal-typical colonial case. Shared territory is an "intrinsic," quasi-permanent factor around which shifts in ethnic consciousness can ebb and flow. In situations of high primordial consciousness, furthermore, it allows ethnicity to be connected to the political and economic interests of every sector of the excluded group. Territory has clearly been central, for example, in the most recent movement for Scottish secession from England in which the shifting economic opportunities of center and periphery have quickly become the focus of a new, more ethnically conscious political strategy (Thompson 1978). Such factors must interact, in turn, with external circumstances. In Ireland, for example, the secessionist drive developed much earlier and more intensively than it did in Scotland because autonomous territory was combined with the kinds of highly rigid external factors described above.

The second crucial factor in moving ethnically conscious groups from inclusive to secessionist strategies is a more idiosyncratic one: the international climate. If secessionist nationalism appears to be "the order of the day" in the mid-twentieth century and, more recently, in industrialized countries, it establishes a normative reference that will inevitably affect perceptions of the actual situation. This "demonstration effect" (Bendix 1976) or cultural diffusion (Smith 1978) is as significant for twentieth-century as it was for nineteenth-century nationalism (Kohn 1962:61–126); the anticolonial nationalism of the postwar world is as important for explaining the timing of the European secessionist movements of the 1960s and 1970s as the upsurge in Italian nationalism was for explaining the Irish Home Rule movement in the 1860s. The international context can also have highly important material effects, not just moral ones, when an outside power supplies arms or financial support to national insurgents.

As the present analysis begins to indicate, the relation between "structural" position—in an internal and external sense—and ideological outcome is mediated in any historical situation by a series of more specific intervening variables (see Smelser 1962). Thus, although the general relation obtains, any single out-group in the course of its development will actually experience all three of the movements described above. American Judaism, for example, continues to include factions that advocate Zionist secession, ethnically conscious inclusion, and assimilation. Furthermore, the movement toward a "structurally appropriate" strategy is never chronologically linear. American black consciousness about primordiality, for example, actually began to increase during the civil rights drives of the 1960s, when the assimilative standard of "equal opportunity" was dominant and the legal and political orders were finally becoming differentiated from biological, particularistic standards. The particular time order of ideological strategies depends upon a series of such historically specific factors, and on this more specific level conflict itself becomes an independent variable. One also wants to consider the effects of the distinction between leadership and the masses. Since strong and independent political leadership so often emerges primarily from middle classes and highly educated strata, certain initial advances toward inclusion—no matter how ultimately ephemeral—will usually occur before secessionist movements can forcefully emerge.

A similar issue concerns the actual motivations of solidary out-groups themselves. Certainly there are periods when excluded groups do not actively desire inclusion, and a few groups never want it. The degree to which an out-group experiences the desire for inclusion relates, in part, to the same internal volitional factors that affect core group receptivity to the excluded party; it also depends upon the length of time of mutual exposure and on the degree to which the external environment of the interaction is differentiated. Where the primordial gap is extreme, the external environment rigid, and the period of mutual exposure relatively short, exclusion is less likely to produce demands for inclusion. Even in this case, however, instrumental self-interest will usually produce demands for equal treatment, if not solidarity, as a strategy to alleviate unsatisfactory external conditions.

Conclusion

Given their rationalist bias, theories of nation building generally ignore the role of solidarity in societal development. Among those theorists who have discussed the integration problem, moreover, an evolutionary bias leads most to underestimate significantly the permanent importance of primordial definitions of the national community. In contrast to these prevailing perspectives, I have argued that because most nations are founded by solidary core groups, and because societal development after this founding is highly uneven, strains toward narrow and exclusive national solidarity remain at the center of even the most "civil" nation-state. Differences in national processes of ethnic inclusion—even in the industrial world—are enormous. To encompass this variation while retaining systematicity, I have proposed a multidimensional model. On the internal axis, inclusion varies according to the degree of primordial complementarity between core group and solidary out-group. On the external axis, inclusion varies according to the degree of institutional differentiation in the host society. It is in response to variations in these structural conditions that ethnic out-groups develop different incorporative strategies —assimilation, ethnically conscious inclusion, and nationalist secession—as well as different stratificational principles to justify their demands.

In applying this general model primarily to special aspects of the inclusion process in the United States I have elaborated it in important ways. Yet this effort is merely a first approximation; much further work remains before the model could truly become a theory of the middle range. For example, it would eventually have to be specified for different classes of empirical events. Therefore, within the general external and internal constraints established, inclusion seems to vary systematically according to the different modes of out-group contact: indentured servitude versus slavery, economic versus military colonization, colonization over groups within contiguous territories versus more territorially distinct occupation, and so forth.[9] This variation in turn affects the kind of external variable that is most significant in any given situation: the state, the economy, religion, or law.[8] This factor weighting is undoubtedly also affected by the kinds of historically specific "differentation combinations" encountered in particular national societies, i.e., which institutional sectors lead and which lag. Finally, different kinds of internal combinations might also be specified; for example, a white Anglo-Saxon Catholic core group will differ in predictable ways from a WASP one and a white Catholic southern European core group from a northern European one.

I hope that it is clear, however, how such further conceptualization can fruitfully draw upon the hypotheses already set forth in this paper. At the very least the model proposed here demonstrates not only that fundamental cleavages in developed societies can be nonutilitarian in scope and proceed along nonlinear paths, but also that within a multidimensional framework such complex strains can be conceptualized in a systematic comparative and historical manner.

Notes

1. At its extreme, such purely behavioral participation by out-groups forms the basis of "plural societies," in the terminology developed by Kuper and Smith (1969, Kuper 1978). In their terms, I am dealing in this essay with the causes and consequences of different degrees of pluralization in the industrial West, a subject to which plural societies theory has not yet devoted significant attention.

2. Although few of the treatments of these mechanisms sufficiently relate them to the distinctive problem of solidarity, the last mechanism I have cited, civic ritualization, is rarely given any attention at all. By civic ritual I refer to the affectively charged, rhetorically simplified occasions through which a society affirms the solidary bonds of its terminal community. Such consensual rituals, microcosms of which are repeated in local milieu, include everything from the funeral ceremonies of powerful leaders to the televised dramas of national political crises and the spectacles of national sports championships. One crucial symbolic element often invoked by these rituals is directly relevant to the crucial historical position of any society's core group, namely, the element of "national ancestors." Every system of national symbolism involves a myth of creation, and these narrative stories must be personified in terms of actual historical persons. These ancestors become an ascriptive "family" for the members of the terminal community, as, in America, George Washington is viewed as the "father" of the American nation. As the personification of the founding core group, the ethnic composition of these symbolic national ancestors is crucial, and the solidary history of a nation can be traced in terms of shifts in their purported ethnicity. In the United States, for example, there has been a struggle over whether the black leader, Martin Luther King, will be accorded such symbolic founding status. The creation of a national holiday honoring his birthday may have resolved this in the affirmative, but it is still too early for a definitive answer.

3. Even when anticivil developments are acknowledged, they tend to be treated as deviant eruptions from the purely civil mode, as in Nolte's penetrating analysis of fascism as an "antitranscendent" ideology or in Mosse's analysis of blood as the common denominator of German "Volk" culture (Nolte 1965; Mosse 1964).

4. This general statement must be modified in applying this model to developing rather than to developed nations. Although every society does have an historical, solidary core, the artificiality of the creation of many postcolonial societies leaves several founding ethnic blocs in primordial competition rather than a single founding group.

5. In terms of contemporary sociological theory, then, the animus of this paper is directed in several directions.

(1) While in one sense I am further developing the functionalist approach to differentiation theory, I am arguing for a much more serious recognition of group interest, differential power, uneven development, and social conflict than has usually characterized this tradition. My "neofunctionalist" argument begins, for example, from the intersection between neo-Marxist and Shilsian center-periphery theory and one aspect of Parsons' system theory, while modifying the former and energizing the latter. I also distance myself from the conflation of ideology, model, and empirical explanation that often characterizes Parsons' work.

(2) On the other hand, by stressing the necessity for analytic differentiation and

multidimensional causality, I am arguing against Marxist and structuralist analyses, which even when they formally recognize the independence of ethnic phenomena—whose inequality they rightly insist upon—continually try to root it in "last instance" arguments. Thus, even in his sophisticated version of Marxist analysis, John Rex (1970) never accepts religion or ethnicity as truly independent variables, nor, more fundamentally, does he view the problem of solidarity as an independent dimension of social life. Concentrating mainly on the activities of labor and work, ethnic domination per se becomes for Rex an extrinsic variable.

Very much the same instrumental theoretical bias reduces the value of Lieberson's (1980) impressive empirical study. In his effort to explain the relative lack of success of postslavery blacks as compared with white immigrants in the United States after 1880, Lieberson tries to conceive of the "heritage of slavery" simply as a structural barrier, i.e., one that affects only the external conditions of the competition between the two groups. In this way, despite his occasional recognition of their importance (e.g., p. 366), the subjective perception of differences experienced by the groups themselves—and by the other ethnic communities involved—becomes a residual category.

> I am suggesting a general process that occurs when racial and ethnic groups have an inherent conflict—and certainly competition for jobs, power, position, maintenance of different subcultural systems, and the like are such conflicts. Under the circumstances, there is a tendency for the competitors to focus on differences between themselves. The observers (in this case the sociologists) may then assume that those differences are the sources of conflict. In point of fact, the rhetoric involving such differences may indeed inflame them, but we can be reasonably certain that the conflict would have occurred in their absence. . . . Differences between blacks and whites (for example) enter into the rhetoric of race and ethnic relations, but they are ultimately secondary to the conflict for society's goodies. . . . Much of the antagonism toward blacks was based on racial features, but one should not interpret this as the ultimate cause. Rather the racial emphasis resulted from the use of the most obvious feature(s) of the group to support the intergroup conflict generated by a fear of blacks based on their threat as economic competitors. (pp. 382–83)

Without a multidimensional framework that takes cultural patterns as constraining structures in their own right Lieberson is necessarily forced to conceive of subjective "discrimination" as an individualistic variable. Indeed, he links the use of discrimination not only to supposedly "psychological" studies of attitude formation but also to analyses that find inherent racial qualities of the victims themselves to be the cause for their oppression.

(3) Finally, by stressing the strong possibility for social and cultural differentiation in Western societies and the distinction and relative autonomy of the external and internal axes of ethnic conflict, I argue against contemporary "internal colonialist" theory. This approach too often refers to domination in an undifferentiated and diffuse way and, conversely, underemphasizes the variations that characterize the histories of oppressed groups by virtue of their distinctive primordial relations to the core group and their different external environments.

(4) For the relation between the present argument and plural society theory—which still remains relatively unsystematized—see note 1 above.

6. A complete picture of the U.S. situation would have to include also the core group conquest of the native North American Indian civilization and the incorporation of the Mexican population of the southwestern United States. Although I believe that these more explicitly colonial situations can be analyzed within the framework presented here, specific variations must be introduced. See the following section of this paper.

7. For a discussion of independent political effects in the South African case, see Kuper 1965:42–56.

8. These are the kinds of variables that Schermerhorn 1970 makes the central focus of his analysis, virtually to the exclusion of the factors I have discussed above.

References

Ahlstrom, Sydney E. 1972. *A Religious History of the American People.* New Haven, Conn.: Yale University Press.

Alexander, Jeffrey C. (1978). "Formal and Substantive Voluntarism in the Work of Talcott Parsons: A Theoretical and Ideological Reinterpretation." *American Sociological Review* (April), v. 43:177–98.

——1983. *The Modern Reconstruction of Classical Thought: Talcott Parsons* vol. 4 of *Theoretical Logic in Sociology.* Berkeley: University of California Press.

Banfield, Edward C. 1959. *The Moral Basis of a Backward Society.* New York: Free Press.

Bean, Walton, 1968. *California.* New York: McGraw-Hill.

Beckett, J. C. 1966. *The Making of Modern Ireland, 1603–1923.* New York: Knopf.

Bellah, Robert N. 1970. *Beyond Belief.* New York: Harper and Row.

——1975. *The Broken Covenant.* New York: Seabury.

Bendix, Reinhard, 1977 (1964). *Nation Building and Citizenship.* Berkeley: University of California Press.

——1976. "The Mandate To Rule: An Introduction." *Social Forces* (December), (2):252–56.

Blauner, Robert, 1972. *Racial Oppression in America.* New York: Harper and Row.

Blumer, Herbert, 1965. "Industrialization and Race Relations." In Guy Hunter, ed., *Industrialization and Race Relations,* pp. 220–53. New York: Oxford University Press.

Bourhis, Richard Y., Howard Giles, and Henri Tajfel. 1973, "Language as a Determinant of Welsh Identity." *European Journal of Social Psychology* 3 (4):447–60.

Bulpitt, Him, 1976. "The Making of the United Kingdom: Aspects of English Imperialism." P.S.A. Workgroup on United Kingdom Politics, University of Strathclyde (September).

Coulton, G. G. 1935. "Nationalism in the Middle Ages." *Cambridge Historical Journal* 5 (1):15–40.

Doxey, G. V. 1961. *The Industrial Colour Bar in South Africa.* New York: Oxford University Press.

Durkheim, Emile, 1947 (1893). *The Division of Labor in Society.* New York: Free Press.

Eisenstadt, S. N. 1954. *The Absorption of Immigrants.* London: Routledge and Kegan Paul.

——1963. *The Political System of Empires.* New York: Free Press.

——1973. *Tradition, Change, and Modernity.* New York: Wiley.

Elkins, Stanley. 1969. "Slavery in Capitalist and Non-Capitalist Countries." In Laura Foner and Eugene D. Genovese, eds., *Slavery in the New World,* pp. 8–26. Englewood, N.J.: Prentice-Hall.

Friedrichs, Carl J. 1964. *Transcendent Justice: The Religious Dimension of Constitutionalism.* Durham, N.C.: Duke University Press.

Geertz, Clifford. 1973a. *The Interpretation of Cultures*. New York: Basic Books.

——1973b. "The Integration Revolution: Primordial Sentiments and Civil Politics in the New States." In Clifford Geertz, *The Interpretation of Cultures*, pp. 255–310.

Gergen, Kenneth. 1968. "The Significance of Skin Color in Human Relations." In John Hope Franklin, ed., *Color and Race*, pp. 112–28. Boston, Mass.: Beacon Press.

Glazer, Nathan. 1975. *Affirmative Discrimination*. New York: Basic Books.

Glazer, Nathan and Daniel Patrick Moynihan. 1963. *Beyond the Melting Pot*. Cambridge, Mass.: MIT Press.

Goode, William J. 1963. *World Revolution and Family Patterns*. New York: Free Press.

Gordon, Milton M. 1964. *Assimilation in American Life*. London: Oxford University Press.

Handling, Oscar. 1957. *Race and Nationality in American Life*. New York: Doubleday.

——1973 (1951). *The Uprooted*. Boston, Mass.: Little, Brown.

Hanham, Harold J. 1969. *Scottish Nationalism*. London: Faber and Faber.

Hansen, Marvin Lee. 1940. *The Immigrant in American History*. Cambridge, Mass.: Harvard University Press.

Harris, Marvin. 1964. *Patterns of Race in the Americas*. New York: Walker.

Hartz, Louis. 1955. *The Liberal Tradition in America*. New York: Harcourt, Brace and Jovanovich.

Hechter, Michael. 1975. *Internal Colonialism: The Celtic Fringe in British Development, 1536–1966*. Berkeley: University of California Press.

Hentoff, Nat. 1964. "Reaching Equality by Special Treatment." In *The New Equality*. New York: Viking.

Higham, John. 1969. *Strangers in the Land*. New York: Atheneum.

Howe, Irving. 1976. *World of Our Fathers*. New York: Harcourt, Brace, Jovanovich.

Jordon, Winthrop D. 1968. *White Over Black*. Durham: University of North Carolina Press.

Kohn, Hans. 1962. *The Age of Nationalism*. New York: Harper and Row.

Kuper, Leo. 1960. "The Heightening of Racial Tension." *Race* (November), 2:24–32.

——1962. *An African Bourgeoisie*. New Haven, Conn.: Yale University Press.

——1969. "Political Change in White Settler Societies: The Possibility of Peaceful Democratization." In Kuper and Smith, *Pluralism in Africa*, pp. 169–93.

——1978. "The Theory of Plural Society: Race and Conquest." Unpublished manuscript.

Kuper, Leo and M. G. Smith, eds. 1969. *Pluralism in Africa*. Berkeley: University of California Press.

Landes, David. 1969. *The Unbound Prometheus*. London: Cambridge University Press.

Lieberson, Stanley. 1980. *A Piece of the Pie*. Berkeley and Los Angeles: University of California Press.

Light, Ivan. 1972. *Ethnic Enterprise in America*. Berkeley: University of California Press.

Lipset, Seymour Martin. 1965. *The First New Nation*. New York: Vintage.

Lipset, Seymour Martin and Stein Rokkan. 1967. "Cleavage Structures, Party Systems, and Voter Alignments: An Introduction." In Seymour Martin Lipset and Stein Rokkan, eds., *Party Systems and Voter Alignments*, pp. 1–64. New York: Free Press.

Lipset, Seymour Martin and Reinhard Bendix. 1960. *Social Mobility in Industrial Society*. Berkeley: University of California Press.

Little, David. 1969. *Religion, Order, and Law*. New York: Harper Torchbook.

Lyman, Stanford M. 1970. "Strangers in the Cities: The Chinese on the Urban Frontier." In Charles Wollenberg, ed., *Ethnic Conflict in California History*, pp. 61–100. Los Angeles, Calif.: Tinnon-Brown.

Marx, Karl. 1955. (1848). *The Communist Manifesto*. Samuel Beer, ed., Northbrook, Ill.: AHM.

Mead, Sidney E. 1963. *The Lively Experiment*. New York: Harper and Row.

Miller, Perry. 1956. *Errand Into the Wilderness*. Cambridge, Mass.: Harvard University Press.

——1967. *Nature's Nation*. Cambridge, Mass.: Harvard University Press.

Mitchison, Rosalind. 1970. *A History of Scotland*. London: Methuen.

Modell, John. 1970. "Japanese-Americans: Some Costs of Group Achievement." In Charles Wollenberg, ed., *Ethnic Conflict in California History*, pp. 101–20. Los Angeles, Calif.: Tinnon-Brown.

Mosse, George L. 1964. *The Crisis of German Ideology*. New York: Grosset and Dunlap.

Nakane, Chie. 1970. *Japanese Society*. Berkeley: University of California Press.

Nolte, Ernst. 1965. *The Three Faces of Fascism*. New York: Mentor.

Norman, E. R. 1968. *Anti-Catholicism in Victorian England*. London: George Allen and Unwin.

Parsons, Talcott. 1967a. "On the Concept of Influence." In Talcott Parsons, ed., *Sociological Theory and Modern Society*, pp. 355–82. New York: Free Press.

——1967b. "Full Citizenship for the Negro American?" In Talcott Parsons, ed., *Sociological Theory and Modern Society*, pp. 422–65. New York: Free Press.

——1971. *The System of Modern Society*. Englewood Cliffs, N.J.: Prentice-Hall.

Philip, Alan Butt. 1975. *The Welsh Question*. Cardiff: University of Wales Press.

Prager, Jeffrey. 1978. "Equal Opportunity and Equal Protection: Ideas and Interpretation in Flux." Presentation to the annual meeting of the American Sociological Association, San Francisco, California, August, 1978.

Raab, Earl.1972. "Quotas by Any Other Name." *Commentary* (January), pp. 41–45.

Rex, John. 1970. *Race Relations in Sociological Theory*. New York: Schocken.

Rokkan, Stein. 1975. "Dimensions of State Formation and Nation Building: A Possible Paradigm for Research on Variations within Europe." In Charles Tilly, ed., *The Formation of Nation States in Western Europe*, pp. 562–600. Princeton, N.J.: Princeton University Press.

Rose, Richard. 1970. "The United Kingdom as a Nation-State." Survey Research Center Occasional Paper No. 6, University of Strathclyde, Glasgow.

——1971. *Governing without Consensus*. London: Faber and Faber.

Royal Institute of International Affairs. 1939. *Nationalism*. Oxford: Oxford University Press.

Schermerhorn, R. A. 1970. *Comparative Ethnic Relations*. New York: Random House.

Schooler, Carmi. 1976. "Serfdom's Legacy: An Ethnic Continuum." *American Journal of Sociology* 81(6):1265–86.

Shils, Edward A. 1975a. "The Integration of Societies." In Edward A. Shils, ed., *Center and Periphery: Essays in Macro-Sociology*, pp. 48–90. Chicago, Ill.: University of Chicago Press.

——1975b. "Primordial, Personal, Sacred, and Civil Ties." In Edward A. Shils, ed., *Center and Periphery: Essays in Macro-Sociology*, Chicago, Ill.: University of Chicago Press

Shils, Edward A. and Young, Michael. 1975 (1956). "The Meaning of the Coronation." In Edward A. Shils, ed., *Center and Periphery: Essays in Macro-Sociology*, pp. 135–52. Chicago, Ill.: University of Chicago University Press.

Smelser, Neil J. 1962. *Theory of Collective Behavior*. New York: Free Press.

——1971. "Stability, Instability, and the Analysis of Political Corruption." In Bernard Barber and Alex Inkeles, eds., *Stability and Social Change*, pp. 7–29. Boston, Mass.: Little, Brown.

Smith, Anthony. 1978. "The Diffusion of Nationalism: Some Historical and Sociological Perspectives." *British Journal of Sociology* 29(2): 234–48.

Tannenbaum, Frank. 1969. "Slavery, the Negro, and Racial Prejudice." In Laura Foner and E. D. Genovese, eds., *Slavery in the New World*, pp. 3–7. Englewood Cliffs, N.J.: Prentice-Hall.

Thernstrom, Stephen. 1974. "Socialism and Social Mobility." In John H. M. Laslett and Seymour Martin Lipset, eds., *Failure of a Dream?* pp. 509–27. New York: Doubleday.

Thompson, Seamus. 1978. *Dual Incorporation in British Politics: A Theory of Class and Ethnic Mobilization*. Ph.D. dissertation. University of California (Los Angeles).

Tocqueville, Alexis de. 1945 (1835). *Democracy in America*. Vol. 1. New York: Random House.

Toennies, Ferdinand. 1957 (1887). *Community and Society*. East Lansing, Mich.: Michigan State University Press.

Vallier, Ivan. 1971. "Empirical Comparison of Social Structure: Leads and Lags." In Ivan Vallier, ed., *Comparative Method in Sociology*, pp. 203–63. Berkeley: University of California Press.

Van den Berghe, Pierre L. 1965. *South Africa: A Study in Conflict*. Middletown, Conn.: Wesleyan University Press.

Van der Horst, Sheila T. 1965. "The Effects of Industrialization on Race Relations in South Africa." In Guy Hunter, ed., *Industrialization and Race Relations*, pp. 97–140. New York: Oxford University Press.

Walzer, Michael. 1965. *The Revolution of the Saints*. Cambridge, Mass.: Harvard University Press.

Weber, Eugen. 1976. *Peasants Into Frenchmen: The Modernization of Rural France, 1870–1914*. Stanford, Calif.: Stanford University Press.

Weber, Max. 1958a (1904). "Class, Status, and Party." In Hans Gerth and C. Wright Mills, eds., *From Max Weber*, pp. 180–95. London: Oxford University Press.

——1958b. *The City*. New York: Free Press.

9

The Differentiation of the Solidary Public

Leon Mayhew

No sociological issue is closer to the center of confrontation between liberal and radical ideologies than the question of the nature and sources of solidarity. The liberal defense of modernity is founded on the assertion that new and valuable forms of differentiated solidarity emerge with modernization. Radical attacks on bourgeois modernity assert, to the contrary that capitalist "freedom" destroys traditional solidarity and produces disorganization. In the vocabulary of evolutionary theory, radical ideology insists that the "differentiation" of solidarity cannot occur until unity is reestablished in a fragmented, divided society by a socialist or communist state acting on behalf of collective interests. Modern solidary institutions are deliberately created, as it were, as a matter of state interest.

Shorn of the complications of dialectical terminology, the radical perspective is the more commonsensical view. It is easy to understand how the release of individual interests can unleash forces that destroy the traditional loyalties of kin, clan, and community. Heroic action to reassert the collective seems the ready path out of the jumble of modern life. Liberals, then, are on the ideological defensive; it is necessary for them to identify new and subtle organizing principles that, once seen, make modern society appear no less solidary than earlier social orders.

Market theory constitutes one approach to a defense of liberalism, but its emphasis on economic calculation makes classical market theory more suited to the defense of rational allocation of resources than of rational production of solidarity. Durkheim, approaching the problem from a more sociological starting place, emphasizes the differentiation of new norms for the institutional regulation of the marketplace and views these new normative patterns as indicative of a new solidarity. Durkheim was the first to emphasize that the new order is no less solidary than the old. His very emphasis on two types of solidarity is the lexical clue to his agenda.

Drawing upon Durkheim's institutional approach, Parsons has extended the analysis of the "organic solidarity" of modern society by calling attention to the institutional framework within which citizens freely and voluntarily form solidary relations with one another. The resulting "societal community" can be described as "differentiated," for the new solidary order does not simply replace kinship but rather emerges as a new level of solidarity with specialized functions and distinct modes of relationships to other components of the social order (Parsons 1971:86–121; Mayhew 1984a; Alexander 1983:96–102, 250–59).

In the present essay I will seek to develop the foregoing line of argument by:

(1) examining the concept of solidarity as typically expressed in social thought, especially in schemes that assert polarity between traditional solidary society and modern atomistic society;

(2) defining an alternative approach to solidarity as an aspect of communication;

(3) explicating Parsons' concept of the differentiation of societal community as an example of a communicative approach to solidarity;

(4) amplifying Parsons' account of the historical emergence of differentiated community; and

(5) extending Parsons' theory of societal community by outlining a concept of the stratification of the public and of public communication. The public is founded on the institutionalization of community in established social processes. These processes prevent the monopolization of communication but, at the same time, regulate public discourse and stratify access to public debate.

Solidarity and Gemeinschaft

For several decades, beginning in the late nineteenth century, social thought was dominated by polar conceptions of social evolution. Clusters of attributes of traditional social orders were said to be replaced by clusters of opposite attributes of modernity. Whether the dimension of change was labeled *GesellschaftGemeinschaft*, sacred-secular, or folk-urban, communal forms of social relations are placed at the traditional, premodern pole. Modernization, then, becomes a process of dissolving communal ties. Social mobility, population density, secular attitudes and, above all, the market nexus destroy face-to-face personal ties and loyalties and replace them with the more tenuous, brittle, selfish interpersonal interests created by trade, urban life, and large-scale association. Among these polar schemes, Toennies' distinction between *Gemeinschaft* (sometimes translated as "community") and *Gesellschaft* is the most paradigmatic and influential (Toennies 1957 [1887]). It also bears the most directly on the problem of modern community and clearly displays the moral and ideological burden of this sort of conceptual approach.

For Toennies, *Gemeinschaft* rests upon "natural will"; it is a community of spontaneous attraction—warm, natural fellow feeling—in which association is valued for its own sake and not as a means to some end beyond the relationship itself. *Gesellschaft*, on the other hand, rests on "artificial will," that is, calculation. One determines whether association with another within a market nexus is instrumental with respect to one's own goals. In a *Gesellschaft*, the motivation to associate is essentially ulterior.

The critical implication of this scheme is that instrumental action is not and cannot be solidary. Just as *Gemeinschaft* and *Gesellschaft* are polar opposites and mutually exclusive forms of social organization, so instrumental and solidary action become polar opposites and mutually exclusive forms of conduct. Instrumental motivation essentially excludes authentic solidarity; indeed, it cannot even be ethical. As much as Toennies may have wanted to deny that he was creating a value-laden moral theory, within the context of traditional German critical theory, *Gemeinschaft* is clearly superior to *Gesellschaft* from an ethical standpoint, for one form of the Kantian ethical imperative is: always treat others as ends in themselves, never as means to something else. Within this framework, then, modernity is suspect from the outset, for its characteristic forms of organization involve instrumental relationships. Such relationships, apart from their fundamentally suspect character, are also less warm, less supported by emotional bonds, more fragile and mobile—in short, less solidary.

During the 1960s, the sociology of development began to question polar evolutionary schemes, attacking their implications of linear developmental movement and their assumptions that tradition and modernity are mutually exclusive (Mayhew 1968). Nevertheless, common thinking about modernity and change have not always shaken the heritage of polar thought, especially as regards the assumption that authentic community must rest on natural bonds: kin, clan, and community, supported in the last analysis by inescapable common fate and reinforced by traditional cultural forms and ceremonies.

Such background assumptions have clouded the thinking of even sophisticated historians writing about the very origins of such forms of modern solidarity as rest more upon choice than nature. When, for example, Christopher Hill, writing on the significance of preaching in Puritan thought, claims that "the direct appeal to the heart of the individual believer as against the traditional ceremonial procession and the miracle of the mass contributed unconsciously to atomize the parish," he betrays a deep suspicion of inherent opposition between individual choice and community (Hill 1967:486). Or, when Michael Walzer asserts that the Puritan's attempt to make "natural connections"—local loyalty, kinship, and marriage—"subject to human will" sowed the seeds of loss of community, he falls into a similar habit of thought (Walzer 1965:193–94).

The Puritans thought that they were creating rather than destroying community. Community based upon mere natural connection was not community at all, for true community rests upon spiritual union, which in turn flows from preaching and reading—from communication.

I have written elsewhere on the foundations of liberal ideology in Puritan conceptions of communion (Mayhew 1984a, 1984b). These arguments need not be rehearsed here in detail. In the present context the point is that both Puritan thought and later liberal social thought proceed from a conception that is diametrically opposed to the idea that communal solidarity is destroyed by forms of association that express will and choice. The key to both Puritan and to subsequent liberal thought (and, as we shall see later, to Parsonian thought) on this subject is the idea that solidarity is or can be created by communication.

Solidarity, Instrumental Action, and Communication

It is appropriate at this point to define "solidarity." Formal, precise definitions of terms are beyond the scope of this essay, but it is necessary to establish boundaries for the rather broad range of concepts placed under the rubric of solidarity. I do not propose to stray far from the meaning of the term in common parlance. The word was borrowed from the French in the mid-nineteenth century and is commonly defined in dictionaries (along the lines of its French origins) as a quality of "perfect" unity within a community. This unity need not be total, in the sense of embracing unity in all things; unity in various respects, whether of interests, sympathies, aspirations, or any other unifying forces, qualifies as solidarity. According to this tradition, let us refer to "solidarity" as a form of social bond founded on a feeling of common membership in a group united by some commonality. Common culture, common residence, common fate, common faith, nationality, or ancestry all qualify, but nothing in this definition— the simple dictionary definition—excludes common instrumental aims. Nothing in the definition proposes that "natural" unities are more solidary than instrumental alliances, a notion that comes from the ideological overlay of romantic concepts of community, not from the ordinary meaning of the term.

From the sociological perspective, this terminological confusion should be clarified through the recognition that there are no "natural" solidarities. All solidarities, whether based upon kinship or upon deliberate, purposeful union, are founded upon a process of communication by which uniting commonalities are discovered or created. Such bonds derive from both verbal and nonverbal communication. Gestures and, indeed, outright acts of nurturance, starting with parental love and sustenance, start a deep bonding process. Yet humans, with their penchant for laying on levels of interpretation, significance, meaning, and conceptual frameworks, bring an additional cultural and creative dimension to the process that allows us, in saying that "uniting commonalities are discovered or created," to lay the emphasis on the creative process. Moreover, because human beings influence each other in the meanings and interpretations that they attach to things, they are open to persuasion. As we shall see, the fundamental insight that Parsons brings to his analysis of the differentiation of solidarity flows from his emphasis on persuasive communication as the foundation of new differentiated solidarities that do not rest on primal nurturant acts. In brief, persons can be persuaded that they have common interests and should be loyal to the solidary ties that these interests imply. It is the task of those who trace the development of this species of solidarity to show the structural forces that bring it about and the institutional foundations that sustain it.

Before explicating Parsons' technical concept of differentiated solidarity, it will be illuminating to establish one more point about the creation of solidarity in the everyday terms that I have employed so far.

Suppose that, through communication, two people discover not a unity of purpose, but a complementarity of purpose. They wish to form a relationship not because they share instrumental aims but because they want to use each other instrumentally in a mutually agreeable manner. John, a banana grower, wants his fence painted; Jim wants bananas. John and Jim do not, then, have a common interest in building a fence; John is interested in a fence, Jim in bananas. So they strike a bargain to exchange labor for bananas. This relationship of complementarity expressed in exchange is a discovered and created bond, but it does not, from this analytical perspective, count as solidarity, for it lacks unifying commonality. This, of course, is what critics of instrumental market organization have against the market as a form of bond: it is not per se solidary.

In this sense, Durkheim's initial definition of organic solidarity as based upon complementarity within a division of labor appears to stretch the meaning of the term "solidarity." Durkheim goes on, however, to stress that market organization based upon the mutuality of calculated self-interest would in fact be unstable; there must be an institutional framework outside individual contractual arrangements to give such arrangements solidity and force (Durkheim 1933:70–132). One way of expressing this insight so as to elucidate the concept of solidarity (in common usage as I have defined it) is to say that contracting partners have a common interest beyond the complementary interest that brought them together and became expressed in the terms of their bargained agreement: (1) they have a common interest in the stability and solidity of the relationship itself, which must last long enough to accomplish mutual complementary purposes; (2) they have a common interest in maintaining the institutional systems (e.g., the legal system) through which contractual relations are established and stabilized; and (3) they have a common interest in sustaining the solidarity of the larger community, whose interrelations are expressed in the contractual order and supported by its institutions. Thus there are three layers of solidarity based upon common interest outside the mutual, reciprocal, and instrumental interests of parties to bargained agreements, levels that can be called the "relational," the "institutional," and the "communal." I take this line of thought to be at the heart of Durkheim's development of the concept of "organic" solidarity.

Similar layers of solidarity surround *alliances* based upon common interests and *bargains* based upon complementary interests. Indeed, the distinction is analytical; concrete human bonds usually contain elements of both. Most alliances require bargained compromises, gives and takes, in order to establish a bond, even when the common interests of the parties are strong. In any event, alliances, like bargained contracts, create interests in sustaining relationships, institutional arrangements, and communities of support for such arrangements. Hence, in analyzing the rise of modern solidary structures founded on discovering and creating common interests, one must simultaneously examine four levels of solidary structure: patterns of common interests, solidary relationships, institutions of solidarity, and supporting communities.

Talcott Parsons on Solidarity

Among recent social theorists Talcott Parsons has made the most important contributions to the analysis of the differentiation of solidarity. His work places the concept of solidarity as communication within the framework of both his famous scheme of fourfold functional classification and his historical analysis of the rise of Western culture and society as an evolutionary process of differentiation (Parsons 1971:86–121, 1963:37–62).

Schemes of social evolution that emphasize differentiation were not, of course, new with Parsons. Nineteenth-century evolutionary doctrine—Spencer's for example—took differentiation to be the engine of evolutionary change and the hallmark of modernity. Parsons, however, from the very beginning of his career was suspicious of polar schemes of evolution. For example, he fully accepted Durkheim's critique of Spencer's notion that a regime of market-driven contracts could *replace* other forms of solidarity. Moreover, in his famous note on Toennies in *The Structure of Social Action*, Parsons takes exception to the assumption that in modern market-organized economies *all* action becomes progressively instrumental. Indeed, the pattern variables were originally designed to show that the elements usually assumed to be characteristic of modern social roles vary independently and that various newly differentiated integrative roles, e.g., professional roles, are not governed entirely by the normative rules of *Gesellschaft* (Parsons 1937:686–94).

It was not until the development of the "influence paradigm" in the 1960s that Parsons fully exploited the potential inherent in his theoretical apparatus by applying his emerging functional scheme to processes of mutual influence. He could then begin to describe the differentiation of solidary institutions in terms far more powerful and illuminating than had been available in the notion of integrative or professional roles. In brief outline, Parsons begins with a fourfold classification of the means by which actors influence other actors: (1) *inducement* or offer of reward; (2) *deterrence* or threat; (3) *persuasion;* and (4) invocation of moral *commitments.* To these four modes correspond four "media" or "generalized capacities" to employ each mode: *money* represents a generalized capacity to offer inducement, and *power* represents a generalized capacity to deter; a generalized capacity to invoke moral commitments is referred to as *"value commitment"* (Parsons 1968). Finally, Parsons refers to a generalized capacity to persuade as *"influence"* (using the word in this context in a specialized sense rather than in the general sense in which all mutual interpersonal effects are the subject of the "influence paradigm").

In an analogy to money, all of these generalized capacities are called "symbolic media" and are said to mediate the flow of interchanges between the various subsystems of society. Each of the media correspond to one of the four functional subsystems suggested by Parsons' fourfold classification of functions. Money, of course, corresponds to the economy (or adaptive subsystem), power to the polity (or goal-attainment subsystem), and value commitment to the pattern maintenance subsystem. Influence corresponds to the integrative subsystem, and this classification clearly places communication, persuasion, and processes of influence at the heart of the integration of society. The scheme clearly puts Parsons solidly in the tradition of communication theories of solidarity.

Persuasion and influence are, for Parsons, at the heart of modern systems of solidarity because, within this paradigm, any act of pure persuasion—without inducement or threat, and without evocation of a prior moral commitment—must rest on establishing a common interest. One party persuades another party to an action by convincing the second party that such action is in both of their interests. Thus the act of persuasion discovers or creates a common interest and hence, by definition, a solidarity; influencers and those who they influence form a solidary alliance. By the same token, analysis of pure persuasion provides a clue to what is involved in the "differentiation of solidarity."

In the early part of this essay I have sought to emphasize ordinary English usage in order to provide a clear context before seeking to establish several finer points regarding institutions of solidarity in modern society. The sole exception has been the phrase "differentia-

tion of solidarity." This phrase connotes rather little in ordinary parlance and may, indeed, convey relatively little even to sophisticated
readers. The idea of differentiation is fairly obvious as applied to the
differentiation of roles; the increasing intensity of the division of labor
is part of our everyday experience. Institutional differentiation, in the
sense of the separation of the economy from traditional patterns of
production and exchange, is a clear enough concept. The differentiation of the political sphere in the rise of the modern bureaucratic
state, with its monopolization of the legitimate use of force, is also
part of our conventional vocabulary. "The differentiation of solidarity," however, has a less clear conventional meaning. Parsons' usage,
within the framework of the influence paradigm, suggests a possible
meaning. Differentiated solidarity occurs when the social system comes
to be integrated through solidary alliances created by persuasion and
influence rather than by traditional culturally defined ties. This can
come about only with the concomitant development of institutional
arrangements allowing and sustaining the creation of such alliances.
Parsons has provided several important analytical and historical
starting points for the analysis of the development of this institutional
analysis. His work did not, however, develop this line of thought in
depth and, moreover, the rather metaphorical analogy of money and
"influence" as media of interchange may be as confusing as it is
suggestive.

Is Influence Like Money?

Analysis of the evocative but somewhat misleading analogy between
money and influence as generalized media provides a useful starting
point for the examination of communicative solidarity in modern
societies. If persuasion works by showing, through mutually acceptable terms of argument (i.e., without force), that the persuader and
the persuaded have a common interest, then influence, considered as
a *generalized* capacity, is the ability to persuade without providing a
fully acceptable argument. The persuader relies in part upon argument, but the process also involves reliance on belief or trust, within
an audience, that the persuader could make a fully acceptable argument if challenged. Hence—and herein lies both the irony and much
of the theoretical interest of Parsons' scheme—persuasion through
influence does not rest on force, but it does rest on status.

Parsons' notion of what sort of status backs influence is ambiguous.
It is either faith in the persuader's expertise—belief that a rational

and persuasive argument could be constructed—or it is faith in the persuader's good will. In the latter case, what the objects of influence take for granted is that the holder of influence does share a common interest and would, therefore, not deliberately mislead. It is not clear that one must make a choice between these conceptions, for influence clearly works both ways: if we are willing to accept assertion rather than proof, we are, in effect, presuming both the good will and the expert analysis of the person who makes the assertion (Baum 1976).

We may now ask whether influence, conceived as a generalized capacity to persuade (backed by trust in a certain sort of status), is indeed like money, which is a generalized capacity to induce (backed by trust in the value of money).

Certain aspects of the analogy are clear and intriguing. Both are generalized and therefore adaptable—i.e., not committed in advance to specific purchases or arguments. Both are based on trust that can be challenged or "called," the parallel to a "run on the bank" being spreading demands that persons of influence prove their claims in detail. Both are symbolic in the sense that money is a token of value rather than a valuable thing and influence involves symbolic labels that define communications as trustworthy and informative. Influence rests on assertions about factual states of affairs rather than the states themselves.

Money, on the other hand, has certain obvious features that make it quite different from influence: it has a quantitative unit of value, so that its users know what value to place on transactions that employ money as a medium. Those engaging in such transactions are well aware that they are employing symbolic monetary value as a measure of value mediating an underlying exchange. Influence not only lacks a quantitative unit of value, but it is by no means clear that persons employing or accepting influence have any concept that in so doing they are accomplishing an exchange of other resources, using influence as a medium. That such an exchange is taking place is an analytical construction of the theoretical observer, who interprets the systematic implications of patterns of influence as interchanges between subsystems of society.

Second, money is a more generalized medium than influence. In an advanced society, there are not a variety of differentially valued currencies. Even the variety of credit instruments that circulate in a highly differentiated society can be bought and sold in central markets at rates fixed in units of the basic societal currency. Influence, on the other hand, is an inherently segmental medium. Influence extends only to particular audiences that trust particular sorts of expertise or accept the status of persons who speak on behalf of particular constituencies and alliances. Being status based in particular solidary groups, influence reflects the structure of crosscutting solidarities that constitute the glue of modern solidary orders. Indeed, it is the very fact of the rise of legitimate plural solidarities that makes modern, democratic influence systems work. The same cannot be said of plural monetary communities.

A third important special characteristic of influence in that, unlike money, it has an inherent tendency to asymmetrical transactions. People with quantities of money use it to purchase items from other persons with a great deal of money or from persons with very little money. The value of a spender's money does not vary with his or her status, but influence, by definition, flows from status. To accept another's influence is to say, in effect; you know *better* than I do what is in my interests.

Taking these three respects in which influence is *unlike* money as background, we are in a position to discuss the forms of communicative solidarity in modern society. It will be helpful, though, to review one more analogy that Parsons made between influence and money, an analogy that I take to be essentially correct and important: just as credit creates money by the process we refer to generically as banking, so does crediting others' expertise and good will create influence. There are not fixed quantities of the media of interchange: the media are themselves created by social processes. In the case of money, its creation takes place in well-organized, specialized, clearly identifiable, and well-known institutions: banks and similar financial institutions. The creation of influence and its resulting solidarities rests on processes and institutional frameworks that are less well understood. My theses are (1) that influence is created in direct rather than mediated social transactions; (2) that such transactions usually create solidarities within groups smaller than the entire society but, secondarily, create societal solidarities through the establishment of the public as a solidary group; and (3) that such transactions are hierarchical in the sense that influentials have a status higher than that of their audiences. In brief, influence (and therefore communication solidarity) is created when persons exchange leadership for the ratification of their status. This takes place when leaders act as "prolocutors," that is, persons who purport or claim to speak on behalf of social groups (on the concept of "prolocutorship" see Mayhew 1971:75–78). The remainder of this paper is devoted to exploring these concepts, to outlining the institutional machinery that allowed this process to develop in Western democracies, and to examining the implications of this aspect of modernity for social stratification.

The Prolocutor

When a speaker claims to represent a constituency—whether a limited interest group or the public at large—and purports to speak on behalf of the common interests of that group, we may refer to the speaker as a "prolocutor." To act as a prolocutor is to make a bid for leadership. Successful leadership may be defined as (a) speaking effectively, that is, with effect, on behalf of one's constituents and (b) achieving acceptance among this constitutency as a legitimate spokesperson. When a person acts as a successful leader in this sense, influence and communicative solidarity have been created.

Note that this conception of the creation of communicative solidarity by successful bids for leadership implicitly refers to communication to two different audiences. This duality of the influence process is the key to understanding the structure of solidarity in modern societies. Leaders seek to speak effectively to others on behalf of the groups they represent, and this implies speaking persuasively to a wide audience. At the same time their arguments must have appeal to the constituency whose support or ratification is being sought; hence the same arguments are also directed internally to the solidary group. Looked at from another perspective, the leader is trying to create both solidarities within the group being led and also solidary alliances with other wider groups. Leaders are thus central integrative figures in modern solidary structures.

Such leadership is by no means easy to accomplish and requires a delicate balancing act. Nevertheless, the balance is necessary, for without effective impact on the larger society, the constituency gets nothing in return for its ratification of the leader's bid; on the other hand, without effective persuasion of the constituency group, a leader will not achieve ratification of leadership status in the form of associational or symbolic affirmations of loyalty.

Because the exchange of effective leadership for ratification of status inherently involves simultaneous appeal to two audiences, the process tends to universalize the terms of rhetoric. Leaders appeal to the common good or the public interest; they appeal to reason. More generally, they speak as prolocutors with the assumption that, to some extent, both of their audiences share a common framework of discourse—both live in a common society, have potentially discoverable common interests, and employ mutually comprehensible concepts for reference to public events and public goods. Prolocutors, then, create the public as a solidary group through discourse. Ironically, their appeals for greater solidarity, recognition, and valued outcomes for their special constituencies implicitly strengthen the realm of public discourse and hence the public itself—a solidary group of speakers and actors who share a civic life and can formulate policies for the public good.

To return to the vocabulary established earlier in this paper, prolocutors, even though they aspire to leadership of particular constituencies, have an interest in sustaining *relational, institutional,* and *communal* solidarities, in that they are benefited (1) by sustaining relations with leaders of other constituencies that permit the formation of mutually effective alliances; (2) by an institutional order that permits both public advocacy and the associational life on which such advocacy depends; and (3) by the solidarity of the larger community within which such institutionally controlled discourse takes place.

Institutionalization of the Public

Three Strands of Cultural Differentiation. If the "differentiation of solidarity" refers to the rise of multiple, created solidarities arising from a process of social leadership, we must identify the institutional frameworks that sustain and support this process and ask how they came about. Parsons usually referred to this institutional apparatus with the shorthand phrase "freedom of association" (Parsons 1963:50ff), emphasizing in this choice of words both the value premise that legitimizes associational solidarity and also a parallel to free markets in the economic realm. The phrase provides a valuable clue, but we must recognize that a great deal of complex institutional history lies behind it; moreover, the term "free" tends to obscure the stratification embedded in modern solidary institutions, just as the phrase "free markets" ideologically softens the actual constraints that stratify a market economy.

1. *The differentiation of willed community.* The first stage of the differentiation of solidarity involved differentiations at the cultural level. In traditional society the right to be a prolocutor resides exclusively in the state and its official religious functionaries. Concepts of

public good and community welfare are deeply rooted in the Western philosophical tradition and its political vocabulary, but in early modern Europe, the right to enunciate the public good had been largely monopolized by central officials. The seeds of change were sown early, however, for the long history of conflict between church and state implies potential debate over who speaks most effectively on behalf of the welfare of the people.

The decisive development occurred when Protestant theology came to emphasize the associational principle of solidary. Weber, in his account of sectarian Christianity, rightly emphasizes this theme, although he did not provide an extensive account of the particular roots of secular associational solidarity in Puritan theology. In his famous essay on the Protestant ethic he located the roots of the secular economic ethic in the doctrine of predestination (Weber 1930). Had he accomplished a comparable study of the associational principle, he could have located the Puritan doctrine of "communion of the saints" as the equivalent in the solidary realm to predestination in economic life (Mayhew 1984b).

"Communion of the saints" in Catholic theology had referred to a communion between saints living and dead. It was a sacramental concept that suggested that communion is achieved when one performs a ritual on behalf of deceased relatives. Luther, Calvin, and their more radical successors developed a more secular concept of communion of the saints, emphasizing the obligation of each Christian to an active community of mutual assistance on earth—a community that could not be achieved by sacramental means but only by mutually beneficial association. The most essential means to communion is the preaching of the Word. Significantly, preaching—a form of persuasive communication—came to be an element in the Puritan's conception of a church: "a company called together by the voice of a preacher" (Seaver 1970:24).

Ironically, this spiritual conception of communion, founded ultimately upon Pauline Christianity, came to legitimize secular association; what the Puritan preachers stressed, in effect, was a voluntaristic, associational concept of community. Community is based not on mere common living together, or on a natural tie of kinship, but on concurrence of wills. The differentiation, then, of associational community rests on a prior cultural differentiation, at the philosophical level, of community in the sense of the natural group from community in the sense of like-minded persons who share a common purpose.

2. *The differentiation of rational rhetoric.* The differentiation of rational rhetoric arose in the historical aftermath of a prior cultural

differentiation of philosophical analysis of common cultural values. Important as the "philosophic breakthrough" was—and we should remember that Parsons accords considerable evolutionary signifi- cance to the differentiation of speculation about cultural absolutes, abstracted from their social contexts—it is also important to recall that shortly after its birth in the Greek polis, philosophical specula- tion came to be institutionalized in a contemplative rather than an activist version. Aristotle's emphasis upon contemplation as the high- est good, as it was received into Thomistic ethics, resulted in the downgrading of the rhetorical tradition. Rhetoric, once viewed as a rationalistic approach to civic life, came to be ethically subordinate to pure contemplation. "Philosophical" intellectual approaches con- tended with "rhetoric." Only with the rebirth of the rhetorical tradi- tion in secular humanism did differentiated institutions promoting learning and rational thought toward secular ends begin to flourish and to form the social basis of intellectual life. We see here another cultural differentiation in support of the valuation of rational persua- sion. The cultural foundation of systems of communicative solidarity rests on this value.

3. *The differentiation of individual authority.* A third cultural differ- entiation prerequisite to the rise of a differentiated solidary public provides legitimation to prolocutorship. Prolocutorship cannot be in- stitutionalized without the legitimation of free speech and publica- tion. That is, the citizen must have a right to bid for support from potentially solidary groups and alliances, without presuming that such a bid is per se disloyal to the larger society. This is a particularly difficult concept to institutionalize and, at the level of political philos- ophy, developed more slowly on the Continent than in Anglo-Ameri- can thought. It developed first in the wake of a differentiation of the grounds of cultural authority away from official spokespersons (for established doctrines) and toward the individual. In this sense, "indi- vidualism" is deeply implicated in liberal philosophy, but reference to individualism can be very misleading, if liberalism is viewed as a philosophy of freedom for the individual from collective constraints. Rather, it is a philosophy of freedom of individual thought and com- mitment from the constraints of force. The individual must be freed not *from* community but freed *to form* community, for the deepest communal ties come from individual commitment driven by reason and choice. As such, liberalism constitutes a celebration of persuasion as much as a plea for individualism. Community must flow, say the spokespersons of liberal thought, from the free play of processes of persuasion. This line of argument can be traced from the radical

Puritan theologians through Locke to John Stuart Mill's classic essay *On Liberty* (Mayhew 1984b). From the beginning of its origin in the doctrine of communion of the saints, Anglo-American arguments for freedom of expression were based on the notion that communion must rest on the free flow of communication—freedom to preach and receive the Word, with the Spirit as the only test of truth. It took only a replacement of reason for spirit in the Puritan formula for communion to create liberal consensus on the value of freedom of speech and publication. This complex is, in effect, another form of the valuation of persuasive communication and constitutes the third strand in the complex thread of cultural differentiations that laid the groundwork for the creation of the differentiated public.

Three Social Conditions. 1. *Free-floating commitments.* The emergence of differentiated cultural grounds of commitment did not, by itself, create a solidary public; it only provided resources for legitimizing freely chosen attachments to solidary associations. The development of the public as a solidary group followed a series of fundamental social changes that facilitated the institutionalization of a politically relevant associational life.

The first such development was the rise of "free-floating commitments." The societal community must contain persons who are ready to make commitments to interest-oriented associations and memberships. This development implies a diversity of interests with various commonalities that can bring cross-sections together. Complexity in the underlying pattern of roles and statuses is the foundation for such diversity.

These various and diverse interests must be attainable within the framework of a state without the transfer of sovereignty to their own interest groups; that is, if groups must (or think that they must) either totally control the state or secede from it in order to achieve their ends—create their own state, so to speak—then the terms of argument are not terms of persuasion but terms of a struggle for power. An arena for influence exists—a *public* in this sense—only when citizens believe that association and alliance can secure interests within a constitutional framework.

One condition that fosters such a social base for the development of a public is the crosscutting bases of diverse interest. Specifically, when economic development creates a division of labor and a consequent diversity of roles and interests, but these new interests do not exactly correspond to religious, regional, local, and other solidary groupings, conditions favoring the rise of the public emerge. Economic development within the framework of preexisting solidary divisions in a sovereign nation is a catalyst for the creation of free-floating commitments.

Seventeenth-century England provided precisely such a setting. The interests of the rising entrepreneurial class were stronger in some regions than in others, stronger among Puritans, and stronger among anticourt factions in the political arena, but were by no means limited to particular groups. Ultimately, and for a time, English society could not stand the strains produced by new bids for political power and representation. The constitutional order faltered, and a period of civil war and relatively rapid constitutional change ensued. Nevertheless, even in the midst of this conflict (and during subsequent conflicts at the end of the seventeenth century), the institutions of the new public order were becoming established. As polarized sides developed—the Parliamentarians and the royalists—there emerged a sense that each citizen must choose his loyalties and that these loyalties were not fixed by prior group memberships. Both sides reached out and asked for commitments from persons able to attach their loyalties in response to processes of persuasion.

The battle of the pamphlets began. The germ of the idea that communication creates a public was already implicit in the idea that a congregation is created by the voice of a preacher, but during the 1640s seventeenth-century Englishmen began to act on the parallel premise that a *civil* public is created by the voice of the press. The number of pamphlets published in England went from 20 in 1640 to 1916 in 1642 (Hill 1977:65). Advocates began to take their causes to the tribunal of public opinion, sometimes meeting with initial controversy or feeling misgivings over the propriety of such a radical approach to politics. The Grand Remonstrance of 1641 provides a first illustration. There was heated debate over a successful motion to publish the remonstrance, which was ostensibly a petition directed from Parliament to the king. The traditional mode of parliamentary argument invoked a universalistic claim to represent all the people as council to the king and hence to express the public interest as against the necessarily partial advice of the king's *private* counselors. As Sir Edward Dering said of the Grand Remonstrance, "I thought to represent unto the King the wicked counsels of pernicious counsellors. . . . I did not dream that we should remonstrate downward, tell stories to the people, and talk of the King as of a third person (Hill 1961:125). But remonstrate they did and the precedent was powerful.

When Thomas Goodwin and his associates saw their national Assembly of Divines headed inexorably toward agreement on a presbyterian mode of ecclesiastical government in 1644, they took their case for congregationalism to the public in *An Apologeticall Narration* (Goodwin 1644). When the levelers debated with the leaders of the army over the terms of settlement of the war, they also published their proposals for more democratic forms of representation (Woodhouse 1951). When Cromwell and his associates determined to execute the king, they took care to have a public trial reported in the nascent newspapers of the day (Wedgwood 1970). One can find rather little explicit seventeenth-century theory about a new entity called "the public," but as civic consciousness developed, the course of practical political action came more and more to take the existence of such a body for granted (Zagorin 1970:203–6; Gunn 1969).

The public is not merely a body to which a practical politician appeals; it is also the bearer of the public interest. The idea of the common good or common weal or public good is deeply rooted in medieval and early modern political and social thought, and, as we have seen, it is one of the elements of the Puritan conception of communion. There is an equally long history behind the notion that the ruler comes to know the common good through a process of advice (Ferguson 1965). When used merely as a definition of the purpose of government, this idea of public interest does not necessarily have democratic implications, but the concept moves decisively in a democratic direction when theorists begin to assert that a free public is the best judge of its own interest. The latter idea emerged as a byproduct of the aforementioned distinction between *private* and *public* advice to the king.

The advice or *concilium feudum* given the king or lord ought not to be a mere reflection of the private interests of the counselor. By the same token, if the advisee wants sound advice, he ought not to interfere with the free speech of the adviser. Even Hobbes insists that "he that giveth counsel to his sovereign . . . when he asketh it, cannot in equity be punished for it" (Hobbes 1962 [1641], II-25, p. 192). We see here another strand of development of the idea that free discussion produces truth—ultimately, in the case of parliamentary counsel, a true account of the public interest. Parliament, advising in the public interest, gives a true account of the public weal; private advisers—a group of "flatterers" or otherwise evil counselors—do not. Once one accepts the premise that the best judge of the public interest is the public itself, or, more commonly, a Parliament that represents the public, it is but a small step to the idea that in matters affecting the common good, the king must act solely on the advice of Parliament. But Parliament was, de facto, a diverse body representing and collat-

ing a variety of emergent free-floating interests. It became, then, a
focal institution within the developing communicative public. During
the course of these early parliamentary struggles, the emergent theory
was expressed rather forcefully by Henry Parker in a manner that
provides important insight into the nascent development of a fully
utilitarian but nonetheless collective concept of the public interest.
According to Henry Parker, the advice of Parliament to the king constitutes an *infallible* statement of the public interest, for the people,
who are all virtually represented in Parliament, cannot be mistaken
about their own best public interests any more than individuals can
be mistaken about their best private interests. By the same token,
private advice to the king is wrong because it is partial and *necessarily*
founded on the personal private interest of the adviser (Parker 1640:
35–36).

The doctrine that representative bodies necessarily express the
common good became a central dogma for Harrington, one of the
principal founders of seventeenth-century liberalism, who even more
explicitly attributed the true expression of public will to a collective
process of communication (see Zagorin 1954:137–38; Macpherson
1962:184). His view has been aptly restated by Pocock:

> To Harrington, the term "public interest" was perfectly intelligible, and
> meant that when the personal experience of the many and the reflective
> capacity of the few were associated in the *ordini* of a republic, there ensued a
> dialogue within the whole, in which the body politic developed a knowledge
> of what was good for it. . . . For Harrington, rationality was a civic process in
> which two partners discovered their interconnectedness. (Pocock 1977:87)

In short, discussion produces truth in representative public deliberative bodies just as it does in printed public discussion. Public
reason is dialogical, a collective product embodied in a process of
communication. It cannot be viewed as a mere instrument of individual will, for it expresses the solidarity of the community.

What I am stressing here is that seventeenth-century political philosophy, shaped in concrete constitutional battles over the nature of
the English constitution, came to reflect an emergent social reality—
an emergent solidary public. Within this public, individuals were free
to distribute their loyalties according to their interests. This need not
create chaos, for the process of allocating such loyalties takes place in
the framework of public discussion of the common good, discussion
that is accountable to orderly processes and standards of universalistic reason.

2. *Prolocutors: the entrepreneurs of influence.* Parsons, in applying

his fourfold paradigm of functions to the factors of production, assigns the integrative function to entrepreneurs. Entrepreneurs combine or organize mobilized factors of production—land, labor, and capital—into a productive process. In a parallel argument, Eisenstadt has noted that social differentiations are initiated and consolidated by leaders who are capable of mobilizing newly liberated resources in powerful new combinations. Historians frequently recognize this process implicitly even when they do not employ theoretical labels. Douglas, for example, in his classic biography of William the Conqueror, describes William as a leader who was able to mobilize and consolidate both the rising power of the great aristocratic magnates and a wave of religious enthusiasm, deftly manipulating his traditional powers of office. Based on this combination of resources he built a more systematic and politically potent feudal order than existed elsewhere in Europe (Eisenstadt 1963; Douglas 1964).

In seventeenth-century England a new type of leader arose who also combined newly liberated resources in novel permutations. Prolocutors began to use influence as a resource base. Starting from a powerful structural position, and from that vantage point combining a variety of newly liberated free-floating commitments under the rubric of novel formulas of legitimation, leaders created fundamental public institutions. Two prolocutorial roles emerged that permitted this sort of leadership to come forth: the publicist and the parliamentarian.

Publicists fully supported by a cash market for writing did not emerge before the eighteenth century. Aristocratic and political patronage remained the principal forms of support for seventeenth-century journalists. The rise of newspapers and widely circulated pamphlets in the 1640s does nevertheless imply the emergence of the publicists' role—the appearance, that is, of a substantial number of people who wrote for public readers. Moreover, these writers pursued their vocation on the presumption that their pamphlets and treatises affected public opinion in meaningful ways. What I have referred to above as the "differentiation of rational rhetoric" required not only cultural legitimation but the development of a group of persons committed to political writing who hoped to create new allegiances (and hence new solidarities) by publishing pleas for support for this or that policy or action. In the early modern period such publicists could not expect to support themselves from sales of their works, but writing was nonetheless a meaningful vocation.

For example, the idea of writing for the public as a meaningful vocation is manifest in the career of John Milton, the most illustrious if not the most widely read of the Puritan propagandists. Milton was an early transitional figure in the long-term movement from patronage to writing for the public. On the eve of the English civil wars, he made the traditional Italian journey common in the training of young men who aspired to careers as Latin scholars and humanistic men of the Renaissance. While in Italy he earned the high regard of the noted Italian patron John Baptistia Manso. For Milton, Manso's sponsorship constituted a strong ratification of his intellectual status. During this period he harbored the ambition of writing a great Christian epic in the classical tradition. Yet, stirred by the impending political struggles in his native England, he returned home and began two decades of composing pamphlets on behalf of the republican cause, putting off *Paradise Lost* until the Restoration brought his political writing to an end (Daiches 1959:58).

Milton, his colleagues, and his pamphleteering opponents must be viewed as a new group of prolocutors who, as intellectual entrepreneurs, created novel combinations of arguments and appeals designed to bring together new publics in support of political reorganization.

For some writers, pamphleteering was an aspect of their careers as parliamentarians. The rise of the power of Parliament and its emergence as the central locus of opposition—ultimately armed opposition—to the Crown provided the setting for the most important new prolocutorial leadership. The principal parliamentary leaders—John Pym, for example—managed to package a combination of free-floating interests, including Puritan religious commitments, gentry opposition to the royal taxation policy, and free traders' opposition to the Crown. It is worth noting that Pym had led the first election campaign in parliamentary history, riding around the country promoting the election of "the puritanical bretheren" (Wood 1691:73). At the same time, he owed his central position in the Commons to aristocratic patronage. His career provides a ready illustration of the entrepreneurial combination of several emergent and mobilizable forces, not the least of which was the rise of a public capable of exercising power through the electoral process. To repeat the formula I used above, Pym was clearly among those who used a powerful structural position on an influence base to combine a variety of newly liberated free-floating commitments under the rubric of novel formulas of legitimation.

3. *The expansion of political capacity.* The third realistic condition for the emergence of an effective solidary public is the rise of political capacity among a citizenry, including the extension of literary and political education and the issue of to what degree the development

of political capacity constitutes the emergence of democracy. Historical research tends to establish and reestablish the relative smallness of the politically emancipated stratum. Scholars discover how few could vote and conclude that there was so little authentic democracy that it can not be said to have had a causal force. This argument confuses ethical arguments about how much democracy there should be with analytical and historical arguments regarding how marginal changes altered the terms of political discourse and action.

This is not an appropriate setting for rehearsing historians' controversies over the extent of literacy and the franchise at the time of the English civil wars or for discussing the even more vexing and possibly unanswerable question of how "democratic" the Puritan revolution was in origin and outcome. It is sufficient to point out that by modern standards, to say nothing of contemporary political ideals, the literate class was quite small and the enfranchised public even smaller. Even at the cultural level of formulas of legitimation, the idea of universal suffrage, passed in the late 1640s by the left wing of the revolutionary movement, was considered radical by the leaders in charge. The demands of the "Levellers" were emphatically rejected by "democratic" theorists who believed that the distribution of political power should follow the extent of citizens' stake in the social order. Democracy in the fullest sense seemed incompatible with the protection of the institution of property. (See Woodhouse 1951, which reprints both the Leveller proposals and existing records of the public debates about them.)

Let us then stipulate a very limited political enablement among the English population in the mid-seventeenth century. Nevertheless, there was a reading public sufficient to consume the massive output of political pamphlets that began in the 1640s, and there was an electorate sufficient to make electioneering and playing to one's constituents a plausible political strategy. In other words, for the political actors of the time, the public existed as a political force. A critical mass of politically capacitated persons, although far short of a literal mass public, was sufficient to allow the differentiation of the solidary public as a constituent element of the social and political order.

This is a point of considerable theoretical importance. It underscores the analytical independence of the solidary public, on the one hand, and authentic mass political democracy on the other. The differentiation and institutionalization of the public as a modern solidary institution is consistent with very considerable social stratification.

Social Stratification and the Public

My extended discussion of the origins of the public frames the most
fundamental point at issue between defenders of the liberal public
and critics of liberal democracy. To what extent do defenses of liberalism, including Parsons' sophisticated use of the influence paradigm,
serve to justify a high level of social stratification by proposing idealized views of the value of merely conceptual legal rights? The prototypical illustration of this critique is provided by Anatole France's
famous aphorism to the effect that "the law, in its magestic equality,
forbids the rich as well as the poor to sleep under bridges." As applied
to the contemporary public, most notably by Jürgen Habermas, this
radical critique emphasizes the corruption of communication. A true
communicative public would be founded on "undominated communication," that is, dialogue among authentically equal communication partners, none of whom enjoy status advantages. Each partici-
pant is under an obligation to be clear and sincere and, on request, to
justify all statements and arguments. According to Habermas, whose
earliest research was on the origins of the public, the institutionalization of an authentic public began to emerge with the rise of liberal
democracy, but was soon debased by institutions of dominated communication. Today, with the rise of a technocratic society, egalitarian
communication is undermined by the status advantage of the expert,
who can rely on social position to brook no argument. Such technologically dominated communication distorts and disguises the discussion of underlying values and policies. Discussion is readily captured
by the power elite, making an authentic communicating public, as
visualized in liberal theory, a hollow ideal far removed from contemporary reality. Habermas' argument is sophisticated and challenging,
and the foregoing brief summary hardly does it justice. Nevertheless,
enough has been stated to allow us to define the issue.

The public, as I have conceptually defined it using Parsons' approach to influence, is inherently a stratified entity. It exists because
persons exercise influence based upon their status. Because people
respect prestige and they trust the assertions of prestigious individuals, stores of influence are generated and solidary groups within the
public are created and sustained. The differentiated public emerged
in the West in early modern times because strategically located prolocutors successfully bid for support and, having gained such support,
mobilized groups on behalf of public ends. The differentiated public
could not have emerged without a system of status in support of the

prestige of those who made bids for public support. Nor did the creation of the public destroy the system of status from which it sprang. Rather, it emerged as a new differentiated system of status based upon control of a new resource. Moreover, the system cannot operate without differential access to and control over such resources. Systems of influence imply influential people.

The alternative—a completely egalitarian system of communication—implies an impossible burden of dialogue. It is always more efficient to take a certain amount for granted. For example, it would not be useful to rethink each morning what would be the very best way to tie one's shoes. Habits—investments of both time and emotion in what one has already learned—allow normal action to take place. It is the same with dialogue and the processes of persuasion. It would be most difficult for a leader—even a progressive leader—to mobilize free-floating commitments on behalf of policies and movements if the leader were questioned about every assumption, made to provide evidence for every statement, and asked to prove every inference. Indeed, if one's followers asked for such justification, one would not, by definition, be a leader; the very trust that allows the leader to be taken on faith founds the leadership. The hallmark of a liberal system is that followers, actual and potential, are allowed to ask questions and insist upon justifications, but, ironically, if everyone always did so, the system would break down. Moreover, according to the Parsonian analogy to money, each request for justification is at least potentially deflationary; it is like a trip to the bank to ask for cash. On the other hand, banking systems cannot be said to be working if no depositors can ask for cash without threat to the system. The enterprise presumes a certain normal level of movement in and out of accounts. Applying the analogy in a rough way, complex systems of modern public solidarity presume that free-floating commitments will be given and withdrawn as interests change and also as faith in leaders waxes and wanes. A constant process of challenge—of insistence on justification—is presumed. It is only when the demand for justification reaches the point that there is so much critique of argument that it undermines the capacity of the system to create and sustain working coalitions that we can say that the influence system has become "depressed."

By the same token I suspect that Habermas would not insist that all communication always be subject to far-reaching and detailed critique. A measure of presumptive legitimacy is acceptable. Habermas would insist that fundamental claims be challengeable and that challenge have effects; but then, so too would Parsons. Where, then, is the issue? Is it just a matter of emphasis? The influence paradigm emphasizes that the system rests on successful status claims, even though it concedes that influence attempts must ultimately rest on solid argument or the system will suffer from chronic inflation. Habermas' concept of communicative action emphasizes that all parties must have comparable rights to speak and to challenge, but concedes that in any given dialogue some premises will be taken for granted.

In some respects the theories do not seem so different, but discussions of the relative open and effective or closed and dominated character of the public and its institutions of communication rarely escape a substantial ideological burden. Various observers' views about whether the system is really working depend on their sense of whether important demands are being expressed and heard to good effect. The "importance" of the various demands depend on the perspective and values of the observer. If what any given critic takes to be important demands, real or potential, are not effectively aggregated, that critic concludes that the system suppresses expression. If a critic supposes that the most important potential demands are the interests of "the people" in creating an entirely new and different social and political system, the critic's conclusion about whether communication is dominated is a foregone conclusion. If the entire system is viewed as fundamentally corrupt, discussion within the bounded framework of that system is essentially meaningless. If revolution is the only allowable evidence of an effective system of communication, such a system cannot, by definition, exist within a stable society. It is not difficult to understand why radical critique would be unsympathetic to a conception that takes the public to be an influence system structured by the prestige of leaders within an established social structure.

It is more difficult to accept the radical presumption that social change through the mobilization of public sentiment requires egalitarian communication. The entire history of the differentiation of the public as a political instrument argues against such a supposition. The critical question is: what institutions (or what institutional reforms) allow new prolocutors to make novel appeals to emergent constituencies who are coming to have political capacity? Answering this question requires studying its component parts: What is happening in society to allow new entrepreneurs of influence to assume leadership roles as prolocutors? What new institutionalized processes or forums provide platforms for such persons to speak? What newly released free-floating commitments create potential groups for such leaders to establish by their public communication? What groups are coming, by their education, social participation, and potential political leverage to form new constituent groups within the public? These questions cannot be analyzed in detail within the boundaries of the present essay. It is appropriate, however, to point out that these questions all relate, at the theoretical level, to the fundamental nature of the differentiation of the public.

The differentiation of the public involves the creation of (a) new loyalties that are "free floating" in the sense that they are not ascribed to locations in a traditional social structure and (b) leaders whose influence base rests on the mobilization of these loyalties rather than their position in traditional order.

It is characteristic of Parsonian sociology to overestimate the differentiation of modern societies and the strength of evolutionary forces pressing toward differentiation. Parsons emphasized the adaptive social capacity created by emancipating social action from ascriptive constraints through differentiation. These forces are assumed to destroy ascriptive elements of the social structure. In fact, ascriptive forces have substantial staying power because they have an economy of their own (Mayhew 1968). Entrepreneurs, including the special sorts of political entrepreneurs of influence I have been discussing, are not constrained by institutional norms calling only for action in support of the differentiation of the influence system from its ascriptive base. On the contrary, as entrepreneurs, their fundamental strategy is to create combinations and alliances from as many sources as possible. If these combinations include the support of traditional groups, including traditional elites, so much the better. If their influence base is supported by their own traditional elite status and contacts, the institutional norms of the influence market do not prohibit using such prestige to good advantage. In consequence, the differentiation of modern influence systems from a society's system of stratification is always partial and imperfect. The two systems remain implicated by each other. The public is itself stratified in any prestige-based system of influence; hence communication is, in this sense, "dominated" and not entirely egalitarian. The public is constituted by *institutionalized* processes of communication. To be "institutionalized" is to be established, and what comes to be established reflects the interests of the participants. Market organization frees rather than suppresses interests—including, ironically, both traditional and stratified interests.

The vanguard institution of full differentiation—the strongest egalitarian force—within an emerging differentiated public is the rise of the specialized leadership role. In this context a "specialized" leader is one whose livelihood and career is solely dependent on appeals to the influence market and not on the sponsorship of elite patrons or on his or her own status in a system of stratification. Pym was not a specialized leader in this sense because he was very dependent on aristocratic patronage. This is, perhaps, as good an indicator of the primitive level of differentiation in the early seventeenth-century public as was the limited extension of literacy and the franchise on which it rested. By the same token the study of the differentiation and egalitarian character of the public in contemporary modern society can be given considerable theoretical focus by emphasizing this structural feature of differentiation. The fully differentiated public would be led by free-lance careerists—for better or for worse. Empirical studies of the public could well focus on the careers of such persons as Ralph Nader, Martin Luther King, John Gardner, and Barry Commoner, with special attention to their relative independence, their success in creating constituencies, and the extent of their effectiveness in producing social change. Among specialists in communication, the effectiveness of the more prominent television newscasters in creating a sense of public solidarity around a middle-of-the-road, apparently objective, and potentially critical perspective would also provide materials for an informative study. Such studies would elucidate how, in contemporary American society, a relatively differentiated public exists—one that is by no means unstratified but, on the other hand, is organized around established processes that prevent the complete monopolization of communication. Such studies, if they were realistic, would also show that the public, by its very nature, involves appeals to prestige, including the prestige that flows from high positions in other social institutions. Hence the public is not entirely differentiated but reproduces the stratification of the larger society in its own structure. Discourse comes, then, to be regulated by the presuppositions that dominate discussion in various institutional settings, and access to public debate is correspondingly limited. The measure of differentiation is the extent to which potential leaders can make successful bids for access to the markets of communication and influence, even if they lack the support of established, hierarchically organized interests. To the extent that such a fully differentiated system develops, the Parsonian analogy of influence to money becomes progressively accurate. Sheer force of argument is effective within the public arena in the same sense that "all money is green." Money will command goods whoever offers it. Influence markets are differentiated to the extent that forceful argument correctly identifies constellations of interests, and new politically effective solidary groups arise around those who have the capacity to envision such coalitions and speak effectively on their behalf.

References

Alexander, Jeffrey C. 1983. *Theoretical Logic in Sociology*. Vol. 4: *The Modern Reconstruction of Classical Thought: Talcott Parsons*. Berkeley: University of California Press.

Baum, Rainer C. 1976. Introduction to "Generalized Media in Action." In Jan L. Laubser, Rainer C. Baum, Andrew Effrat, and Meyer Lidz, eds., *Explorations in General Theory in Social Science: Essays in Honor of Talcott Parsons*, pp. 448–69. New York: Free Press.

Daiches, David. 1959. *Milton*. London: Hutchinson University Library.

Douglas, David. C. 1964. *William the Conqueror*. Berkeley: University of California Press.

Durkheim, Emile. 1933. *The Division of Labor in Society*. George Simpson, tr. and ed. New York: Macmillan.

Eisenstadt, S. N. 1963. *The Political Systems of Empires*. New York: Free Press.

Ferguson, Arthur B. 1965. *The Articulate Citizen and the English Renaissance*. Durham, N.C.: Duke University Press.

Goodwin, Thomas et al. 1644. *An Apologetical Narration*.

Gunn, J. A. W. 1969. *Politics and the Public Interest in the Seventeenth Century*. London: Routledge and Kegan Paul.

Habermas, Jürgen. 1974. "The Public Sphere." *New German Critique* 3:49–55.

Hill, Christopher. 1961. *The Century of Revolution, 1603–1714*. New York: Norton.

——1967. *Society and Puritanism in Pre-Revolutionary England*. 2d ed. New York: Schocken Books.

——1977. *Milton and the English Revolution*. Harmondsworth, Middlesex, England: Penguin.

Hobbes, Thomas. 1962. *Leviathan: On the Matter, Forme and Power of a Commonwealth Ecclesiastical and Civil*. New York: Collier. Originally published in 1641.

Macpherson, C. B. 1962. *The Political Theory of Possessive Individualism: Hobbes to Locke*. London: Oxford University Press.

Mayhew, Leon. 1968. "Ascription in Modern Society." *Sociological Inquiry* (spring), 38:105–20.

——1971. *Society: Institutions and Activity*. Glenview, Ill.: Scott, Foresman.

——1984a. "In Defense of Modernity: Talcott Parsons and Utilitarian Tradition." *American Sociological Review* (May), 89:1273–1305.

——1984b. *The Public Spirit: On the Origins of Liberal Thought*. Davis, Calif.: Library Associates.

Parker, Henry. 1640. *The Case of Shipmony Briefly Discoursed*. STC 19215.

Parsons, Talcott. 1937. *The Structure of Social Action*. New York: McGraw Hill.

——1963. "On the Concept of Influence." *Public Opinion Quarterly* (spring), pp. 37–62.

——1968. "On the Concept of Value Commitment." *Sociological Inquiry* 38:135–60.

——1971. *The Systems of Modern Societies*. Englewood Cliffs, N.J.: Prentice-Hall.

Pocock, J. G. A. 1977. *The Political Works of James Harrington*. Cambridge: Cambridge University Press.

Seaver, Paul S. 1970. *The Puritan Lectureships: The Politics of Religious Dissent.* Stanford, Calif.: Stanford University Press.

Toennies, Ferdinand. 1957. *Community and Society.* Charles P. Loomis, ed. and tr. East Lansing, Mich.: Michigan State University Press. Originally published in German as *Gemeinschaft und Gesellschaft* (1887).

Walzer, Michael. 1965. *The Revolution of the Saints.* Cambridge, Mass.: Harvard University Press.

Weber, Max. 1930. *The Protestant Ethic and the Spirit of Capitalism.* Talcott Parsons, tr. New York: Scribner's.

Wedgwood, C. V. 1970. "The Trial of Charles I." In R. H. Parry, ed., *The English Civil War and After, 1642–1658,* pp. 41–58. Berkeley: University of California Press.

Wood, Anthony A. 1691. *Athenic Oxoniensis.* Vol. 3. Oxford.

Woodhouse, A. S. P. 1951. *Puritanism and Liberty.* Chicago, Ill.: University of Chicago Press.

Zagorin, Perez. 1954. *A History of Political Thought in the English Revolution.* London: Routledge and Kegan Paul.

——1970. *The Court and the Country: The Beginning of the English Revolution.* New York: Atheneum.

10

The Mass News Media in Systemic, Historical, and, Comparative Perspective

Jeffrey C. Alexander

In its search for greater precision and causal specificity, contemporary sociology has tended to neglect "society" as such—a point of reference whose empirical significance is often matched only by its theoretical obscurity. To speak of the whole invites generality and historical scope, qualities that undermine the assurance of exact verification, yet it is precisely generality and historical perspective that are necessary if the components and boundaries of society are to be understood. If ignoring the whole creates difficulty in every area of "special" sociological focus, it is particularly dangerous in the attempt to understand those institutions whose "function" is actually to address society as a general unit.[1] The mass media is such an institution.

I am interested in making a theoretical statement about the mass news media that is both thoroughly general and abstract and at the same time directly specifiable in empirical terms. I locate the media in terms of, first, a theory of the social system and, second, a theory of social differentiation that provides both an historical and comparative perspective. By linking that analysis of the news media to these

For their earlier comments on this paper, I thank Robert N. Bellah, Ruth H. Bloch, Donald N. Levine, Jeffrey Prager, and Neil J. Smelser.

broader theoretical traditions, I hope to enrich sociological thinking about the relation of the media to the operation of other social institutions and to issues of social change, subjects that are usually underplayed by more micro studies of mass communication. I hope also to throw a different light on broader implications of media practices that are either interpreted narrowly or simply taken for granted. Finally, in the course of carrying out this analysis, I hope to illuminate certain problematic moral and political issues that have been the focus of ideological debate about the role of news media in social life.

The Mass News Media in the Social System

The mass media produce symbolic patterns that create the invisible tissues of society on the cultural level just as the legal system creates the boundaries of the community on a more concrete and "real" one. In a modernizing and differentiating society, the media are a functional substitute for concrete group contact, for the now impossible meeting-of-the-whole. Indeed, as I argue below, media emerge only with social differentiation itself, and the more "modern" a society is the more important its media. This dialectic between media integration and differentiation forcibly struck visitors to the early American nation. Tocqueville (1835: part 1, ch. 11) described newspapers as "the power which impels the circulation of political life through all the districts of that vast [American] territory," and Thomas Hamilton (1833: 72–73) another visitor to the United States in the early nineteenth century, testified that "the influence and circulation of newspapers is great beyond anything ever known in Europe. . . . In truth, nine-tenths of the population read nothing else. . . . Every village, nay, almost every hamlet, has its press. . . . Newspapers penetrate to every crevice of the nation." It is certainly true, as I emphasize below, that mass media have a certain atomizing effect on the perception of social life. Yet such fragmentation hardly exhausts its function. To the contrary, this effect is what allows the integrating power of the media to exercise its distinctive scope.

If cultural patterns can be differentiated into cognitive, expressive, and evaluative strands (Parsons 1951: 24–112, 1961), the mass media can be divided into cognitive and expressive components. In the category of expressive media I include the narrative stories found most frequently on television. By the cognitive dimension of media I refer to news stories that occur in newspapers as well as in television news programs. Because of these different foci, entertainment and news media have sharply different social functions; they depend on very different kinds of social resources and must be judged according to what are often contradictory criteria of success (Fass 1976). I limit myself in this effort to the news media and the cognitive dimension.

But a question immediately presents itself that touches on a critical problem in the sociological literature: is "cognitive" in fact a sufficient designation for the orientation of news reporting? Cognitive patterns are typically understood to concern objective definitions of social reality, definitions that are directed toward the object itself rather than toward the subject's feeling about that object (that feeling, by contrast, defining the expressive patterns) or toward the relation between subject and object (an orientation that defines moral or evaluative patterns). The perception of news as providing "information" indicates this cognitive status in both lay and sociological parlance. However, as recent postpositivist discussion in the philosophy and history of science has emphasized, even the most radically cognitive statements are bound to have evaluative or moral dimensions that, although secondary, are nonetheless significant. The empirical perceptions of scientists are influenced by their group commitments, as well as by their more general moral, cultural, and metaphysical concerns (Polanyi 1958; Kuhn 1969; Holton 1973). Professional disciplinary self-scrutiny cannot eliminate the nonempirical aspect of scientific observation; it can only change the nature of noncognitive constraint (Toulmin 1972). It follows logically that news judgments, as less controlled exercises in empirical observation, are also bound to be partly evaluative (see Gans 1979: 39–42, 201–2).

To focus primarily on the impact of overt political bias on news reporting or on the problem of journalistic ethics, as a vast literature on the media has done (e.g., Noelle-Neumann 1978), obscures the fact that a major function of the news media is actually to produce "bias," to create through the framework of cognitive statements certain nonempirical evaluations. The problems of reportorial bias and professional ethics concern the cognitive dimensions of news, but if we accept the notion that the production of moral bias is also a "good" and necessary social function (see Missika 1986, 1987), the empirical and theoretical focus of analysis shifts. The problem becomes discovering what particular kinds of evaluative judgments the news media produce and under what conditions they do so, and, perhaps formulating the ideal and pathological conditions for the performance of this task.

There are two possible orientations of evaluative symbolic judgments: the level of values and the level of norms. Norms occupy an intermediate position between general value patterns and the "raw data" or "plain facts" that are continually being produced in the course of human activity. If we do not accept the view of human life as thoroughly atomistic and discrete, we must assume that "just doing it" cannot be a major mode of self-explanation in any society (see Bellah 1970:261). More general and significant justifications and legitimations are necessary. Yet at the same time it is true that social life is too variegated, too fluid, too profane to be organized in a manner strictly consistent with the broad sacred tenets that provide the generalized integration that forms value patterns. A more flexible form of integration is provided by "normative" patterns, which although sharing in the generality of the value dimension are nonetheless more specific and contingent, more open to continuous reformulaiton in relation to shifting social exigencies.

What is most conspicuous about the news media is their focus on this normative level. Just as individuals continually try to organize their experience in terms of formulating different normative explanations, newspapers do this for the—or at least for "a"—society at large. News stories and news commentaries can be understood as a continuous processing of raw information that makes the experience of a society comprehensible in terms of more general categories. In the early nineteenth century a writer for the *Boston Daily Advertiser* made this link between the need for individual integration and interpretation and the functional necessity for institutional interpretation very clear. "The insatiable appetite for *news*," he wrote in 1814 (quoted in Mott 1941:202; original italics), "has given rise to a general form of salutation on the meeting of friends and strangers: *What's the news?*" A news story, in other words, is a situationally specific, extraordinarily flexible kind of nonempirical evaluation.

It has, of course, been phenomenology that has conceptualized the ordering to contingency from the standpoint of the individual. As Husserl (1977 [1931]) and, later, Garfinkel (1967) suggested, individuals view external events as documenting, or elaborating, prior perceptions. The news media, I am suggesting, can be understood as linking such individual documentation to social events that an individual never directly encounters. They do so by reporting events in terms of more general categories.[2] Reporters employ this "documentary" method in their own perceptions of events, and the products of their investigations—the stories they file—allow the categories they have chosen to "document events" for their readers. The cognitive implication of "categories" is intended. News provides the social component of rational judgments about the nature of everyday life, and it does so in a uniquely standardizing way.[3] Law, by contrast, provides the social, standardizing framework for judgements about the morality of everyday life. Because it is expressed in what are apparently transparently cognitive terms, the normative element of news judgments is not nearly as visible as the normative component of legal ones. News, in other words, camouflages its nonempirical interpretive aspect in the same way as science.

The categories that news stories evoke emerge from previously articulated norms and from more general values about what to expect from social life. Both this interpretive character and the nesting in broader patterns are manifest in any reporting that is subject to conflicting interpretations and therefore becomes an object of at least covertly political contention. In March 1978, for example, twenty-one of the thirty-seven members of the House International Relations Committee of the U.S. Congress wrote a letter urging the president of the United States to reconsider his controversial arms package deal with Israel, Egypt, and Saudi Arabia. In an article reporting this event, the *Washington Post* linked it to the actions of a number of pro-Israeli groups, describing it as part of a "determined campaign to block the package deal" (*Near East Report* 1978:46). The *Washington Post* had characterized these congressional representatives as acting in terms of their ascriptive political bias rather than as responding to their constitutional duties or their individual consciences. It is likely that five years earlier—when American sympathies for Israel were more firmly rooted—this "fact" would have emerged in an entirely different light, if indeed it would have been viewed as sufficiently interesting to have been reported as news at all.

A similarly revealing incident was disclosed by former Israeli defense minister Ariel Sharon's libel suit against *Time* magazine for its report on his involvement in the massacre of Lebanese civilians in September 1982 (*Los Angeles Times*, January 14, 1985, part 1). In this case two distinct levels of interpretation were involved. *Time* had reported that Sharon had "discussed ... the need for revenge" with Lebanese leaders the day before the massacre and that the discussion was cited in a secret appendix of the special Israeli government commission's report on the incident. In the libel trial, Sharon's attorneys were able to force *Time*'s Jerusalem correspondent, David Halevy, to admit under oath that, while he had been told about conversations between Sharon and Lebanese leaders, he had never actually been told that the crucial meeting between them was detailed in the appendix. Rather, Halevy said, he had "inferred" this after hearing a description of what sort of material the appendix contained. Halevy could have made such an inference only because he was looking at these Israeli events within a preexisting framework that supplied him with expectations unfavorable to Sharon. The trial did, in fact, reveal that Halevy sympathized with anti-Sharon groups in Israeli politics, although these connections were, per se, no different from those that any active reporter usually maintains. In Halevy's case such expectations quite naturally led him to see the references made to the appendix as documenting his suspicions and allowing him to make connections between "facts" as the basis of a story. The broad story he perceived, moreover, meshed perfectly not only with his own expectations but also with the outrage of his audience. Americans had reacted forcefully against the Israeli invasion, and *Time*—its earlier leanings notwithstanding—was swept along in the outrush of public feeling. It was, after all, a member of another quite different solidary community—that of Ariel Sharon—who brought the suit against *Time;* Sharon's quite different normative expectations allowed him to perceive a different way in which the "facts" could have been put together.

That suspicions of Sharon and outrage at the massacre led to one particular interpretation among possible others is made even more clear in a second level of documentation revealed by the suit. All newspapers and news magazines submit news stories for editing by the home desk. In this case, it was revealed, the *Time* writer in New York had changed the Jerusalem dispatches in distinctive ways. Where the dispatch had read "we understand [that the meeting is cited in Appendix B]," the New York editor had changed that to "*Time* has learned." Where Halevy had reported that Sharon "gave them [the Lebanese leaders] the feeling . . . that he understood their need to take revenge," the home editor rewrote it to read that Sharon "reportedly discussed with . . . [Lebanese leaders] their need to take revenge." In a purely factual sense, understanding that a conversation has taken place is not different from having learned that it did so. Both phrasings assume that such a conversation occurred. The second way of putting this information, however, implies a more authoritative objectivity than Halevy may have desired, given his own preceding interpretive leap. Since *Time*'s New York editor knew nothing about the internal interpretation that had produced this earlier documentation of objective phenomena, he had no more reason to hesitate before a more active formulation than his readers themselves would have. Much the same can be said for the second rewriting I have noted. How could Sharon have given the Lebanese such an impression without having discussed it with them? The brute "facts" do not differ, but the frames used to explain them, and that they implicitly document, contrast in a subtle but significant way.

Another typical example of how "objective" news reporting actually places raw data in a preexisting normative framework, and of how this acts upon the documentary method of journalist's common sense activities, is revealed by a controversy generated in Canada by Canadian reporting of a visit by the French prime minister, in 1979. The prime minister of Quebec and ardent French nationalist, René Levesque, hosted a visit by French prime minister Raymond Barré. Canada's English-language papers described Levesque's behavior throughout the trip as an embarrassment, reporting that he frequently drank too much and engaged in "erratic behavior." The French-language press viewed the visit differently. Levesque's behavior, when mentioned at all, was usually treated as good fun, evidence of his informality and high spirits. The *Toronto Globe and Mail*, a leading English-language paper, accused the French-language press of a cover-up. Michel Roy, editor of Montreal's *Le Devoir*, argued instead that the reporting of the specific incident revealed contrasting general orientations:

The secrets and travels of Margaret Trudeau have never had the place of honor in the French-language press that they have had in the newspapers of our colleagues. . . . What comes out of the anecdote, out of private behavior, out of the digressions of conduct of a public figure—without being submitted to censorship for an instant—interests the French press much less [than the English]. (*Los Angeles Times* 1979)

To the French journalist and editors, Roy is arguing, the "incidents" had simply not been news: they had not violated their general expectations of personal behavior for public figures, especially when those figures were their own.

Although the newspaper and magazine reports from which I have drawn my information treated these controversies as deviant cases, as departures from standard professional conduct, I have presented them in a way that reveals their typical features. Critics of a specific piece of reporting—be they interested observers or academic analysts —usually charge its author with bias. The primordial fact that in producing a news story all atomized pieces of data must be normatively organized is conveniently ignored. What is really happening in such instances is that these critics are arguing against a bias of which they do not approve, not against bias per se. This is not to say that one cannot differentiate good reporting from bad—there is, after all, "thick" versus "thin" interpretation (Geertz 1973)—nor is it to say that the notion of journalistic bias must be dispensed with. Later in this paper I develop a theory of "biased" and "unbiased" reporting that accepts interpretation as a primordial fact. It is to say, however, that the ordering of disparate information is an inherent feature of news reporting and that, despite the examples I have used, it is not limited to international reporting or to specifically political issues. Events must be reconstructed in an orderly and relatively coherent way, day in and day out, even when such logicality is not actually apparent.

Although the study conducted by Paletz, Reichert, and McIntire of city council news coverage in Durham, North Carolina emphasizes the specifically political bias of news reporting, it can just as accurately be viewed as documenting the more neutral function of news as a normative organizer and interpreter in a "typical" domestic situation. The study concludes that news reports on the city council's activities invested events with a "rationality, causality, and temporal coherence" that was not inherent in the events themselves. Its conclusions are worth quoting directly:

> Conventional journalism includ[es] condensing and summarizing; investing events with rationality and coherence (even though the events may be confusing to the participants, and the reporter himself may not fully comprehend both what has occurred and its meaning); emphasizing the council's decisions at the expense of other activities[;] . . . and treating the council and its members with respect. (Paletz, Reichert, and McIntire 1971:81)

The idiosyncratic aspects of news writing and its professional mores can be viewed as geared to this intermediate level of normative production.[4] For example, an examination of news leads indicates that they are cognitively oriented not only to the "five w's"—that is, to the traditional injunction to identify "who, what, when, where, and why"; they invariably make a strong normative and moral point, and this latter function is, indeed, the implicit criterion by which good lead writing is distinguished from bad. The lead seems to be a device for summing up the significance of the data/event by relating it, implicitly, to what people would have expected to happen in similar situations or to more general value judgments that would normally be applicable.

The clarifying, and by implication the interpretive, function of news writing is revealed by journalists' self-imposed strictures about style. The style books used by major news organizations universally stress simplicity of language in the service of communicability. To achieve such simplicity, of course, important details must be selected from a wide range of facts. As Harold Evans (1972:25, italics added), former editor of the London Sunday *Times,* writes in *Newsman's English:* "Sentences should assert. The newspaper reader above all does not want to be told what is not. *He should be told what is."* As Evans makes clear in the rules he lays down for copy editors, to be simple and precise is at the same time to identify facts that are significant to an individual's social life. The copy editor, he writes,

> must insist on language which is specific, emphatic, and concise. Every work must be understood by the ordinary man, every sentence must be clear at one glance, and every story must say something about people. *There must never be a doubt about its relevance to our daily life.* (ibid: 17, italics added)

The close relation between the interpretive function of news and its peculiar linguistic style is also revealed in the following admoniton by Curtis McDougall (1968:104, italics added), professor emeritus of journalism at Northwestern University:

> Vagueness and indefiniteness are avoided, and clarity obtained, by placing important ideas at the beginnings of sentences. Also by *playing up the action, significance, result or feature of the paragraph or story,* by avoiding vague and indefinite words and eliminating superfluous details, words, phrases, and clauses.

Of course, these latent functions of news style are contrary to the self-conscious, manifest professional rationale, which views stylistic simplicity simply as a means to more powerfully communicate neutral and objective truth. Sometimes this contradiction is revealed quite plainly, as when Hogenberg (1978:100), author of *The Professional Journalist,* argues, on the one hand, that instead of using platitudes and jargon the writer should just provide "a clear, simple story of what happened" and, on the other (ibid.:440), that the journalist must be an interpreter who "applies the rule of reason to the news" (see Harris 1978).

In fact, the entire professional concentration on what is "newsworthy" and "fresh" as opposed to "stale," as well as the stratification of rewards according to the ability to make news "discoveries," can be viewed as flowing from this normative function. For only by continually finding new, unfiltered, and unforeseen societal experiences can the media effectively perform their normative function. This normative function also explains the occupational character and psychology of the role of the news reporter. The "tough," "cynical" quality of the role is usually taken as an indication that reporters have become jaded by the inundation of social experience and are concerned, as a result, only with recording the "facts" on the most pragmatic and empirical level of analysis. I would suggest, to the contrary, that reporters remain committed to evaluate judgment and that their "tough-minded" cynicism is a professional role demand requiring the particular kinds of judgments they must produce—particularized and flexible normative evaluations rather than the more generalized, self-important, and "religious" judgments that characterize spokesmen in institutions concerned with broader cultural patterns. Gans observes that American reporters seek to exclude "conscious values" from their work:

The news media I have studied seem to attract people who keep their values to themselves. . . . They have no prior values about the topics which become news, nor do they always develop them about topics on which they are working. . . . They did not become journalists to advocate values or to reform society. (Gans 1979:184)

Still, Gans insists that "unconscious values" continue to underlie these reporters' judgments, no matter how pragmatic or situationally specific they "consciously" try to be. Indeed, this continued occupational commitment to normative evaluation is reflected in what is actually an inherent gullibility of the reportorial role, which is shown, for example, in the way newspapers are always open to accepting "the hoax" (Shaw 1975). It is also reflected in the continual strain toward journalistic "advocacy" and activism, even under the conditions of media differentiation.

Institutions in every social sector can be associated with different kinds of social control—can be understood as providing society with certain kinds of resources with which to respond to social strain and social conflict. The legal system is the institution commonly associated with social control in the normative sector. Laws present contingent formulations that are consistent with more general values and at the same time allow society to change and evolve in response to developing strain and conflict. In distinguishing the news media from the law, the significant point is the media's flexibility. By daily exposing and reformulating themselves vis-à-vis changing values, group formations, and objective economic and political conditions, the news media allow "public opinion" to be organized responsively on a mass basis. By acting as an information conduit and normative organizer, the news media provide the normative dimension of society with great flexibility in dealing with social strains. In exchange for this flexibility, the news media must, in effect, eschew certain attributes that allow social control to be exercised in other ways; they cannot, for example, attain the self-consciousness, legitimacy, and enforceability of the norms associated with the legal system. Between the news media, on one side, and the legal system, on the other, a continuum of other institutions make other kinds of normative contributions. Political parties, for example, are more explicitly normative than the news media and at the same time significantly less flexible in response to social events; in relation to the legal system, parties produce norms that are more flexible and responsive although less legitimate and enforceable.

American news coverage of the Vietnam War strikingly illustrates these distinctive characteristics: the noncognitive dimension of news judgments, the particular character of normative versus value statements, and the flexibility this function provides in terms of the operation of social control. It can be argued that throughout the long American involvement in Asia, the "facts" of the war remained relatively constant. With the passage of time, however, the war was reported on very differently and came to seem like a different war. If the empirical event had not changed, what had altered were the nonempirical inputs to the American news media, particularly the normative definitions of those solidary groups that came to oppose the war and the more general value orientations supplied by the intellectual community. In a secondary but nonetheless significant manner, the news media were also responding to the domestic economic and political strains created by the war, which were filtered through intellectual and solidary groups. Because of these changing inputs the "news facts" about the Vietnam War—the headlines, leads, interviews, and reports on direct observations—became more critical. In a symbiotic fashion, such "new" facts contributed to the restructuring of public opinion concerning the "old" facts of the war.

Perhaps the most spectacular illustration of this shifting process of interpretation can be seen in the American news media's coverage of the 1968 Tet offensive in Vietnam. Baestrup (1978) has shown that American war reporters' perceptions of the massive strength of the North Vietnamese army after Tet had much to do with the changing framework through which they filtered their experience of the war: their growing distrust for official U.S. military sources in Saigon; their increasing alienation from U.S. governmental authority in general; and their ever more firmly rooted pessimism about any successful outcome of the U.S. war effort. For these reasons, U.S. reporters' descriptions of the Tet offensive emphasized the "psychological defeat" suffered by the United States and South Vietnam instead of focusing on the more purely military side of the U.S. response. In terms of the latter, Tet could, in fact, have been interpreted as a standoff or even as a limited U.S. victory given the military objectives of the North Vietnamese. The domestic impact of Tet "news" was, of course, tremendous. It was undoubtedly in part responsible for the decision of Lyndon Johnson not to seek a second term in office and indirectly contributed, therefore, to the election of Richard Nixon.

This incident demonstrates the potential autonomy that news interpretation possesses vis-à-vis other institutions and other normative pressures. Still, these war correspondents' judgments were themselves highly responsive to the changing positions of other institutions and other authoritative interpreters of public events. There is a symbiotic relationship among the reporting of news, the discovery of new facts, the opinions of intellectuals (both elite and dissident) as expressed in intellectual journals, the contents of "little magazines," and the stories in mass news magazines. In one sense, the intellectual journals and little magazines may be seen as the creators, and the mass weeklies and daily news media as the distributors, of new orientations (see Hirsch 1978). On the other hand, these sources of opinion are interdependent; they are closely linked through personal networks as well as through channels of information to institutions in other sectors of the social system (see Kadushin 1975).

Another striking overt illustration of the theoretical position taken here is the American reporting of the Watergate scandal. Throughout the Watergate period, battle raged between different social groups over the proper normative framework for interpreting the break-in and electoral violations, ranging from the Republican administration's characterization (a third-rate burglary) to the Left's portrayal (a reactionary neofascist plot). Because of the balance of social groups and normative definitions that existed before the 1972 presidential election, a situation I discuss later in this essay in a different context, the "facts" that appeared as Watergate news before the election supported the former moderate "observations." Only afterward, when events had changed and more universalistic national definitions had begun to reassert themselves, could the version of Watergate now accepted as real be reported as news. In retrospect, it is clear that the facts about Watergate are not facts at all without the framework provided by notions of "constitutionalism," "impersonal higher authority," and other similar kinds of generalized value commitments. Only the combination of these emergent definitions with the raw data of changing events allowed the more critical normative conclusions to be drawn in the form of "fast-breaking" new reports.

In concluding this section, I relate the theory presented here to an approach that appears to be its diametrical opposite, the understanding of news media presented by mass society theory and, more recently, by "critical" theory (Mills 1956:298–324; Benjamin 1973:112–13; Hall and Whannel 1964:364–86; Mueller 1973:86–126; Dahlgren 1978; Golding 1978). According to this perspective, rather than performing an integrative function the news media actually produce atomism and inhibit rather than facilitate the exercise of independent, rational, and principled social action. While the sense of atomization often produced by mass news coverage is an undeniable fact, two responses to this mass society critique seem in order. First, the diverse pieces of news information are not, in fact, as disorganized as they appear, for as normative evaluations they are always informed by more general patterns of value orientation. Second, the lack of overall coherence among these pieces faithfully represents the actual conditions of a differentiated society. From the perspective I have outlined, atomization should be seen as the result of the commitment of the news media to organizing information at a normative level in as flexible a manner as possible. To maintain flexibility, these norms cannot be tied directly to any particular sacred value or to any particular organizational form, even though either of these connections would contribute to a greater sense of overall coherence. I am arguing, in other words, that the sense of disorder created by the front page of a newspaper or by a half-hour of network news is actually composed of a series of normative statements, each of which provides integration at a situationally specific level. A sense of overall disorder is necessary if the mass news media are to perform effectively their function of "covering" with a normative net the wide range of national societal experience. Moreover, we shall see that far from creating passivity and resignation, as the mass society critics and critical theorists assume, this mode of integration creates the possibility for effective voluntary action and for the assertion of individual rights.

This recent emphasis by mass society and critical theory on the enormous power of the media to suppress reflexivity and to enforce passivity rests upon a theoretical logic that must be strongly rejected. These theories imply that individuals can create their own interpretations of the external world without reference to social norms. Thus the very fact that consumers of modern mass media make political interpretations linked to supraindividual "social facts" (in Durkheim's sense) is considered by critical theory to be prima facie evidence of the repressive character of the effect of mass media. I assume, to the contrary, that all individual decisions occur in a normatively defined environment. For this reason, the decisive issue becomes not whether, but how and what: that is, what is the nature of this normative institution and how does it affect action? This question introduces an historical and comparative perspective on the question of reflexivity and autonomy that is absent from most of the recent media literature informed by critical theory.

Whereas this recent "strong media" approach overemphasizes the power of the media vis-à-vis individuals (and, correspondingly, virtually eliminates the reality of secondary institutional life), earlier classical media studies like the two-step flow model of communication (Katz and Lazarsfeld 1955) created a "weak media" model that was unrealistic in the other extreme. These studies focused on whether the media could influence short-run political events—and on whether media effects can be isolated from the social context—rather than on their specific cultural impact on normative perception. Certainly the media are impotent if they depart too radically from the socialized values of their audience and its primary groups (see Shils and Janowitz (1975 [1948]). The critical sociological contribution of such studies is precisely to relate these background values to the vast array of particular incidents that unfold in the daily life of a modern society. The relevant theoretical question at this stage of media research is not that of primary groups *versus* mass media but rather the specific function performed by mass media vis-à-vis primary groups, secondary institutions, and ongoing social events.

The third theoretical tradition of mass media research that I polemically address in this paper is the more orthodox Marxist or ruling class model whereby the media are viewed as instruments for the dominant economic elite to control information for their own instrumental interests (for an attempt to make this argument for the Canadian case, see Clement 1973:270ff). The fundamental theoretical weakness of this perspective is that it overlooks the pivotal role of voluntary action in the media process—the fact that the judgments expressed in news stories are much more the result of the socialized value orientations of reporters than of the instrumental control of media owners. In historical terms, as I demonstrate below, the general movement of Western media has been to separate themselves from direct client relationships with social groups (for the Canadian case, see Baldwin's [1977] argument against Clement). The ruling class model argues, to the contrary, not only that the media have retained their tight linkage to social interests but also that any historical analysis of the media position should focus principally on social classes (see Golding 1974:23–29). I insist, by contrast, on a multidimensional analysis: the media have a variable and potentially independent relation to every major institutional subsystem. This leads to the historical and comparative discussion that follows.

The Mass News Media in Historical and Comparative Perspective

Although I have thus far described the mass news media in purely systemic terms, the exercise of this function is dependent on certain unique historical conditions, and the comparative variation in the performance of the news function can be explained in reference to the variation in these historical conditions. The very possibility of flexible normative production, for example, as distinguished from normative production per se, is dependent on the autonomy of news media from control by groups and institutions in other social subsystems. If the news is controlled by political authorities it will be much more rigid in its interpretation of political events because it will be unable to incorporate other political and normative perspectives. In addition to political differentiation, of course, the news media may also be independent, in a relative sense, of more general value-producing institutions like the church, university, and political parties. Finally, there may be differentiation from structures in the economic dimension, particularly from social classes.

Fusion and Autonomy: A Developmental Model. This differentiation of the mass news media is a developmental process parallel to the classic cases of differentiation that have traditionally been the focus of attention, the emergence of the autonomous economic market, the independent state, and independent religious and cultural activities (see Parsons and White 1969; Alexander 1978). It should be viewed not as an event but as a process. Differentiation of the news media begins with the creation of the first news institution, or collectivity, where there had previously been only the circulation of rumors or improvised publication by broadside. The emergence and circulation of *La Chanson de Roland*, the epic poem of medieval France, illustrates how public opinion is organized about a political event—Charlemagne's campaigns in A.D. 778–779—where public discussion has not yet taken a differentiated institutional form as "news." The relationship of such epics, and of rumor and broadsides as well, to the later media is the same as the relation of court cliques to political parties in political life, trading fairs to markets in the economic sphere, and early monotheistic religions to transcendental religion in the cultural world. The earliest institutions of mass news may be traced to the *canards* in fifteenth- and sixteenth-century France (see Seguin 1961, 1964). These proto-news sheets combined a religious-magical world view with standards about "objective" reporting that typify a more modern, differentiated media. On the one hand, *canards* regularly reported fantastic events like miracles, visions, and various manifestations of the divine will on earth; at the same time, they tried to "verify" them, in good reportorial style, by providing impressive lists of eyewitnesses —for whom age and profession would be presented—and by providing legitimating texts from religious and secular authorities.

Even after the actual institution of a newspaper first emerged, however, differentiation in anything other than the most minimal, concrete sense did not yet exist. Despite this concrete structural differentiation, these first newspapers were tied rather directly to—in fact, they usually emerged in response to—efforts to realize specific group aims such as class demands, party commitments, or religious values. Only gradually was there movement toward more substantive autonomy, as not only institutional structures but also the goals themselves became differentiated (for this distinction, see Eisenstadt 1969:13–32). One step in this process is the creation of a free press in the legal sense, but differentiation involves freedom from more informal but equally powerful forces in the religious, solidary, economic, and political subsystems.

Because of differences in specific historical development, the mass media of different Western nations were attached to, and promoted by, different kinds of groups and institutions. Media differentiation has proceeded, therefore, at enormously different rates and with widely varying results. In France, the first real newspapers were organs of the absolutist state, to which the Church soon responded with papers of its own (Albert and Terrou 1970). In the United States, on the contrary, the differentiated state as such never had its own media, and the most important early papers were promoted by independent bourgeois such as the Franklin brothers and later by political parties (Mott 1941). The relationship between institutional independence and legal freedom is similarly uneven. Whereas in the United States legal freedom of the press preceded any real institutional independence, the institutional autonomy of certain newspapers in nineteenth century France—at least the ability of newspapers to disagree with one another and the government, to present, that is, divergent interpretations of unfolding events—preceded the legal freedom that arrived only with the Third Republic.

The emergence of more independent news media can be interpreted as the creation of an "autonomous regulatory mechanism" for the integrative dimension of society in the same manner that the emergence of representation, party formation, and constitutionalism indicates the development of regulatory mechanisms in the political sphere. And just as the resulting "generalization" of political power is basic for the achievement of substantive freedom and reformist types of social control (Eisenstadt 1969; Alexander 1978), so can the differentiation of mass news media be regarded as the generalization of normative resources. Such generalization provides society with an enormously increased flexibility in responding to changing events and contributes in a fundamental way to the attainment of increased freedom in the society at large. With political and cultural differentiation, the legitimation of political power moves from the unconditional forms of traditional support to the conditional forms of what Weber called, somewhat misleadingly "rational-legal" legitimation. As the result of this development, the response of other social sectors to the activities of national government becomes increasingly significant for the maintenance of that power. It should be clear that the differentiation of mass news media is basic to such nontraditional legitimation, for it allows the continuous "regulation" of government action according to the more general value commitments produced by intellectual and cultural groups, as well as by the activities of political, economic, and solidary groups outside of the government itself. It is no wonder that in democratic societies the media are in constant struggle with the state: they confront the state as the populist counterpart to constitutional legal controls.

In rational-legal societies, this struggle between state and media will be a fight for position and relative strength with each side retaining its relative freedom of movement. In societies where regimes are neither fully traditional nor fully rational-legal, on the other hand, the state will become interventionist and impinge on the internal functioning of the press itself. The governments in such societies will confront the media in different ways, depending on the nature of the particular resources they possess. In various forms of political dictatorship, the governments of nineteenth-century France relied on direct political force of one kind or another. Napoleon established the first left-wing control of media with his "Décret du 27 Nivôse" on January 17, 1780, which tried to institutionalize general ideological values from which newspapers could not deviate. It forbade journals to publish articles "contrary to the social compact, to the sovereignty of the people and the glory of the armies" (Albert and Terrou 1970:30). The purpose of this tactic was to control the effects of social differentiation by preventing any independent interpretive intercession between the government and newly emerging social groups. This rationale was articulated very precisely by Napoleon in his memoirs written at Saint-Hélène. As he wrote about his government-controlled newspaper, *Le Moniteur* (see Albert and Terrou 1970:31): "J'ai fait du *Moniteur* l'âme et al force de mon gouvernement ansi que mon intermédiare avec l'opinion public du dedans comme du dehors. . . . C'était le mot d'ordre pour les partisans du gouvernement" (I made the *Moniteur* the soul and the power of my government as well as my intermediary with public opinion inside and outside the country. . . . It laid down the "word of order" for the supporters of the government).

Later, when the French government of the Second Empire could not control the increase in newspapers in the face of rapid and widespread social differentiation and its own weakened control, the regulation it did achieve was still established through political means: first, by establishing "authorization" for opposition media, demanding the rights to prepublication readings *(prélables)*, and by sponsoring its own official media in Havin's *Le Siècle*, the "monitor of the opposition." Despite these precautions, the existence of the "authorized" opposition papers contributed massively to the fall of the regime in the late 1860s and early 1870s.

By contrast, in a liberal if not fully democratic regime, like that in late eighteenth- and early nineteenth-century England, the government seeks to control opposition media in more voluntary ways. Thus, between 1815 and 1855 Britain's government imposed high taxes that made British papers the most expensive in Europe—three times as expensive as the French ones. The effect of this indirect economic control was, nonetheless, much the same as with direct political control: it cut off the ability of competing leadership to reach the masses and thereby enforced a more strongly stratified political community (Albert and Terrou 1970:50).

The social forces that produce and inhibit differentiation of the news media are the same as those that create differentiation in other spheres. On the structural level, media differentiation is produced by the demands for more universalistic information that oppressed groups make in the course of their demands for societal inclusion and support —for example, in the demands for the end of "antiworkingman" reporting in late nineteenth-century America or the demand by black groups for "community" coverage in American society in the 1960s and 1970s. As long as state control does not become absolute—as in the ideal-typical Fascist or Communist state—social differentiation will produce (and be created by) new social groups whose position vis-à-vis other groups and unfolding events must be articulated and whose demands must be internally integrated and standardized. These tasks can be achieved only if the group has its own news medium. For this reason, in nineteenth-century France, despite the unfree status of the press, the number and varieties of newspapers increased dramatically, as did the total circulation, which grew from 150,000 to 1,000,000 between 1852 and 1870, a period when the French were under authoritarian government control. Every new rupture in French society during the 1860s, even that between the government and its natural supporters like the Catholics, created new papers. By 1870 even the *Normaliens* had their own organ, *Le Courier du Dimanche* (Bellet 1967).

Another structural factor producing media differentiation is the growth of professional norms and self-regulation within the journalistic profession itself, a development that leads to demands for increased prestige and autonomy in journalistic work. The growth of a journalistic profession illustrates how role differentiation must accompany institutional differentiation. In eighteenth-century America, the first newspapers were established and written by printers, who performed a number of different tasks in their local communities. The typical editor

had other affairs besides his newspaper on his hands. He was a job-printer and usually a publisher of books and pamphlets . . . often the local postmaster, sometimes a magistrate, in many cases public printer . . . frequently kept a bookstore . . . [and] occasionally branched out into general merchandise lines. (Mott 1941:47)

There seem to have been three phases of role differentiation in the history of American media. In the first, printers themselves performed all the principal tasks involved. In the second phase, which extended from the first days of the nation into the late nineteenth century, the printers were, on the one hand, differentiated from general editors, who directed all editorial policy and were usually also the owners of the paper, and from writers on the other. Writers in this period were usually highly educated intellectuals. In the third phase, owners and editors were differentiated from each other, and correspondingly the journalist's role became more specialized and professional and relatively more insulated from the personal intervention of the owner

(Schudson 1978:61–87). These differentiating processes manifest themselves in a number of different ways, for example, in changes in policies for hiring reporters, or in the editorial changes that often accompany generational shifts in newspaper ownership within the same family. One can also observe that there has been a significant differentiation of content along with role and institution. The contents of newspapers themselves became increasingly differentiated as they sought to integrate and interpret the events and institutions of an increasingly differentiated society. From the last nineteenth century, the sections of newspapers throughout Western nations have become increasingly specialized into sports sections; home sections; religion and book review supplements; and business, leisure, and travel sections. Editorial coverage has been differentiated into national, local, and foreign news.

On the cultural level, the crucial variable in producing media differentiation is the degree of universalism in national civic cultures, which depends on a range of factors from national religion to the structure of the educational system. In England, for example, the universalistic religious categories of Puritanism gave a tremendous push to the development of early English news pamphlets (Walzer 1965:255). The transcendent and impersonal orientation of the Puritans made them distrust traditional, personal sources of information, particularly as they related to outside events like foreign wars and the progress of the international Protestant movement. To remedy this situation, the Puritans issued their own more objective news pamphlets. This early development in the mass news media also served to define the self-consciousness of a newly emerging social group, the English gentry.

This kind of multidimensional analysis of sources of differentiation makes it possible to understand a fact that is commonly misinterpreted in the literature on media, namely the impact of decreasing economic competition among newspapers and television stations. The fact that this historical development has been accompanied by a perception of increased news objectivity indicates that although economic competition is certainly a facilitating factor, it is only one economic factor among several others in contributing to media independence. Indeed, economic competition is not nearly as important as the differentiation of media institutions from other strategic elites and from institutions in other societal sectors. Directed by a strategic elite oriented toward a unique function, the news media need enormous financial resources to support their independence from other sectors in the society, even from the industrial-corporate one. Thus the paradox: in the period of late capitalism the media became corporatized and their markets oligopolistic. These developments, however, allowed media institutions to save themselves from domination by certain forms of economic power and from a dominant economic class.[5]

The French case is interesting in this regard, for it can be argued that one of the primary reasons for the historical lack of independence of the French press from various social groups and classes was its inability to procure advertising. British and U.S. (see Schudson 1978:14–31) papers relied heavily on advertising to expand circulation and news coverage and to generate capital internally; in this way, they became more independent of personal wealth and direct control. In France, however, the strong cultural bias against "bourgeois commercialization" for a long time made it impossible for newspapers to both publish advertisements and be accepted as objective media (Albert and Terrou 1970). The differences between this French situation and the American one could not be more striking. In America the early papers were often started precisely for the purpose of advertising, the "news" representing a later editorial addition. The felt antinomy between advertising and objectivity was virtually nonexistent in America. A vast number of newspapers in the early nineteenth century were in fact called "advertisers" even when they were principally devoted to news reporting and to political affairs (e.g., the *Boston Daily Advertiser*). The "penny press," which appeared in the 1830s, was even more openly dependent on mass advertising; yet this penny press virtually invented the modern concept of "news" as a detached and relatively independent medium (Schudson 1978:22). This perceived complementarity between news and advertising is evidenced by the announcement in the *Baltimore Sun* of 1837 of its intention "to lay out before the public, at a price within the means of everyone, all the news of the day, and at the same time afford an advantageous medium for advertising" (quoted in Schudson 1978:21).

By contrast to the aristocratic distrust of commercialization ingrained in French culture, individualism informs the positive American attitude toward media advertising. As the *Boston Daily Times* replied to its critics in 1837:

Some of our readers complain of the great number of patent medicines advertised in this paper. . . . Whether the articles advertised are what they purport to be . . . is an inquiry for the reader who feels interested in the matter, and not for us, to make. It is sufficient for our purpose that the advertisements are paid for. . . . One man has as good a right as another to have his wares, his goods, his panaceas, his profession published to the world in a newspaper, provided he pays for it. (quoted in Mott 1941:301)

At the risk of simplification, this abstract general argument can be stated succinctly in the following way. The problem of the differentiation of the news media is the problem of the realization of a democratic social order or, to use a term I have developed in other contexts (Alexander 1978, 1983a), substantive freedom. To the degree that the news media are tied to religious, ideological, political, or class grouping, they are not free to form and reform public events in a flexible way. Without this flexibility, public opinion becomes "artificial" and "biased": it will be keyed to a part over the whole.

Fusion and Autonomy: Comparative Perspectives. We are now in a position to return to the general perspective stated at the outset of this paper and to place it in a more comparative perspective. Charges of "news bias" must not be viewed as the failure of a reporter to report what is true, to indulge in the provision of moral judgment as opposed to cognitive information. It should, rather, be understood as the failure of an activity that has a normative and evaluative character to achieve sufficiently differentiated social status. Strains produced by such fusion, dedifferentiation, and the consequent perception of "bias" are endemic, in various degrees, in all modern societies. If the mass media are "superimposed" upon (Dahrendorf 1959:206–40), rather than differentiated from, specific religious, class, political, economic, or regional groupings, they will continuously recreate these particularistic formations instead of "society" itself. The informational inputs to the media will be partial and shielded, and the normative outputs will be rooted in particularistic perspectives. Because flexibility in creating evaluative judgment is diminished, the social control function of the media is rigidified. Because opinion will be formed on the basis of partial information, efforts at reform will be less successful, strain will be increasingly unresolved, and social polarization will be exacerbated.

In such less differentiated situations, the normative definitions produced by the mass media—the news that they report as fact—are no longer perceived as objective fact, as "news," by the society as a whole. Only the members of those communities directly associated with the particular medium consider the reporting to be accurate; it is regarded as biased by all other groups, which in turn have their own version of the facts supplied by their own "client" media.

We can view this problem in static terms, comparing different Western media and relating degrees of differentiation to degrees of national acceptance of news as fact or fiction. In the United States, one newspaper, the *New York Times*, is accepted as a factual arbiter by a wide spectrum of social opinion, with certain exceptions to be discussed below. In England, there is less unanimity, and the *London Times* reports facts that are often in direct contention with those reported by the more Labor- or Social Democratic–oriented *Guardian* and *Observer*. In Continental countries, dedifferentiation is often more pronounced. Both national news channels in Italian television, according to Hallin and Mancini (1984:830), "have partisan and ideological attachments" that are religious and political. One is pro-Catholic, "employing managers and journalists close to the Christian Democratic party; the other is secular, and close to the parties of the noncommunist left." The more general comparison these observers draw between Italian and American media is particularly to the point.

Many of the print media in Italy are oriented toward providing political commentary, a function that they share with the other institutions of political debate. And if print journalism in Italy shares the functions of the political parties, television journalism serves them. The Italian television journalist is, both in training and in terms of actual power relations, a party functionary. The journalist is trained in the party apparatus, and can be transferred by the party if his or her work displeases its leadership. American journalism, by contrast, has developed into a separate political institution, with a set of functions and an ideology that are more or less its own. American journalists are not only free of direct political control, their political loyalty is primarily to journalism itself rather than to any distinct political tendencies. (Hallan and Mancini 1984:842)

Only after World War I did the papers of France move from direct "party" affiliations to the representation of "tendencies" (Albert and Terrou 1970:94), and the particularistic association between medium and political orientation still remains strikingly apparent. In the typical coverage of a single event in the Parisian press, one often sees very little overlap in "facts" among the several papers, which span the political spectrum from right to left. For example, on Sunday, July 30, 1978, most papers reported that the French government planned to support Spain's entry into the European Common Market. The conservative *Le Figaro* ran the news as a major front-page story, but it focused entirely on what it described as the dishonest, unscrupulous manner in which Socialist leaders had opposed the government's decision under the banner of support for southern French agricultural workers. The Communist paper, *L'Humanité*, played the story in an equally big way, but its "news" focused on the "intolerable" and irresponsible aspect of the government's decision, which was purportedly taken without "rational" consultation with the agricultural groups affected. Equally important to its front-page story was the announcement by Communist groups of the elaborate demonstrations against Spanish entry to be held by the agricultural workers in southern France. *Le Matin,* then the moderate Socialist daily, barely referred to the government's decision, focusing almost completely in its front-page news coverage on the new political conflict the decision had triggered between the Socialists and Communists. *Le Monde* placed the story on page 20, presenting without elaboration the press releases of the government, the Socialists, and the Communists. As this brief recounting begins to indicate, the fact that interpretation occurs in France in a still relatively fused context makes it difficult to get a sense of the nature of the actual event without reading the report in every paper. In the weekend edition of *Le Figaro,* July 29–30, 1978, five out of six front-page stories were basically editorial commentaries. With the exception of the Common Market story referred to above, the first news reports appeared on page 3.

Left-wing totalitarian governments present, of course, a systematically different and much more primitive kind of media fusion. There the lack of differentiation between state and society has pushed the media less into the role of party newspaper than of party-state ideological organ. There is, however, a direct link between such a media position and the dominance of party papers in the prerevolutionary periods. Bolshevik papers began, for example, as the instruments of a struggling party, organs that, correctly, viewed bourgeois papers as similarly particularistic and ideological in orientation. The Russian Revolution, then, simply substituted one dominant class bias for another. As Lenin wrote in 1921:

Capitalism has transformed journals into capitalist enterprises, into instruments of gain for informing and amusing the rich, and as a means of duping and undermining the mass of workers. . . . *We* have begun to make the journals an instrument for instructing the masses, to teach them to live and to build their economy without the financial interests and the capitalists. (quoted in Conte 1973, italics added)

This perspective is firmly in place today. As a leading journalist, V. Kudraiavtsev, wrote in *Izvestiia* on August 25, 1968: "Even the very term 'truth' has a class content" (quoted in Conte 1973). In 1969, 77 percent of the more than 11,000 students entering Soviet journalism schools were party members. As I have indicated by calling them ideological organs rather than party newspapers, the Soviet press actually performs more a generalized value function than a specific normative one. They are more interested in the underlying "meaning" of events—in putting the events directly into the general ideological context of Soviet Marxism-Leninism and Russian national culture— than in the nature of the unfolding events themselves and in their immediate relation to other events in the society. It seems possible that the more detailed and concrete function of day-to-day integration and interpretation is performed by other Soviet institutions, for example by the elaborate and profuse "letters to the editor" sections contained in many newspapers.

Fusion and Autonomy: Specific Historical Paths. We can also view this problem of "biased," clientlike relationships between media and particular social groups and institutions in historical terms. The different paths toward development and the uneven, discontinuous advances toward differentiation taken by different Western mass media must be seen against the background of divergent national social structures and cultures.

From the early 1600s to the revolution, the French *ancien régime* established strong censorship and a directly political tradition of news reporting. (In this discussion of a French case, I am drawing upon Manévy 1955; Deniel 1965; Boussel 1960; Bellanger et al. 1969–1976; Bellet 1967; Albert and Terrou 1970.) Thus, in the first period of the formally free press, 1789–1792, the perspective of the revolutionaries was that newspapers were not to be unattached but were, rather, to instruct. As Brissot wrote of the press: "It is the unique means of instruction for a large nation little accustomed to read and wanting to leave ignorance and bondage behind" (quoted in Albert and Terrou 1970:26–27). New journals formed around individual radical political leaders, expressing their personal points of view and closely connected to revolutionary clubs and societies. Equally personal counterrevolutionary news organs soon established themselves. After the end of Napoleon's rigid governmental control, the regulation became less intense, but Restoration papers continued to view themselves mainly as adjuncts to parties, classes, regions, and religious groups, and they reported news from a similarly personal editorial outlook. The Catholic Right, for example, had its own weekly journals and daily papers that regulated and interpreted its relation to the government, to the republicans, and to the Church itself vis-à-vis unfolding daily events. These interpretations occurred against the background of certain general value commitments, supplied particularly by Pauline texts as they were articulated by Bonald, Maîstre, and Lamenais. Thus, the reporting by the Catholic press of such mundane and specific events as parliamentary debates reflected the general themes of hierarchical authority, the organic unity of the state, and the need for religion in public life.

The revolutionary period of 1848 repeated this pattern of personal political journalism, this time shifting toward the Left: George Sand, Raspail, Lamartine, Hugo, and Proudhon all had their own news organs. And despite the broadening mass audience in the later nineteenth century, political and social conditions ensured the continuation of this sectarian style. In the Third Republic, serious senatorial candidates would often start their own newspapers as a means of bolstering their chances for election, and even in this democratic period government authority continued to interfere directly with the media's autonomy. The Republic's press law of 1881 continued to outlaw "offenses against the President of the Republic, defamations against the army and its leaders, attacks against the regime, and calls to dissolve the laws" (Manévy 1955:69). In the 1890s, this law was used freely against Socialist and anarchist papers. In the Dreyfus case, newspapers were highly politicized. Zola, after all, had initiated the affair with his famous "J'accuse" in *L'Amore* in 1898, for which he spent one month in prison. During each day of the trial, newspapers of different political persuasions devoted their pages to the task of exposing the errors and contradictions of the opposing side. At the time of the outbreak of World War I, fully forty of the fifty major French newspapers were frankly and openly propagandistic for different political factions. Although partisanship subsided to some degree between the wars, it was revived during the early postwar years primarily because of the effects of the Resistance, during which highly personalized and political journals flourished around individual leaders.

The American media experience differed drastically from the French for a number of reasons: (1) Although both colonial America and prerevolutionary France were enmeshed in patrimonial political systems with nondemocratic states, the American experience in this regard was significantly more conducive to media autonomy. America's colonial separation made it much more difficult for England to enforce its royal restrictions than for the French king to enforce the writs of the *ancien régime*. Equally important, the English form of patrimonial rule was significantly more differentiated and controlled than the French; it left more room for decentralized, independent estates and for dissent. (2) The subsequent revolutionary experiences of the two nations were also far different. In France, the highly personalized attacks of the dissenting newspapers on traditional authority were strongly linked to particular ideological positions; this particularism set the stage for a vicious circle of personalized journalism to continue unabated into the postrevolutionary phases. In the United States the equally personalized attacks on authority were carried out in the name of "freedom of the press," since the colonial rebellion was one that united the whole nation and was conducted in part under the ideology of neutral "due process." The revolutionary victory, therefore, set the stage for a future American journalism that, while still highly personalistic, could be carried out under the legal auspices of a free press. (3) Postrevolutionary France remained significantly traditional and highly polarized through the early twentieth century, with more or less primordially defined religious, economic, and political groups vying for control of the state. The United States, by contrast, despite continuing polarization and the early history of confrontation between North and South, maintained a rational-legal state throughout its subsequent history and had a certain level of diffuse civil consensus.

Just as the ideal-typical model I have articulated for media development was specified in a particular way in France, it must be modified for the American case (I draw here on Mott 1941; Commager 1950; and Schudson 1978).

The first newspaper in the U.S. colonies was published in 1689 in Massachusetts as the spokesman for the religious-political leadership of the colony; the first opposition paper, published in the early eighteenth century by the older Franklin brother, can be seen as representing the protests of the newly independent artisan group against elite control. The famous Zenger case in 1735 set the crucial course for public attitudes toward newspapers throughout the colonial struggle for independence: prosecuted by the colonial governor for printing anti-English material, Zenger published pro-American news from his jail cell throughout the nine months of his pretrial incarceration, all in the name of "freedom of the press." At the end of this time he was freed because the local grand jury would not convict him for his patriotic action. This case combined two of the factors that made American media development distinct: the relatively legal-rational English system (trial by jury, due process) and the independence provided by America's colonial status (the local grand jury). During the Revolutionary period, this same pattern was reinforced. In the name of "freedom of the press," American colonialists engaged relatively freely in the very kind of extremely partisan and personalized journalism that in the French—and, as we shall see, in the German—situation would have been suppressed immediately, and that would have reinforced ideological, more personalized notions of journalism. Thus the lead of the March 12, 1770 *Boston Gazette*'s story on the Boston "massacre" was the following: "The Town of Boston affords a recent and melancholy Demonstration of the destructive Consequences of quartering Troops among Citizens in a Time of Peace." Only after two-thirds of a column of such editorializing did it actually begin its news: the "circumstantial Account of the tragical Affair on Monday Night last" (quoted in Mott 1941:102).

The first daily newspapers appeared in the postrevolutionary period in response to two kind of pressures: (1) the need of the mercantile class for up-to-the-minute and wide-ranging information on sailing vessels and import offerings; and (2) the need of newly emerging political parties to interpret events to their respective audiences. Freneau's *National Gazette*, for example, was initiated by Thomas Jefferson and significantly widened the breach between Federalists and their Republican opposition in the 1790s. In 1798, the Alien and Sedition Acts, passed under the Federalist administration, sought among other things to directly link the media with state control under the umbrella of conservative political ideology. Although the law failed for a number of reasons, its inability specifically to control news reporting had a revealing sidelight. In order to suppress a news report, the law stipulated that malicious intent had to be proven, thereby acknowledging the existence—even in the early period—of a relatively institutionalized normative standard of universalistic truth against which any partisan statement could be judged. This acknowledgment simply was never made in relationship to the French media, not even by the Third Republic.

The "penny press," an inexpensive paper well within the reach of most Americans, first appeared in the pre–Civil War years. Responding to the emergence of mass middle and working classes on the American scene, this press was sharply opposed by economic and party papers, which wanted to maintain their monopoly on information. Significantly, the penny press first pursued the "plain old news" of everyday life, and it could do so only because it was the first news medium to conceive of itself as being in a relatively differentiated position. This ambition was trumpeted by the *Baltimore Sun* in a particularly lofty manner.

We shall give no place to religious controversy nor to political discussions of merely partisan character. On political principles, and questions involving the interests of honor of the whole country, it will be free, firm, and temperate. Our object will be the common good, without regard to that of sects, factions, or parties; and for this object we shall labor without fear or partiality. (quoted in Schudson 1978:22)

Despite the emergence of this relative independence, however, the vast majority of papers in this period continued to link their "news" to economic-merchant and political-personal interests. As a spokesman for the Democratic party press wrote in 1852, "every shade of political persuasion has its organ. . . . Each of these organs is a propagandist after its own fashion" (quoted in Mott 1941:253). In the 1850 census, only 5 percent of the country's papers were listed as neutral or independent. Although the Civil War experience continued to support the legal freedom and differentiation of the press, the particularistic style of party papers remained in full force after the war. It was an informal association of newspaper editors that gained Andrew Greely, the famous editor of the *Herald Tribune*, the Democratic nomination for president in 1872, and when Ochs bought the *New York Times* in 1896 he tied it publicly to the antisilver campaign. By the last decades of the century news media were becoming more differentiated, not just in terms of how they viewed their product, but institutionally as well. What contemporaries of the period called the "new journalism" was intricately tied up with sensationalism and the attempt to create for the growing industrial classes an apolitical paper that would sell. More general factors were involved than the "capitalist" factor of the potentially wider market, as any comparative reference reveals. Although native-language ethnic papers often served as protosocialist organs for first-generation immigrant groups and partisan worker-oriented papers were a constant feature of nineteenth-century social history, it is extremely significant that there were no "labor" papers attached to working-class parties that emerged on a mass scale in the United States. By 1880, one-quarter of American papers were independent or neutral, and by 1890 one-third were. Papers developed *"human* interest" stories, and for the first time defined the reporter's role as actively seeking out "news." They launched "crusades" in the name of the "public interest" against corrupt groups like New York's Tweed ring. This transition in content coincided with the birth of journalistic professionalization and the emergence of newspapers as big business. By the turn of the twentieth century, the notion of the news media as a public institution was, then, beginning to be institutionalized. The major exception to this tendency was the relation of the news media to racial groups. American media remained tighly linked to the white core group of American society until at least the mid-twentieth century.

Although I have developed this contrast in the historical specification of media development in terms of French versus American media history, nineteenth-century Germany presents a case where newspapers were even more sharply polarized around class and party than were the French newspapers. As a result of its more rigid patrimonial structure and the lateness of its indutrialization, Germany produced a confrontation between proletarian and middle-class papers that was unmatched anywhere in Europe and that contributed to the increasing social rigidity that led to that nation's fateful social conflict (Roth 1963:243–48). In 1873, for example, the German Social Democratic newspaper reported that the typhoid epidemic then sweeping Germany was actually a bourgeois conspiratorial tool against the working class! In their turn, middle-class papers so distorted the activities of working-class groups that their readers could learn virtually nothing of the positive sides of and real political justifications for the Socialist movement. The Social Democrats responded in a revealing way. They decided to start party papers only in areas where middle-class papers already existed; only in this way, they reasoned, could middle-class readers compare news reports of the same event. But while the sectarian nature of Socialist papers certainly served the vital intraparty function of bolstering members' self-images in the face of often degrading and offensive characterizations in the middle-class press, such papers obviously presented a significant barrier to expanding the Social Democratic following. Even though more space was given to "news" and less to party affairs after the expansion of membership in the 1890s, these papers never moved beyond a highly sectarian orientation that alienated many workers, and particularly a large number of workers' wives, who remained relatively integrated with the dominant culture (particularly the religion) of the Reich. Fully 80 percent of the editors of Social Democratic papers were from the working classes, and the party prohibited its members from working for the bourgeois press.

Fusion and Autonomy: A Dynamic Process.   Finally, the problem of media "bias" can be seen not only in comparative or historical terms but also as a dynamic process that ebbs and flows with the episodic polarization produced by the strains that inevitably occur within the modernizing process of every nation, no matter how differentiated its media are in comparative or historical terms. For example, in the United States in the late 1960s and early 1970s, spokespersons for the national government acceptably portrayed the "Eastern establishment" press as presenting a biased and distorted picture of American social life. The success of this characterization was tied to the polarization of the national normative community into sharply opposed particularistic groupings (see Sciulli, this volume). From this perspective it is clear why, as Bernstein and Woodward reported (1974), the Nixon administration was not worried about the Watergate problem before the 1972 presidential election. They believed, quite correctly, that a sufficiently large number of Americans would not accept the news reported by the *Washington Post* as "factual." A large group of Americans perceived the *Post* as biased because, in the preceding years of social turmoil, that newspaper had become the normative spokesman of a liberal community no longer in the national majority. During this period of social conflict most of the national news media were not perceived as strongly differentiated from the positions and perspectives of particular social groups. Only after the 1972 presidential election, with the defeat of McGovern and the ensuing depolarization of American society, did the national media once again begin to receive the more broadly based inputs of support that allowed it to produce news about Watergate that could be judged as fact rather than opinion.

Although the parallel is not exact, a similar relationship can be seen between a later period of intense polarization in France and the emergence there of more particularistic media. In September 1977, when it appeared that the French Left coalition would come to power in the March 1979 national elections, a potentially powerful new paper, *J'informe*, appeared on the national scene. Published by a former cabinet minister close to President Giscard-D'Estaing and financed by a number of large industrial interests, the paper immediately assumed the role of spokesperson and interpreter for the government's center-Right coalition (with an initial circulation of 150,000). Although *J'informe*'s short-run purpose was to contribute to the government's reelection, its long-range goal was to provide a forum for Giscard's party and, presumably, for the social interests attached to it, after the Left took control. Once the Left coalition split apart in late 1977, and the prospect of a left-wing government receded, the need for the new and self-consciously propagandistic paper no longer existed. On December 18, 1977, *J'informe* ceased publication; its financial backers had withdrawn the necessary support (*New York Times*, December 18, 1977).

I would conclude by noting that whereas social scientists have studied "cleavage" problems extensively in regard to the economic, political, and cultural subsystems of society, they have rarely investigated the impact of cleavage on the integrative dimension and the production of norms. This lack of attention is largely the result of the fact that, in contrast to these other sectors, processes in the normative dimension have rarely been theoretically articulated (see Alexander 1978). In this section I have indicated that sharp cleavage situations are explosive not only because they produce broadly defined economic, political, and cultural conflicts, but also because, through their impact on the news media, they produce less cognitive agreement about the "factual" nature of the social world itself. The more this kind of disagreement occurs, the more social strains will become exacerbated and prove immutable to social reform.

Structured Strain in Differentiated Societies

I have argued that the news media's success in performing their normative "function" is dependent on certain distinctive kinds of historical conditions. In the modern period, three ideal-typical situations may be identified: (1) a single newspaper or news network that is the voice of official state ideology; (2) news institutions representing specific social perspectives of relatively autonomous groups; and (3) news media that are structurally free of directly inhibiting economic, political, solidary, and cultural entanglements.[6] Only in the third situation does the national public perceive the news media as providing "facts," and only in this situation can the media's normative function be performed in a manner that maximizes the public's flexibility.

Yet even though such a differentiated situation is in a certain sense ideal, it produces certain distinctive social conflicts and is open to certain ideological criticisms. I describe these as "structured strains" or "contradictions," which are inherent in the relation between a differentiated mass news medium and its social system environment. Although my treatment of such strains cannot be exhaustive, I will elaborate the problematic relationships I have in mind.

On the micro level of role conflict, the existence of differentiation must by its very nature continually raise the problem of collusion between a news reporter and his or her sources. In order to function as normative organizers, news reporters must extend their access into the "socially unknown," which means establishing intimate and trustworthy contacts through which to gain information that otherwise would remain private and "unregulated." Yet if to discover is to engage, to evaluate is to withdraw, and only if the latter occurs can the information garnered by the reporter be processed and judged according to independent norms. This problem must be regarded as a dilemma inherent in the very structure of the differentiated system. "Selling out" is a possibility only because differentiation has first established the partners for the transaction. On the other side of this conflict, the differentiated and legally protected status of the journalist's role raises the possibility that the narrow interest in finding "what's news" enters into conflict with important public interests, as when journalists protect the idenity of illegal sources. This kind of strain has manifested itself in the increasingly acrimonious conflict between courts and media that is occurring in most Western nations.

Another more general structural problem for even the most ideally differentiated media is the antagonism between government and news agencies that generates efforts at news distortion and manipulation by the government and, in turn, occasional episodes of irresponsible criticism of the government by the media. If, as Neustadt, for example, has maintained (1960:42–63), the American president is himself a "normative" figure engaged in persuasion, as well as in command, the government's political goals become directly competitive with the goals of the mass media, for each seeks to place public events within a more general evaluative framework. The president and the media are in continual battle over the normative definitions of events. The norms the president seeks to impose, however, are those of a particular segment of the national community. In other words, precisely because the power of the state is thoroughly differentiated from the news media, the latter become vulnerable to an enormously potent political force whose aim, paradoxically, is to dedifferentiate, or fuse, the relationship. Although the prize in this battle is influence rather than power, the struggle is in deadly earnest, and to minimize the stakes in the conflict between democratically elected governments and the free press—as critical theorists of the "bourgeois" press inevitably do—is a serious mistake.

In periods of political polarization, of course, this conflict is particularly acute. In his first four years in office, Richard Nixon devoted strenuous legal and illegal efforts to restrict the autonomous judgments of news reporters (Porter 1976). But even in relatively tranquil times, the war continues. When Ronald Reagan began his second term in office in January 1985, he announced that the White House would launch its own news service to distribute presidential speeches and announcements. While liberal opponents of the conservative president's first term had viewed Reagan as having successfully tamed a now docile White House press corps, this was not Reagan's own view at all. According to the Associated Press report on the rationale for the news service (*Los Angeles Times*, January 7, 1985), "Reagan has complained to reporters that they misinterpret his words and distort his views." As one White House official explained, the president would be more effective if his views were "unfiltered" by the independent media. The effort, quite clearly, was to avoid the primordial fact of news interpretation, which in the American situation is carried out by a body with a structured antagonism to central power. In the American case, it should be mentioned, this strain goes back to the founding of the nation itself. In 1789, the U.S. Congress sharply restricted journalists' access to the Senate because of what they regarded as the latter's "misrepresentations" of recent senatorial debates (quoted in Mott 1941:143).

The controversy that developed in the early 1970s in France between *Le Monde* and its veteran economic reporter, Philippe Simmonet, offers an example of such structured conflict in a different national media environment. Claiming that Simmonet had discovered and intended to print information embarrassing to the government's relation to the international oil companies, the French government brought suit to prevent publication. Its strength in this situation is revealed by the fact that *Le Monde*'s editors easily surrendered to government pressure. In fact, they joined the government's campaign to pressure Simmonet to reveal his sources, and when he would not do so they fired him without a hearing. The firing, of course, immediately became politicized. Socialist and Communist trade union representatives joined Simmonet's suit to regain his position, and the story was interpreted in particularistic ways. It is revealing that the message Simmonet took away from his experience (Simmonet 1977) is that the idea of a "liberal" independent journal in a capitalist society is hypocritical and that newspapers should seek to develop consistent, all-encompassing political perspectives on everyday events. To the degree that this does occur, however, governments simply seek to control news media in a more direct manner. Simmonet's reaction clearly illustrates how the structured strain in a differentiated situation can lead, under certain conditions, to a powerful argument for undermining media differentiation itself.

The third and most general kind of contradiction I mention concerns the manner in which the differentiated position of the media makes them vulnerable to pressures for the "inflation" (Parsons 1967) of its social system role. I describe this strain in relation to several of its specific manifestations.

Theorists from Aristotle to Marx and Weber have emphasized that the achievement of intellectual insight proceeds most effectively along a dialectical path, through the head-on dialogue of opposing perspectives. Yet, by a logic that would be contradictory to the entire implication of the preceding argument, it appears that the conditions for such dialogue occur only in societies in which the news media are less rather than more differentiated, for only in relatively undifferentiated situations do the media produce sharply divergent perspectives of public events. This logic is apparently fortified by the charges made by intellectuals critical of the American press, who describe it as bland and simplistic, who assert that by not "facing the issues" the press contributes to the political and moral stagnation of American society. Of course, to continue the science analogy used earlier, the knowledge created by such polarized media would be subject to a high degree of paradigm conflict. Still, media differentiation appears, paradoxically, to be inversely related to the sharpness of public thought and the quality of intellectual insight available to the society at large.

But this connection between the relative impoverishment of public dialogue and media differentiatioin is, indeed, only apparent. Social scientists drawing such a connection misunderstand the media's social function, and when the same error is committed by the public at large the media become vulnerable to serious damage. The news media's peculiar social position means that they "reflect" the conditions of the society around them, and in this respect they are, as conventional wisdom would have it, "slaves to the facts," if that phrase is taken in a noncognitive sense. Because of its very flexibility and integrative power a differentiated news medium cannot be an explicit "organizer" of norms in the way that institutions in other dimensions often are: it cannot formulate basic goals, which is a political responsibility, or basic values, which is a cultural one. In my view, the lack of sharp political focus and perspective in American political news is not a dire commentary on the impact of differentiation on the news media but rather a reflection of the inadequate autonomy achieved by the American political system, as manifest by such structural weaknesses as the atomization of executive and legislative functions and particularly the inability of political parties to articulate and maintain distinctive political positions (see Huntington 1968:93–139; Hardin 1974).

This specific problem provides an opportunity for formulating in more general terms the contradiction with which I am concerned. To the degree that the mass media sustain a differentiated position, they will absorb the weaknesses and reflect the distortions created by inadequate structural development in other social sectors. Social differentiation is always an "uneven and combined" process of development, and in one society certain sectors "lead" where in other societies these same sectors "lag" (Smelser 1970:7). The peculiarly American combination of a highly differentiated news media and less thoroughly differentiated political and intellectual institutions produces certain distinctive problems. In this situation, precisely because the media have been such effective normative organizers, they will be "blamed" for the weaknesses of these other sectors.

Such a double-bind situation creates strong centrifugal pressure for the inflation of the media's social function, which can lead ultimately to an equally radical deflation. The media will be asked to perform, and may well accept, a political or cultural role, and because they do not actually possess the functional resources for performing such tasks they are bound to fail.

Illustrations of this inflationary-deflationary spiral abound in the recent history of the news media in America. In social crises, for example in the 1960s, when the weaknesses of the American political system are exacerbated, pressure mounts for the media to expand their functions, to engage in critical or radical political judgment, and to investigate and "clean up" the government and the society as a whole. But because the government has itself been unable to accomplish this task, in responding to these demands the media open themselves to devastating political criticism about their lack of objectivity.

"Media politics" present another example of the manner in which effective media performance can be undercut by weaknesses in the political sector. By media politics I mean a range of politically degenerate phenomena: the generation of political support on the basis of presentation of self rather than the articulation of public issues; presidential use of television to create the charismatic, Caesarist domination of political opposition; and the volatility of public opinion, which encourages the mercurial ascension of untried, inexperienced, and often incompetent political leadership. Yet once again these problems relate to the deficiencies of the American political system interacting with the peculiar functional position of the media, not to the problem of differentiation in the media themselves. Although the differentiation of news media does introduce a high degree of fluidity into political communication, it need not necessarily dominate other forms of political influence as it tends to do in the United States. The real problem in the U.S. case is not the differentiation of the integrative dimension but the lack of differentiation of the political system. Because the institutions that should produce self-conscious political norms cannot do so—cannot, in terms of systemic logic, provide certain kinds of competing inputs to the media—political candidates gain popularity without articulating explicit positions. In the same manner, although "presidential politics" are facilitated by a differentiated media, the failure of organizational opposition prevents the creation of alternative, competing political symbolization. And, once again, the pervasive public criticism of what are mistakenly regarded as instances of inflation of the media's political role can result in the deflation of what is, in itself, a relatively "healthy" social institution.

This inflationary-deflationary dilemma can occur in regard to the cultural as well as the political dimension. In certain situations of extreme social strain, the news media's normative orientation becomes legitimately transformed into a "value" function, although even this more generalized role is performed in a flexible and differentiated way. Such a generalization of function characterized television news at crucial points in the Watergate period, particularly during the congressional hearings, when television served a key function in the ritualistic invocation of the civic culture that was one of the fundamental responses to the strain of that time. After such episodes (see Lang and Lang 1968), however, the danger is that the news media will be expected to assume the permanent role of, and will accept responsibility for, value arbiter rather than norm organizer. But this inflation can occur only to the degree that deficiencies exist in the cultural dimension itself, if moral leadership cannot generate sufficient clarity and relevance to provide the news media with the value inputs they would normally "register" in a normative manner. The performance of this inflated function makes the news media particularly vulnerable and opens up the possibility of the destructive deflation of their normative scope, for example in the public support for presidential legislation restricting the media's flexibility.

Finally, if our system reference shifts from the national to the international level, we can see quite clearly that even the most differentiated national medium will usually be closely linked to particularistic national loyalties in terms of its relationship to extranational events. One way of comparing the international and national communities is in the degree to which their normative structures are, first, widely shared and, second, universalistic. On the international level there is radically less commonality and radically more particularism. Consequently, whereas the direct link between newspapers and a particular social group remains a distinct possibility on the national level, the dedifferentiated identification of newspapers with the interests of a particular national community is standard practice at the level of international social relations. Although many a national newspaper may succeed in differentiating itself from a particular government's "line" on the interpretation of an international event, it will rarely succeed in differentiating itself from the norms and values of the nation as a normative community. Events in the international arena are, as a result, almost always interpreted from the particularistic perspective of the nation within which the news medium operates. Thus, when the Western powers moved to establish wire services in the mid-nineteenth century—the Wolffe Agency in Germany, Reuters in England, L'Agence Havas in France, and the Associated Press in the United States—it was precisely in order to gain control over the information conveyed to their respective citizenries about the rapidly developing international economic and political relations of the day (for the French case, see Frédérix 1959). International particularism is revealed in a particularly acute way by the lies that are so often told, wittingly and unwittingly, by reporters during wars (Knightley 1978). But it extends to the mundane as well. When the first American landed on the moon, the event was covered in strikingly different ways by French, Italian, and Russian newspapers (Tudesq 1973).

The fusion of the national community and national media in terms of international news means that little "regulation" over government policy in this area is exercised by democratic media. The bias is not simply the result of such factors as reportorial ethics or an overreliance on government sources. It constitutes a major independent factor in the creation and exacerbation of international conflict. Although the problem of national media particularism is not created by media differentiation—as are the other strains I have mentioned—it is certainly a structured strain that such differentiation does nothing to resolve.

In this paper I have presented the outlines of a general theory of the mass news media in society. The media produce certain normative definitions, and the "success" of this production depends on the degree to which they have achieved autonomy from other social institutions and groups. Dependent media—the products of an unevenly differentiated, relatively fused society—can themselves become a significant source of social polarization and rigidification of social control. Moreover, the flexibility of the news media is such that even in a highly differentiated condition they can become a focal point of great social strain, for their very transparency makes them a highly visible conduit for the weaknesses of their external social environment. Although my argument has been abstract and condensed it provides, I hope, a relatively specific model for future empirical elaboration and debate.

Notes

1. My use of the concept of "function" here and elsewhere in this paper is a shortand form that makes it easier to situate the cultural and "structural" aspects of the mass news media—their causes, effects, and institutional character—in the social system. I believe that the following discussion demonstrates that there is nothing teleological, conservative, or static about functionalist analysis when it is conducted in a certain way. This is not to say, however, that functionalism is simply "good sociology" by another name (see Alexander 1985).

2. In his later writings, Goffman (1974:17) understood the news media in precisely this kind of phenomenological way. Although he limits his remarks specifically to the press's reporting of human interest stories, they hold good, it seems to me, for news as such:

> Our understanding of the world precedes these stories, determining which ones reporters will select and how the ones that are selected will be told. . . . The design of these reported events is fully responsive to our demands—which are not for facts but for typifications. Their telling demonstrates the power of our conventional understandings to cope with the bizarre potentials of social life, the furthest reaches of experience. What appears, then, to be a threat to our way of making sense of the world turns out to be an ingeniously selected defense of it.

This position ignores, of course, the possibility that the media might also contribute to social change or to the achievement of rationality. That is the price of adopting a purely phenomenological understanding, and I try to avoid it below.

3. Parsons (1961) provides a precise conceptual discussion of the ways in which the normative sphere of culture—which he also identifies with the integrative sphere in the social system—provides regulation over cognitive as well as expressive and explicitly ethical judgments.

4. As the phrase "normative production" indicates, I am looking at the normative function of the media in terms of the theory of interchange that Parsons developed in his later work (Alexander 1983b:73–118). According to this model of the social system, fundamentally different kinds of activities—economic life, political life, integrative and norm-setting activities, value maintenance, and socialization—can be conceived as subsystems that produce important resources (outputs) upon which the others depend. Each subsystem relies on receiving suitable inputs in turn. This model makes it possible to conduct a fully multidimensional analysis of social system life, because it differentiates analytically the interdependence of various social system activities that in "real life" are interpenetrating and interact simultaneously. The emphasis on reciprocity and exchange, moreover, makes this systemic analysis dynamic rather than static. My use of interchange theory differs from Parsons' own, however, in my insistence that it is an abstract model rather than an actual description of social system processes. In opposition to Parsons' "conflated" usage (Alexander 1983:186–276; cf. Eisenstadt, this volume), I focus here on concrete institutional processes, social groups and their interested activity, structural fusion (as resulting from functional interchange), the uneven develop-

ment of different sectors, and the possibility that social strain and even pathology are attendant on the differentiation process.

5. This is not to say, of course, that the pressure to sell papers (or media time) is always supportive of the media's interpretive function. It is to say, however, that the results of capitalist pressures on the media have usually been greatly exaggerated, both in terms of their distorting and their dominative tendencies.

Raymond Williams is perhaps the most influential analyst of the media who has taken up the neo-Marxist position I am criticizing here. Describing the corporatization of the mass media as one of the "two major factors in the modern history of communication" (Williams 1962), he condemns it as fundamentally antidemocratic. Whereas I have described the separation of editorial control from financial ownership as a phase of role differentiation that allowed news reporting to be increasingly autonomous vis-à-vis particularistic opinion, Williams (1962) describes it as having allowed "the methods and attitudes of capitalist business to have established themselves at the centre of public communications." Corporatization, according to Williams, means the reliance on advertising sales to finance papers, i.e., a newly economic bottom line. Relying on Marx's commodification theory, Williams (1962:25) suggests that in these conditions communications are produced not for "use" but for exchange, a development tantamount in his view to eroding the capacity for truth.

Williams overlooks here the multidimensional context of media development, which necessitates looking not only at the media's economic links but also at political, cultural, and solidary links. This change in ownership, for example, occurred more or less simultaneously with another central phenomenon, namely professionalization. The result was that, during the purported period of commodificaiton, the work of the actual producer of communication—the reporting of news—was pushed toward greater concern with use. Increasingly, the reporter's work became subject to a wide range of normative controls that revolved around creating more "rational" and "truthful" news.

More generally, Williams has not developed a viable sociological understanding of the conditions for "media truth." In the first place, autonomy vis-à-vis capital is only one of several major forms of differentiation that must be accomplished, as my discussions of the relations between media and religious groups, intellectuals, ethnic communities, and political parties indicate. Second, it is not the autonomy vis-à-vis capital per se that has been crucial historically but the autonomy of one institutional source of capital in relation to the capital of others. I have laid out the reasons for this earlier in this paper. In the text that follows I suggest, indeed, that wide reliance on advertising actually helped American newspapers to become more democratic—e.g., more responsive to wide segments of the reading public, more flexible in its evaluations of ongoing events—than the privately controlled newspapers in France, where the possibilities for advertising were quite limited.

6. I stress that these are ideal types. The concrete arrangements in each national case are idiosyncratic and blur these analytic distinctions in various ways. One important source of this blurring is state ownership of national news organizations. In a vulgar sense, all such institutions would have to represent the "state." In democratic societies, however, there is a distinction between the solidary community of citizens, which is constitutionally endowed with a range of power-enhancing public skills, and the actual state apparatus. The democratic situation creates the possibility for an autonomous news organization within a state-owned system—usually called "public ownership"—but it does not necessitate it. Thus,

the English BBC has been relatively independent of particular governments, whereas the French national news has not. In Italy, there is a different situation still, with state ownership being combined with at least two competing party-affiliated organizations. Because the present essay has been so historical in scope, televised news has not been a primary focus. Insofar as it becomes so—despite the recent trends toward deregulation and privatization—the factor of state ownership becomes important, for it mediates the phenomena of fusion and autonomy in situationally specific ways—for example, contrasting cultural milieux make legal control by government different in every case. For an analysis of privately owned television news that correlates fairly closely with the model suggested here, see Gans' (1979) extended research on the relationship between values and objectivity in American television news and on the often tense relationship between American news organizations and their surrounding environments.

References

Albert, P. and F. Terrou, 1970. *Histoire de la presse*. Paris: Presses Universitaires de France.

Alexander, Jeffrey C. 1978. "Formal and Substantive Voluntarism in the Work of Talcott Parsons: A Theoretical and Ideological Reinterpretation." *American Sociological Review* (April), 43:177–98.

—— 1980. "Core Soliclarity, Ethnic Outgroup, and Social Differentiation: A Multi-Dimensional Model of Inclusion in Modern Societies." In Jacques Dofny and Akinsola Akinono, eds., *National and Ethnic Movements*. Beverly Hills, Calif. and London: Sage.

—— 1983a. "Max Weber, la théorie de la rationalisation et le marxisme." *Sociologie et Sociétés* 14(2):33–43.

—— 1983b. *The Modern Reconstruction of Classical Thought: Talcott Parsons*. Vol. 4 of *Theoretical Logic in Sociology*. Berkeley and Los Angeles: University of California Press.

—— 1985. "Introduction." In Jeffrey C. Alexander, ed., *Neofunctionalism*, pp. 7–20. Beverly Hills, Calif. and London: Sage.

Baestrup, Peter. 1978. *Big Story: How the American Press and Television Reported and Interpreted the Crisis of Tet 1968 in Vietnam and Washington*. New York: Doubleday.

Baldwin, Elizabeth. 1977. "The Mass Media and the Corporate Elite: A Re-Analysis of the Overlap Between the Media and Economic Elites." *Canadian Journal of Sociology* 2(1):1–27.

Bellah, Robert N. 1970. "The Systematic Study of Religion." In Robert N. Bellah, *Beyond Belief*, pp. 260–80. New York: Harper and Row.

Bellanger, Claude, Jacques Godechot, Pierre Guiral, and Fernand Terrou. 1969–1976. *Histoire générale de les presses françaises*. 5 vols. Paris: Presses Universitaires de France.

Bellet, Roger. 1967. *Presse et journalisme sous le Deuxième Empire*. Paris: Armand Colin.

Benjamin, Walter. 1973. *Charles Baudelaire: A Cynic Poet in the Era of High Capitalism*. London: New Left Review Books.

Bernstein, Carl and Bob Woodward. 1974. *All the President's Men*. New York: Simon and Schuster.

Boussel, Patrice. 1960. *L'Affaire Dreyfus et la presse*. Paris: Armand Colin.

Clement, Wallace. 1973. *The Canadian Corporate Elite*. Toronto: McClelland and Stewart.

Commager, Henry Steele. 1950. *The American Mind*. New Haven, Conn.: Yale University Press.

Conte, A. 1973. "La presse soviètique et le premier débarquement Americain sur la lune."P p. 117–45 in A.-J. Judesq, ed., *La presse et l'événement*. Paris: Mouton.

Dahlgren, Peter. 1978. "TV News and the Suppression of Reflexivity." Paper delivered at the Ninth World Congress of Sociology, Uppsala, Sweden (August).

Dahrendorf, Ralph. 1959. *Class and Class Conflict in the Industrial Revolution*. Stanford, Calif.: Stanford University Press.

Deniel, Raymond. 1965. *Une image de la famille et de la société sous la Reconstruction*. Paris: Les Editions Ouvrières.

Eisenstadt, S. N. 1969. *The Political System of Empires*. 2d ed. New York: Free Press.

Evans, Harold. 1972. *Newsman's English*. New York: Holt, Rinehart and Winston.

Fass, Paula S. 1976. "Television as a Cultural Document: Promises and Problems." In *Television as a Cultural Force*, pp. 37–58. New York: Praeger.

Frédérix, Pierre. 1959. *Un siècle de chausse aux nouvelles: De l'Agence d'Information Havas à l'Agence France Presse, 1835–1957*. Paris: Flammarion.

Gans, Herbert. 1979. *Deciding What's News: A Study of CBS Evening News, NBC Nightly News, Newsweek, and Time*. New York: Pantheon.

Garfinkel, Harold. 1967. *Studies in Ethnomethodology* Englewood, Cliffs, N.J.: Prentice-Hall.

Geertz, Clifford. 1973. "Thick Description." In Clifford Geertz, *The Interpretation of Cultures*, pp. 3–32. New York: Basic Books.

Goffman, Erving. 1974. *Frame Analysis*. New York: Harper and Row.

Golding, Peter. 1974. *Mass Media*. London: Longman.

—— 1978. "The Missing Dimensions—News Media and the Management of Social Change." Paper delivered at the Ninth World Congress of Sociology, Uppsala, Sweden (August).

Hall, Stuart and Paddy Whannel. 1964. *The Popular Arts: A Critical Guide to the Mass Media*. Boston, Mass.: Beacon.

Hallin, Daniel and Paolo Mancini. 1984. "Speaking of the President: Political Structure and Representational Form in U.S. and Italian Television News. *Theory and Society* 13:829–51.

Hamilton, Thomas. 1833 (1968). *Men and Manners in America*. New York: Johnson Reprint.

Hardin, Charles M. 1974. *Presidential Power and Accountability: Toward a New Constititution*. Chicago, Ill.: University of Chicago Press.

Harris, William F. 1978. "Government Without Newspapers?" Paper delivered at the Ninth World Congress of Sociology, Uppsala, Sweden (August).

Hirsch, Paul M. 1978. "Institutional Functions of Elite and Mass Media." Paper delivered at the Ninth World Congress of Sociology, Uppsala, Sweden (August).

Hohenberg, John. 1978. *The Professional Journalist*, 4th ed. New York: Holt, Rinehart and Winston.

Holton, Gerald. 1973. *The Thematic Origins of Science: From Kepler to Einstein*. Cambridge, Mass.: Harvard University Press.

Huntington, Samuel P. 1968. *Political Order in Changing Societies*. New Haven, Conn.: Yale University Press.

Husserl, Edmund. 1977 (1931). *Cartesian Meditations.* The Hague: Martinus Nijhoff.

Kadushin, Charles. 1975. *The American Intellectual Elite.* Boston, Mass.: Little, Brown.

Katz, Elihu and Paul F. Lazarsfeld. 1955. *Personal Influence.* New York: Free Press.

Kinghtley, Phillip. 1978. *The First Casualty.* New York: Harcourt, Brace, Jovanovich.

Kuhn, Thomas. 1970. *The Structure of Scientific Revolutions.* 2d ed., Chicago: University of Chicago Press.

Lang, Kurt and Gladys Engel Lang. 1968. *Politics and Television.* Chicago, Ill.: Quadrangle.

Manévy, Raymond. 1955. *La Presse de la Trosième Republique.* Paris: J. Foret.

McDougall, Curtis D. 1968. *Interpretive Reporting.* 5th ed. New York: Macmillan.

Mills, C. Wright. 1956. *The Power Elite.* London: Oxford University Press.

Missika, Jean-Louis. 1986. "Abstracts for Decision: The Parsimonious Elements of Public Choice in Public Controversy." *European Journal of Communication* 1:27–42.

—— 1987. "Selecting Political Controversies: Mass Media, Parties, and Public Opinion During the March 1986 Legislative Campaign in France." *European Journal of Communication,* vol. 2.

Mott, Frank Luther. 1941. *American Journalism.* New York: Macmillan.

Mueller, Claus. 1973. *The Politics of Communication.* New York: Oxford University Press.

Near East Report. 1978. *Washington Letter on American Policy in the Near East* (March 15), Vol. 22, no. 11.

Neustadt, Richard E. 1960. *Presidential Power.* New York: Wiley.

Noelle-Neumann, Elisabeth. 1978. "Mass Media and Social Change in Developed Societies." Paper delivered at the Ninth World Congress of Sociology, Uppsala, Sweden (August).

Paletz, David, Peggy Reichert, and Barbara McIntyre. 1971. "How the Media Support Local Governmental Authority." *Public Opinion Quarterly* (spring), 35:80–92.

Parsons, Talcott. 1951. *The Social System.* New York: Free Press.

—— 1961. "Introduction to Culture and the Social System." In Talcott Parsons, Kasper D. Naegele, Edward A. Shils, and Jess R. Pitts, eds., *Theories of Society,* pp. 967–93. New York: Free Press.

—— 1967. "On the Concept of Influence." In Talcott Parsons, *Sociological Theory and Modern Society,* pp. 355–82. New York: Free Press.

Parsons, Talcott and Winston White. 1969. "The Mass Media and the Structure of American Society." In Talcott Parson, *Politics and Social Structure,* pp. 241–51. New York: Free Press.

Polanyi, Michael. 1958. *Personal Knowledge.* New York: Harper and Row.

Porter, William E. 1976. *Assault on the Media: The Nixon Years.* Ann Arbor: University of Michigan Press.

Roth, Guenther. 1963. *The Social Democrats in Imperial Germany.* New York: Bedminster Press.

Schudson, Michael. 1978. *Discovering the News.* New York: Basic Books.

Seguin, Jean-Paul. 1961. *L'information en France: De Louis XII à Henri II.* Geneva: E. Droz.

—— 1964. *L'information en France avant le périodique: 517 Canards imprimés entre 1529 et 1631.* Paris: G.-P. Maisonneuve et Larose.

Shaw, David. 1975. "Hoax: A Risk That Haunts Newspapers." *Los Angeles Times,* July 7.

Shils, Edward and Morris Janowitz. 1975 (1948). "Cohesion and Disintegration in the Wehrmacht in World War II." Reprinted in Edward Shils, ed., *Center and Periphery: Essays in Macrosociology*, pp. 345–83. Chicago, Ill.: University of Chicago Press.

Simmonet, Philippe. 1977. *"Le Monde" et le pouvior.* Paris: Les Presses d'Aujourd'hui.

Smelser, Neil J. 1970. "Stability, Instability, and the Analysis of Political Corruption." In Bernard Barber and Alex Inkeles, eds., *Stability and Change*, pp. 7–29. Boston, Mass.: Little, Brown.

Tocqueville, Alexis de. 1835. (1945) *Democracy in America*, vol. I. New York: Random House.

Tudesq, André-Jean. 1973. "La Presse soviètique et la première débarquement américain sur la lune." In André-Jean Tudesq, ed., *La presse et L'événment*, pp. 117–36. Paris: Mouton.

Toulmin, Stephen. 1972. *Human Understanding.* Princeton, N.J.: Princeton University Press.

Walzer, Michael. 1965. *Revolution of the Saints.* Cambridge, Mass.: Harvard University Press.

Williams, Raymond. 1962. *Communications.* London: Penguin.

Woodward, Bob and Carl Berstein. 1976. *The Final Days.* New York: Simon and Schuster.

11

Differentiation and Collegial Formations: Implications of Societal Constitutionalism

David Sciulli

Societal constitutionalism specifies procedural institutions that must be in evidence within modern societies in order for actors' nonauthoritarian social integration to be a possiblity in practice (Sciulli Forthcoming ch. 2 on the distinction between social control and social integration). The presence of these institutions—across governmental agencies, divisions of corporations, and sectors of interest associations and social movements—literally offers actors and researchers alike the possibility of simply distinguishing, for instance, between latently authoritarian social control (or the mass manipulation of mere subjective legitimation) and genuine social integration. In particular, if systemic pressures of social change cause organizations and institutions to drift toward inadvertently violating the integrity of either the "collegial form of organization" or the norms of "procedural legality,"[1] then arbitrariness and authoritarianism cannot possibly be restrained within modern societies[2] and social order cannot possibly be based upon actors' possible social integration but can only be based upon actors' social control.

Societal constitutionalism is designed to establish, therefore, not only whether particular instances of purposeful exercises of arbitrary power are increasing or decreasing within social life, but also whether inadvertent instances of manipulation or latent coercion are increasing or decreasing.[3] The procedural restraints on arbitrary power specified by societal constitutionalism cannot be relativized or dismissed. Moreover, their further differentiation and institutionalization by actors, in practice, is not merely one policy option among others. Rather, if actors fail to further differentiate and institutionalize these restraints within extant liberal democracies, then these societies will drift invariably toward increasing arbitrariness in social relations, and then possibly toward authoritarianism. (Of course, if the same restraints are not instituted within third world and Eastern bloc societies, they will remain authoritarian). This will be the case regardless of policymakers' particular motivations and beliefs within particular societies, and regardless of each society's distinct traditions.

I read Jürgen Habermas, Talcott Parsons, and Lon Fuller as converging upon this thesis of the importance of procedural institutions within contemporary societies, despite all of their remaining significant disagreements (see also Hayek 1973–1979; Arendt 1951, 1963; and Lowi 1969, among other theorists as diverse as, e.g., Vile 1967; Friedrich 1937, 1963, 1974; and Dahl since the mid-1970s, e.g., 1977, 1982). Societal constitutionalism's status as an "Archimedean point" that separates actors' mere social control from the possibility of their genuine social integration rests upon a synthesis of Habermas' *idealized* standard of procedural reason, Parsons' *analytical* standard of procedural institutionalization, and Fuller's *empirical* standard of procedural legality.[4]

Parsons' view of systemic "drift" toward authoritarianism is reviewed first, along with some basic criticisms of contemporary interest group politics in the United States. Parsons' view is consistent with these criticisms and with related diagnoses of liberal democracies by social theorists as diverse as Friedrich Hayek and Hannah Arendt. The following section addresses Parsons' own response to the problem of drift. For him, if existing normative restraints on drift are to be maintained ("pattern maintenance"), contemporary social change ("functional differentiation") must include "procedural institutionalization" in general and the institutionalization of "collegial formations" in particular.

Parsons' response is reformulated in a later section, however, by noting explicitly that the collegial form of organization elaborates and extends Fuller's principles of "procedural legality." Moreover, by pushing Parsons and Fuller in directions that neither developed independently, and especially by pushing Parsons' treatment of collegial formations to its inescapable practical implication as normative restraints upon the drift of purposive-rational social change itself, the status of societal constitutionalism's normative restraints comes into view. They specify a procedural threshold that separates actors' mere social control from their possible genuine social integration (for discussions of the synthesis see Sciulli 1985, 1986, 1988, and forthcoming).

In the last section, prescriptions proposed by Hayek, Arendt, and Lowi respectively for restraining authoritarianism are reviewed in order to illustrate a few of the policy implications of societal constitutionalism: the legislative assembly, the council system, and juridical democracy. At the same time societal constitutionalism helps to clarify each prescription and to assist each one in finally overcoming shortcomings of vagueness or impracticality from which it otherwise suffers. (On Arendt see Wolf 1961; Habermas 1977; Hill 1979. On Hayek see Meikeljohn 1980. On Hayek and Lowi see Bensel 1980.) I propose in my conclusion, that the issue of firmly institutionalizing the procedural restraints of societal constitutionalism can be expected to become explicitly adopted not only by broad-based and sustained social movements across the Western liberal democracies, but also by such movements across selected Eastern bloc countries (e.g., Poland, East Germany, and Yugoslavia) and even across certain "advanced" third world countries (e.g., Brazil, Mexico, Cuba, and South Korea).

Systemic Drift: Purposive-Rational Social Change and Authoritarianism

Social Change as Entropic Drift. Parsons agreed with Weber and Pareto that modern social change "drifts" toward (a) the increasing pluralism or substantive differentiation of group interests and (b) authorities' increasing reliance upon bureaucratically organized, specialized agencies of enforcement to maintain social order despite these group divisions.

The emergence of [adventurers' capitalism] is due to a process of emancipation from ethical control, the setting free of interests and impulses from normative limitations, traditional or [value-] rationally ethical. . . . This is the centrifugal "bombardment of interests and appetites," their tendency to escape control. . . . It is essentially the process involved in Pareto's process of transition from dominance of the residues of persistence to those of combination, equally in Durkheim's transition from solidarity or integration to anomie. It is a process the possibility of which is inherent in the voluntaristic conception of action as such. (Parsons 1968c [1937]:685–86, 710)

With the exception of his works of the early 1950s (especially 1951; see Parsons 1964c), Parsons treated rationalization as an "entropic" and "anomic" systemic force.[5] It pressures organizations and institutions to "adapt" in ways that are largely unplanned and inadvertent. Each cycle of social change takes place, that is, under less and less normative guidance, and actors experience these cycles as "drift." They experience each cycle as a steady diminishing of earlier, shared senses of direction.

For Parsons the potential for dissensus and conflict between contemporary groups increases incrementally with every *unmediated* extension of purposive-rational action into new areas of life:

The institutions of citizenship and nationality can nevertheless render the societal community vulnerable if the bases of pluralism are exacerbated into sharply structured cleavages. Since the typical modern community unifies a large population over a large territory, for example, its solidarity may be severely strained by regional cleavages. This is particularly true where the regional cleavages coincide with ethnic and/or religious divisions. *Many* modern societies have disintegrated before varying combinations of these bases of cleavage. . . . [Even] where societal solidarity is emancipated from the more primordial bases of religion, ethnicity and territoriality, it tends to foster other types of internal differentiation and pluralization. (1971:22, my emphasis; see also pp. 12–14, 98ff, 106–7)

Parsons purposely overstated and telescoped the empirical disruptions that would accompany the most unmediated extensions of purposive-rational action in order to establish a "limiting case" standard of drift as "entropy" (see also Habermas 1975 on legitimation and motivation crises; and Merton and Barber 1976 on ambivalence in social roles). Unlike Weber and Marx and their contemporary followers, however, Parsons refused to convert this limiting case in thought experiment into a theory of crisis in practice. Put differently, he refused to follow other theorists in condemning every aspect of contemporary social change in vague and romanticist terms as unnecessary, "capitalistic" encroachments against actors' presumed essential being or shared "life-world" (*Lebenswelt*) (Husserl 1970 [1934–1937]; Horkheimer and Adorno 1944; Paci 1972; and Habermas 1984 take the latter approach).

In Parsons' terminology, pressures of purposive-rational social change are comprised of (1) adaptive and goal attainment functions and (2) the concomitant (albeit more broadly defined) belief system that he called "instrumental activism." Adaptive functions (A), or the economy subsystem, encompass all *analytical* aspects of social actions that unambiguously increase a group's or a society's efficiency in material production (see, e.g., Parsons and Smelser 1969). Goal attainment functions (G), or the political subsystem, encompass all aspects that unambiguously increase a group's or a society's effectiveness in organizing personnel (see, e.g., Parsons 1958, 1969b, 1969d, 1969e). Instrumental activism, then, is the belief system that actors adopt that accords priority to adaptation and goal attainment even as these activities, if left unmediated, undermine the integrity of normative principles that earlier generations of actors accepted as exemplary qualities of social life (Parsons 1958, 1969d:336–37; Parsons and White 1961; Parsons and Platt 1973:41ff). Commonplace examples of the undermining of such principles, taken merely from the last three decades in the United States, include the erosion of "blue laws" that once prohibited commercial transactions on the sabbath and the proliferation of state and city lotteries and other extensions of state-sanctioned gambling.

Against the limiting case standard of unmediated purposive-rational social change, therefore, Parsons concentrated upon specifying (1) those analytical aspects of social action that can possibly integrate actors either within groups or across a society as a whole, that is, the "societal community" or the integrative (I) subsystem; and (2) other analytical aspects that can possibly maintain a group's or a society's normative principles generally, that is, the "fiduciary" or the latency (L) subsystem. The question is whether normative principles can be specified that could allow even heterogeneous actors within pluralist groups to simply recognize which restraints on drift are genuinely integrative and which restraints revitalize "traditional" obstacles to social change, along with latent or manifest practices of authoritarian social control.

In Parsons' view, nonauthoritarian social integration today requires the institutionalization of normative restraints that are procedural mediations *of* social change, and not exclusively the institutionalization of those restraints that are direct substantive limitations *against* social change. Parsons thereby explicitly questioned the view shared by Durkheimians, Kantians, and neo-Aristotelians, viz., that social integration requires actors to internalize shared substantive beliefs (or to act upon shared motivations).[6] Yet Parsons' suggestions regarding "procedural institutions" must be specified and reformulated as well as elaborated in order to appreciate the point that may be found buried in his writings.

Specifying Drift: Interest Group Politics in the United States.   Despite their quite different and often incompatible approaches to the study of politics and society, Hayek, Arendt, and Lowi share Parsons' view of drift. Unlike Parsons, however, each condemns unhesitatingly the decline of Western institutions' fidelity to principle and the concomitant decline of the integrity and autonomy of governmental agencies, professional, cultural, and civic associations, and socioeconomic enterprises. Each insists that these organizations and institutions are already resorting or acceding to exercises of arbitrary power and that they are thereby either accommodating the relatively unmediated bargaining of group interests (in the United States) or else they are accommodating the relatively unmediated policy agendas of mass political parties (in Western Europe) within a general social context of systemic, purposive-rational drift.

Political scientists insist, for instance, that the key to understanding contemporary politics within the United States is the interrelationship between interest group pressures and the "policy process." In contrast to the pessimism of the three theorists just mentioned, however, they portray the erosion of both substantive and procedural norms as a virtue of this group "pluralism." For them the steady movement away from strict normative principles is a manifestation of the United States' (and any other liberal democracy's) flexibility, adaptability, and maturity. (Truman 1953; Dahl 1956, 1971, 1967; and Polsby 1963 remain the most influential pluralist arguments. Dahl has since become critical; see, e.g., 1977, 1982).

Indeed, political scientists insist that the *only* due process that is necessary today to maintain democracy and actors' freedoms is the "countervailing" pressures between interest associations that are permitted to mobilize and compete for political influence. As long as all potential interest associations have access, at least in principle, to means by which they can influence policymakers and power holders, that is, as long as their access is not hampered by any de jure blockages, then their very competition automatically prevents any faction or coalition of interests from becoming hegemonic. The problem of systemic drift, however, or the problem of where the otherwise unrestrained competition between and accommodation of group interests may lead, is ignored altogether. By contrast to the skepticism of theorists in the 1920s and 1930s (which Parsons shared), political scientists in the postwar era simply assume that drift *is* "progress" (see, e.g., Huntington 1971: esp. 290). They assume that the United States is a "mature" democracy that could not possibly suffer the "regressions" experienced on the Continent in the 1920s. However, they offer neither evidence for nor any theoretical grounding in support of such grand assumptions.

As part of the "public philosophy" of the United States, pluralism updates classical liberalism. (The remainder of this section draws upon Lowi 1969; for a popular reappraisal see Reich 1985.) The latter is best applied to *individuals* (whether entrepreneurs, investors, laborers, or consumers) prior to the onset of unionization, urbanization, and the administrative welfare state. Individuals' economic competition within a marketplace comprised of "sovereign consumers" was assumed to be sufficient to prevent monopolistic pricing (except for "externalities"). Steering of the socioeconomic order by the state required justification.[7]

By contrast, pluralism applies to quite different units of competition: urban social movements, public and private bureaucracies, oligopolistic corporations, mass political parties, single-issue and broad-based group interests, and civic and professional associations. Moreover, pluralism does not treat the administrative state's steering of the economy as encroachments that require justification. Rather, governmental steering becomes an ideal incubator of new group interests. Additional group pressures, in turn, can only help to countervail those group interests already found within the socioeconomic order and within the policymaking process (Lipset 1960:64–86; see Galbraith 1967 for a now classic statement).

But like liberals' notion of the "hidden hand," pluralists simply assume that group competition over policymaking (and directly or indirectly over corporate investment strategies) literally embodies "justice" or "fairness" as such (see Friedland and Sanders 1985 on groups' influence over macro investment strategies). Political scientists rightly point out that *substantive* norms or standards of justice can no longer secure acceptance across group interests independently of the group competition itself. Natural law standards of "the good life," for instance, no longer instruct groups in practice. Rather, norms of justice and fairness are reduced in practice, and by default, to the temporary compromises established between groups over particular sets of issues (Lowi 1969:47–54, 68–79, 85–97). The groups' lack of rebellion, as well as the government's infrequent resort to manifest coercion, remain pluralist theorists' strongest "evidence" that social order within the United States is genuinely integrative rather than manipulated or based upon latent coercion.

Lowi has conveniently summarized major criticisms of the pluralist model of interest group politics. (Other influential criticisms include those by Schattschneider 1960; McConnell 1966; Bachrach and Baratz 1970; Balbus 1971; Sennett 1978; and Dahl 1977, 1982. Parsons sounds similar on occasions; see, e.g., 1962b:59–60, 1968a:50.)[8] The same criticisms are shared by Hayek and Arendt, given their own criticisms of the declining integrity of the "rule of law." Lowi's very choice of words in describing interest group politics conveys the radical, un-compromising quality of all three theorists' criticisms of interest group politics: "The corruption of modern democratic government began with the emergence of interest-group liberalism as the public philos-ophy. Its corrupting influence takes at least four important forms, four counts, therefore, of an indictment. . . . Also to be indicted . . . is the philosophic component of the ideology, pluralism."

First, interest group liberalism "deranges and confuses expecta-tions about democratic institutions . . . by treating all values in the process [whether substantive or procedural] as equivalent interests" that may be compromised by bargains and negotiation. Second, inter-est group liberalism "renders government impotent" to administer services according to plan. Administrative agencies are not guided by clear ends or standards but are subjected to group pressures. Third, interest group liberalism "demoralizes government because liberal governments cannot achieve justice." Lowi is not referring to justice in some ideal substantive sense found in political theory from Plato to Marx. Rather, he is concerned about justice in a more practicable and irreducible sense as those preconditions necessary for any credi-ble aspiration to realize *any possible* substantive ideal of the good life. Finally, interest group liberalism "corrupts democratic government" by weakening "the capacity of government to live by democratic formalism"; interest group politics "oppos[es] formal procedures with informal bargaining." (See Lowi 1969:287–93 for the four indict-ments.)

The Convergent Diagnosis: Latent Authoritarianism in the West. In terms as explicit as Lowi's, Hayek and Arendt do not merely insist that the contemporary liberal democracies are drifting toward authoritarian-ism. They argue instead that the liberal democracies are already latently authoritarian. In their view the absence of resilient norma-tive restraints on exercises of collective power is not yet self-evident only because some institutions in the West continue to draw support that is habitual and manipulated (see also Habermas 1973, 1984). To be sure, Hayek (1944: 1973–1979) focuses upon the latent authoritarianism of governmental agencies, whereas Arendt (1969) insists that it is corporate behavior within the socioeconomic order that undermines normative principles. Regardless, each theorist insists that legislatures already lack institutional integrity in the face of the "bastard pragmatism" of group politics (the phrase is Hurst's; see Parsons 1962b; also Drew 1983; Etzioni 1984). For instance, Hayek wrote his three volumes on law and liberty with the following outlook in mind:

> The reader will probably gather that the whole book has been inspired by a growing apprehension about the direction in which the political order of what used to be regarded as the most advanced countries is tending. The growing conviction . . . that this threatening development towards a totalitarian state is made inevitable by certain deeply entrenched defects of construction of the generally accepted type of "democratic" government has forced me to think through alternative arrangements. . . . I am becoming more and more convinced that we are moving towards an impasse from which political leaders will offer to extricate us by desperate means. Where the present volume leads up to is a proposal of basic alteration of the structure of democratic government, which is meant to provide a set of intellectual stand-by equipment for the time, which may not be far away, when the breakdown of the existing institutions becomes unmistakable and when I hope it may show a way out (1979, Vol. 3:xiii)

Still, Hayek, Arendt, and Lowi fail in their independent attempts to specify and clarify how necessary procedural restraints may be revitalized. Only by reading Fuller's and Parsons' conceptual distinctions into each theorist's prescriptions can the latter be specified and clarified. The same exercise brings the implications of societal constitutionalism into view.

Parsons' Response to Drift: Procedural Institutions

Restraints on Rationalization: Latent Qualities of Pattern Maintenance. An especially important characteristic and indicator of contemporary social integration and procedural institutionalization for Parsons was whether the integrity of the distinctive "collegial" *form* of organization is being maintained. He pointed to enterprises within the "fiduciary subsystem" that are chosen to bear responsibility for maintaining the integrity of collegial formations (Parsons 1969a; Parsons and Platt 1973). Initially called the "pattern maintenance" or "latency" subsystem, the fiduciary subsystem's specialization (or differentiated social function) is to maintain the integrity of groups' normative principles, despite the pressures of purposive-rational social change and group bargaining. Its success remains always "latent" or indirect, however. It *maintains* (rather than institutes) the integrity of groups' normative and "nonrational" patterns of social action. The latter, in turn, restrain social change and group bargaining from adapting more immediately to pressures of rationalization.

Norms of social bonding are inherently nonrational or not purposive-rational. That is, some norms are qualities of life that in principle cannot simply be reduced to the means and ends of purposive-rational action. Parsons insisted that if actors' nonauthoritarian social integration is to be a practicable possiblity, roles and enterprises bearing specialized responsibility for maintaining the integrity of latent qualities of social bonding must also become increasingly differentiated and institutionalized in practice, like all other functions in a society (see Parsons 1962a:63–64ff, 1968a:51, 1968b:471–72, 1971; Parsons and Platt 1973:12, 50–58, 97, 109, 131–32, 149ff). More specifically, professions must become specialized in taking responsibility for maintaining the integrity of certain normative principles. By so doing they indirectly or latently prevent the drift of social change from indifferently accommodating pressures of marketplace competition and efficient production (A); administrative hierarchies of command and effective organization (G); or democratized bargaining between influential group interests (I).

In this way Parsons responded to Weber's and Pareto's insights rather than turning to some updated liberal notion, whereby social order is treated as the product of mechanisms of a "hidden hand," or else turning with pluralists to the view that advanced societies (and the United States in particular) conveniently and automatically revolve around some equilibrium of group interests. Parsons' well-known optimism about the prospects for actors' social integration, in fact, rested upon his openness to empirical possibilities that Continental theorists (and especially Weber and Marx) were "too rigid" to incorporate into their own social theories (see Parsons 1961:311–18). Parsons considered Continental theorists' pessimism to be a product of their simplistic and romanticist understanding of solidarity or community and their concomitantly simplistic disappointment upon being confronted with the undeniable realization that modern societies are not conforming to their categorizations—despite the elegance of their works and despite the passion with which they presented their ideas to contemporaries (see Parsons and Platt 1973:282–91; on Marx and Weber, see also Alexander 1982b, 1983a).

By contrast Parsons rejected any and all romanticist expectations of a radical leap to a new ideal of substantive community or substantive nationhood (to say nothing of a class's solidarity as a substantive way of life). He pointed instead to the possibility—and not the inevitability—that contemporary professionals employed within government, the courts, universities, public and private research centers, professional associations, and intellectual and artistic networks could become and remain organized within "collegial" formations. Parsons insisted that in principle the collegial form of organization embodies a distinctive "normative orientation." This orientation, in turn, overarches the diverse normative motivations and material interests of any set of individual professionals within the formation. However, he failed to specify that this normative orientation also contributes a procedural restraint upon, or mediation of, purposive-rational social change itself.

In my view it is the normative orientation that inheres in the collegial form that allows actors and researchers alike the very possibility of simply recognizing in common when collective power within modern societies is being exercised arbitrarily. Put differently, actors' shared recognition of arbitrary power is no longer possible within modern societies once professionals become predominantly organized in any other type of formation. Thus, should professionals fail to maintain their own organizations' and institutions' integrity and autonomy by failing to establish and then maintain the collegial form of organization, and should they thereby fail to maintain the normative orientation that is distinctive to this formation and to professionals' own practices, then the social orders of advanced societies can be expected to become riddled by increasing manifestations of interest dissensus and normative entropy and to become vulnerable to increasing instances of bureaucratic-authoritarian social control.

Against the romanticism of Continental theorists, therefore, a methodical exploration of the "functions" (or the social duties) of collegial formations within nonauthoritarian social orders literally transforms, for instance, what is meant by "community" itself. The fundamentalism and ethnocentrism of earlier references to community is jettisoned. Community becomes reformulated as particular types of social enterprises that can be both functionally specified and procedurally institutionalized. Stated differently, the institutionalization of collegial formations across a social order is consistent with increasing functional differentiation. By contrast, the attempted institutionalization of substantive communities across a modern social order is a prescription for "consociationalism." It would invariably spawn the dangerous arrangements of rigid, communal cleavages that are based upon actors' ethnicity, religion, or region (see Lijphart 1977; Young 1976, 1980; Barth 1969; Smith 1975; and Katznelson 1972 for an early review).[9] In short, collegial formations render "community": functional rather than spatial in its "site" or in its "place" in social life; achieved (or generalizable) rather than ascriptive (or ethnocentric) in its memberships' shared status; and irreducibly procedural (and qualitative) rather than exclusively substantive.

Three points may be presented now that will be elaborated in the remainder of this paper. First, collegial formations can be expected to become more and more pervasive and influential across professional enterprises within nonauthoritarian social orders. Second, actors' increasing heterogeneity of substantive motivations and groups' increasing pluralism of substantive beliefs and material interests may potentially be overarched by the procedural orientation that is institutionalized by the collegial form. Third, the normative orientation of fidelity to procedural norms, which can be shared even by heterogeneous actors within collegial formations, may allow both heterogeneous actors and pluralist groups to at least broadly recognize, and then to broadly direct, how organizations and institutions adapt to purposive-rational pressures of social change, regardless of actors' and groups' remaining (and possibly even increasing) differences in substantive beliefs and interests.

But several questions remain. First, what are collegial formations? Second, why is the collegial form so critical as a restraint upon or mediation of authoritarianism, rather than some other form of organization—say, the democratic form? Third, how can researchers or actors know when professional associations, universities, or the other bodies mentioned above are indeed maintaining their own institutional integrity or are maintaining the distinctive normative orientation of restraint? Fourth, what is the connection between the latency or indirectness of pattern maintenance and collegial formations?

Procedural Restraints and the "Public Interest." A necessary precondition for actors' nonauthoritarian social integration, in terms of Parsons' social theory, is the institutionalization of enterprises that are specialized in pattern maintenance (see Habermas 1984). However, Parsons himself referred more generically to social order rather than emphasizing that his social theory really only applies to *nonauthoritarian* social order. One result of this is that he failed to see that even the successful institutionalization of the function of pattern maintenance does not somehow guarantee that arbitrary power and authoritarianism will actually be restrained in practice. Failure to institutionalize pattern maintenance does indeed guarantee that authoritarianism cannot be avoided. But the successful institutionalization of pattern maintenance does not guarantee that actors will be genuinely integrated. For instance, actors may zealously maintain the integrity of a substantive way of life through specialized institutions of pattern maintenance. Yet this may foster authoritarianism by stultifying social change and creating unnecessary obstacles. Parsons saw that such instances of "dedifferentiation" lead to dysfunctions (or structural crises), and most likely culminate in bureaucratic-authoritarian social control (see Parsons 1964, 1966, 1967, 1971). But he failed to distinguish sharply between differentiated and dedifferentiated pattern maintenance.

It is not very likely, nor is it necessary, that actors within nonauthoritarian modern societies internalize sets of substantive norms that are the same as their own (shared) belief systems (see Rossi and Berk 1985). Modern societies are not characterized by actors' lifestyle homogeneity, actors' shared practices in socializing children, or actors' shared deference to particular life-styles. This is why it is so difficult for them, after all, to specify areas of social life that they absolutely prohibit from being changed and adapted in substance in response to pressures of rationalization.

> For a modern society there is no possibility of uniformity in roles, personalities, and styles of life; tolerance of diversity must exist in a pluralized environment. The maintenance of such diversity is dependent upon the institutionalization of procedural rules. . . . Such procedural rules sustain the differentiation of the [academic] system while acting to integrate it also. . . . Disregard of the procedural rules would be tantamount to suppression of cognitive processes at their highest levels of expression. (Parsons and Platt 1973:199)

The major dilemma facing all modern societies, therefore, is that *there is no possible coalition of substantive interests that embodies, represents, or administers the public interest.* (See Huntington 1968:24–32 for a decidedly simplistic approach to the "public interest". See Giddens 1968:265, 1984:257 for an equally simplistic approach to "sectional interests.") There is no modern equivalent to Aristotle's vision of the good life, or the telos. (MacIntrye 1981 accepts this, but fails to turn to procedural norms as the basis for what he calls "a practice"; see Mara 1985.) There is no detailed ranking of substantive "virtues," social aspirations, or phenomenologies of "needs" whose integrity can be recognized unambiguously, and without procedural mediation, across the memberships of pluralist group interests (see phenomenological Marxists such as Enzo Paci, Pier Aldo Rovatti, and Paul Piccone; and others such as Agnes Heller and Ferenc Feher).

Collegial Formation: Fiduciary Responsibility for Procedural Norms. Parsons emphasized, beginning in the 1930s, that one of the most distinctive and irreversible characteristics of contemporary social life is the differentiation between and proliferation of professions (see, e.g., Parsons 1964b). Professionally trained specialists may be found today within the technocracy and governmental agencies, to say nothing of public and private research centers, academic departments, and intellectual networks. But Parsons radicalized this point, at least conceptually, by the 1960s and 1970s (see Parsons 1969d, 1977b; Parsons and Platt 1973; Parsons and Gerstein 1977). By simply maintaining the integrity of their own distinctive collegial form of organization in the workplace against encroachments by either bureaucratic coercion or marketplace inducements, professionals and their associations may "orient" social change overall to restrain unnecessary bureaucratization, commercialization, and democratized "leveling" and may simultaneously restrain contemporary pressures to drift toward authoritarianism.[10]

Collegial formations are very distinctive. Whether their integrity is being maintained at any given moment reflects not merely whether professionals in particular are continuing to honor the procedural norms of research and practice. It also represents a social interest that is much broader than the mere self-interests of the professionals involved. That is, professionals' continued fidelity to procedural norms and to the collegial form inherently interrelates their particular interests (their self-interests in maintaining the integrity and autonomy of their own research and practice) with more generalizable interests (a social interest in restraining arbitrary power across the social order). This interrelationship exists regardless of professionals' personal motivations or substantive beliefs. Indeed, the continued integrity and autonomy of collegial formations within any work environment rests primarily upon professionals' shared recognition of unambiguous thresholds of procedural restraints on arbitrary power. It can then rest only secondarily upon professionals' common internalization of particular substantive beliefs or motivations.

Nonauthoritarian social integration does not depend, therefore, upon professionals' altruistic or selfless motivations to personally confront power holders who wield or threaten to wield arbitrary power.[11] This is as unnecessary in principle as it is unlikely to occur in practice (cf. Hirsch's 1976 vagueness in addressing this problem). *Rather, the continued integrity of collegial formations interrelates the self-interests of all practicing professionals and also interrelates the institutional interests of their work organizations or divisions and professional associations and the integrity of latent restraints on both purposeful and inadvertent exercises of arbitrary collective power.*

Parsons correctly insisted, therefore, that collegial formations are neither traditional nor anachronistic (by contrast to Weber's references to "collegiate bodies"; See, e.g., Weber 1968 [1914–1920]:271–84, 994–98, 1089). He nonetheless accepted with Weber that collegial formations are nonbureaucratic, and invariably "nonrational." A corollary that goes beyond Weber's ideal types, however, was at best only intimated by Parsons: precisely because they are nonrational, or not purposive-rational, the very presence of collegial formations within any society is inherently inconsistent with, and thereby invariably mediates or restrains, organizations' and institutions' tendencies to adapt more immediately to pressures of purposive-rational social change. Conversely, the collegial form is so distinctive that it literally ceases to exist whenever the integrity of its procedural qualities becomes subordinated to any substantive enterprise that adapts more immediately to pressures of purposive rationalization. It loses its integrity as a distinct formation and becomes steadily transformed under the presures of rationalization into a bureaucratic, democratized, or patron-client form of organization (on the latter, see Schmidt et al. 1977; Eisenstadt and Roniger 1984).

Thus even corporate research divisions or sections of the "technocracy" may fall analytically as much within the nonrational realm of pattern maintenance (by maintaining the integrity of procedural norms and the collegial form) as within the purposive-rational realm of efficient production or effective administration. Examples of such divisions or sectors may be found, for instance, within Bell Laboratories, General Electric, General Motors, International Business Machines, and Ferme Laboratories. Regardless of their personal self-understandings at any given point in time, therefore, professionals possess not only the potential to maintain the integrity or distinctiveness of collegial formations despite the pressures of rationalization; they also possess the potential to even more widely institutionalize collegial formations as the professions themselves proliferate across the organizations and institutions of modern societies.

The potential that professionals possess to both establish and maintain this social context provides some basis for Parsons' optimism regarding the prospects for integrative social change in the West, and especially within the United States. Yet Parsons' own works fail to clearly present this basis. Unlike the bargaining that takes place between bureaucratic interest associations within the societal community, for instance, the procedural norms that are distinctive to collegial formations do not orient professionals to negotiate between and accommodate formally equal substantive interests. Nor, certainly, are collegial formations like economic enterprises or political agencies, which orient their memberships to most efficiently and effectively secure quantifiable ends. Rather, the activity of maintaining the integrity of professionals' bodies and forums of deliberation and interpretation is an inherently voluntaristic or contingent social enterprise (see Sciulli 1986 on voluntaristic action in this sense).

Societal Constitutionalism: Elaborating the Collegial Form

Collegial Formations: From Residual Category to Functional Restraint.
Beyond condemning one-sided bureaucratization (and one-sided democratization), however, Parsons failed to carry through the implications of his insights on collegial formations. In particular, his failure to provide a positive definition of collegial formations closed him off, in short, from exploring the full range of its contributions to nonauthoritarian social order (see, e.g., Parsons 1969d:508ff, 1971:98ff; Parsons and Platt 1973:127–28, 142ff, 151–52, 284ff). He tended rather to define the collegial form negatively or residually as the not-bureaucratized and the not-democratized:

The collegial association . . . is prominent in the fiduciary sector of the society, as one of four possible types, the other three being the economic market, the democratic association, and administrative bureaucracy. (Parsons and Platt 1973:284 n. 26)

This "collegial" pattern, modifying bureaucracy in an associational direction, involves membership roles that are occupational; participation is a "full-time job." Collegial responsibilities cannot be specified in the fashion that line authority ordains for primarily bureaucratic organizations. Nor are they peripheral and segmental as are membership responsibilities in associations more generally, including the political component of citizenship. (Parsons 1971:105)

I have elsewhere (Sciulli 1986) presented a tripartite definition of collegial formations. This definition ranges from an empirical category, which merely describes the formation as an extant organization, to an ideal type, which emphasizes the formation's distinctive procedural norms, to a "functional" specialization or analytical category, which emphasizes the formation's inherent contribution (or function) of procedural restraint. For my present purposes I concentrate exclusively upon, and elaborate, this third part of the definition: collegial formations are differentiated functionally, and they specialize in maintaining normative patterns of a certain kind. Put more specifically, the proliferation of collegial formations across a society's institutions and organizations performs three "functions" of restraint. Taken together, these restraints are irreducibly necessary to the very possibility of nonauthoritarian social order within modern societies as such.

(1) Strictly out of self-interest, professionals within each collegial formation may protect the formation's integrity and autonomy against pressures of drift, toward either bureaucratization or democratization. They need not be *motivated* by any generalizable interest, nor, certainly, by any shared sense of altruistic activism.

(2) All professionals across all collegial formations share this interest in pattern maintenance by virtue of their very presence within the formations themselves. They share the additional interest of mobilizing broader social support for extending the social duty of honoring the integrity of procedural norms to as many rule-making and rule-enforcing bodies in the social order as possible, regardless of the latter bodies' forms of organization.

(3) The very presence of a multiplicity of collegial formations within and across a social order creates the social context in which even the most heterogeneous actors and most pluralistic group interests retain the possibility of recognizing in common when bureaucratic agencies or corporate enterprises (or social movements) are either exercising power arbitrarily or are enforcing legitimate social duties within legitimate jurisdictions.

I am not simply positing ad hoc these three specialized activities of nonauthoritarian pattern maintenance. I am also not arguing that they are burdens that personnel within extant collegial formations "ought" to bear, should they become bonded by some presumed collective conscience, categorical obligation, or internalized consensus (see Münch 1981a, 1981b, 1982 on norms as categorical imperatives). Neither am I arguing that these burdens constitute altruistic, dispassionate, or selfless moral commitments that the membership of collegial formations may bear for others in society should they be so motivated. Rather, I insist that the three "functions" of restraint are unique and that they are inherently interrelated. They represent the most irreducible, and the most "calculating" and "strategic," *institutional* "self-interests" that personnel within extant collegial formations can possibly have—if they are simply to maintain the integrity of this distinctive form of organization at their own work sites. The three goals specify the normative *orientation* that inheres in collegial formations *as a form of organization,* or regardless of their substantive activities.

Put more specifically, collegial formations *must* first and foremost maintain fidelity to Lon Fuller's eight procedural principles (the ideal-typical definition). In addition, they *must* also institutionalize their distinctive duty *and* aspiration of maintaining this fidelity by attempting to perform all three "functions" of restraint. I have discussed Fuller's notion of procedural legality elsewhere (see, especially, Sciulli 1988, on the relationship between duty and aspiration in Fuller, but also Sciulli 1986, 1985).

Fuller's eight principles of procedural legality are important because they specify the distinctiveness of collegial forms vis-à-vis all other possible forms of organization. Members of bureaucratic agencies who are engaged in effectively enforcing social control, for instance, may ignore these principles, and yet they may nonetheless maintain the integrity of the bureaucratic form of organization. Indeed, it is precisely because of this that bureaucratization is so easily (over)extended into more and more areas of social life. Bureaucratization subordinates the integrity and autonomy of deliberative bodies by compelling more and more actors to obey enforcers' decrees, regardless of whether the actors (or even the enforcers) mutually recognize and understand what the decrees are that are being announced and enforced. Weber ultimately reduced law to such a narrow standard of social control:

Law [is an order] externally guaranteed by the probability that physical or psychological coercion will be applied by a *staff* of people in order to bring about compliance or avenge violation. (Weber 1968:34)

A "legal order" shall ... be said to exist wherever coercive means, of a physical or psychological kind, are available ... in other words, wherever we find a consociation specifically dedicated to the purpose of "legal coercion." (Weber 1968:317)

As against Weber, Fuller insisted that if a governmental agency or a division of a "private" corporation violates *any* of his eight principles by any collective undertaking, one cannot call its enforced rules "law" at all.[13] Its enforced rules are rather manifestations of arbitrary exercises of collective power. But beyond Fuller's own writings, the eight principles of procedural legality and the collegial *form* of organization are in practice inherently interrelated. Unlike bureaucratic or other forms of organization, a presumed "collegial formation" that markedly violates any of the eight procedural principles becomes simply an oxymoron.

The latter point can be clarified by looking at it from a different angle. In order for actors to consistently maintain the integrity of the eight procedural principles in practice, this activity of pattern maintenance, like any other consistently performed social activity, must be institutionalized or routinized. Institutions are needed, however, that are organized, at least in a quite distinctive formation. Neither top-down chains of command nor popular plebiscites can be relied upon to institutionalize this integrity. Taken together, therefore, the procedures and the collegial form present a clear threshold of procedural restraint and pattern maintenance. The presence of collegial formations across the major institutions and organizations of a modern society is the irreducible organizational expression of consistent restraints on arbitrary exercises of collective power anywhere in social life, and this can best be termed societal constitutionalism. The very presence of collegial formations within any modern society counterbalances the drift of purposive-rational social change, and it does so regardless of the beliefs, interests, and motivations of the actors working within those formations (see Sciulli 1986, in preparation, for the theoretical rationale for this point).

Thus societal constitutionalism specifies the indirect or latent and yet irreducible social duties of nonauthoritarian social integration. It does not dictate more specifically how actors must live beyond their activities of simply maintaining these shared social duties. Once actors have firmly institutionalized procedural restraints on purposeful exercises of arbitrary collective power as well as on the drift of social change and inadvertent exercises of collective power, societal constitutionalism cannot directly instruct actors regarding which particular actions they must or should undertake together in order to secure the best way of life. But then, neither can any extant social or political theory today. Unlike competing theories, however, societal constitutionalism does indeed specify an "Archimedean point" with regard to which heterogeneous actors and pluralist groups may possibly share an appreciation of the irreducible threshold of, and the ineluctable contingency of maintaining, the organizational and institutional infrastructure of nonauthoritarian social integration. Given the irreducibility of this threshold, even the most heterogeneous actors and most pluralistic group interests may at least share a recognition and understanding of how they may escape the most threatening manifestations of purposive-rational social change.

The Implications of Societal Constitutionalism

Linking Practice and Research. The social enterprise of maintaining the integrity of collegial formations provides the basis for addressing two problems of nonauthoritarian social order that had been posed by Parsons even before he had developed the concept, and even before he had fully developed his analysis of the pattern maintenance or fiduciary subsystem. First, actors within nonauthoritarian social orders must establish (that is, they must further differentiate and institutionalize) certain mechanisms of restraint in order to: ensure their own shared recognition and understanding of social duties, despite systematic pressures that lead to misunderstanding and purposeful and inadvertent deviance (Parsons 1962a:63–64ff); or ensure the generalizability of at least some (procedural) aspects of value institutionalization (Parsons 1969c:471–72). Second, at least some of these additional procedural restraints must be "protected," both from interest group bargaining and from pressures to adapt more immediately to purposive-rational social change (Parsons 1962a:51ff, 1969).

The only identifiable "public interest" to be found within nonauthoritarian modern societies today, in short, is actors' shared social duty to maintain the resilience of procedural restraints that are irreducible to their own possibility of being genuinely integrated. The "public interest" cannot possibly be attached to any particular substantive interest or aspiration that contradicts this duty (such as "totality"; see, e.g., Jay 1984). Moreover, the integrity of procedural social duties may be upheld by sanctions without this leading to authoritarian social control. By contrast, sanctions that compel actors to attain substantive ends by violating the integrity of the procedural duties cannot escape drifting into authoritarian social control (Sciulli in preparation).

But if authoritarianism is to be restrained despite the systemic pressures of purposive-rational social change, professionals must become much more mobilized, sophisticated, and aggressive. To be sure, other group interests on both the Right and the Left will resist and oppose this mobilization precisely because the activity of maintaining the integrity of collegial formations crosscuts and transcends (mediates) any and all substantive interests in society that are based more immediately upon actors' class and status positions. Yet, regardless, one practical implication of the discussion of functional differentiation and collegial formations is that participants within extant collegial formations in universities, public and corporate research centers, governmental agencies, courts, and intellectual networks must become much more reflective. They must actively and purposefully advocate and promote their shared institutional interest in simply maintaining the integrity of their collegial formations.

The crisis of the Western formal democracies as well as of "advanced" third world countries (e.g., Brazil, Mexico, Cuba) is in no small part the crisis of professionals' lack of vision regarding what is possible in political practice; the ineptness or shortsightedness of their associations' leadership even on matters of immediate concern to their membership; and a social, political, and economic context that generally disregards the integrity of normative principles in the face of interest groups' substantive demands that all institutions and organizations accommodate more immediately the pressures of purposive-rational social change. In particular, the major problem faced by professionals today is not the demands placed upon professionals by working-class, consumer, and underclass interests. Rather, the major problem is the demands and pressures placed upon professionals by corporate actors who are engaged in relatively unrestrained competition (Hirsch 1976) and by outright corruption within corporate enterprises (Clinard and Yeager 1980), and how this eventually affects both the legislative and executive branches of government (Drew 1983; and see Etzioni 1984 on the political manifestations).

Societal constitutionalism's specification of the procedural interests that are shared by high- and low-income professionals alike in maintaining the integrity of a particular form of organization and that broadly orient all professionals qua professionals moves beyond the issues of class, work, property, and even political and civil rights that have been posed by Marxists, liberals, or conservatives. First, societal constitutionalism moves beyond these social theories in its implications for practice. The activity of maintaining the integrity of procedural restraints may be rendered consistent with the substantive interests of a great diversity of citizens' groups and associations (including the nonauthoritarian working class and underclass). It also opens up the possibility of revitalizing the ideals and "sense of right" of disillusioned governmental officials and professionals in the public and private sectors and in universities and institutes. Professionals' training and earliest commitments remain distinguished from the marketplace calculations of efficiency that unite middle management and corporate elites. They also remain distinguished from calculations of maximizing effective social control by enforcement agencies within the government.

Many professionals remain committed to their nonrational "ideals" despite the pressures of commercialism and bureaucratization. But they have understandably lost the shared sense of direction that is necessary to either become effective politically or remain reasoned and responsible rather than being drawn into the eschatological programs of the Right or the Left. Societal constitutionalism offers professionals the Archimedean point upon which they may recognize institutional development and decay and thereby escape both frustration and eschatology as they become more politically sophisticated and effective.

Second, societal constitutionalism moves beyond Marxism, liberalism, and conservatism in its implications for empirical research in the social sciences. It offers researchers in comparative political sociology an Archimedean point that enables them to describe and evaluate the social and political practices of extant regimes in the West, the Eastern bloc, and "advanced" third world countries (especially Latin America—e.g., Brazil, Mexico, Cuba, and Argentina). The same basis, of course, also allows researchers to describe and evaluate the practices of social movements that are seeking to change particular regimes. Rather than basing comparative research upon relativistic empirical generalizations (regarding, for instance, resource mobilization), or upon some substantive grounding that is promoted in absolutist ways (for example, liberalism's free market ideal, neo-Marxism's concepts of disalienation and totality, Weberians' notions of substantive rationality, and even Habermas' unmediated concept of the "ideal speech situation"), the basis of comparison becomes a standard of institutional integrity that is practicable, intersubjectively recognizable, and very likely operationalizable empirically. This standard of institutional integrity may be found in the demands of social movements throughout the contemporary world, whether of blacks in South Africa, the Solidarity movement and Catholics in Poland, the middle class in Brazil, intellectuals in Cuba and the Soviet Union, or more sophisticated environmentalists, consumer advocates and tax protesters, and religious minorities within the United States and Western Europe.

Because many extant professions and universities have lost (or are losing) their own sense of institutional integrity, however, and because many of them concentrate more and more exclusively upon protecting and promoting narrower and more immediate material interests, policymakers in government have increasingly recognized that they may treat the former interests the way they treat those promoted by any other groups in society. There seems to be no clear reason why policymakers should accord professionals' interests more authority than that accorded to the demands of labor unions, corporations, single-issue lobbies (such as the National Rifle Association), environmental groups, or any other bureaucratized interest association. The rise of malpractice suits in medicine, psychiatry, and law, as well as the rise of corporate crime in the research divisions of major corporations (see Braithwaite 1984), is a manifestation of more deep-seated organizational defects of professional practice (and research). The leadership of professional associations has become incapable of establishing and maintaining even the most minimal standards of professional duty among their membership. As one result they have been unable to establish sufficient trust among the public and its elected officials to continue to regulate their own membership (see Barber 1983). By default, the courts have been increasingly compelled to intervene between the public and the professions.

Societal constitutionalism represents neither an absolutist critique of current social and political practices nor a critique that lacks an unambiguous "audience" or identifiable agents of social change (as was the case, for example, with the first generation of the Frankfurt school). I turn in conclusion to three prescriptions that are consistent with societal constitutionalism and that begin to illustrate the policy agenda that is available to professionals. Each prescription would revitalize the integrity of deliberative bodies within government as well as the integrity of professional enterprises in society. Two of the prescriptions are radical. They pose a direct threat to elites (that is, Hayek's legislative assembly and Arendt's council system). The third is reformist (that is, Lowi's juridical democracy). Whether Lowi's strictly reformist prescriptions become institutionalized offers professionals a clear, practicable standard by which they may evaluate their ongoing success. But the successful institutionalization of the reformist prescription cannot alone restrain or mediate the pressures of drift that were noted earlier.

Prescriptions from Hayek, Arendt, and Lowi. Regardless of their differences in characterizing social change, Hayek, Arendt, and Lowi concur with Parsons, Fuller, and Habermas in insisting that only new procedural institutions can restrain the contemporary pressures of the drift toward unmediated commercialism, bureaucratization, and (latent or manifest) authoritarianism. Yet none of the first three writers mentioned developed conceptual distinctions as specific as those found in Fuller and Parsons. Instead, each refers vaguely to the need to revitalize the "rule of law," and each writer's terminology is misleading at times.

Such failures by Hayek in particular account for his continued insistence that the marketplace should remain largely unrestrained, rather than his seeing Parsons' (and Hannah Arendt's) point that the unrestrained marketplace is as much a manifestation of arbitrary collective power as are the unrestrained activities of governmental agencies. In addition, Hayek and Arendt both treat restraint (or the rule of law) as resting ultimately upon actors' sincerity, or upon actors' strength of will or personal integrity. By relying too heavily upon actors' mere subjective resolve, without specifying the form and procedures that must frame this resolve, they readily move their claims well beyond what is practicable even in terms of their own social theories. In this way and others, each fails to see the most compelling implications of his/her own prescriptions. Each writer's prescriptions are then easily exposed to criticism for being vague, impractical, or elitist.

Once the procedural threshold of societal constitutionalism is injected into Hayek's prescriptions, however, the latter become specified and justified, detached from an overreliance upon the sincerity of actors' motivations, and thereby rendered practicable. Hayek basically calls for further differentiation and institutionalization of Fuller's eighth principle: that enforcement remain congruent with legislative intent. Like pluralist theorists, Hayek sees mass social movements and political parties, interest group politics, and the administrative welfare state as transforming the workings of the legislative branch. He sees the latter evolving inadvertently from a deliberative body that broadly frames the context for social action into a regulatory body that increasingly concentrates upon the details of public administration (see also Parsons 1962a:50). The major defect of the liberal democracies today, in Hayek's view, is that everywhere the same legislative body is called upon to engage simultaneously in two activities that are fundamentally incompatible.

First, the legislature establishes and oversees the enforcement of the specific tasks of government. This encompasses the latter's activities of substantive policymaking and administration. As discussed earlier, the policymaking process and the administration of law are today directly subjected to the competition of interest groups, political parties, and administrative subdivisions. All of the latter, in turn, are subordinated to systemic pressures of purposive-rational social change. Habermas refers to these pressures as "capitalistic modernization"; Parsons addressed them as "instrumental activism." Second, the same legislative body is also expected to restrain arbitrary exercises of collective power by government agencies by upholding the integrity of some relatively permanent framework of rules. This is what Hayek, Arendt, and Lowi refer to broadly as the "rule of law."

Hayek acknowledges that the Supreme Court in the United States mitigates to at least some degree the thorough subordination of all procedural standards to pluralist competition over policymaking (1979 Vol. 3:11, 26). But he insists nonetheless that even in the United States the courts and most certainly the legislative branch can reestablish their integrity only if their current pattern of overextension is reversed by a new institution of restraint: a new national legislative body.

Thus Hayek proposes that a "legislative assembly" become differentiated from extant "governmental assemblies" in order to perform a single specialized task. Its mandate would be to veto any and all governmental actions (whether by administrative agencies, national or state legislatures, or the federal or state courts themselves) that violate the integrity of the "rule of law." Its only task or specialty, therefore, would be pattern maintenance. It would lack the authority to initiate any substantive piece of legislation. In this way its jurisdiction would be far more restricted than that of any extant legislature. But within its narrow jurisdiction the legislative assembly would have superordinate power and authority; it would have the sovereignty of restraint.

> Government subject to the control of a parliamentary assembly will assure a government under the law only if that assembly merely restrains the power of the government by general rules but does not itself direct the actions of government, and by doing so make legal anything it orders government to do. The existing situation is such that even the awareness has been lost of the distinction between law in the sense of rules of just conduct and law in the sense of the expression of the majority's will on some particular matter. (Hayek 1979 Vol. 3:25–6, also 2–4)

Hayek sees that different legislative bodies must today perform each of the two activities of lawmaking precisely because these two activities have indeed become differentiated in practice. Put differently, *governmental institutionalization has simply not kept pace with this already irreversible social change,* even within the so-called "developed" or "advanced" societies. Hayek notes that a differentiation of legislative bodies may have been approximated at selected moments in history. But it has never been institutionalized. Nor has it ever been codified by explicit constitutional provision: "Peoples have approached this . . . only temporarily thanks to the prevailing of certain strong political traditions" (Vol. 3:1979:26). In short, governmental institutions within "developed societies" are underdeveloped or backward.

Actors' shared recognition and understanding of their inherited traditions of the rule of law, however, have today been undermined and rendered ambiguous by extant legislatures' drift toward accommodating contemporary interest group pressures. Without a new governmental institution whose specialized mandate is explicitly specified by constitutional provision, Hayek fears that the Western liberal democracies will accede to the pressures of this drift and become manifestly authoritarian: "The effect of the existing institutional setup has been progressively to destroy what had remained of the tradition of the rule of law" (1979 Vol. 3:26, also 107–8). The problem is that Hayek never sharply specifies what he means by the rule of law. Even worse, his only elaborate discussion of the legislative assembly focuses upon how its membership is to be recruited rather than how its form of organization and its activities restrain drift (1979 Vol. 3:111–19).

In terms of my earlier discussion of societal constitutionalism, only collegial formations can possibly uphold the integrity of the rule of law despite the pressures of purposive-rational social change. Using Fuller's eight principles to specify what Hayek means by the rule of law, and then treating the legislative assembly as a collegial formation that bears the ultimate fiduciary responsibility for maintaining the integrity of this procedural threshold's restraint on arbitrary exercises of collective power across a society, Hayek's entire discussion becomes specified, clarified, and strengthened on several counts. It also becomes radicalized, however, in a manner that most certainly would displease Hayek himself.

In the sixteenth and seventeenth centuries, traditional governmental constitutionalists concentrated, like Hayek today, exclusively on the problem of how to institutionalize procedural restraints on the arbitrary power of government. But societal constitutionalism emphasizes that the potential arbitrariness of broad social changes (in addition to the continuing threat of authoritarian government) is today a permanent, systemic threat. Hayek's legislative assembly is a specific, procedural institution that must be given the mandate to evaluate and restrain the arbitrary actions of decision-making bodies within large corporations—not only the mandate to evaluate and restrain the arbitrary actions of decision-making bodies and adminsitrative agencies within government. In order to keep major organizations and institutions in society from adapting more immediately to the systemic pressures of drift, specialized institutions of procedural restraint must today be formally differentiated far beyond government; they must be extended formally beyond governmental institutions into so-called "private" institutions of the social and economic orders.

Because societal constitutionalism responds directly to the broader systemic threat posed by inadvertent exercises of arbitrary collective power in society, it renders sociological the intent of traditional constitutionalists. It pushes political theory toward social theory and thereby exposes the former's inherent limitations. For instance, societal constitutionalism shifts the focus of Hayek's prescription away from actors' qualifications for, and the mechanisms by which they are recruited to, the legislative assembly; away from individual members' motivations within the legislative assembly; and away from the assumption that the end of the legislative assembly is to directly protect individuals' liberties or what Hayek calls individuals' "domains" in society or in private life. Societal constitutionalism shifts the focus to the issue of the integrity of the legislative assembly's own collegial form of organization and how it can develop and maintain broad-based social support for its activities of restraint.

This shift in focus places the emphasis upon how the maintaining of its own collegial form and that of other collegial formations within society can be the only truly distinctive end of the legislative assembly. It also places the emphasis on how the assembly's own collegial form itself provides its members with a common overarching normative orientation that can mediate the great diversity of each individual member's motivations. This means, of course, that the mechanisms by which members are recruited are of secondary importance. They may remain always negotiable from society to society. What is not negotiable, however, is that the legislative assembly must maintain the integrity of its own collegial form against any and all social interests and systemic pressures of social change that would either purposefully or inadvertently transform it. It must also maintain and sanction all other organizations' and institutions' fidelity to procedural legality as the necessary precondition for possibly protecting and extending collegial formations across the social or economic orders.

To see the end of the legislative assembly in any other light would overemphasize the importance of the proper motivations of its members as they attempt to prohibit encroachments against citizens' individual "domains" of freedom. Or else it would move the legislative assembly to particularistic positions on substantive policy issues, and thereby compromise its own claim to a basis of authority that is generalizable. The former focuses theory and practice upon the "sincerity" of actors' personal commitment to individual liberties, rather than upon the integrity of forms and procedures which is irreducibly necessary to restrain arbitrary exercises of collective power. The latter transforms the legislative assembly into a direct policy advocate. This would lead invariably to its being lobbied by interest groups like any other legislative body, and to its internal voting being controlled, in time, by mass political parties.

Turning now to Arendt, she insists that the possibility of nonauthoritarian social order today requires that large segments of the citizenry become organized within deliberative bodies so that a "system" of "councils" is created that spans a society. In her view, the latter alone can establish and maintain the popular support that is needed to uphold the integrity of the "rule of law." In essence, Arendt updates earlier governmental constitutionalists' understanding of the "constituent power." During periods of "good" (that is, limited) government, the constituent group remains a latent and unorganized potential "power" within the population. When government begins to wield power arbitrarily, this amorphous, constituent force coalesces into the "constituent group" in order to assume responsibility for again establishing limited government. Once this responsibility has been successfully borne, however, the group is to again revert to the unorganized "constituent power" (see Friedrich 1937:129–55).

The problem today, however, is that given the enormously large corporate and functionally differentiated units of contemporary social orders, the capacity of each of these units to exercise collective power arbitrarily has itself become institutionalized or rendered permanent rather than remaining an infrequent or periodic possibility. In essence, therefore, Arendt's "council system" is one proposal for differentiating and permanently institutionalizing the constituent power as a standing, constituent group in order to counterbalance the systemic threats that are today permanent features of social life in advanced societies. Like Hayek, however, Arendt failed to specify what she meant by the "rule of law," and, even worse, failed to say much at all about the council system's distinctive forms and activities.

Rather, she explored the historical moments when councils emerged unexpectedly (especially during the American, French, and Russian Revolutions, during 1963, and during the "Hungarian revolution" against Soviet domination; see Arendt 1969:ch. 8). She then addressed the seemingly insuperable difficulties that are involved in any attempt to institutionalize them into a permanent system of popular representation. But the reason that the institutionalization of the

councils seems impracticable to many critics is that Arendt failed to
see that: the councils' form of organization must be the collegial form;
professionals constitute the only "communities" of actors in society
that could turn her prescription into a *sustained* or *resilient* social and
political movement; and professionals could do so as much out of self-
interest as out of any altruistic concern about the greater good.

Theodore Lowi calls for "juridical democracy" to replace interest
group liberalism in the United States. The problem with his prescription is not its impracticality but rather the phrase he uses to label it:
he should have used the term "collegiality" instead of "democracy,"
and he should have used "fiduciary" instead of "juridical." Lowi's
terminology conveys the impression that he is calling either for additional litigation or for some vague alternative of participatory democracy. But if one substitutes the term "collegial" for Lowi's use of the
term "democratic," as is done in the following passage, his own proposed alternative become specified and clarified:

[Collegial] forms were supposed to precede and accompany the formulation
of policies so that policies could be implemented authoritatively and firmly.
. . . Interest-group liberalism fights the [restraints of collegial formations] but
succeeds only in taking away its authoritativeness. Whether it is called "creative federalism" by President Johnson, "cooperation" by the farmers, "local
autonomy" by the Republicans, or "participatory democracy" by the New
Left, the interest-group liberal effort does not create [collegial restraint] but
rather negates it. (1969:293)

Unlike Arendt and Hayek, Lowi at least specifies the "ends" of
juridical democracy (again, I would substitute "fiduciary collegiality"). First, he insists that the *"Schechter* rule" be revived: rather than
the Supreme Court continuing to give "official and complete faith and
credit to all expressions formally passed along by the legislature," the
Schechter rule would allow it to "declar[e] invalid and unconstitu-
tional any delegation of power to an administrative agency that is not
accompanied by clear standards of implementation" (Lowi 1969:297–
98). The last time the Court actually did this was in 1935, however, in
A. L. A. Schechter Poultry Corporation v. *United States,* 295 U.S. 495.[14]

Second, Lowi offers a proposal to "deal with the slippage [that
occurs] within the dictates of the rule of law" when "social pressure
for some kind of quick action prevents a full search for a proper rule
in a statute" or "an early and frequent administrative rule-making"
(1969:299). Rather than administrative agencies interpreting the legislature's general rules case by case, Lowi argues that general rules
would have to be given clarity by administrative agencies' *rules* ahead

of time, based upon "examples drawn up with the known cases in mind." In this way, "administrative centralization and responsibility can be achieved by centralization around rules: lesser authority can be subject to higher authority through criteria relevant to the programs themselves" (1969:300, 302).

I would add that if the extant legislature is again expected to draft clear statutes (which itself would streamline interest group competition); if the Court is again expected to concentrate upon upholding the procedural integrity of law; and if administrative agencies are then expected to provide examples in advance of how law will be applied, then Hayek's legislative assembly could monitor collective power anywhere along the governmental chain. It could specify when this power is being exercised in ways that are arbitrary or that encroach against the integrity of extant collegial formations either within government or within society. Lowi's proposals are reformist, however, because they are consistent with the ongoing "drift" of social change.[15] They specify interim steps that could help to revitalize genuine procedural restraints. Lowi, however, sees his reforms as ends in themselves.

Conclusions

Each of the three theorist's ideas reviewed above are of interest because they are consistent with the differentiation and institutionalization of collegial formations. First, the legislative assembly could mediate the substantive programs of governmental agencies and of corporate enterprises alike in terms of procedural principles. Second, the council system would operate at the local level of citizens' associations and provide the legislative assembly with a necessary base of popular support. Third, juridical democracy (that is, fiduciary collegiality) would specify the political and administrative "means" linking national and local collegial formations, and thereby protect the integrity of the collegial form at each level. Still, none of the three theorists uses the term "collegial formation." Nor do any of them offer a supporting conceptual framework as sophisticated as Parsons' work on functional differentiation.

Once the terminology and conceptual framework of societal constitutionalism is brought to their prescriptions, there emerges a remarkable agreement between Hayek, Arendt, Lowi, and Parsons (along with Habermas and Fuller): unless a more radical functional differentiation of procedural institutions becomes a policy issue of new social movements, the Western formal democracies can be expected to drift inadvertently toward (latent or manifest) authoritarianism. The maintaining of the integrity of extant collegial formations is itself a precondition for successfully upholding the rule of law, and for thereby protecting individual actors' current rights and freedoms within the liberal democracies. In fact, given the rationalization and bureaucratization of modern social life, these rights and freedoms are best exercised within collegial formations (For example, within research centers, universities, deliberative committees, and Hayek's and Arendt's citizens' groupings). In Parsons' terminology, the collegial form is the precondition for "institutionalized individualism." It is quite inconsistent with classical liberalism's doctrine of the natural rights of the preinstitutionalized individual.

Notes

1. The term "procedural legality" is from Lon Fuller (1975). The phrase "collegial formations" increasingly appears in Talcott Parsons' writings beginning in 1969 (1978:508ff).

2. Of course, institutions within a particular social order may violate this integrity and retain popularity. This may also allow them at given moments to be latently authoritarian (or manipulative) rather than becoming manifestly coercive. But empirical indices of popularity or of infrequent uses of repression are not, in and of themselves, reliable indicators of genuine social integration (as Habermas correctly insists—e.g., 1973, 1975, 1984).

3. Societal constitutionalism responds directly to the problem of manipulation and "systematically distorted communication" that Habermas (1984) has been exploring for over a decade. Habermas is the first social theorist to methodically expose the pervasiveness of manipulation within contemporary social orders. In my view, however, he overextends his concept of communicative action analytically, overextends the charge of manipulation, and thereby misreads the possible scope of application of his own concept.

4. Habermas' critique of neopositivism and the resulting communication theory and consensus theory of truth provides the metatheoretical grounding for the generalizability of societal constitutionalism, or for its transcendence of relativism.

5. In both *The Structure of Social Action* (1968c [1937]) and *Economy and Society* (Parsons and Smelser 1969), Parsons treated the increased pluralism of groups as "the bombardment of interests" against normative integration. By the early 1960s (e.g., 1962b:559–60), in fact, he took over J. W. Hurst's view that the "bastard pragmatism" of interest group bargaining was a persistent and increasing threat to normative "directionality" (e.g., 1969e:337–38; 1968a:51ff; 1968b:461ff; 1977c:623; 1977a:16–19, 23–26; 1971:12–14, 22, 98ff, 106–7; 1977d:382ff, 389ff; 1977b: esp. 40). But Parsons had taken a "wrong turn" in the late 1940s and early 1950s. Parsons' works of the early 1950s, especially *The Social System* (1964c [1951]) and *Toward a General Theory of Action* (1951), but including also *Working Papers* (1953) and his essays of the period, had reversed his central thesis as I reconstruct it in

the text. That is, Parsons momentarily replaced his longstanding emphasis on the drift toward entropy or group dissensus with a hypostasization of social consensus based upon actors' supposedly shared internalization of substantive norms. Unfortunately, it is these works of "the middle period" upon which Parsons' reputation in social theory had been established, and upon which it unfortunately rests to this day. In my view, these works are not only Parsons' poorest and most confused contributions to social theory, and they not only manifestly contradict his earlier works. They were also explicitly corrected by Parsons himself in his later works, beginning with his 1956 collaboration with Neil Smelser. This autocritique by Parsons has largely escaped the notice of his students and exegetes. Critics have rightly ridiculed this hypostasization in Parsons' works. But they have failed to see that this middle period is not consistent with either his earlier or later works. I am not suggesting, however, that we undertake a periodization of Parsons' works, like that done in the 1960s with Marx regarding whether and when the concept of alienation drops out of his works and whether and when Marx becomes "scientific." This is not necessary with Parsons since he noted repeatedly that he had to substantially reformulate his ideas of the middle period; by contrast, one cannot find comparable explicit corrections by Parsons of his works of the 1930s or of his later works beginning in 1956 (although one can indeed find extensions and elaborations of themes).

6. (See Parsons 1962b:564; 1966; 1968a,b; 1969c,d; 1970a; 1970c; 1977c:67; 1971; 1974:9; 1977d:225–27; 1977b: esp. 23ff, 41ff; Parsons and Platt 1973:47, 119–20, 139–40, 156–62; Parsons and Gerstein 1977:45, 48, 53.) Münch errs (1981a, 1981b, 1982) in thinking that the integrative subsystem can somehow restrain entropic drift and, therefore, is "the highest" subsystem cybernetically rather than the pattern maintenance or fiduciary. This error is due in turn to Münch's: (1) overestimation of the importance of *The Social System* (1951) in Parsons' fifty years of publication, and Münch's own acceptance of Parsons' momentary hypostasization of actors' internalization of shared substantive norms; (2) oversight of Parsons' own explicit later corrections and criticisms of this work and others of his middle period of the early 1950s; and (3) failure to see the importance of the early connection Parsons drew between the pressures of rationalization and possibilities for entropy or normative breakdown, and how this thesis reappears in all of Parsons' later works beginning with *Economy and Society* (with Smelser 1969, [1956]) until his death in 1979.

7. On externalities see, e.g., Alchian and Allen (1972:243–47); Heilbroner and Thurow (1978:229–35, 239). Milton Friedman's term is "neighborhood effects" (1962: ch. 2). For treatments of the rise of the welfare state, see Hirsch (1976); Janowitz (1976); Skocpol (1980); Weir and Skocpol (1983).

8. The criticisms may be extended to "corporatist" sociopolitical orders, wherein interest groups are created or directly controlled by state administrative agencies, e.g., in continental Europe or Brazil (see Schmitter 1971, 1981, and 1982 on the distinction between pluralism and corporatism).

9. Part of the fiduciary subsystem does indeed remain tied to substantive norms, and it is not addressed in this paper. It can no longer account for nonauthoritarian social integration within modern societies. It is best referred to by the older term, "pattern maintenance." Moreover, it is itself subdivided into those groupings that are pansocietal or cultural (e.g., religion, nation, ethnicity) and all other groupings that are subsocietal or primary (e.g., community, neighborhood, family). Many premodern professions, in fact, once relied upon substantive (or lived) qualities of

integrity (as examples, living in cloistered settings, undergoing physical cleansing ceremonies through fasting and rigorous physical and mental training, or remaining celibate). But contemporary collegial formations can only retain their "moral" influence today by demonstrating a scrupulous respect for the integrity of certain procedures and forms. By contrast, any revitalization of the substantive ways of life just mentioned would symbolize a profession's withdrawal from the larger society, and it would symbolize as well their internal authoritarianism and external abandonment of fiduciary responsibility for the organizational and institutional infrastructure of possible social integration.

10. It is important to be blunt in posing this point, due to the widespread misunderstanding of Parsons' original position and the possibility that readers may casually carry this over to their reading of societal constitutionalism: forms and procedures do not "determine" social integration. Rather, forms and procedures are absolutely irreducible manifestations of, and indicators of, the possibility of actors' social integration. That is, integration within a modern social order that has not institutionalized the forms and procedures is an impossibility; it becomes a contradiction. Such "integration" is either latently authoritarian (that is, manipulative or based upon arbitrary uses of power that are nonetheless popularly accepted) or manifestly authoritarian (that is, arbitrary as well as repressive of popular expression). Moreover, for at least four related reasons, the integrity of even this less rigid procedural mediation remains always threatened by the ongoing disruptions of functional differentiation and the continuing relativism of actors' substantive norms and the pluralism of their group interest. First, the maintaining of procedural norms and procedural institutions is an inherently "voluntaristic" or contingent enterprise. It can never become systemically guaranteed, like a hidden hand equilibrium (Sciulli 1986; Loubser 1976; Luhmann 1976). Second, even *successful* restraint on arbitrary exercises of social power, or the possibility of nonauthoritarian social integration, remains always a "latent" social enterprise. The importance of procedural mediation is not routinely politicized (on this meaning of politicization, see Parsons 1968b:453). Third, the integrity of all substantive norms or ways of life in modern societies continues to be subordinated to the systemic "necessity" of ceaselessly increasing efficiency in production and effectiveness in organization. Thus, procedural norms and institutions may never secure a steady base of broad support in actors' substantive beliefs and motivations. Fourth, pluralist believers and competing interest groups can in time become indifferent to or uncertain regarding whether the integrity of particular patterns of norms are being maintained, regardless of whether the normative patterns are substantive or procedural.

11. Alexander, for instance (1983b:105–7, 120ff, 236ff, 385–87 n. 44, 453 n. 40), treats collegiality in terms of participants' *internalized* commitments, or in terms of their "basic rights" to participate in the societal community, rather than in terms of a formation's "function" of latent (procedural) restraint.

12. Fuller's work is important because rather than being satisfied with a residual and negative definition of law's procedural foundations as nonpurposive-rational, he specified eight procedural principles that are irreducible to the possibility of rendering laws, or shared social duties of any kind, understandable to heterogeneous actors who bring diverse motivations to any collective enterprise. Regardless of their substance or content, laws proper or genuinely shared normative duties of any kind: must comprise general statements rather than ad hoc dictums; must be publicized or made available to all affected by them; must be

(with few exceptions) prospective, rather than retroactive; must be clear and understandable at least to those trained in rule making; must be free from contradiction or demanding opposite actions from the citizenry; must be possible for the citizenry to perform; must not be frequently changed; and must be congruent with the actual administration of the rules (Fuller 1975:46–84). These eight procedural principles provide actors with the possibility of simply *recognizing and understanding* in common *what* their shared social duties are. They do not guarantee that actors will comply with or accept these duties in practice. Rather, they offer actors the possibility of mutually recognizing and understanding the duties, and then of possibly mutually recognizing and understanding what acts of compliance and acts of noncompliance can be.

13. For a few of Parsons' direct references to Fuller, see 1968a, 1971, and 1977b. Neither Alexander nor Münch mentions Fuller. Alexander insists, rather, that Parsons "relies heavily" upon Weber's view of law (see, e.g., Alexander 1983:100, also 75, 96–98, 242–43, 253–54, 369 n. 102). Parsons (e.g., 1977b) states bluntly that he does not. He is also blunt in stating that Weber's treatment of law is irremediably defective.

14. Regarding the *Schechter* rule, Lowi noted in 1969 (1969:126) that "the last major statute invalidated [by the Supreme Court] for involving too broad a delegation to either public agencies or private associations was the 'sick chicken case' of 1935. The 1935 decision has never been reversed, but the Supreme Court has not seen fit to apply it since that time." Lowi footnotes: "*A.L.A. Schechter Poultry Corporation* v. *United States*, 295 U.S. 495. The Court held that the National Industrial Recovery Act, in giving the President the authority to promulgate codes of fair competition, had gone too far in delegating lawmaking power which was 'unconfined and vagrant . . . not canalized within banks to keep it from overflowing.' The ruling was confirmed in a major case in 1936 but not seriously applied thereafter."

15. All of Lowi's other proposed "ends" of reform are more piecemeal: a truly independent senior civil service; an increase in the functions performed by "regional government"; the use of "fiscal policy as an instrument of control" rather than the use of transfer payments; and the placing of a time limit (five to ten years) on statutes that establish agencies in order to compel serious review (1969:303–10).

References

Alchian, A. A., and W. R. Allen. 1972. *University Economics: Elements of Inquiry.* 3d ed. Belmont, Calif.: Wadsworth.

Alexander, J. C. 1982a. *Positivism, Presuppositions, and Current Controversies.* Vol. 1 of *Theoretical Logic in Sociology.* Berkeley: University of California Press.

——1982b. *The Antinomies of Classical Thought: Marx and Durkheim.* Vol. 2 of *Theoretical Logic in Sociology.* Berkeley: University of California Press.

——1983a. *The Classical Attempt at Theoretical Synthesis: Max Weber.* Vol. 3 of *Theoretical Logic in Sociology.* Berkeley: University of California Press.

——1983b. *The Modern Reconstruction of Classical Thought: Talcott Parsons.* Vol. 4 of *Theoretical Logic in Sociology.* Berkeley: University of California Press.

Arendt, H. 1969 (1951). The Origins of Totalitarianism. Cleveland, Ohio: Meredian.

——1963. *On Revolution.* New York: Vintage.

Bachrach, P. and M. S. Baratz. 1970. *Power and Poverty: Theory and Practice.* New York: Oxford University Press.

Balbus, I. 1971. "The Concept of Interest in Pluralist and Marxian Analysis." *Politics and Society* (February), pp. 151–77.

Barber, B. 1983. *The Logic and Limits of Trust.* New Brunswick, N.J.: Rutgers University Press.

Barth, F., ed. 1969. *Ethnic Groups and Boundaries: The Social Organization of Culture Difference.* Boston, Mass.: Little, Brown.

Bensel, R. F. 1980. "Creating the Statutory State: The Implications of a Rule of Law Standard in American Politics." *American Political Science Review* 74(3):734–44.

Braithwaite, J. 1984. *Corporate Crime in the Pharmaceutical Industry.* London: Routledge and Kegan Paul.

Clinard, M. and P. C. Yeager. 1980. *Corporate Crime.* New York: Free Press.

Dahl, R. 1956. *Preface to Democratic Theory.* Chicago, Ill.: University of Chicago Press.

——1967. *Pluralist Democracy in the United States.* Chicago, Ill.: Rand McNally.

——1970. *After the Revolution?* New Haven, Conn.: Yale University Press.

——1971 (1961). *Who Governs? Democracy and Power in an American City.* New Haven, Conn.: Yale University Press.

——1973 (1971). *Polyarchy: Participation and Opposition.* New Haven, Conn.: Yale University Press.

——1977. "On Removing Certain Impediments to Democracy in the United States." *Political Science Quarterly* 92:1–20.

——1982. *Dilemmas of Pluralist Democracy: Autonomy vs. Control.* New Haven, Conn.: Yale University Press.

Drew, E. 1983. *Politics and Money: The New Road to Corruption.* New York: Macmillan.

Eisenstadt, S. N. and L. Roniger. 1984. *Patrons, Clients and Friends: Interpersonal Relations and the Structure of Trust in Society.* Cambridge: Cambridge University Press.

Etzioni, A. 1984. *Capital Corruption: The New Attack on American Democracy.* New York: Harcourt, Brace, Jovanovich.

Friedland, R. and J. Sanders. 1985. "The Public Economy and Economic Growth in Western Market Economies." *American Sociological Review* 50:421–37.

Friedman, M. 1962. *Capitalism and Freedom.* Chicago, Ill.: University of Chicago Press.

Friedrich, C. J. 1937. *Constitutional Government and Politics.* Boston, Mass.: Little, Brown.

——1963. *Man and His Government: An Empirical Theory of Politics.* New York: McGraw-Hill.

——1974. *Limited Government: A Comparison.* Englewood Cliffs, N.J.: Prentice-Hall.

Fuller, L. L. 1975 (1969). *The Morality of Law.* Rev. ed. New Haven, Conn.: Yale University Press.

Galbraith, J. K. 1967. *The New Industrial State.* Boston, Mass.: Houghton Mifflin.

Giddens, A. 1968. " 'Power' in the Recent Writings of Talcott Parsons." *Sociology* (September), pp. 257–72."

——1984. *The Constitution of Society.* London: Polity.

Habermas, J. 1973 (1971). "Some Difficulties in the Attempt to Link Theory and Practice." In *Theory and Practice*, pp. 1–40. Boston, Mass.: Beacon.

——1975. (1973). *Legitimation Crisis.* Boston, Mass.: Beacon.

——1977. "Hannah Arendt's Communications Concept of Power." *Social Research* 44:3–24.

——1984 (1981). *The Theory of Communicative Action.* Vol. 1: *Reason and the Rationalization of Society.* Boston, Mass.: Beacon.

Hayek, F. A. 1944. *The Road to Serfdom.* Chicago, Ill.: University of Chicago Press.

——1973–1979. *Law, Legislation and Liberty: A New Statement of the Liberal Principles of Justice and Political Economy.* 3 vols. Chicago, Ill.: University of Chicago Press.

Heilbroner, R. and L. Thurow. 1978. *The Economic Problem.* Englewood Cliffs, N.J.: Prentice-Hall.

Hill, M. A., ed. 1979. *Hannah Arendt: The Recovery of the Public World.* New York: St. Martin's.

Hirsch, F. 1976. *Social Limits of Growth.* Cambridge, Mass.: Harvard University Press.

Horkheimer, M. and T. W. Adorno. 1944. *Dialectic of Enlightenment.* New York: Herder and Herder.

Huntington, S. P. 1968. *Political Order in Changing Societies.* New Haven, Conn.: Yale University Press.

——1971. "The Change to Change: Modernization, Development and Change." *Comparative Politics* 3:283–322.

Husserl, E. 1970 (1934–1937). *The Crisis of European Sciences and Transcendental Phenomenology.* Evanston, Ill.: Northwestern University Press.

Janowitz, M. 1976. *Social Control of the Welfare State.* New York: Elsevier

Jay, M. 1984. *Marxism and Totality.* Berkeley: University of California Press.

Kasfir, N. 1976. *The Shrinking Political Arena.* Berkeley: University of California Press.

Katznelson, I. 1972. "Comparative Studies of Race and Ethnicity: Plural Analysis and Beyond." *Comparative Politics* (October), pp. 135–45.

Lijphart, A. 1977. *Democracy in Plural Societies: A Comparative Exploration.* New Haven, Conn.: Yale University Press.

Lipset, S. M. 1960. *Political Man.* New York: Vintage.

Loubser, J. J. 1976. "Action and Experience." In J. J. Loubser, R. C. Baum, A. Effrat, and V. M. Lidz, eds., *Explorations in General Theory in Social Science* 1:240–63. New York: Free Press.

Lowi, T. J. 1969. *The End of Liberalism.* New York: Vintage.

Luhmann, N. 1976. "Generalized Media and the Problem of Contingency." In J. J. Loubser, R. C. Baum, A. Effrat, and V. M. Lidz, eds., *Explorations in General Theory in Social Science* 2:507–532. New York: Free Press.

MacIntrye, A. 1981. *After Virtue: A Study in Moral Theory.* Notre Dame, Ill.: University of Notre Dame Press.

Mara, G. M. 1985. "After Virtue, Autonomy: Jürgen Habermas and Greek Political Theory." *Journal of Politics* 47:1036–61.

McConnell, G. 1966. *Private Power and American Democracy.* New York: Knopf.

Meikeljohn, D. 1980. "Democracy and the Rule of Law." *Ethics* 91:117–24.

Merton, R. K. and E. Barber. 1976 (1963). "Sociological Ambivalence." In R. K. Merton, ed., *Sociological Ambivalence and Other Essays*, pp. 3–31, New York: Free Press.

Münch, R. 1981a. "Talcott Parsons and the Theory of Action, I: The Structure of the Kantian Core." *American Journal of Sociology* 86:709–39.

——1981b. "Socialization and Personality Development from the Point of View of Action Theory: The Legacy of Emile Durkheim." *Sociological Inquiry* 51:311–54.

——1982. "Talcott Parsons and the Theory of Action, II. The Continuity of Development. *American Journal of Sociology* 87:771–826.

Paci, E. 1972 (1963). *The Function of the Sciences and the Meaning of Man.* Evanston: Northwestern University Press.

Parsons, T. 1935. "The Place of Ultimate Values in Sociological Theory. *International Journal of Ethics* 45:282–316.

——1958. "Authority, Legitimation, and Political Action." In Carl J. Friedrich, ed. Nomos I: Authority. Cambridge: Harvard University Press.

——1961. "The Point of View of the Author." In Max Black, ed. *The Social Theories of Talcott Parsons*, pp. 311–363. Carbondale, Ill.: Southern Ilinois University Press.

——1962a (1956). "Law and Social Control." In W. M. Evan, ed. *Law and Sociology: Exploratory Essays*, pp. 57–72. New York: Free Press.

——1962b. "Review of Law and Social Process by Hurst." *Journal of the History of Ideas* 27:558–65.

——1964a (1952). "A Sociologist Looks at the Legal Profession." In *Essays in Sociological Theory.* New York: Free Press.

——1964b (1939). "The Professions and Social Structure." In *Essays in Sociological Theory* (rev. ed.), pp. 370–85. New York: Free Press.

——1964c (1951). *The Social System.* New York: Free Press.

——1966. *Societies: Evolutionary and Comparative Perspectives.* Englewood Cliffs, N.J.: Prentice-Hall.

——1967 (1964). "Evolutionary Universals in Sociology." In *Sociological Theory and Modern Society*, pp. 500–514. New York: Free Press.

——1968a. "Law and Sociology: A Promising Courtship?" In A. E. Sutherland, ed. *The Path of the Law from 1967.* Cambridge: Harvard Law School.

——1968b. Introduction to the paperback edition of *Structure and Social Action.* New York: Free Press.

——1968c (1937). *The Structure of Social Action.* 2 vols. New York: Free Press.

——1969 (1966). "The Political Aspect of Social Structure and Process." In *Politics and Social Structure* New York: Free Press.

——1969a (1963). "On the Concept of Influence." In *Politics and Social Structure*, pp. 405–38. New York: Free Press.

——1969b (1963). "On the Concept of Political Power." In *Politics and Social Structure*, pp. 352–54. New York: Free Press.

——1969c. (1968). "On the Concept of Value Commitments." In *Politics and Social Structure.* New York: Free Press.

——1969d. "Polity and Society: Some Considerations." In *Politics and Social Structure*, pp. 473–522. New York: Free Press.

——1970. "the Impact of Technology on Culture and Emerging New Modes of Behavior." *International Social Science Journal* 22:607–27.

——1971. *The System of Modern Societies.* Englewood Cliffs, N.J.: Prentice-Hall.

——1974. "The Institutional Function in Organization Theory." *Organization and Administrative Science* 5:3–16.

——1977a (1970). "Equality and Inequality in Modern Society, or Social Stratification Revisited, pp. 321–80. In *Social Systems and the Evolution of Action Theory*. New York: Free Press.

——1977b. "Law as an Intellectual Stepchild." *Sociological Inquiry* 47:11–58.

——1977c (1970). "On Building Social System Theory: A Personal History." In *Social Systems and the Evolution of Action Theory*. New York: Free Press.

——1977d (1975). "Some Theoretical Considerations on the Nature and Trends of Ethnicity. In *Social Systems and the Evolution of Action Theory*. New York: Free Press.

——1978 (1969). "Belief, Unbelief and Disbelief." In *Action Theory and the Human Condition*, pp. 233–63. New York: Free Press.

Parsons, T., R. F. Bales, and E. A. Shils. 1953. *Working Papers in the Theory of Action*. New York: Free Press.

Parsons, T. and D. R. Gerstein. 1977. "Two Cases of Social Deviances: Addition to Heroin, Addition to Power." In Edward Sagarin, ed. *Deviance and Social Change*. Beverly Hills, Calif.: Sage.

Parsons, T. and G. M. Platt. 1973. *The American University* Cambridge: Harvard University Press.

Parsons, T. and N. J. Smelser. 1969 (1956). *Economy and Society*. New York: Free Press.

Parsons, T. and W. White. 1961. "The Link Between Character and Society." In S. M. Lipset and L. Lowenthal, eds. *Culture and Social Character, pp. 89–135*. New York: Free Press.

Polsby, N. W. 1969 (1963). *Community Power and Political Theory*. New Haven, Conn.: Yale University Press.

Reich, R. 1985. "Toward a New Public Philosophy." *Atlantic Monthly* 255:68–79.

Rossi, P. H. and R. A. Berk. 1985. "Varieties of Normative Consensus." *American Sociological Review* 50:333–47.

Schattschneider, E. E. 1960. *The Semi-Sovereign People: A Realists's View of Democracy in America*. New York: Holt, Rinehart and Winston.

Schmitter, P. C. 1971. *Interest Conflict and Political Change in Brazil*. Stanford, Calif.: Stanford University Press.

Schmidt, S. W. et al., eds. 1977. *Friends, Followers and Factions*. Berkeley: University of California Press.

Sciulli, D. 1985. "The Practical Groundwork of Critical Theory: Bringing Parsons to Habermas (and Vice Versa)." In J. C. Alexander, ed., *Neofunctionalism*, pp. 21–50. Beverly Hills, Calif.: Sage.

——1986. "Voluntaristic Action as a Distinct Concept: Theoretical Foundations of Societal Constitutionalism." *American Sociological Review* 51:743–66.

——1988. "Toward Societal Constitutionalism: Principles from Communicative Action and Procedural Legality." *British Journal of Sociology*.

——Forthcoming. "Theory of Societal Constitutionalism: Foundations of a Non-Marxist Critical Theory."

Sennett, R. 1978 (1974). *The Fall of Public Man: On the Social Psychology of Capitalism*. New York: Vintage.

Skocpol, T. 1979. *States and Social Revolutions*. New York: Cambridge University Press.

——1980. "Political Response to Capitalist Crisis: Neo-Marxist Theories of the State and the Case of the New Deal." *Politics and Society*.

Truman, D. 1953. *The Governmental Process*. New York: Knopf.

Collegial Formations **405**

Vile, M. J. C. 1967. *Constitutionalism and the Separation of Powers.* London: Clarendon.

Weber, M. 1968 (1914–1920). *Economy and Society.* New York: Bedminster.

Weir, M. and T. Skocpol. 1983. "State Structures and Social Keynesianism: Responses to the Great Depression in Sweden and the United States." *International Journal of Comparative Sociology* 24:4–29.

Wolff, Kurt. 1961. "On the Significance of Hannah Arendt's *The Human Condition* for Sociology." *Inquiry* 4:67–106.

Young, C. 1976. *The Politics of Cultural Pluralism.* Madison: State University of Wisconsin Press.

——1980. "Patterns of Social Conflict: State, Class and Ethnicity." *Daedalus* 11:71–98.

FOUR

Differentiation and Metatheory

12

The Paradox of System Differentiation and the Evolution of Society

Niklas Luhmann

Ever since there has been sociological theory it has been concerned with social differentiation (Luhmann 1985b). In fact, all of the criticism that has been aimed at this concept and its application in different social theories has been unable to eliminate it completely, no matter how justified the individual arguments may have been. The concept of (social) differentiation simply proved irreplaceable. So the question must be asked: why?

If sociology intends to maintain itself within the context of the sciences as one discipline among others then it has to present an object of research of its own. Its unity as a separate domain of research can be justified only by means of the unity of its own object of research.[1] This is accomplished by the introduction of the concept of society which, accordingly, has to be construed in a new way, i.e., no longer identified with the traditional concepts of *societas, communitas perfecta*, or the ideological concepts of the nineteenth century. Something like an all-encompassing concept of society is required—but one established in a theoretically fruitful way. It must contain directions for analysis in order to stimulate both theory and research; and the concept of social differentiation was the first to do so.

As paradoxical as it may sound (even though this has been known for a long time), *society* is accurately characterized as a *differentiated unity*. This concept implies a difference of logical levels (or "types" in the sense of Russell and Whitehead) which allows it to participate in its own unity. Consequently, the level of differentiated unity (society) has to be distinguished from that of its parts, which are differentiated with respect to one another. Both levels reciprocally presuppose each other, and this constitutes the paradox. They mirror each other without being reduced to each other. The totality of the differentiated relationships is (and yet is not) the unity of the system. The unity of the system itself finds no place within the system. It is not a part of it. And so the parts of the system cannot be the unity of the system, neither individually nor taken together. Nor is system unity "more" than the sum of its parts. For where is this "more" to be found, inside or outside the system?

The distinction of levels is only one of the many possibilities of the logical treatment and refinement of the basic paradox of a *unitas multiplex*. Another possibility reintroduces the unity within itself as a part. This solution has been connected for a long time with the concept of "representation," either through the assumption of a behavioral "representation" of the unity by means of distinctive organs designed for this purpose or through the idea of a conceptually distinguished *representatio identitatis*.[2] In the first case, the distinction of levels helps in the observation and description of the differentiated system, while the representation solution establishes a capacity to decide and act. Nevertheless, both forms of resolving the paradox conceal problems of their own. The distinction of levels leaves unclear just how the unity of this difference is to be conceived and how the one level is to be made accessible to the other. The representation of the system within itself must specify both its necessary position in it and its types of operations and, at the same time, make clear that it is not identical with what it represents. Thus, on the level of system parts, it has to distinguish itself from the other parts. The introduction of the unity of the system within itself *is therefore a differentiation itself*. It produces difference because it desires unity. (This is made very clear in Gauchet 1976.)

Just because of this paradox of a "tangled" (Hofstadter 1979) hierarchy the concept of differentiated unity tries to present itself as conceptual unity—simply to provoke theoretical attempts at undoing the conceptual paradox. The trick in the theory's design resides in concealing this problem—perhaps in saying that the only solution to the problem is the one presented by the theory or by saying that this corresponds to the unity of the differentiated unity without admitting any other possibilities. So, the paradox has continued throughout the history of sociological theory—e.g., in interpreting society either as a unity or as the totality of its parts, either as system or collective, either in respect to the conditions of the possibility of its conception or as the web (i.e., as formed by the web) of social relations. These opposed interpretations remain necessarily distinct. But any theoretical achievement resides precisely in denying this. The basic paradox of a unity decomposed into parts (but which arises out of them and, at the same time, is something other than them) has to be reworked if the paradoxical unity of the concept of society is to attain theoretical practicality. This problem presents every attempt at a solution with other functionally equivalent possibilities.

The hypothesis that the whole is more than the sum of its parts had been discussed extensively by the time liberal thought used it for the purpose of concealing a paradox of its own. An essential part of this was the discovery of a difference between individual and social rationality that was closely connected with the development of trade and industry and "political economy." Not the first but perhaps the most famous interpretation was that of Bernard Mandeville (1728). According to him, certain vices of the wealthy (luxurious needs, envy, unrestrained drive for acquisition) are the indispensable stimuli of business and, at the same time, beneficial to the whole of society. Thus the argument presupposes modern society and, at the same time, emphasizes a new basic differentiation vis-à-vis established ones: the rich and the poor. Only the wealthy can cultivate their vices for the good of the whole of society. The poor would ruin their labor capacity by doing so. For the latter, morality counts at face value, and they cannot be counted on to replace religion with enlightened reason. It is evident, then, how a new formula for difference mediated previous ones by offering a new reconstruction of the old paradox that the whole is more than the sum of its parts.

I will leave open at present the question of whether the self-reference of a differentiated society can be construed as the relation of a whole to its parts. If such is the case, then certain ways of eliminating its paradox are already indicated. Mandeville's text proceeds along one of these paths when it facetiously exposes the paradox as a moral one (private vices, public virtues) and reveals it as an illusion. In the way it is *formulated* the paradox is still shocking but basically harmless. It does not proclaim the impossiblity of social life (nor its possibility through grace alone) but rather, conversely, *how it is possible as order*.

As the reflection of the paradox of differentiated unity Mandeville's text cannot approximate this paradox. Its achievement is not its paradoxical truth but the elimination of the paradox. And this requires the removal of certain problems.[3] In the moral paradox of wealth, political economy itself is represented. The actions of the wealthy represent society as a functional paradox. But the question of how it happens that a part of the whole comes to represent the whole as such is never raised. Only later, especially for political representation, does this question become topical. "In France, the king calls himself the state, parliament calls itself the state, the aristocracy calls itself the state. But none of them can say what this is nor if it is" (Linguet 1778:13). And the superformula of a *volonte generale* only remystifies the problem.

The eighteenth century sought a very similarly structured solution in the distinction between private and public. But it concealed the paradox of differentiation. The distinction that once expressed the difference between domestic and political matters (Spontone 1599:181ff) now confronts system differentiation directly and intercepts the collapse of the old order and the uncertainty about the new through a semantic overburdening of the public domain (Holmes 1984:241ff). The whole is represented by what is public. But the latter fulfills this function only if it restricts itself to reason. This restriction is attained through the liberated expression of private opinion, i.e., through freedom. Freedom of the autonomous private person becomes the highest goal of the politicosocial order because this is the only way to secure the effectiveness of reason. What is private is necessary to constitute what is public. The more private an individual becomes, the greater the chance that the possible consensus is rational and can realize the interests of all—a remarkable construction capable of convincing only in an historical situation that sought to solve the paradox of differentiation in a way other than stratification (Habermas 1962). The whole is therefore expressed *within* the private/public distinction as the public, while the distinction itself is applied to the ideal relation of freedom and reason and thereby legitimated.

Only because the private domain is free can the public domain represent the whole within the whole. Therefore, if the conditions of a representative public domain are pursued, the result is unexpectedly the opposite: the private domain. In this case, a distinction supplants the paradox of the differentiated unity. The public domain is not the unity of the many private ones. Nor is it a (public) whole that is the sum of its (private) parts. The substitution of private/public for part/whole merely pushes the paradox into another formulation and lets it appear here under different conditions of plausibility. One may assume then that this maneuver of liberal theory (and I have provided just a few examples for many similar cases) accompanied and helped complete the transition from a stratified to a functional differentiation of the social system. But the basic problem of the *unitas multiplex* was not formulated as such in the completion of the transformation. So, the concept of hierarchy or rank order had to be abandoned as the solution to the paradox of a differentiated unity. But at the same time there was nothing to put in its place.

The nineteenth century was not able to solve this problem any better. Although here utopian formulas of unity make a virtue out of necessity: the "aesthetic state" of tasteful communication (Schiller), social "solidarity" (Fourier), and the "classless society" (Marx). Such formulas take time. They projectd the problem into the future after the French Revolution had shown that it could not be solved at one stroke. In view of existing differences the unity was transferred into the future and the behavioral directives for the present were drawn from there—whether in the form of education, moral-literary publicity, or another revolution at some future time. Only in the second half of the nineteenth century did the belief in time as the medium of problem solving collapse. Only then did a "sociology" arise that could discover its own unity as a differentiated one.

After the collapse of the utopian beliefs in the future that guided Comte, Marx, and Spencer (even if their differences lay only in the scope of the social changes they deemed necessary to reach a better future), classical sociology consolidated itself by means of a structural description of society. Differentiation was interpreted by Simmel and Durkheim and indirectly by Weber as the *result* of social development, and thus became a central theme of social theory. On the one hand this resulted in the interpretation of evolution as increasing differentiation, and thereby social Darwinism could be separated from formulas of selection such as the "survival of the fittest" and "struggle for existence." On the other hand interest in the future was characterized by the investigation of the consequences of social differentiation and, consequently, utopian belief in the future could be abandoned. Henceforth the *structural* theme of differentiation determined the view of *history*. Yet structure did not take the place of process, as misleading polemics often assume, nor did it produce a static point of view that ignored dynamics and history. Rather, the description of contemporary society as highly differentiated forms was the hinge that mediated past and future. The result was that the modern period became an object simultaneously of admiration and criticism. It was interpreted as the irreversible result of history, while its future was viewed with complete skepticism. For Simmel as well as for Weber highly developed *form* is one of the correlates of differentiation. The prominence of individuality is another. But at the same time form cannot be purchased without a considerable loss of meaning. It always presents itself as restriction and renunciation at the same time. And individuality does *not* confer on the individual what it would like to be but produces a sense of alienation instead. With distinctive individuality the awareness of what is *not* given to the individual increased and, since the end of the nineteenth century, the result has taken the form of different theories: of the plural self, of a conflict between social and personal identity, of conflicting socialization or individual self-programming.

A theory that brought so many different types of things together and, in its descriptions, provided so many plausible points of connection found it easy to occupy the then open field now called sociology. But its conceptual and theoretical efforts were limited and hardly even noticed at first. Talcott Parsons was the first to address the problems that appear when an attempt is made to formulate the *unity* of this theory. And through him the endeavor acquired a form to which much of sociology reacted with disbelief and misunderstanding. For Parsons the assumption of social differentiation remains the starting point for theory formation. The concern of presenting the unity of classical theory leads to questions about the object of this differentiation. Formerly, differentiation had been applied explicitly or implicitly—at any rate without considering other possibilities—to society. Parsons applies differentiation to actions.[4] Action is analyzed as the emergent product of a plurality of components,[5] while the evolution of action is interpreted as the history of this emergence. The evolution of action is the unfolding of the structural differentiation of the action system. Differentiation leads to this system's greater complexity in such a way that the necessary action components are differentiated as relatively independent reference points (functions) for the establishment of the subsystems of the encompassing action system. And these subsystems themselves are guided primarily by their respective functions. Ultimately every subsystem makes a contribution to the emergence of action. For the unity of the theory's object as well as the theory itself the emergence of action requires more than just one such contribution and, in the case of all functional specification, it becomes increasingly dependent on the use of the other necessary functions. The alternative is not the collapse of highly developed society; it is much more radical: the disappearance of action. It works only in conjunction with the organism capable of behavior (A), the personal system (G), the social system (I), and culture (L). So the evolution of differentiation means that each of the subsystems is guided primarily by its own function and is thereby more clearly distinguished from the others. No further functions can be added because the emergence of action requires no more and no less. All further differentiation has to be achieved within the subsystems through repetition of the same pattern. In the final analysis, nothing else can bring and hold the necessary components of action together. As in the case of the general theory of evolution, the complexity that results from this is the epigenetic product of evolution. It is not an intended goal in itself. So without knowing and wanting to, Parsons carries with him the inheritance of classical sociology: the ability to treat differentiation only as fatality. This means that it presents itself as an historical result. If emergent action appears in the process of general evolution, then it is its result. Differentiation is the *fait sociale* simpliciter, the *fait accompli* of modern society. Only the results of this structure can be judged and eventually disposed of—perhaps for the sake of more solidarity or rationality. A society without differentiation would be a society without facticity, a utopia (although one not even worth pursuing).

Although Parsons often expressed himself as if he viewed modern society (particularly in its American variant) as an historical result and as superior to all others, his own theory actually prevents him from doing this. According to this theory, goals and values, goal attainment and latent pattern maintenance, are particular functions among others. They are nothing more than contributions to the emergence of action. Action sets its own goals and evaluates itself. It would be impossible for it to be any other way. The fact that immense complexity and functionally structural differentiation results from this in the process of evolution and that, in this way, typical traits of modern society are realized, therefore, cannot be viewed and evaluated as goal attainment. After all, which action could be a constitutive part of this goal attainment or valuation: the observation and description of society? an action outside the system? Every application of goal concepts and value judgments—which Parsons designates as subsystems—to the *unitas multiplex*, to the totality of differentiation, involves this theory in the above-mentioned paradox of differentiation. Every value judgment about the end result of previous evolution, immense complexity, or functional differentiation, indeed about the emergence of the action simpliciter becomes, for this theory, one of those "stange loops" that, according to Douglas Hofstadter (1979), betrays a "tangled hierarchy." The presentation of the differentiated system's unity employs semantic forms that are permissible only as components of differentiation and are, so to say, consumed in this way. Every judgment about action becomes a factor in the constitution of action and every judgment about society becomes a judgment in the society.

Of course, one can say that there is no way out of this paradox and that it ought to be treated as a theoretical mistake. But this only brings us back to the theory: how it becomes aware of the paradox, how it handles it, how it aspires to eliminate the paradox, and how it can control what it does in this regard. In this respect, Parsons' contribution enjoys classical status. It structures the theory as the "cybernetic hierarchy" of the self-control of its object. Therefore the unity of the differentiated system takes the form of a hierarchy for which every level makes its own contribution to emergence and conditioning when it behaves in accordance with its position. But the paradox that results when level concepts like goals and values are applied to the hierarchy as a whole becomes unmanageable. In effect, the theory is forced to do what it cannot allow itself to do. Parsons never dealt with this side of the self-reflection of his theory. A theoretical discussion of this framework would have to be conducted as one that connects what is known to it, viz., the AGIL hierarchy, with what has to remain unknown.

We could also ask why we have to enter upon such an artificial reflection as such. It is evident that every assumption of a hierarchical order has this effect. It is also evident that the assumption of a *unitas multiplex* requires an observer and creates a paradox for him that can be localized precisely. The question is then whether this insight can be used to rethink the entire theory design anew.

In the following discussion the concept of differentiation will be restricted to *system differentiation.** By the latter I do not mean the

TRANSLATOR'S NOTE: Luhmann uses the word "differentiation" in three different connnotations. He talks about "differentiation" [*Differenzierung* of *Systemdifferenzierung*] simpliciter. This refers to differentiation in general. But he also uses the terms *"Ausdifferenzierung"* and *"Innendifferenzierung."* I have translated these terms as "differentiation" when any further explanation of them was unnecessary and the sense of the translation was not distorted in any way. This could be done because, although the original German terms are different, they really in effect refer to the same process viewed from two different perspectives. *"Ausdifferenzierung"* refers to the process by which a function system (law, religion, politics, education, etc.) separates itself from other function systems through the development of its own (binary) code and programs for the use of this code. *"Innendifferenzierung"* is this same process but viewed from the perspective of the entire system of society. So *"Ausdifferenzierung"* and *"Innendifferenzierung"* are the same variety of persons or tastes, the multiplicity and distinctiveness of technical processes, or role differentiations. I do not even mean structural differentiation as such. All of this will come under consideration at the appropriate time, but only as a dependent variable, i.e., only to the extent that it depends on the kind and extent of system differentiation. This method enjoys the advantage of restriction, enriching, and revaluing the concept of differentiation with the findings of systems research. It presupposes that the evolution of system differentiation is of decisive importance for the constitution of complexity and for everything that depends on it (see also Luhmann 1980a:9ff, 1982).

The most important theoretical innovations in systems analysis have an implicit connection with the whole/parts paradox. They do not dismiss the paradox but reinterpret it in a way that is more favorable to research and permits more complexity to accrue than the does model of a whole comprised of its parts. Summarized briefly,[6] four viewpoints can be distinguished:

(1) The *unity* of the whole, as the main theoretical issue, is replaced by the *difference* between system and environment. For all observation (including self-observation and scientific analysis), the distinction between system and environment is taken as basic; statements about systems have meaning only when systems distinguish themselves from their environment and attempt to reproduce themselves under the condition of the exclusion of their environment.

(2) Self-reference must be the starting point in the analysis of systems that produce themselves under these conditions. Among other things this means that systems can steer themselves within their own boundaries according to the difference between system and environment. Self-referential systems *are* not only something different from their environment. The performance of their own operations not only differentiates them in the actual carrying out of these operations, but the difference between system and environment can also, *as a premise,* form the basis of the *selection of operations* so that the system itself determines its relation to the environment, i.e., regulates and improves itself. In this sense the system enjoys not only factual (autopoietic) but also regulative autonomy.

---

process: *"Ausdifferenzierung"* for the separate function systems and *"Innendifferenzierung"* for society as a whole.

Corresponding to this is the distinction between external and internal boundaries. The external boundary refers to the difference between society as a whole and its environment (whatever is not social). Internal boundaries occur within society as the difference between function systems.—JOHN BEDNARZ

(3) Correspondingly, every systems-theoretical statement presupposes the *choice of a system reference*. But this does not mean that something in the world becomes an object of interest (like apples can be a focus of interest rather than potatoes). The choice of a system reference only determines the system from whose point of view everything else is environment. Thus, the choice of a system reference only determines a boundary line that reflects or transforms all designations: determines the distinction by which the world observes itself (Günther 1976:249–328; Brown 1972:105). So the choice of a system reference excludes no objects, only other distinctions, as the presupposition of determinability.[7] The paradox of the *unitas multiplex* is reinterpreted to mean that all determination presupposes a previous distinction and cannot be derived from a previous unity—either emanatively or deductively. In this way, the unregulatable choice of a system reference becomes the application of a form of paradox elimination. With it, the world is transformed from an implex (see Valéry 1960:195–275) to a complex one.

(4) As the difference between system and environment, every system reference is arranged *asymmetrically*. It is impossible for it to be symmetrical and reversible because this is the way it distinguishes itself from system-to-system relations. The environment is not a system for it, nor even an encompassing whole. It is the open complexity of everything else that results from distinguishing the system and that can be viewed only from the latter. Only through a bifurcation in its environment can a subsystem realize that it belongs to another encompassing system and coordinate its own system reference to it. Then it has to distinguish the internal environment of the encompassing system—in our case, society—from its external environment, e.g., as politics are distinguished from, say, iron and blood. Despite all of the possibilities for gradated differentiations, the environment remains an open complexity. It contains not only countless other possibilities but also their overlapping environments. In addition, their endless iteration is a quasi-endless internal multiplication. Therefore, the only point of departure for an observation and for the reduction of complexity is the system of its own system reference.

These basic points also apply to the formation of systems within systems, i.e., to (internal) system differentiation.

The operation of fixing a system reference is repeatable and forms the basis of connections. Although constantly new and different system references cannot be chosen, a choice can be held constant and further system references can be determined within a presupposed distinction between system and environment. This can occur when, within the environment of a system, systems are constituted that refer to environments to which the initial system belongs. Or it can occur when a system is identified within the initial system/environment distinction and is used as the unity of a system/environment difference within the system (like a world that determines itself through an internal difference between system and environment). This last case is that of system differentiation.

Accordingly, system differentiation is nothing more than the reapplication of system formation to itself, as the repetition of system formation within itself. In this way system formation means the establishment, at any time, of a difference between system and environment. The formation of subsystems reconstructs the whole system within systems—in part as subsystem and in part as the internal environment of the system, seen from the subsystem. Thus, every subsystem of society, together with its internal social environment, is the whole society. And, together with its (socially internal and socially external) environment it is also the world, viewed and treated from a differentiated perspective.

This explains why for all differentiation the reference to the whole is retained and why not only more things *(res)* develop but also why the *unity* of the whole becomes more complex. It is precisely through differentiation that the *unitas multiplex* results—whether as the world or as a differentiated system (but not one without the other). In this sense, complexity does not merely mean that a multitude of things coexist and entertain certain relations among themselves. The multiplication refers to system/environment differences. Above all, this means that the ability to observe grows correspondingly. The unity of every subsystem/environment difference is, at any time, the whole system. But the environment of every subsystem/environment difference always contains other subsystems with corresponding environments—as in the case of other tribes in the environment of the tribes of tribal societies, or the peasantry in the environment of the nobility, or the economy, science, and the education system with their system-specific, particular environments in the environment of the political system of modern society. Therefore, in an exploration of their specific environments, subsystems encounter themselves as determinate parts of the environments of the other subsystems of their own environment. They experience themselves not only in the operations of observing and acting but also as observed, acted on. And this only increases as the system differentiation increases. The system is, so to say, forced into reflection. But in this case reflection occurs only on the level of subsystems because only subsystems are observed and acted on in the environment of other subsystems. The unity of the entire society as the unity of the totality of all system-environment differences within the system slips from view. Its reflection becomes more difficult with an increasing complexity of system differentiation. And its presentation becomes theoretical, i.e., contingent and disputable. Society itself can be brought to reflection only through its environment. And perhaps, at present, we are experiencing the beginnings of this process.

In any event, the plurality of subsystem perspectives that reconstruct the unity of society through an internal system/environment difference does not question the unity of the system of society itself. This would be the case if the reconstruction stopped at the boundaries of the social system and left its environment unconsidered.[8] But this is by no means the case. However inadequate their theory, all subsystems can distinguish between men and animals or between chemical and communicative processes. Society's descriptions of itself from the viewpoint of its respective subsystems may diverge, but this does not affect its unity, which resides in the distinction of its own system from its environment.

Not only the preconditions of society's descriptions of itself but also the preconditions of its evolution are connected with system differentiation. On the one hand, system differentiation is employed in evolution as the form of stabilization of evolutionary achievements. It orders and preserves the complexity that has been attained. On the other hand, it is easy to achieve almost by chance. It *presupposes no total plan*—unlike the one that the theory of the whole and its parts, with its ideas about *divisio* and *partitio*, had suggested. It can begin almost anywhere in the system and then reinforce the deviation that occurs. The deviation itself then becomes a factor that, as positive feedback, develops the resulting difference and makes it irreversible (see Maruyama 1963:233–41). Among many settlements a prominent, preferred location develops which provides the mutual advantages of centralization in such a way that a new difference between city and country results. Only then do the remaining settlements become "villages" in distinction to the city and adapt to the idea that a city presents them with the possibility of a different life than the one led in the village and that, as the environment of the village, the city influences its possibilities.

To the extent that social differentiation occurs the mere coming into being of subsystems sets in motion a self-perpetuating development. Every new formation of and every change in a subsystem is, at the same time, a change in the environment of other subsystems.

Whatever happens happens doubly or multiply, viz., in a system and in the environment of other systems. Therefore every structurally relevant event triggers different causal processes depending on whether the events that are connected with it are organized as the reaction of a system to itself or as the reaction of many different systems to a change in their environment. Thus a rapid decrease in the need for labor power in the economy, for cyclical or technological reasons, may signify an increase in rationality or profitability. But as an environmental change for other systems it may have quite different effects on, e.g., the political system, the affected families, the education system, or the new research theme of science. In this sense, differentiation multiplies the causal effect of individual events and creates a self-effecting causal dynamics that cannot be conceived according to the traditional model of a causal law, whether this is a necessary or a statistical-probable model. At best one may raise the question of whether and how in such turbulent and explosive causal relations the structures of the entire system of society still hold and continue, and finally whether society exists only as a collection of self-effecting subsystems in which basic functional domains can break down at any time.

If the entire society is viewed as a differentiated system then what must be explained are the special conditions under which subsystems within the social system not only come into being and die out, but also restructure their environment and, with this, create the conditions under which the new and more rigorously differentiated system can continue.

The exceptional system—e.g., a particularly wealthy family, a group of religious fanatics—may and will normally remain without extensive consequences and thereby constitute an evolutionary variation that is neither selected nor stabilized, i.e., a variation that has no structural effects that change society and that is quickly eliminated. If this is the normal case, what makes exceptions possible? And what explains the fact that systems in the system's environment adjust themselves to the existence of the differentiated unity and thereby transform themselves?[9] In somewhat different words we can ask: under what conditions does society accept a difference as the reconstruction of its own unity? A theoretically rigorous, i.e., deductive answer to this question is not in sight. I suspect that a complexity has to be found to compensate for the increase of complexity that accompanies increased differentiation.

Increasing differentiation changes the conditions under which society as the unity of the internal system/environment differences can be realized. Subsystems continually effect society with their own operations and refer to an environment that, likewise, is society for them. Thus, the difference cannot be expanded to an absolute indifference. "Some relations of derivation," to follow Durkheim (1973:xx), result from the fact that this is a matter of social differentiation. Once again we encounter the paradox of the differentiated unity, but now with the question: how can the unity reappear within the difference? This requires relatively simple forms that abstract from details and reduce the complexity accompanying differentiation.

Until recently, i.e., until the sociology of a Durkheim or a Parsons and the discussion about "civil religion" or basic values, a normative answer to this question was sought—as if participation in society led to the assumption of a minimum of obligation. At the same time the argument that increasing differentiation leads to an increasing generalization of these "shared symbolic patterns," norms, and values gained acceptance. As a consequence their directive value decreases when the complexity of society increases. This argument is not necessarily false, only insufficient. The bourgeois theory of the eighteenth century had already argued that the idea of an integration of society through natural law, social contract, or morality extends the boundaries of a rational politics much too far, and that the rational treatment of property together with the consequences of a sharp difference between the rich and the poor entails much sharper limitations. Quite rightfully one might raise the question today whether the idea of a normative integration of society—an idea that is unable to find general recognition, no less realization—is strong and determinate enough to formulate the real conditions that a highly differentiated society puts upon all social communication.

Besides, we know that the communication of a norm permits both the negation of and deviation from the norm—so that this form of integration constantly undermines itself. In this way the call for the rejection of the society in which we live is placative. It is pronounced with an appeal to the values and norms of humanity that is the same as the appeal to affirmation and conformity. Neither is capable of performing a "critique" in the sense of a diagnosis. Neither produces prognostically or strategically useful distinctions that would even to a small degree approximate the complexity of the real relations. The more aggressively progressive and conservative ideologies turn against each other, the more obvious the insufficiency of the common basis of their opposition becomes for the observer: the assumption that normative claims can be addressed to the unity of society.

I will therefore replace the assumption of a normative integration of society with the argument that the unity of society is expressed by the *forms of system differentiation.* Society by no means exists as a unity in the weak form of counterfactual expectations that are maintained even when they are disappointed. It exists as the form that solves the paradox and complexity of a *unitas multiplex.* Society exists as the form through which subsystems can recognize and handle their difference from the socially internal environment as society. The (evolutionary) selection of such a form has consequences that reach all the way into the details of structures and processes. What kinds of morality, values, law, and normative culture are possible depends to a great extent upon the respective form of differentiation. The argument for a normative integration of society therefore does not necessarily lead to the very structure that actually determines a type of society. It adheres only to a dependent variable.

Only a few forms of differentiation have revealed and proved themselves so far in evolution. So, in this case, there is also a "law of limited possibilities." Four of these different possibilities have attained prominence:

(1) *Segmentary differentiation*, understood as the equality of every social subsystem with every other subsystem in its internal social environment.

(2) *Differentiation*, understood as center and periphery. In this instance *one* case of inequality is permitted—the central location, the city, the palace, the temple, the fortress—that orders all other subsystems in relation to one another as equal in relation to the other.

(3) *Stratificatory differentiation*, understood as the inequality of rank of all subsystems. The unity of society appears in this case as inequality, i.e., as rank. This requires at least a threefold hierarchy to document the universality of the principle and to avoid the reversibility of precedence within any relation of two members of this order. Equality is possible only within one level. But because of this, stratification organizes equality as the principle of the formation of subsystems in distinction to their social environment.

(4) *Functional differentiation*, likewise understood as inequality, but rejecting the unity of society as a relation of rank. Society itself is realized now only through the nonarbitrariness of the selection of functions that are important for the formation of subsystems and in the institution of the primacy of a single function for any specific subsystem. The relation among the subsystems are given over to evolution.

In all four cases the social typology of internal system-environment relations is defined by the typology of *relations among subsystems*. System-environment relations are too open, too indeterminate, too dependent on the reduction of a gradient of complexity to be able to have model effect. The form in which unity appears as differentiation can be attained by means of a further reduction. In this case, other systems in the environment of the subsystem take the place of its environment.[10] This is a requirement of the acquisition of form. System and environment can never be "equal." They can never enter into a relationship of rank and can never specialize in different functions. All of these form-concepts require a comparison of different systems. Every subsystem is forced to determine its relation to the internal social environment according to its relation to the other subsystems in the environment—a highly successful simplification where, e.g., the increasingly important problem of the interdependencies among these subsystems is overlooked. A self-differentiating society, however, depends on such a simplification and, with it, loses control over itself.[11]

The different forms of system differentiation are not necessarily mutually exclusive.[12] Whether and to what extent they all can be combined and actualized depends on the complexity of the social system, which in turn depends on the primary form of differentiation and the evolutionary exhaustion of its possibilities. Nevertheless, a form of differentiation can characterize a type of social system: it can do so precisely when the primary division of society—the primary level of the formation of subsystems—clearly follows one of these forms of differentiation and excludes others on this level (which, as I said earlier, does not have to mean that they cannot occur in society). There is no logical or empirical compulsion for every social system to decide for one and only one of these possibilities of primary differentiation. Even the empirical plurality of phenomena (viz., in tribal, late archaic, peasant societies and then particularly in late medieval Europe) speaks against such an argument. But clear advantages are connected with the univocality of such a structural decision because the problems that would result from the other possibilities of order (e.g., the impossibility of binding decisions concerning disputes in purely segmentary societies) can be shelved. I will therefore begin from the position that society's production of clearly distinguishable social formations is connected with an acceptance of the primacy of a determinate form of differentiation (in which case the acceptance is to be explained evolutionarily).

This leads us to a further consideration. If decisions of this type about primacy are made, history can be observed as the transforma-

tion of one social type into another. A general progression from segmentary to stratified to functionally differentiated systems is recognizable in which an ordering on the model of center and periphery—
especially in the formation of cities—enables the transition to advanced civilization and, consequently, stratification, and then shapes
the reality of these stratified societies into the modern period.[13] The
sequence is constructed like a Guttman scale (it can occur only in this
way). And the actualization of any type of system differentiation presupposes the actualization of all of those that came before it. With
almost demographic inevitability, segmentary differentiation is possible only on the basis of settlement or familial relationships. Levels
develop only when existing segments (families) distinguish themselves as unequal to others. Functional differentiation develops only
when functional systems separate themselves from identification with
determinate levels (castes, classes: e.g., priests, soldiers, merchants,
peasants, and servants) and establish themselves autonomously as a
kind of counterdifferentiation vis-à-vis all relationships of rank. Instead, they bind themselves to the primacy of their own function. The
one order outgrows the other. And there are precisely specifiable,
already prepared breaks that make the transition possible. If the old
order did not have unsolvable problems, new orders would not arise.
This transition, too, is possible only because of a law of restricted
possibilities. If an unmanageable form of inequality arises, it is either
eliminated or it becomes the starting point of a differentiation of its
own.

Therefore, in such a development the representation of the unity of
society within the system is shifted from equality to inequality. The
difference that achieves the unity of the system as system differentiation is, so to speak, more different. It becomes less probable, less
intuitive—it increasingly depends on a supporting semantics, i.e., on
a theory of the system within the system. Equality provides more
information more quickly about the society than does inequality, for
one needs only to consider one's own house in order to know how
things are elsewhere. And then everything not corresponding to this
can be rejected simply as hostile. But if the internal difference follows
a principle of inequality this possibility has to be rejected and one has
to explore the environment before one can know how to handle it.

Since the system's range of combinations can be increased by means
of inequality, the structure is opened for greater complexity, and
evolution gradually fills out this range of possibilities. A new beginning under another form of differentiation may appear as the reversal
of differentiation *(Entdifferenzierung)*—as the reduction of old, unnec-

essary complexities. The second half of the eighteenth century is full of ideas about simplification, especially in law, the economy, and politics. The physiocrats are a good example of this. But the new order is superior precisely because it relaxes structural restrictions in order to acquire greater complexity. This cannot happen in any way whatever; for example, it cannot happen through a return to an origin or through making the system chaotic. A new form of differentiation must already stand ready, must have proved itself, if the change is to succeed. The transition to functional differentiation within the most important functional domains had already been in preparation for centuries, if not completed, when the second half of the eighteenth century recognized and rejected the traditional class system as dead wood.

The reversal of the internal differentiation (and with it of the operative unity) of the system from equality to inequality is connected with the rejection of classes. It risks greater uncertainties on the basis of already managed, standardized uncertainties. Precisely because of this, neither a planning of the succeeding state nor of the transition is possible. The orientation remains historical. Its certainty is that things are no longer as they were before. The opposing differentiations say almost nothing about the form of differentiation that now occurs. This is true for the distinction of *oikos* and *polis* in the structural differentiation of the Greek state. It is even true for the opposing differentiations of the eighteenth century: nature/civilization, morality/legality, private/public, or economy/society. No transformation of the social system's form of differentiation had been capable of observing itself because this required the replacement of the basic distinctions.

One of the most important hypotheses that can be reached with the help of the distinction between different forms of differentiation concerns the relation between external differentiation *(Ausdifferenzierung)* and the internal differentiation of society. An "in itself" undifferentiated unity cannot distinguish itself from its environment because this operation would already introduce a system differentiation. Only an observer with a figure/ground pattern can perceive such a system. But internal differentiation also creates the possibility of disagreement with the environment for the system itself. The relation of internally differentiated situations, operations, roles, and inevitably subsystems no longer corresponds to the environment—even if an attempt had been made to construct such a correspondence, e.g., to present the struggles of men as the struggle of the gods.

The form of internal differentiation and what is at the same time triggered by it differentiates society from its external environment. And the evolutionary change of the forms of differentiation reinforces this process of separation. To the extent that internal differentiation switches from equality to inequality, the burdens of control and consequences increase and society distinguishes itself ever more sharply from its environment. Segmentary societies live in an anthropomorphically understood environment that exists without a clear delimitation of its own domains. Stratified societies celebrate their particularity vis-à-vis the domain of the animals or savages as developmental progress. They recognize their distinctiveness. But they still base this distinction upon a cosmologically/religiously founded continuum of meaning. They find the meaning of the world in their perfection and from this position they can judge, exploit, and proselytize their environment without being plagued by doubt. Only for a functionally differentiated society does this cosmological continuum of meaning break down. Religion is reduced to one social function among others and condemned to a kind of faithless belief. Only then can society understand itself in a theoretically reformed sense as the self-referentially closed communication system that is still only "ecologically" embedded in its environment and that operates its own autopoiesis in a necessarily autonomous way. The maximum level of internal inequality and autonomy of the subsystems, at the same time, conditions a maximum of difference between society and the environment. But in terms of external differentiation this does not mean a maximum of independence. Instead it means an increase of dependence and independence together. More than ever before the relations between society and its environment are in need of order. And through this they become the object of social reflection.

The result of all of this is a framework for conceptual premises and empirical hypotheses. As can readily be seen, empirical verification or a correction resulting from research would require an immense amount of work. In the following I can undertake only a few steps in this direction. I will, therefore, distinguish segmentary, stratified, and functionally differentiated societies as the empirical types of social evolution and attempt to discover how far the attainable state of knowledge is able to support the argument of the decisive significance of system differentiation. This procedure involves a very selective treatment of the existing literature, and in this regard exposes itself to criticism.

These system-theoretical analyses by themselves do not explain how the evolution of the forms of social differentiation takes place. It is not enough to conceive of evolution as a goal-directed development (progress) or as the mere sequence of types or phases of social development. At present the concept of evolution is used in the same sense as the one conferred on it by Darwin. Just like systems theory, evolution theory is a theory that begins from *difference* and not from *unity*. Evolution results from the differentiation between variation, selection, and restabilization. According to this theory, differentiation means the dependence of transitions upon chance. In other words, variation is not directed toward selection, and selection is not directed toward restabilization. The connection is produced neither by planning nor by means of a coordination performed by an encompassing system—i.e., not by an "invisible hand." "Chance" means the "absence of system coordination." It also means that the evolution that begins from any system-state is improbable. What evolution theory ultimately tries to explain is the becoming probable of what is improbable.

In biology as well as sociology such a task means that evolution theory and systems theory have to work together.[14] The improbable result of evolution is nothing more than the external differentiation (*Ausdifferenzierung*) of systems. And the same is true for the condition of the possibility of evolution, i.e., for the condition of the possibility of differentiating variation, selection, and restabilization. Accordingly, systems theory has to explain how and under what conditions territorial are transformed into larger units (lineages, clans, villages), and these again into still larger ones (tribes). In this case the social bond, dependence, and "controllability" decrease with the increasing size of the unit. Inclusive hierarchies are, as it were, natural forms of system formation. They are cybernetically favorable forms of the reduction of complexity and are also widespread in other domains (Bronson 1995:7–25; Simon 1969; Mesarovic 1969; White, Wilson, and Wilson 1969; Pattee 1973; Pollatschek 1977:147–51). Therefore it is not surprising that human societies developed first in this direction.

The transition from segmentary to stratificatory differentiation requires a *reversal of this principle into its opposite*. Symmetry must produce asymmetry. Inclusive must produce exclusive hierarchies, i.e., orders of rank among the mutually exclusive subsystems (figure 12.1 produces figure 12.2). How is this possible, and how can evolution theory explain such an upheaval (if it is already an evident fact that it was possible)?

First to be noted is that a latent possibility for asymmetry, whether of performances or levels, is present but not used in segmentary societies. Indeed, it is resisted and continually releveled.[18] The possi-

<table>
<tr><td></td><td></td><td></td><td></td></tr>
<tr><td></td><td></td><td></td><td></td></tr>
<tr><td></td><td></td><td></td><td></td></tr>
<tr><td></td><td></td><td></td><td></td></tr>
</table>

Figure 12.1

bility of asymmetry is reproduced together with its inhibition. It signifies that performances cannot be resisted indefinitely and that they therefore lead to a statuslike indebtedness. Surpluses that are collected in individual households due to favorable circumstances have to be spent or even squandered. And within the semantics of these societies, giving and helping are not stylized as "voluntary," as kindnesses that demand thanks even if they were intended and received in this manner, but as social duties. They cannot be presented as instruments of indebtedness, but only as expressions of social solidarity (see the pertinent remarks of Service 1966:16f). Every tendency toward asymmetrization is treated and suppressed as a deviation from the valid order and the typology of correct behavior. Precisely because segmentation, reciprocity, and inclusive hierarchies are already evolutionary achievements every effort is made to preserve them. The system does not look for development; instead it stabilizes its form of differentiation.

The evolution of another social formation based on asymmetry is therefore a mistake to begin with. Whatever is normally improbable and impeded may, nevertheless, occur in exceptional cases. Latently present but inhibited possibilities are disinhibited and set free. And then, suddenly, it may become clear that possibilities for order reside

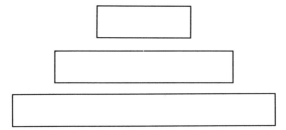

Figure 12.2

even in structural asymmetries, e.g., in the structure of a stratified system. An upper stratum differentiates itself through the centralization of resources and endogamy. It can then employ performances that were impossible in the previous order. The old order of segmentation, reciprocity, and even the morality of generosity and obliging beneficence is retained within the stratum.[19] The stratum does not concern persons but households, i.e., segments. The old order is incorporated, but no longer serves as the structural law of society. The unity of society is now expressed by a difference of rank and/or a center/periphery difference. Both of these mutually support each other. The unity of society can then be represented within the society—either by a position of supreme authority, the upper stratum, or the center (city) (see Spahn 1980:529–64).

For this type of evolution theory the investigation of "decisive causes" is meaningless, even if it occurs, successfully or unsuccessfully, in the literature concerned with the "origin of the state" or the origin of "class societies" (see also Flannery 1972:399–426). It is also not enough to introduce additional causes to construct more complex models or to relativize their validity. What is needed is a theory that can explain under what specific conditions accidents acquire the quality of structure-changing causes.

The case of the infrequent, occasional transition from segmentary to stratified societies discussed above suggests the following contributions:

(1) Change must begin with *distinctive structures*. It cannot simply transform something indeterminate into something determinate or something diffuse into something specific. In the present case, the starting point is the emphasis of reciprocity and hierarchical inclusion.

(2) In the transition, change must not present itself as a "better possibility." An evolutionary transition cannot depend on an insight into the superiority of new solutions to problems. It rests on the possibility of *putting up with mistakes and deviations*.

(3) The change must comprehend the already present possibilities. It must be able to *disinhibit what is inhibited*. It cannot create something new out of nothing. New possibilities are discovered and exploited only secondarily in the already practiced structures. Only selection can make stabilization possible through the enrichment of meaning, semantic decoration, and the assumption of new functions.

(4) Separate developments triggered by chance lead to a *bifurcation:* in addition to the old social orders new types develop. The occurrence of the bifurcation is insignificant and hardly noticeable

and can be left to chance. A bifurcation can establish a starting point for a differential history, which becomes irreversible.

(5) The explanation for this lies in possibilities for the *reinforcement of deviation* (see Maruyama 1963:233–41). In other words, evolution presupposes a kind of deviation that can become a codeterminant of its own continuation and of an increase in bifurcation.

If these considerations are accepted, evolution is neither a structural determination (law) nor a purely chance accumulation of accidents. Instead it selects systems that are structured so that they can change themselves in a way conditioned by chance. In this connection, a cooperation between order and disorder, information and noise, and closure and pertubation has already been indicated (see van Foerster 1960:31–48; Atlan 1979:39 ff; Wilden 1980:395 ff; Varela 1983:147–64). Without chance there is no evolution. But a second condition is also necessary: the system's structure must be in a position to derandomize chance and exploit it for morphogenesis.

The same theoretical concept can be used to explain the transition from the traditional stratified society to the modern one. Of course, we have to assume that modern society cannot be characterized by individual traits such as the capitalistic mode of production or the form of social rationality. Instead it distinguishes itself from all previous societies through the form of its differentiation. Its distinguishing mark is the form that triggers the paradox of differentiated unity and nevertheless makes it possible to act socially within society by means of subsystems. Modern society is characterized by differentiating its primary subsystems according to specific functions and by attributing primacy to these functions (e.g., to politics or to science, to law or to health care, to the economy or to art) vis-à-vis all other functions, even if society is not able to bring these functions or the functional systems into a universal, transitive order of rank. Every subsystem is the society for itself because it fulfills a specific function under the condition of immense sensitivity to changes in the internal social environment. To the extent that functional systems (e.g., as market or as democracy) produce immense sensitivity to their environment they can persuade themselves that, as this difference between system and environment, they are society itself and bring society to reflection along their boundaries. Nevertheless this remains only one reconstruction of society among others. No subsystem can take the place of another because no subsystem can be a functional equivalent for any other. It is impossible to order all of them together from a central position or a position of supreme authority. There is no other guarantee of the unity of society than the combination of functional closure and sensible openness to the environment on the level of the individual functional systems. This is the order that reproduces the ever-increasing complexity and lability of modern society.

Viewed retrospectively, in the high Middle Ages the beginnings of the transformation are already discernible: the removal of ecclesiastical organization from the domestic economy of the aristocracy through celibacy, the beginning differentiation of territorial dominions, the rapidly increasing money economy, and the economic-legal-political independence of cities. But within the context of a primarily religiomoral cosmology this increasing structural complexity can only be experienced as an explosion of sin (see Delumeau 1983). In this way religion itself comes under the pressure to adapt. Theology reacts in part through the internalization of the demands of morality and through the reinforcement of controls, i.e., through the institutionalization of penance (Hahn 1982:408–34), and in part through greater abstraction (i.e., nominalism, contingency-philosophy, and a theology of the will—Duns Scotus, Ockham). In the domain of popular piety, belief in miracles increases and with it belief in the cult of the saints, the Blessed Virgin, relics, exorcisms, and other theologically semilegitimate practices (see Spangenberg 1984). Obviously the need for relief from sins must be met, particularly when the possibility that sinfulness is no longer an article of faith has to be suppressed or self-certain religious minorities split off. The guiding semantics becomes ambivalent. The devil as the defense attorney in the litigation for the just punishment of sins vies with the Blessed Virgin for souls. A lack of merit can be compensated for with piety or through spontaneous prayer in times of peril. The need grows for the explanation of exceptions in terms of miracles. And the byways to eternal life become the highways. Salvation becomes purchasable. The system oscillates between justice and grace. The overburdening and "involutive" (in the sense of Geertz 1963) development of religion is noticeable in countless places. Only the Reformation introduces a clear counterdifferentiation that is directed specifically against religious commercialization that finally ends in religion's retreat to its specific function and in a release of its social environment for "secularization." (For the connection between functional differentiation and secularization see Luhmann 1977:225ff.) It is not exalted moral scrupulousness and anxiety over salvation, as Weber thought, that clear the way for a new economic rationality. Instead it is the clearer differentiation of religious and economic interests that relieves religion from thinking about the economy. In comparison with the Middle Ages, when almost everything was for sale, modern society is distinguished by a more severely restricted possibility of spending money. And this is the only reason that internal economic "constraints" can regulate the economy.[20]

In a parallel fashion politics was also gradually withdrawn from religious control. Before the sixteenth and seventeenth centuries religion had to cope with an almost necessary amorality; the justification of the murder of John Huss by the Council of Constance is an example. In this respect Machiavelli introduces nothing new (see Mattei 1969). The only innovation is that moral indignation regarding Machiavelli makes it possible to reduce the necessary offenses against law and religion to a privilege of political authority and to justify them as *jus eminens* instead of theologically.[21]

In summary it can be said that religiomoral cosmology tries to avoid the perception of new kinds of structural complexity or tries to direct it back into the system. In this case theoretical radicalizations, religious radicalizations, and semantic ambivalences result. But at the same time these also clarify points at which the autonomy requirements of the functional systems diverge and introduce a bifurcation. For a long time the theory of the "just price" had merely been a moral garb for the market price (see de Roover 1958:418–34; Grice-Hutchinson 1978). It was abandoned as soon as it was discovered that (and how) price is determined within the economy. Early natural science was aware of its points of interference with the religiously clad cosmology; and depending on temperament—i.e., depending on chance—it chose avoidance, appeasement, or conflict. And this was not just a history of famous names such as Copernicus and Galileo but a history of the daily practice of theory formation, metaphors, and the choice of words and concepts.[22] In particular arguments against a theologically oriented cosmology were accompanied by an awareness that this tentative model of explanation all too often was directed at theological needs.[23]

But these phenomena of bending and breaking are revealed not only in the religiomoral cosmology. The presentation of the social corpus and its stratification bears the same pressure.[24] The late Middle Ages invented the theory of the three estates in order to hold onto something that no longer corresponded to reality.[25] In the theory of the social corpus or of the *communitas perfecta* the prince was often described as the soul of the body (with the peculiarity that this soul could be killed and that precautions for the sake of the state had to be taken against it). The problem is expressed more clearly if the prince is related to the social corpus as a physician whose task it is to promote the health of the latter (see Archambault 1967:21–53, esp. 38 ff).

These few remarks have to suffice to indicate that even in the transition from stratification to functional differentiation involution and evolution intertwine (for a further example see Luhmann 1980b:72–161). The dynamics of already differentiated functional domains, especially of the money economy of the cities and territorial political dominion, made their presence felt. Distant trade increased. The complicated dual system of currency (foreign currency/domestic currency) of the Middle Ages encountered difficulties and demanded new financial solutions. The political bureaucracy separated itself from the household of the prince and recruited less and less with regard to class. Nevertheless, well into the seventeenth century the problems of complexity resulting from all of this were still directed back into the old forms. Increasing uncertainty and awareness of failure were the consequences.[26] But this is exactly where the signals for the accompanying new formation of modern consciousness are to be found: for an anthropology that develops out of the negation of negativity (see Luhmann 1980a:162–234) and for a cosmology that grounds the hopes of stability and change in transitoriness and technical controllability of the elements (while for the former way of thinking, control of the elements was a privilege of God or the gods). These new ideas about order were not initially formulated for a functionally differentiated society. But they were clearly "preadaptive advances" insofar as the requirements of the negation of the negative and of the exploitation of the ephemeral and transient already implicitly referred to functional systems.

Even in the case of this transition, it is a question of an evolution that is blind to the future. Here too bifurcations and deviation reinforcements occur at prominent points of the existing social order. And transformation is propelled by concerns about their prevention. The old order: the continuum of rationality combining being, thought, and action; the unity of a religiously grounded morality; and the unity of the hierarchical order of social positions becomes of increasing, almost desperate concern. But now all of this promotes the *dissolution* of the old order because the relationships are much more complex and flexible than in the case of the origin of urban and stratified societies. The history of ideas and the semantic presentation of the world and society also assumed a greater role, which the invention of printing further reinforced. In the eighteenth century theories of reflection within the individual functional systems assumed the task of defining modern society. Epistemology did this for the sciences and their theoretical programs, while the theory of the division of labor and the formation of capital, the market, and finally state intervention did so for the economy. And the theory of the state and constitution, leading all the way to the crisis theories of the welfare state, did so for politics. The unity of the social system was still brought to reflection only at the boundaries of the functional systems, and thereby appeared unavoidably as crisis.

The paradox of a differentiated unity receded behind the impenetrable veil of complexity. The functional systems satisfied themselves with surveying the unity of society as the unintelligible complexity of their environmental relations and adapting themselves structurally to a turbulent environment. The reduction rather than the unity of complexity became their problem. The most important functional systems are codified under this premise and in this way attain a performative capacity that is historically without parallel. Admittedly, religion was to a certain extent left behind by all of this—as if to help to remind us that complexity is not the only formulation of paradox and that the reduction of complexity itself can, once again, become a problem (see Luhmann 1985a).

Notes

1. That the question immediately arises of an adequate method and its relation theory can be detected from the disputes over method at the beginnings of sociology. But this concerns only the internal reconstruction of sociology—a secondary problem vis-à-vis the principal question of the unity of the object.

2. The origin of this concept seems to be the conciliar movement of the fifteenth century directed against the Pope's claim to be sole representative. Thus it arose out of a conflict over the Church's legitimate representation within the Church.

3. See the somewhat larger scale reconstruction of the "texte de la tradition liberale," in Dumouchel (1979:211ff). The task of such a test is to intermix knowledge with what is unknowable and irreducible to it. For Dumouchel, of course, the paradox does not lie in the differentiated unity but in a conflict à la René Girard: in the conflict with the model of one's own needs that one imitates.

4. As in The Structure of Social Action (Parsons 1937). This basic decision has never been revised despite all the further development of action theory in terms of systems theory in the later work of Parsons. Parsons had received the stimulus for this from his reading of Max Weber. This concealed for Parsons, at the same time, the full dimension of differentiation. Parsons viewed his work within the continuity of classical theory and as the further development of its internal unity, while in reality it refers to an object formulated entirely differently.

5. In The Structure of Social Action (Parsons 1937), actor, end, situation, and normative orientation are still named relatively traditionally (pp. 44ff). They are later developed into the functional schema of adaption, goal attainment, and latent pattern maintenance that Parsons holds as his genuine theoretical discovery.

6. This is amplified in Luhmann (1984), especially pp. 33ff.

7. This determinability is usually simply presupposed as a property of the world. As when, e.g., phenomenology maintains that "indeterminacy means necessarily a determinacy of a rigidly prescribed style" (Husserl 1950:100). With this, at the same time, the possibility is ignored that the world as a differentiated unity could itself be paradoxical and that every operation of determination could be blocked by this.

8. Pierre Livet supports his objection to this interpretation of a self-referentially closed social system: this would lead to the theory of a system without unity (unicite).

9. Perhaps the first classical example of such a process is found in the preface to the second edition of Emile Durkheim, de la division du travail social. Before the rise of associations there are only families. Through the development of associations the families did not remain what they had been previously. They adapted themselves to the difference between family and association. Oikos and polis were reciprocally determined by this difference. See also a theoretically abstract argument that does not consider the system/environment problem. Parsons (1971:100ff). Differentiation is described here as the "basic unifier of evolutionary and comparative aspects. Since these differences are conceived to have emerged by a process of change in a system which I interpret to mean in some dense within the framework of the system, the presumption is that the differentiated parts are comparable in the sense of being systematically related to each other, both because they still belong within the same system and, through their interrelations, to their antecedents." As is well known, Durkheim had also considered differentiation to be the basis of "certain relations of antecedence" of what is differentiated (Durkheim 1973:xx) and thereby of solidarity too. To this interpretation I add the thesis of evolutionary improbability and selection, i.e., I combined these with the previously discussed theory of evolution and investigate the particular conditions of a differentiation that successfully transforms the whole society.

10. As can be seen, the practically simpler solution requires a theoretically more complex formulation.

11. This is just another formulation of the above statement that differentiation cannot succeed as the standard of a plan for the whole.

12. This counts even more when the differentiation between situations, roles, terminologies, etc. is brought into consideration over and beyond the analysis of system differentiation. It then becomes evident that even the simplest segmentary societies can already specify and distinguish situations and roles.

13. Insofar as the designation "stratified society," in keeping with the trend, adopts the upper-class ideas of order. While the lower classes, above all the mass of farmers and peasants, live precisely in a "one-class society" (according to Laslett 1971) and are guided by the difference between centery and periphery.

14. In biological research this has long since been observed and now is formulated as a research program. See, e.g., Verela (1982).

15. See, for an early society not yet ordered primarily according to segmentation, Barth (1975).

16. This is often described. See, e.g., Sahlins (1968:14ff).

17. This concept is found in Southall (1956).

18. This could be described via the concept of "potentialization." The possibilities are kept in the state of mere possibilities and their actualization is prevented. See Barel (1979:185).

19. For the Japanese institution of giri see Shiro (1974). In the European tradition a clearly anti-economic way of thinking can be demonstrated as the norm for the aristocracy, which naturally did not exclude an interest in possession. At the end of the eighteenth century a surprising presence of discussions of monetary matters could still be heard in the salons. It was experienced as the "decline" that already belonged to a different order of social differentiation. See, e.g., de Meilhan (1787:323).

20. The beginning of a corresponding theoretical development in the sixteenth and seventeenth centuries at the same time make clear which "accidental" events— an abundance of precious metals in America, problems of British foreign trade, the spectacular and unexplainable economic success of the Dutch—gave impetus to this. And the theory also showed that it was not a matter of good will, ambition, or qualitatively superior production but of the balance of trade and the laws of economics. See, for this, Appleby (1978).

21. See, for much of this, Spontone (1599:17ff). "Il pefido Nicolo Machiavelli," on the one hand, and "La ragione di Stato e un certo privilegio che lo Scetto concede a i Principi" on the other.

22. E.g., one may speak of the "circulation" of the blood (Harvey) where hitherto the circle as the perfect figure was reserved for the heavens and, besides, does not really correspond to the system of the blood vessels? Here is a provocation indeed!

23. This, of course, did not have to be said. It is self-evident. See, e.g., the (quite shocking at its time) "Discours anatomiques" of Guillaume Lamy (Lamy 1679).

24. See, specifically, from the viewpoint of differentiation of the system of law, Little (1969). See Luhmann (1984).

25. See, explicitly, Heers (1974:11). For more detail on the theory of the estates see Mohl (1978).

26. See, perhaps, Norden (1577) (with a remarkably optimistic undercurrent, e.g., fol. 113: "nothing has come into being or gone out at all, but through the passing of time increases and amends or becomes more complex." Secondary analyses include: Williamson (1935) or Harris (1949).

References

Appleby, Joyce O. 1978. *Economic Thought and Ideology in Seventeenth-Century England*. Princeton, N.J.: Princeton University Press.

Archambault, Paul. 1967. "The Analogy of the Body in Renaissance Political Literature." *Bibliotheque d'humanisme et Renaissance* 29:21–53.

Atlan, Henri. 1979. *Entre le cristal et la fumée*. Paris: Seuil.

Barel, Yves. 1979. *La paradoxe et le système: Essai sur le fantastique social*. Grenoble: Press Universitaires.

Barth, Fredrick. 1975. *Ritual and Knowledge Among the Baktaman of New Guinea*. Oslo: Universitets Forlaget.

Blute, Marion. 1979. "Sociocultural Evolutionism: An Untried Theory." *Behavioral Science* 24:46–59.

Bronson, Gordon. 1965. "The Hierarchical Organization of the Central Nervous System: Implications for Learning Processes and Critical Periods in Early Development." *Behavioral Science* 10:7–25.

Brown, George Spencer. 1972. *Laws of Form*. 2d ed. New York: Julian Press.

Delumeau, Jean. 1983. *Le peche et la peur: La culpabilisation en Occident XIIIe–XVIII3 siecles.* Paris: Fayard.

de Mattei, Rodolpho. 1969. *Dal Premachiavellismo al Antimachiavellismo europeo del Cinquecento.* Firenze: Sansoni.

de Meilhan, Senac. 1787. *Considerations sur l'esprit et les moeurs.* London.

de Roover, Raymond. 1958. "The Concept of Just Price: Theory and Economic Policy." *Journal of Economic History* 18:418–34.

Dumouchel, Paul. 1979. "L'ambivalence de la rareté." In Paul Dumouchel and Jean-Pierre Dupuy, eds., *L'enfer des choses: Rene Girard et la logique de l'economie,* pp. 135–254. Paris: Seuil.

Durkheim, Emile. 1973. *De la division du travail social.* 2d ed. Presses Universitaires.

Flannery, Kent V. 1972. "The Cultural Evolution of Civilization." *Annual Review of Ecology and Systematics* 3:399–426.

Foerster, Heinz von. 160. "On Self-Organizing Systems and Their Environments." In Marshall C. Yovits and Scott Cameron, eds., *The Self-Organizing System,* pp. 31–48. Oxford: Pergamon Press.

Gauchet, Marcel. 1976. "L'experience totalitaire et la pensée politique." *Esprit* (July/August), pp. 3–28.

Geertz, Clifford. 1963. *Agrarian Involution: The Process of Ecological Changes in Indonesia.* Berkeley: University of California Press.

Grice-Hutchinson, Marjorie. 1978. *Early Economic Thought in Spain, 1170–1740.* London: Allen and Unwin.

Günther, Gotthard. 1976. "Cybernetic Ontology and Transjunctional Operations." In Gotthard Günther, *Beitrage zur Grundlegung einer operationsfaehigen Dialektik.* Vol. 1. Hamburg: Meiner, pp. 249–328.

Habermas, Jürgen. 1962. *Strukturwandel der Oeffentlichkeit.* Neuwied: Luchterhand.

Hahn, Alois. 1982. "Zur Soziologie der Beichte und anderen Formen institutionalisierter Bekenntnisse: Selbstthematisierung und Zivilisationsprozess." *Koelner Zeitschrift für Soziologie und Sozialpsychologie* 34:408–34.

Harris, Victor. 1949. *All Coherence Gone: A Study of the Seventeenth-Century Controversy Over Disorder and Decay in the Universe.* Chicago, Ill: University of Chicago Press.

Heers, Jacques. 1974. *Le clan familiale au Moyen Age: Etude sur les structures politiques et sociales des milieus urbains.* Paris: Presses Universitaires.

Hofstadter, Douglas. 1979. *Goedel, Escher, Bach: An Eternal Golden Braid.* Hassocks, Sussex, England: Harvester.

Holmes, Stephen. 1984. *Benjamin Constant and the Making of Modern Liberalism.* New Haven, Conn.: Yale University Press.

Husserl, Edmund. 1950. *Ideen zu einer reinen Phaenomenologie und phaenomenologischen Philosophie.* Vol. 1. The Hague: Nijhoff.

Lamy, Guillaume. 1769. *Discours anatomiques.* 2d ed. Brussels: Frict.

Laslett, Peter. 1971. *The World We Have Lost.* 2d ed. London: Methuen.

Le Roy, Loys. 1577. *De la vicissitude ou varieté des choses en l'univers . . .* Paris: L'Huillier.

Linguet, Simon Nicolas-Henri. 1778. "Tableu de l'état politique actuel du globe." In Simon Nicolas-Henri Linguet, *Mélanges de politique et de la litterature, extraits des Annales,* p. 13.

Little, David. 1969. *Religion, Order, and Law: A Study of Pre-Revolutionary England*. New York: Harper.

Livet, Pierre. 1983. "La fascination de auto-organisation." in Paul Dumouchel and Jean-Pierre Dupuy, eds., *Auto-organisation: De la physique au politique*, pp. 165–71. Paris: Seuil.

Luhmann, Niklas. 1977. *Die Funktion der Religion*. Frankfurt: Suhrkamp.

—— 1980a. *Gesellschaftstruktur und Semantik*. Vol. 1. Frankfurt: Suhrkamp.

—— 1980b. "Interaktion in Oberschichten: Zur Transformation ihrer Semantik im 17. und 18. Jahrhundert." *Gesselschaftstruktur und Semantik* 1:72–161.

—— 1982. *The Differentiation of Society*. New York: Columbia University Press.

—— 1984. Die Theorie des Ordnung und dis natürlicher (The Theory of Order and Natural Rights.) *Rechtshistorisches Journal* 3:133–49.

—— 1985a. "Society, Meaning, Religion: Based on Self-Reference." *Sociological Analysis*, vol. 46.

Luhmann, Niklas, ed. 1985b. *Soziale Differenzierung: Zur Geschichte einer Idee*. Opladem: West Jurbihe Verlag.

Mandeville, Bernard. 1924 (1728). *The Fable of the Bees*. 2d ed. F. B. Kaye, ed. Oxford: Clarendon.

Maruyama, Magoroh. 1963. "The Second Cybernetics: Deviation-Amplifying Mutual Causal Processes." *General Systems* 8:233–41.

Mesarovic, Mihajlo D., et al. 1969. *Theory of Multilevel Hierarchical Systems*. New York: Academic Press.

Mohl, Ruth. 1962 (1933). *The Three Estates in Medieval and Renaissance Literature*. New York: Ungar.

Mousnier, Roland. 1978. "Les concepts d"ordre,' d"états,' de 'fidelité' et de 'monarchie' absolute en France, de la fin du XVe siecle à la fin du XVIIIe." *Revue historique no. 247 l'imaginaire du Feodalisme*. Paris, pp. 289–312.

Norden, John. 1600. *Vicissitudo Rerum: An Elegiacal Poeme of the Interchangeable Courses and Varietie of Things in This World*. London: Stafford.

Parsons, Talcott. 1937. *The Structure of Social Action*. New York: McGraw-Hill.

—— 1971. "Comparative Studies and Evolutionary Change." In Ivan Vallier, ed., *Comparative Methods in Sociology: Essays on Trends and Applications*, pp. 97–139. Berkeley: University of California Press.

Pollatschek, M. A. 1977. "Hierarchical Systems and Fuzzy-Set Theory." *Kybernetes* 8:147–51.

Roth, Gerhard. 1982. "Conditions of Evolution and Adaption in Organisms as Autopoietic Systems." In D. Mossakowski and Gerhard Roth, *Environmental Adaption and Evolution*, pp. 37–48. Stuttgart.

Sahlins, Marshall D. 1968. *Tribesmen*. Englewood Cliffs, N.J.: Prentice-Hall.

Schwer, Wilhelm. 1952. *Stand und Staendeordnung im Weltbild des Mittelalters: Die geistes- und gesellschaftsgeschichtlichen Grundlagen der berufsstaendischen Idee*. 2d ed. Paderborn: Schöningh.

Service, Elman R. 1966. *The Hunters*. Englewood Cliffs, N.J.: Prentice-Hall.

Shiro, Ishii. 1974. "Pre-Modern Law and the Tokugawa Political Structure." *The East* 10(7):20–27.

Simon, Herbert A. 1969. *The Sciences of the Artificial*. Cambridge, Mass.: Harvard University Press.

Southall, Aidan W. 1956. *Alur Society: A Study in Process and Types of Domination.* Cambridge: Cambridge University Press.

Spahn, Peter. 1980. "Oikos unds Polis: Beobachtungen zum Prozess der Polisbildung bei Hesiod, Solon und Aischylos." *Historische Zeitschrift* 231:529–64.

Spangenberg, Peter-Michael. 1987. *Maria ist immer und überal: Die Alltagswelten des spaetmittelalterlichen Mirakels.* Frankfurt: Suhrkamp.

Spontone, Ciro. 1599. *Dodici libri del governo di stato.* Verona: Pigozzo de Rossi.

Valéry, Paul. 1960. "L'idée fixe ou deux hommes à la mer." In Paul Valéry, *Oeuvres,* 2:195–275. Paris: Gallimard.

Varela, Francisco J. 1982. *Principles of Biological Autonomy.* New York: North-Holland.

——— 1983. "L'auto-organisation: de l'apparence au mecanisme." In Paul Dumouchel and Jean-Pierre Dupuy, eds., *L'auto-organisation: De la physique au politique,* pp. 147–64. Parus: Seuil.

Whyte, Lancelot L., Albert G. Wilson, and Dona Wilson, eds., *Hierarchy Theory: The Challenge of Complex Systems.* New York: Elsevier.

Wilden, Anthony. 1980. *Systems and Structure: Essays in Communication and Exchange.* 2d ed. London: Tavistock.

Williamson, George. 1935. "Mutability, Decay and Seventeenth-Century Melancholy." *Journal of English Literary History* 2:121–50.

13

Differentiation, Rationalization, Interpenetration: The Emergence of Modern Society

Richard Münch

Theoretical debates characterized German sociology both during its emergence at the turn of the century and during its resurgence after World War II. The debates concerning both historical and idealistic or nomological and naturalistic social science and the question of value judgments dominated the rise of sociology in Germany. Its reconstruction after the war initially saw a small debate on role theory and its view of the individual actor, with Ralf Dahrendorf and Friedrich Tenbruck as the main protagonists. The 1960s saw the very heated controversy between "neopositivism" and its much more sophisticated successor "critical rationalism," on the one hand, and the Frankfurt school of critical theory on the other. The radical movement of the late 1960s led to a short-term dominance of a more orthodox Marxism, which, however, was not able to maintain this position and tended rather to decline in the 1970s. Orthodox Marxism believed that it could not learn anything from "bourgeois" sociology, as non-Marxist sociology was called in the late 1960s; this orthodox Marxism of the late 1960s and the early 1970s is now out of the theoretical discussion. The 1970s had a new theoretical topic: the discussion between Luhmann and Habermas on sociology as a social technology or as a critical theory of society.

The 1980s are characterized by yet another theoretical goal: constructing a theory of society and explaining and understanding the basic structures, roots, and developments of modern societies. Major contributions to this discussion have been provided by Niklas Luhmann's systems theory, Jürgen Habermas' theory of communicative action, Wolfgang Schluchter's interpretation of Max Weber's theory of rationalization, and the theory of action developed out of Talcott Parsons' approach. The great classics who contributed to a global perspective on modern society hav ˙en rediscovered, particularly Weber, Durkheim, and Parsons. They .e used as more or less stable building blocks for a theory of society and an understanding of modernity. Luhmann plays a special role here. He conceives of his own theory as a revolution that cannot continue with the ballast of old theorists. This does not mean that the other contributions to this debate are only recapitulations of the classical figures. The interpretation of the classics is dominated by the perspective of rational theoretical reconstruction. In this case the contemporary authors have their own conception of a comprehensive social theory and they make use of the classics only insofar as they fit into the new theory. That means that an attitude simultaneously of learning from and critical distance to the classics is present. This characterizes Habermas' interpretation of Weber, Durkheim, and Parsons, just as it does Schluchter's Weberianism and the extended Parsonianism. A further and not insubstantial aspect of this debate is convergence between opposing positions, and a willingness to understand opposing positions, as was not the case in earlier controversies. Everybody knows that the truth is not on one of the opposing sides, but that approaching truth can only be the long-term outcome of mutual criticism. This is at least partly an effect of the institutionalizing activities of the theory section of the German Sociological Association which began with regular meetings in the mid-1970s.

The starting point of the new debate is Weber's theory of rationalization of modern society into spheres that are guided to an increasing extent by their own inner laws (Weber 1951, 1958, 1968, 1976, 1981). This theory of rationalization has been combined—by Schluchter and Habermas—with the theory of functional differentiation as it was formulated by Luhmann. We can distinguish at least four interrelated questions that are answered differently by the different approaches described above. The first question is directed toward the meaning of differentiation and rationalization of spheres of action in modern societies, and the second toward how this process of differentiation and rationalization has to be generally explained; the third is oriented to the effects of this process on the chances of maintaining social order, and the fourth to the question of how social order is possible at all under modern conditions.

Increasing Complexity and the Differentiation of Systems

In Luhmann's (1970, 1980, 1984) systems perspective the differentiation of society is the result of growing complexity which is itself produced by factors such as population growth, societal inclusion of groups and their social participation, and cultural changes such as the change from the legitimacy of inequality to the legitimacy of equality. As these factors grow, action and decision making can no longer claim validity for every sphere of action, every group and every actor. Otherwise, complete anomie would result. Action and decision making have to be confined to ever smaller systems of interaction. Religious fervor and intellectual ideas only produce conflict under these conditions when they are applied to political decision making. The search for truth is appropriate in science; in politics it results in the paralysis of decision making and/or in the imposition of unchangeable ideological positions upon decisions that are nevertheless selections from among a great many alternatives. This is not to say that the ideals of the intellectual are completely irrelevant to the political process. They provide the material that politicians use in accordance with the rules of politics, in the sense that they build their campaigns on the basis of great values in order to win votes.

The process of differentiation for its own part increases complexity and thus makes further differentiation necessary. It is a self-perpetuating process. Differentiation means the growing autonomy of subsystems of interaction which have their own rules. It is explained by growing complexity. These are Luhmann's answers to the first and second of the questions posed above. Regarding the third question about the chances for social order under these conditions Luhmann's answer is a simple and surprising one: differentiation is itself the only possible way of ordering action in modern societies. He prefers to speak of the coordination of action. This order is only endangered by claims reaching beyond specific subsystems of action. Thus, if priests, for example, confine themselves to the definition of meaning in a completely autonomous sphere of religious action and intellectuals confine themselves to the discussion of the validity of ideas as such, everything is in order; things only go wrong when priests and intellectuals claim to have the right and concrete answers to political problems such as the handling of internal and external conflicts, the maintenance of peace, welfare politics, environmental politics, and so on.

As to the fourth question, this differentiated order refuses to adopt any basic moral principles regarding its foundation. Order is completely "demoralized." However, Luhmann has to admit that at least the principle that every sphere is completely autonomous and indifferent to all other spheres, which is a problem in itself, is a principle that has to claim validity for the whole of society. Otherwise it would break down in conflict between spheres and groups of action. The only basic principle of modern society is Luhmann's theory itself. The concept of autopoiesis is Luhmann's new theoretical device in founding a theory of differentiated society. Society is compartmentalized into a growing number of autopoietical—that is, self-regulating—systems which treat each other as environments to which they have to adapt actively. Thus intellectual ideas have no direct legitimating quality for political procedures and decisions; they can only be dealt with as environmental facts that have to be processed within the political system according to its own inner laws of effective decision making.

The Occidental Process of Rationalization

A combination of Luhmann's differentiation theory with Weber's theory of rationalization has been presented by Wolfgang Schluchter (1976, 1979). He first conceives of religious evolution as a process of rationalization, with Calvinism as its point of culmination, leading off to a complete secularization of life in which religion is replaced and destroyed by modern science. In this process Calvinism is caught in the paradox of rationalization. Insofar as it approached the world by striving for its complete domination according to rational ethical standards, Calvinism set free a process of rationalization of different spheres of the world in which these spheres gained more and more dominance, thus destroying their religious origin. Capitalism follows its own nonmoral laws and no longer has any need for a Puritan ethics; bureaucracy develops a logic of world domination without any ethical control; modern science makes the questioning of everything its own principle, thus leaving no room for religion, which always has to sacrifice the intellect. In this view, rationalization means—referring to the first question—the development of ever more sharply differentiated spheres of life which are guided by their own inner laws, making them more efficient in solving their problems but at the same time producing effects that appear irrational from the points of view of the other (outside) spheres of action. The economy, politics, and science are rational in themselves but at least partly irrational for each other. The origin of rationalization—the second question—is the process of rationalization of religion which leads to the rationalization of each societal sphere. Religion becomes rationalized as soon as it is guided by the rules of intellectual interpretation of the world. With regard to the third question—the consequences for order —this perspective does not give a promising answer. Religion and morals have been destroyed by the intellectual questioning of everything, which ultimately leads to the complete demagicalization of the world (disenchantment). The modern world does not allow a binding moral order; it is divided by the irreconcilable conflict of values and spheres of life.

Weber leaves us with no answer to the fourth question: there is ultimately no binding order that is possible. Schluchter tries to escape this blind alley in Weber's position by construing Weber's concept of an ethic of responsibility as a new center for a modern social order. He interprets this ethic in his *The Rise of Western Rationalism* (1981) as a rule of pure contingency and comes very close to Luhmann's solution, not realizing that in his Weberian view this would leave the world with its value conflicts and a principle that "anything goes." Without a certain ethical principle having primacy over all others, power remains the only means available for making rules of action binding. Thus, without any consensual basis the Hobbesian power struggle will be the fate of modern society. And as we know, Weber never overcame this view of politics in his political writings. In sum, according to Schluchter's logic or argumentation, order will only be possible when there is a complete one-sidedness of the distribution of power and it will be a mere factual order lacking any ethical and consensual quality.

From Cognitive-Instrumental to Communicative Rationalization

Habermas (1981) begins with Schluchter's interpretation of Weber and tries to avoid its negative outlook with his theory of communicative rationality. He also thinks of rationalization in terms of a process of growing autonomy for the spheres of action (the first question), which is advanced (the second question) by an inner logic of the intellectual rationalization of religion leading, first of all, to the cultural rationalization and differentiation of science, art, and morality from their religious source. In the next step this cultural rationalization sets free the societal rationalization of capitalism, bureaucracy, and the legal system. The result is the differentiation of these technologically rationalized systems from communication in the context of the life-world. The actual process of rationalization in the West has produced systems which to an increasing extent dominate even life-world contexts: that is to say, the world is becoming increasingly economized, bureaucratized, and juridified; the life-world is suppressed as a result of colonization by the systems. There is an order in modern societies (the third question), but an order that is based only on a naturalistic systems integration and that lacks *social* integration from the life-world.

However, Habermas points to a way out of this dilemma of rationalization (the fourth question). The rationalization of systems as it proceeded in the West is itself an effect of cultural life-world rationalization that still has to be advanced, because it has been restricted to the dimension of cognitive-instrumental rationality. To the extent that we can overcome this constriction of rationality, we can break the domination of systems rationality. The solution is offered in Habermas' theory of communicative rationality. In this theory the procedure of discourse is the basis of consensus formation; this is itself the criterion for the validity not only of cognitive propositions but also of aesthetic judgments and moral norms. We have a concept of rationality that is based on consensus and contains morality, thus opening up the chances for a rational and at the same time moral order in modern societies, two features that were in complete contradiction in Weber's view.

The question, however, is whether the coincidence of rationality and morality in the possible order of modern societies advocated by Habermas relies on a presupposed constriction of rationality within the confines of a consensually born life-world. We may indeed conceive of rational progress not only in cognitive science but also in normative ideas, expressive systems, and meaning constructions as far as they progress in ordering contingent action, in providing identity in a complexity of expressive feelings, or in constructing meaning in a complexity of life views. However, this progress is based on a never-ending process of criticism, of questioning every proposition, and effecting "dissensus," which leaves no room for any consensus. The objective validity of moral rules can only be approached—never attained—in this dissensus-creating process. Their unquestioned and binding application in concrete action, however, is on the contrary based on a consensus that does not allow any articulation of dissensus-creating questions. The home of this consensus is the traditionally given life-world of a community with a clearly confined horizon of thinking. This binding character is always attained in connection with the particularization of norms. We have a consensual and moral order in this case, but a particularistic one. Thus we are caught upon the horns of the dilemma on the rationality of *universally* valid but never concretely consensually born norms and the bindingness of particularistic norms. Habermas' solution underestimates this dilemma, never really addressing its importance in his reconciliation of rationality and order.

Differentiation, Rationalization, and Interpenetration

Let me now outline the approach I propose from a European, radicalized, and partly reformulated and changed architectonic of Parsonian action theory (Münch 1982, 1984, 1986). In this view I conceive of "differentiation" as a process in which action increasingly steps beyond the boundaries of regulated action within a closed community, leading to a separation of economic exchange, political action based on the use of power, and intellectual thought about the world from communal action based on relationships of solidarity. Differentiation is a process that starts from a closed community—in terms of the theory of action, from a closed system of interaction strictly regulated by norms, which closes the scope for action (I. integration, closing), and this process brings about the emergence of systems of interaction outside the boundaries of communal interaction, as follows: economic exchange, which in terms of action theory is a system that opens the scope for action based on voluntarily chosen action according to the individual's utility calculations (A. adaptation, opening); political action based on the use of power, which in terms of action theory is a system specifying the scope for action and directing action toward specific goals (G. goal attainment, specification); and rational discourse as specialized thinking about the world based on argumentation, which in terms of action theory is a system generalizing the scope for action by subsuming action under general ideas (L. latent pattern maintenance, generalization).

The process of rationalization has to be differentiated into two steps in this perspective. It first means transcending the boundaries of communal action in the direction of establishing intellectual thinking about the world for its own sake: the emergence of rational discourse as a form of interaction emancipated from community ties. Thus, rationalization covers only one of three dimensions of differentiation. In the second step rationalization has the meaning of permeating the spheres of action that are outside rational discourse through rational thinking about the world. Community life (I), political action (G), and economic action (A) come under the pressure of rationalization in the sense of rational choice of associations, rational justification of decisions, and rational calculation of opportunities for satisfying needs. Thus far I have outlined the meaning of differentiation and rationalization. Let me now look at the explanation of these processes.

What we call "primitive societies" are societies in which action approaches to a higher degree than in any other society the model of action taking place only within the boundaries of a closed community. The members of such a community are tied to one another through relationships of solidarity between equals and of piety between unequals (leaders and followers, older and younger people). Every action is regulated through the shared norms of the community. Violations of the norms are violations of the community that cause emotional reactions of anger and repressive sanctions from community members. Membership in the community closes out membership in other communities. Thus, a strict regulation of communal action through shared norms, based on solidarity between equals and piety between unequals, enforced through repressive sanctions, and accompanied by magic, traditional law, and ethical particularism characterizes action within the boundaries of a community (see figure 13.1).

Even if every known society has transcended the boundaries of a pure community, we can conceive of differentiation as a process that transgresses the boundaries of community life. And we can at least say that those societies that we term traditional—located above the level of those that we term primitive—are distinctive in that they display the quality of transcending the boundaries of community life to a much higher degree than do primitive societies. How then can this process be explained? (See figure 13.2.)

In terms of action, it is the emergence of interactions with strangers outside the community that leads to the differentiation of noncommunal spheres of interaction from communal interaction. This is true for all three dimensions of differentiation that I have distinguished. Insofar as members of a community come into contact with members of another community and exchange goods, try to establish their supremacy over a given territory against other communities, and realize that there are other forms of thinking about the world outside their community, economic exchange, political action, and intellec-

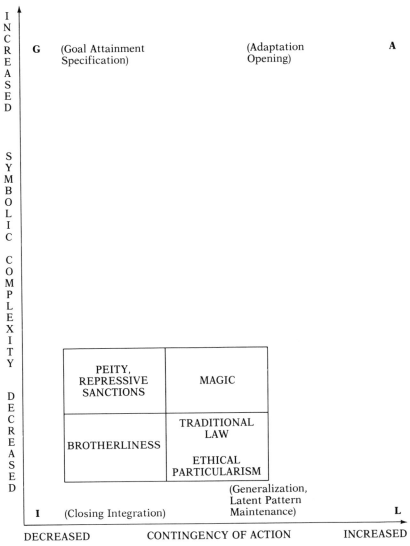

Figure 13.1

tual thinking about the world begin to arise as new forms of interactions that are not covered by the internal regulations of the community. There are no communal norms for economic exchange with strangers, for political action establishing supremacy over strangers or fighting back against such supremacy, and for purely intellectual reasoning outside the boundaries of traditional belief.

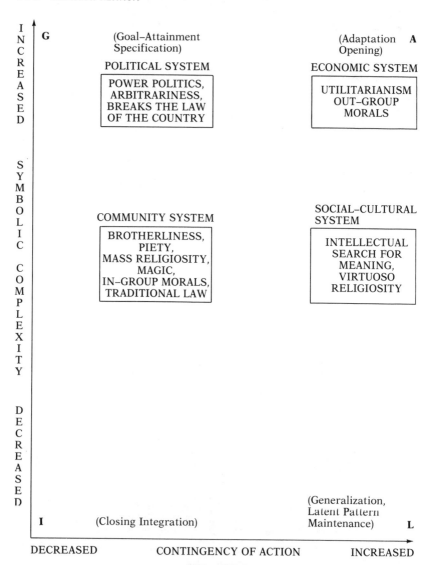

Figure 13.2

Economic exchange is in the first place interaction between strangers. What we call "differentiation of in-group morals and out-group morals" characterizes this situation. Because the traditional norms of community life do not apply to economic exchange between strangers, action is completely free, following only calculations of individual utility. Thus, utilitarianism becomes the major principle of economic exchange, separating it from the rules of brotherliness and piety within community life. And it is a feature of this utilitarianism that the application and fear of deceit are always involved in economic exchange; therefore, mistrust reigns and hinders the establishment of a common regulation of economic exchange through norms. The same is true with political action toward strangers. There also, the traditional norms do not apply, so that power politics and a corresponding mutual fear of strangers reigns. In communication between strangers mutual misunderstanding dominates. The purely intellectual thinking about the world that evolves out of this misunderstanding becomes alienated from the traditional norms of the community and results in the search for meaning for its own sake, which is clearly separated from widespread magical beliefs.

Thus far I have not explained the differentiation of economic exchange, political action, and intellectual thinking about the world as results of the adaptation of a system to a changing environment. I conceive of these processes as results of the extension of social interaction beyond the boundaries of the community, establishing forms of interaction between strangers that are not regulated by community norms and thus follow their own principles: it can be by chance that such contacts occur, but insofar as they have occurred the differentiation of spheres of action takes place. In this sense I explain the differentiation of the economic, political, and intellectual spheres of action as nonintended effects of social interaction between strangers. This is an explanation of differentiation in terms neither of action theory nor of systems theory.

Max Weber had a clear view of the processes of differentiation just described. And he attributed these processes in the first place to the *traditional* societies he studied using the examples of the Oriental cultures of China and India. Thus, contrary to the prevailing sociological interpretation, differentiation is in Weber's perspective the defining character of *traditional* societies. And at the same time Weber pointed out that something completely different characterizes the emergence of modern Western culture: the replacement of utilitarianism, power politics, and the pure search for meaning by new regulated forms of economic and political action and of intellectual thought (see figure 13.3).

Weber says that economic exchange in traditional societies is based on the complete separation of the in-group morals of the community and the out-group morals of economic action: "At first, free exchange does not occur but with the world outside of the neighborhood or the personal association" (Weber 1968: 637). "What is prohibited in rela-

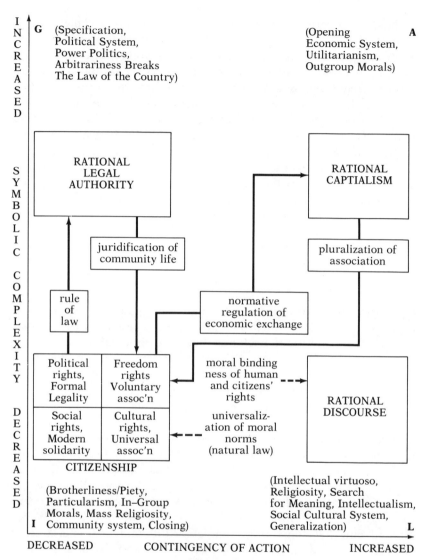

Figure 13.3

tion to one's brothers is permitted in relation to strangers" (Weber 1968:614). Economic exchange is without any regulation and makes deceit and mistrust a common feature of economic action. Weber pointed out this feature particularly with reference to China, where a unique contrast prevailed between traditionally regulated communal action within the boundaries of the clan and utilitarian economic action between strangers:

All communal action there remained engulfed and conditioned by purely personal, above all, by kinship relations. This applied also to occupational associations. (Weber 1951:241, also 236)

In conjunction with the tremendous density of population in China, a calculating mentality and self-sufficient frugality of unexampled intensity developed under the influence of worldly-minded utilitarianism and belief in the value of wealth as a universal means of moral perfection. (Weber 1951: 242)

It is of considerable economic consequence whether or not confidence, which is basic to business, rests upon purely personal, familial, or semi-familial relationships as was largely the case in China. . . . The economic ramifications of universal and mutual distrust must probably be rated high, though we have no yardstick for this. Thus, universal distrust resulted from the official and exclusive sway of conventional dishonesty and from the Confucian emphasis on keeping face. (Weber 1951:237)

In contradistinction to this peculiarity of traditional societies, overcoming the separation of in-group and out-group morals is a feature of modern Western culture that leads to a new form of regulated economic action which Weber calls "rational capitalism": "Unlimited greed for gain is not in the least identical with capitalism, and is still less its spirit. Capitalism *may* even be identical with the restraint, or at least a rational tempering, of this irrational impulse" (Weber 1976:17). Along with the emergence of rational capitalism communal action becomes transformed into a form of association that is open for individual decisions and economic calculation. Association is not based on ascriptive ties, but is voluntarily and rationally chosen: "Thus, a rational association takes the place of the 'natural' participation in the household's social action with its advantages and obligations" (Weber 1968:377, also 375–80; 1951:241). Thus, there evolves a plurality of voluntarily chosen associations. Even the family acquires features of voluntariness, freedom of individual decisions and economic calculation. Thus we have a form of communal association of individuals that is much more open than primordial communities and pluralistic in character. On the other hand economic action is regulated by norms. This is the result of a process of interpenetration of communal association and economic action leading to a mutual reshaping at their zones of interpenetration: voluntary and pluralistic association, and normatively regulated economic action. As we can read in the script of Weber's Munich lecture on economic history the traditional contradiction between in-group and out-group morals is resolved by rational forms of communal association and normatively regulated forms of acquisitive drives:

> Originally, two opposite attitudes toward the pursuit of gain exist in combination. Internally, there is attachment to tradition and to the pietistic relations of fellow members of tribe, clan, and house-community, with the exclusion of the unrestricted quest of gain within the circle of those bound together by religious ties; externally, there is absolutely unrestricted play of the gain spirit in economic relations, every foreigner being originally an enemy in relation to whom no ethical restrictions apply; that is, the ethics of internal and external relations are categorically distinct. The course of development involves on the one hand the bringing of calculation into the traditional brotherhood, displacing the old religious relationship. As soon as accountability is established within the family community, and economic relations are no longer strictly communistic, there is an end of the naive piety and its repression of the economic impulse. This side of the development is especially characteristic in the west. At the same time there is a tempering of the unrestricted quest of gain with the adoption of the economic principle into the internal economy. The result is a regulated economic life with the economic impulse functioning within bounds. (Weber 1981:356)

Several factors that had no counterparts in Oriental cultures contributed to the Occidental process of interpenetration of communal association and economic action: The universalization of the Christian community contributed to breaking the boundaries of clan particularism. It formed the universal cultural foundation for voluntarily chosen forms of association (Weber 1951:237; 1968:1244). The emergence of citizenship in the medieval town constituted a new form of political association. It provided the political foundations for voluntary associations (Weber 1968:1226–65). The rise of the market community in the medieval town and the corresponding formation of legal regulations for economic trading by lawyers established a new form of economic association. It provided the economic foundations for voluntary associations (Weber 1968:635–40, 666–752, 1212–36, 1322–39, 1353–54).

Weber also describes the enormous degree to which pure power politics exists in traditional societies, particularly in India. A defining feature of his view of traditional authority is the fact that it lacks predictability (!) because it always oscillates between tradition and arbitrariness of decisions (Weber 1968:227, 239, 1006–22; 1951:100–4). "Arbitrariness (of the ruler) breaks the law of the country" is Weber's formulation, meaning that the extension of the domination of a ruler beyond the confines of his original home rule or an *oikos* breaks the traditional law of communities under his new rule through the application of pure and arbitrarily applied power (Weber 1951:100, 148–49). Weber says that in India a pure Machiavellian power politics predominated:

And as in the Hellenic *polis* of classical times, so the princes, as early as the epic and the Maurya epoch and more so in later times, practiced as a matter of course the most naked "Machiavellism" without objections on ethical grounds [I have adapted this translation with reference to the original]. (Weber 1958:146, also 3)

Thus, it is a characteristic feature of traditional societies that action within the narrow confines of clan and neighborhood communities is regulated by common norms, but that action that applies power and transgresses these boundaries lacks any control by norms. In contrast to this character of traditional politics it is a feature of modern Western culture to have established a type of authority that reaches beyond the boundaries of communal life and that is nevertheless normatively regulated. This is rational-legal authority, based on the rules of a constitution that binds both rulers and ruled to common norms. In other words, the emergence of constitutional authority and the "rule of law" in politics is as much a peculiarity of modern Western culture as the emergence of rational capitalism:

In fact, the State itself, in the sense of a political association with a rational, written constitution, rationally ordained law, and an administration bound to rational rules or laws, administered by trained officials, is known, in this combination of characteristics, only in the Occident, despite all other approaches to it. (Weber 1976:16–17; see also 1968:217–26, 956–1005).

This peculiarity of modern political authority is again a result of interpenetration, namely of the interpenetration of communal association and political action. In this process political action becomes normatively regulated; guidance through a constitution and through law, constitutionality, and legality are part of political action. On the other hand, formal legality permeates communal association. Even in communities like the family formal rights and less primordial ties guide the actions of community members. What is nowadays discussed under the concept of juridification is the permeation of primordial relationships of solidarity by positive law.

England took a lead in establishing the rule of law well ahead of the emergence of rational capitalism. A major part was played by the mutual assimilation of the aristocracy and the bourgeoisie. We can see here an economic foundation for the rule of law (Moore 1966:21–61). The process of establishing the common law contributed to submitting political authority to the rule of law. This is a cultural foundation of the rule of law (Little 1970). The emergence of citizenship as a new form of universalistic and voluntary association provided political foundations for the rule of law (Marshall 1964).

The terms in which Weber described the separation of communal association and the intellectual search for meaning in the traditional societies of Oriental culture are expressed in the phrase "separation of the religiosity of the intellectual virtuoso and of the masses" (Weber 1968:500–18).

The religiosity of the intellectuals (the "virtuoso"), as a separated status group, tended toward the search for meaning for its own sake in highly abstract terms. This applies particularly to the Indian Brahmins and their shaping of Hinduism, and to the Buddhist intellectuals: "Asia, and that is to say, again, India is the typical land of intellectual struggle singly and alone for a *Weltanschauung*, in the particular sense of the word, for the 'meaning' of life in the world [I have adapted the translation in line with the original]" (Weber 1958:331). In contrast to this abstraction of intellectual religiosity the religiosity of the masses remains linked to magical belief: "Therefore, not the 'miracle,' but the 'magic formula' remained the core substance of mass religiosity, particularly of the peasants and the working class, but also of the middle class" (translation of Weber 1972:370; see also 1951:226, 233, 240).

Without any rationalization communal action remains tied to the particularism of piety norms for unequals and norms of brotherliness for equals. Indian society was divided into different communities that were alien to each other: the castes, the local communities, and the families, with their own norms for behavior. No universal norms existed that could have been applied for everybody in the same way: "There was no universally valid ethic, but only a status compartmentalization of private and social ethic" (Weber 1958:144). Again Weber points to a feature that completely distinguishes modern Western culture from this separation of intellectual abstraction and communal particularism. He says that the Oriental cultures did not develop a concept of natural law that claims the validity and bindingness of universal norms for every human being, as became established in Occidental culture:

All the problems which the concept of "natural law" called into being in the Occident were completely lacking. There simply was no "natural" equality of man before any authority, least of all before a super-worldly god.

This is the negative side of the case. Most important, it excluded forever the rise of social criticism, of rationalistic speculation, and abstractions of natural law type, and hindered the development of any sort of idea of "human rights." (Weber 1958:144; see also 1951: 147–50)

In contradistinction to this it is a characterizing feature of modern Western natural law to define the rights of every human individual (Weber 1968:865–80). Natural law formulates moral principles that bring together rational justification and rootedness in community life. This quality of modern Western natural law is the result of the inter- penetration of rational discourse and communal action. On the one hand, universal norms for communal association emerge, claiming validity for the association between every human being and breaking communal particularism. On the other hand, rational discourse is directed toward the formulation of a basic morality for the existing society, binding it to the society and preventing its aberration into the pure search for meaning.

A major part in bringing about the interpenetration of rational discourse and community life was played by the involvement of intel- lectuals in societal associations with practical aims. The inclusion of the religious intellectuals in the Christian community and, later on, the inclusion of the philosophers of the enlightenment in the bour- geoisie contributed to the cultural foundations of natural law (Weber 1968:507–18). The participation of lawyers in the regulation of eco- nomic trading provided economic foundations; their participation in the formation of political constitutions formed political foundations (Weber 1968:784–808, 865–80).

In the process of interpenetration both elements involved have changed their character. Economic exchange, political action, and intellectual abstraction have been linked to the normative regulation of behavior. Contractual norms of exchange, constitutions and the rule of law, and the universalistic morals of natural law are the results. Community life has lost its domination of the individual through norms of brotherliness and piety and through repressive sanctions. And it has overcome its primordial particularism. Com- munity life has become more and more based on voluntary and plu- ralistic association, formal rights and legality, and universal norms of morality (Marshall 1964).

The core of modern communal association is citizenship as an as- sociation of individuals. It is voluntarily chosen and allows a plurality of specific associations, and it is based on rationality and on rights of freedom and equality. It implies formal legality of associational rela- tionships, and it is based on political rights. The solidarity of citizens is shaped by these aspects; it combines freedom, formal legality, and universality at the same time. The social rights of solidarity are molded in this way and are therefore different from the particularistic brotherliness of a clan society. This complex nature of modern citizenship and its many preconditions make it improbable that it will develop outside modern Western culture. This is the one feature of modernity that most developing societies lack to the highest degree, regardless of their economic, political, and intellectual "differentiation." Even if we acknowledge that the emergence of citizenship has not gone far enough in modern Western culture, it *is* its distinguishing feature, and this feature together with the regulation of the differentiated spheres of the economy, polity, and intellectualism can only be sufficiently explained if we have a clear view of the interpenetration of already differentiated spheres as its basic source. And even if we lament, as Weber does in his concluding remarks to his Protestant ethic study, at the heartless and mindless working of the modern systems of capitalism and bureaucracy after the height of Puritanism's reign, it cannot be denied that the extension of citizenship rights, the normative regulation of the economy and polity, and the development of the moral bindingness of human rights is a process that has advanced considerably since Weber's days in the core Western societies. This is simply an undeniable fact. No sociological theory of differentiation has thus far adequately grasped and explained this fundamental feature of modern Western culture.

In the perspective outlined above the consequence of differentiation is the emergence of normatively unregulated spheres of action, possibly leading to a breakdown of order in the differentiated society as a whole. The solution to this new problem of order is not the return to community life, but the interpenetration of the differentiated spheres, leading to a differentiated yet integrated complex and contingent order (See Münch 1984).

The outlined view of differentiation and interpenetration also throws light on the process of rationalization in the two steps that I have distinguished, resulting in a position where it explains in a new way the possibility of social order under modern conditions.

Rationalization is a feature of modern Western culture, approaching—but never attaining—objective validity (truth) of meaning constructions, norms, expressions, and cognitions. This process is not confined to the cognitive sciences. It advances as far as culture is shaped by intellectuals according to the logic of argumentation. A distinctive feature of the Judeo-Christian religion compared to the other world religions, however, is much less its intellectual rationalization (which had other sources such as Hellenism and the secular Enlightenment) than its central position of *shaping the world* according to religious-cultural ideas. This represented a link between cultural ideas and societal and worldly spheres of life that had never been attained to the same extent anywhere else. The religious-cultural permeation of the world was the distinctive character of the development of Judeo-Christian religion. Strictly conceived of, this cultural permeation of the world did not primarily set free a logic of development in the inner laws of societal spheres because this would mean a culture-free economizing of the economy resulting in pure utilitarian calculation, a politicizing of politics resulting in pure power politics, and a communalizing of communal association resulting in particularistic group cohesion. The opposite is true: these spheres, which were particularly developed according to their inner laws in India, were submitted to the shaping influence of religious-cultural ideas. Communal action was submitted to the pressure of universalization, economic action to the pressure of ethical control, and political action to the pressure of realizing universal values. But this was not a one-way process. The more religious culture approached the world the more it had to take the logic of the worldly spheres as material that had to be formed. In this process a converse permeation of culture by the worldly spheres developed (see figure 13.4).

The mutual penetration of rational thought and the pursuance of collective and political goals and decisions has been thematized by Weber under the concept of rational-ethical subduing and mastering of the world. In one direction, this means the realization of values in pursuing goals and in the other direction the selection of ideas and of interpretations of ideas according to goals: "From the relation between the supra-mundane God and the creaturally wicked, ethically irrational world there resulted, however, the absolute unholiness of tradition and the truly endless task of ethically and rationally subduing and mastering the given world, i.e., rational, objective 'progress' (Weber 1951:240, also 235, 248). The dynamic forces that made possible this development were the Judeo-Christian conception of a ruler-god and the significance of ethical prophecy in Judeo-Christian religion.

The mutual penetration of rational thought and economic action has been considered by Weber under the concept of methodical-rational and practical-rational conduct of life. Here economic motives became submitted to rationally calculated control; in the opposite direction ideas are adapted to changing situations and economic motives: "For though the development of economic rationalism is partly

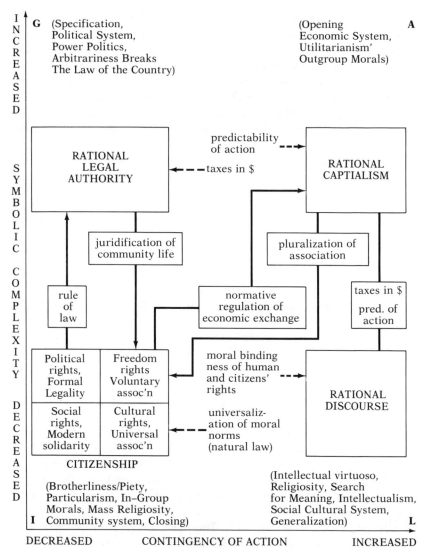

Figure 13.4

dependent on rational technique and law, it is at the same time determined by the ability and disposition of men to adopt certain types of practical rational conduct" (Weber 1976:26, also 155–80; 1951:245–47).

The foundations of economic rationalism in Puritan inner-worldly asceticism are the main interest of Weber's study on Protestantism.

The mutual penetration of rational thought and communal action —as has been demonstrated—has been illuminated by Weber under the concept of natural law. In this context the moral norms of the community become universalized and the cultural ideas of human rights and the rights of citizens become established as morally binding norms (Weber 1968:865–80).

We can also find formulations in Weber's work for the last mutual penetration of subsystems of social action according to our model, for the interpenetration of the economy and the polity. He says that capitalism is dependent on the predictability of the actions of individuals and of the state which is provided by the legislation and administration of rational-legal authority. In the opposite direction, collecting taxes in terms of money is a precondition for rational politics: "For modern rational capitalism has need . . . of a calculable legal system and of administration in terms of formal rules" (Weber 1976:25; see also 1981:339; 1968:311–19, 333–38, 666–752, 963–69, 975). A precipitating function for the development of a predictable order through legislation and administration was fulfilled by the emergence of rational legislation and administration in the collaboration of absolutism and the legal profession.

Whether the outlined development led in every case to a balanced *interpenetration* or to a complete domination of culture by the worldly spheres is a question that has to be answered differently for different steps of development and different societies. At any rate the rationalization of the modern West did not mean a direct translation of cultural rationalization into societal rationalization. At the heart of Western development lies a feature that is contrary to a pure dynamic of rationalization and differentiation according to the internal logic of systems of action: interpenetration. This process of interpenetration calls for another explanation. It is not so much the intellectualization of religion that is the origin of this development, but the Judeo-Christian transgression beyond culture into the world.

This different explanation of the Western development also leads to a different answer to the questions of the chances for and character of order in modern societies. The interpenetration of subsystems of action is a device for integrating spheres as distant from one another as intellectual discourse, communal solidarity, political decision making, and economic calculation. In this way a complex and contingent order emerges that can indeed combine rationality and order as Habermas wants it, not by conceptually equating rationality and consensus but by linking them as two very different processes in zones of interpenetration located between them. Rationality as based in dissensus creation, consensus as based in communal solidarity, and decision making, for example, have to be linked together in an institutionalized public discussion which lives on these different resources and performs the function of transmitting the products from one system to the other. What is culturally valid is, according to this perspective, also valid in political action. In this respect I can follow Habermas and reject Luhmann's theory of compartmentalized systems differentiation. But the valid cultural ideas leave open different ways of applying them which have to be decided upon politically. Here I have to follow Luhmann and to reject Habermas. I have to draw equally careful distinctions between specific arguments offered by Habermas and Weber. First, consensus is possible in modern societies. Here I deviate from Weber and follow Habermas. This consensus, however, is grounded in solidarity and not in rational discussion, so at this point I must part company with Habermas. Rationality is also possible in the development of norms, which again is to concur with Habermas and argue against Weber. Yet this rationality is accompanied by permanent dissensus. In this respect I differ from Habermas and stand on the side of Weber. The character that the modern order approaches according to this model is a combination of factual, normative, and voluntary features. What we need are not simple solutions, but increasingly complex ones.

Concluding Remarks

The theories of Luhmann, Schluchter, and Habermas on the differentiation and rationalization of society do not adequately conceive of differentiation as starting out from a state where action is limited by primordial communal ties and then leading on to the development of spheres of action beyond the boundaries of community life. They do not precisely conceive of rationalization as a subtype of differentiation developing in two steps, from community life to rational discourse and from rational discourse back to community life and economic and political action. The explanations these theories provide for differentiation and rationalization are pure developmental logics, in the shape of a logic of increasing complexity of environment and systems, of a logic of intellectual rationalization, or of a logic of rationalization of societal systems. The consequences they draw from differentiation and rationalization either run too smoothly toward integration, as in Luhmann's identification of differentiation and integration, or they lead unavoidably to the collapse of rationality into irrationality, as in Schluchter's Weber interpretation, or else they are inconsistently reduced to a mere empirical incompleteness as in Habermas' Weber interpretation. As to the problem of order under modern conditions the different theories offer either a too simple solution, as does Luhmann's theory, or no solution at all, as does Schluchter's, or a too rationalistic one, as does Habermas'. They all have in common that they have no access to the process of interpenetration as the feature that distinguishes modern Western culture from all cultures existing previously and/or elsewhere.

In the perspective I propose, differentiation is a process of establishing spheres of action outside the boundaries of community life. Rationalization is first one dimension of differentiation and second a spreading of differentiated culture to other spheres of action. Differentiation has to be explained as a nonintended consequence of interactions between strangers that occur by chance. The consequence is differentiated spheres of action with no interlinking order. This is precisely what is brought out in Max Weber's comparative historical studies as a feature of traditional societies. The interpenetration of the differentiated spheres with the establishment of new interlinking mechanisms is again clearly recognized by Weber as a distinguishing feature of modern Western culture. And apart from the answer to the question of how far this process of interpenetration has gone, it is the only possible answer to the problem of social order under modern conditions.

References

Habermas, Jürgen. 1981. *Theorie des kommunikativen Handelns.* 2 vols. Frankfurt: Suhrkamp.

Little, David. 1970. *Religion, Order and Law: A Study in Pre-Revolutionary England.* Oxford: Blackwell.

Luhmann, Niklas. 1970. *Soziologische Aufklärung.* Vol. 1. Opladen: Westdeutscher Verlag.

—— 1980. *Gesellschaftsstruktur und Semantik.* Frankfurt: Suhrkamp.

—— 1984. *Soziale Systeme.* Frankfurt: Suhrkamp.

Marshall, T. H. 1964. *Class, Citizenship and Social Development.* Garden City, N.Y.: Doubleday.

Moore, B. 1966. *Social Origins of Dictatorship and Democracy: Lord and Peasant in the Making of the Modern World.* Boston, Mass.: Beacon.

Münch, Richard. 1982. *Theorie des Handelns.* Frankfurt: Suhrkamp.

—— 1984. *Die Struktur der Moderne.* Frankfurt: Suhrkamp.

—— 1986. *Die Entwicklung der Moderne: England, Amerika, Frankreich und Deutschland.* Frankfurt: Suhrkamp.

Schluchter, Wolfgang. 1976. "Die Paradoxie der Rationalisierung: Zum Verhältnis von 'Ethik' und 'Welt' bei Max Weber." *Zeitschrift für Soziologie* 5:256–84.

—— 1979. "The Paradox of Rationalization: On the Relation of Ethics and World." in Guenther Roth and Wolfgang Schluchter, *Max Weber's Vision of History* pp. 11–64. Los Angeles and Berkeley: University of California Press.

—— 1981. *The Rise of Western Rationalism.* Berkeley: University of California Press.

Weber, Max. 1951. *The Religion of China.* H. H. Gerth, ed. and tr. New York: Free Press.

—— 1958. *The Religion of India.* H. H. Gerth and D. Martindale, trs. and eds. New York: Free Press.

—— 1968. *Economy and Society.* 3 vols. G. Roth and C. Wittich, eds. New York: Bedminster Press.

—— 1972. *Gesammelte Aufsätze zur Religionssoziologie.* Vol. 2. Tübingen: Mohr Siebeck.

—— 1976. *The Protestant Ethic and the Spirit of Capitalism.* T. Parsons, tr. A. Giddens, ed. New York: Scribner's.

—— 1981. *General Economic History.* I. J. Cohen, ed. New Brunswick, N.J.: Transaction Books.

Conclusion

Revisions and Progress in Differentiation Theory

Paul Colomy

This collection of essays exhibits extraordinary substantive diversity: alongside an examination of the structural and cultural characteristics of Axial Age civilizations there is an investigation of recent developments in the higher educational systems of England, France, Sweden, and the United States; a detailed study of Tlingit society is followed by the application of an abstract model of dedifferentiation to the Chinese cultural revolution, the Iranian revolution, and American fundamentalism. Nevertheless, there is unity in this diversity. Each contribution draws upon a common theoretical tradition—differentiation theory—and pushes that tradition in new and promising directions.

This concluding chapter specifies how each paper extends differentiation theory. These extensions of the theory, it is argued, can be understood as responses to several previous critiques leveled against the functionalist approach to change, and represent efforts to revise the theory in order to save it. I begin with an overview of the initial version of modern differentiation theory, which is then employed as a baseline to assess the changes, alterations, and progress introduced by the articles contained in this volume. These essays, I contend, revise the original theory in four general ways: first, they extend the empirical scope of differentiation theory; second, they lay the theoretical foundation for a more comprehensive explanation of structural differentiation; third, they present a more incisive treatment of the consequences of differentiation; and finally, they directly address the ideological ramifications of differentiation theory. After describing these theoretical elaborations, some predictions about the directions of subsequent theorizing and research in this tradition are tendered.

The Emergence of Modern Differentiation Theory

Sociological theories often grow and develop in response to criticisms formulated by those outside the particular theory group. Frequently, it is a school's competitors who are especially attuned to the theoretical and empirical weaknesses of a given approach. Critics often provide a school with a theoretical and research agenda, and a theory's progress can be measured by its ability to produce satisfactory revisions.

The initial formulation and subsequent refinements of modern differentiation theory can be partially understood as responses to criticisms directed at functional theory. With respect to functionalism's approach to social change, these "external" criticisms appeared in two overlapping waves. In response to each surge, functionalism initiated significant extensions or modifications of its model.

In the mid-1950s, functionalism provoked several critical rejoinders, with Lockwood (1956), Mills (1959), Coser (1956), and Dahrendorf (1958, 1959) issuing the sharpest and most polemical rebukes. These critiques claimed that structural functionalism, premised on value consensus and the internalization of norms, was inherently conservative and could not account for either social change or conflict. They also asserted that action theory was excessively abstract and could not be applied empirically. Although these charges were not entirely correct (see Parsons 1942, 1947, 1951:480–535; Baum and Lechner 1981; Alexander 1981), they nevertheless quickly achieved a virtually unimpeachable status. Indeed, such claims have become cardinal tenets of the discipline's folklore and persist in the face of overwhelmingly contradictory evidence.

Partially in response to such criticisms, scholars aligned with the functionalist approach initiated systematic theorizing and empirical research on the issue of change.[1] Differentiation theory was the product of this collective intellectual endeavor, and its early formulation rested on three fundamental tenets.

First, this approach described a "master trend" of social change. The master trend of differentiation identified the replacement of multifunctional institutions and roles by more specialized units as one of the most theoretically and empirically significant aspects of modern social change. Parsons (1966, 1971) described this trend for "total societies," arguing that sociocultural evolution has traversed primitive, archaic, intermediate, and modern stages. Several other scholars documented the trend toward greater specialization in distinctive functional spheres: Parsons and Smelser (1956:246–94) for economic roles; Smelser (1959) for familial and work roles; Eisenstadt (1963) for the emergence of historic bureaucratic empires; Keller (1963) for leadership roles; and Bellah (1964) for religious ideas, institutions, and action.

Second, when modern differentiation theory was not used primarily as a classificatory device, ordering institutions and societies in terms of their relative complexity, it typically invoked a societal need explanatory framework to account for the transition from a multifunctional unit to more specialized structures. Often that societal need model was tied to the idea of structural strain, the contention being that when functional prerequisites were not being effectively met, strain appeared which, in turn, prompted the creation of more efficient, differentiated arrangements.

Smelser (1959) presented the most sophisticated version of the strain-produces-differentiation argument. Adopting a problem-solving model of society, Smelser maintained that differentiation was precipitated by an inadequately functioning structure that generated widespread dissatisfaction. A given episode of change concluded with the institutionalization of a more differentiated and effective unit. Indeed, the more efficient performance of a given function was presumed to be a motive force behind the impulse to create more differentiated structures. In addition, the model presumed a single dominant value system which served to legitimate the initial dissatisfaction and, subsequently, to sanctify the more efficient innovation. The model also sharply distinguished between those who expressed dissatisfaction and a "disinterested" authority structure which handled and channeled disturbances. Finally, it was assumed that more effective, differentiated arrangements produced widespread satisfaction.

The third tenet of differentiation theory asserted that the institutionalization of more specialized structures increases the adaptive capacity of a social system or subsystem (Parsons 1964). In addition, it was argued that high levels of differentiation are correlated with value generalization, greater inclusion, and the emergence of specialized integrative institutions (Parsons 1966, 1971; Parsons and Smelser 1956:101–84; Smelser 1959:313–83). The latter processes promote the reintegration of a system grown more complex through differentiation (Parsons 1961; Smelser 1968).

Formulated, in part, as a response to critics who charged that functionalism could not analyze change, this initial version of differentiation theory instigated, in turn, a second round of criticism which indicted the theory on four grounds. First, there were several criticisms aimed at the empirical breadth and scope of differentiation theory. In particular, critics argued that the functionalist theory of change lacked historical and empirical specificity and presumed, unjustifiably, that modernity is associated with a radically complete break from the past (e.g., Bendix 1967; Nisbet 1969:268–70, 1972:40–5; Smith 1973:151–54; Stinchcombe 1978:77–104; Turner and Maryanski 1979:109–13). Second, functionalism's explanatory framework was attacked. Opponents maintained that the functionalist model of differentiation suffered from three maladies: an idealist bias which undermined the explanation of transitions between evolutionary stages; a failure to examine the impact of concrete social groups; and a neglect of power and conflict (e.g., Rueschemeyer 1977; Smith 1973:42–50; Abrahamson 1978:40–48). Third, the theory's analysis of the consequences of differentiation was questioned. According to critics, differentiation theory falsely assumed that structural change invariably increases systemic adaptiveness, was unable to describe specific integrative mechanisms, and tended to treat the absence of integration in highly differentiated systems in a residual way (e.g., Granovetter 1979; Rueschemeyer 1977; Smith 1973:70–76). Finally, the ideological charge that functionalism and its theoretical progeny, including differentiation theory, were inherently conservative was more forcefully articulated and infused with a greater sense of moral indignation and urgency (e.g., Gouldner 1970).

Acknowledging the partial legitimacy of these objections, the essays collected in this volume respond to each criticism and in so doing introduce significant revisions of differentiation theory. First, they elaborate the empirical scope of the original model, supplementing descriptions of the master trend with the identification of patterned departures from that trend. Second, they open up the explanatory framework of differentiation theory, specifying the cultural and structural parameters conditioning structural differentiation in a more multidimensional manner, and giving greater attention both to how concrete groups affect the course of change and to the role of power, conflict, and contingency in structural differentiation. Third, the original characterization of the effects of differentiation is modified, with reintegration and greater efficiency now being treated as a subset of a much larger array of possible consequences. Finally, the still widely accepted ideological charge of conservatism is challenged and the rudiments of a "critical modernism" are outlined.

Extending the Empirical Scope of Differentiation Theory

Fertile macrosociological theories of change invariably posit a conceptual master trend which serves as a guide for subsequent theorizing and research. Although critically important for any theory of social change, the identification of a master trend constitutes only the first step in a fully satisfactory theory. In order to advance, a theory must incorporate the study of patterned departures from its postulated master trend. The ultimate product of this approach is a more theoretically variegated and empirically fruitful conception of change.

Like other sociological approaches, differentiation theory postulates an analytic master trend. That trend presumes that a significant aspect of social change is the replacement of multifunctional institutions and roles by more specialized units. Critics, on the other hand, contend that differentiation theory's preoccupation with abstract depictions of societal and institutional master trends sacrifices historical specificity and ignores empirical variation. In response to these charges, several essays collected in this volume push differentiation theory toward a more comprehensive conception of change.

This revisionist effort should not be interpreted as a rejection of differentiation theory's master trend. To the contrary, much of the work assembled here identifies movement toward differentiation either in total societies or in a particular functional sphere. However, in contrast to earlier work in this tradition, the identification of a master trend in these essays is supplemented with the explicit recognition of variations and departures from the trend. For example, Mayhew maintains that the differentiation of an autonomous public sphere from a society's broader stratification system is never complete. The latter invariably intrudes upon public discourse and debate. Similarly, Alexander asserts that inclusion is a master trend of change in modern solidary relations but notes that the degree of inclusion varies for different racial and ethnic groups, and that despite progress toward greater inclusion many "exclusive" practices and sentiments endure. Finally, Luhmann's description of a Guttman scale–like sequence of structural change is coupled with the recognition that the different forms of system differentiation may be combined. Thus, even when the investigation of a master trend is a central concern, these essays exhibit a heightened sensitivity to the incomplete institutionalization of modern differentiated structures.

Although acknowledging the analytic significance of a master trend, several essays are explicitly concerned with expanding differentiation theory's empirical scope. These papers supplement differentiation theory's master trend in two ways. First, detailed historical accounts and empirically grounded comparative approaches highlight patterned departures from the master trend and underscore considerable variation in the amount of differentiation both within and between societies. Recognition of these variations has generated new concepts that extend differentiation theory's analytic description of change. Second, it is argued that the master trend toward differentiation often engenders resistance and "discontents," and patterns of change arising in opposition to institutional differentiation are identified. This work suggests a possible shift in the pertinent unit of analysis, from a near exclusive focus on the master trend to the investigation of sequences of change that combine both differentiation and the backlash movements it provokes. A brief review of several contributions to this volume substantiates each of these revisions.

Smelser's discussion of English mass education in the first three-quarters of the nineteenth century provides a rich historical-sociological account of what can be called "blunted differentiation." During this period, the establishment and institutionalization of primary education for children of working-class and poor parents were impeded by a concatenation of social forces that pulled mass education in opposing directions. Educational reformers, politicians, and ruling-class elements promoted education as a means of stabilizing an evolving class system. Similarly, religious leaders and organizations also promoted working-class education, but tensions between Church and Dissenting factions and concern for their respective religious position in society made each party suspicious of massive state intervention in education. The most significant obstacle to mass education, however, was economic. The demands of early British capitalism, as mediated through the working-class "family economy," promoted children's early withdrawal and irregular attendance. The bulk of Smelser's paper presents a detailed examination of how the pattern of economic constraints and opportunities confronting working-class families undermined mass education. Despite the sustained efforts of reformers and politicians, mass education did not become fully established until a series of economic and political developments made it both more affordable and more difficult to evade.

Champagne's analysis of Tlingit society describes a pattern of "unequal differentiation." That term denotes an unequal rate and degree of differentiation across distinct functional spheres. Thus, Champagne notes that largely in response to Western encroachment the Tlingit economy and polity experienced considerable differentiation from traditional kinship structures. On the other hand and in contrast to the extensive differentiation of the economy and polity, the solidary and cultural subsystems continue to be infused with traditionalism. His discussion suggests that despite variations in their degree of differentiation, these subsystems exhibit a relatively stable pattern of accommodation.

A more comparative focus is evident in my study of political change and continuity in the antebellum United States. I introduce the term "uneven differentiation" to designate the varying rate and degree of differentiation of a single institutional sector or role structure within a society. That concept is used to examine variations in the rate and degree of mass party development in the antebellum period. The essay indicates that antebellum New York exhibited the highest degree of political differentiation, featuring a relatively specialized political elite, an extensive party organization, and the articulation of new rules of the political game that sanctified party loyalty and discipline. South Carolina, on the other hand, displayed the least amount of political differentiation, retaining a diffuse, gentry ruling class, a minimal degree of mass party development, and a near-compulsive adherence to the classic political virtues of statesmanship and stewardship. Both Massachusetts and Virginia fell between these extremes, each state generating extensive party organization and articulating the rudiments of a distinctly political normative framework, while retaining significant elements of gentry class leadership and traditional political culture.

Several other papers analyze cross-societal developments. Alexander, for example, describes the contrasting developmental paths of France, Germany, and the United States toward a more differentiated news media. Similarly, Rhoades' essay highlights variations in the responses to growth of French, English, Swedish, and American systems of higher education through the 1960s and 1970s. Finally, Eisenstadt analyzes differences in the mode of structural differentiation in African societies, historic cities, and Axial Age civilizations.

Although exhibiting remarkable substantive diversity, these historically informed and comparatively oriented essays make a similar analytic point, viz., the need to examine variations in the degree, rate, and sequencing of structural change. This recommendation broadens the empirical scope of differentiation theory and, as I will argue later, provides an incentive to generate a more comprehensive explanation of differentiation that can account for both the master trend and patterned departures from it.

A second set of analytic amendations extends differentiation theory by enlarging the unit of analysis. Earlier formulations provided illuminating descriptions of the greater complexity of differentiated social systems and subsystems relative to more traditional configurations. By contrast, contributions to this volume argue that differentiation is often fruitfully regarded as one element in a broader pattern of change.[2]

In chapter 4, for example, I identify a "double-movement" sequence. I argue that newly differentiated institutions seek to consolidate their material position and solidify their cultural authority. However, this drive toward consolidation frequently impinges upon the interests and authority of established or emerging institutions and groups. In an effort to protect their own niche, individuals and groups may take steps designed to contain what they regard as the excesses of the consolidating institution. Thus, structural differentiation often assumes the character of a double movement, where the drive toward consolidation is opposed by a loose coalition seeking to defend both specific subsystem interests and a more amorphous public welfare. Assuming that a minimal degree of preexisting cultural and structural differentiation exists, I hypothesize that the breadth and intensity of opposition to institutional differentiation are greatest when the new structure has been most successful in its drive toward consolidation. A burgeoning structure's very success in extending its sphere of influence over domains previously controlled by other institutions and groups usually prompts vigorous attacks from those so threatened and thereby instigates a broadly based resistance designed to temper the focal structure's perceived excesses and undermine its legitimacy.

I garner empirical support for this argument through an analysis of party development in the antebellum United States. Attacks on political parties were most intense and broadly based in New York, precisely where mass parties had been most successful in consolidating their position. In the Empire state, a loose coalition including "dispossessed" elements of the gentry class, religious leaders, humanitarian reformers, disillusioned members of the working class, and intellectuals launched a material and ideological assault on mass parties. These developments, I conclude, are consistent with the double-movement hypothesis and underscore the utility of coupling analyses of institutional differentiation with the study of the resistance differentiation engenders.

In a more analytic way, Lechner argues that modernization engenders discontents centered about problems in the meaningful organization of action. His essay demonstrates how value generalization, one correlate of high levels of differentiation, spawns "reductionist" movements designed to restore meaningful order on the basis of an absolute, substantive value principle. More formally, he characterizes fundamentalism as collective action aimed at resolving problems inherent in value generalization by means of dedifferentiation across the levels of action on the basis of pattern maintenance as the primary value principle. Distinguishing between controlling and dynamizing subsystems and maintaining that a variety of different relations between these subsystems may obtain, Lechner describes fundamentalism as a form of "oversteering" wherein controlling subsystems dominate dynamizing subsystems. An abstract model is devised to specify the systemic logic of this type of dedifferentiation, and the unique features of fundamentalism are discussed by tracing the implications of value absolutism through Parsons' AGIL schema. General cultural and social conditions necessary for the emergence of fundamentalist syndromes and factors shaping possible trajectories of those movements are identified. The model is then applied to three empirical instances of dedifferentiation—the Chinese cultural revolution, the Iranian revolution, and fundamentalism in the United States. The more general point of Lechner's argument should not be lost. He contends that reductionist movements must be understood as one part of a sequence of structural change where high levels of differentiation and value generalization render order problematic and make dedifferentiating movements aimed at restoring or reconstructing that order a recurrent possibility.

The two types of revisions reviewed above elaborate functionalism's conception of change in a number of ways. First, distinctive patterns of change—including blunted, unequal, and uneven differentiation and dedifferentiation—are identified. Further, these patterns suggest that the assumption of a radically complete break with the past that is implicit in differentiation theory's master trend must be rejected. Rather than presuming that there is a perfect inverse relation between advancing differentiation and eroding traditionalism, that more efficient specialized units completely supplant less effective, diffuse structures, these essays (see, especially, Smelser, Lechner, Alexander,

Champagne, Luhmann, and my first paper) indicate that vestiges or enclaves of traditionalism persist even in quintessentially modern societies. At the same time, this more inclusive conception of change also recognizes that those traditionalist patterns and practices that manage to persist despite encroaching modernity are, nevertheless, likely to experience significant strains (see Lechner).

Second, these papers broaden the scope of differentiation theory by arguing that differentiation often represents only one step in a more encompassing pattern of change. Both Lechner's paper and my first essay recommend that differentiation be examined in conjunction with the discontents and resistance it engenders.

Finally, these revisions impart a greater sense of empirical specific-ity and variation to differentiation theory and provide an impetus to create a more general explanation that can account for both the master trend of differentiation and patterned departures from it.

Elaborating the Explanatory Framework of Differentiation Theory

The inclusion of greater historical specificity, empirical variations, and encompassing sequences of structural change extends the scope of differentiation theory and represents an important advance. In addition to constructing a more variegated description of change, the papers in this book lay the theoretical foundation for a more compre-hensive explanation of differentiation. These papers take aim at the charges that functionalist explanations of differentiation suffer from an inherent idealist bias, that they fail to examine how concrete groups affect change, and that they ignore conflict and power.

Considered as a whole, this volume suggests that two general sets of elements are necessary for a comprehensive and persuasive expla-nation of differentiation and its subsidiary patterns. First, several discussions identify relatively intractable parameters—i.e., struc-tural contradictions or strains, and configurations of opportunities and constraints—that precipitate change and establish broad limits on the types of possible transformations. These "structural" analyses convey a rigorous multidimensional thrust, the authors insisting that both material and ideal factors, economic as well as cultural forces, must be accorded equal analytic status in explanations of differentia-tion. In several of the papers this general multidimensional orienta-tion is refracted across a more specified systemic model, and in this manner the impact of concrete structural elements (e.g., values, solidary relations, economic forces, and political formations) upon differentiation is assessed.

Second, voluntaristic elements are also discussed. A number of essays investigate how concrete groups affect the course of differentiation. Cognizant of the structuring properties of social and cultural systems, these papers argue that within the limits established by these parameters considerable variation is possible. The general contention is that competing and contesting groups and processes of group mobilization, coalition formation, and intergroup conflict contribute to the "selection" of a particular mode of differentiation from an array of possible alternatives.

Alexander's analysis of ethnic relations and Champagne's discussion of Tlingit society construct multidimensional structural models to explain patterns of uneven and unequal differentiation. In contrast to the optimistic evolutionary bias of earlier theorists, Alexander contends both that the process of inclusion is uneven and that primordial definitions of the societal community persist even in the most civil, modern nation-state. His paper also outlines a multidimensional model to explain variations in the processes of ethnic inclusion. The model is organized around two factors: the degree of differentiation evident in the host society's economic, political, and cultural institutions; and the degree of primordial complementarity between the core group and the solidary out-group. His broad-ranging overview of ethnic relations in the United States indicates that European immigrants encountered a social environment characterized by a relatively high degree of institutional differentiation manifest in structural openings that these groups employed to their advantage. In addition, European out-groups evinced some degree of primordial commonality—whether on the basis of color, language, or religion—with the WASP core group, and this fostered their relatively successful inclusion. On the other hand, Alexander argues that blacks and Asians confronted a substantially less differentiated social environment and suffered a more intense primordial aversion, both factors operating to exclude them from the terminal community. Finally, Alexander demonstrates how distinctive combinations of both structural and primordial factors promote disparate strategies—assimilative, nationalist, and secessionist—to equalize an out-group's position vis-à-vis the core.

A multidimensional approach is also readily apparent in Champagne's contribution. His theoretically ambitious analysis brings together several purportedly hostile intellectual traditions in an historically rich investigation of Tlingit society. He devises a comprehensive structural model of change that combines Parsons' discussion of internally open systems with neo-Marxist treatments of externally open systems. This intriguing synthesis is employed to trace the impact of exogenous and endogenous material and ideal factors upon Tlingit society. His substantive discussion indicates that economic incorporation by the world market, political and administrative subordination to the United States, and the penetration of American values stimulated substantial differentiation within Tlingit society. The most significant changes occurred in Tlingit economic and political institutions. The encroachment of the world market resulted in the expropriation of traditional subsistence economic resources, the "semiproletarianization" of the work force, and substantial differentiation of economic organization from the traditional kinship structure. American political and administrative domination promoted the differentiation of educational and judicial functions and established incentives for creating a differentiated political center capable of articulating and aggressively pursuing Tlingit interests vis-à-vis American economic, political, and administrative structures. The penetration of Western values (and Champagne notes the considerable overlap between Tlingit and Western beliefs) and changes in the Tlingit's economic and political infrastructure contributed to a more expansive solidary community and somewhat more universalistic cultural orientations.

Despite these various movements toward greater differentiation, remnants of traditional solidary relations, rituals, and values endure. The potlatch complex continues to be extremely important, and social rank is still partially determined by potlatch contributions. The core of Tlingit society remains in the clan-moiety system, and there is a complex and intimate relation between the kinship system and more differentiated economic and political institutions. The ubiquitous presence of the Raven and the Eagle—powerful emblems of the Tlingit's two major moieties—and the elaborate rituals to honor clan ancestors testify to the persistence of traditional beliefs. In sum, Champagne's multidimensional and externally and internally open structural model provides a compelling explanation of this instance of unequal differentiation.

In an effort to explain distinctive patterns of differentiation, several other papers formulated structural models that give equal analytic status to both material and ideal factors. Eisenstadt, for example, is particularly sensitive to how both political and economic or resource considerations as well as cultural orientations affect the nature of structural differentiation. Similarly, Mayhew identifies a conjuncture of cultural and structural forces that "loaded the dice" in favor of the institutionalization of the public sphere.

In conjunction with the development of multidimensional structural models of change, this volume also includes several essays that emphasize the impact of social groups and the processes of group competition and conflict on differentiation. Analytically, the impetus for this type of theorizing and research is the admission that differentiation cannot be fully understood as a natural, inevitable response to social strain or as an immanent systemic impulse toward greater efficiency. Acknowledging that the conceivable array of structural alterations is limited by relatively impermeable parameters, the question becomes: given a system's configuration of opportunities and constraints, what determines which particular option, from that delimited set of alternatives, is selected in response to structural contradictions and strains? The emphasis on concrete groups evident in several contributions to this book represents an attempt to address this issue.

Eisenstadt (1964, 1965, 1971, 1973, 1980) has taken the lead in wedding notions of group mobilization and conflict to differentiation theory.[3] His theoretical and empirical studies explicitly recognize that strain alone does not automatically and invariably produce higher levels of differentiation. While acutely sensitive to the structuring properties of cultural and social systems, Eisenstadt also gives considerable attention to the processes of group mobilization, coalition formation, control over pertinent resources, and conflict as factors affecting the specific course of institutional change.

His theorizing about the significance of groups and group conflict became more formal in his notion of "institutional entrepreneurs." He uses the term to refer to small groups of individuals who crystallize broad symbolic orientations, articulate specific and innovative goals, establish new normative and organizational frameworks for the pursuit of those goals, and mobilize the resources necessary to achieve them. Eisenstadt argues that the very occurrence of structural change and the specific direction it takes are shaped by the activities of institutional entrepreneurs. Moreover, these innovating groups are not disinterested altruistic agents of greater systemic adaptiveness. To the contrary, their advocacy of more highly differentiated structures is partially informed by their own interests. Frequently these groups seek to carve out an institutional or organizational niche where they can realize those specific interests. However, institutional entrepreneurs do not simply impose their will on the larger community.

Their "particularistic" interests are typically blunted and compromised by the frequently countervailing interests of their coalition partners, by the larger cultural patterns in terms of which they seek to legitimate their institutional quest, by the surrounding social structure that conditions their activities, resources, and sources of potential support, and by the conflicting interests of their opponents. A fully adequate explanation of institutional differentiation, he suggests, must examine these factors.

Eisenstadt's contribution to this volume extends his earlier discussions of institutional entrepreneurs by focusing on the impact of distinct elites and linking their activities and orientations to three core dimensions of social order: constructing trust and solidarity, regulating power, and providing meaning and legitimation. Treating elite activities as an autonomous aspect of institutionalization, he argues that they influence the particular form structural differentiation assumes at a given level of social evolution. The visions and activities of elites are directly tied to a society's cultural orientations or codes, and distinct elites (he distinguishes between solidary, political, and cultural elites) are carriers of different types of orientations. He also notes that elites' control over pertinent social resources varies. The particular formation structural differentiation assumes is shaped, then, not only by general structural and value patterns but also by elites' cultural orientations, coalitions, control over or access to social resources, and confrontations with opposition groups. Eisenstadt concretizes this general model by applying it to examinations of the early state in African societies, "historic" cities, and Axial Age civilizations.

My second paper also extends the notion of institutional entrepreneurs. My study of political differentiation in the antebellum United States asserts that states with similar patterns of cleavage structures, cultural codes, and constitutional frameworks nevertheless exhibited significant variations in the degree to which differentiated mass political organizations and distinctively "political" rules of the game emerged. I argue that this pattern of uneven differentiation was partially attributable to the orientations, activities, and organization of distinct leadership groups in different states. This finding prompted a generalization of Eisenstadt's concept of institutional entrepreneurs to the more inclusive notion of strategic groups. The latter term designates collectivities whose members assume leadership roles in directing the course of institutional development. This general concept includes an array of distinct leadership groups including institutional entrepreneurs, institutional followers, institutional conservatives, and institutional accommodationists. I argue that the pattern of uneven political differentiation realized in antebellum Massachusetts, New York, South Carolina, and Virginia is partially accounted for by the relative strength and resources of these distinct types of strategic groups.

I go on to point out that these leadership groups encountered substantial opposition, and that processes and patterns of group conflict had a significant impact upon the creation of differentiated institutions. For example, I note that one pattern of conflict, "institutionalization through opposition," fostered the construction of differentiated mass politics. In antebellum New York and Virginia, entrepreneurs' efforts to garner the support and resources necessary for differentiated party structures engendered conservative opposition. Initially, conservatives vigorously opposed the entrepreneurs' proposed organizational and normative innovations and sought to mobilize a large constituency in defense of traditional deferential patterns. However, on the basis of these conventional standards and practices conservatives were unable to compete effectively with the more differentiated party organizations devised by entrepreneurs and, consequently, lost many elections. By 1840, however, segments of the conservative leadership not only adopted but improved upon the innovations introduced by entrepreneurs. These segments of conservatism, then, ultimately served as agents for the institutionalization of the more differentiated political structures that they had originally opposed. At the same time, the paper points out, several conservatives refused to adopt entrepreneurs' innovations. Many of these "principled" conservatives became critics of the burgeoning party system and inhibited its complete institutionalization.

An emphasis on concrete groups and the processes of coalition formation and conflict is evident in Rhoades' comparative examination of academic drift in France, England, Sweden, and the United States. He underscores the importance of academic groups, external "lay" groups, internal professional administrators, and the state in accounting for the relative absence of substantial structural differentiation despite the presence of significant enrollment growth from 1960 to 1980 and the accompanying strain placed on higher educational institutions. Noting that attempts to produce further structural differentiation were usually instigated by lay groups rather than by institutionally conservative academics, Rhoades found that differentiation was most likely to occur when, as in the United States, administrators and representatives of the state (e.g., politicians and legislators) were strong relative to academics and when they were also receptive to both pressure from and the concerns of lay groups. Further, differentiation was least likely to occur when, as in England, academics possessed relative strength at both the institutional and national levels, while lay groups were comparatively weak. Moreover, when the implementation of proposed reforms was left to the professoriate, as was true in all of the European countries examined in his study, academics tended to twist new structures to conventional academic purposes. One might note parenthetically, as it were, that unlike earlier studies that treated the polity as a "disinterested bystander" that benignly channeled and handled disturbances, Rhoades' analysis attributes to the state (or at least to specific groups within the state apparatus) an activitist and leading role in fomenting differentiation.

A voluntaristic element is suggested or implied in several other papers in this book: Mayhew's discussion of publicists and parliamentarians illustrates the role of "intellectual entrepreneurs" in establishing a differentiated solidary public; Champagne's description of Tlingit political and economic leaders also highlights a voluntaristic component in his explanation of unequal differentiation; finally, Alexander's distinction between different strategies available to ethnic out-groups clearly implies a role for leadership in mobilizing a constituency behind one or more of these options.

More generally, the studies described above reflect contemporary differentiation theory's increasing attention to the impact of social groups and conflict on institutional transformations and its concern for the historical and empirical details of how structural change actually occurs. In a broad analytic sense, these revisions introduce a "political" element into the functionalist explanation of change. It is noteworthy, in this regard, that in a recently published paper one of the contributors to this book coupled the acknowledgment that many earlier versions of the theory posited a systemic propensity toward greater adaptiveness as a motive force behind the master trend toward differentiation with the claim that such a "problem-solving explanatory model" should now be supplemented with an "interest model" that recognizes that differentiation is partially contingent on the relative strength and position of contending groups (Smelser 1985). According to the latter model, which is generally consistent with the Eisenstadt, Colomy, and Rhoades contributions to this volume, specific instances of structural differentiation partially reflect the outcome of a political struggle between groups vying for advantage and seeking to fashion structures consistent with the "particularistic" interests.

Nonetheless, this "interest model" is not reducible to a simple struggle for power. Indeed, the groups who fight over the form and content of more differentiated institutions rarely seek power as an end in itself. More commonly, power is sought as a means for realizing a particular institutional vision or ensuring that a given institution pursues a specific mission, goal, or function. Analytically, then, the ensuing political struggle is multidimensional and involves a battle waged over both conflicting material and ideal interests.

The examination of group contention and its impact on structural change is, simultaneously, an effort to lend differentiation theory greater empirical specificity. However, differentiation theorists have also studied conflict at higher levels of abstraction with sustained attention being given to the potential structural contradictions associated with differentiation within and between cultural, social, and personality systems. Thus, Alexander (1978, 1982) suggests that differentiation theory is a conflict theory that holds that high levels of differentiation increase the amount of conflict but reduce its scope. Similarly, Luhmann's contribution to this volume underscores the fragile unity of highly differentiated systems. References to concrete collectivities and "political" struggles are often oblique or only implied with this innovative work, but the increasing preoccupation with systemic conflicts suggest several parallels with more group-oriented investigations.

For example, the principle of "leads and lags" describes how a particular pattern of differentiation fosters systemic strains. When concentrated in a single institutional subsystem, rapid change can "outstrip" the responsive capacity of interdependent subsystems. Depending on the prevailing configuration of historical and social circumstances, this tension-inducing disjunction can produce a wide variety of consequences. Employing a specified version of the lead and lag principle, Alexander's investigation of the American mass media contends that differentiated institutions are constantly susceptible to cycles of inflation and deflation. He maintains that inadequate structural developments in other spheres, especially in political and cultural institutions, are commonly displaced onto the media. Such displacement generates strong pressure for the inflation of the media's systemic role and it may be pressed to perform a political or cultural function even though it lacks the necessary resources. That "double-bind" situation often results in radical deflation, with charges of bias and distortion undermining the media's credibility.

In addition, Alexander identifies three other structural sources of conflict in the relation between a differentiated mass media and its environing social system. A differentiated press generates tensions over possible collusion between news reporters and their sources. Further, there is an inherent antagonism between the government and news agencies with, for example, the president and the media continually battling over the normative definition of events. Finally, at the international level the media is typically dedifferentiated, and by rigidly espousing the nation's "party line" in foreign affairs the media reinforces international tensions.

I have focused on Alexander's analysis of the structural sources of systemic conflict. However, the observant reader will have noticed that similar analyses of systemic strains and contradictions are evident in Lechner's work on dedifferentiation, Smelser's study of English mass education, Alexander's investigation of ethnic inclusion, Champagne's examination of Tlingit society, my elaboration of the notion of double movements, Sciulli's treatment of societal constitutionalism, Eisenstadt's overview of traditional civilizations, and Luhmann's analysis of the relations between functional subsystems.

In sum, contributors to this volume have begun to construct a more comprehensive explanatory framework. On a general level, these papers aspire to construct an approach sensitive to the confluence of structural and voluntaristic factors. On the one hand, several essays outline a multidimensional structural model to identify the material and ideal factors that condition differentiation. Other essays devote considerable attention to specific groups mobilized for and against differentiation. Both types of models emphasize conflict and the struggle over material and ideal interests. They also belie the still widely accepted charge that functionalist theories are inherently idealist and incapable of explaining or incorporating conflict. Moreover, each set of these contributions is open to the explanatory models proposed by the other, and in many essays (see, for example, Champagne and Eisenstadt) there are interesting and explicit parallels and "crossovers" between the structuralist and voluntarist frameworks. In short, these elaborations of differentiation theory have begun to provide a better understanding of the processes associated with structural differentiation. The construction of a more general model to incorporate both structural and voluntaristic considerations is clearly a priority for future work in differentiation theory.

Reconceptualizing the Consequences of Differentiation

Earlier renditions of differentiation theory concentrated on two primary consequences of structural change: increased efficiency and reintegration. Increased structural specialization, it was argued, fostered greater efficiency and augmented a system's capacity to adapt flexibly to its environment. Moreover, some formulations implied that a systemic imperative for greater efficiency was a primary impetus to structural differentiation. Those early discussions also acknowledged that the master trend toward differentiation made social integration more problematic. The appearance of more general cultural codes and specialized "integrative" institutions purportedly served to integrate relatively complex sociocultural systems.

Treating increased efficiency and integration as theoretically and empirically possible but not invariable outcomes, the analyses collected in this volume provide a broader conception of the consequences of differentiation. Accordingly, the contention that differentiation automatically increases systemic efficiency and effectiveness is rejected. By contrast it is argued that differentiated institutions establish new bases of interest around which groups may rally when confronted with perceived threats. Structural innovations produce new roles, each of which constitutes the basis for the formation of collectivities that may become "political" constituencies concerned with maintaining or advancing their interests (Smelser 1985). As Rhoades' discussion of institutionally conservative academics suggests, a preoccupation with protecting vested interests introduces an element of rigidity and inflexibility into a system and thereby reduces its capacity for adaptation to a changing environment.

In an analogous fashion, the notion of reintegration has also been supplemented and refined. Münch's work identifies several distinct forms that the relations between relatively autonomous subsystems may assume. Distinguishing between regulative or controlling subsystems and dynamizing subsystems and asserting that there are fundamental tensions between distinct subsystems of action, Münch has argued that several possible relations may actually obtain between subsystems. "Interpenetration" denotes that "form of relation through which opposed spheres or subsystems can both expand without thereby creating mutual interference. Interpenetration is the mechanism by which the potential of every system is converted into actuality" (Münch 1982:772–73). He rejects Parsons' assumption that interpenetration is the modal concrete relation between differentiated subsystems, and claims that many different types of relations may obtain empirically. Therefore, Münch treats interpenetration analytically, as one possible subsystem relation among an array of alternatives, which include: the accommodation of the potentially controlling subsystem to the dynamizing subsystem; their mutual isolation; and the one-sided domination of the potentially dynamizing subsystem by the controlling one. Münch's revisions, then, transcend earlier discussions of conflict versus integration, and provide a powerful analytic lens for examining empirical variation and tensions in the relations between differentiated subsystems.

Münch's contribution to this volume describes the theoretical utility of the concept of interpenetration in the context of recent German debates over differentiation and rationalization. In contrast to the argument that differentiation produces normatively unregulated spheres of action that lead to social breakdown, Münch contends that the interpenetration of differentiated spheres promotes a complex and contingent society that combines rationality and order. He illustrates the usefulness of the interpenetration concept (and the corollary notion of zones of interpenetration) through illuminating discussions of economic, political, and intellectual action. Finally, he notes that the process of interpenetration is a feature that distinguishes Western society from many previous and existing social orders.

Sciulli's notion of "societal constitutionalism" represents another intriguing reconceptualization of integrative processes in highly differentiated systems. He maintains that the entropic drift toward arbitrary power and bureaucratic authoritarianism initiated by "purposive rationalization" in the political and socioeconomic orders can be most effectively controlled by "collegial formations" premised on procedural norms. The standard of societal constitutionalism eschews exclusive reliance on internalized substantive beliefs as the sole basis for reintegration, and maintains that shared recognition of procedural restraints and the institutionalization of collegial formations across differentiated social functions establishes the possibility that actors can determine collectively when power is being exercised arbitrarily. Sciulli argues that contemporary modern societies are threatened by a drift toward bureaucratic authoritarianism and calls upon professionals in a variety of institutional and organizational settings to battle against that threat by revitalizing their collegial formations. To combat purposive rationalization more effectively he also recommends radical and reformative structural alterations.

Mayhew's analysis of the solidary public is an innovative effort to specify a distinctive form of integration in highly differentiated systems. In contrast to traditional social orders where solidarity is premised primarily on primordial principles, modern societies employ communication to establish unifying commonalities: "Differentiated solidarity occurs when the social system comes to be integrated through solidary alliances created by persuasion and influence rather than by traditional, culturally defined ties" (Mayhew, chapter 9). It is through public debate and discourse that new solidarities are discovered and affirmed. Pursuant to an intriguing comparison of the parallels and differences between money and influence as media of exchange, Mayhew discusses how a specialized leadership role—the prolocutor—produces communicative solidarity. The prolocutor occupies a dual position, speaking to the larger society on behalf of a constituency group, and serving as a central integrative figure in modern solidary structures. The prolocutor's dual position fosters appeals to the public good and to reason generally, and in this fashion creates the public as a solidary group through discourse. Mayhew also offers a corrective to Parsons, who tended to overestimate the amount of differentiation in modern societies, by observing that the public is never completely differentiated from the larger status order: "The differentiation of modern influence systems from a society's system of stratification is always partial and imperfect. The two systems remain implicated in each other" (Mayhew, chapter 9). In brief, Mayhew argues that integration in liberal democracies is secured in part by the institutionalization of a differentiated structure, the public, in which appeals to universal values and reason create a new form of solidarity.

In some respects, Luhmann goes even further than the others in his reconceptualization of integration. Indeed, Luhmann appears to eschew the notion of integration, especially when it is presented as value generalization and shared symbolic patterns. He prefers to speak of the "unity of society," and maintains that such unity inheres in distinctive forms of system differentiation which, in turn, are defined by the relations that obtain between subsystems. While his paper identifies four forms of system differentiation—segmentary, center and periphery, stratificatory, and functional—his primary concern is with the latter, the form that defines modern societies. Luhmann strongly emphasizes the autonomy, both autopoietic and regulative, of functional subsystems in modern societies. The emergence of modern society, as Luhmann describes it, revolves around the "liberation" of functional subsystems from the meddlesome interference of other systems, particularly religion. A central feature of modernity is that each subsystem, including religion, is increasingly organized around the performance of its respective function. Each subsystem is confronted with an "internal social environment" composed of the other subsystems. At the same time, each subsystem exhibits a heightened sensitivity to its environment. One consequence of the conjunction of a highly differentiated society and the heightened sensitivity of its constituent subsystems is that the causal impact of individual events reverberates throughout the subsystems, often exerting significantly different effects on each subsystem. Given the often "turbulent and explosive" causal relations between subsystems, the unity of society is regularly subject to strain and the threat of breakdown.

In light of these studies, it is readily apparent that the reintegration or unity of differentiated and rationalized systems continues to be an important issue in differentiation theory. In contrast to earlier discussions, however, the analyses presented here are distinctive in three ways. First, they explicitly recognize that integration is not the only or even the necessary outcome of differentiation. Thus, Münch notes that fundamentally opposed relations between differentiated subsystems may obtain, while Sciulli contends that modern societies are endangered by a drift toward bureaucratic authoritarianism. Second, they argue that integration and conflict, whether through public debate or the aggressive pursuit of mundane interests, are not mutually exclusive. Modern societies promote both integrative and conflictual processes, and one distinctive characteristic of these social orders is their ability to cohere despite substantial conflict. The unity of modern societies is, as Luhmann might put it, a precarious one. Finally, these essays, particularly those of Münch, Sciulli, and Mayhew, present conceptually incisive and exciting specifications of how integration works. In the place of abstruse references to value generalization, value implementation, and inclusion, the concepts of interpenetration, societal constitutionalism, and the solidary public identify more specific integrative mechanisms.

Toward a Critical Modernism

In the preceding sections I have argued that the contributions to this volume revise functionalism in response to earlier critiques. The opposition to functionalism has never been based solely on narrow scholarly grounds, however. In each of the two critical waves, strictly scientific objections were combined with ideological attacks. In the 1950s, functionalism was assailed for its unwillingness to give systematic attention to change or conflict. The reluctance to investigate those issues, critics charged, reflected both a preoccupation with stability, system equilibrium, value consensus, and internalization and an inclination to conceptualize instances of change as irrational disturbances or as deviance. It was summarily determined that functionalism's purportedly scientific predilection for equilibrium and stasis masked a deeper ideological commitment to the status quo.

In the polarized 1960s and 1970s, the ideological critique was elaborated. Gouldner (1970) forcefully articulated the reigning sensibility of the day with his claim that functionalism was "essentially conservative in character." Further, he said, functional theorists, congenitally disposed to support the "establishment," were devoted to maintaining current social arrangements. Functionalism treated extant institutions as given, proposed "Band-Aid" remedies to improve institutional functioning rather than devising genuine alternatives, and counseled resignation to the powers that be.

In the social and ideological climate of that era, the radical Left assumed the high moral ground and the "burden of proof" was dumped onto functionalists. They did not shoulder the load well, adopting the denial and avoidance of ideological issues as primary strategies. Many functionalists were convinced that in order to advance, a science had to separate itself from ideology. Thus, in response to charges of conservatism, many functionalists asserted that the theory was ideologically neutral and value free. In a polarized social context, however, claims of standing above or outside the fray are always suspect. The argument that different functionalists could be found on all sides of the political spectrum and that, therefore, an individual's ideological convictions were independent of his or her scientific commitments did little to persuade those who were already strongly predisposed to disbelieve such "politically naive" assertions.

Today, with charges of conservatism now an accepted part of the discipline's folklore about functionalism, evasive maneuvers continue to be employed. For example, intending to highlight the suppleness of functionalist concepts and thereby undercut the claim that this approach is inherently conservative, it is sometimes observed that self-proclaimed critical and neo-Marxist theorists incorporate elements of a Parsonian-inspired systemic framework in their own work. Though partially true, such observations do not address the issue directly.

A more aggressive approach to this dilemma is beginning to emerge and promises to lift functionalism out of the neutral corner into which earlier adherents had painted themselves. There are three elements in this burgeoning response. First, it is conceded that every perspective in the social sciences contains an ideological component that is partially autonomous from its presuppositions, theoretical models, and empirical propositions (Alexander 1982). Second, it is asserted that functionalism's ideological commitment is not to social stability, system equilibrium, or the status quo, as widely alleged, but to individual autonomy (Bourricaud 1981). Voluntarism or individual freedom is to be understood multidimensionally and obtains "to the extent that the concrete person exercizes autonomy vis-à-vis both the normative and conditional aspects of his situation" (Alexander 1978:84). Finally, and particularly germane to the articles in this volume, it is suggested that institutionalized individualism is more likely to flourish in particular social and historical circumstances than in others. Specifically, voluntarism increases in societies characterized by high levels of cultural, social, and psychological differentiation (Alexander 1982, 1983). The ideological implications of this argument are straightforward. Material and normative arrangements, whether existing, emerging, or only conceived, that increase levels of differentiation and thereby foster greater voluntarism are supported or promoted. Conversely, developments that threaten to undermine institutionalized individualism pose a threat to freedom and should be subject to critical attack.

Several chapters in this book elaborate the argument. Sciulli's paper is the most explicitly ideological. He maintains that modern life is characterized by ceaseless pressure toward purposive rationalization, especially in the "material" spheres of the economy and the polity. These pressures encourage an entropic drift toward bureaucratic authoritarianism. This drift toward arbitrary power can be averted, Sciulli contends, by the further differentiation and institutionalization of procedural restraints and collegial formations. His synthetic standard of societal constitutionalism brings together Fuller's notion of "procedural legality" and Parsons' treatment of the collegial forms of organization into a threshold which, in turn, clearly separates genuine social integration from bureaucratic domination. In terms of practice, societal constitutionalism provides a socially grounded and recognizable Archimedian point that actors can employ to evaluate and critique social, political, and institutional developments that depart from it. Further, this standard encourages activities that promote the integrity and autonomy of collegial formations and procedural restraints: "if authoritarianism is to be restrained despite the systemic pressures of purposive-rationalization, professionals must become much more mobilized, sophisticated and aggressive" (Sciulli, chapter 11). In addition, maintaining "the integrity of extant collegial formations is itself a precondition for successfully upholding the rule of law and thereby for protecting individual actors' rights and freedoms" (Sciulli, chapter 11). In Parsons' terminology, the collegial form is a precondition for institutionalized individualism. Sciulli concludes his paper with three prescriptions, each of them refracted through the clarifying and specifying lens of societal constitutionalism: a differentiated legislative assembly, a differentiated council system, and a juridical democracy or fiduciary collegiality. In brief, Sciulli demonstrates the ideological potential of a critical modernism and some of the ways in which it can inform practice.

Mayhew's contribution also contains an ideological core, though in comparison to Sciulli's his argument is somewhat less apocalyptic about the dangers confronting modern society. He rejects the radical (and the commonsense) claim that bourgeois modernity destroys traditional solidarity and produces social disorganization. According to the radical critique, capitalism unleashes forces that destroy traditional loyalties of kin, clan, and community. If solidarity is to be restored, according to this view, drastic transformations (e.g., the inauguration of a socialist or communist state) are necessary. Mayhew argues, in contrast, that the new order is no less solidary than the old. Accepting the Durkheimian critique of the classic market theory of solidarity and moving beyond both Durkheim's and Parsons' respective identification of new regulatory norms and the societal community as bases of modern integration, Mayhew contends that the institutionalization of a differentiated public sphere establishes an apparatus where a new type of social bond can be forged. Further, he critiques Habermas' conception of a "true public," where discourse among authentically equal communicative partners flourishes, as utopian and as implying an impossible burden of dialogue. To the contrary, he asserts, the public is inherently stratified, for it constitutes an influence system structured by the prestige of leaders within an established social structure. Still, the public and the new hierarchies it generates are constantly subject to deflationary pressures: "The hallmark of a liberal system is that followers, actual and potential, are allowed to ask questions and to insist upon justifications, but, ironically, if everyone always did so, the system would break down" (Mayhew, chapter 9). Mayhew's paper, then, can be read, ideologically, as a liberal defense of modernity against the radical critique.

Although Mayhew maintains that the modern solidary public needs to be preserved and extended, it should also be readily apparent that the public is a structural mechanism that promotes social change. It is through public discourse that critical evaluations of policies, existing institutional practices, and entire societies are formulated and debated, that new solidarities are created, and that collectivities are mobilized for practical action. In defending the solidary public, then, Mayhew supports an institution that foments change.

Other articles in this volume also have ideological implications. For example, Münch's notion of interpenetration can be treated as a standard for evaluating and criticizing relations between subsystems, while Alexander's treatment of the media implies that the media operates most effectively as a "normative organizer" when other functional spheres, especially the cultural and the political spheres, are more strongly differentiated.

Finally, it should also be clear that while many of these essays are informed by a critical modernism, the particular ideological commitments and the practical recommendations emanating from them vary. For example, while Sciulli proposes radical alterations (or additions) of structure as safeguards against encroaching bureaucratic authoritarianism, Mayhew presents a resounding defense of the modern public sphere and cautions that the protection of that arena is essential for modernity. Nonetheless, the outlines of a critical modernism are now visible, and future work in this tradition will elaborate this position in greater detail. The emergence of this explicitly critical ideological perspective effectively undermines the charge that functionalism is inherently conservative.

Conclusion

Arguing that differentiation theory has developed, in part, as a response to two waves of criticism, this concluding essay has provided an analytic review of the contributions to this volume. In brief, these essays revise differentiation theory by outlining a more variegated conception of change, presenting a more comprehensive and empirically grounded explanatory framework, elaborating a more expansive approach to the consequences of differentiation, and articulating the rudiments of a critical modernism.

The immediate future of differentiation theory cannot be precisely determined. Nonetheless, three general developments appear likely. First, there will be an increasing emphasis on empirical research. A sophisticated and comprehensive analytic framework has always been functionalism's great strength. However, a truly successful theory requires empirical specification, and the research collected here testifies to a burgeoning consensus among functionalists about the need to establish a cumulative research program.

Second, the evolutionary framework of differentiation theory will be modified. Beyond disengaging the theory from its parochial Western bias, the determinist thrust of the theory will be superceded by a more flexible approach that acknowledges both the contingent nature of change and the role of concrete groups, mobilization, leadership, and intergroup conflict.

Finally, it is likely that differentiation theory will increase its conceptual richness and empirical specificity by borrowing from other intellectual traditions. Such borrowing has a long history in functionalism and contemporary students of change have readily adopted the practice of their predecessors. Accordingly, concepts and research associated with purportedly hostile traditions have been borrowed and adapted by differentiation theorists. This cross-fertilization reflects both a modest decline in the level of discord between sociological traditions and a broadly based effort on the part of some functionalists to revise their approach in a way that remedies perceived weaknesses and extends existing areas of strength.

With regard to this last point, it should be evident that my effort in this concluding essay has been to describe, by means of an analytic summary, how the contributions to this volume improve differentiation theory. Toward that end, I have highlighted the complementary advances introduced by the contributors. There are, of course, important dissimilarities among some of the papers, and I would be remiss if I failed to acknowledge some of the more pronounced differences. The attentive reader will have observed, for example, that the papers by Luhmann and Münch differ from the others in significant ways. They proceed at a more general analytic level, giving considerably less attention to the details of historical and comparative development than do many of the other contributors. Where their work is oriented toward delineating general models, many of the other essays attempt to specify differentiation theory through analyses of particular cases.

For many of the American contributors, differentiation theory can be advanced only by moving beyond Parsons' heavy reliance on general systemic properties; structural and contingent elements must be combined and variable patterns of differentiation explained. Münch and Luhmann, by contrast, continue to be systems oriented; they employ organicist metaphors and evolutionary principles to analyze differentiation and its consequences. One finds much less concern in their work with the question of how the course of differentiation is shaped by historical actors, either collective or individual. In response to the American effort to incorporate group action and conflict, for example, Münch (1985) has argued that such factors can be most fruitfully treated from a systems and evolutionary perspective; the pertinent dimensions of group conflict should be analyzed in terms of a system's "selective criteria," which determine the survival of institutional patterns. Münch wonders whether, if the American pattern is continued, "anything remains to be done by the sociologist" (1985:226), suggesting that attention to group action has made American students of differentiation excessively historical.

For the editors of this book, however, it seems clear that recent American research and theorizing have neither abandoned systemic notions in favor of an individualistic approach nor rejected sociology in favor of history. It has taken as the central issue, rather, the challenge of explaining how configurations of systemic conditions combine with patterns of corporate and individual action to produce historically specific outcomes of institutional change. Simply to "pluralize" systemic, selective criteria—as Münch proposes—is not sufficient, particularly since institutional survival is an unsatisfactory and overgeneralized term. Because systemic criteria are often subject to change, inconsistent with one another, internally ambiguous, and susceptible to diverse interpretations, the problem of specification is chronic and paramount. It is precisely because the connection between "selective criteria" and institutional patterns is tenuous and loose that the "contributions" of concrete actors to the process of structural differentiation must be assessed. This approach maintains, then, that within the broad limits established by systemic parameters, corporate action and group conflict specify the pattern of differentiation that ultimately obtains. Although this type of explanatory theory requires historically and empirically grounded research, it does not in any way mean that sociology has been supplanted by history.

Recent German writing about social change has increasingly taken differentiation as its referent. In the process, the German debate has become relatively self-contained. Münch's analysis of interpenetration, for instance, is more a critical reaction to Luhmann's description of autonomous and self-referential systems than a response to the path of American work. One of the interesting issues confronting contemporary differentiation theory is whether the distinctive national intellectual styles of post-Parsonian theorizing will interpenetrate or continue to diverge. While the German debate has certainly contributed to our understanding of differentiation and modernity, at this point it has not developed a close linkage to the post-Parsonian movement in the United States.

The thesis of this concluding essay has been that modern differentiation theory can be partially understood as a response to "external" critiques. Recent developments, particularly the reemergence of German theorizing, however, suggest the possibility that during the next several years differentiation theory will flourish as much in response to an "internal dialogue" among those who share many assumptions about the nature of change and modernity as in reaction to externally generated criticism. The increasing appeal of differentiation theory to an ever larger number of innovative and thoughtful scholars, whose similar perspectives on social change are nevertheless often informed by other diverse intellectual commitments, may well constitute an additional dynamic in the development of differentiation theory. In short, this approach to change and modernity has attracted a critical mass of very capable scholars, and its future has never looked more promising.

Notes

1. The role of "external" critiques in stimulating revisions and extensions of a particular sociological tradition is often quite subtle. Nonetheless, there is evidence suggesting that the early formulations of differentiation theory were instigated, in part, by such critiques. Describing the intellectual milieu surrounding his collaborative work with Parsons in *Economy and Society* and his own dissertation and subsequent monograph, *Social Change in the Industrial Revolution*, Smelser (1969:160–61) recounts: "As I recall, the mid-1950's were the heyday of two types of criticisms of the theory of action (though these criticisms have continued to this day). The first is the criticism that the theory of action focuses almost exclusively on static phenomena, and is unable to shed light on processes of conflict and change. The second is the criticism that the theory of action is too abstract and 'grand,' and is unable to be applied systematically to empirical problems and empirical data. I felt then—and continue to feel—that many variants of these criticisms are erroneous or misplaced. On the other hand, I was—and continue to be—keenly aware of the general significance and partial validity of these lines of criticism of existing action theory. I envisioned my study of structural differentiation as an effort to do something constructive in response to these criticisms. I wanted to assess the potential of the theory of action for analyzing social dynamics in a concrete historical setting."

Similarly, much of the work featured in this volume refers to critical assessments of differentiation theory and attempts to revise the theory in a way that redresses legitimate objections.

2. Previous work, it must be acknowledged, often treated differentiation as part of a broader pattern of change, viz., differentiation cum reintegration. However, that research frequently neglected other systemic responses to structural differentiation, and it is my contention that a comprehensive conception of change must incorporate the diversity of reactions engendered by differentiation.

3. Eisenstadt's theoretical and empirical revisions of functionalism and the "openings" his work presents to other sociological traditions are discussed in Alexander and Colomy (1985a, 1985b).

References

Abrahamson, Mark. 1978. *Functionalism.* Englewood Cliffs, N.J.: Prentice-Hall.

Alexander, Jeffrey C. 1978. "Formal and Substantive Voluntarism in the Work of Talcott Parsons: A Theoretical and Ideological Reinterpretation." *American Sociological Review* 43:177–98.

—— 1981. "Revolution, Reaction, and Reform: The Change Theory of Parsons' Middle Period." *Sociological Inquiry* 52:267–80.

—— 1982. *Positivism, Presuppositions, and Current Controversies.* Berkeley: University of California Press.

—— 1983. *The Modern Reconstruction of Classical Thought: Talcott Parsons.* Berkeley: University of California Press.

Alexander, Jeffrey C. and Paul Colomy. 1985a. "Institutionalization and Collective Behavior: Points of Contact Between Eisenstadt's Functionalism and Symbolic Interactionism." In E. Cohen, M. Lissak, and U. Almagor, eds., *Comparative Social Dynamics*, pp. 337–45. Boulder, Colo.: Westview.

—— 1985b. "Toward Neofunctionalism: Eisenstadt's Change Theory and Symbolic Interactionism." *Sociological Theory* 2:11–23.

Baum, Rainer C. 1981. *The Holocaust and the German Elite: Genocide and National Suicide in Germany, 1871–1945.* Totowa, N.J.: Rowman and Littlefield.

Baum, Rainer C. and Frank J. Lechner. 1981. "National Socialism: Toward an Actional-Theoretical Interpretation." *Sociological Inquiry* 51:281–308.

Bellah, Robert. 1964. "Religious Evolution." *American Sociological Review* 29:358–74.

Bendix, Reinhard. 1967. "Tradition and Modernity Reconsidered." *Comparative Studies in Society and History* 9:292–346.

Bourricaud, François. 1981. *The Sociology of Talcott Parsons.* Chicago, Ill.: University of Chicago Press. Originally published in French in 1977.

Coser, Lewis A. 1956. *The Functions of Social Conflict.* New York: Free Press.

Dahrendorf, Ralf. 1958. "Out of Utopia." *American Journal of Sociology* 64:115–27.

—— 1959. *Class and Class Conflict in Industrial Society.* Stanford, Calif.: Stanford University Press.

Eisenstadt, S. N. 1963. *The Political System of Empires.* New York: Free Press.

—— 1964. "Social Change, Differentiation and Evolution." *American Sociological Review* 29:235–47.

—— 1965. *Essays on Comparative Institutions.* New York: Wiley.

—— 1971. "Introduction." In S. N. Eisenstadt, ed., *Weber: On Charisma and Institution Building.* Chicago, Ill.: University of Chicago Press.

—— 1973. *Tradition, Change and Modernity.* New York: Wiley.

—— 1980. "Cultural Orientations, Institutional Entrepreneurs, and Social Change: Comparative Analyses of Traditional Civilizations." *American Journal of Sociology* 85:840–69.

Eisenstadt, S. N. and M. Curelaru. 1976. *The Form of Sociology: Paradigm and Crises.* New York: Wiley.

Gould, Mark. 1986. *Revolution in the Development of Capitalism*. Berkeley: University of California Press.

Gouldner, Alvin. 1970. *The Coming Crisis of Western Sociology*. New York: Free Press.

Granovetter, Mark. 1979. "Notes on Evolutionary Theory." *American Journal of Sociology* 85:489–515.

Keller, Suzanne. 1963. *Beyond the Ruling Class*. New York: Random House.

Lockwood, David. 1956. "Some Remarks on the Social System." *British Journal of Sociology* 7:134–45.

Mills, C. Wright. 1959. *The Sociological Imagination*. London: Oxford University Press.

Münch, Richard. 1981. "Talcott Parsons and the Theory of Action I: The Structure of Kantian Lore." *American Journal of Sociology* 86:709–39.

—— 1982. "Talcott Parsons and the Theory of Action II: The Continuity of Development." *American Journal of Sociology* 87:771–826.

—— 1985. "Differentiation, Consensus, and Conflict." In Jeffrey C. Alexander, ed., *Neofunctionalism*, pp. 225–37. Beverly Hills, Calif.: Sage.

Nisbet, Robert A. 1969. *Social Change and History*. London: Oxford University Press.

—— 1972. *Social Change*. New York: Harper and Row.

Parsons, Talcott. 1942. "Some Sociological Aspects on the Fascist Movements." *Social Forces* 21:138–47.

—— 1947. "Certain Primary Sources and Patterns of Aggression in the Social Structure of the Western World." *Psychiatry* 10:167–81.

—— 1951. *The Social System*. New York: Free Press.

—— 1961. "Some Considerations on the Theory of Social Change." *Rural Sociology* 26:219–39.

—— 1964. "Evolutionary Universals in Society." *American Sociological Review* 29:339–57.

—— 1966. *Societies: Evolutionary and Comparative Perspectives*. New York: Free Press.

—— 1971. *The System of Modern Societies*. Englewood Cliffs, N.J.: Prentice-Hall.

Parsons, Talcott and Neil J. Smelser. 1956. *Economy and Society*. New York: Free Press.

Polanyi, Karl. 1944. *The Great Transformation*. Boston, Mass.: Beacon Press.

Rueschemeyer, Dietrich. 1977. "Structural Differentiation, Efficiency and Power." *American Journal of Sociology* 83:1–25.

Smelser, Neil J. 1959. *Social Change in the Industrial Revolution*. Chicago, Ill.: University of Chicago Press.

—— 1968. *Essays in Sociological Explanation*. Englewood Cliffs, N.J.: Prentice-Hall.

—— 1969. "Some Personal Thoughts on the Pursuit of Sociological Problems." *Sociological Inquiry* 39:155–67.

—— 1985. "Evaluating the Model of Structural Differentiation in Relation to Educational Change in the Nineteenth Century." In J. Alexander, ed., *Neofunctionalism*, pp. 113–29. Beverly Hills, Calif.: Sage.

Smith, Anthony D. 1973. *The Concept of Social Change: A Critique of the Functionalist Theory of Social Change*. London: Routledge and Kegan Paul.

Stinchcombe, Arthur L., 1978. *Theoretical Methods in Social History*. New York: Academic Press.

Turner, Jonathan and Alexandra Maryanski. 1979. *Functionalism*. Menlo Park, Calif.: Benjamin and Cummings.

Index of Names

Subject Index